THE LIFE OF JOHNSON

By JAMES BOSWELL

ABRIDGED AND EDITED, WITH AN INTRODUCTION

By CHARLES GROSVENOR OSGOOD

The Life of Johnson
By James Boswell

Print ISBN 13: 978-1-4209-6729-6
eBook ISBN 13: 978-1-4209-6730-2

Cover Image: a detail of an illustration of Samuel Johnson and others, by Joseph Ratcliffe Skelton, from *English Literature for Boys and Girls* by H. E. Marshall, published by Frederick A. Stokes Company, c. 1910.

Please visit *www.digireads.com*

CONTENTS

Preface

In making this abridgement of Boswell's *Life of Johnson* I have omitted most of Boswell's criticisms, comments, and notes, all of Johnson's opinions in legal cases, most of the letters, and parts of the conversation dealing with matters which were of greater importance in Boswell's day than now. I have kept in mind an old habit, common enough, I dare say, among its devotees, of opening the book of random, and reading wherever the eye falls upon a passage of especial interest. All such passages, I hope, have been retained, and enough of the whole book to illustrate all the phases of Johnson's mind and of his time which Boswell observed.

Loyal Johnsonians may look upon such a book with a measure of scorn. I could not have made it, had I not believed that it would be the means of drawing new readers to Boswell, and eventually of finding for them in the complete work what many have already found—days and years of growing enlightenment and happy companionship, and an innocent refuge from the cares and perturbations of life.

PRINCETON, June 28, 1917.

Introduction

Phillips Brooks once told the boys at Exeter that in reading biography three men meet one another in close intimacy—the subject of the biography, the author, and the reader. Of the three the most interesting is, of course, the man about whom the book is written. The most privileged is the reader, who is thus allowed to live familiarly with an eminent man. Least regarded of the three is the author. It is his part to introduce the others, and to develop between them an acquaintance, perhaps a friendship, while he, though ever busy and solicitous, withdraws into the background.

Some think that Boswell, in his *Life of Johnson*, did not sufficiently realize his duty of self-effacement. He is too much in evidence, too bustling, too anxious that his own opinion, though comparatively unimportant, should get a hearing. In general, Boswell's faults are easily noticed, and have been too much talked about. He was morbid, restless, self-conscious, vain, insinuating; and, poor fellow, he died a drunkard. But the essential Boswell, the skilful and devoted artist, is almost unrecognized. As the creator of the *Life of Johnson* he is almost as much effaced as is Homer in the *Odyssey*. He is indeed so closely concealed that the reader suspects no art at all. Boswell's performance looks easy enough—merely the more or less coherent stringing together of a mass of memoranda. Nevertheless it was rare and difficult, as is the highest achievement in art. Boswell is primarily the artist, and he has created one of the great masterpieces of the world.* He created nothing else, though his head was continually filling itself with literary schemes that came to nought. But into his *Life of Johnson* he poured all his artistic energies, as Milton poured his into *Paradise Lost*, and Vergil his into the Æneid.

First, Boswell had the industry and the devotion to his task of an artist. Twenty years and more he labored in collecting his material. He speaks frankly of his methods. He recorded the talk of Johnson and his associates partly by a rough shorthand of his own, partly by an exceptional memory, which he carefully trained for this very purpose. 'O for shorthand to take this down!' said he to Mrs. Thrale as they listened to Johnson; and she replied: 'You'll carry it all in your head; a long head is as good as shorthand.' Miss Hannah More recalls a gay meeting at the Garricks', in Johnson's absence, when Boswell was bold enough to match his skill with no other than Garrick himself in an imitation of Johnson. Though Garrick was more successful in his Johnsonian recitation of poetry, Boswell won in reproducing his familiar conversation. He lost no time in perfecting his notes both mental and stenographic, and sat up many a night followed by a day of headache, to write them in final form, that none of the freshness and glow might fade. The sheer labor of this process, not to mention the difficulty, can be measured only by one who attempts a similar feat. Let him try to report the best conversation of a lively evening, following its course, preserving its point, differentiating sharply the traits of the participants, keeping the style, idiom, and exact words of each. Let him reject all parts of it, however diverting, of which the charm and force will evaporate with the occasion, and retain only that which will be as amusing, significant, and lively as ever at the end of one hundred, or, for all that we can see, one thousand years. He will then, in some measure, realize the difficulty of Boswell's performance. When his work appeared Boswell himself said: 'The stretch of mind and prompt assiduity by which so many conversations are preserved, I myself, at some distance of time, contemplate with wonder.'

He was indefatigable in hunting up and consulting all who had known parts or aspects of Johnson's life which to him were inaccessible. He mentions all told more than fifty names of men and women whom he consulted for information, to which number many others should be added of those who gave him nothing that he could use. 'I have sometimes been obliged to run half over London, in order to fix a date correctly.' He agonized over his work with the true devotion of an artist: 'You cannot imagine,' he says, 'what labor, what perplexity, what vexation I have endured in arranging a prodigious multiplicity of materials, in supplying omissions, in searching for papers buried in different masses, and all this besides the exertion of composing and polishing.' He despairs of making his picture vivid or full enough, and of ever realizing his preconception of his masterpiece.

Boswell's devotion to his work appears in even more extraordinary ways. Throughout he repeatedly offers himself as a victim to illustrate his great friend's wit, ill-humor, wisdom, affection, or goodness. He never spares himself, except now and then to assume a somewhat diaphanous anonymity. Without regard for his own dignity, he exhibits himself as humiliated, or drunken, or hypochondriac, or inquisitive, or resorting to petty subterfuge—anything for the accomplishment of his one main purpose. 'Nay, Sir,' said Johnson, 'it was not the wine that made your head ache, but the sense that I put into it.' 'What, Sir,' asks the hapless Boswell, 'will sense make the head ache?' 'Yes, Sir, when it is not used to it.'

Boswell is also the artist in his regard for truth. In him it was a passion. Again and again he insists upon his authenticity. He developed an infallible gust and unerring relish of what was genuinely Johnsonian in speech, writing, or action; and his own account leads to the inference that he discarded, as worthless, masses of diverting material which would have tempted a less scrupulous writer beyond resistance. 'I observed to him,' said Boswell, 'that there were very few of his friends so accurate as that I could venture to put down in writing what they told me as his sayings.' The faithfulness of his portrait, even to the minutest details, is his unremitting care, and he subjects all contributed material to the sternest criticism.

Industry and love of truth alone will not make the artist. With only these Boswell might have been merely a tireless transcriber. But he had besides a keen sense of artistic values. This appears partly in the unity of his vast work. Though it was years in the making, though the details that demanded his attention were countless, yet they all centre consistently in one figure, and are so focused upon it, that one can hardly open the book at random to a line which has not its direct bearing upon the one subject of the work. Nor is the unity of the book that of an undeviating narrative in chronological order of one man's life; it grows rather out of a single dominating personality exhibited in all the vicissitudes of a manifold career. Boswell often speaks of his work as a painting, a portrait, and of single incidents as pictures or scenes in a drama. His eye is keen for contrasts, for picturesque moments, for dramatic action. While it is always the same Johnson whom he makes the central figure, he studies to shift the background, the interlocutors, the light and shade, in search of new revelations and effects. He presents a succession of many scenes, exquisitely wrought, of Johnson amid widely various settings of Eighteenth-Century England. And subject and setting are so closely allied that each borrows charm and emphasis from the other. Let the devoted reader of Boswell ask himself what glamor would fade from the church of St. Clement Danes, from the Mitre, from Fleet Street, the Oxford coach, and

Lichfield, if the burly figure were withdrawn from them; or what charm and illumination, of the man himself would have been lost apart from these settings. It is the unseen hand of the artist Boswell that has wrought them inseparably into this reciprocal effect.

The single scenes and pictures which Boswell has given us will all of them bear close scrutiny for their precision, their economy of means, their lifelikeness, their artistic effect. None was wrought more beautifully, nor more ardently, than that of Johnson's interview with the King. First we see the plain massive figure of the scholar amid the elegant comfort of Buckingham House. He is intent on his book before the fire. Then the approach of the King, lighted on his way by Mr. Barnard with candles caught from a table; their entrance by a private door, with Johnson's unconscious absorption, his sudden surprise, his starting up, his dignity, the King's ease with him, their conversation, in which the King courteously draws from Johnson knowledge of that in which Johnson is expert, Johnson's manly bearing and voice throughout—all is set forth with the unadorned vividness and permanent effect which seem artless enough, but which are characteristic of only the greatest art.

Boswell's *Life of Johnson* is further a masterpiece of art in that it exerts the vigorous energy of a masterpiece, an abundance of what, for want of a better word, we call personality. It is Boswell's confessed endeavor to add this quality to the others, because he perceived that it was an essential quality of Johnson himself, and he more than once laments his inability to transmit the full force and vitality of his original. Besides artistic perception and skill it required in him admiration and enthusiasm to seize this characteristic and impart it to his work. His admiration he confesses unashamed: 'I said I worshipped him . . . I cannot help worshipping him, he is so much superior to other men.' He studied his subject intensely. 'During all the course of my long intimacy with him, my respectful attention never abated.' Upon such intensity and such ardor and enthusiasm depend the energy and animation of his portrait.

But it exhibits other personal qualities than these, which, if less often remarked, are at any rate unconsciously enjoyed. Boswell had great social charm. His friends are agreed upon his liveliness and good nature. Johnson called him 'clubbable,' 'the best traveling companion in the world,' 'one Scotchman who is cheerful,' 'a man whom everybody likes,' 'a man who I believe never left a house without leaving a wish for his return.' His vivacity, his love of fun, his passion for good company and friendship, his sympathy, his amiability, which made him acceptable everywhere, have mingled throughout with his own handiwork, and cause it to radiate a kind of genial warmth. This geniality it may be which has attracted so many readers to the book. They find themselves in good company, in a comfortable, pleasant place, agreeably stimulated with wit and fun, and cheered with friendliness. They are loth to leave it, and would ever enter it again. This rare charm the book owes in large measure to its creator.

The alliance of author with subject in Boswell's *Johnson* is one of the happiest and most sympathetic the world has known. So close is it that one cannot easily discern what great qualities the work owes to each. While it surely derives more of its excellence than is commonly remarked from the art of Boswell, its greatness after all is ultimately that of its subject. The noble qualities of Johnson have been well discerned by Carlyle, and his obvious peculiarities and prejudices somewhat magnified and distorted in Macaulay's brilliant refractions. One quality only shall I dwell upon, though that may be the sum of all the rest. Johnson had a supreme capacity for human relationship. In him this capacity amounted to genius.

In all respects he was of great stature. His contemporaries called him a colossus, the literary Goliath, the Giant, the great Cham of literature, a tremendous companion. His frame was majestic; he strode when he walked, and his physical strength and courage were heroic. His mode of speaking was 'very impressive,' his utterance 'deliberate and strong.' His conversation was compared to 'an antique statue, where every vein and muscle is distinct and bold.' From boyhood throughout his life his companions naturally deferred to him, and he dominated them without effort. But what overcame the harshness of this autocracy, and made it reasonable, was the largeness of a nature that loved men and was ever hungry for knowledge of them. 'Sir,' said he, 'I look upon every day lost in which I do not make a new acquaintance.' And again: 'Why, Sir, I am a man of the world. I live in the world, and I take, in some degree, the color of the world as it moves along.' Thus he was a part of all that he met, a central figure in his time, with whose opinion one must reckon in considering any important matter of his day.

His love of London is but a part of his hunger for men. 'The happiness of London is not to be conceived but by those who have been in it.' 'Why, Sir, you find no man at all intellectual who is willing to leave London: No, Sir, when a man is tired of London, he is tired of life; for there is in London all that life can afford.' As he loved London, so he loved a tavern for its sociability. 'Sir, there is nothing which has yet been contrived by man, by which so much happiness is produced as by a good tavern.' 'A tavern chair is the throne of human felicity.'

Personal words are often upon his lips, such as 'love' and 'hate,' and vast is the number, range, and variety of people who at one time or another had been in some degree personally related with him, from Bet Flint and his black servant Francis, to the adored Duchess of Devonshire and the King himself. To no one who passed a word with him was he personally indifferent. Even fools received his personal attention. Said one: 'But I don't understand you, Sir.' 'Sir, I have found you an argument. I am not obliged to find you an understanding.' 'Sir, you are irascible,' said Boswell; 'you have no patience with folly or absurdity.'

But it is in Johnson's capacity for friendship that his greatness is specially revealed. 'Keep your friendships in good repair.' As the old friends disappeared, new ones came to him. For Johnson seems never to have sought out friends. He was not a common 'mixer.' He stooped to no devices for the sake of popularity. He pours only scorn upon the lack of mind and conviction which is necessary to him who is everybody's friend.

His friendships included all classes and all ages. He was a great favorite with children, and knew how to meet them, from little four-months-old Veronica Boswell to his godchild Jane Langton. 'Sir,' said he, 'I love the acquaintance of young people, . . . young men have more virtue than old men; they have more generous sentiments in every respect.' At sixty-eight he said: 'I value myself upon this, that there is nothing of the old man in my conversation.' Upon women of all classes and ages he exerts without trying a charm the consciousness of which would have turned any head less constant than his own, and with their fulsome adoration he was pleased none the less for perceiving its real value.

But the most important of his friendships developed between him and such men of genius as Boswell, David Garrick, Oliver Goldsmith, Sir Joshua Reynolds, and Edmund Burke. Johnson's genius left no fit testimony of itself from his own hand. With all the greatness of his mind he had no talent in sufficient measure by which fully to express himself. He had no ear for music and no eye for painting, and the finest qualities in the creations of Goldsmith were lost upon him. But his genius found its talents in others, and through the talents of his personal friends expressed itself as it were by proxy. They rubbed their minds upon his, and he set in motion for them ideas which they might use. But the intelligence of genius is profounder and more personal than mere ideas. It has within it something energetic, expansive, propulsive from mind to mind, perennial, yet steady and controlled; and it was with such force that Johnson's almost superhuman personality inspired the art of his friends. Of this they were in some degree aware. Reynolds confessed that Johnson formed his mind, and 'brushed from it a great deal of rubbish.' Gibbon called Johnson 'Reynolds' oracle.' In one of his *Discourses* Sir Joshua, mindful no doubt of his own experience, recommends that young artists seek the companionship of such a man merely as a tonic to their art. Boswell often testifies to the stimulating effect of Johnson's presence. Once he speaks of 'an animating blaze of eloquence, which roused every intellectual power in me to the highest pitch'; and again of the 'full glow' of Johnson's conversation, in which he felt himself 'elevated as if brought into another state of being.' He says that all members of Johnson's 'school' 'are distinguished for a love of truth and accuracy which they would not have possessed in the same degree if they had not been acquainted with Johnson.' He quotes Johnson at length and repeatedly as the author of his own large conception of biography. He was Goldsmith's 'great master,' Garrick feared his criticism, and one cannot but recognize the power of Johnson's personality in the increasing intelligence and consistency of Garrick's interpretations, in the growing vigor and firmness of Goldsmith's stroke, in the charm, finality, and exuberant life of Sir Joshua's portraits; and above all in the skill, truth, brilliance, and lifelike spontaneity of Boswell's art. It is in such works as these that we shall find the real Johnson, and through them that he will exert the force of his personality upon us.

Biography is the literature of realized personality, of life as it has been lived, of actual achievements or shortcomings, of success or failure; it is not imaginary and embellished, not what might be or might have been, not reduced to prescribed or artificial forms, but it is the unvarnished story of that which was delightful, disappointing, possible, or impossible, in a life spent in this world.

In this sense it is peculiarly the literature of truth and authenticity. Elements of imagination and speculation must enter into all other forms of literature, and as purely creative forms they may rank superior to biography; but in each case it will be found that their authenticity, their right to our attention and credence, ultimately rests upon the biographical element which is basic in them, that is, upon what they have derived by observation and experience from a human life seriously lived. Biography contains this element in its purity. For this reason it is more authentic than other kinds of literature, and more relevant. The thing that most concerns me, the individual, whether I will or no, is the management of myself in this world. The fundamental and essential conditions of life are the same in any age, however the adventitious circumstances may change. The beginning and the end are the same, the average length the same, the problems and the prize the same. How, then, have others managed, both those who failed and those who succeeded, or those, in far greatest number, who did both? Let me know their ambitions, their odds, their handicaps, obstacles, weaknesses, and struggles, how they finally fared, and what they had to say about it. Let me know a great variety of such instances that I may mark their disagreements, but more especially their agreement about it. How did they play the game? How did they fight the fight that I am to fight, and how in any case did they lose or win? To these questions biography gives the direct answer. Such is its importance over other literature. For such reasons, doubtless, Johnson 'loved' it most. For such reasons the book which has been most cherished and revered for well-nigh two thousand years is a biography.

Biography, then, is the chief text-book in the art of living, and preeminent in its kind is the *Life of Johnson*. Here is the instance of a man who was born into a life stripped of all ornament and artificiality. His equipment in mind and stature was Olympian, but the odds against him were proportionate to his powers. Without fear or complaint, without boast or noise, he fairly joined issue with the world and overcame it. He scorned circumstance, and laid bare the unvarying realities of the contest. He was ever the sworn enemy of speciousness, of nonsense, of idle and insincere speculation, of the mind that does not take seriously the duty of making itself up, of neglect in the gravest consideration of life. He insisted upon the rights and dignity of the individual man, and at the same time upon the vital necessity to him of reverence and submission, and no man ever more beautifully illustrated their interdependence, and their exquisite combination in a noble nature.

Boswell's *Johnson* is consistently and primarily the life of one man. Incidentally it is more, for through it one is carried from his own present limitations into a spacious and genial world. The reader there meets a vast number of people, men, women, children, nay even animals, from George the Third down to the cat Hodge. By the author's magic each is alive, and the reader mingles with them as with his acquaintances. It is a varied world, and includes the smoky and swarming courts and highways of London, its stately drawing-rooms, its cheerful inns, its shops and markets, and beyond is the highroad which we travel in lumbering coach or speeding postchaise to venerable Oxford with its polite and leisurely dons, or to the staunch little cathedral city of Lichfield, welcoming back its famous son to dinner and tea, or to the seat of a country squire, or ducal castle, or village tavern, or the grim but hospitable feudal life of the Hebrides. And wherever we go with Johnson there is the lively traffic in ideas, lending vitality and significance to everything about him.

A part of education and culture is the extension of one's narrow range of living to include wider possibilities or actualities, such as may be gathered from other fields of thought, other times, other men; in short, to use a Johnsonian phrase, it is 'multiplicity of consciousness.' There is no book more effective through long familiarity to such extension and such multiplication than Boswell's *Life of Johnson*. It adds a new world to one's own, it increases one's acquaintance among people who think, it gives intimate companionship with a great and friendly man.

The *Life of Johnson* is not a book on first acquaintance to be read through from the first page to the end. 'No, Sir, do *you* read books through?' asked Johnson. His way is probably the best one of undertaking this book. Open at random, read here and there, forward and back, wholly according to inclination; follow the practice of Johnson and all good readers, of 'tearing the heart' out of it. In this way you most readily come within the reach of its charm and power. Then, not content with a part, seek the unabridged whole, and grow into the infinite possibilities of it.

But the supreme end of education, we are told, is expert discernment in all things—the power to tell the good from the bad, the genuine from the counterfeit, and to prefer the good and the genuine to the bad and the counterfeit. This is the supreme end of the talk of Socrates, and it is the supreme end of the talk of Johnson. 'My dear friend,' said he, 'clear your mind of cant; . . . don't *think* foolishly.' The effect of long companionship with Boswell's *Johnson* is just this. As Sir Joshua said, 'it brushes away the rubbish'; it clears the mind of cant; it instills the habit of singling out the essential thing; it imparts discernment. Thus, through his friendship with Boswell, Johnson will realize his wish, still to be teaching as the years increase.

The Life of Samuel Johnson

Had Dr. Johnson written his own life, in conformity with the opinion which he has given, that every man's life may be best written by himself; had he employed in the preservation of his own history, that clearness of narration and elegance of language in which he has embalmed so many eminent persons, the world would probably have had the most perfect example of biography that was ever exhibited. But although he at different times, in a desultory manner, committed to writing many particulars of the progress of his mind and fortunes, he never had persevering diligence enough to form them into a regular composition. Of these memorials a few have been preserved; but the greater part was consigned by him to the flames, a few days before his death.

As I had the honour and happiness of enjoying his friendship for upwards of twenty years; as I had the scheme of writing his life constantly in view; as he was well apprised of this circumstance, and from time to time obligingly satisfied my inquiries, by communicating to me the incidents of his early years; as I acquired a facility in recollecting, and was very assiduous in recording, his conversation, of which the extraordinary vigour and vivacity constituted one of the first features of his character; and as I have spared no pains in obtaining materials concerning him, from every quarter where I could discover that they were to be found, and have been favoured with the most liberal communications by his friends; I flatter myself that few biographers have entered upon such a work as this, with more advantages; independent of literary abilities, in which I am not vain enough to compare myself with some great names who have gone before me in this kind of writing.

Instead of melting down my materials into one mass, and constantly speaking in my own person, by which I might have appeared to have more merit in the execution of the work, I have resolved to adopt and enlarge upon the excellent plan of Mr. Mason, in his Memoirs of Gray. Wherever narrative is necessary to explain, connect, and supply, I furnish it to the best of my abilities; but in the chronological series of Johnson's life, which I trace as distinctly as I can, year by year, I produce, wherever it is in my power, his own minutes, letters or conversation, being convinced that this mode is more lively, and will make my readers better acquainted with him, than even most of those were who actually knew him, but could know him only partially; whereas there is here an accumulation of intelligence from various points, by which his character is more fully understood and illustrated.

Indeed I cannot conceive a more perfect mode of writing any man's life, than not only relating all the most important events of it in their order, but interweaving what he privately wrote, and said, and thought; by which mankind are enabled as it were to see him live, and to 'live o'er each scene' with him, as he actually advanced through the several stages of his life. Had his other friends been as diligent and ardent as I was, he might have been almost entirely preserved. As it is, I will venture to say that he will be seen in this work more completely than any man who has ever yet lived.

And he will be seen as he really was; for I profess to write, not his panegyrick, which must be all praise, but his Life; which, great and good as he was, must not be supposed to be entirely perfect. To be as he was, is indeed subject of panegyrick enough to any man in this state of being; but in every picture there should be shade as well as light, and when I delineate him without reserve, I do what he himself recommended, both by his precept and his example.

I am fully aware of the objections which may be made to the minuteness on some occasions of my detail of Johnson's conversation, and how happily it is adapted for the petty exercise of ridicule, by men of superficial understanding and ludicrous fancy; but I remain firm and confident in my opinion, that minute particulars are frequently characteristick, and always amusing, when they relate to a distinguished man. I am therefore exceedingly unwilling that any thing, however slight, which my illustrious friend thought it worth his while to express, with any degree of point, should perish.

Of one thing I am certain, that considering how highly the small portion which we have of the table-talk and other anecdotes of our celebrated writers is valued, and how earnestly it is regretted that we have not more, I am justified in preserving rather too many of Johnson's sayings, than too few; especially as from the diversity of dispositions it cannot be known with certainty beforehand, whether what may seem trifling to some, and perhaps to the collector himself, may not be most agreeable to many; and the greater number that an authour can please in any degree, the more pleasure does there arise to a benevolent mind.

SAMUEL JOHNSON was born at Lichfield, in Staffordshire, on the 18th of September, N. S., 1709; and his initiation into the Christian Church was not delayed; for his baptism is recorded, in the register of St. Mary's parish in that city, to have been performed on the day of his birth. His father is there stiled *Gentleman*, a circumstance of which an ignorant panegyrist has praised him for not being proud; when the truth is, that the appellation of Gentleman, though now lost in the indiscriminate assumption of *Esquire*, was commonly taken by those who could not boast of gentility. His father was Michael Johnson, a native of Derbyshire, of obscure extraction, who settled in Lichfield as a bookseller and stationer. His mother was Sarah Ford, descended of an ancient race of substantial yeomanry in Warwickshire. They were well advanced in years when they married, and never had more than two children, both sons; Samuel, their first born, who lived to be the illustrious character whose various excellence I am to endeavour to record, and Nathanael, who died in his twenty-fifth year.

Mr. Michael Johnson was a man of a large and robust body, and of a strong and active mind; yet, as in the most solid rocks veins of unsound substance are often discovered, there was in him a mixture of that disease, the nature of which eludes the most minute enquiry, though the effects are well known to be a weariness of life, an unconcern about those things which agitate the greater part of mankind, and a general sensation of gloomy wretchedness. From him then his son inherited, with some other qualities, 'a vile melancholy,' which in his too strong expression of any disturbance of the mind, 'made him mad all his life, at least not sober.' Michael was, however, forced by the narrowness of his circumstances to be very diligent in business, not only in his shop, but by occasionally resorting to several towns in the neighbourhood, some of which were at a considerable distance from Lichfield. At that time booksellers' shops in the provincial towns of England were very rare, so that there was not one even in Birmingham, in which town old Mr. Johnson used to open a shop every market-day. He was a pretty good Latin scholar, and a citizen so creditable as to be made one of the magistrates of Lichfield; and, being a man of good sense, and skill in his trade, he acquired a reasonable share of wealth, of which however he afterwards lost the greatest part, by engaging unsuccessfully in a manufacture of parchment. He was a zealous high-church man and royalist, and retained his attachment to the unfortunate house of Stuart, though he reconciled himself, by casuistical arguments of expediency and necessity, to take the oaths imposed by the prevailing power.

Johnson's mother was a woman of distinguished understanding. I asked his old school-fellow, Mr. Hector, surgeon of Birmingham, if she was not vain of her son. He said, 'she had too much good sense to be vain, but she knew her son's value.' Her piety was not inferiour to her understanding; and to her must be ascribed those early impressions of religion upon the mind of her son, from which the world afterwards derived so much benefit. He told me, that he remembered distinctly having had the first notice of Heaven, 'a place to which good people went,' and hell, 'a place to which bad people went,' communicated to him by her, when a little child in bed with her; and that it might be the better fixed in his memory, she sent him to repeat it to Thomas Jackson, their man-servant; he not being in the way, this was not done; but there was no occasion for any artificial aid for its preservation.

There is a traditional story of the infant Hercules of toryism, so curiously characteristick, that I shall not withhold it. It was communicated to me in a letter from Miss Mary Adye, of Lichfield:

'When Dr. Sacheverel was at Lichfield, Johnson was not quite three years old. My grandfather Hammond observed him at the cathedral perched upon his father's shoulders, listening and gaping at the much celebrated preacher. Mr. Hammond asked Mr. Johnson how he could possibly think of bringing such an infant to church, and in the midst of so great a crowd. He answered, because it was impossible to keep him at home; for, young as he was, he believed he had caught the publick spirit and zeal for Sacheverel, and would have staid for ever in the church, satisfied with beholding him.'

Nor can I omit a little instance of that jealous independence of spirit, and impetuosity of temper, which never forsook him. The fact was acknowledged to me by himself, upon the authority of his mother. One day, when the servant who used to be sent to school to conduct him home, had not come in time, he set out by himself, though he was then so near-sighted, that he was obliged to stoop down on his hands and knees to take a view of the kennel before he ventured to step over it. His school-mistress, afraid that he might miss his way, or fall into the kennel, or be run over by a cart, followed him at some distance. He happened to turn about and perceive her. Feeling her careful attention as an insult to his manliness, he ran back to her in a rage, and beat her, as well as his strength would permit.

Of the power of his memory, for which he was all his life eminent to a degree almost incredible, the following early instance was told me in his presence at Lichfield, in 1776, by his step-daughter, Mrs. Lucy Porter, as related to her by his mother. When he was a child in petticoats, and had learnt to read, Mrs. Johnson one morning put the common prayer-book into his hands, pointed to the collect for the day, and said, 'Sam, you must get this by heart.' She went up stairs, leaving him to study it: But by the time she had reached the second floor, she heard him following her. 'What's the matter?' said she. 'I can say it,' he replied; and repeated it distinctly, though he could not have read it more than twice.

But there has been another story of his infant precocity generally circulated, and generally believed, the truth of which I am to refute upon his own authority. It is told, that, when a child of three years old, he chanced to tread upon a duckling, the eleventh of a brood, and killed it; upon which, it is said, he dictated to his mother the following epitaph:

> 'Here lies good master duck,
>   Whom Samuel Johnson trod on;
> If it had liv'd, it had been *good luck*,
>   For then we'd had an *odd one*.'

There is surely internal evidence that this little composition combines in it, what no child of three years old could produce, without an extension of its faculties by immediate inspiration; yet Mrs. Lucy Porter, Dr. Johnson's stepdaughter, positively maintained to me, in his presence, that there could be no doubt of the truth of this anecdote, for she had heard it from his mother. So difficult is it to obtain an authentick relation of facts, and such authority may there be for errour; for he assured me, that his father made the verses, and wished to pass them for his child's. He added, 'my father was a foolish old man; that is to say, foolish in talking of his children.'

Young Johnson had the misfortune to be much afflicted with the scrophula, or king's evil, which disfigured a countenance naturally well formed, and hurt his visual nerves so much, that he did not see at all with one of his eyes, though its appearance was little different from that of the other. There is amongst his prayers, one inscribed '*When, my* EYE *was restored to its use*,' which ascertains a defect that many of his friends knew he had, though I never perceived it. I supposed him to be only near-sighted; and indeed I must observe, that in no other respect could I discern any defect in his vision; on the contrary, the force of his attention and perceptive quickness made him see and distinguish all manner of objects, whether of nature or of art, with a nicety that is rarely to be found. When he and I were travelling in the Highlands of Scotland, and I pointed out to him a mountain which I observed resembled a cone, he corrected my inaccuracy, by shewing me, that it was indeed pointed at the top, but that one side of it was larger than the other. And the ladies with whom he was acquainted agree, that no man was more nicely and minutely critical in the elegance of female dress.

When I found that he saw the romantick beauties of Islam, in Derbyshire, much better than I did, I told him that he resembled an able performer upon a bad instrument. It has been said, that he contracted this grievous malady from his nurse. His mother yielding to the superstitious notion, which, it is wonderful to think, prevailed so long in this country, as to the virtue of the regal touch; a notion, which our kings encouraged, and to which a man of such inquiry and such judgement as Carte could give credit; carried him to London, where he was actually touched by Queen Anne. Mrs. Johnson indeed, as Mr. Hector informed me, acted by the advice of the celebrated Sir John Floyer, then a physician in Lichfield. Johnson used to talk of this very frankly; and Mrs. Piozzi has preserved his very picturesque description of the scene, as it remained upon his fancy. Being asked if he could remember Queen Anne, 'He had (he said) a confused, but somehow a sort of solemn recollection of a lady in diamonds, and a long black hood.' This touch, however, was without any effect. I ventured to say to him, in allusion to the political principles in which he was educated, and of which he ever retained some odour, that 'his mother had not carried him far enough; she should have taken him to ROME.'

He was first taught to read English by Dame Oliver, a widow, who kept a school for young children in Lichfield. He told me she could read the black letter, and asked him to borrow for her, from his father, a bible in that character. When he was going to Oxford, she came to take leave of him, brought him, in the simplicity of her kindness, a present of gingerbread, and said, he was the best scholar she ever had. He delighted in mentioning this early compliment: adding, with a smile, that 'this was as high a proof of his merit as he could conceive.' His next instructor in English was a master, whom, when he spoke of him to me, he familiarly called Tom Brown, who, said he, 'published a spelling-book, and dedicated it to the UNIVERSE; but, I fear, no copy of it can now be had.'

He began to learn Latin with Mr. Hawkins, usher, or under-master of Lichfield school, 'a man (said he) very skilful in his little way.' With him he continued two years, and then rose to be under the care of Mr. Hunter, the headmaster, who, according to his account, 'was very severe, and wrong-headedly severe. He used (said he) to beat us unmercifully; and he did not distinguish between ignorance and negligence; for he would beat a boy equally for not knowing a thing, as for neglecting to know it. He would ask a boy a question; and if he did not answer it, he would beat him, without considering whether he had an opportunity of knowing how to answer it. For instance, he would call up a boy and ask him Latin for a candlestick, which the boy could not expect to be asked. Now, Sir, if a boy could answer every question, there would be no need of a master to teach him.'

It is, however, but justice to the memory of Mr. Hunter to mention, that though he might err in being too severe, the school of Lichfield was very respectable in his time. The late Dr. Taylor, Prebendary of Westminster, who was educated under him, told me, that 'he was an excellent master, and that his ushers were most of them men of eminence; that Holbrook, one of the most ingenious men, best scholars, and best preachers of his age, was usher during the greatest part of the time that Johnson was at school. Then came Hague, of whom as much might be said, with the addition that he was an elegant poet. Hague was succeeded by Green, afterwards Bishop of Lincoln, whose character in the learned world is well known.'

Indeed Johnson was very sensible how much he owed to Mr. Hunter. Mr. Langton one day asked him how he had acquired so accurate a knowledge of Latin, in which, I believe, he was exceeded by no man of his time; he said, 'My master whipt me very well. Without that, Sir, I should have done nothing.' He told Mr. Langton, that while Hunter was flogging his boys unmercifully, he used to say, 'And this I do to save you from the gallows.' Johnson, upon all occasions, expressed his approbation of enforcing instruction by means of the rod. 'I would rather (said he) have the rod to be the general terrour to all, to make them learn, than tell a child, if you do thus, or thus, you will be more esteemed than your brothers or sisters. The rod produces an effect which terminates in itself. A child is afraid of being whipped, and gets his task, and there's an end on't; whereas, by exciting emulation and comparisons of superiority, you lay the foundation of lasting mischief; you make brothers and sisters hate each other.'

That superiority over his fellows, which he maintained with so much dignity in his march through life, was not assumed from vanity and ostentation, but was the natural and constant effect of those extraordinary powers of mind, of which he could not but be conscious by comparison; the intellectual difference, which in other cases of comparison of characters, is often a matter of undecided contest, being as clear in his case as the superiority of stature in some men above others. Johnson did not strut or stand on tiptoe; He only did not stoop. From his earliest years his superiority was perceived and acknowledged. He was from the beginning Αναξάνδρών, a king of men. His school-fellow, Mr. Hector, has obligingly furnished me with many particulars of his boyish days: and assured me that he never knew him corrected at school, but for talking and diverting other boys from their business. He seemed to learn by intuition; for though indolence and procrastination were inherent in his constitution, whenever he made an exertion he did more than any one else. His favourites used to receive very liberal assistance from him; and such was the submission and deference with which he was treated, such the desire to obtain his regard, that three of the boys, of whom Mr. Hector was sometimes one, used to come in the morning as his humble attendants, and carry him to school. One in the middle stooped, while he sat upon his back, and one on each side supported him; and thus he was borne triumphant. Such a proof of the early predominance of intellectual vigour is very remarkable, and does honour to human nature. Talking to me once himself of his being much distinguished at school, he told me, 'they never thought to raise me by comparing me to any one; they never said, Johnson is as good a scholar as such a one; but such a one is as good a scholar as Johnson; and this was said but of one, but of Lowe; and I do not think he was as good a scholar.'

He discovered a great ambition to excel, which roused him to counteract his indolence. He was uncommonly inquisitive; and his memory was so tenacious, that he never forgot any thing that he either heard or read. Mr. Hector remembers having recited to him eighteen verses, which, after a little pause, he repeated *verbatim*, varying only one epithet, by which he improved the line.

He never joined with the other boys in their ordinary diversions: his only amusement was in winter, when he took a pleasure in being drawn upon the ice by a boy barefooted, who pulled him along by a garter fixed round him; no very easy operation, as his size was remarkably large. His defective sight, indeed, prevented him from enjoying the common sports; and he once pleasantly remarked to me, 'how wonderfully well he had contrived to be idle without them.' Mr. Hector relates, that 'he could not oblige him more than by sauntering away the hours of vacation in the fields, during which he was more engaged in talking to himself than to his companion.'

Dr. Percy, the Bishop of Dromore, who was long intimately acquainted with him, and has preserved a few anecdotes concerning him, regretting that he was not a more diligent collector, informs me, that 'when a boy he was immoderately fond of reading romances of chivalry, and he retained his fondness for them through life; so that (adds his Lordship) spending part of a summer at my parsonage house in the country, he chose for his regular reading the old Spanish romance of *Felixmarte* of *Hircania*, in folio, which he read quite through. Yet I have heard him attribute to these extravagant fictions that unsettled turn of mind which prevented his ever fixing in any profession.'

1725: ÆTAT. 16.—After having resided for some time at the house of his uncle, Cornelius Ford, Johnson was, at the age of fifteen, removed to the school of Stourbridge, in Worcestershire, of which Mr. Wentworth was then master. This step was taken by the advice of his cousin, the Reverend Mr. Ford, a man in whom both talents and good dispositions were disgraced by licentiousness, but who was a very able judge of what was right. At this school he did not receive so much benefit as was expected. It has been said, that he acted in the capacity of an assistant to Mr. Wentworth, in teaching the younger boys. 'Mr.

Wentworth (he told me) was a very able man, but an idle man, and to me very severe; but I cannot blame him much. I was then a big boy; he saw I did not reverence him; and that he should get no honour by me. I had brought enough with me, to carry me through; and all I should get at his school would be ascribed to my own labour, or to my former master. Yet he taught me a great deal.'

He thus discriminated, to Dr. Percy, Bishop of Dromore, his progress at his two grammar-schools. 'At one, I learnt much in the school, but little from the master; in the other, I learnt much from the master, but little in the school.'

He remained at Stourbridge little more than a year, and then returned home, where he may be said to have loitered, for two years, in a state very unworthy his uncommon abilities. He had already given several proofs of his poetical genius, both in his school-exercises and in other occasional compositions.

He had no settled plan of life, nor looked forward at all, but merely lived from day to day. Yet he read a great deal in a desultory manner, without any scheme of study, as chance threw books in his way, and inclination directed him through them. He used to mention one curious instance of his casual reading, when but a boy. Having imagined that his brother had hid some apples behind a large folio upon an upper shelf in his father's shop, he climbed up to search for them. There were no apples; but the large folio proved to be Petrarch, whom he had seen mentioned in some preface, as one of the restorers of learning. His curiosity having been thus excited, he sat down with avidity, and read a great part of the book. What he read during these two years he told me, was not works of mere amusement, 'not voyages and travels, but all literature, Sir, all ancient writers, all manly: though but little Greek, only some of Anacreon and Hesiod; but in this irregular manner (added he) I had looked into a great many books, which were not commonly known at the Universities, where they seldom read any books but what are put into their hands by their tutors; so that when I came to Oxford, Dr. Adams, now master of Pembroke College, told me I was the best qualified for the University that he had ever known come there.'

That a man in Mr. Michael Johnson's circumstances should think of sending his son to the expensive University of Oxford, at his own charge, seems very improbable. The subject was too delicate to question Johnson upon. But I have been assured by Dr. Taylor that the scheme never would have taken place had not a gentleman of Shropshire, one of his schoolfellows, spontaneously undertaken to support him at Oxford, in the character of his companion; though, in fact, he never received any assistance whatever from that gentleman.

He, however, went to Oxford, and was entered a Commoner of Pembroke College on the 31st of October, 1728, being then in his nineteenth year.

The Reverend Dr. Adams, who afterwards presided over Pembroke College with universal esteem, told me he was present, and gave me some account of what passed on the night of Johnson's arrival at Oxford. On that evening, his father, who had anxiously accompanied him, found means to have him introduced to Mr. Jorden, who was to be his tutor.

His father seemed very full of the merits of his son, and told the company he was a good scholar, and a poet, and wrote Latin verses. His figure and manner appeared strange to them; but he behaved modestly, and sat silent, till upon something which occurred in the course of conversation, he suddenly struck in and quoted Macrobius; and thus he gave the first impression of that more extensive reading in which he had indulged himself.

His tutor, Mr. Jorden, fellow of Pembroke, was not, it seems, a man of such abilities as we should conceive requisite for the instructor of Samuel Johnson, who gave me the following account of him. 'He was a very worthy man, but a heavy man, and I did not profit much by his instructions. Indeed, I did not attend him much. The first day after I came to college I waited upon him, and then staid away four. On the sixth, Mr. Jorden asked me why I had not attended. I answered I had been sliding in Christ-Church meadow. And this I said with as much *nonchalance* as I am now talking to you. I had no notion that I was wrong or irreverent to my tutor. BOSWELL: 'That, Sir, was great fortitude of mind.' JOHNSON: 'No, Sir; stark insensibility.'

He had a love and respect for Jorden, not for his literature, but for his worth. 'Whenever (said he) a young man becomes Jorden's pupil, he becomes his son.'

Having given a specimen of his poetical powers, he was asked by Mr. Jorden, to translate Pope's Messiah into Latin verse, as a Christmas exercise. He performed it with uncommon rapidity, and in so masterly a manner, that he obtained great applause from it, which ever after kept him high in the estimation of his College, and, indeed, of all the University.

It is said, that Mr. Pope expressed himself concerning it in terms of strong approbation. Dr. Taylor told me, that it was first printed for old Mr. Johnson, without the knowledge of his son, who was very angry when he heard of it.

The 'morbid melancholy,' which was lurking in his constitution, and to which we may ascribe those particularities, and that aversion to regular life, which, at a very early period, marked his character, gathered such strength in his twentieth year, as to afflict him in a dreadful manner. While he was at Lichfield, in the college vacation of the year 1729, he felt himself overwhelmed with an horrible hypochondria, with perpetual irritation, fretfulness, and impatience; and with a dejection, gloom, and despair, which made existence misery.

From this dismal malady he never afterwards was perfectly relieved; and all his labours, and all his enjoyments, were but temporary interruptions of its baleful influence. He told Mr. Paradise that he was sometimes so languid and inefficient, that he could not distinguish the hour upon the town-clock.

Johnson, upon the first violent attack of this disorder, strove to overcome it by forcible exertions. He frequently walked to Birmingham and back again, and tried many other expedients, but all in vain. His expression concerning it to me was 'I did not then know how to manage it.' His distress became so intolerable, that he applied to Dr. Swinfen, physician in Lichfield, his god-father, and put into his hands a state of his case, written in Latin. Dr. Swinfen was so much struck with the extraordinary acuteness, research, and eloquence of this paper, that in his zeal for his godson he shewed it to several people. His daughter, Mrs. Desmoulins, who was many years humanely supported in Dr. Johnson's house in London, told me, that upon his discovering that Dr. Swinfen had communicated his case, he was so much offended, that he was never afterwards fully reconciled to him. He indeed had good reason to be offended; for though Dr. Swinfen's motive was good, he inconsiderately betrayed a matter deeply interesting and of great delicacy, which had been entrusted to him in confidence; and exposed a complaint of his young friend and patient, which, in the superficial opinion of the generality of mankind, is attended with contempt and disgrace.

To Johnson, whose supreme enjoyment was the exercise of his reason, the disturbance or obscuration of that faculty was the evil most to be dreaded. Insanity, therefore, was the object of his most dismal apprehension; and he fancied himself seized by it, or approaching to it, at the very time when he was giving proofs of a more than ordinary soundness and vigour of judgement. That his own diseased imagination should have so far deceived him, is strange; but it is stranger still that some of his friends should have given credit to his groundless opinion, when they had such undoubted proofs that it was totally fallacious; though it is by no means surprising that those who wish to depreciate him, should, since his death, have laid hold of this circumstance, and insisted upon it with very unfair aggravation.

The history of his mind as to religion is an important article. I have mentioned the early impressions made upon his tender imagination by his mother, who continued her pious care with assiduity, but, in his opinion, not with judgement. 'Sunday (said he) was a heavy day to me when I was a boy. My mother confined me on that day, and made me read "The Whole Duty of Man," from a great part of which I could derive no instruction. When, for instance, I had read the chapter on theft, which from my infancy I had been taught was wrong, I was no more convinced that theft was wrong than before; so there was no accession of knowledge. A boy should be introduced to such books, by having his attention directed to the arrangement, to the style, and other excellencies of composition; that the mind being thus engaged by an amusing variety of objects, may not grow weary.'

He communicated to me the following particulars upon the subject of his religious progress. 'I fell into an inattention to religion, or an indifference about it, in my ninth year. The church at Lichfield, in which we had a seat, wanted reparation, so I was to go and find a seat in other churches; and having bad eyes, and being awkward about this, I used to go and read in the fields on Sunday. This habit continued till my fourteenth year; and still I find a great reluctance to go to church. I then became a sort of lax *talker* against religion, for I did not much *think* against it; and this lasted till I went to Oxford, where it would not be *suffered*. When at Oxford, I took up Law's *Serious Call to a Holy Life*, expecting to find it a dull book (as such books generally are), and perhaps to laugh at it. But I found Law quite an overmatch for me; and this was the first occasion of my thinking in earnest of religion, after I became capable of rational inquiry.' From this time forward religion was the predominant object of his thoughts; though, with the just sentiments of a conscientious Christian, he lamented that his practice of its duties fell far short of what it ought to be.

The particular course of his reading while at Oxford, and during the time of vacation which he passed at home, cannot be traced. Enough has been said of his irregular mode of study. He told me that from his earliest years he loved to read poetry, but hardly ever read any poem to an end; that he read Shakspeare at a period so early, that the speech of the ghost in Hamlet terrified him when he was alone; that Horace's Odes were the compositions in which he took most delight, and it was long before he liked his Epistles and Satires. He told me what he read *solidly* at Oxford was Greek; not the Grecian historians, but Homer and Euripides, and now and then a little Epigram; that the study of which he was the most fond was Metaphysicks, but he had not read much, even in that way. I always thought that he did himself injustice in his account of what he had read, and that he must have been speaking with reference to the vast portion of study which is possible, and to which a few scholars in the whole history of literature have attained; for when I once asked him whether a person, whose name I have now forgotten, studied hard, he answered 'No, Sir; I do not believe he studied hard. I never knew a man who studied hard. I conclude, indeed, from the effects, that some men have studied hard, as Bentley and Clarke.' Trying him by that criterion upon which he formed his judgement of others, we may be absolutely certain, both from his writings and his conversation, that his reading was very extensive. Dr. Adam Smith, than whom few were better judges on this subject, once observed to me that 'Johnson knew more books than any man alive.' He had a peculiar facility in seizing at once what was valuable in any book, without submitting to the labour of perusing it from beginning to end. He had, from the irritability of his constitution, at all times, an impatience and hurry when he either read or wrote. A certain apprehension, arising from novelty, made him write his first exercise at College twice over; but he never took that trouble with any other composition; and we shall see that his most excellent works were struck off at a heat, with rapid exertion.

No man had a more ardent love of literature, or a higher respect for it than Johnson. His apartment in Pembroke College was that upon the second floor, over the gateway. The enthusiasts of learning will ever contemplate it with veneration. One day, while he was sitting in it quite alone, Dr. Panting, then master of the College, whom he called 'a fine Jacobite fellow,' overheard him uttering this soliloquy in his strong, emphatick voice: 'Well, I have a mind to see what is done in other places of learning. I'll go and visit the Universities abroad. I'll go to France and Italy. I'll go to Padua.—And I'll mind my business. For an *Athenian* blockhead is the worst of all blockheads.'

Dr. Adams told me that Johnson, while he was at Pembroke College, 'was caressed and loved by all about him, was a gay and frolicksome fellow, and passed there the happiest part of his life.' But this is a striking proof of the fallacy of appearances, and how little any of us know of the real internal state even of those whom we see most frequently; for the truth is, that he was then depressed by poverty, and irritated by disease. When I mentioned to him this account as given me by Dr. Adams, he said; 'Ah, Sir, I was mad and violent. It was bitterness which they mistook for frolick. I was miserably poor, and I thought to fight my way by my literature and my wit; so I disregarded all power and all authority.'

The Bishop of Dromore observes in a letter to me,

'The pleasure he took in vexing the tutors and fellows has been often mentioned. But I have heard him say, what ought to be recorded to the honour of the present venerable master of that College, the Reverend William Adams, D.D., who was then very young, and one of the junior fellows; that the mild but judicious expostulations of this worthy man, whose virtue awed him, and whose learning he revered, made him really ashamed of himself, "though I fear (said he) I was too proud to own it."

'I have heard from some of his cotemporaries that he was generally seen lounging at the College gate, with a circle of young students round him, whom he was entertaining with wit, and keeping from their studies, if not spiriting them up to rebellion against the College discipline, which in his maturer years he so much extolled.'

I do not find that he formed any close intimacies with his fellow-collegians. But Dr. Adams told me that he contracted a love and regard for Pembroke College, which he retained to the last. A short time before his death he sent to that College a present of all his works, to be deposited in their library; and he had thoughts of leaving to it his house at Lichfield; but his friends who were about him very properly dissuaded him from it, and he bequeathed it to some poor relations. He took a pleasure in boasting of the many eminent men who had been educated at Pembroke. In this list are found the names of Mr. Hawkins the Poetry Professor, Mr. Shenstone, Sir William Blackstone, and others; not forgetting the celebrated popular preacher, Mr. George Whitefield, of whom, though Dr. Johnson did not think very highly, it must be acknowledged that his eloquence was powerful, his views pious and charitable, his assiduity almost incredible; and, that since his death, the integrity of his character has been fully vindicated. Being himself a poet, Johnson was peculiarly happy in mentioning how many of the sons of Pembroke were poets; adding, with a smile of sportive triumph, 'Sir, we are a nest of singing birds.'

He was not, however, blind to what he thought the defects of his own College; and I have, from the information of Dr. Taylor, a very strong instance of that rigid honesty which he ever inflexibly preserved. Taylor had obtained his father's consent to be entered of Pembroke, that he might be with his schoolfellow Johnson, with whom, though some years older than himself, he was very intimate. This would have been a great comfort to Johnson. But he fairly told Taylor that he could not, in conscience, suffer him to enter where he knew he could not have an able tutor. He then made inquiry all round the University, and having found that Mr. Bateman, of Christ Church, was the tutor of highest reputation, Taylor was entered of that College. Mr. Bateman's lectures were so excellent, that Johnson used to come and get them at second-hand from Taylor, till his poverty being so extreme that his shoes were worn out, and his feet appeared through them, he saw that this humiliating circumstance was perceived by the Christ Church men, and he came no more. He was too proud to accept of money, and somebody having set a pair of new shoes at his door, he threw them away with indignation. How must we feel when we read such an anecdote of Samuel Johnson!

The *res angusta domi* prevented him from having the advantage of a complete academical education. The friend to whom he had trusted for support had deceived him. His debts in College, though not great, were increasing; and his scanty remittances from Lichfield, which had all along been made with great difficulty, could be supplied no longer, his father having fallen into a state of insolvency. Compelled, therefore, by irresistible necessity, he left the College in autumn, 1731, without a degree, having been a member of it little more than three years.

And now (I had almost said *poor*) Samuel Johnson returned to his native city, destitute, and not knowing how he should gain even a decent livelihood. His father's misfortunes in trade rendered him unable to support his son; and for some time there appeared no means by which he could maintain himself. In the December of this year his father died.

Johnson was so far fortunate, that the respectable character of his parents, and his own merit, had, from his earliest years, secured him a kind reception in the best families at Lichfield. Among these I can mention Mr. Howard, Dr. Swinfen, Mr. Simpson, Mr. Levett, Captain Garrick, father of the great ornament of the British stage; but above all, Mr. Gilbert Walmsley, Register of the Prerogative Court of Lichfield, whose character, long after his decease, Dr. Johnson has, in his Life of Edmund Smith, thus drawn in the glowing colours of gratitude:

'Of Gilbert Walmsley, thus presented to my mind, let me indulge myself in the remembrance. I knew him very early; he was one of the first friends that literature procured me, and I hope that, at least, my gratitude made me worthy of his notice.

'He was of an advanced age, and I was only not a boy, yet he never received my notions with contempt. He was a whig, with all the virulence and malevolence of his party; yet difference of opinion did not keep us apart. I honoured him and he endured me.

'At this man's table I enjoyed many cheerful and instructive hours, with companions, such as are not often found—with one who has lengthened, and one who has gladdened life; with Dr. James, whose skill in physick will be long remembered; and with David Garrick, whom I hoped to have gratified with this character of our common friend. But what are the hopes of man! I am disappointed by that stroke of death, which has eclipsed the gaiety of nations, and impoverished the publick stock of harmless pleasure.'

In these families he passed much time in his early years. In most of them, he was in the company of ladies, particularly at Mr. Walmsley's, whose wife and sisters-in-law, of the name of Aston, and daughters of a Baronet, were remarkable for good breeding; so that the notion which has been industriously circulated and believed, that he never was in good company till late in life, and, consequently had been confirmed in coarse and ferocious manners by long habits, is wholly without foundation. Some of the ladies have assured me, they recollected him well when a young man, as distinguished for his complaisance.

In the forlorn state of his circumstances, he accepted of an offer to be employed as usher in the school of Market-Bosworth, in Leicestershire, to which it appears, from one of his little fragments of a diary, that he went on foot, on the 16th of July.

This employment was very irksome to him in every respect, and he complained grievously of it in his letters to his friend Mr. Hector, who was now settled as a surgeon at Birmingham. The letters are lost; but Mr. Hector recollects his writing 'that the poet had described the dull

sameness of his existence in these words, "*Vitam continet una dies*"
(one day contains the whole of my life); that it was unvaried as the note
of the cuckow; and that he did not know whether it was more
disagreeable for him to teach, or the boys to learn, the grammar rules.'
His general aversion to this painful drudgery was greatly enhanced by a
disagreement between him and Sir Wolstan Dixey, the patron of the
school, in whose house, I have been told, he officiated as a kind of
domestick chaplain, so far, at least, as to say grace at table, but was
treated with what he represented as intolerable harshness; and, after
suffering for a few months such complicated misery, he relinquished a
situation which all his life afterwards he recollected with the strongest
aversion, and even a degree of horrour. But it is probable that at this
period, whatever uneasiness he may have endured, he laid the
foundation of much future eminence by application to his studies.

Being now again totally unoccupied, he was invited by Mr. Hector
to pass some time with him at Birmingham, as his guest, at the house of
Mr. Warren, with whom Mr. Hector lodged and boarded. Mr. Warren
was the first established bookseller in Birmingham, and was very
attentive to Johnson, who he soon found could be of much service to
him in his trade, by his knowledge of literature; and he even obtained
the assistance of his pen in furnishing some numbers of a periodical
Essay printed in the newspaper, of which Warren was proprietor. After
very diligent inquiry, I have not been able to recover those early
specimens of that particular mode of writing by which Johnson
afterwards so greatly distinguished himself.

He continued to live as Mr. Hector's guest for about six months,
and then hired lodgings in another part of the town, finding himself as
well situated at Birmingham as he supposed he could be any where,
while he had no settled plan of life, and very scanty means of
subsistence. He made some valuable acquaintances there, amongst
whom were Mr. Porter, a mercer, whose widow he afterwards married,
and Mr. Taylor, who by his ingenuity in mechanical inventions, and his
success in trade, acquired an immense fortune. But the comfort of being
near Mr. Hector, his old school-fellow and intimate friend, was
Johnson's chief inducement to continue here.

His juvenile attachments to the fair sex were very transient; and it
is certain that he formed no criminal connection whatsoever. Mr.
Hector, who lived with him in his younger days in the utmost intimacy
and social freedom, has assured me, that even at that ardent season his
conduct was strictly virtuous in that respect; and that though he loved
to exhilarate himself with wine, he never knew him intoxicated but
once.

In a man whom religious education has secured from licentious
indulgences, the passion of love, when once it has seized him, is
exceedingly strong; being unimpaired by dissipation, and totally

concentrated in one object. This was experienced by Johnson, when he became the fervent admirer of Mrs. Porter, after her first husband's death. Miss Porter told me, that when he was first introduced to her mother, his appearance was very forbidding: he was then lean and lank, so that his immense structure of bones was hideously striking to the eye, and the scars of the scrophula were deeply visible. He also wore his hair, which was straight and stiff, and separated behind: and he often had, seemingly, convulsive starts and odd gesticulations, which tended to excite at once surprize and ridicule. Mrs. Porter was so much engaged by his conversation that she overlooked all these external disadvantages, and said to her daughter, 'this is the most sensible man that I ever saw in my life.'

Though Mrs. Porter was double the age of Johnson, and her person and manner, as described to me by the late Mr. Garrick, were by no means pleasing to others, she must have had a superiority of understanding and talents, as she certainly inspired him with a more than ordinary passion; and she having signified her willingness to accept of his hand, he went to Lichfield to ask his mother's consent to the marriage, which he could not but be conscious was a very imprudent scheme, both on account of their disparity of years, and her want of fortune. But Mrs. Johnson knew too well the ardour of her son's temper, and was too tender a parent to oppose his inclinations.

I know not for what reason the marriage ceremony was not performed at Birmingham; but a resolution was taken that it should be at Derby, for which place the bride and bridegroom set out on horseback, I suppose in very good humour. But though Mr. Topham Beauclerk used archly to mention Johnson's having told him, with much gravity, 'Sir, it was a love marriage on both sides,' I have had from my illustrious friend the following curious account of their journey to church upon the nuptial morn:

9*th* July:—'Sir, she had read the old romances, and had got into her head the fantastical notion that a woman of spirit should use her lover like a dog. So, Sir, at first she told me that I rode too fast, and she could not keep up with me; and, when I rode a little slower, she passed me, and complained that I lagged behind. I was not to be made the slave of caprice; and I resolved to begin as I meant to end. I therefore pushed on briskly, till I was fairly out of her sight. The road lay between two hedges, so I was sure she could not miss it; and I contrived that she should soon come up with me. When she did, I observed her to be in tears.'

This, it must be allowed, was a singular beginning of connubial felicity; but there is no doubt that Johnson, though he thus shewed a manly firmness, proved a most affectionate and indulgent husband to the last moment of Mrs. Johnson's life: and in his *Prayers and Meditations*, we find very remarkable evidence that his regard and fondness for her never ceased, even after her death.

He now set up a private academy, for which purpose he hired a large house, well situated near his native city. In the *Gentleman's Magazine* for 1736, there is the following advertisement:

'At Edial, near Lichfield, in Staffordshire, young gentlemen are boarded and taught the Latin and Greek languages, by SAMUEL JOHNSON.'

But the only pupils that were put under his care were the celebrated David Garrick and his brother George, and a Mr. Offely, a young gentleman of good fortune who died early. The truth is, that he was not so well qualified for being a teacher of elements, and a conductor in learning by regular gradations, as men of inferiour powers of mind. His own acquisitions had been made by fits and starts, by violent irruptions into the regions of knowledge; and it could not be expected that his impatience would be subdued, and his impetuosity restrained, so as to fit him for a quiet guide to novices.

Johnson was not more satisfied with his situation as the master of an academy, than with that of the usher of a school; we need not wonder, therefore, that he did not keep his academy above a year and a half. From Mr. Garrick's account he did not appear to have been profoundly reverenced by his pupils. His oddities of manner, and uncouth gesticulations, could not but be the subject of merriment to them; and, in particular, the young rogues used to listen at the door of his bed-chamber, and peep through the key-hole, that they might turn into ridicule his tumultuous and awkward fondness for Mrs. Johnson, whom he used to name by the familiar appellation of *Tetty* or *Tetsey*, which, like *Betty* or *Betsey*, is provincially used as a contraction for *Elisabeth*, her christian name, but which to us seems ludicrous, when applied to a woman of her age and appearance. Mr. Garrick described her to me as very fat, with a bosom of more than ordinary protuberance, with swelled cheeks of a florid red, produced by thick painting, and increased by the liberal use of cordials; flaring and fantastick in her dress, and affected both in her speech and her general behaviour. I have seen Garrick exhibit her, by his exquisite talent of mimickry, so as to excite the heartiest bursts of laughter; but he, probably, as is the case in all such representations, considerably aggravated the picture.

Johnson now thought of trying his fortune in London, the great field of genius and exertion, where talents of every kind have the fullest scope, and the highest encouragement. It is a memorable circumstance that his pupil David Garrick went thither at the same time,[1] with

---

[1] Both of them used to talk pleasantly of this their first journey to London. Garrick, evidently meaning to embellish a little, said one day in my hearing, 'we rode and tied.' And the Bishop of Killaloe informed me, that at another time, when Johnson and Garrick were dining together in a pretty large company, Johnson humorously ascertaining the chronology of something, expressed himself thus: 'that was the year when I came to

intention to complete his education, and follow the profession of the law, from which he was soon diverted by his decided preference for the stage.

They were recommended to Mr. Colson, an eminent mathematician and master of an academy, by the following letter from Mr. Walmsley:

'TO THE REVEREND MR. COLSON.

'Lichfield, March 2,1737.

'DEAR SIR, I had the favour of yours, and am extremely obliged to you; but I cannot say I had a greater affection for you upon it than I had before, being long since so much endeared to you, as well by an early friendship, as by your many excellent and valuable qualifications; and, had I a son of my own, it would be my ambition, instead of sending him to the University, to dispose of him as this young gentleman is.

'He, and another neighbour of mine, one Mr. Samuel Johnson, set out this morning for London together. Davy Garrick is to be with you early the next week, and Mr. Johnson to try his fate with a tragedy, and to see to get himself employed in some translation, either from the Latin or the French. Johnson is a very good scholar and poet, and I have great hopes will turn out a fine tragedy-writer. If it should any way lie in your way, doubt not but you would be ready to recommend and assist your countryman.

'G. WALMSLEY.'

How he employed himself upon his first coming to London is not particularly known.'[2]

He had a little money when he came to town, and he knew how he could live in the cheapest manner. His first lodgings were at the house of Mr. Norris, a staymaker, in Exeter-street, adjoining Catharine-street, in the Strand. 'I dined (said he) very well for eight-pence, with very good company, at the Pine Apple in New-street, just by. Several of them had travelled. They expected to meet every day; but did not know one another's names. It used to cost the rest a shilling, for they drank wine; but I had a cut of meat for six-pence, and bread for a penny, and gave the waiter a penny; so that I was quite well served, nay, better

---

London with two-pence half-penny in my pocket.' Garrick overhearing him, exclaimed, 'eh? What do you say? with two-pence half-penny in your pocket?'—JOHNSON, 'Why yes; when I came with two-pence half-penny in *my* pocket, and thou, Davy, with three half-pence in thine.'—BOSWELL.

[2] One curious anecdote was communicated by himself to Mr. John Nichols. Mr. Wilcox, the bookseller, on being informed by him that his intention was to get his livelihood as an authour, eyed his robust frame attentively, and with a significant look, said, 'You had better buy a porter's knot.' He however added, 'Wilcox was one of *my* best friends.'—BOSWELL.

than the rest, for they gave the waiter nothing.' He at this time, I believe, abstained entirely from fermented liquors: a practice to which he rigidly conformed for many years together, at different periods of his life.

His Ofellus in the *Art of Living in London*, I have heard him relate, was an Irish painter, whom he knew at Birmingham, and who had practised his own precepts of oeconomy for several years in the British capital. He assured Johnson, who, I suppose, was then meditating to try his fortune in London, but was apprehensive of the expence, 'that thirty pounds a year was enough to enable a man to live there without being contemptible. He allowed ten pounds for clothes and linen. He said a man might live in a garret at eighteen-pence a week; few people would inquire where he lodged; and if they did, it was easy to say, "Sir, I am to be found at such a place." By spending three-pence in a coffeehouse, he might be for some hours every day in very good company; he might dine for six-pence, breakfast on bread and milk for a penny, and do without supper. On *clean-shirt-day* he went abroad, and paid visits.' I have heard him more than once talk of this frugal friend, whom he recollected with esteem and kindness, and did not like to have one smile at the recital. 'This man (said he, gravely) was a very sensible man, who perfectly understood common affairs: a man of a great deal of knowledge of the world, fresh from life, not strained through books. He amused himself, I remember, by computing how much more expence was absolutely necessary to live upon the same scale with that which his friend described, when the value of money was diminished by the progress of commerce. It may be estimated that double the money might now with difficulty be sufficient.'

Amidst this cold obscurity, there was one brilliant circumstance to cheer him; he was well acquainted with Mr. Henry Hervey, one of the branches of the noble family of that name, who had been quartered at Lichfield as an officer of the army, and had at this time a house in London, where Johnson was frequently entertained, and had an opportunity of meeting genteel company. Not very long before his death, he mentioned this, among other particulars of his life, which he was kindly communicating to me; and he described this early friend, 'Harry Hervey,' thus: 'He was a vicious man, but very kind to me. If you call a dog HERVEY, I shall love him.'

He told me he had now written only three acts of his *Irene*, and that he retired for some time to lodgings at Greenwich, where he proceeded in it somewhat further, and used to compose, walking in the Park; but did not stay long enough at that place to finish it.

In the course of the summer he returned to Lichfield, where he had left Mrs. Johnson, and there he at last finished his tragedy, which was not executed with his rapidity of composition upon other occasions, but was slowly and painfully elaborated. A few days before his death, while burning a great mass of papers, he picked out from among them the original unformed sketch of this tragedy, in his own hand-writing, and gave it to Mr. Langton, by whose favour a copy of it is now in my possession.

Johnson's residence at Lichfield, on his return to it at this time, was only for three months; and as he had as yet seen but a small part of the wonders of the Metropolis, he had little to tell his townsmen. He related to me the following minute anecdote of this period: 'In the last age, when my mother lived in London, there were two sets of people, those who gave the wall, and those who took it; the peaceable and the quarrelsome. When I returned to Lichfield, after having been in London, my mother asked me, whether I was one of those who gave the wall, or those who took it. *Now* it is fixed that every man keeps to the right; or, if one is taking the wall, another yields it; and it is never a dispute.'

He now removed to London with Mrs. Johnson; but her daughter, who had lived with them at Edial, was left with her relations in the country. His lodgings were for some time in Woodstock-street, near Hanover-square, and afterwards in Castle-street, near Cavendish-square.

His tragedy being by this time, as he thought, completely finished and fit for the stage, he was very desirous that it should be brought forward. Mr. Peter Garrick told me, that Johnson and he went together to the Fountain tavern, and read it over, and that he afterwards solicited Mr. Fleetwood, the patentee of Drury-lane theatre, to have it acted at his house; but Mr. Fleetwood would not accept it, probably because it was not patronized by some man of high rank; and it was not acted till 1749, when his friend David Garrick was manager of that theatre.

The Gentleman's Magazine, begun and carried on by Mr. Edward Cave, under the name of SYLVANUS URBAN, had attracted the notice and esteem of Johnson, in an eminent degree, before he came to London as an adventurer in literature. He told me, that when he first saw St. John's Gate, the place where that deservedly popular miscellany was originally printed, he 'beheld it with reverence.'

It appears that he was now enlisted by Mr. Cave as a regular coadjutor in his magazine, by which he probably obtained a tolerable livelihood. At what time, or by what means, he had acquired a competent knowledge both of French and Italian, I do not know; but he was so well skilled in them, as to be sufficiently qualified for a translator. That part of his labour which consisted in emendation and improvement of the productions of other contributors, like that employed in levelling ground, can be perceived only by those who had an opportunity of comparing the original with the altered copy. What we certainly know to have been done by him in this way, was the Debates in both houses of Parliament, under the name of 'The Senate of

Lilliput,' sometimes with feigned denominations of the several speakers, sometimes with denominations formed of the letters of their real names, in the manner of what is called anagram, so that they might easily be decyphered. Parliament then kept the press in a kind of mysterious awe, which made it necessary to have recourse to such devices. In our time it has acquired an unrestrained freedom, so that the people in all parts of the kingdom have a fair, open, and exact report of the actual proceedings of their representatives and legislators, which in our constitution is highly to be valued; though, unquestionably, there has of late been too much reason to complain of the petulance with which obscure scribblers have presumed to treat men of the most respectable character and situation.

This important article of the *Gentlemen's Magazine* was, for several years, executed by Mr. William Guthrie, a man who deserves to be respectably recorded in the literary annals of this country. The debates in Parliament, which were brought home and digested by Guthrie, whose memory, though surpassed by others who have since followed him in the same department, was yet very quick and tenacious, were sent by Cave to Johnson for his revision; and, after some time, when Guthrie had attained to greater variety of employment, and the speeches were more and more enriched by the accession of Johnson's genius, it was resolved that he should do the whole himself, from the scanty notes furnished by persons employed to attend in both houses of Parliament. Sometimes, however, as he himself told me, he had nothing more communicated to him than the names of the several speakers, and the part which they had taken in the debate.[3]

But what first displayed his transcendent powers, and 'gave the world assurance of the MAN,' was his *London, a Poem, in Imitation of the Third Satire of Juvenal:* which came out in May this year, and burst forth with a splendour, the rays of which will for ever encircle his name. Boileau had imitated the same satire with great success, applying it to Paris; but an attentive comparison will satisfy every reader, that he is much excelled by the English Juvenal. Oldham had also imitated it, and applied it to London; all which performances concur to prove, that great cities, in every age, and in every country, will furnish similar topicks of satire. Whether Johnson had previously read Oldham's imitation, I do not know; but it is not a little remarkable, that there is scarcely any coincidence found between the two performances, though upon the very same subject.

Johnson's *London* was published in May, 1738; and it is

---

[3] Johnson later told Boswell that 'as soon as he found that the speeches were thought genuine he determined that he would write no more of them: for "he would not be accessory to the propagation of falsehood." And such was the tenderness of his conscience, that a short time before his death he expressed his regret for his having been the authour of fictions which had passed for realities.'—Ed.

remarkable, that it came out on the same morning with Pope's satire, entitled '1738;' so that England had at once its Juvenal and Horace as poetical monitors. The Reverend Dr. Douglas, now Bishop of Salisbury, to whom I am indebted for some obliging communications, was then a student at Oxford, and remembers well the effect which London produced. Every body was delighted with it; and there being no name to it, the first buz of the literary circles was 'here is an unknown poet, greater even than Pope.' And it is recorded in the *Gentleman's Magazine* of that year, that it 'got to the second edition in the course of a week.'

One of the warmest patrons of this poem on its first appearance was General Oglethorpe, whose 'strong benevolence of soul,' was unabated during the course of a very long life; though it is painful to think, that he had but too much reason to become cold and callous, and discontented with the world, from the neglect which he experienced of his publick and private worth, by those in whose power it was to gratify so gallant a veteran with marks of distinction. This extraordinary person was as remarkable for his learning and taste, as for his other eminent qualities; and no man was more prompt, active, and generous, in encouraging merit. I have heard Johnson gratefully acknowledge, in his presence, the kind and effectual support which he gave to his *London*, though unacquainted with its authour.

Pope, who then filled the poetical throne without a rival, it may reasonably be presumed, must have been particularly struck by the sudden appearance of such a poet; and, to his credit, let it be remembered, that his feelings and conduct on the occasion were candid and liberal. He requested Mr. Richardson, son of the painter, to endeavour to find out who this new authour was. Mr. Richardson, after some inquiry, having informed him that he had discovered only that his name was Johnson, and that he was some obscure man, Pope said; 'he will soon be *déterré.*' We shall presently see, from a note written by Pope, that he was himself afterwards more successful in his inquiries than his friend.

While we admire the poetical excellence of this poem, candour obliges us to allow, that the flame of patriotism and zeal for popular resistance with which it is fraught, had no just cause. There was, in truth, no 'oppression;' the 'nation' was *not* 'cheated.' Sir Robert Walpole was a wise and a benevolent minister, who thought that the happiness and prosperity of a commercial country like ours, would be best promoted by peace, which he accordingly maintained, with credit, during a very long period. Johnson himself afterwards honestly acknowledged the merit of Walpole, whom he called 'a fixed star;' while he characterised his opponent, Pitt, as 'a meteor.' But Johnson's juvenile poem was naturally impregnated with the fire of opposition, and upon every account was universally admired.

Though thus elevated into fame, and conscious of uncommon powers, he had not that bustling confidence, or, I may rather say, that animated ambition, which one might have supposed would have urged him to endeavour at rising in life. But such was his inflexible dignity of character, that he could not stoop to court the great; without which, hardly any man has made his way to a high station. He could not expect to produce many such works as his *London*, and he felt the hardships of writing for bread; he was, therefore, willing to resume the office of a schoolmaster, so as to have a sure, though moderate income for his life; and an offer being made to him of the mastership of a school, provided he could obtain the degree of Master of Arts, Dr. Adams was applied to, by a common friend, to know whether that could be granted him as a favour from the University of Oxford. But though he had made such a figure in the literary world, it was then thought too great a favour to be asked.

Pope, without any knowledge of him but from his *London*, recommended him to Earl Gower, who endeavoured to procure for him a degree from Dublin.

It was, perhaps, no small disappointment to Johnson that this respectable application had not the desired effect; yet how much reason has there been, both for himself and his country, to rejoice that it did not succeed, as he might probably have wasted in obscurity those hours in which he afterwards produced his incomparable works.

About this time he made one other effort to emancipate himself from the drudgery of authourship. He applied to Dr. Adams, to consult Dr. Smalbroke of the Commons, whether a person might be permitted to practice as an advocate there, without a doctor's degree in Civil Law. 'I am (said he) a total stranger to these studies; but whatever is a profession, and maintains numbers, must be within the reach of common abilities, and some degree of industry.' Dr. Adams was much pleased with Johnson's design to employ his talents in that manner, being confident he would have attained to great eminence.

As Mr. Pope's note concerning Johnson, alluded to in a former page, refers both to his *London*, and his *Marmor Norfolciense*, I have deferred inserting it till now. I am indebted for it to Dr. Percy, the Bishop of Dromore, who permitted me to copy it from the original in his possession. It was presented to his Lordship by Sir Joshua Reynolds, to whom it was given by the son of Mr. Richardson the painter, the person to whom it is addressed. I have transcribed it with minute exactness, that the peculiar mode of writing, and imperfect spelling of that celebrated poet, may be exhibited to the curious in literature. It justifies Swift's epithet of 'Paper-sparing Pope,' for it is written on a slip no larger than a common message-card, and was sent to Mr. Richardson, along with the *Imitation of Juvenal*.

'This is imitated by one Johnson who put in for a Publick-school in

Shropshire, but was disappointed. He has an infirmity of the convulsive kind, that attacks him sometimes, so as to make him a sad Spectacle. Mr. P. from the Merit of this Work which was all the knowledge he had of him endeavour'd to serve him without his own application; & wrote to my Ld gore, but he did not succeed. Mr. Johnson published afterw^ds another Poem in Latin with Notes the whole very Humerous call'd the Norfolk Prophecy. P.'

Johnson had been told of this note; and Sir Joshua Reynolds informed him of the compliment which it contained, but, from delicacy, avoided shewing him the paper itself. When Sir Joshua observed to Johnson that he seemed very desirous to see Pope's note, he answered, 'Who would not be proud to have such a man as Pope so solicitous in inquiring about him?'

The infirmity to which Mr. Pope alludes, appeared to me also, as I have elsewhere observed, to be of the convulsive kind, and of the nature of that distemper called St. Vitus's dance; and in this opinion I am confirmed by the description which Sydenham gives of that disease. 'This disorder is a kind of convulsion. It manifests itself by halting or unsteadiness of one of the legs, which the patient draws after him like an ideot. If the hand of the same side be applied to the breast, or any other part of the body, he cannot keep it a moment in the same posture, but it will be drawn into a different one by a convulsion, notwithstanding all his efforts to the contrary.' Sir Joshua Reynolds, however, was of a different opinion, and favoured me with the following paper.

'Those motions or tricks of Dr. Johnson are improperly called convulsions. He could sit motionless, when he was told so to do, as well as any other man; my opinion is that it proceeded from a habit which he had indulged himself in, of accompanying his thoughts with certain untoward actions, and those actions always appeared to me as if they were meant to reprobate some part of his past conduct. Whenever he was not engaged in conversation, such thoughts were sure to rush into his mind; and, for this reason, any company, any employment whatever, he preferred to being alone. The great business of his life (he said) was to escape from himself; this disposition he considered as the disease of his mind, which nothing cured but company.

'One instance of his absence and particularity, as it is characteristick of the man, may be worth relating. When he and I took a journey together into the West, we visited the late Mr. Banks, of Dorsetshire; the conversation turning upon pictures, which Johnson could not well see, he retired to a corner of the room, stretching out his right leg as far as he could reach before him, then bringing up his left leg, and stretching his right still further on. The old gentleman observing him, went up to him, and in a very courteous manner assured him, that though it was not a new house, the flooring was perfectly safe. The Doctor started from his reverie, like a person waked out of his sleep, but spoke not a word.'

While we are on this subject, my readers may not be displeased with another anecdote, communicated to me by the same friend, from the relation of Mr. Hogarth.

Johnson used to be a pretty frequent visitor at the house of Mr. Richardson, authour of *Clarissa*, and other novels of extensive reputation. Mr. Hogarth came one day to see Richardson, soon after the execution of Dr. Cameron, for having taken arms for the house of Stuart in 1745-6; and being a warm partisan of George the Second, he observed to Richardson, that certainly there must have been some very unfavourable circumstances lately discovered in this particular case, which had induced the King to approve of an execution for rebellion so long after the time when it was committed, as this had the appearance of putting a man to death in cold blood, and was very unlike his Majesty's usual clemency. While he was talking, he perceived a person standing at a window in the room, shaking his head, and rolling himself about in a strange ridiculous manner. He concluded that he was an ideot, whom his relations had put under the care of Mr. Richardson, as a very good man. To his great surprise, however, this figure stalked forwards to where he and Mr. Richardson were sitting, and all at once took up the argument, and burst out into an invective against George the Second, as one, who, upon all occasions was unrelenting and barbarous; mentioning many instances, particularly, that when an officer of high rank had been acquitted by a Court Martial, George the Second had with his own hand, struck his name off the list. In short, he displayed such a power of eloquence, that Hogarth looked at him with astonishment, and actually imagined that this ideot had been at the moment inspired. Neither Hogarth nor Johnson were made known to each other at this interview.

1740: ÆTAT. 31.]—In 1740 he wrote for the *Gentleman's Magazine* the 'Preface,' 'Life of Sir Francis Drake,' and the first parts of those of 'Admiral Blake,' and of 'Philip Baretier,' both which he finished the following year. He also wrote an 'Essay on Epitaphs,' and an 'Epitaph on Philips, a Musician,' which was afterwards published with some other pieces of his, in Mrs. Williams's *Miscellanies*. This Epitaph is so exquisitely beautiful, that I remember even Lord Kames, strangely prejudiced as he was against Dr. Johnson, was compelled to allow it very high praise. It has been ascribed to Mr. Garrick, from its appearing at first with the signature G; but I have heard Mr. Garrick declare, that it was written by Dr. Johnson, and give the following account of the manner in which it was composed. Johnson and he were sitting together; when, amongst other things, Garrick repeated an Epitaph upon this Philips by a Dr. Wilkes, in these words:

'Exalted soul! whose harmony could please
The love-sick virgin, and the gouty ease;
Could jarring discord, like Amphion, move
To beauteous order and harmonious love;
Rest here in peace, till angels bid thee rise,
And meet thy blessed Saviour in the skies.'

Johnson shook his head at these common-place funereal lines, and said to Garrick, 'I think, Davy, I can make a better.' Then, stirring about his tea for a little while, in a state of meditation, he almost extempore produced the following verses:

'Philips, whose touch harmonious could remove
The pangs of guilty power or hapless love;
Rest here, distress'd by poverty no more,
Here find that calm thou gav'st so oft before;
Sleep, undisturb'd, within this peaceful shrine,
Till angels wake thee with a note like thine!'

1742: ÆTAT. 33.]—In 1742 he wrote . . . 'Proposals for Printing Bibliotheca Harleiana, or a Catalogue of the Library of the Earl of Oxford.' He was employed in this business by Mr. Thomas Osborne the bookseller, who purchased the library for 13,000*l.*, a sum which Mr. Oldys says, in one of his manuscripts, was not more than the binding of the books had cost; yet, as Dr. Johnson assured me, the slowness of the sale was such, that there was not much gained by it. It has been confidently related, with many embellishments, that Johnson one day knocked Osborne down in his shop, with a folio, and put his foot upon his neck. The simple truth I had from Johnson himself. 'Sir, he was impertinent to me, and I beat him. But it was not in his shop: it was in my own chamber.'

1744: ÆTAT. 35.]—He produced one work this year, fully sufficient to maintain the high reputation which he had acquired. This was *The Life of Richard Savage*; a man, of whom it is difficult to speak impartially, without wondering that he was for some time the intimate companion of Johnson; for his character was marked by profligacy, insolence, and ingratitude: yet, as he undoubtedly had a warm and vigorous, though unregulated mind, had seen life in all its varieties, and been much in the company of the statesmen and wits of his time, he could communicate to Johnson an abundant supply of such materials as his philosophical curiosity most eagerly desired; and as Savage's misfortunes and misconduct had reduced him to the lowest state of wretchedness as a writer for bread, his visits to St. John's Gate naturally brought Johnson and him together.

It is melancholy to reflect, that Johnson and Savage were sometimes in such extreme indigence,[4] that they could not pay for a lodging; so that they have wandered together whole nights in the streets. Yet in these almost incredible scenes of distress, we may suppose that Savage mentioned many of the anecdotes with which Johnson afterwards enriched the life of his unhappy companion, and those of other Poets.

He told Sir Joshua Reynolds, that one night in particular, when Savage and he walked round St. James's-square for want of a lodging, they were not at all depressed by their situation; but in high spirits and brimful of patriotism, traversed the square for several hours, inveighed against the minister, and 'resolved they would *stand by their country.*'

In Johnson's Life of Savage, although it must be allowed that its moral is the reverse of—'*Respicere exemplar vitae morumque jubebo,*' a very useful lesson is inculcated, to guard men of warm passions from a too free indulgence of them; and the various incidents are related in so clear and animated a manner, and illuminated throughout with so much philosophy, that it is one of the most interesting narratives in the English language. Sir Joshua Reynolds told me, that upon his return from Italy he met with it in Devonshire, knowing nothing of its authour, and began to read it while he was standing with his arm leaning against a chimney-piece. It seized his attention so strongly, that, not being able to lay down the book till he had finished it, when he attempted to move, he found his arm totally benumbed. The rapidity with which this work was composed, is a wonderful circumstance. Johnson has been heard to say, 'I wrote forty-eight of the printed octavo pages of the *Life of Savage* at a sitting; but then I sat up all night.'

It is remarkable, that in this biographical disquisition there appears a very strong symptom of Johnson's prejudice against players; a prejudice which may be attributed to the following causes: first, the imperfection of his organs, which were so defective that he was not susceptible of the fine impressions which theatrical excellence produces upon the generality of mankind; secondly, the cold rejection of his tragedy; and, lastly, the brilliant success of Garrick, who had been his pupil, who had come to London at the same time with him, not in a much more prosperous state than himself, and whose talents he undoubtedly rated low, compared with his own. His being outstripped by his pupil in the race of immediate fame, as well as of fortune,

---

[4] Soon after Savage's *Life* was published, Mr. Harte dined with Edward Cave, and occasionally praised it. Soon after, meeting him, Cave said, 'You made a man very happy t'other day.'—'How could that be.' says Harte; 'nobody was there but ourselves.' Cave answered, by reminding him that a plate of victuals was sent behind a screen, which was to Johnson, dressed so shabbily, that he did not choose to appear; but on hearing the conversation, was highly delighted with the encomiums on his book—MALONE.

probably made him feel some indignation, as thinking that whatever might be Garrick's merits in his art, the reward was too great when compared with what the most successful efforts of literary labour could attain. At all periods of his life Johnson used to talk contemptuously of players; but in this work he speaks of them with peculiar acrimony; for which, perhaps, there was formerly too much reason from the licentious and dissolute manners of those engaged in that profession. It is but justice to add, that in our own time such a change has taken place, that there is no longer room for such an unfavourable distinction.

His schoolfellow and friend, Dr. Taylor, told me a pleasant anecdote of Johnson's triumphing over his pupil David Garrick. When that great actor had played some little time at Goodman's fields, Johnson and Taylor went to see him perform, and afterwards passed the evening at a tavern with him and old Giffard. Johnson, who was ever depreciating stage-players, after censuring some mistakes in emphasis which Garrick had committed in the course of that night's acting, said, 'The players, Sir, have got a kind of rant, with which they run on, without any regard either to accent or emphasis.' Both Garrick and Giffard were offended at this sarcasm, and endeavoured to refute it; upon which Johnson rejoined, 'Well now, I'll give you something to speak, with which you are little acquainted, and then we shall see how just my observation is. That shall be the criterion. Let me hear you repeat the ninth Commandment, "Thou shalt not bear false witness against thy neighbour."' Both tried at it, said Dr. Taylor, and both mistook the emphasis, which should be upon *not* and *false witness*. Johnson put them right, and enjoyed his victory with great glee.

Johnson's partiality for Savage made him entertain no doubt of his story, however extraordinary and improbable. It never occurred to him to question his being the son of the Countess of Macclesfield, of whose unrelenting barbarity he so loudly complained, and the particulars of which are related in so strong and affecting a manner in Johnson's life of him. Johnson was certainly well warranted in publishing his narrative, however offensive it might be to the lady and her relations, because her alledged unnatural and cruel conduct to her son, and shameful avowal of guilt, were stated in a *Life of Savage* now lying before me, which came out so early as 1727, and no attempt had been made to confute it, or to punish the authour or printer as a libeller: but for the honour of human nature, we should be glad to find the shocking tale not true; and, from a respectable gentleman connected with the lady's family, I have received such information and remarks, as joined to my own inquiries, will, I think, render it at least somewhat doubtful, especially when we consider that it must have originated from the person himself who went by the name of Richard Savage.

1746: ÆTAT. 37.]—It is somewhat curious, that his literary career appears to have been almost totally suspended in the years 1745 and

1746, those years which were marked by a civil war in Great-Britain, when a rash attempt was made to restore the House of Stuart to the throne. That he had a tenderness for that unfortunate House, is well known; and some may fancifully imagine, that a sympathetick anxiety impeded the exertion of his intellectual powers: but I am inclined to think, that he was, during this time, sketching the outlines of his great philological work.

1747: ÆTAT. 38.]—This year his old pupil and friend, David Garrick, having become joint patentee and manager of Drury-lane theatre, Johnson honoured his opening of it with a Prologue, which for just and manly dramatick criticism, on the whole range of the English stage, as well as for poetical excellence, is unrivalled. Like the celebrated Epilogue to the *Distressed Mother*, it was, during the season, often called for by the audience.

But the year 1747 is distinguished as the epoch, when Johnson's arduous and important work, his DICTIONARY OF THE ENGLISH LANGUAGE, was announced to the world, by the publication of its Plan or *Prospectus*.

How long this immense undertaking had been the object of his contemplation, I do not know. I once asked him by what means he had attained to that astonishing knowledge of our language, by which he was enabled to realise a design of such extent, and accumulated difficulty. He told me, that 'it was not the effect of particular study; but that it had grown up in his mind insensibly.' I have been informed by Mr. James Dodsley, that several years before this period, when Johnson was one day sitting in his brother Robert's shop, he heard his brother suggest to him, that a Dictionary of the English Language would be a work that would be well received by the publick; that Johnson seemed at first to catch at the proposition, but, after a pause, said, in his abrupt decisive manner, 'I believe I shall not undertake it.' That he, however, had bestowed much thought upon the subject, before he published his *Plan*, is evident from the enlarged, clear, and accurate views which it exhibits; and we find him mentioning in that tract, that many of the writers whose testimonies were to be produced as authorities, were selected by Pope; which proves that he had been furnished, probably by Mr. Robert Dodsley, with whatever hints that eminent poet had contributed towards a great literary project, that had been the subject of important consideration in a former reign.

The booksellers who contracted with Johnson, single and unaided, for the execution of a work, which in other countries has not been effected but by the co-operating exertions of many, were Mr. Robert Dodsley, Mr. Charles Hitch, Mr. Andrew Millar, the two Messieurs Longman, and the two Messieurs Knapton. The price stipulated was fifteen hundred and seventy-five pounds.

The *Plan*, was addressed to Philip Dormer, Earl of Chesterfield, then one of his Majesty's Principal Secretaries of State; a nobleman who was very ambitious of literary distinction, and who, upon being informed of the design, had expressed himself in terms very favourable to its success. There is, perhaps in every thing of any consequence, a secret history which it would be amusing to know, could we have it authentically communicated. Johnson told me, 'Sir, the way in which the *Plan* of my *Dictionary* came to be inscribed to Lord Chesterfield, was this: I had neglected to write it by the time appointed. Dodsley suggested a desire to have it addressed to Lord Chesterfield. I laid hold of this as a pretext for delay, that it might be better done, and let Dodsley have his desire. I said to my friend, Dr. Bathurst, "Now if any good comes of my addressing to Lord Chesterfield, it will be ascribed to deep policy, when, in fact, it was only a casual excuse for laziness."'

Dr. Adams found him one day busy at his *Dictionary*, when the following dialogue ensued. 'ADAMS. This is a great work, Sir. How are you to get all the etymologies? JOHNSON. Why, Sir, here is a shelf with Junius, and Skinner, and others; and there is a Welch gentleman who has published a collection of Welch proverbs, who will help me with the Welch. ADAMS. But, Sir, how can you do this in three years? JOHNSON. Sir, I have no doubt that I can do it in three years. ADAMS. But the French Academy, which consists of forty members, took forty years to compile their Dictionary. JOHNSON. Sir, thus it is. This is the proportion. Let me see; forty times forty is sixteen hundred. As three to sixteen hundred, so is the proportion of an Englishman to a Frenchman.' With so much ease and pleasantry could he talk of that prodigious labour which he had undertaken to execute.

For the mechanical part he employed, as he told me, six amanuenses; and let it be remembered by the natives of North-Britain, to whom he is supposed to have been so hostile, that five of them were of that country. There were two Messieurs Macbean; Mr. Shiels, who we shall hereafter see partly wrote the *Lives of the Poets* to which the name of Cibber is affixed; Mr. Stewart, son of Mr. George Stewart, bookseller at Edinburgh; and a Mr. Maitland. The sixth of these humble assistants was Mr. Peyton, who, I believe, taught French, and published some elementary tracts.

To all these painful labourers, Johnson shewed a never-ceasing kindness, so far as they stood in need of it. The elder Mr. Macbean had afterwards the honour of being Librarian to Archibald, Duke of Argyle, for many years, but was left without a shilling. Johnson wrote for him a Preface to *A System of Ancient Geography*; and, by the favour of Lord Thurlow, got him admitted a poor brother of the Charterhouse. For Shiels, who died of a consumption, he had much tenderness; and it has been thought that some choice sentences in the *Lives of the Poets* were supplied by him. Peyton, when reduced to penury, had frequent aid from the bounty of Johnson, who at last was at the expense of burying both him and his wife.

While the *Dictionary* was going forward, Johnson lived part of the time in Holborn, part in Gough-square, Fleet-street; and he had an upper room fitted up like a counting-house for the purpose, in which he gave to the copyists their several tasks. The words, partly taken from other dictionaries, and partly supplied by himself, having been first written down with spaces left between them, he delivered in writing their etymologies, definitions, and various significations. The authorities were copied from the books themselves, in which he had marked the passages with a black-lead pencil, the traces of which could easily be effaced. I have seen several of them, in which that trouble had not been taken; so that they were just as when used by the copyists. It is remarkable, that he was so attentive in the choice of the passages in which words were authorised, that one may read page after page of his *Dictionary* with improvement and pleasure; and it should not pass unobserved, that he has quoted no authour whose writings had a tendency to hurt sound religion and morality.

The necessary expense of preparing a work of such magnitude for the press, must have been a considerable deduction from the price stipulated to be paid for the copy-right. I understand that nothing was allowed by the booksellers on that account; and I remember his telling me, that a large portion of it having by mistake been written upon both sides of the paper, so as to be inconvenient for the compositor, it cost him twenty pounds to have it transcribed upon one side only.

He is now to be considered as 'tugging at his oar,' as engaged in a steady continued course of occupation, sufficient to employ all his time for some years; and which was the best preventive of that constitutional melancholy which was ever lurking about him, ready to trouble his quiet. But his enlarged and lively mind could not be satisfied without more diversity of employment, and the pleasure of animated relaxation. He therefore not only exerted his talents in occasional composition very different from Lexicography, but formed a club in Ivy-lane, Paternoster-row, with a view to enjoy literary discussion, and amuse his evening hours. The members associated with him in this little society were his beloved friend Dr. Richard Bathurst, Mr. Hawkesworth, afterwards well known by his writings, Mr. John Hawkins, an attorney, and a few others of different professions.

1749: ÆTAT. 40.]—In January, 1749, he published *The Vanity of Human Wishes, being the Tenth Satire of Juvenal imitated.* He, I believe, composed it the preceding year. Mrs. Johnson, for the sake of country air, had lodgings at Hampstead, to which he resorted occasionally, and there the greatest part, if not the whole, of this *Imitation* was written. The fervid rapidity with which it was produced, is scarcely credible. I have heard him say, that he composed seventy lines of it in one day, without putting one of them upon paper till they were finished. I remember when I once regretted to him that he had not given us more of Juvenal's *Satires*, he said he probably should give more, for he had them all in his head; by which I understood that he had the originals and correspondent allusions floating in his mind, which he could, when he pleased, embody and render permanent without much labour. Some of them, however, he observed were too gross for imitation.

The profits of a single poem, however excellent, appear to have been very small in the last reign, compared with what a publication of the same size has since been known to yield. I have mentioned, upon Johnson's own authority, that for his London he had only ten guineas; and now, after his fame was established, he got for his *Vanity of Human* Wishes but five guineas more, as is proved by an authentick document in my possession.

His *Vanity of Human Wishes* has less of common life, but more of a philosophick dignity than his *London*. More readers, therefore, will be delighted with the pointed spirit of *London*, than with the profound reflection of *The Vanity of Human Wishes*. Garrick, for instance, observed in his sprightly manner, with more vivacity than regard to just discrimination, as is usual with wits: 'When Johnson lived much with the Herveys, and saw a good deal of what was passing in life, he wrote his *London*, which is lively and easy. When he became more retired, he gave us his *Vanity of Human Wishes*, which is as hard as Greek. Had he gone on to imitate another satire, it would have been as hard as Hebrew.'

Garrick being now vested with theatrical power by being manager of Drury-lane theatre, he kindly and generously made use of it to bring out Johnson's tragedy, which had been long kept back for want of encouragement. But in this benevolent purpose he met with no small difficulty from the temper of Johnson, which could not brook that a drama which he had formed with much study, and had been obliged to keep more than the nine years of Horace, should be revised and altered at the pleasure of an actor. Yet Garrick knew well, that without some alterations it would not be fit for the stage. A violent dispute having ensued between them, Garrick applied to the Reverend Dr. Taylor to interpose. Johnson was at first very obstinate. 'Sir, (said he) the fellow wants me to make Mahomet run mad, that he may have an opportunity of tossing his hands and kicking his heels.' He was, however, at last, with difficulty, prevailed on to comply with Garrick's wishes, so as to allow of some changes; but still there were not enough.

Dr. Adams was present the first night of the representation of *Irene*, and gave me the following account: 'Before the curtain drew up, there were catcalls whistling, which alarmed Johnson's friends. The Prologue, which was written by himself in a manly strain, soothed the audience, and the play went off tolerably, till it came to the conclusion, when Mrs. Pritchard, the heroine of the piece, was to be strangled upon the stage, and was to speak two lines with the bowstring round her neck. The audience cried out "*Murder! Murder!*" She several times attempted to speak; but in vain. At last she was obliged to go off the stage alive.' This passage was afterwards struck out, and she was carried off to be put to death behind the scenes, as the play now has it. The Epilogue, as Johnson informed me, was written by Sir William Yonge. I know not how his play came to be thus graced by the pen of a person then so eminent in the political world.

Notwithstanding all the support of such performers as Garrick, Barry, Mrs. Cibber, Mrs. Pritchard, and every advantage of dress and decoration, the tragedy of *Irene* did not please the publick. Mr. Garrick's zeal carried it through for nine nights, so that the authour had his three nights' profits; and from a receipt signed by him, now in the hands of Mr. James Dodsley, it appears that his friend Mr. Robert Dodsley gave him one hundred pounds for the copy, with his usual reservation of the right of one edition.

When asked how he felt upon the ill success of his tragedy, he replied, 'Like the Monument;' meaning that he continued firm and unmoved as that column. And let it be remembered, as an admonition to the *genus irritabile* of dramatick writers, that this great man, instead of peevishly complaining of the bad taste of the town, submitted to its decision without a murmur. He had, indeed, upon all occasions, a great deference for the general opinion: 'A man (said he) who writes a book, thinks himself wiser or wittier than the rest of mankind; he supposes that he can instruct or amuse them, and the publick to whom he appeals, must, after all, be the judges of his pretensions.'

On occasion of his play being brought upon the stage, Johnson had a fancy that as a dramatick authour his dress should be more gay than what he ordinarily wore; he therefore appeared behind the scenes, and even in one of the side boxes, in a scarlet waistcoat, with rich gold lace, and a gold-laced hat. He humourously observed to Mr. Langton, 'that when in that dress he could not treat people with the same ease as when in his usual plain clothes.' Dress indeed, we must allow, has more effect even upon strong minds than one should suppose, without having had the experience of it. His necessary attendance while his play was in rehearsal, and during its performance, brought him acquainted with many of the performers of both sexes, which produced a more favourable opinion of their profession than he had harshly expressed in his *Life of Savage*. With some of them he kept up an acquaintance as long as he and they lived, and was ever ready to shew them acts of kindness. He for a considerable time used to frequent the *Green Room*, and seemed to take delight in dissipating his gloom, by mixing in the sprightly chit-chat of the motley circle then to be found there. Mr. David Hume related to me from Mr. Garrick, that Johnson at last denied himself this amusement, from considerations of rigid virtue; saying, 'I'll come no more behind your scenes, David; for the silk stockings and white bosoms of your actresses excite my amorous propensities.'

1750: ÆTAT. 41.]—In 1750 he came forth in the character for which he was eminently qualified, a majestick teacher of moral and religious wisdom. The vehicle which he chose was that of a periodical paper, which he knew had been, upon former occasions, employed with great success. *The Tatler, Spectator*, and *Guardian*, were the last of the kind published in England, which had stood the test of a long trial; and such an interval had now elapsed since their publication, as made him justly think that, to many of his readers, this form of instruction would, in some degree, have the advantage of novelty. A few days before the first of his *Essays* came out, there started another competitor for fame in the same form, under the title of *The Tatler Revived*, which I believe was 'born but to die.' Johnson was, I think, not very happy in the choice of his title, *The Rambler*, which certainly is not suited to a series of grave and moral discourses; which the Italians have literally, but ludicrously translated by *Il Vagabondo*; and which has been lately assumed as the denomination of a vehicle of licentious tales, The *Rambler's Magazine*. He gave Sir Joshua Reynolds the following account of its getting this name: 'What *must* be done, Sir, *will* be done. When I was to begin publishing that paper, I was at a loss how to name it. I sat down at night upon my bedside, and resolved that I would not go to sleep till I had fixed its title. *The Rambler* seemed the best that occurred, and I took it.'

With what devout and conscientious sentiments this paper was undertaken, is evidenced by the following prayer, which he composed and offered up on the occasion: 'Almighty GOD, the giver of all good things, without whose help all labour is ineffectual, and without whose grace all wisdom is folly; grant, I beseech Thee, that in this undertaking thy Holy Spirit may not be with-held from me, but that I may promote thy glory, and the salvation of myself and others: grant this, O LORD, for the sake of thy son JESUS CHRIST. Amen.'

The first paper of *The Rambler* was published on Tuesday the 20th of March, 1750; and its authour was enabled to continue it, without interruption, every Tuesday and Friday, till Saturday the 17th of March, 1752, on which day it closed. This is a strong confirmation of the truth of a remark of his, which I have had occasion to quote elsewhere, that 'a man may write at any time, if he will set himself doggedly to it;' for, notwithstanding his constitutional indolence, his depression of spirits, and his labour in carrying on his *Dictionary*, he answered the stated calls of the press twice a week from the stores of his mind, during all that time.

Posterity will be astonished when they are told, upon the authority of Johnson himself, that many of these discourses, which we should suppose had been laboured with all the slow attention of literary leisure, were written in haste as the moment pressed, without even being read over by him before they were printed. It can be accounted for only in this way; that by reading and meditation, and a very close inspection of life, he had accumulated a great fund of miscellaneous knowledge, which, by a peculiar promptitude of mind, was ever ready at his call, and which he had constantly accustomed himself to clothe in the most apt and energetick expression. Sir Joshua Reynolds once asked him by what means he had attained his extraordinary accuracy and flow of language. He told him, that he had early laid it down as a fixed rule to do his best on every occasion, and in every company; to impart whatever he knew in the most forcible language he could put it in; and that by constant practice, and never suffering any careless expressions to escape him, or attempting to deliver his thoughts without arranging them in the clearest manner, it became habitual to him.

As *The Rambler* was entirely the work of one man, there was, of course, such a uniformity in its texture, as very much to exclude the charm of variety; and the grave and often solemn cast of thinking, which distinguished it from other periodical papers, made it, for some time, not generally liked. So slowly did this excellent work, of which twelve editions have now issued from the press, gain upon the world at large, that even in the closing number the authour says, 'I have never been much a favourite of the publick.'

Johnson told me, with an amiable fondness, a little pleasing circumstance relative to this work. Mrs. Johnson, in whose judgement and taste he had great confidence, said to him, after a few numbers of *The Rambler* had come out, 'I thought very well of you before; but I did not imagine you could have written any thing equal to this.' Distant praise, from whatever quarter, is not so delightful as that of a wife whom a man loves and esteems. Her approbation may be said to 'come home to his *bosom*;' and being so near, its effect is most sensible and permanent.

Mr. James Elphinston, who has since published various works, and who was ever esteemed by Johnson as a worthy man, happened to be in Scotland while *The Rambler* was coming out in single papers at London. With a laudable zeal at once for the improvement of his countrymen, and the reputation of his friend, he suggested and took the charge of an edition of those Essays at Edinburgh, which followed progressively the London publication.

This year he wrote to the same gentleman upon a mournful occasion.

'TO MR. JAMES ELPHINSTON.

September 25, 1750.

'DEAR SIR, You have, as I find by every kind of evidence, lost an excellent mother; and I hope you will not think me incapable of partaking of your grief. I have a mother, now eighty-two years of age, whom, therefore, I must soon lose, unless it please GOD that she rather should mourn for me. I read the letters in which you relate your mother's death to Mrs. Strahan, and think I do myself honour, when I tell you that I read them with tears; but tears are neither to *you* nor to *me* of any further use, when once the tribute of nature has been paid. The business of life summons us away from useless grief, and calls us to the exercise of those virtues of which we are lamenting our deprivation. The greatest benefit which one friend can confer upon another, is to guard, and excite, and elevate his virtues. This your mother will still perform, if you diligently preserve the memory of her life, and of her death: a life, so far as I can learn, useful, wise, and innocent; and a death resigned, peaceful, and holy. I cannot forbear to mention, that neither reason nor revelation denies you to hope, that you may increase her happiness by obeying her precepts; and that she may, in her present state, look with pleasure upon every act of virtue to which her instructions or example have contributed. Whether this be more than a pleasing dream, or a just opinion of separate spirits, is, indeed, of no great importance to us, when we consider ourselves as acting under the eye of GOD: yet, surely, there is something pleasing in the belief, that our separation from those whom we love is merely corporeal; and it may be a great incitement to virtuous friendship, if it can be made probable, that that union that has received the divine approbation shall continue to eternity.

'There is one expedient by which you may, in some degree, continue her presence. If you write down minutely what you remember of her from your earliest years, you will read it with great pleasure, and receive from it many hints of soothing recollection, when time shall remove her yet farther from you, and your grief shall be matured to veneration. To this, however painful for the present, I cannot but advise you, as to a source of comfort and satisfaction in the time to come; for all comfort and all satisfaction is sincerely wished you by, dear Sir, your most obliged, most obedient, and most humble servant,

'SAM. JOHNSON.'

The Rambler has increased in fame as in age. Soon after its first folio edition was concluded, it was published in six duodecimo volumes; and its authour lived to see ten numerous editions of it in London, beside those of Ireland and Scotland.

The style of Johnson was, undoubtedly, much formed upon that of the great writers in the last century, Hooker, Bacon, Sanderson, Hakewell, and others; those 'GIANTS,' as they were well characterised by A GREAT PERSONAGE, whose authority, were I to name him, would stamp a reverence on the opinion.

Johnson assured me, that he had not taken upon him to add more than four or five words to the English language, of his own formation; and he was very much offended at the general licence, by no means 'modestly taken' in his time not only to coin new words, but to use many words in senses quite different from their established meaning, and those frequently very fantastical.

Sir Thomas Brown, whose life Johnson wrote, was remarkably fond of Anglo-Latin diction; and to his example we are to ascribe Johnson's sometimes indulging himself in this kind of phraseology. Johnson's comprehension of mind was the mould for his language. Had his conceptions been narrower, his expression would have been easier. His sentences have a dignified march; and, it is certain, that his example has given a general elevation to the language of his country, for many of our best writers have approached very near to him; and, from the influence which he has had upon our composition, scarcely any thing is written now that is not better expressed than was usual before he appeared to lead the national taste.

Though *The Rambler* was not concluded till the year 1752, I shall, under this year, say all that I have to observe upon it. Some of the translations of the mottos by himself are admirably done. He acknowledges to have received 'elegant translations' of many of them from Mr. James Elphinston; and some are very happily translated by a Mr. *F. Lewis*, of whom I never heard more, except that Johnson thus described him to Mr. Malone: 'Sir, he lived in London, and hung loose upon society.'

His just abhorrence of Milton's political notions was ever strong. But this did not prevent his warm admiration of Milton's great poetical merit, to which he has done illustrious justice, beyond all who have written upon the subject. And this year he not only wrote a Prologue, which was spoken by Mr. Garrick before the acting of *Comus* at Drury-lane theatre, for the benefit of Milton's grand-daughter, but took a very zealous interest in the success of the charity.

1751: ÆTAT. 42.]—In 1751 we are to consider him as carrying on both his *Dictionary* and *Rambler*.

Though Johnson's circumstances were at this time far from being easy, his humane and charitable disposition was constantly exerting itself. Mrs. Anna Williams, daughter of a very ingenious Welsh physician, and a woman of more than ordinary talents and literature, having come to London in hopes of being cured of a cataract in both her eyes, which afterwards ended in total blindness, was kindly received as a constant visitor at his house while Mrs. Johnson lived; and after her death, having come under his roof in order to have an operation upon her eyes performed with more comfort to her than in lodgings, she had an apartment from him during the rest of her life, at all times when he had a house.

1752: ÆTAT. 43.]—In 1752 he was almost entirely occupied with his *Dictionary*. The last paper of his *Rambler* was published March 2, this year; after which, there was a cessation for some time of any exertion of his talents as an essayist. But, in the same year, Dr. Hawkesworth, who was his warm admirer, and a studious imitator of his style, and then lived in great intimacy with him, began a periodical paper, entitled *The Adventurer*, in connection with other gentlemen, one of whom was Johnson's much-beloved friend, Dr. Bathurst; and, without doubt, they received many valuable hints from his conversation, most of his friends having been so assisted in the course of their works.

That there should be a suspension of his literary labours during a part of the year 1752, will not seem strange, when it is considered that soon after closing his *Rambler*, he suffered a loss which, there can be no doubt, affected him with the deepest distress. For on the 17th of March, O.S., his wife died.

The following very solemn and affecting prayer was found after Dr. Johnson's decease, by his servant, Mr. Francis Barber, who delivered it to my worthy friend the Reverend Mr. Strahan, Vicar of Islington, who at my earnest request has obligingly favoured me with a copy of it, which he and I compared with the original:

'April 26, 1752, being after 12 at Night of the 25th.

'O Lord! Governour of heaven and earth, in whose hands are embodied and departed Spirits, if thou hast ordained the Souls of the Dead to minister to the Living, and appointed my departed Wife to have care of me, grant that I may enjoy the good effects of her attention and ministration, whether exercised by appearance, impulses, dreams or in any other manner agreeable to thy Government. Forgive my presumption, enlighten my ignorance, and however meaner agents are employed, grant me the blessed influences of thy holy Spirit, through Jesus Christ our Lord. Amen.'

That his love for his wife was of the most ardent kind, and, during the long period of fifty years, was unimpaired by the lapse of time, is evident from various passages in the series of his Prayers and Meditations, published by the Reverend Mr. Strahan, as well as from other memorials, two of which I select, as strongly marking the tenderness and sensibility of his mind.

'March 28, 1753. I kept this day as the anniversary of my Tetty's death, with prayer and tears in the morning. In the evening I prayed for her conditionally, if it were lawful.'

'April 23, 1753. I know not whether I do not too much indulge the vain longings of affection; but I hope they intenerate my heart, and that when I die like my Tetty, this affection will be acknowledged in a happy interview, and that in the mean time I am incited by it to piety. I will, however, not deviate too much from common and received methods of devotion.'

Her wedding ring, when she became his wife, was, after her death, preserved by him, as long as he lived, with an affectionate care, in a little round wooden box, in the inside of which he pasted a slip of paper, thus inscribed by him in fair characters, as follows:

'Eheu!
Eliz. Johnson
Nupta Jul. 9 1736,
Mortua, eheu!
Mart. 17 1752.'

After his death, Mr. Francis Barber, his faithful servant and residuary legatee, offered this memorial of tenderness to Mrs. Lucy Porter, Mrs. Johnson's daughter; but she having declined to accept of it, he had it enamelled as a mourning ring for his old master, and presented it to his wife, Mrs. Barber, who now has it.

I have, indeed, been told by Mrs. Desmoulins, who, before her marriage, lived for some time with Mrs. Johnson at Hampstead, that she indulged herself in country air and nice living, at an unsuitable expense, while her husband was drudging in the smoke of London, and that she by no means treated him with that complacency which is the most engaging quality in a wife. But all this is perfectly compatible with his fondness for her, especially when it is remembered that he had a high opinion of her understanding, and that the impressions which her beauty, real or imaginary, had originally made upon his fancy, being continued by habit, had not been effaced, though she herself was doubtless much altered for the worse. The dreadful shock of separation took place in the night; and he immediately dispatched a letter to his friend, the Reverend Dr. Taylor, which, as Taylor told me, expressed grief in the strongest manner he had ever read; so that it is much to be regretted it has not been preserved. The letter was brought to Dr. Taylor, at his house in the Cloisters, Westminster, about three in the morning; and as it signified an earnest desire to see him, he got up, and went to Johnson as soon as he was dressed, and found him in tears and in extreme agitation. After being a little while together, Johnson requested him to join with him in prayer. He then prayed extempore, as did Dr. Taylor; and thus, by means of that piety which was ever his primary object, his troubled mind was, in some degree, soothed and composed.

The next day he wrote as follows:

'TO THE REVEREND DR. TAYLOR.

'DEAR SIR,—Let me have your company and instruction. Do not live away from me. My distress is great.

'Pray desire Mrs. Taylor to inform me what mourning I should buy for my mother and Miss Porter, and bring a note in writing with you.

'Remember me in your prayers, for vain is the help of man. I am, dear Sir, &c.

'March 18, 1752.'

'SAM. JOHNSON.'

That his sufferings upon the death of his wife were severe, beyond what are commonly endured, I have no doubt, from the information of many who were then about him, to none of whom I give more credit than to Mr. Francis Barber, his faithful negro servant, who came into his family about a fortnight after the dismal event. These sufferings were aggravated by the melancholy inherent in his constitution; and although he probably was not oftener in the wrong than she was, in the little disagreements which sometimes troubled his married state, during which, he owned to me, that the gloomy irritability of his existence was more painful to him than ever, he might very naturally, after her death, be tenderly disposed to charge himself with slight omissions and offences, the sense of which would give him much uneasiness. Accordingly we find, about a year after her decease, that he thus addressed the Supreme Being: 'O LORD, who givest the grace of repentance, and hearest the prayers of the penitent, grant that by true contrition I may obtain forgiveness of all the sins committed, and of all duties neglected in my union with the wife whom thou hast taken from me; for the neglect of joint devotion, patient exhortation, and mild instruction.' The kindness of his heart, notwithstanding the impetuosity of his temper, is well known to his friends; and I cannot trace the smallest foundation for the following dark and uncharitable assertion by Sir John Hawkins: 'The apparition of his departed wife was altogether of the terrifick kind, and hardly afforded him a hope that she was in a state of happiness.' That he, in conformity with the opinion of many of the most able, learned, and pious Christians in all ages, supposed that there was a middle state after death, previous to the time at which departed souls are finally received to eternal felicity, appears, I think, unquestionably from his devotions: 'And, O LORD, so far as it may be lawful in me, I commend to thy fatherly goodness *the soul of my departed wife*; beseeching thee to *grant* her whatever is best in her *present state*, and *finally to receive her to eternal happiness.*' But this state has not been looked upon with horrour, but only as less gracious.

He deposited the remains of Mrs. Johnson in the church of Bromley, in Kent, to which he was probably led by the residence of his friend Hawkesworth at that place. The funeral sermon which he composed for her, which was never preached, but having been given to Dr. Taylor, has been published since his death, is a performance of uncommon excellence, and full of rational and pious comfort to such as are depressed by that severe affliction which Johnson felt when he wrote it. When it is considered that it was written in such an agitation of mind, and in the short interval between her death and burial, it cannot be read without wonder.

From Mr. Francis Barber I have had the following authentick and artless account of the situation in which he found him recently after his wife's death:

'He was in great affliction. Mrs. Williams was then living in his house, which was in Gough-square. He was busy with the Dictionary. Mr. Shiels, and some others of the gentlemen who had formerly written for him, used to come about him. He had then little for himself, but frequently sent money to Mr. Shiels when in distress. The friends who visited him at that time, were chiefly Dr. Bathurst, and Mr. Diamond, an apothecary in Cork-street, Burlington-gardens, with whom he and Mrs. Williams generally dined every Sunday. There was a talk of his going to Iceland with him, which would probably have happened had he lived. There were also Mr. Cave, Dr. Hawkesworth, Mr. Ryland, merchant on Tower Hill, Mrs. Masters, the poetess, who lived with Mr. Cave, Mrs. Carter, and sometimes Mrs. Macaulay, also Mrs. Gardiner, wife of a tallow-chandler on Snow-hill, not in the learned way, but a worthy good woman; Mr. (now Sir Joshua) Reynolds; Mr. Millar, Mr. Dodsley, Mr. Bouquet, Mr. Payne of Paternoster-row, booksellers; Mr. Strahan, the printer; the Earl of Orrery, Lord Southwell, Mr. Garrick.'

Many are, no doubt, omitted in this catalogue of his friends, and, in particular, his humble friend Mr. Robert Levet, an obscure practiser in physick amongst the lower people, his fees being sometimes very small sums, sometimes whatever provisions his patients could afford him; but of such extensive practice in that way, that Mrs. Williams has told me, his walk was from Hounsditch to Marybone. It appears from Johnson's diary that their acquaintance commenced about the year 1746; and such was Johnson's predilection for him, and fanciful estimation of his moderate abilities, that I have heard him say he should not be satisfied, though attended by all the College of Physicians, unless he had Mr. Levet with him. Ever since I was acquainted with Dr. Johnson, and many years before, as I have been assured by those who knew him earlier, Mr. Levet had an apartment in his house, or his chambers, and waited upon him every morning, through the whole course of his late and tedious breakfast. He was of a strange grotesque appearance, stiff and formal in his manner, and seldom said a word while any company was present.

The circle of his friends, indeed, at this time was extensive and various, far beyond what has been generally imagined. To trace his acquaintance with each particular person, if it could be done, would be a task, of which the labour would not be repaid by the advantage. But exceptions are to be made; one of which must be a friend so eminent as Sir Joshua Reynolds, who was truly his *dulce decus*, and with whom he maintained an uninterrupted intimacy to the last hour of his life. When Johnson lived in Castle-street, Cavendish-square, he used frequently to visit two ladies, who lived opposite to him, Miss Cotterells, daughters of Admiral Cotterell. Reynolds used also to visit there, and thus they met. Mr. Reynolds, as I have observed above, had, from the first reading of his *Life of Savage*, conceived a very high admiration of Johnson's powers of writing. His conversation no less delighted him; and he cultivated his acquaintance with the laudable zeal of one who was ambitious of general improvement. Sir Joshua, indeed, was lucky enough at their very first meeting to make a remark, which was so much above the common-place style of conversation, that Johnson at once perceived that Reynolds had the habit of thinking for himself. The ladies were regretting the death of a friend, to whom they owed great obligations; upon which Reynolds observed, 'You have, however, the comfort of being relieved from a burthen of gratitude.' They were shocked a little at this alleviating suggestion, as too selfish; but Johnson defended it in his clear and forcible manner, and was much pleased with the *mind*, the fair view of human nature, which it exhibited, like some of the reflections of Rochefaucault. The consequence was, that he went home with Reynolds, and supped with him.

Sir Joshua told me a pleasant characteristical anecdote of Johnson about the time of their first acquaintance. When they were one evening together at the Miss Cotterells', the then Duchess of Argyle and another lady of high rank came in. Johnson thinking that the Miss Cotterells were too much engrossed by them, and that he and his friend were neglected, as low company of whom they were somewhat ashamed, grew angry; and resolving to shock their supposed pride, by making their great visitors imagine that his friend and he were low indeed, he addressed himself in a loud tone to Mr. Reynolds, saying, 'How much do you think you and I could get in a week, if we were to *work as hard as we could*?'—as if they had been common mechanicks.

His acquaintance with Bennet Langton, Esq. of Langton, in Lincolnshire, another much valued friend, commenced soon after the conclusion of his *Rambler*; which that gentleman, then a youth, had read with so much admiration, that he came to London chiefly with the view of endeavouring to be introduced to its authour. By a fortunate chance he happened to take lodgings in a house where Mr. Levet frequently visited; and having mentioned his wish to his landlady, she introduced him to Mr. Levet, who readily obtained Johnson's permission to bring Mr. Langton to him; as, indeed, Johnson, during the whole course of his life, had no shyness, real or affected, but was easy of access to all who were properly recommended, and even wished to see numbers at his *levee*, as his morning circle of company might, with strict propriety, be called. Mr. Langton was exceedingly surprised when the sage first appeared. He had not received the smallest intimation of his figure, dress, or manner. From perusing his writings, he fancied he should see a decent, well-drest, in short, remarkably decorous philosopher. Instead of which, down from his bed-chamber, about noon, came, as newly risen, a huge uncouth figure, with a little dark wig which scarcely covered his head, and his clothes hanging loose about him. But his conversation was so rich, so animated, and so forcible, and his religious and political notions so congenial with those in which Langton had been educated, that he conceived for him that veneration and attachment which he ever preserved. Johnson was not the less ready to love Mr. Langton, for his being of a very ancient family; for I have heard him say, with pleasure, 'Langton, Sir, has a grant of free warren from Henry the Second; and Cardinal Stephen Langton, in King John's reign, was of this family.'

Mr. Langton afterwards went to pursue his studies at Trinity College, Oxford, where he formed an acquaintance with his fellow student, Mr. Topham Beauclerk; who, though their opinions and modes of life were so different, that it seemed utterly improbable that they should at all agree, had so ardent a love of literature, so acute an understanding, such elegance of manners, and so well discerned the excellent qualities of Mr. Langton, a gentleman eminent not only for worth and learning, but for an inexhaustible fund of entertaining conversation, that they became intimate friends.

Johnson, soon after this acquaintance began, passed a considerable time at Oxford. He at first thought it strange that Langton should associate so much with one who had the character of being loose, both in his principles and practice; but, by degrees, he himself was fascinated. Mr. Beauclerk's being of the St. Alban's family, and having, in some particulars, a resemblance to Charles the Second, contributed, in Johnson's imagination, to throw a lustre upon his other qualities; and, in a short time, the moral, pious Johnson, and the gay, dissipated Beauclerk, were companions. 'What a coalition! (said Garrick, when he heard of this;) I shall have my old friend to bail out of the Round-house.' But I can bear testimony that it was a very agreeable association. Beauclerk was too polite, and valued learning and wit too much, to offend Johnson by sallies of infidelity or licentiousness; and Johnson delighted in the good qualities of Beauclerk, and hoped to correct the evil. Innumerable were the scenes in which Johnson was amused by these young men. Beauclerk could take more liberty with him, than any body with whom I ever saw him; but, on the other hand, Beauclerk was not spared by his respectable companion, when reproof was proper. Beauclerk had such a propensity to satire, that at one time Johnson said to him, 'You never open your mouth but with intention to give pain; and you have often given me pain, not from the power of what you said, but from seeing your intention.' At another time applying to him, with a slight alteration, a line of Pope, he said,

'Thy love of folly, and thy scorn of fools—

Every thing thou dost shews the one, and every thing thou say'st the other.' At another time he said to him, 'Thy body is all vice, and thy mind all virtue.' Beauclerk not seeming to relish the compliment, Johnson said, 'Nay, Sir, Alexander the Great, marching in triumph into Babylon, could not have desired to have had more said to him.'

Johnson was some time with Beauclerk at his house at Windsor, where he was entertained with experiments in natural philosophy. One Sunday, when the weather was very fine, Beauclerk enticed him, insensibly, to saunter about all the morning. They went into a church-yard, in the time of divine service, and Johnson laid himself down at his ease upon one of the tomb-stones. 'Now, Sir, (said Beauclerk) you are like Hogarth's Idle Apprentice.' When Johnson got his pension, Beauclerk said to him, in the humorous phrase of Falstaff, 'I hope you'll now purge and live cleanly like a gentleman.'

One night when Beauclerk and Langton had supped at a tavern in London, and sat till about three in the morning, it came into their heads to go and knock up Johnson, and see if they could prevail on him to join them in a ramble. They rapped violently at the door of his chambers in the Temple, till at last he appeared in his shirt, with his little black wig on the top of his head, instead of a nightcap, and a poker in his hand, imagining, probably, that some ruffians were coming to attack him. When he discovered who they were, and was told their errand, he smiled, and with great good humour agreed to their proposal: 'What, is it you, you dogs! I'll have a frisk with you.' He was soon drest, and they sallied forth together into Covent-Garden, where the greengrocers and fruiterers were beginning to arrange their hampers, just come in from the country. Johnson made some attempts to help them; but the honest gardeners stared so at his figure and manner, and odd interference, that he soon saw his services were not relished. They then repaired to one of the neighbouring taverns, and made a bowl of that liquor called *Bishop*, which Johnson had always liked; while in joyous contempt of sleep, from which he had been roused, he repeated the festive lines,

'Short, O short then be thy reign,
And give us to the world again!'

They did not stay long, but walked down to the Thames, took a boat, and rowed to Billingsgate. Beauclerk and Johnson were so well pleased with their amusement, that they resolved to persevere in dissipation for the rest of the day: but Langton deserted them, being engaged to breakfast with some young Ladies. Johnson scolded him for 'leaving his social friends, to go and sit with a set of wretched *un-idea'd* girls.' Garrick being told of this ramble, said to him smartly, 'I heard of your frolick t'other night. You'll be in the Chronicle.' Upon which Johnson afterwards observed, '*He* durst not do such a thing. His *wife* would not *let* him!'

1753: ÆTAT. 44.]—He entered upon this year 1753 with his usual piety, as appears from the following prayer, which I transcribed from that part of his diary which he burnt a few days before his death:

'Jan. 1, 1753, N.S. which I shall use for the future.

'Almighty GOD, who hast continued my life to this day, grant that, by the assistance of thy Holy Spirit, I may improve the time which thou shalt grant me, to my eternal salvation. Make me to remember, to thy glory, thy judgements and thy mercies. Make me so to consider the loss of my wife, whom thou hast taken from me, that it may dispose me, by thy grace, to lead the residue of my life in thy fear. Grant this, O LORD, for JESUS CHRIST'S sake. Amen.'

He now relieved the drudgery of his *Dictionary*, and the melancholy of his grief, by taking an active part in the composition of *The Adventurer*, in which he began to write April 10.

In one of the books of his diary I find the following entry:

'Apr. 3, 1753. I began the second vol. of my Dictionary, room being left in the first for Preface, Grammar, and History, none of them yet begun.

'O GOD, who hast hitherto supported me, enable me to proceed in this labour, and in the whole task of my present state; that when I shall render up, at the last day, an account of the talent committed to me, I may receive pardon, for the sake of JESUS CHRIST. Amen.'

1754: ÆTAT. 45.]—The *Dictionary*, we may believe, afforded Johnson full occupation this year. As it approached to its conclusion, he probably worked with redoubled vigour, as seamen increase their exertion and alacrity when they have a near prospect of their haven.

Lord Chesterfield, to whom Johnson had paid the high compliment of addressing to his Lordship the *Plan* of his *Dictionary*, had behaved to him in such a manner as to excite his contempt and indignation. The world has been for many years amused with a story confidently told, and as confidently repeated with additional circumstances, that a sudden disgust was taken by Johnson upon occasion of his having been one day kept long in waiting in his Lordship's antechamber, for which the reason assigned was, that he had company with him; and that at last, when the door opened, out walked Colley Cibber; and that Johnson was so violently provoked when he found for whom he had been so long excluded, that he went away in a passion, and never would return. I remember having mentioned this story to George Lord Lyttelton, who told me, he was very intimate with Lord Chesterfield; and holding it as a well-known truth, defended Lord Chesterfield, by saying, that 'Cibber, who had been introduced familiarly by the back-stairs, had probably not been there above ten minutes.' It may seem strange even to entertain a doubt concerning a story so long and so widely current, and thus implicitly adopted, if not sanctioned, by the authority which I have mentioned; but Johnson himself assured me, that there was not the least foundation for it. He told me, that there never was any particular incident which produced a quarrel between Lord Chesterfield and him; but that his Lordship's continued neglect was the reason why he resolved to have no connection with him. When the *Dictionary* was upon the eve of publication, Lord Chesterfield, who, it is said, had flattered himself with expectations that Johnson would dedicate the work to him, attempted, in a courtly manner, to sooth, and insinuate himself with the Sage, conscious, as it should seem, of the cold indifference with which he had treated its learned authour; and further attempted to conciliate him, by writing two papers in *The World*, in recommendation of the work; and it must be confessed, that they contain some studied compliments, so finely turned, that if there had been no previous offence, it is probable that Johnson would have been highly delighted.[5] Praise, in general, was pleasing to him; but by praise from a man of rank and elegant accomplishments, he was peculiarly gratified.

This courtly device failed of its effect. Johnson, who thought that 'all was false and hollow,' despised the honeyed words, and was even indignant that Lord Chesterfield should, for a moment, imagine that he could be the dupe of such an artifice. His expression to me concerning Lord Chesterfield, upon this occasion, was, 'Sir, after making great professions, he had, for many years, taken no notice of me; but when my *Dictionary* was coming out, he fell a scribbling in *The World* about it. Upon which, I wrote him a letter expressed in civil terms, but such as might shew him that I did not mind what he said or wrote, and that I had done with him.'

This is that celebrated letter of which so much has been said, and about which curiosity has been so long excited, without being gratified.

---

[5] Boswell could not have read the second paper carefully. It is silly and indecent and was certain to offend Johnson.—Ed.

I for many years solicited Johnson to favour me with a copy of it, that so excellent a composition might not be lost to posterity. He delayed from time to time to give it me; till at last in 1781, when we were on a visit at Mr. Dilly's, at Southill in Bedfordshire, he was pleased to dictate it to me from memory. He afterwards found among his papers a copy of it, which he had dictated to Mr. Baretti, with its title and corrections, in his own handwriting. This he gave to Mr. Langton; adding that if it were to come into print, he wished it to be from that copy. By Mr. Langton's kindness, I am enabled to enrich my work with a perfect transcript of what the world has so eagerly desired to see.

'TO THE RIGHT HONOURABLE THE EARL OF CHESTERFIELD

'February 7, 1755.

'MY LORD, I have been lately informed, by the proprietor of *The World*, that two papers, in which my Dictionary is recommended to the publick, were written by your Lordship. To be so distinguished, is an honour, which, being very little accustomed to favours from the great, I know not well how to receive, or in what terms to acknowledge.

'When, upon some slight encouragement, I first visited your Lordship, I was overpowered, like the rest of mankind, by the enchantment of your address; and could not forbear to wish that I might boast myself *Le vainqueur du vainqueur de la terre*;—that I might obtain that regard for which I saw the world contending; but I found my attendance so little encouraged, that neither pride nor modesty would suffer me to continue it. When I had once addressed your Lordship in publick, I had exhausted all the art of pleasing which a retired and uncourtly scholar can possess. I had done all that I could; and no man is well pleased to have his all neglected, be it ever so little.

'Seven years, my Lord, have now past, since I waited in your outward rooms, or was repulsed from your door; during which time I have been pushing on my work through difficulties, of which it is useless to complain, and have brought it, at last, to the verge of publication, without one act of assistance, one word of encouragement, or one smile of favour. Such treatment I did not expect, for I never had a Patron before.

'The shepherd in Virgil grew at last acquainted with Love, and found him a native of the rocks.

'Is not a Patron, my Lord, one who looks with unconcern on a man struggling for life in the water, and, when he has reached ground, encumbers him with help? The notice which you have been pleased to take of my labours, had it been early, had been kind; but it has been delayed till I am indifferent, and cannot enjoy it; till I am solitary, and cannot impart it; till I am known, and do not want it. I hope it is no very cynical asperity not to confess obligations where no benefit has been received, or to be unwilling that the Publick should consider me as owing that to a Patron, which Providence has enabled me to do for myself.

'Having carried on my work thus far with so little obligation to any favourer of learning, I shall not be disappointed though I should conclude it, if less be possible, with less; for I have been long wakened from that dream of hope, in which I once boasted myself with so much exultation, my Lord, your Lordship's most humble, most obedient servant,

'SAM. JOHNSON.'

'While this was the talk of the town, (says Dr. Adams, in a letter to me) I happened to visit Dr. Warburton, who finding that I was acquainted with Johnson, desired me earnestly to carry his compliments to him, and to tell him that he honoured him for his manly behaviour in rejecting these condescensions of Lord Chesterfield, and for resenting the treatment he had received from him, with a proper spirit. Johnson was visibly pleased with this compliment, for he had always a high opinion of Warburton. Indeed, the force of mind which appeared in this letter, was congenial with that which Warburton himself amply possessed.'

There is a curious minute circumstance which struck me, in comparing the various editions of Johnson's imitations of Juvenal. In the tenth Satire, one of the couplets upon the vanity of wishes even for literary distinction stood thus:

> 'Yet think what ills the scholar's life assail,
> Pride, envy, want, the *garret*, and the jail.'

But after experiencing the uneasiness which Lord Chesterfield's fallacious patronage made him feel, he dismissed the word *garret* from the sad group, and in all the subsequent editions the line stands—

> 'Pride, envy, want, the *patron*, and the jail.'

That Lord Chesterfield must have been mortified by the lofty contempt, and polite, yet keen satire with which Johnson exhibited him to himself in this letter, it is impossible to doubt. He, however, with that glossy duplicity which was his constant study, affected to be quite unconcerned. Dr. Adams mentioned to Mr. Robert Dodsley that he was sorry Johnson had written his letter to Lord Chesterfield. Dodsley, with the true feelings of trade, said 'he was very sorry too; for that he had a property in the *Dictionary*, to which his Lordship's patronage might have been of consequence.' He then told Dr. Adams, that Lord Chesterfield had shewn him the letter. 'I should have imagined (replied

Dr. Adams) that Lord Chesterfield would have concealed it.' 'Poh! (said Dodsley) do you think a letter from Johnson could hurt Lord Chesterfield? Not at all, Sir. It lay upon his table; where any body might see it. He read it to me; said, "this man has great powers," pointed out the severest passages, and observed how well they were expressed.' This air of indifference, which imposed upon the worthy Dodsley, was certainly nothing but a specimen of that dissimulation which Lord Chesterfield inculcated as one of the most essential lessons for the conduct of life. His Lordship endeavoured to justify himself to Dodsley from the charges brought against him by Johnson; but we may judge of the flimsiness of his defence, from his having excused his neglect of Johnson, by saying that 'he had heard he had changed his lodgings, and did not know where he lived;' as if there could have been the smallest difficulty to inform himself of that circumstance, by inquiring in the literary circle with which his Lordship was well acquainted, and was, indeed, himself one of its ornaments.

Dr. Adams expostulated with Johnson, and suggested, that his not being admitted when he called on him, was, probably, not to be imputed to Lord Chesterfield; for his Lordship had declared to Dodsley, that 'he would have turned off the best servant he ever had, if he had known that he denied him to a man who would have been always more than welcome;' and, in confirmation of this, he insisted on Lord Chesterfield's general affability and easiness of access, especially to literary men. 'Sir (said Johnson) that is not Lord Chesterfield; he is the proudest man this day existing.' 'No, (said Dr. Adams) there is one person, at least, as proud; I think, by your own account, you are the prouder man of the two.' 'But mine (replied Johnson, instantly) was *defensive* pride.' This, as Dr. Adams well observed, was one of those happy turns for which he was so remarkably ready.

Johnson having now explicitly avowed his opinion of Lord Chesterfield, did not refrain from expressing himself concerning that nobleman with pointed freedom: 'This man (said he) I thought had been a Lord among wits; but, I find, he is only a wit among Lords!' And when his *Letters* to his natural son were published, he observed, that 'they teach the morals of a whore, and the manners of a dancing master.'

On the 6th of March came out Lord Bolingbroke's works, published by Mr. David Mallet. The wild and pernicious ravings, under the name of *Philosophy*, which were thus ushered into the world, gave great offence to all well-principled men. Johnson, hearing of their tendency, which nobody disputed, was roused with a just indignation, and pronounced this memorable sentence upon the noble authour and his editor. 'Sir, he was a scoundrel, and a coward: a scoundrel, for charging a blunderbuss against religion and morality; a coward, because he had not resolution to fire it off himself, but left half a crown to a beggarly Scotchman, to draw the trigger after his death!'

Johnson this year found an interval of leisure to make an excursion to Oxford, for the purpose of consulting the libraries there.

Of his conversation while at Oxford at this time, Mr. Warton preserved and communicated to me the following memorial, which, though not written with all the care and attention which that learned and elegant writer bestowed on those compositions which he intended for the publick eye, is so happily expressed in an easy style, that I should injure it by any alteration:

'When Johnson came to Oxford in 1754, the long vacation was beginning, and most people were leaving the place. This was the first time of his being there, after quitting the University. The next morning after his arrival, he wished to see his old College, *Pembroke*. I went with him. He was highly pleased to find all the College-servants which he had left there still remaining, particularly a very old butler; and expressed great satisfaction at being recognised by them, and conversed with them familiarly. He waited on the master, Dr. Radcliffe, who received him very coldly. Johnson at least expected, that the master would order a copy of his Dictionary, now near publication: but the master did not choose to talk on the subject, never asked Johnson to dine, nor even to visit him, while he stayed at Oxford. After we had left the lodgings, Johnson said to me, "*There* lives a man, who lives by the revenues of literature, and will not move a finger to support it. If I come to live at Oxford, I shall take up my abode at Trinity." We then called on the Reverend Mr. Meeke, one of the fellows, and of Johnson's standing. Here was a most cordial greeting on both sides. On leaving him, Johnson said, "I used to think Meeke had excellent parts, when we were boys together at the College: but, alas!

'Lost in a convent's solitary gloom!'

I remember, at the classical lecture in the Hall, I could not bear Meeke's superiority, and I tried to sit as far from him as I could, that I might not hear him construe."

'As we were leaving the College, he said, "Here I translated Pope's Messiah. Which do you think is the best line in it?—My own favourite is,

'Vallis aromaticas fundit Saronica nubes.'"

I told him, I thought it a very sonorous hexameter. I did not tell him, it was not in the Virgilian style. He much regretted that his *first* tutor was dead; for whom he seemed to retain the greatest regard. He said, "I once had been a whole morning sliding in Christ-Church Meadow, and missed his lecture in logick. After dinner, he sent for me to his room. I expected a sharp rebuke for my idleness, and went with a beating heart. When we were seated, he told me he had sent for me to drink a glass of wine with him, and to tell me, he was *not* angry with me for missing his lecture. This was, in fact, a most severe reprimand. Some more of the boys were then sent for, and we spent a very pleasant afternoon." Besides Mr. Meeke, there was only one other Fellow of Pembroke now resident: from both of whom Johnson received the greatest civilities during this visit, and they pressed him very much to have a room in the College.

'In the course of this visit (1754), Johnson and I walked, three or four times, to Ellsfield, a village beautifully situated about three miles from Oxford, to see Mr. Wise, Radclivian librarian, with whom Johnson was much pleased. At this place, Mr. Wise had fitted up a house and gardens, in a singular manner, but with great taste. Here was an excellent library; particularly, a valuable collection of books in Northern literature, with which Johnson was often very busy. One day Mr. Wise read to us a dissertation which he was preparing for the press, intitled, "A History and Chronology of the fabulous Ages." Some old divinities of Thrace, related to the Titans, and called the CABIRI, made a very important part of the theory of this piece; and in conversation afterwards, Mr. Wise talked much of his CABIRI. As we returned to Oxford in the evening, I out-walked Johnson, and he cried out *Sufflamina*, a Latin word which came from his mouth with peculiar grace, and was as much as to say, *Put on your drag chain*. Before we got home, I again walked too fast for him; and he now cried out, "Why, you walk as if you were pursued by all the CABIRI in a body." In an evening, we frequently took long walks from Oxford into the country, returning to supper. Once, in our way home, we viewed the ruins of the abbies of Oseney and Rewley, near Oxford. After at least half an hour's silence, Johnson said, "I viewed them with indignation!" We had then a long conversation on Gothick buildings; and in talking of the form of old halls, he said, "In these halls, the fire place was anciently always in the middle of the room, till the Whigs removed it on one side."—About this time there had been an execution of two or three criminals at Oxford on a Monday. Soon afterwards, one day at dinner, I was saying that Mr. Swinton the chaplain of the gaol, and also a frequent preacher before the University, a learned man, but often thoughtless and absent, preached the condemnation-sermon on repentance, before the convicts, on the preceding day, Sunday; and that in the close he told his audience, that he should give them the remainder of what he had to say on the subject, the next Lord's Day. Upon which, one of our company, a Doctor of Divinity, and a plain matter-of-fact man, by way of offering an apology for Mr. Swinton, gravely remarked, that he had probably preached the same sermon before the University: "Yes, Sir, (says Johnson) but the University were not to be hanged the next morning."

'I forgot to observe before, that when he left Mr. Meeke, (as I have told above) he added, "About the same time of life, Meeke was left behind at Oxford to feed on a Fellowship, and I went to London to get my living: now, Sir, see the difference of our literary characters!"'

The degree of Master of Arts, which, it has been observed, could not be obtained for him at an early period of his life, was now considered as an honour of considerable importance, in order to grace the title-page of his *Dictionary*; and his character in the literary world being by this time deservedly high, his friends thought that, if proper exertions were made, the University of Oxford would pay him the compliment.

TO THE REVEREND THOMAS WARTON.

'DEAR SIR,—I am extremely sensible of the favour done me, both by Mr. Wise and yourself. The book[6] cannot, I think, be printed in less than six weeks, nor probably so soon; and I will keep back the title-page, for such an insertion as you seem to promise me. . . .

'I had lately the favour of a letter from your brother, with some account of poor Collins, for whom I am much concerned. I have a notion, that by very great temperance, or more properly abstinence, he may yet recover. . . .

'You know poor Mr. Dodsley has lost his wife; I believe he is much affected. I hope he will not suffer so much as I yet suffer for the loss of mine.

Ο'ίμοι. Τί δ' ο'ίμοι; Θνήτα γάρ πεπόνθαμεν.

I have ever since seemed to myself broken off from mankind; a kind of solitary wanderer in the wild of life, without any direction, or fixed point of view: a gloomy gazer on a world to which I have little relation. Yet I would endeavour, by the help of you and your brother, to supply the want of closer union, by friendship: and hope to have long the pleasure of being, dear Sir, most affectionately your's,
'[London.] Dec. 21, 1754.'
'SAM. JOHNSON.'

1755: ÆTAT. 46.]—In 1755 we behold him to great advantage; his degree of Master of Arts conferred upon him, his *Dictionary* published, his correspondence animated, his benevolence exercised.

Mr. Charles Burney, who has since distinguished himself so much in the science of Musick, and obtained a Doctor's degree from the University of Oxford, had been driven from the capital by bad health,

---

[6] 'His Dictionary'—WARTON.

and was now residing at Lynne Regis, in Norfolk. He had been so much delighted with Johnson's *Rambler* and the *Plan* of his *Dictionary*, that when the great work was announced in the news-papers as nearly finished,' he wrote to Dr. Johnson, begging to be informed when and in what manner his *Dictionary* would be published; intreating, if it should be by subscription, or he should have any books at his own disposal, to be favoured with six copies for himself and friends.

In answer to this application, Dr. Johnson wrote the following letter, of which (to use Dr. Burney's own words) 'if it be remembered that it was written to an obscure young man, who at this time had not much distinguished himself even in his own profession, but whose name could never have reached the authour of *The Rambler*, the politeness and urbanity may be opposed to some of the stories which have been lately circulated of Dr. Johnson's natural rudeness and ferocity.'

'TO MR. BURNEY, IN LYNNE REGIS, NORFOLK.

'SIR,—If you imagine that by delaying my answer I intended to shew any neglect of the notice with which you have favoured me, you will neither think justly of yourself nor of me. Your civilities were offered with too much elegance not to engage attention; and I have too much pleasure in pleasing men like you, not to feel very sensibly the distinction which you have bestowed upon me.

'Few consequences of my endeavours to please or to benefit mankind have delighted me more than your friendship thus voluntarily offered, which now I have it I hope to keep, because I hope to continue to deserve it.

'I have no *Dictionaries* to dispose of for myself, but shall be glad to have you direct your friends to Mr. Dodsley, because it was by his recommendation that I was employed in the work.

'When you have leisure to think again upon me, let me be favoured with another letter; and another yet, when you have looked into my *Dictionary*. If you find faults, I shall endeavour to mend them; if you find none, I shall think you blinded by kind partiality: but to have made you partial in his favour, will very much gratify the ambition of, Sir, your most obliged and most humble servant,

'SAM. JOHNSON.'

'Gough-square, Fleet-street, April 8,1755.'

The *Dictionary*, with a *Grammar and History of the English Language*, being now at length published, in two volumes folio, the world contemplated with wonder so stupendous a work achieved by one man, while other countries had thought such undertakings fit only for whole academies. Vast as his powers were, I cannot but think that his imagination deceived him, when he supposed that by constant application he might have performed the task in three years.

The extensive reading which was absolutely necessary for the accumulation of authorities, and which alone may account for Johnson's retentive mind being enriched with a very large and various store of knowledge and imagery, must have occupied several years. The Preface furnishes an eminent instance of a double talent, of which Johnson was fully conscious. Sir Joshua Reynolds heard him say, 'There are two things which I am confident I can do very well: one is an introduction to any literary work, stating what it is to contain, and how it should be executed in the most perfect manner; the other is a conclusion, shewing from various causes why the execution has not been equal to what the authour promised to himself and to the publick.'

A few of his definitions must be admitted to be erroneous. Thus, *Windward* and *Leeward*, though directly of opposite meaning, are defined identically the same way; as to which inconsiderable specks it is enough to observe, that his Preface announces that he was aware there might be many such in so immense a work; nor was he at all disconcerted when an instance was pointed out to him. A lady once asked him how he came to define *Pastern* the *knee* of a horse: instead of making an elaborate defence, as she expected, he at once answered, 'Ignorance, madam, pure ignorance.' His definition of *Network*[7] has been often quoted with sportive malignity, as obscuring a thing in itself very plain. But to these frivolous censures no other answer is necessary than that with which we are furnished by his own Preface.

His introducing his own opinions, and even prejudices, under general definitions of words, while at the same time the original meaning of the words is not explained, as his *Tory, Whig, Pension, Oats, Excise,*[8] and a few more, cannot be fully defended, and must be placed to the account of capricious and humorous indulgence. Talking to me upon this subject when we were at Ashbourne in 1777, he mentioned a still stronger instance of the predominance of his private feelings in the composition of this work, than any now to be found in it. 'You know, Sir, Lord Gower forsook the old Jacobite interest. When I came to the word *Renegado*, after telling that it meant "one who deserts to the enemy, a revolter," I added, *Sometimes we say a* GOWER. Thus it went to the press; but the printer had more wit than I, and struck it out.'

---

[7] Any thing reticulated or decussated, at equal distances, with interstices between the intersections.'—Ed.

[8] Tory. 'One who adheres to the ancient constitution or the state and the apostolical hierarchy of the church or England, opposed to a whig.' Whig. 'The name of a faction.' Pension. 'An allowance made to any one without an equivalent. In England it is generally understood to mean pay given to a state hireling for treason to his country.' Oats. 'A grain which in England is generally given to horses, but in Scotland supports the people.' Excise. 'A hateful tax levied upon commodities, and adjudged not by the common judges of property, but wretches hired by those to whom excise is paid.'—Ed.

Let it, however, be remembered, that this indulgence does not display itself only in sarcasm towards others, but sometimes in playful allusion to the notions commonly entertained of his own laborious task. Thus: 'Grub-street, the name of a street in London, much inhabited by writers of small histories, dictionaries, and temporary poems; whence any mean production is called *Grub-street.*'—'*Lexicographer*, a writer of *dictionaries, a harmless drudge.*'

It must undoubtedly seem strange, that the conclusion of his Preface should be expressed in terms so desponding, when it is considered that the authour was then only in his forty-sixth year. But we must ascribe its gloom to that miserable dejection of spirits to which he was constitutionally subject, and which was aggravated by the death of his wife two years before. I have heard it ingeniously observed by a lady of rank and elegance, that 'his melancholy was then at its meridian.' It pleased GOD to grant him almost thirty years of life after this time; and once, when he was in a placid frame of mind, he was obliged to own to me that he had enjoyed happier days, and had many more friends, since that gloomy hour than before.

It is a sad saying, that 'most of those whom he wished to please had sunk into the grave;' and his case at forty-five was singularly unhappy, unless the circle of his friends was very narrow. He said to Sir Joshua Reynolds, 'If a man does not make new acquaintance as he advances through life, he will soon find himself left alone. A man, Sir, should keep his friendship *in constant repair.*'

In July this year he had formed some scheme of mental improvement, the particular purpose of which does not appear. But we find in his *Prayers and Meditations*, p. 25, a prayer entitled 'On the Study of Philosophy, as an Instrument of living;' and after it follows a note, 'This study was not pursued.'

On the 13th of the same month he wrote in his *Journal* the following scheme of life, for Sunday:

'Having lived' (as he with tenderness of conscience expresses himself) 'not without an habitual reverence for the Sabbath, yet without that attention to its religious duties which Christianity requires;

'1. To rise early, and in order to it, to go to sleep early on Saturday.

'2. To use some extraordinary devotion in the morning.

'3. To examine the tenour of my life, and particularly the last week; and to mark my advances in religion, or recession from it.

'4. To read the Scripture methodically with such helps as are at hand.

'5. To go to church twice.

'6. To read books of Divinity, either speculative or practical.

'7. To instruct my family.

'8. To wear off by meditation any worldly soil contracted in the week.'

1756: ÆTAT. 47.]—In 1756 Johnson found that the great fame of his *Dictionary* had not set him above the necessity of 'making provision for the day that was passing over him.' No royal or noble patron extended a munificent hand to give independence to the man who had conferred stability on the language of his country. We may feel indignant that there should have been such unworthy neglect; but we must, at the same time, congratulate ourselves, when we consider that to this very neglect, operating to rouse the natural indolence of his constitution, we owe many valuable productions, which otherwise, perhaps, might never have appeared.

He had spent, during the progress of the work, the money for which he had contracted to write his *Dictionary*. We have seen that the reward of his labour was only fifteen hundred and seventy-five pounds; and when the expence of amanuenses and paper, and other articles are deducted, his clear profit was very inconsiderable. I once said to him, 'I am sorry, Sir, you did not get more for your *Dictionary*.' His answer was, 'I am sorry, too. But it was very well. The booksellers are generous, liberal-minded men.' He, upon all occasions, did ample justice to their character in this respect. He considered them as the patrons of literature; and, indeed, although they have eventually been considerable gainers by his *Dictionary*, it is to them that we owe its having been undertaken and carried through at the risk of great expence, for they were not absolutely sure of being indemnified.

He this year resumed his scheme of giving an edition of *Shakspeare* with notes.[9] He issued Proposals of considerable length, in which he shewed that he perfectly well knew what a variety of research such an undertaking required; but his indolence prevented him from pursuing it with that diligence which alone can collect those scattered facts that genius, however acute, penetrating, and luminous, cannot discover by its own force. It is remarkable, that at this time his fancied activity was for the moment so vigorous, that he promised his work should be published before Christmas, 1757. Yet nine years elapsed before it saw the light. His throes in bringing it forth had been severe and remittent; and at last we may almost conclude that the Caesarian operation was performed by the knife of Churchill, whose upbraiding satire, I dare say, made Johnson's friends urge him to dispatch.

> 'He for subscribers bates his hook,
> And takes your cash; but where's the book?
> No matter where; wise fear, you know,
> Forbids the robbing of a foe;
> But what, to serve our private ends,
> Forbids the cheating of our friends?'

[9] First proposed in 1745—Ed.

About this period he was offered a living of considerable value in Lincolnshire, if he were inclined to enter into holy orders. It was a rectory in the gift of Mr. Langton, the father of his much valued friend. But he did not accept of it; partly I believe from a conscientious motive, being persuaded that his temper and habits rendered him unfit for that assiduous and familiar instruction of the vulgar and ignorant which he held to be an essential duty in a clergyman; and partly because his love of a London life was so strong, that he would have thought himself an exile in any other place, particularly if residing in the country. Whoever would wish to see his thoughts upon that subject displayed in their full force, may peruse *The Adventurer*, Number 126.

1757: ÆTAT. 48.]—MR. BURNEY having enclosed to him an extract from the review of his *Dictionary* in the *Bibliothèque des Savans*, and a list of subscribers to his Shakspeare, which Mr. Burney had procured in Norfolk, he wrote the following answer:

'TO MR. BURNEY, IN LYNNE, NORFOLK.

'SIR,—That I may shew myself sensible of your favours, and not commit the same fault a second time, I make haste to answer the letter which I received this morning. The truth is, the other likewise was received, and I wrote an answer; but being desirous to transmit you some proposals and receipts, I waited till I could find a convenient conveyance, and day was passed after day, till other things drove it from my thoughts; yet not so, but that I remember with great pleasure your commendation of my Dictionary. Your praise was welcome, not only because I believe it was sincere, but because praise has been very scarce. A man of your candour will be surprised when I tell you, that among all my acquaintance there were only two, who upon the publication of my book did not endeavour to depress me with threats of censure from the publick, or with objections learned from those who had learned them from my own Preface. Your's is the only letter of goodwill that I have received; though, indeed, I am promised something of that sort from Sweden.

'How my new edition will be received I know not; the subscription has not been very successful. I shall publish about March.

'If you can direct me how to send proposals, I should wish that they were in such hands.

'I remember, Sir, in some of the first letters with which you favoured me, you mentioned your lady. May I enquire after her? In return for the favours which you have shewn me, it is not much to tell you, that I wish you and her all that can conduce to your happiness. I am, Sir, your most obliged, and most humble servant,

SAM. JOHNSON.'

'Gough-square, Dec. 24, 1757.'

In 1758 we find him, it should seem, in as easy and pleasant a state of existence, as constitutional unhappiness ever permitted him to enjoy.

'TO BENNET LANGTON, ESQ., AT LANGTON, LINCOLNSHIRE.

'DEAREST SIR,—I must indeed have slept very fast, not to have been awakened by your letter. None of your suspicions are true; I am not much richer than when you left me; and, what is worse, my omission of an answer to your first letter, will prove that I am not much wiser. But I go on as I formerly did, designing to be some time or other both rich and wise; and yet cultivate neither mind nor fortune. Do you take notice of my example, and learn the danger of delay. When I was as you are now, towering in the confidence of twenty-one, little did I suspect that I should be at forty-nine, what I now am.

'But you do not seem to need my admonition. You are busy in acquiring and in communicating knowledge, and while you are studying, enjoy the end of study, by making others wiser and happier. I was much pleased with the tale that you told me of being tutour to your sisters. I, who have no sisters nor brothers, look with some degree of innocent envy on those who may be said to be born to friends; and cannot see, without wonder, how rarely that native union is afterwards regarded. It sometimes, indeed, happens, that some supervenient cause of discord may overpower this original amity; but it seems to me more frequently thrown away with levity, or lost by negligence, than destroyed by injury or violence. We tell the ladies that good wives make good husbands; I believe it is a more certain position that good brothers make good sisters.

'I am satisfied with your stay at home, as Juvenal with his friend's retirement to Cumae: I know that your absence is best, though it be not best for me.

> '*Quamvis digressu veteris confusus amici,*
> *Laudo tamen vacuis quod sedem figere Cumis*
> *Destinet, atque unum civem donare Sibylloe.*'

'*Langton* is a good Cumae, but who must be Sibylla? Mrs. Langton is as wise as Sibyl, and as good; and will live, if my wishes can prolong life, till she shall in time be as old. But she differs in this, that she has not scattered her precepts in the wind, at least not those which she bestowed upon you.

'The two Wartons just looked into the town, and were taken to see

Cleone, where, David[10] says, they were starved for want of company to
keep them warm. David and Doddy[11] have had a new quarrel, and, I
think, cannot conveniently quarrel any more. *Cleone* was well acted by
all the characters, but Bellamy left nothing to be desired. I went the first
night, and supported it, as well as I might; for Doddy, you know, is my
patron, and I would not desert him. The play was very well received.
Doddy, after the danger was over, went every night to the stage-side,
and cried at the distress of poor Cleone.

'I have left off housekeeping, and therefore made presents of the
game which you were pleased to send me. The pheasant I gave to Mr.
Richardson,[12] the bustard to Dr. Lawrence, and the pot I placed with
Miss Williams, to be eaten by myself. She desires that her compliments
and good wishes may be accepted by the family; and I make the same
request for myself.

'Mr. Reynolds has within these few days raised his price to twenty
guineas a head, and Miss is much employed in miniatures. I know not
any body [else] whose prosperity has increased since you left them.

'Murphy is to have his *Orphan of China* acted next month; and is
therefore, I suppose, happy. I wish I could tell you of any great good to
which I was approaching, but at present my prospects do not much
delight me; however, I am always pleased when I find that you, dear
Sir, remember, your affectionate, humble servant,

SAM. JOHNSON.'

'Jan. 9, 1758.'

Dr. Burney has kindly favoured me with the following
memorandum, which I take the liberty to insert in his own genuine easy
style. I love to exhibit sketches of my illustrious friend by various
eminent hands.

'Soon after this, Mr. Burney, during a visit to the capital, had an
interview with him in Gough-square, where he dined and drank tea
with him, and was introduced to the acquaintance of Mrs. Williams.
After dinner, Mr. Johnson proposed to Mr. Burney to go up with him
into his garret, which being accepted, he there found about five or six
Greek folios, a deal writing-desk, and a chair and a half. Johnson giving
to his guest the entire seat, tottered himself on one with only three legs
and one arm. Here he gave Mr. Burney Mrs. Williams's history, and
shewed him some volumes of his *Shakspeare* already printed, to prove
that he was in earnest. Upon Mr. Burney's opening the first volume, at
the *Merchant of Venice*, he observed to him, that he seemed to be more
severe on Warburton than Theobald. "O poor Tib.! (said Johnson) he

---

[10] Mr. Garrick—BOSWELL.
[11] Mr. Dodsley, the Authour of Cleone.—BOSWELL.
[12] Mr. Samuel Richardson, authour of Clarissa.—BOSWELL.

was ready knocked down to my hands; Warburton stands between me and him." "But, Sir, (said Mr. Burney,) you'll have Warburton upon your bones, won't you?" "No, Sir; he'll not come out: he'll only growl in his den." "But you think, Sir, that Warburton is a superiour critick to Theobald?" "O Sir he'd make two-and-fifty Theobalds, cut into slices! The worst of Warburton is, that he has a rage for saying something, when there's nothing to be said." Mr. Burney then asked him whether he had seen the letter which Warburton had written in answer to a pamphlet addressed "To the most impudent Man alive." He answered in the negative. Mr. Burney told him it was supposed to be written by Mallet. The controversey now raged between the friends of Pope and Bolingbroke; and Warburton and Mallet were the leaders of the several parties. Mr. Burney asked him then if he had seen Warburton's book against Bolingbroke's *Philosophy*? "No, Sir, I have never read Bolingbroke's impiety, and therefore am not interested about its confutation."'

On the fifteenth of April he began a new periodical paper, entitled *The Idler*, which came out every Saturday in a weekly news-paper, called *The Universal Chronicle, or Weekly Gazette*, published by Newbery. These essays were continued till April 5, 1760. Of one hundred and three, their total number, twelve were contributed by his friends.

The Idler is evidently the work of the same mind which produced *The Rambler*, but has less body and more spirit. It has more variety of real life, and greater facility of language. He describes the miseries of idleness, with the lively sensations of one who has felt them; and in his private memorandums while engaged in it, we find 'This year I hope to learn diligence.' Many of these excellent essays were written as hastily as an ordinary letter. Mr. Langton remembers Johnson, when on a visit at Oxford, asking him one evening how long it was till the post went out; and on being told about half an hour, he exclaimed, 'then we shall do very well.' He upon this instantly sat down and finished an *Idler*, which it was necessary should be in London the next day. Mr. Langton having signified a wish to read it, 'Sir, (said he) you shall not do more than I have done myself.' He then folded it up and sent it off.

1759: Ætat. 50.]—In 1759, in the month of January, his mother died at the great age of ninety, an event which deeply affected him; not that 'his mind had acquired no firmness by the contemplation of mortality;' but that his reverential affection for her was not abated by years, as indeed he retained all his tender feelings even to the latest period of his life. I have been told that he regretted much his not having gone to visit his mother for several years, previous to her death. But he was constantly engaged in literary labours which confined him to London; and though he had not the comfort of seeing his aged parent, he contributed liberally to her support.

Soon after this event, he wrote his *Rasselas, Prince of Abyssinia*; concerning the publication of which Sir John Hawkins guesses vaguely and idly, instead of having taken the trouble to inform himself with authentick precision. Not to trouble my readers with a repetition of the Knight's reveries, I have to mention, that the late Mr. Strahan the printer told me, that Johnson wrote it, that with the profits he might defray the expence of his mother's funeral, and pay some little debts which she had left. He told Sir Joshua Reynolds that he composed it in the evenings of one week, sent it to the press in portions as it was written, and had never since read it over. Mr. Strahan, Mr. Johnston, and Mr. Dodsley purchased it for a hundred pounds, but afterwards paid him twenty-five pounds more, when it came to a second edition.

Voltaire's *Candide*, written to refute the system of Optimism, which it has accomplished with brilliant success, is wonderfully similar in its plan and conduct to Johnson's *Rasselas*; insomuch, that I have heard Johnson say, that if they had not been published so closely one after the other that there was not time for imitation, it would have been in vain to deny that the scheme of that which came latest was taken from the other. Though the proposition illustrated by both these works was the same, namely, that in our present state there is more evil than good, the intention of the writers was very different. Voltaire, I am afraid, meant only by wanton profaneness to obtain a sportive victory over religion, and to discredit the belief of a superintending Providence; Johnson meant, by shewing the unsatisfactory nature of things temporal, to direct the hopes of man to things eternal. *Rasselas*, as was observed to me by a very accomplished lady, may be considered as a more enlarged and more deeply philosophical discourse in prose, upon the interesting truth, which in his *Vanity of Human Wishes* he had so successfully enforced in verse.

I would ascribe to this year the following letter to a son of one of his early friends at Lichfield, Mr. Joseph Simpson, Barrister, and authour of a tract entitled *Reflections on the Study of the Law*.

'TO JOSEPH SIMPSON, ESQ.

'DEAR SIR,—Your father's inexorability not only grieves but amazes me: he is your father; he was always accounted a wise man; nor do I remember any thing to the disadvantage of his good-nature; but in his refusal to assist you there is neither good-nature, fatherhood, nor wisdom. It is the practice of good-nature to overlook faults which have already, by the consequences, punished the delinquent. It is natural for a father to think more favourably than others of his children; and it is always wise to give assistance while a little help will prevent the necessity of greater.

'If you married imprudently, you miscarried at your own hazard, at an age when you had a right of choice. It would be hard if the man might not choose his own wife, who has a right to plead before the Judges of his country.

'If your imprudence has ended in difficulties and inconveniences, you are yourself to support them; and, with the help of a little better health, you would support them and conquer them. Surely, that want which accident and sickness produces, is to be supported in every region of humanity, though there were neither friends nor fathers in the world. You have certainly from your father the highest claim of charity, though none of right; and therefore I would counsel you to omit no decent nor manly degree of importunity. Your debts in the whole are not large, and of the whole but a small part is troublesome. Small debts are like small shot; they are rattling on every side, and can scarcely be escaped without a wound: great debts are like cannon; of loud noise, but little danger. You must, therefore, be enabled to discharge petty debts, that you may have leisure, with security to struggle with the rest. Neither the great nor little debts disgrace you. I am sure you have my esteem for the courage with which you contracted them, and the spirit with which you endure them. I wish my esteem could be of more use. I have been invited, or have invited myself, to several parts of the kingdom; and will not incommode my dear Lucy by coming to Lichfield, while her present lodging is of any use to her. I hope, in a few days, to be at leisure, and to make visits. Whither I shall fly is matter of no importance. A man unconnected is at home every where; unless he may be said to be at home no where. I am sorry, dear Sir, that where you have parents, a man of your merits should not have an home. I wish I could give it you. I am, my dear Sir, affectionately yours,

'SAM. JOHNSON.'

He now refreshed himself by an excursion to Oxford, of which the following short characteristical notice, in his own words, is preserved

'* * * is now making tea for me. I have been in my gown ever since I came here. It was, at my first coming, quite new and handsome. I have swum thrice, which I had disused for many years. I have proposed to Vansittart, climbing over the wall, but he has refused me. And I have clapped my hands till they are sore, at Dr. King's speech.'

His negro servant, Francis Barber, having left him, and been some time at sea, not pressed as has been supposed, but with his own consent, it appears from a letter to John Wilkes, Esq., from Dr. Smollet, that his master kindly interested himself in procuring his release from a state of life of which Johnson always expressed the utmost abhorrence. He said, 'No man will be a sailor who has contrivance enough to get himself into a jail; for being in a ship is being in a jail, with the chance of being drowned.' And at another time, 'A man in a jail has more room, better food, and commonly better company.' The letter was as follows:—

'Chelsea, March 16, 1759.

'DEAR SIR, I am again your petitioner, in behalf of that great CHAM of literature, Samuel Johnson. His black servant, whose name is Francis Barber, has been pressed on board the Stag Frigate, Captain Angel, and our lexicographer is in great distress. He says the boy is a sickly lad, of a delicate frame, and particularly subject to a malady in his throat, which renders him very unfit for his Majesty's service. You know what manner of animosity the said Johnson has against you; and I dare say you desire no other opportunity of resenting it than that of laying him under an obligation. He was humble enough to desire my assistance on this occasion, though he and I were never cater-cousins; and I gave him to understand that I would make application to my friend Mr. Wilkes, who, perhaps, by his interest with Dr. Hay and Mr. Elliot, might be able to procure the discharge of his lacquey. It would be superfluous to say more on the subject, which I leave to your own consideration; but I cannot let slip this opportunity of declaring that I am, with the most inviolable esteem and attachment, dear Sir, your affectionate, obliged, humble servant,

'T. SMOLLET.'

Mr. Wilkes, who upon all occasions has acted, as a private gentleman, with most polite liberality, applied to his friend Sir George Hay, then one of the Lords Commissioners of the Admiralty; and Francis Barber was discharged, as he has told me, without any wish of his own. He found his old master in Chambers in the Inner Temple, and returned to his service.

1760: ÆTAT. 51.]—I take this opportunity to relate the manner in which an acquaintance first commenced between Dr. Johnson and Mr. Murphy. During the publication of *The Gray's-Inn Journal*, a periodical paper which was successfully carried on by Mr. Murphy alone, when a very young man, he happened to be in the country with Mr. Foote; and having mentioned that he was obliged to go to London in order to get ready for the press one of the numbers of that *Journal*, Foote said to him, 'You need not go on that account. Here is a French magazine, in which you will find a very pretty oriental tale; translate that, and send it to your printer.' Mr. Murphy having read the tale, was highly pleased with it, and followed Foote's advice. When he returned to town, this tale was pointed out to him in *The Rambler*, from whence it had been translated into the French magazine. Mr. Murphy then waited upon Johnson, to explain this curious incident. His talents, literature, and gentleman-like manners, were soon perceived by Johnson, and a friendship was formed which was never broken.

1762: ÆTAT. 53.]—A lady having at this time solicited him to obtain the Archbishop of Canterbury's patronage to have her son sent to the University, one of those solicitations which are too frequent, where people, anxious for a particular object, do not consider propriety, or the opportunity which the persons whom they solicit have to assist them, he wrote to her the following answer, with a copy of which I am favoured by the Reverend Dr. Farmer, Master of Emanuel College, Cambridge.

'MADAM,—I hope you will believe that my delay in answering your letter could proceed only from my unwillingness to destroy any hope that you had formed. Hope is itself a species of happiness, and, perhaps, the chief happiness which this world affords: but, like all other pleasures immoderately enjoyed, the excesses of hope must be expiated by pain; and expectations improperly indulged, must end in disappointment. If it be asked, what is the improper expectation which it is dangerous to indulge, experience will quickly answer, that it is such expectation as is dictated not by reason, but by desire; expectation raised, not by the common occurrences of life, but by the wants of the expectant; an expectation that requires the common course of things to be changed, and the general rules of action to be broken.

'When you made your request to me, you should have considered, Madam, what you were asking. You ask me to solicit a great man, to whom I never spoke, for a young person whom I had never seen, upon a supposition which I had no means of knowing to be true. There is no reason why, amongst all the great, I should chuse to supplicate the Archbishop, nor why, among all the possible objects of his bounty, the Archbishop should chuse your son. I know, Madam, how unwillingly conviction is admitted, when interest opposes it; but surely, Madam, you must allow, that there is no reason why that should be done by me, which every other man may do with equal reason, and which, indeed no man can do properly, without some very particular relation both to the Archbishop and to you. If I could help you in this exigence by any proper means, it would give me pleasure; but this proposal is so very remote from all usual methods, that I cannot comply with it, but at the risk of such answer and suspicions as I believe you do not wish me to undergo.

'I have seen your son this morning; he seems a pretty youth, and will, perhaps, find some better friend than I can procure him; but, though he should at last miss the University, he may still be wise, useful, and happy. I am, Madam, your most humble servant,

'SAM. JOHNSON.'

'June 8, 1762.'

'TO MR. JOSEPH BARETTI, AT MILAN.

'London, July 20, 1762.

'SIR, However justly you may accuse me for want of punctuality in correspondence, I am not so far lost in negligence as to omit the opportunity of writing to you, which Mr. Beauclerk's passage through Milan affords me.

'I suppose you received the *Idlers*, and I intend that you shall soon receive *Shakspeare*, that you may explain his works to the ladies of Italy, and tell them the story of the editor, among the other strange narratives with which your long residence in this unknown region has supplied you.

'As you have now been long away, I suppose your curiosity may pant for some news of your old friends. Miss Williams and I live much as we did. Miss Cotterel still continues to cling to Mrs. Porter, and Charlotte is now big of the fourth child. Mr. Reynolds gets six thousands a year. Levet is lately married, not without much suspicion that he has been wretchedly cheated in his match. Mr. Chambers is gone this day, for the first time, the circuit with the Judges. Mr. Richardson is dead of an apoplexy, and his second daughter has married a merchant.

'My vanity, or my kindness, makes me flatter myself, that you would rather hear of me than of those whom I have mentioned; but of myself I have very little which I care to tell. Last winter I went down to my native town, where I found the streets much narrower and shorter than I thought I had left them, inhabited by a new race of people, to whom I was very little known. My play-fellows were grown old, and forced me to suspect that I was no longer young. My only remaining friend has changed his principles, and was become the tool of the predominant faction. My daughter-in-law, from whom I expected most, and whom I met with sincere benevolence, has lost the beauty and gaiety of youth, without having gained much of the wisdom of age. I wandered about for five days, and took the first convenient opportunity of returning to a place, where, if there is not much happiness, there is, at least, such a diversity of good and evil, that slight vexations do not fix upon the heart. . . .

'May you, my Baretti, be very happy at Milan, or some other place nearer to, Sir, your most affectionate humble servant,

'SAM. JOHNSON.'

The accession of George the Third to the throne of these kingdoms, opened a new and brighter prospect to men of literary merit, who had been honoured with no mark of royal favour in the preceding reign. His present Majesty's education in this country, as well as his taste and beneficence, prompted him to be the patron of science and the arts; and early this year Johnson, having been represented to him as a very learned and good man, without any certain provision, his Majesty was pleased to grant him a pension of three hundred pounds a year. The Earl of Bute, who was then Prime Minister, had the honour to announce this instance of his Sovereign's bounty, concerning which, many and various stories, all equally erroneous, have been propagated: maliciously representing it as a political bribe to Johnson, to desert his avowed principles, and become the tool of a government which he held to be founded in usurpation. I have taken care to have it in my power to refute them from the most authentick information. Lord Bute told me, that Mr. Wedderburne, now Lord Loughborough, was the person who first mentioned this subject to him. Lord Loughborough told me, that the pension was granted to Johnson solely as the reward of his literary merit, without any stipulation whatever, or even tacit understanding that he should write for administration. His Lordship added, that he was confident the political tracts which Johnson afterwards did write, as they were entirely consonant with his own opinions, would have been written by him though no pension had been granted to him.

Mr. Thomas Sheridan and Mr. Murphy, who then lived a good deal both with him and Mr. Wedderburne, told me, that they previously talked with Johnson upon this matter, and that it was perfectly understood by all parties that the pension was merely honorary. Sir Joshua Reynolds told me, that Johnson called on him after his majesty's intention had been notified to him, and said he wished to consult his friends as to the propriety of his accepting this mark of the royal favour, after the definitions which he had given in his *Dictionary* of *pension* and *pensioners*. He said he would not have Sir Joshua's answer till next day, when he would call again, and desired he might think of it. Sir Joshua answered that he was clear to give his opinion then, that there could be no objection to his receiving from the King a reward for literary merit; and that certainly the definitions in his *Dictionary* were not applicable to him. Johnson, it should seem, was satisfied, for he did not call again till he had accepted the pension, and had waited on Lord Bute to thank him. He then told Sir Joshua that Lord Bute said to him expressly, 'It is not given you for anything you are to do, but for what you have done.' His Lordship, he said, behaved in the handsomest manner, he repeated the words twice, that he might be sure Johnson heard them, and thus set his mind perfectly at ease. This nobleman, who has been so virulently abused, acted with great honour in this instance and displayed a mind truly liberal. A minister of a more narrow and selfish disposition would have availed himself of such an opportunity to fix an implied obligation on a man of Johnson's powerful talents to give him his support.

Mr. Murphy and the late Mr. Sheridan severally contended for the distinction of having been the first who mentioned to Mr. Wedderburne that Johnson ought to have a pension. When I spoke of this to Lord Loughborough, wishing to know if he recollected the prime mover in the business, he said, 'All his friends assisted:' and when I told him that Mr. Sheridan strenuously asserted his claim to it, his Lordship said, 'He rang the bell.' And it is but just to add, that Mr. Sheridan told me, that when he communicated to Dr. Johnson that a pension was to be granted him, he replied in a fervour of gratitude, 'The English language does not afford me terms adequate to my feelings on this occasion. I must have recourse to the French. I am *pénétré* with his Majesty's goodness.' When I repeated this to Dr. Johnson, he did not contradict it.

This year his friend Sir Joshua Reynolds paid a visit of some weeks to his native country, Devonshire, in which he was accompanied by Johnson, who was much pleased with this jaunt, and declared he had derived from it a great accession of new ideas. He was entertained at the seats of several noblemen and gentlemen in the West of England; but the greatest part of the time was passed at Plymouth, where the magnificence of the navy, the ship-building and all its circumstances, afforded him a grand subject of contemplation. The Commissioner of the Dock-yard paid him the compliment of ordering the yacht to convey him and his friend to the Eddystone, to which they accordingly sailed. But the weather was so tempestuous that they could not land.

Reynolds and he were at this time the guests of Dr. Mudge, the celebrated surgeon, and now physician of that place, not more distinguished for quickness of parts and variety of knowledge, than loved and esteemed for his amiable manners; and here Johnson formed an acquaintance with Dr. Mudge's father, that very eminent divine, the Reverend Zachariah Mudge, Prebendary of Exeter, who was idolised in the west, both for his excellence as a preacher and the uniform perfect propriety of his private conduct. He preached a sermon purposely that Johnson might hear him; and we shall see afterwards that Johnson honoured his memory by drawing his character. While Johnson was at Plymouth, he saw a great many of its inhabitants, and was not sparing of his very entertaining conversation. It was here that he made that frank and truly original confession, that 'ignorance, pure ignorance,' was the cause of a wrong definition in his *Dictionary* of the word *pastern*, to the no small surprise of the Lady who put the question to him; who having the most profound reverence for his character, so as almost to suppose him endowed with infallibility, expected to hear an explanation (of what, to be sure, seemed strange to a common reader,) drawn from some deep-learned source with which she was unacquainted.

Sir Joshua Reynolds, to whom I was obliged for my information concerning this excursion, mentions a very characteristical anecdote of Johnson while at Plymouth. Having observed that in consequence of the Dock-yard a new town had arisen about two miles off as a rival to the old; and knowing from his sagacity, and just observation of human nature, that it is certain if a man hates at all, he will hate his next neighbour; he concluded that this new and rising town could not but excite the envy and jealousy of the old, in which conjecture he was very soon confirmed; he therefore set himself resolutely on the side of the old town, the *established* town, in which his lot was cast, considering it as a kind of duty to *stand by* it. He accordingly entered warmly into its interests, and upon every occasion talked of the *dockers*, as the inhabitants of the new town were called, as upstarts and aliens. Plymouth is very plentifully supplied with water by a river brought into it from a great distance, which is so abundant that it runs to waste in the town. The Dock, or New-town, being totally destitute of water, petitioned Plymouth that a small portion of the conduit might be permitted to go to them, and this was now under consideration. Johnson, affecting to entertain the passions of the place, was violent in opposition; and, half-laughing at himself for his pretended zeal where he had no concern, exclaimed, 'No, no! I am against the *dockers*; I am a Plymouth man. Rogues! let them die of thirst. They shall not have a drop!'

1763: ÆTAT. 54.]—This is to me a memorable year; for in it I had the happiness to obtain the acquaintance of that extraordinary man whose memoirs I am now writing; an acquaintance which I shall ever esteem as one of the most fortunate circumstances in my life. Though then but two-and-twenty, I had for several years read his works with delight and instruction, and had the highest reverence for their authour, which had grown up in my fancy into a kind of mysterious veneration, by figuring to myself a state of solemn elevated abstraction, in which I supposed him to live in the immense metropolis of London. Mr. Gentleman, a native of Ireland, who passed some years in Scotland as a player, and as an instructor in the English language, a man whose talents and worth were depressed by misfortunes, had given me a representation of the figure and manner of DICTIONARY JOHNSON! as he was then generally called; and during my first visit to London, which was for three months in 1760, Mr. Derrick the poet, who was Gentleman's friend and countryman, flattered me with hopes that he would introduce me to Johnson, an honour of which I was very ambitious. But he never found an opportunity; which made me doubt that he had promised to do what was not in his power; till Johnson some years afterwards told me, 'Derrick, Sir, might very well have introduced you. I had a kindness for Derrick, and am sorry he is dead.'

In the summer of 1761 Mr. Thomas Sheridan was at Edinburgh, and delivered lectures upon the English Language and Publick Speaking to large and respectable audiences. I was often in his company, and heard him frequently expatiate upon Johnson's extraordinary knowledge, talents, and virtues, repeat his pointed sayings, describe his particularities, and boast of his being his guest sometimes till two or three in the morning. At his house I hoped to have many opportunities of seeing the sage, as Mr. Sheridan obligingly assured me I should not be disappointed.

When I returned to London in the end of 1762, to my surprise and regret I found an irreconcilable difference had taken place between Johnson and Sheridan. A pension of two hundred pounds a year had been given to Sheridan. Johnson, who, as has been already mentioned, thought slightingly of Sheridan's art, upon hearing that he was also pensioned, exclaimed, 'What! have they given *him* a pension? Then it is time for me to give up mine.'

Johnson complained that a man who disliked him repeated his sarcasm to Mr. Sheridan, without telling him what followed, which was, that after a pause he added, 'However, I am glad that Mr. Sheridan has a pension, for he is a very good man.' Sheridan could never forgive this hasty contemptuous expression. It rankled in his mind; and though I informed him of all that Johnson said, and that he would be very glad to meet him amicably, he positively declined repeated offers which I made, and once went off abruptly from a house where he and I were engaged to dine, because he was told that Dr. Johnson was to be there.

This rupture with Sheridan deprived Johnson of one of his most agreeable resources for amusement in his lonely evenings; for Sheridan's well-informed, animated, and bustling mind never suffered conversation to stagnate; and Mrs. Sheridan was a most agreeable companion to an intellectual man. She was sensible, ingenious, unassuming, yet communicative. I recollect, with satisfaction, many pleasing hours which I passed with her under the hospitable roof of her husband, who was to me a very kind friend. Her novel, entitled Memoirs of *Miss Sydney Biddulph*, contains an excellent moral while it inculcates a future state of retribution; and what it teaches is impressed upon the mind by a series of as deep distress as can affect humanity, in the amiable and pious heroine who goes to her grave unrelieved, but resigned, and full of hope of 'heaven's mercy.' Johnson paid her this high compliment upon it: 'I know not, Madam, that you have a right, upon moral principles, to make your readers suffer so much.'

Mr. Thomas Davies the actor, who then kept a bookseller's shop in Russel-street, Covent-garden, told me that Johnson was very much his friend, and came frequently to his house, where he more than once invited me to meet him; but by some unlucky accident or other he was prevented from coming to us.

Mr. Thomas Davies was a man of good understanding and talents, with the advantage of a liberal education. Though somewhat pompous, he was an entertaining companion; and his literary performances have no inconsiderable share of merit. He was a friendly and very hospitable man. Both he and his wife, (who has been celebrated for her beauty,) though upon the stage for many years, maintained an uniform decency of character; and Johnson esteemed them, and lived in as easy an intimacy with them, as with any family which he used to visit. Mr. Davies recollected several of Johnson's remarkable sayings, and was one of the best of the many imitators of his voice and manner, while relating them. He increased my impatience more and more to see the extraordinary man whose works I highly valued, and whose conversation was reported to be so peculiarly excellent.

At last, on Monday the 16th of May, when I was sitting in Mr. Davies's back-parlour, after having drunk tea with him and Mrs. Davies, Johnson unexpectedly came into the shop; and Mr. Davies having perceived him through the glass-door in the room in which we were sitting, advancing towards us,—he announced his aweful approach to me, somewhat in the manner of an actor in the part of Horatio, when he addresses Hamlet on the appearance of his father's ghost, 'Look, my Lord, it comes.' I found that I had a very perfect idea of Johnson's figure, from the portrait of him painted by Sir Joshua Reynolds soon after he had published his *Dictionary*, in the attitude of sitting in his easy chair in deep meditation, which was the first picture his friend did for him, which Sir Joshua very kindly presented to me, and from which an engraving has been made for this work. Mr. Davies mentioned my name, and respectfully introduced me to him. I was much agitated; and recollecting his prejudice against the Scotch, of which I had heard much, I said to Davies, 'Don't tell where I come from.'—'From Scotland,' cried Davies roguishly. 'Mr. Johnson, (said I) I do indeed come from Scotland, but I cannot help it.' I am willing to flatter myself that I meant this as light pleasantry to sooth and conciliate him, and not as an humiliating abasement at the expence of my country. But however that might be, this speech was somewhat unlucky; for with that quickness of wit for which he was so remarkable, he seized the expression 'come from Scotland,' which I used in the sense of being of that country; and, as if I had said that I had come away from it, or left it, retorted, 'That, Sir, I find, is what a very great many of your countrymen cannot help.' This stroke stunned me a good deal; and when we had sat down, I felt myself not a little embarrassed, and apprehensive of what might come next. He then addressed himself to Davies: 'What do you think of Garrick? He has refused me an order for the play for Miss Williams, because he knows the house will be full, and that an order would be worth three shillings.' Eager to take any opening to get into conversation with him, I ventured to say, 'O, Sir, I cannot think Mr. Garrick would grudge such a trifle to you.' 'Sir, (said he, with a stern look,) I have known David Garrick longer than you have done: and I know no right you have to talk to me on the subject.' Perhaps I deserved this check; for it was rather presumptuous in me, an entire stranger, to express any doubt of the justice of his animadversion upon his old acquaintance and pupil.[13] I now felt myself much mortified, and began to think that the hope which I had long indulged of obtaining his acquaintance was blasted. And, in truth, had not my ardour been uncommonly strong, and my resolution uncommonly persevering, so rough a reception might have deterred me for ever from making any further attempts. Fortunately, however, I remained upon the field not wholly discomfited.

I was highly pleased with the extraordinary vigour of his conversation, and regretted that I was drawn away from it by an engagement at another place. I had, for a part of the evening, been left alone with him, and had ventured to make an observation now and then, which he received very civilly; so that I was satisfied that though there was a roughness in his manner, there was no ill-nature in his disposition. Davies followed me to the door, and when I complained to him a little of the hard blows which the great man had given me, he kindly took upon him to console me by saying, 'Don't be uneasy. I can see he likes you very well.'

A few days afterwards I called on Davies, and asked him if he thought I might take the liberty of waiting on Mr. Johnson at his Chambers in the Temple. He said I certainly might, and that Mr. Johnson would take it as a compliment. So upon Tuesday the 24th of May, after having been enlivened by the witty sallies of Messieurs Thornton, Wilkes, Churchill and Lloyd, with whom I had passed the morning, I boldly repaired to Johnson. His Chambers were on the first floor of No. 1, Inner-Temple-lane, and I entered them with an impression given me by the Reverend Dr. Blair, of Edinburgh, who had been introduced to him not long before, and described his having 'found the Giant in his den;' an expression, which, when I came to be pretty well acquainted with Johnson, I repeated to him, and he was diverted at this picturesque account of himself. Dr. Blair had been presented to him by Dr. James Fordyce. At this time the controversy concerning the pieces published by Mr. James Macpherson, as translations of *Ossian*, was at its height. Johnson had all along denied their authenticity; and, what was still more provoking to their admirers, maintained that they had no merit. The subject having been introduced by Dr. Fordyce, Dr. Blair, relying on the internal evidence of their antiquity, asked Dr. Johnson whether he thought any man of a modern age could have written such poems? Johnson replied, 'Yes, Sir, many

---

[13] That this was a momentary sally against Garrick there can be no doubt; for at Johnson's desire he had, some years before, given a benefit-night at his theatre to this very person, by which she had got two hundred pounds. Johnson, indeed, upon all other occasions, when I was in his company praised the very liberal charity of Garrick. I once mentioned to him, 'It is observed, Sir, that you attack Garrick yourself, but will suffer nobody else to do it.' Johnson, (smiling) 'Why, Sir, that is true.'—BOSWELL.

men, many women, and many children.' Johnson, at this time, did not know that Dr. Blair had just published a *Dissertation*, not only defending their authenticity, but seriously ranking them with the poems of *Homer* and *Virgil*; and when he was afterwards informed of this circumstance, he expressed some displeasure at Dr. Fordyce's having suggested the topick, and said, 'I am not sorry that they got thus much for their pains. Sir, it was like leading one to talk of a book when the authour is concealed behind the door.'

He received me very courteously; but, it must be confessed, that his apartment, and furniture, and morning dress, were sufficiently uncouth. His brown suit of cloaths looked very rusty; he had on a little old shrivelled unpowdered wig, which was too small for his head; his shirt-neck and knees of his breeches were loose; his black worsted stockings ill drawn up; and he had a pair of unbuckled shoes by way of slippers. But all these slovenly particularities were forgotten the moment that he began to talk. Some gentlemen, whom I do not recollect, were sitting with him; and when they went away, I also rose; but he said to me, 'Nay, don't go.' 'Sir, (said I,) I am afraid that I intrude upon you. It is benevolent to allow me to sit and hear you.' He seemed pleased with this compliment, which I sincerely paid him, and answered, 'Sir, I am obliged to any man who visits me.' I have preserved the following short minute of what passed this day:—

'Madness frequently discovers itself merely by unnecessary deviation from the usual modes of the world. My poor friend Smart shewed the disturbance of his mind, by falling upon his knees, and saying his prayers in the street, or in any other unusual place. Now although, rationally speaking, it is greater madness not to pray at all, than to pray as Smart did, I am afraid there are so many who do not pray, that their understanding is not called in question.'

Concerning this unfortunate poet, Christopher Smart, who was confined in a mad-house, he had, at another time, the following conversation with Dr. Burney:—BURNEY. 'How does poor Smart do, Sir; is he likely to recover?' JOHNSON. 'It seems as if his mind had ceased to struggle with the disease; for he grows fat upon it.' BURNEY. 'Perhaps, Sir, that may be from want of exercise.' JOHNSON. 'No, Sir; he has partly as much exercise as he used to have, for he digs in the garden. Indeed, before his confinement, he used for exercise to walk to the ale-house; but he was *carried* back again. I did not think he ought to be shut up. His infirmities were not noxious to society. He insisted on people praying with him; and I'd as lief pray with Kit Smart as any one else. Another charge was, that he did not love clean linen; and I have no passion for it.'—Johnson continued. 'Mankind have a great aversion to intellectual labour; but even supposing knowledge to be easily attainable, more people would be content to be ignorant than would take even a little trouble to acquire it.'

Talking of Garrick, he said, 'He is the first man in the world for sprightly conversation.'

When I rose a second time he again pressed me to stay, which I did.

He told me, that he generally went abroad at four in the afternoon, and seldom came home till two in the morning. I took the liberty to ask if he did not think it wrong to live thus, and not make more use of his great talents. He owned it was a bad habit. On reviewing, at the distance of many years, my journal of this period, I wonder how, at my first visit, I ventured to talk to him so freely, and that he bore it with so much indulgence.

Before we parted, he was so good as to promise to favour me with his company one evening at my lodgings; and, as I took my leave, shook me cordially by the hand. It is almost needless to add, that I felt no little elation at having now so happily established an acquaintance of which I had been so long ambitious.

I did not visit him again till Monday, June 13, at which time I recollect no part of his conversation, except that when I told him I had been to see Johnson ride upon three horses, he said, 'Such a man, Sir, should be encouraged; for his performances shew the extent of the human powers in one instance, and thus tend to raise our opinion of the faculties of man. He shews what may be attained by persevering application; so that every man may hope, that by giving as much application, although perhaps he may never ride three horses at a time, or dance upon a wire, yet he may be equally expert in whatever profession he has chosen to pursue.'

He again shook me by the hand at parting, and asked me why I did not come oftener to him. Trusting that I was now in his good graces, I answered, that he had not given me much encouragement, and reminded him of the check I had received from him at our first interview. 'Poh, poh! (said he, with a complacent smile,) never mind these things. Come to me as often as you can. I shall be glad to see you.'

I had learnt that his place of frequent resort was the Mitre tavern in Fleet-street, where he loved to sit up late, and I begged I might be allowed to pass an evening with him there soon, which he promised I should. A few days afterwards I met him near Temple-bar, about one o'clock in the morning, and asked if he would then go to the Mitre. 'Sir, (said he) it is too late; they won't let us in. But I'll go with you another night with all my heart.'

A revolution of some importance in my plan of life had just taken place; for instead of procuring a commission in the foot-guards, which was my own inclination, I had, in compliance with my father's wishes, agreed to study the law, and was soon to set out for Utrecht, to hear the lectures of an excellent Civilian in that University, and then to proceed on my travels. Though very desirous of obtaining Dr. Johnson's advice and instructions on the mode of pursuing my studies, I was at this time so occupied, shall I call it? or so dissipated, by the amusements of London, that our next meeting was not till Saturday, June 25, when happening to dine at Clifton's eating-house, in Butcher-row I was surprized to perceive Johnson come in and take his seat at another table. The mode of dining, or rather being fed, at such houses in London, is well known to many to be particularly unsocial, as there is no Ordinary, or united company, but each person has his own mess, and is under no obligation to hold any intercourse with any one. A liberal and full-minded man, however, who loves to talk, will break through this churlish and unsocial restraint. Johnson and an Irish gentleman got into a dispute concerning the cause of some part of mankind being black. 'Why, Sir, (said Johnson,) it has been accounted for in three ways: either by supposing that they are the posterity of Ham, who was cursed; or that GOD at first created two kinds of men, one black and another white; or that by the heat of the sun the skin is scorched, and so acquires a sooty hue. This matter has been much canvassed among naturalists, but has never been brought to any certain issue.' What the Irishman said is totally obliterated from my mind; but I remember that he became very warm and intemperate in his expressions; upon which Johnson rose, and quietly walked away. When he had retired, his antagonist took his revenge, as he thought, by saying, 'He has a most ungainly figure, and an affectation of pomposity, unworthy of a man of genius.'

Johnson had not observed that I was in the room. I followed him, however, and he agreed to meet me in the evening at the Mitre. I called on him, and we went thither at nine. We had a good supper, and port wine, of which he then sometimes drank a bottle. The orthodox high-church sound of the MITRE,—the figure and manner of the celebrated SAMUEL JOHNSON,—the extraordinary power and precision of his conversation, and the pride arising from finding myself admitted as his companion, produced a variety of sensations, and a pleasing elevation of mind beyond what I had ever before experienced. I find in my journal the following minute of our conversation, which, though it will give but a very faint notion of what passed, is in some degree a valuable record; and it will be curious in this view, as shewing how habitual to his mind were some opinions which appear in his works.

'Colley Cibber, Sir, was by no means a blockhead; but by arrogating to himself too much, he was in danger of losing that degree of estimation to which he was entitled. His friends gave out that he *intended* his birth-day *Odes* should be bad: but that was not the case, Sir; for he kept them many months by him, and a few years before he died he shewed me one of them, with great solicitude to render it as perfect as might be, and I made some corrections, to which he was not very willing to submit. I remember the following couplet in allusion to the King and himself:

> "Perch'd on the eagle's soaring wing,
> The lowly linnet loves to sing."

Sir, he had heard something of the fabulous tale of the wren sitting upon the eagle's wing, and he had applied it to a linnet. Cibber's familiar style, however, was better than that which Whitehead has assumed. *Grand* nonsense is insupportable. Whitehead is but a little man to inscribe verses to players.

'Sir, I do not think Gray a first-rate poet. He has not a bold imagination, nor much command of words. The obscurity in which he has involved himself will not persuade us that he is sublime. His *Elegy in a Church-yard* has a happy selection of images, but I don't like what are called his great things. His *Ode* which begins

> "Ruin seize thee, ruthless King,
> Confusion on thy banners wait!"

has been celebrated for its abruptness, and plunging into the subject all at once. But such arts as these have no merit, unless when they are original. We admire them only once; and this abruptness has nothing new in it. We have had it often before. Nay, we have it in the old song of Johnny Armstrong:

> "Is there ever a man in all Scotland
> From the highest estate to the lowest degree," &c.

And then, Sir,

> "Yes, there is a man in Westmoreland,
> And Johnny Armstrong they do him call."

There, now, you plunge at once into the subject. You have no previous narration to lead you to it. The two next lines in that *Ode* are, I think, very good:

> "Though fann'd by conquest's crimson wing,
> They mock the air with idle state."'

Finding him in a placid humour, and wishing to avail myself of the opportunity which I fortunately had of consulting a sage, to hear whose wisdom, I conceived in the ardour of youthful imagination, that men filled with a noble enthusiasm for intellectual improvement would gladly have resorted from distant lands;—I opened my mind to him ingenuously, and gave him a little sketch of my life, to which he was pleased to listen with great attention.

I acknowledged, that though educated very strictly in the principles of religion, I had for some time been misled into a certain degree of infidelity; but that I was come now to a better way of thinking, and was fully satisfied of the truth of the Christian revelation, though I was not clear as to every point considered to be orthodox. Being at all times a curious examiner of the human mind, and pleased with an undisguised display of what had passed in it, he called to me with warmth, 'Give me your hand; I have taken a liking to you.' He then began to descant upon the force of testimony, and the little we could know of final causes; so that the objections of, why was it so? or why was it not so? ought not to disturb us: adding, that he himself had at one period been guilty of a temporary neglect of religion, but that it was not the result of argument, but mere absence of thought.

After having given credit to reports of his bigotry, I was agreeably surprized when he expressed the following very liberal sentiment, which has the additional value of obviating an objection to our holy religion, founded upon the discordant tenets of Christians themselves: 'For my part, Sir, I think all Christians, whether Papists or Protestants, agree in the essential articles, and that their differences are trivial, and rather political than religious.'

We talked of belief in ghosts. He said, 'Sir, I make a distinction between what a man may experience by the mere strength of his imagination, and what imagination cannot possibly produce. Thus, suppose I should think that I saw a form, and heard a voice cry "Johnson, you are a very wicked fellow, and unless you repent you will certainly be punished;" my own unworthiness is so deeply impressed upon my mind, that I might *imagine* I thus saw and heard, and therefore I should not believe that an external communication had been made to me. But if a form should appear, and a voice should tell me that a particular man had died at a particular place, and a particular hour, a fact which I had no apprehension of, nor any means of knowing, and this fact, with all its circumstances, should afterwards be unquestionably proved, I should, in that case, be persuaded that I had supernatural intelligence imparted to me.'

Here it is proper, once for all, to give a true and fair statement of Johnson's way of thinking upon the question, whether departed spirits are ever permitted to appear in this world, or in any way to operate upon human life. He has been ignorantly misrepresented as weakly credulous upon that subject; and, therefore, though I feel an inclination to disdain and treat with silent contempt so foolish a notion concerning my illustrious friend, yet as I find it has gained ground, it is necessary to refute it. The real fact then is, that Johnson had a very philosophical mind, and such a rational respect for testimony, as to make him submit his understanding to what was authentically proved, though he could not comprehend why it was so. Being thus disposed, he was willing to inquire into the truth of any relation of supernatural agency, a general belief of which has prevailed in all nations and ages. But so far was he from being the dupe of implicit faith, that he examined the matter with a jealous attention, and no man was more ready to refute its falsehood when he had discovered it. Churchill, in his poem entitled *The Ghost*, availed himself of the absurd credulity imputed to Johnson, and drew a caricature of him under the name of 'POMPOSO,' representing him as one of the believers of the story of a Ghost in Cock-lane, which, in the year 1762, had gained very general credit in London. Many of my readers, I am convinced, are to this hour under an impression that Johnson was thus foolishly deceived. It will therefore surprize them a good deal when they are informed upon undoubted authority, that Johnson was one of those by whom the imposture was detected. The story had become so popular, that he thought it should be investigated; and in this research he was assisted by the Reverend Dr. Douglas, now Bishop of Salisbury, the great detector of impostures; who informs me, that after the gentlemen who went and examined into the evidence were satisfied of its falsity, Johnson wrote in their presence an account of it, which was published in the newspapers and *Gentleman's Magazine*, and undeceived the world.

Our conversation proceeded. 'Sir, (said he) I am a friend to subordination, as most conducive to the happiness of society. There is a reciprocal pleasure in governing and being governed.'

'Dr. Goldsmith is one of the first men we now have as an authour, and he is a very worthy man too. He has been loose in his principles, but he is coming right.'

I complained to him that I had not yet acquired much knowledge, and asked his advice as to my studies. He said, 'Don't talk of study now. I will give you a plan; but it will require some time to consider of it.' 'It is very good in you (I replied,) to allow me to be with you thus. Had it been foretold to me some years ago that I should pass an evening with the authour of *The Rambler*, how should I have exulted!' What I then expressed, was sincerely from the heart. He was satisfied that it was, and cordially answered, 'Sir, I am glad we have met. I hope we shall pass many evenings and mornings too, together.' We finished a couple of bottles of port, and sat till between one and two in the morning.

As Dr. Oliver Goldsmith will frequently appear in this narrative, I shall endeavour to make my readers in some degree acquainted with his singular character. He was a native of Ireland, and a contemporary with Mr. Burke at Trinity College, Dublin, but did not then give much promise of future celebrity. He, however, observed to Mr. Malone, that 'though he made no great figure in mathematicks, which was a study in much repute there, he could turn an Ode of Horace into English better than any of them.' He afterwards studied physick at Edinburgh, and upon the Continent; and I have been informed, was enabled to pursue his travels on foot, partly by demanding at Universities to enter the lists as a disputant, by which, according to the custom of many of them, he was entitled to the premium of a crown, when luckily for him his challenge was not accepted; so that, as I once observed to Dr. Johnson, he *disputed* his passage through Europe. He then came to England, and was employed successively in the capacities of an usher to an academy, a corrector of the press, a reviewer, and a writer for a news-paper. He had sagacity enough to cultivate assiduously the acquaintance of Johnson, and his faculties were gradually enlarged by the contemplation of such a model. To me and many others it appeared that he studiously copied the manner of Johnson, though, indeed, upon a smaller scale.

At this time I think he had published nothing with his name, though it was pretty generally known that *one Dr. Goldsmith* was the authour of *An Enquiry into the present State of polite Learning in Europe*, and of *The Citizen of the World*, a series of letters supposed to be written from London by a Chinese. No man had the art of displaying with more advantage as a writer, whatever literary acquisitions he made. '*Nihil quod tetigit non ornavit.*' His mind resembled a fertile, but thin soil. There was a quick, but not a strong vegetation, of whatever chanced to be thrown upon it. No deep root could be struck. The oak of the forest did not grow there; but the elegant shrubbery and the fragrant parterre appeared in gay succession. It has been generally circulated and believed that he was a mere fool in conversation; but, in truth, this has been greatly exaggerated. He had, no doubt, a more than common share of that hurry of ideas which we often find in his countrymen, and which sometimes produces a laughable confusion in expressing them. He was very much what the French call *un étourdi*, and from vanity and an eager desire of being conspicuous wherever he was, he frequently talked carelessly without knowledge of the subject, or even without thought. His person was short, his countenance coarse and vulgar, his deportment that of a scholar aukwardly affecting the easy gentleman. Those who were in any way distinguished, excited envy in him to so ridiculous an excess, that the instances of it are hardly credible. When accompanying two beautiful young ladies[14] with their mother on a tour in France, he was seriously angry that more attention was paid to them than to him; and once at the exhibition of the Fantoccini in London, when those who sat next him observed with

---

[14] These were the Misses Horneck, known otherwise as 'Little Comedy' and 'The Jessamy Bride.'—Ed.

what dexterity a puppet was made to toss a pike, he could not bear that it should have such praise, and exclaimed with some warmth, 'Pshaw! I can do it better myself.'

He boasted to me at this time of the power of his pen in commanding money, which I believe was true in a certain degree, though in the instance he gave he was by no means correct. He told me that he had sold a novel for four hundred pounds. This was his *Vicar of Wakefield*. But Johnson informed me, that he had made the bargain for Goldsmith, and the price was sixty pounds. 'And, Sir, (said he,) a sufficient price too, when it was sold; for then the fame of Goldsmith had not been elevated, as it afterwards was, by his Traveller; and the bookseller had such faint hopes of profit by his bargain, that he kept the manuscript by him a long time, and did not publish it till after *The Traveller* had appeared. Then, to be sure, it was accidentally worth more money.

Mrs. Piozzi and Sir John Hawkins have strangely misstated the history of Goldsmith's situation and Johnson's friendly interference, when this novel was sold. I shall give it authentically from Johnson's own exact narration:—'I received one morning a message from poor Goldsmith that he was in great distress, and as it was not in his power to come to me, begging that I would come to him as soon as possible. I sent him a guinea, and promised to come to him directly. I accordingly went as soon as I was drest, and found that his landlady had arrested him for his rent, at which he was in a violent passion. I perceived that he had already changed my guinea, and had got a bottle of Madeira and a glass before him. I put the cork into the bottle, desired he would be calm, and began to talk to him of the means by which he might be extricated. He then told me that he had a novel ready for the press, which he produced to me. I looked into it, and saw its merit; told the landlady I should soon return, and having gone to a bookseller, sold it for sixty pounds. I brought Goldsmith the money, and he discharged his rent, not without rating his landlady in a high tone for having used him so ill.'

My next meeting with Johnson was on Friday the 1st of July, when he and I and Dr. Goldsmith supped together at the Mitre. I was before this time pretty well acquainted with Goldsmith, who was one of the brightest ornaments of the Johnsonian school. Goldsmith's respectful attachment to Johnson was then at its height; for his own literary reputation had not yet distinguished him so much as to excite a vain desire of competition with his great Master. He had increased my admiration of the goodness of Johnson's heart, by incidental remarks in the course of conversation, such as, when I mentioned Mr. Levet, whom he entertained under his roof, 'He is poor and honest, which is recommendation enough to Johnson;' and when I wondered that he was very kind to a man of whom I had heard a very bad character, 'He is now become miserable; and that insures the protection of Johnson.'

He talked very contemptuously of Churchill's poetry, observing, that 'it had a temporary currency, only from its audacity of abuse, and being filled with living names, and that it would sink into oblivion.' I ventured to hint that he was not quite a fair judge, as Churchill had attacked him violently. JOHNSON. 'Nay, Sir, I am a very fair judge. He did not attack me violently till he found I did not like his poetry; and his attack on me shall not prevent me from continuing to say what I think of him, from an apprehension that it may be ascribed to resentment. No, Sir, I called the fellow a blockhead at first, and I will call him a blockhead still. However, I will acknowledge that I have a better opinion of him now, than I once had; for he has shewn more fertility than I expected. To be sure, he is a tree that cannot produce good fruit: he only bears crabs. But, Sir, a tree that produces a great many crabs is better than a tree which produces only a few.'

Let me here apologize for the imperfect manner in which I am obliged to exhibit Johnson's conversation at this period. In the early part of my acquaintance with him, I was so wrapt in admiration of his extraordinary colloquial talents, and so little accustomed to his peculiar mode of expression, that I found it extremely difficult to recollect and record his conversation with its genuine vigour and vivacity. In progress of time, when my mind was, as it were, *strongly impregnated with the Johnsonian æther*, I could, with much more facility and exactness, carry in my memory and commit to paper the exuberant variety of his wisdom and wit.

At this time *Miss* Williams, as she was then called, though she did not reside with him in the Temple under his roof, but had lodgings in Bolt-court, Fleet-street, had so much of his attention, that he every night drank tea with her before he went home, however late it might be, and she always sat up for him. This, it may be fairly conjectured, was not alone a proof of his regard for *her*, but of his own unwillingness to go into solitude, before that unseasonable hour at which he had habituated himself to expect the oblivion of repose. Dr. Goldsmith, being a privileged man, went with him this night, strutting away, and calling to me with an air of superiority, like that of an esoterick over an exoterick disciple of a sage of antiquity, 'I go to Miss Williams.' I confess, I then envied him this mighty privilege, of which he seemed so proud; but it was not long before I obtained the same mark of distinction.

On Tuesday the 5th of July, I again visited Johnson.

Talking of London, he observed, 'Sir, if you wish to have a just notion of the magnitude of this city, you must not be satisfied with seeing its great streets and squares, but must survey the innumerable little lanes and courts. It is not in the showy evolutions of buildings, but in the multiplicity of human habitations which are crouded together, that the wonderful immensity of London consists.'

On Wednesday, July 6, he was engaged to sup with me at my lodgings in Downing-street, Westminster. But on the preceding night my landlord having behaved very rudely to me and some company who were with me, I had resolved not to remain another night in his house. I was exceedingly uneasy at the aukward appearance I supposed I should make to Johnson and the other gentlemen whom I had invited, not being able to receive them at home, and being obliged to order supper at the Mitre. I went to Johnson in the morning, and talked of it as a serious distress. He laughed, and said, 'Consider, Sir, how insignificant this will appear a twelvemonth hence.'—Were this consideration to be applied to most of the little vexatious incidents of life, by which our quiet is too often disturbed, it would prevent many painful sensations. I have tried it frequently, with good effect. 'There is nothing (continued he) in this mighty misfortune; nay, we shall be better at the Mitre.'

I had as my guests this evening at the Mitre tavern, Dr. Johnson, Dr. Goldsmith, Mr. Thomas Davies, Mr. Eccles, an Irish gentleman, for whose agreeable company I was obliged to Mr. Davies, and the Reverend Mr. John Ogilvie, who was desirous of being in company with my illustrious friend, while I, in my turn, was proud to have the honour of shewing one of my countrymen upon what easy terms Johnson permitted me to live with him.

Goldsmith, as usual, endeavoured, with too much eagerness, to *shine*, and disputed very warmly with Johnson against the well-known maxim of the British constitution, 'the King can do no wrong;' affirming, that 'what was morally false could not be politically true; and as the King might, in the exercise of his regal power, command and cause the doing of what was wrong, it certainly might be said, in sense and in reason, that he could do wrong.' JOHNSON. 'Sir, you are to consider, that in our constitution, according to its true principles, the King is the head; he is supreme; he is above every thing, and there is no power by which he can be tried. Therefore, it is, Sir, that we hold the King can do no wrong; that whatever may happen to be wrong in government may not be above our reach, by being ascribed to Majesty. Redress is always to be had against oppression, by punishing the immediate agents. The King, though he should command, cannot force a Judge to condemn a man unjustly; therefore it is the Judge whom we prosecute and punish. Political institutions are formed upon the consideration of what will most frequently tend to the good of the whole, although now and then exceptions may occur. Thus it is better in general that a nation should have a supreme legislative power, although it may at times be abused. And then, Sir, there is this consideration, that *if the abuse be enormous, Nature will rise up, and claiming her original rights, overturn a corrupt political system.*' I mark this animated sentence with peculiar pleasure, as a noble instance of that truly dignified spirit of freedom which ever glowed in his heart, though he was charged with slavish tenets by superficial observers; because he was at all times indignant against that false patriotism, that pretended love of freedom, that unruly restlessness, which is inconsistent with the stable authority of any good government.

'Bayle's *Dictionary* is a very useful work for those to consult who love the biographical part of literature, which is what I love most.'

Talking of the eminent writers in Queen Anne's reign, he observed, 'I think Dr. Arbuthnot the first man among them. He was the most universal genius, being an excellent physician, a man of deep learning, and a man of much humour. Mr. Addison was, to be sure, a great man; his learning was not profound; but his morality, his humour, and his elegance of writing, set him very high.'

Mr. Ogilvie was unlucky enough to choose for the topick of his conversation the praises of his native country. He began with saying, that there was very rich land round Edinburgh. Goldsmith, who had studied physick there, contradicted this, very untruly, with a sneering laugh. Disconcerted a little by this, Mr. Ogilvie then took new ground, where, I suppose, he thought himself perfectly safe; for he observed, that Scotland had a great many noble wild prospects. JOHNSON. 'I believe, Sir, you have a great many. Norway, too, has noble wild prospects; and Lapland is remarkable for prodigious noble wild prospects. But, Sir, let me tell you, the noblest prospect which a Scotchman ever sees, is the high road that leads him to England!' This unexpected and pointed sally produced a roar of applause. After all, however, those, who admire the rude grandeur of Nature, cannot deny it to Caledonia.

On Saturday, July 9, I found Johnson surrounded with a numerous levee, but have not preserved any part of his conversation. On the 14th we had another evening by ourselves at the Mitre. It happening to be a very rainy night, I made some common-place observations on the relaxation of nerves and depression of spirits which such weather occasioned; adding, however, that it was good for the vegetable creation. Johnson, who, as we have already seen, denied that the temperature of the air had any influence on the human frame, answered, with a smile of ridicule. 'Why yes, Sir, it is good for vegetables, and for the animals who eat those vegetables, and for the animals who eat those animals.' This observation of his aptly enough introduced a good supper; and I soon forgot, in Johnson's company, the influence of a moist atmosphere.

Feeling myself now quite at ease as his companion, though I had all possible reverence for him, I expressed a regret that I could not be so easy with my father, though he was not much older than Johnson, and certainly however respectable had not more learning and greater abilities to depress me. I asked him the reason of this. JOHNSON. 'Why,

Sir, I am a man of the world. I live in the world, and I take, in some degree, the colour of the world as it moves along. Your father is a Judge in a remote part of the island, and all his notions are taken from the old world. Besides, Sir, there must always be a struggle between a father and son while one aims at power and the other at independence.'

He enlarged very convincingly upon the excellence of rhyme over blank verse in English poetry. I mentioned to him that Dr. Adam Smith, in his lectures upon composition, when I studied under him in the College of Glasgow, had maintained the same opinion strenuously, and I repeated some of his arguments. JOHNSON. 'Sir, I was once in company with Smith, and we did not take to each other; but had I known that he loved rhyme as much as you tell me he does, I should have HUGGED him.'

'Idleness is a disease which must be combated; but I would not advise a rigid adherence to a particular plan of study. I myself have never persisted in any plan for two days together. A man ought to read just as inclination leads him; for what he reads as a task will do him little good. A young man should read five hours in a day, and so may acquire a great deal of knowledge.'

To such a degree of unrestrained frankness had he now accustomed me, that in the course of this evening I talked of the numerous reflections which had been thrown out against him on account of his having accepted a pension from his present Majesty. 'Why, Sir, (said he, with a hearty laugh,) it is a mighty foolish noise that they make.[15] I have accepted of a pension as a reward which has been thought due to my literary merit; and now that I have this pension, I am the same man in every respect that I have ever been; I retain the same principles. It is true, that I cannot now curse (smiling) the House of Hanover; nor would it be decent for me to drink King James's health in the wine that King George gives me money to pay for. But, Sir, I think that the pleasure of cursing the House of Hanover, and drinking King James's health, are amply overbalanced by three hundred pounds a year.'

There was here, most certainly, an affectation of more Jacobitism than he really had. Yet there is no doubt that at earlier periods he was wont often to exercise both his pleasantry and ingenuity in talking Jacobitism. My much respected friend, Dr. Douglas, now Bishop of Salisbury, has favoured me with the following admirable instance from his Lordship's own recollection. One day, when dining at old Mr. Langton's where Miss Roberts, his niece, was one of the company, Johnson, with his usual complacent attention to the fair sex, took her by the hand and said, 'My dear, I hope you are a Jacobite.' Old Mr.

---

[15] When I mentioned the same idle clamour to him several years afterwards, he said, with a smile, 'I wish my pension were twice as large, that they might make twice as much noise.'—BOSWELL.

Langton, who, though a high and steady Tory, was attached to the present Royal Family, seemed offended, and asked Johnson, with great warmth, what he could mean by putting such a question to his niece? 'Why, Sir, (said Johnson) I meant no offence to your niece, I meant her a great compliment. A Jacobite, Sir, believes in the divine right of Kings. He that believes in the divine right of Kings believes in a Divinity. A Jacobite believes in the divine right of Bishops. He that believes in the divine right of Bishops believes in the divine authority of the Christian religion. Therefore, Sir, a Jacobite is neither an Atheist nor a Deist. That cannot be said of a Whig; for *Whiggism is a negation of all principle.*'[16]

He advised me, when abroad, to be as much as I could with the Professors in the Universities, and with the Clergy; for from their conversation I might expect the best accounts of every thing in whatever country I should be, with the additional advantage of keeping my learning alive.

It will be observed, that when giving me advice as to my travels, Dr. Johnson did not dwell upon cities, and palaces, and pictures, and shows, and Arcadian scenes. He was of Lord Essex's opinion, who advises his kinsman Roger Earl of Rutland, 'rather to go an hundred miles to speak with one wise man, than five miles to see a fair town.'

I described to him an impudent fellow from Scotland, who affected to be a savage, and railed at all established systems. JOHNSON. 'There is nothing surprizing in this, Sir. He wants to make himself conspicuous. He would tumble in a hogstye, as long as you looked at him and called to him to come out. But let him alone, never mind him, and he'll soon give it over.'

I added, that the same person maintained that there was no distinction between virtue and vice. JOHNSON. 'Why, Sir, if the fellow does not think as he speaks, he is lying; and I see not what honour he can propose to himself from having the character of a lyar. But if he does really think that there is no distinction between virtue and vice, why, Sir, when he leaves our houses let us count our spoons.'

He recommended to me to keep a journal of my life, full and unreserved. He said it would be a very good exercise, and would yield me great satisfaction when the particulars were faded from my remembrance. I was uncommonly fortunate in having had a previous coincidence of opinion with him upon this subject, for I had kept such a journal for some time; and it was no small pleasure to me to have this

---

[16] He used to tell, with great humour, from my relation to him, the following little story of my early years, which was literally true: 'Boswell, in the year 1745, was a fine boy, wore a white cockade, and prayed for King James, till one of his uncles (General Cochran) gave him a shilling on condition that he should pray for King George, which he accordingly did. So you see (says Boswell) that Whigs of all ages are made the same way.'—BOSWELL.

to tell him, and to receive his approbation. He counselled me to keep it private, and said I might surely have a friend who would burn it in case of my death. From this habit I have been enabled to give the world so many anecdotes, which would otherwise have been lost to posterity. I mentioned that I was afraid I put into my journal too many little incidents. JOHNSON. 'There is nothing, Sir, too little for so little a creature as man. It is by studying little things that we attain the great art of having as little misery and as much happiness as possible.'

Next morning Mr. Dempster happened to call on me, and was so much struck even with the imperfect account which I gave him of Dr. Johnson's conversation, that to his honour be it recorded, when I complained that drinking port and sitting up late with him affected my nerves for some time after, he said, 'One had better be palsied at eighteen than not keep company with such a man.'

On Tuesday, July 18, I found tall Sir Thomas Robinson sitting with Johnson. Sir Thomas said, that the king of Prussia valued himself upon three things;—upon being a hero, a musician, and an authour. JOHNSON. 'Pretty well, Sir, for one man. As to his being an authour, I have not looked at his poetry; but his prose is poor stuff. He writes just as you might suppose Voltaire's footboy to do, who has been his amanuensis. He has such parts as the valet might have, and about as much of the colouring of the style as might be got by transcribing his works.' When I was at Ferney, I repeated this to Voltaire, in order to reconcile him somewhat to Johnson, whom he, in affecting the English mode of expression, had previously characterised as 'a superstitious dog;' but after hearing such a criticism on Frederick the Great, with whom he was then on bad terms, he exclaimed, 'An honest fellow!'

Mr. Levet this day shewed me Dr. Johnson's library, which was contained in two garrets over his Chambers, where Lintot, son of the celebrated bookseller of that name, had formerly his warehouse. I found a number of good books, but very dusty and in great confusion. The floor was strewed with manuscript leaves, in Johnson's own handwriting, which I beheld with a degree of veneration, supposing they perhaps might contain portions of *The Rambler* or of *Rasselas*. I observed an apparatus for chymical experiments, of which Johnson was all his life very fond. The place seemed to be very favourable for retirement and meditation. Johnson told me, that he went up thither without mentioning it to his servant, when he wanted to study, secure from interruption; for he would not allow his servant to say he was not at home when he really was. 'A servant's strict regard for truth, (said he) must be weakened by such a practice. A philosopher may know that it is merely a form of denial; but few servants are such nice distinguishers. If I accustom a servant to tell a lie for *me*, have I not reason to apprehend that he will tell many lies for *himself*.'

Mr. Temple, now vicar of St. Gluvias, Cornwall, who had been my intimate friend for many years, had at this time chambers in Farrar's-buildings, at the bottom of Inner Temple-lane, which he kindly lent me upon my quitting my lodgings, he being to return to Trinity Hall, Cambridge. I found them particularly convenient for me, as they were so near Dr. Johnson's.

On Wednesday, July 20, Dr. Johnson, Mr. Dempster, and my uncle Dr. Boswell, who happened to be now in London, supped with me at these Chambers. JOHNSON. 'Pity is not natural to man. Children are always cruel. Savages are always cruel. Pity is acquired and improved by the cultivation of reason. We may have uneasy sensations from seeing a creature in distress, without pity; for we have not pity unless we wish to relieve them. When I am on my way to dine with a friend, and finding it late, have bid the coachman make haste, if I happen to attend when he whips his horses, I may feel unpleasantly that the animals are put to pain, but I do not wish him to desist. No, Sir, I wish him to drive on.'

Rousseau's treatise on the inequality of mankind was at this time a fashionable topick. It gave rise to an observation by Mr. Dempster, that the advantages of fortune and rank were nothing to a wise man, who ought to value only merit. JOHNSON. 'If man were a savage, living in the woods by himself, this might be true; but in civilized society we all depend upon each other, and our happiness is very much owing to the good opinion of mankind. Now, Sir, in civilized society, external advantages make us more respected. A man with a good coat upon his back meets with a better reception than he who has a bad one. Sir, you may analyse this, and say what is there in it? But that will avail you nothing, for it is a part of a general system. Pound St. Paul's Church into atoms, and consider any single atom; it is, to be sure, good for nothing: but, put all these atoms together, and you have St. Paul's Church. So it is with human felicity, which is made up of many ingredients, each of which may be shewn to be very insignificant. In civilized society, personal merit will not serve you so much as money will. Sir, you may make the experiment. Go into the street, and give one man a lecture on morality, and another a shilling, and see which will respect you most. If you wish only to support nature, Sir William Petty fixes your allowance at three pounds a year; but as times are much altered, let us call it six pounds. This sum will fill your belly, shelter you from the weather, and even get you a strong lasting coat, supposing it to be made of good bull's hide. Now, Sir, all beyond this is artificial, and is desired in order to obtain a greater degree of respect from our fellow-creatures. And, Sir, if six hundred pounds a year procure a man more consequence, and, of course, more happiness than six pounds a year, the same proportion will hold as to six thousand, and so on as far as opulence can be carried. Perhaps he who has a large fortune may not be so happy as he who has a small one; but that must proceed from other causes than from his having the large fortune: for, *cœteris paribus*, he who is rich in a civilized society, must be happier than he who is poor; as riches, if properly used, (and it is a man's own fault if they are not,) must be productive of the highest advantages. Money, to be sure, of itself is of no use; for its only use is to part with it. Rousseau, and all those who deal in paradoxes, are led away by a childish desire of novelty. When I was a boy, I used always to choose the wrong side of a debate, because most ingenious things, that is to say, most new things, could be said upon it. Sir, there is nothing for which you may not muster up more plausible arguments, than those which are urged against wealth and other external advantages. Why, now, there is stealing; why should it be thought a crime? When we consider by what unjust methods property has been often acquired, and that what was unjustly got it must be unjust to keep, where is the harm in one man's taking the property of another from him? Besides, Sir, when we consider the bad use that many people make of their property, and how much better use the thief may make of it, it may be defended as a very allowable practice. Yet, Sir, the experience of mankind has discovered stealing to be so very bad a thing, that they make no scruple to hang a man for it. When I was running about this town a very poor fellow, I was a great arguer for the advantages of poverty; but I was, at the same time, very sorry to be poor. Sir, all the arguments which are brought to represent poverty as no evil, shew it to be evidently a great evil. You never find people labouring to convince you that you may live very happily upon a plentiful fortune.—So you hear people talking how miserable a King must be; and yet they all wish to be in his place.'

It was suggested that Kings must be unhappy, because they are deprived of the greatest of all satisfactions, easy and unreserved society. JOHNSON. 'That is an ill-founded notion. Being a King does not exclude a man from such society. Great Kings have always been social. The King of Prussia, the only great King at present, is very social. Charles the Second, the last King of England who was a man of parts, was social; and our Henrys and Edwards were all social.'

Mr. Dempster having endeavoured to maintain that intrinsick merit *ought* to make the only distinction amongst mankind. JOHNSON. 'Why, Sir, mankind have found that this cannot be. How shall we determine the proportion of intrinsick merit? Were that to be the only distinction amongst mankind, we should soon quarrel about the degrees of it. Were all distinctions abolished, the strongest would not long acquiesce, but would endeavour to obtain a superiority by their bodily strength. But, Sir, as subordination is very necessary for society, and contentions for superiority very dangerous, mankind, that is to say, all civilized nations, have settled it upon a plain invariable principle. A man is born to hereditary rank; or his being appointed to certain offices, gives him a certain rank. Subordination tends greatly to human happiness. Were we all upon an equality, we should have no other enjoyment than mere animal pleasure.'

He took care to guard himself against any possible suspicion that his settled principles of reverence for rank and respect for wealth were at all owing to mean or interested motives; for he asserted his own independence as a literary man. 'No man (said he) who ever lived by literature, has lived more independently than I have done.' He said he had taken longer time than he needed to have done in composing his *Dictionary*. He received our compliments upon that great work with complacency, and told us that the *Academia della Crusca* could scarcely believe that it was done by one man.

At night[17] Mr. Johnson and I supped in a private room at the Turk's Head coffee-house, in the Strand. 'I encourage this house (said he;) for the mistress of it is a good civil woman, and has not much business.'

'Sir, I love the acquaintance of young people; because, in the first place, I don't like to think myself growing old. In the next place, young acquaintances must last longest, if they do last; and then, Sir, young men have more virtue than old men: they have more generous sentiments in every respect. I love the young dogs of this age: they have more wit and humour and knowledge of life than we had; but then the dogs are not so good scholars. Sir, in my early years I read very hard. It is a sad reflection, but a true one, that I knew almost as much at eighteen as I do now. My judgement, to be sure, was not so good; but I had all the facts. I remember very well, when I was at Oxford, an old gentleman said to me, "Young man, ply your book diligently now, and acquire a stock of knowledge; for when years come upon you, you will find that poring upon books will be but an irksome task."'

He again insisted on the duty of maintaining subordination of rank. 'Sir, I would no more deprive a nobleman of his respect, than of his money. I consider myself as acting a part in the great system of society, and I do to others as I would have them to do to me. I would behave to a nobleman as I should expect he would behave to me, were I a nobleman and he Sam. Johnson. Sir, there is one Mrs. Macaulay[18] in this town, a great republican. One day when I was at her house, I put on a very grave countenance, and said to her, "Madam, I am now become a convert to your way of thinking. I am convinced that all mankind are upon an equal footing; and to give you an unquestionable proof, Madam, that I am in earnest, here is a very sensible, civil, well-behaved fellow-citizen, your footman; I desire that he may be allowed to sit down and dine with us." I thus, Sir, shewed her the absurdity of the

---

[17] July 21.

[18] This ONE Mrs. Macaulay was the same personage who afterwards made herself so much known as the celebrated female historian.'—BOSWELL.

levelling doctrine. She has never liked me since. Sir, your levellers wish to level *down* as far as themselves; but they cannot bear levelling *up* to themselves. They would all have some people under them; why not then have some people above them?' I mentioned a certain authour who disgusted me by his forwardness, and by shewing no deference to noblemen into whose company he was admitted. JOHNSON. 'Suppose a shoemaker should claim an equality with him, as he does with a Lord; how he would stare. "Why, Sir, do you stare? (says the shoemaker,) I do great service to society. 'Tis true I am paid for doing it; but so are you, Sir: and I am sorry to say it, paid better than I am, for doing something not so necessary. For mankind could do better without your books, than without my shoes." Thus, Sir, there would be a perpetual struggle for precedence, were there no fixed invariable rules for the distinction of rank, which creates no jealousy, as it is allowed to be accidental.'

He said he would go to the Hebrides with me, when I returned from my travels, unless some very good companion should offer when I was absent, which he did not think probable; adding, 'There are few people to whom I take so much to as you.' And when I talked of my leaving England, he said with a very affectionate air, 'My dear Boswell, I should be very unhappy at parting, did I think we were not to meet again.' I cannot too often remind my readers, that although such instances of his kindness are doubtless very flattering to me; yet I hope my recording them will be ascribed to a better motive than to vanity; for they afford unquestionable evidence of his tenderness and complacency, which some, while they were forced to acknowledge his great powers, have been so strenuous to deny.

He maintained that a boy at school was the happiest of human beings. I supported a different opinion, from which I have never yet varied, that a man is happier; and I enlarged upon the anxiety and sufferings which are endured at school. JOHNSON. 'Ah! Sir, a boy's being flogged is not so severe as a man's having the hiss of the world against him.'

On Tuesday, July 26, I found Mr. Johnson alone. It was a very wet day, and I again complained of the disagreeable effects of such weather. JOHNSON. 'Sir, this is all imagination, which physicians encourage; for man lives in air, as a fish lives in water; so that if the atmosphere press heavy from above, there is an equal resistance from below. To be sure, bad weather is hard upon people who are obliged to be abroad; and men cannot labour so well in the open air in bad weather, as in good: but, Sir, a smith or a taylor, whose work is within doors, will surely do as much in rainy weather, as in fair. Some very delicate frames, indeed, may be affected by wet weather; but not common constitutions.'

We talked of the education of children; and I asked him what he thought was best to teach them first. JOHNSON. 'Sir, it is no matter what you teach them first, any more than what leg you shall put into your breeches first. Sir, you may stand disputing which is best to put in first, but in the mean time your breech is bare. Sir, while you are considering which of two things you should teach your child first, another boy has learnt them both.'

On Thursday, July 28, we again supped in private at the Turk's Head coffee-house. JOHNSON. 'Swift has a higher reputation than he deserves. His excellence is strong sense; for his humour, though very well, is not remarkably good. I doubt whether *The Tale of a Tub* be his; for he never owned it, and it is much above his usual manner.'

'Thomson, I think, had as much of the poet about him as most writers. Every thing appeared to him through the medium of his favourite pursuit. He could not have viewed those two candles burning but with a poetical eye.'

'As to the Christian religion, Sir, besides the strong evidence which we have for it, there is a balance in its favour from the number of great men who have been convinced of its truth, after a serious consideration of the question. Grotius was an acute man, a lawyer, a man accustomed to examine evidence, and he was convinced. Grotius was not a recluse, but a man of the world, who certainly had no bias to the side of religion. Sir Isaac Newton set out an infidel, and came to be a very firm believer.'

He this evening recommended to me to perambulate Spain. I said it would amuse him to get a letter from me dated at Salamancha. JOHNSON. 'I love the University of Salamancha; for when the Spaniards were in doubt as to the lawfulness of their conquering America, the University of Salamancha gave it as their opinion that it was not lawful.' He spoke this with great emotion, and with that generous warmth which dictated the lines in his *London*, against Spanish encroachment.

I expressed my opinion of my friend Derrick as but a poor writer. JOHNSON. 'To be sure, Sir, he is; but you are to consider that his being a literary man has got for him all that he has. It has made him King of Bath. Sir, he has nothing to say for himself but that he is a writer. Had he not been a writer, he must have been sweeping the crossings in the streets, and asking halfpence from every body that past.'

In justice however, to the memory of Mr. Derrick, who was my first tutor in the ways of London, and shewed me the town in all its variety of departments, both literary and sportive, the particulars of which Dr. Johnson advised me to put in writing, it is proper to mention what Johnson, at a subsequent period, said of him both as a writer and an editor: 'Sir, I have often said, that if Derrick's letters had been written by one of a more established name, they would have been thought very pretty letters.' And, 'I sent Derrick to Dryden's relations to gather materials for his life; and I believe he got all that I myself should have got.'

Johnson said once to me, 'Sir, I honour Derrick for his presence of mind. One night, when Floyd, another poor authour, was wandering about the streets in the night, he found Derrick fast asleep upon a bulk; upon being suddenly waked, Derrick started up, "My dear Floyd, I am sorry to see you in this destitute state; will you go home with me to *my lodgings?*"'

I again begged his advice as to my method of study at Utrecht. 'Come, (said he) let us make a day of it. Let us go down to Greenwich and dine, and talk of it there.' The following Saturday was fixed for this excursion.

As we walked along the Strand to-night, arm in arm, a woman of the town accosted us, in the usual enticing manner. 'No, no, my girl, (said Johnson) it won't do.' He, however, did not treat her with harshness, and we talked of the wretched life of such women; and agreed, that much more misery than happiness, upon the whole, is produced by illicit commerce between the sexes.

On Saturday, July 30, Dr. Johnson and I took a sculler at the Temple-stairs, and set out for Greenwich. I asked him if he really thought a knowledge of the Greek and Latin languages an essential requisite to a good education. JOHNSON. 'Most certainly, Sir; for those who know them have a very great advantage over those who do not. Nay, Sir, it is wonderful what a difference learning makes upon people even in the common intercourse of life, which does not appear to be much connected with it.' 'And yet, (said I) people go through the world very well, and carry on the business of life to good advantage, without learning.' JOHNSON. 'Why, Sir, that may be true in cases where learning cannot possibly be of any use; for instance, this boy rows us as well without learning, as if he could sing the song of Orpheus to the Argonauts, who were the first sailors.' He then called to the boy, 'What would you give, my lad, to know about the Argonauts?' 'Sir, (said the boy,) I would give what I have.' Johnson was much pleased with his answer, and we gave him a double fare. Dr. Johnson then turning to me, 'Sir, (said he) a desire of knowledge is the natural feeling of mankind; and every human being, whose mind is not debauched, will be willing to give all that he has to get knowledge.'

We landed at the Old Swan, and walked to Billingsgate, where we took oars, and moved smoothly along the silver Thames. It was a very fine day. We were entertained with the immense number and variety of ships that were lying at anchor, and with the beautiful country on each side of the river.

I talked of preaching, and of the great success which those called Methodists have. JOHNSON. 'Sir, it is owing to their expressing themselves in a plain and familiar manner, which is the only way to do good to the common people, and which clergymen of genius and learning ought to do from a principle of duty, when it is suited to their congregations; a practice, for which they will be praised by men of sense. To insist against drunkenness as a crime, because it debases reason, the noblest faculty of man, would be of no service to the common people: but to tell them that they may die in a fit of drunkenness, and shew them how dreadful that would be, cannot fail to make a deep impression. Sir, when your Scotch clergy give up their homely manner, religion will soon decay in that country.' Let this observation, as Johnson meant it, be ever remembered.

I was much pleased to find myself with Johnson at Greenwich, which he celebrates in his *London* as a favourite scene. I had the poem in my pocket, and read the lines aloud with enthusiasm:

> 'On Thames's banks in silent thought we stood:
> Where Greenwich smiles upon the silver flood:
> Pleas'd with the seat which gave ELIZA birth,
> We kneel, and kiss the consecrated earth.'

Afterwards he entered upon the business of the day, which was to give me his advice as to a course of study.

We walked in the evening in Greenwich Park. He asked me, I suppose, by way of trying my disposition, 'Is not this very fine?' Having no exquisite relish of the beauties of Nature, and being more delighted with 'the busy hum of men,' I answered, 'Yes, Sir; but not equal to Fleet-street.' JOHNSON. 'You are right, Sir.'

I am aware that many of my readers may censure my want of taste. Let me, however, shelter myself under the authority of a very fashionable Baronet in the brilliant world, who, on his attention being called to the fragrance of a May evening in the country, observed, 'This may be very well; but, for my part, I prefer the smell of a flambeau at the playhouse.'

We staid so long at Greenwich, that our sail up the river, in our return to London, was by no means so pleasant as in the morning; for the night air was so cold that it made me shiver. I was the more sensible of it from having sat up all the night before, recollecting and writing in my journal what I thought worthy of preservation; an exertion, which, during the first part of my acquaintance with Johnson, I frequently made. I remember having sat up four nights in one week, without being much incommoded in the day time.

Johnson, whose robust frame was not in the least affected by the cold, scolded me, as if my shivering had been a paltry effeminacy, saying, 'Why do you shiver?' Sir William Scott, of the Commons, told me, that when he complained of a head-ache in the post-chaise, as they were travelling together to Scotland, Johnson treated him in the same manner: 'At your age, Sir, I had no head-ache.'

We concluded the day at the Turk's Head coffee-house very socially. He was pleased to listen to a particular account which I gave him of my family, and of its hereditary estate, as to the extent and population of which he asked questions, and made calculations; recommending, at the same time, a liberal kindness to the tenantry, as people over whom the proprietor was placed by Providence. He took delight in hearing my description of the romantick seat of my ancestors. 'I must be there, Sir, (said he) and we will live in the old castle; and if there is not a room in it remaining, we will build one.' I was highly flattered, but could scarcely indulge a hope that Auchinleck would indeed be honoured by his presence, and celebrated by a description, as it afterwards was, in his *Journey to the Western Islands*.

After we had again talked of my setting out for Holland, he said, 'I must see thee out of England; I will accompany you to Harwich.' I could not find words to express what I felt upon this unexpected and very great mark of his affectionate regard.

Next day, Sunday, July 31, I told him I had been that morning at a meeting of the people called Quakers, where I had heard a woman preach. JOHNSON. 'Sir, a woman's preaching is like a dog's walking on his hinder legs. It is not done well; but you are surprized to find it done at all.'

On Tuesday, August 2 (the day of my departure from London having been fixed for the 5th,) Dr. Johnson did me the honour to pass a part of the morning with me at my Chambers. He said, that 'he always felt an inclination to do nothing.' I observed, that it was strange to think that the most indolent man in Britain had written the most laborious work, *The English Dictionary*.

I had now made good my title to be a privileged man, and was carried by him in the evening to drink tea with Miss Williams, whom, though under the misfortune of having lost her sight, I found to be agreeable in conversation; for she had a variety of literature, and expressed herself well; but her peculiar value was the intimacy in which she had long lived with Johnson, by which she was well acquainted with his habits, and knew how to lead him on to talk.

After tea he carried me to what he called his walk, which was a long narrow paved court in the neighbourhood, overshadowed by some trees. There we sauntered a considerable time; and I complained to him that my love of London and of his company was such, that I shrunk almost from the thought of going away, even to travel, which is generally so much desired by young men. He roused me by manly and spirited conversation. He advised me, when settled in any place abroad, to study with an eagerness after knowledge, and to apply to Greek an hour every day; and when I was moving about, to read diligently the great book of mankind.

On Wednesday, August 3, we had our last social evening at the Turk's Head coffee-house, before my setting out for foreign parts. I had the misfortune, before we parted, to irritate him unintentionally. I mentioned to him how common it was in the world to tell absurd stories of him, and to ascribe to him very strange sayings. JOHNSON. 'What do they make me say, Sir?' BOSWELL. 'Why, Sir, as an instance very strange indeed, (laughing heartily as I spoke,) David Hume told me, you said that you would stand before a battery of cannon, to restore the Convocation to its full powers.' Little did I apprehend that he had actually said this: but I was soon convinced of my errour; for, with a determined look, he thundered out 'And would I not, Sir? Shall the Presbyterian KIRK of Scotland have its General Assembly, and the Church of England be denied its Convocation?' He was walking up and down the room while I told him the anecdote; but when he uttered this explosion of high-church zeal, he had come close to my chair, and his eyes flashed with indignation. I bowed to the storm, and diverted the force of it, by leading him to expatiate on the influence which religion derived from maintaining the church with great external respectability.

On Friday, August 5, we set out early in the morning in the Harwich stage coach. A fat elderly gentlewoman, and a young Dutchman, seemed the most inclined among us to conversation. At the inn where we dined, the gentlewoman said that she had done her best to educate her children; and particularly, that she had never suffered them to be a moment idle. JOHNSON. 'I wish, madam, you would educate me too; for I have been an idle fellow all my life.' 'I am sure, Sir, (said she) you have not been idle.' JOHNSON. 'Nay, Madam, it is very true; and that gentleman there (pointing to me,) has been idle. He was idle at Edinburgh. His father sent him to Glasgow, where he continued to be idle. He then came to London, where he has been very idle; and now he is going to Utrecht, where he will be as idle as ever. I asked him privately how he could expose me so. JOHNSON. 'Poh, poh! (said he) they knew nothing about you, and will think of it no more.' In the afternoon the gentlewoman talked violently against the Roman Catholicks, and of the horrours of the Inquisition. To the utter astonishment of all the passengers but myself, who knew that he could talk upon any side of a question, he defended the Inquisition, and maintained, that 'false doctrine should be checked on its first appearance; that the civil power should unite with the church in punishing those who dared to attack the established religion, and that such only were punished by the Inquisition.' He had in his pocket *Pomponius Mela de situ Orbis*, in which he read occasionally, and seemed very intent upon ancient geography. Though by no means niggardly, his attention to what was generally right was so minute, that having observed at one of the stages that I ostentatiously gave a shilling to the coachman, when the custom was for each passenger to give only six-pence, he took me aside and scolded me, saying that what I had done would make the coachman dissatisfied with all the rest of the passengers, who gave him no more than his due. This was a just reprimand; for in whatever way a man may indulge his generosity or his vanity in spending his money, for the sake of others he ought not to raise the price of any article for which there is a constant demand.

At supper this night[19] he talked of good eating with uncommon satisfaction. 'Some people (said he,) have a foolish way of not minding, or pretending not to mind, what they eat. For my part, I mind my belly very studiously, and very carefully; for I look upon it, that he who does not mind his belly will hardly mind anything else.' He now appeared to me *Jean Bull philosophe*, and he was, for the moment, not only serious but vehement. Yet I have heard him, upon other occasions, talk with great contempt of people who were anxious to gratify their palates; and the 206th number of his *Rambler* is a masterly essay against gulosity. His practice, indeed, I must acknowledge, may be considered as casting the balance of his different opinions upon this subject; for I never knew any man who relished good eating more than he did. When at table, he was totally absorbed in the business of the moment; his looks seemed rivetted to his plate; nor would he, unless when in very high company, say one word, or even pay the least attention to what was said by others, till he had satisfied his appetite, which was so fierce, and indulged with such intenseness, that while in the act of eating, the veins of his forehead swelled, and generally a strong perspiration was visible. To those whose sensations were delicate, this could not but be disgusting; and it was doubtless not very suitable to the character of a philosopher, who should be distinguished by self-command. But it must be owned, that Johnson, though he could be rigidly *abstemious*, was not a *temperate* man either in eating or drinking. He could refrain, but he could not use moderately. He told me, that he had fasted two days without inconvenience, and that he had never been hungry but once. They who beheld with wonder how much he eat upon all occasions when his dinner was to his taste, could not easily conceive what he must have meant by hunger; and not only was he remarkable for the extraordinary quantity which he eat, but he was, or affected to be, a man of very nice discernment in the science of cookery. He used to descant critically on the dishes which had been at table where he had dined or supped, and to recollect very minutely what he had liked. I remember, when he was in Scotland, his praising 'Gordon's palates,' (a dish of palates at the Honourable Alexander Gordon's) with a warmth of expression which might have done honour to more important subjects. 'As for Maclaurin's imitation of a *made dish*, it was a wretched attempt.' He about the same time was so much displeased

---

[19] At Colchester.—Ed.

with the performances of a nobleman's French cook, that he exclaimed with vehemence, 'I'd throw such a rascal into the river, and he then proceeded to alarm a lady at whose house he was to sup, by the following manifesto of his skill: 'I, Madam, who live at a variety of good tables, am a much better judge of cookery, than any person who has a very tolerable cook, but lives much at home; for his palate is gradually adapted to the taste of his cook; whereas, Madam, in trying by a wider range, I can more exquisitely judge.' When invited to dine, even with an intimate friend, he was not pleased if something better than a plain dinner was not prepared for him. I have heard him say on such an occasion, 'This was a good dinner enough, to be sure; but it was not a dinner to *ask* a man to.' On the other hand, he was wont to express, with great glee, his satisfaction when he had been entertained quite to his mind. One day when we had dined with his neighbour and landlord in Bolt-court, Mr. Allen, the printer, whose old housekeeper had studied his taste in every thing, he pronounced this eulogy: 'Sir, we could not have had a better dinner had there been a *Synod of Cooks.*'

While we were left by ourselves, after the Dutchman had gone to bed, Dr. Johnson talked of that studied behaviour which many have recommended and practised. He disapproved of it; and said, 'I never considered whether I should be a grave man, or a merry man, but just let inclination, for the time, have its course.'

I teized him with fanciful apprehensions of unhappiness. A moth having fluttered round the candle, and burnt itself, he laid hold of this little incident to admonish me; saying, with a sly look, and in a solemn but quiet tone, 'That creature was its own tormentor, and I believe its name was BOSWELL.'

Next day we got to Harwich to dinner; and my passage in the packet-boat to Helvoetsluys being secured, and my baggage put on board, we dined at our inn by ourselves. I happened to say it would be terrible if he should not find a speedy opportunity of returning to London, and be confined to so dull a place. JOHNSON. 'Don't Sir, accustom yourself to use big words for little matters. It would *not* be *terrible*, though I *were* to be detained some time here.'

We went and looked at the church, and having gone into it and walked up to the altar, Johnson, whose piety was constant and fervent, sent me to my knees, saying, 'Now that you are going to leave your native country, recommend yourself to the protection of your CREATOR and REDEEMER.'

After we came out of the church, we stood talking for some time together of Bishop Berkeley's ingenious sophistry to prove the non-existence of matter, and that every thing in the universe is merely ideal. I observed, that though we are satisfied his doctrine is not true, it is impossible to refute it. I never shall forget the alacrity with which Johnson answered, striking his foot with mighty force against a large stone, till he rebounded from it, 'I refute it *thus.*'

My revered friend walked down with me to the beach, where we embraced and parted with tenderness, and engaged to correspond by letters. I said, 'I hope, Sir, you will not forget me in my absence.' JOHNSON. 'Nay, Sir, it is more likely you should forget me, than that I should forget you.' As the vessel put out to sea, I kept my eyes upon him for a considerable time, while he remained rolling his majestick frame in his usual manner: and at last I perceived him walk hack into the town, and he disappeared.

1764: ÆTAT. 55.]—Early in 1764 Johnson paid a visit to the Langton family, at their seat of Langton, in Lincolnshire, where he passed some time, much to his satisfaction. His friend Bennet Langton, it will not he doubted, did every thing in his power to make the place agreeable to so illustrious a guest; and the elder Mr. Langton and his lady, being fully capable of understanding his value, were not wanting in attention.

Johnson, during his stay at Langton, had the advantage of a good library, and saw several gentlemen of the neighbourhood. I have obtained from Mr. Langton the following particulars of this period.

He was now fully convinced that he could not have been satisfied with a country living; for, talking of a respectable clergyman in Lincolnshire, he observed, 'This man, Sir, fills up the duties of his life well. I approve of him, but could not imitate him.'

To a lady who endeavoured to vindicate herself from blame for neglecting social attention to worthy neighbours, by saying, 'I would go to them if it would do them any good,' he said, 'What good, Madam, do you expect to have in your power to do them? It is shewing them respect, and that is doing them good.'

So socially accommodating was he, that once when Mr. Langton and he were driving together in a coach, and Mr. Langton complained of being sick, he insisted that they should go out and sit on the back of it in the open air, which they did. And being sensible how strange the appearance must be, observed, that a countryman whom they saw in a field, would probably be thinking, 'If these two madmen should come down, what would become of me?'

Soon after his return to London, which was in February, was founded that CLUB which existed long without a name, but at Mr. Garrick's funeral became distinguished by the title of THE LITERARY CLUB. Sir Joshua Reynolds had the merit of being the first proposer of it, to which Johnson acceded, and the original members were, Sir Joshua Reynolds, Dr. Johnson, Mr. Edmund Burke, Dr. Nugent, Mr. Beauclerk, Mr. Langton, Dr. Goldsmith, Mr. Chamier, and Sir John Hawkins. They met at the Turk's Head, in Gerrard-street, Soho, one evening in every week, at seven, and generally continued their conversation till a pretty late hour. This club has been gradually increased to its present number, thirty-five: After about ten years, instead of supping weekly, it was resolved to dine together once a fortnight during the meeting of Parliament. Their original tavern having been converted into a private house, they moved first to Prince's in Sackville-street, then to Le Telier's in Dover-street, and now meet at Parsloe's, St. James's-street. Between the time of its formation, and the time at which this work is passing through the press, (June 1792,) the following persons, now dead, were members of it: Mr. Dunning, (afterwards Lord Ashburton,) Mr. Samuel Dyer, Mr. Garrick, Dr. Shipley Bishop of St. Asaph, Mr. Vesey, Mr. Thomas Warton and Dr. Adam Smith. The present members are,—Mr. Burke, Mr. Langton, Lord Charlemont, Sir Robert Chambers, Dr. Percy Bishop of Dromore, Dr. Barnard Bishop of Killaloc, Dr. Marlay Bishop of Clonfert, Mr. Fox, Dr. George Fordyce, Sir William Scott, Sir Joseph Banks, Sir Charles Bunbury, Mr. Windham of Norfolk, Mr. Sheridan, Mr. Gibbon, Sir William Jones, Mr. Colman, Mr. Steevens, Dr. Burney, Dr. Joseph Warton, Mr. Malone, Lord Ossory, Lord Spencer, Lord Lucan, Lord Palmerston, Lord Eliot, Lord Macartney, Mr. Richard Burke junior, Sir William Hamilton, Dr. Warren, Mr. Courtenay, Dr. Hinchcliffe Bishop of Peterborough, the Duke of Leeds, Dr. Douglas Bishop of Salisbury, and the writer of this account.

Not very long after the institution of our club, Sir Joshua Reynolds was speaking of it to Garrick. 'I like it much, (said he), I think I shall be of you.' When Sir Joshua mentioned this to Dr. Johnson, he was much displeased with the actor's conceit. '*He'll be of us,* (said Johnson) how does he know we will *permit* him? The first Duke in England has no right to hold such language.' However, when Garrick was regularly proposed some time afterwards, Johnson, though he had taken a momentary offence at his arrogance, warmly and kindly supported him, and he was accordingly elected, was a most agreeable member, and continued to attend our meetings to the time of his death.

It was Johnson's custom to observe certain days with a pious abstraction; viz. New-year's-day, the day of his wife's death, Good Friday, Easter-day, and his own birth-day. He this year says:—'I have now spent fifty-five years in resolving; having, from the earliest time almost that I can remember, been forming schemes of a better life. I have done nothing. The need of doing, therefore, is pressing, since the time of doing is short. O GOD, grant me to resolve aright, and to keep my resolutions, for JESUS CHRIST'S sake. Amen.'

About this time he was afflicted with a very severe return of the hypochondriack disorder, which was ever lurking about him. He was so ill, as, notwithstanding his remarkable love of company, to be entirely averse to society, the most fatal symptom of that malady. Dr. Adams told me, that as an old friend he was admitted to visit him, and that he found him in a deplorable state, sighing, groaning, talking to himself, and restlessly walking from room to room. He then used this emphatical expression of the misery which he felt: 'I would consent to have a limb amputated to recover my spirits.'

Talking to himself was, indeed, one of his singularities ever since I knew him. I was certain that he was frequently uttering pious ejaculations; for fragments of the Lord's Prayer have been distinctly overheard. His friend Mr. Thomas Davies, of whom Churchill says,

'That Davies hath a very pretty wife,'

when Dr. Johnson muttered 'lead us not into temptation,' used with waggish and gallant humour to whisper Mrs. Davies, 'You, my dear, are the cause of this.'

He had another particularity, of which none of his friends ever ventured to ask an explanation. It appeared to me some superstitious habit, which he had contracted early, and from which he had never called upon his reason to disentangle him. This was his anxious care to go out or in at a door or passage by a certain number of steps from a certain point, or at least so as that either his right or his left foot, (I am not certain which,) should constantly make the first actual movement when he came close to the door or passage. Thus I conjecture: for I have, upon innumerable occasions, observed him suddenly stop, and then seem to count his steps with a deep earnestness; and when he had neglected or gone wrong in this sort of magical movement, I have seen him go back again, put himself in a proper posture to begin the ceremony, and, having gone through it, break from his abstraction, walk briskly on, and join his companion. A strange instance of something of this nature, even when on horseback, happened when he was in the isle of Sky. Sir Joshua Reynolds has observed him to go a good way about, rather than cross a particular alley in Leicester-fields; but this Sir Joshua imputed to his having had some disagreeable recollection associated with it.

That the most minute singularities which belonged to him, and made very observable parts of his appearance and manner, may not be omitted, it is requisite to mention, that while talking or even musing as he sat in his chair, he commonly held his head to one side towards his right shoulder, and shook it in a tremulous manner, moving his body backwards and forwards, and rubbing his left knee in the same direction, with the palm of his hand. In the intervals of articulating he made various sounds with his mouth, sometimes as if ruminating, or what is called chewing the cud, sometimes giving a half whistle, sometimes making his tongue play backwards from the roof of his mouth, as if clucking like a hen, and sometimes protruding it against his upper gums in front, as if pronouncing quickly under his breath, *too, too, too*: all this accompanied sometimes with a thoughtful look, but more frequently with a smile. Generally when he had concluded a period, in the course of a dispute, by which time he was a good deal exhausted by violence and vociferation, he used to blow out his breath like a Whale. This I supposed was a relief to his lungs; and seemed in him to be a contemptuous mode of expression, as if he had made the arguments of his opponent fly like chaff before the wind.

1765: ÆTAT. 56.]—TRINITY College, Dublin, at this time surprised Johnson with a spontaneous compliment of the highest academical honours, by creating him Doctor of Laws.

He appears this year to have been seized with a temporary fit of ambition, for he had thoughts both of studying law and of engaging in politics. His 'Prayer before the Study of Law' is truly admirable:—

'Sept. 26, 1765.

'Almighty GOD, the giver of wisdom, without whose help resolutions are vain, without whose blessing study is ineffectual; enable me, if it be thy will, to attain such knowledge as may qualify me to direct the doubtful, and instruct the ignorant; to prevent wrongs and terminate contentions; and grant that I may use that knowledge which I shall attain, to thy glory and my own salvation, for JESUS CHRIST'S sake. Amen.'

This year was distinguished by his being introduced into the family of Mr. Thrale, one of the most eminent brewers in England, and Member of Parliament for the borough of Southwark. Foreigners are not a little amazed when they hear of brewers, distillers, and men in similar departments of trade, held forth as persons of considerable consequence. In this great commercial country it is natural that a situation which produces much wealth should be considered as very respectable; and, no doubt, honest industry is entitled to esteem. But, perhaps, the too rapid advance of men of low extraction tends to lessen the value of that distinction by birth and gentility, which has ever been found beneficial to the grand scheme of subordination. Johnson used to give this account of the rise of Mr. Thrale's father: 'He worked at six shillings a week for twenty years in the great brewery, which afterwards was his own. The proprietor of it had an only daughter, who was married to a nobleman. It was not fit that a peer should continue the business. On the old man's death, therefore, the brewery was to be sold. To find a purchaser for so large a property was a difficult matter; and, after some time, it was suggested, that it would be adviseable to treat with Thrale, a sensible, active, honest man, who had been employed in the house, and to transfer the whole to him for thirty thousand pounds, security being taken upon the property. This was accordingly settled. In eleven years Thrale paid the purchase-money. He acquired a large fortune, and lived to be Member of Parliament for

Southwark. But what was most remarkable was the liberality with which he used his riches. He gave his son and daughters the best education. The esteem which his good conduct procured him from the nobleman who had married his master's daughter, made him be treated with much attention; and his son, both at school and at the University of Oxford, associated with young men of the first rank. His allowance from his father, after he left college, was splendid; no less than a thousand a year. This, in a man who had risen as old Thrale did, was a very extraordinary instance of generosity. He used to say, "If this young dog does not find so much after I am gone as he expects, let him remember that he has had a great deal in my own time.'"

The son, though in affluent circumstances, had good sense enough to carry on his father's trade, which was of such extent, that I remember he once told me, he would not quit it for an annuity of ten thousand a year; 'Not (said he,) that I get ten thousand a year by it, but it is an estate to a family.' Having left daughters only, the property was sold for the immense sum of one hundred and thirty-five thousand pounds; a magnificent proof of what may be done by fair trade in no long period of time.

Mr. Thrale had married Miss Hesther Lynch Salusbury, of good Welsh extraction, a lady of lively talents, improved by education. That Johnson's introduction into Mr. Thrale's family, which contributed so much to the happiness of his life, was owing to her desire for his conversation, is very probable and a general supposition: but it is not the truth. Mr. Murphy, who was intimate with Mr. Thrale, having spoken very highly of Dr. Johnson, he was requested to make them acquainted. This being mentioned to Johnson, he accepted of an invitation to dinner at Thrale's, and was so much pleased with his reception, both by Mr. and Mrs. Thrale, and they so much pleased with him, that his invitations to their house were more and more frequent, till at last he became one of the family, and an apartment was appropriated to him, both in their house in Southwark, and in their villa at Streatham.

Johnson had a very sincere esteem for Mr. Thrale, as a man of excellent principles, a good scholar, well skilled in trade, of a sound understanding, and of manners such as presented the character of a plain independent English Squire. As this family will frequently be mentioned in the course of the following pages, and as a false notion has prevailed that Mr. Thrale was inferiour, and in some degree insignificant, compared with Mrs. Thrale, it may be proper to give a true state of the case from the authority of Johnson himself in his own words.

'I know no man, (said he,) who is more master of his wife and family than Thrale. If he but holds up a finger, he is obeyed. It is a great mistake to suppose that she is above him in literary attainments. She is more flippant; but he has ten times her learning: he is a regular scholar; but her learning is that of a school-boy in one of the lower forms.' My readers may naturally wish for some representation of the figures of this couple. Mr. Thrale was tall, well proportioned, and stately. As for *Madam*, or *my Mistress*, by which epithets Johnson used to mention Mrs. Thrale, she was short, plump, and brisk. She has herself given us a lively view of the idea which Johnson had of her person, on her appearing before him in a dark-coloured gown: 'You little creatures should never wear those sort of clothes, however; they are unsuitable in every way. What! have not all insects gay colours?' Mr. Thrale gave his wife a liberal indulgence, both in the choice of their company, and in the mode of entertaining them. He understood and valued Johnson, without remission, from their first acquaintance to the day of his death. Mrs. Thrale was enchanted with Johnson's conversation, for its own sake, and had also a very allowable vanity in appearing to be honoured with the attention of so celebrated a man.

Nothing could be more fortunate for Johnson than this connection. He had at Mr. Thrale's all the comforts and even luxuries of life; his melancholy was diverted, and his irregular habits lessened by association with an agreeable and well-ordered family. He was treated with the utmost respect, and even affection. The vivacity of Mrs. Thrale's literary talk roused him to cheerfulness and exertion, even when they were alone. But this was not often the case; for he found here a constant succession of what gave him the highest enjoyment: the society of the learned, the witty, and the eminent in every way, who were assembled in numerous companies, called forth his wonderful powers, and gratified him with admiration, to which no man could be insensible.

In the October of this year he at length gave to the world his edition of *Shakspeare*, which, if it had no other merit but that of producing his Preface, in which the excellencies and defects of that immortal bard are displayed with a masterly hand, the nation would have had no reason to complain.

In 1764 and 1765 it should seem that Dr. Johnson was so busily employed with his edition of *Shakspeare*, as to have had little leisure for any other literary exertion, or, indeed, even for private correspondence. He did not favour me with a single letter for more than two years, for which it will appear that he afterwards apologised.

He was, however, at all times ready to give assistance to his friends, and others, in revising their works, and in writing for them, or greatly improving their Dedications. In that courtly species of composition no man excelled Dr. Johnson. Though the loftiness of his mind prevented him from ever dedicating in his own person, he wrote a very great number of Dedications for others. Some of these, the persons who were favoured with them are unwilling should be mentioned, from a too anxious apprehension, as I think, that they might be suspected of having received larger assistance; and some, after all the diligence I have bestowed, have escaped my enquiries. He told me, a great many years ago, 'he believed he had dedicated to all the Royal Family round;' and it was indifferent to him what was the subject of the work dedicated, provided it were innocent. He once dedicated some Musick for the German Flute to Edward, Duke of York. In writing Dedications for others, he considered himself as by no means speaking his own sentiments.

I returned to London in February,[20] and found Dr. Johnson in a good house in Johnson's Court, Fleet-street, in which he had accommodated Miss Williams with an apartment on the ground floor, while Mr. Levet occupied his post in the garret: his faithful Francis was still attending upon him. He received me with much kindness. The fragments of our first conversation, which I have preserved, are these: I told him that Voltaire, in a conversation with me, had distinguished Pope and Dryden thus:—'Pope drives a handsome chariot, with a couple of neat trim nags; Dryden a coach, and six stately horses.' JOHNSON. 'Why, Sir, the truth is, they both drive coaches and six; but Dryden's horses are either galloping or stumbling: Pope's go at a steady even trot.' He said of Goldsmith's *Traveller*, which had been published in my absence, 'There has not been so fine a poem since Pope's time.'

Talking of education, 'People have now a-days, (said he,) got a strange opinion that every thing should be taught by lectures. Now, I cannot see that lectures can do so much good as reading the books from which the lectures are taken. I know nothing that can be best taught by lectures, except where experiments are to be shewn. You may teach chymistry by lectures.—You might teach making of shoes by lectures!'

At night I supped with him at the Mitre tavern, that we might renew our social intimacy at the original place of meeting. But there was now a considerable difference in his way of living. Having had an illness, in which he was advised to leave off wine, he had, from that period, continued to abstain from it, and drank only water, or lemonade.

I told him that a foreign friend of his, whom I had met with abroad, was so wretchedly perverted to infidelity, that he treated the hopes of immortality with brutal levity; and said, 'As man dies like a dog, let him lie like a dog.' JOHNSON. '*If* he dies like a dog, *let* him lie like a dog.' I added, that this man said to me, 'I hate mankind, for I think myself one of the best of them, and I know how bad I am.' JOHNSON. 'Sir, he must be very singular in his opinion, if he thinks himself one of the best of men; for none of his friends think him so.'—He said, 'no honest man could be a Deist; for no man could be so after a fair

---

[20] 1766.

examination of the proofs of Christianity.' I named Hume. JOHNSON. 'No, Sir; Hume owned to a clergyman in the bishoprick of Durham, that he had never read the New Testament with attention.' I mentioned Hume's notion, that all who are happy are equally happy; a little miss with a new gown at a dancing school ball, a general at the head of a victorious army, and an orator, after having made an eloquent speech in a great assembly. JOHNSON. 'Sir, that all who are happy, are equally happy, is not true. A peasant and a philosopher may be equally *satisfied*, but not equally *happy*. Happiness consists in the multiplicity of agreeable consciousness. A peasant has not capacity for having equal happiness with a philosopher.'

Dr. Johnson was very kind this evening, and said to me 'You have now lived five-and-twenty years, and you have employed them well.' 'Alas, Sir, (said I,) I fear not. Do I know history? Do I know mathematicks? Do I know law?' JOHNSON. 'Why, Sir, though you may know no science so well as to be able to teach it, and no profession so well as to be able to follow it, your general mass of knowledge of books and men renders you very capable to make yourself master of any science, or fit yourself for any profession.' I mentioned that a gay friend had advised me against being a lawyer, because I should be excelled by plodding block-heads. JOHNSON. 'Why, Sir, in the formulary and statutory part of law, a plodding block-head may excel; but in the ingenious and rational part of it a plodding block-head can never excel.'

I talked of the mode adopted by some to rise in the world, by courting great men, and asked him whether he had ever submitted to it. JOHNSON. 'Why, Sir, I never was near enough to great men, to court them. You may be prudently attached to great men and yet independent. You are not to do what you think wrong; and, Sir, you are to calculate, and not pay too dear for what you get. You must not give a shilling's worth of court for six-pence worth of good. But if you can get a shilling's worth of good for six-pence worth of court, you are a fool if you do not pay court.'

I talked to him a great deal of what I had seen in Corsica, and of my intention to publish an account of it. He encouraged me by saying, 'You cannot go to the bottom of the subject; but all that you tell us will be new to us. Give us as many anecdotes as you can.'

Our next meeting at the Mitre was on Saturday the 15th of February, when I presented to him my old and most intimate friend, the Reverend Mr. Temple, then of Cambridge. I having mentioned that I had passed some time with Rousseau in his wild retreat, and having quoted some remark made by Mr. Wilkes, with whom I had spent many pleasant hours in Italy, Johnson said (sarcastically,) 'It seems, Sir, you have kept very good company abroad, Rousseau and Wilkes!' Thinking it enough to defend one at a time, I said nothing as to my gay friend, but answered with a smile, 'My dear Sir, you don't call Rousseau bad company. Do you really think *him* a bad man?' JOHNSON. 'Sir, if you are talking jestingly of this, I don't talk with you. If you mean to be serious, I think him one of the worst of men; a rascal who ought to be hunted out of society, as he has been. Three or four nations have expelled him; and it is a shame that he is protected in this country.' BOSWELL. 'I don't deny, Sir, but that his novel may, perhaps, do harm; but I cannot think his intention was bad.' JOHNSON. 'Sir, that will not do. We cannot prove any man's intention to be bad. You may shoot a man through the head, and say you intended to miss him; but the Judge will order you to be hanged. An alleged want of intention, when evil is committed, will not be allowed in a court of justice. Rousseau, Sir, is a very bad man. I would sooner sign a sentence for his transportation, than that of any felon who has gone from the Old Bailey these many years. Yes, I should like to have him work in the plantations.' BOSWELL. 'Sir, do you think him as bad a man as Voltaire?' JOHNSON. 'Why, Sir, it is difficult to settle the proportion of iniquity between them.'

On his favourite subject of subordination, Johnson said, 'So far is it from being true that men are naturally equal, that no two people can be half an hour together, but one shall acquire an evident superiority over the other.'

I mentioned the advice given us by philosophers, to console ourselves, when distressed or embarrassed, by thinking of those who are in a worse situation than ourselves. This, I observed, could not apply to all, for there must be some who have nobody worse than they are. JOHNSON. 'Why, to be sure, Sir, there are; but they don't know it. There is no being so poor and so contemptible, who does not think there is somebody still poorer, and still more contemptible.'

As my stay in London at this time was very short, I had not many opportunities of being with Dr. Johnson; but I felt my veneration for him in no degree lessened, by my having seen *multorum hominum mores et urbes*. On the contrary, by having it in my power to compare him with many of the most celebrated persons of other countries, my admiration of his extraordinary mind was increased and confirmed.

The roughness, indeed, which sometimes appeared in his manners, was more striking to me now, from my having been accustomed to the studied smooth complying habits of the Continent; and I clearly recognised in him, not without respect for his honest conscientious zeal, the same indignant and sarcastical mode of treating every attempt to unhinge or weaken good principles.

One evening when a young gentleman teized him with an account of the infidelity of his servant, who, he said, would not believe the scriptures, because he could not read them in the original tongues, and be sure that they were not invented, 'Why, foolish fellow, (said

Johnson,) has he any better authority for almost every thing that he believes?' BOSWELL. 'Then the vulgar, Sir, never can know they are right, but must submit themselves to the learned.' JOHNSON. 'To be sure, Sir. The vulgar are the children of the State, and must be taught like children.' BOSWELL. 'Then, Sir, a poor Turk must be a Mahometan, just as a poor Englishman must be a Christian?' JOHNSON. 'Why, yes, Sir; and what then? This now is such stuff as I used to talk to my mother, when I first began to think myself a clever fellow; and she ought to have whipt me for it.'

Another evening Dr. Goldsmith and I called on him, with the hope of prevailing on him to sup with us at the Mitre. We found him indisposed, and resolved not to go abroad. 'Come then, (said Goldsmith,) we will not go to the Mitre to-night, since we cannot have the big man with us.' Johnson then called for a bottle of port, of which Goldsmith and I partook, while our friend, now a water-drinker, sat by us. GOLDSMITH. 'I think, Mr. Johnson, you don't go near the theatres now. You give yourself no more concern about a new play, than if you had never had any thing to do with the stage.' JOHNSON. 'Why, Sir, our tastes greatly alter. The lad does not care for the child's rattle, and the old man does not care for the young man's whore.' GOLDSMITH. 'Nay, Sir, but your Muse was not a whore.' JOHNSON. 'Sir, I do not think she was. But as we advance in the journey of life, we drop some of the things which have pleased us; whether it be that we are fatigued and don't choose to carry so many things any farther, or that we find other things which we like better.' BOSWELL. 'But, Sir, why don't you give us something in some other way?' GOLDSMITH. 'Ay, Sir, we have a claim upon you.' JOHNSON. No, Sir, I am not obliged to do any more. No man is obliged to do as much as he can do. A man is to have part of his life to himself. If a soldier has fought a good many campaigns, he is not to be blamed if he retires to ease and tranquillity. A physician, who has practised long in a great city, may be excused if he retires to a small town, and takes less practice. Now, Sir, the good I can do by my conversation bears the same proportion to the good I can do by my writings, that the practice of a physician, retired to a small town, does to his practice in a great city.' BOSWELL. 'But I wonder, Sir, you have not more pleasure in writing than in not writing.' JOHNSON. 'Sir, you *may* wonder.'

He talked of making verses, and observed, 'The great difficulty is to know when you have made good ones. When composing, I have generally had them in my mind, perhaps fifty at a time, walking up and down in my room; and then I have written them down, and often, from laziness, have written only half lines. I have written a hundred lines in a day. I remember I wrote a hundred lines of *The Vanity of Human Wishes* in a day. Doctor, (turning to Goldsmith,) I am not quite idle; I made one line t'other day; but I made no more.' GOLDSMITH. 'Let us hear it; we'll put a bad one to it.' JOHNSON. 'No, Sir, I have forgot it.'

'TO BENNET LANGTON, ESQ., AT LANGTON, NEAR SPILSBY, LINCOLNSHIRE

'DEAR SIR,—What your friends have done, that from your departure till now nothing has been heard of you, none of us are able to inform the rest; but as we are all neglected alike, no one thinks himself entitled to the privilege of complaint.

'I should have known nothing of you or of Langton, from the time that dear Miss Langton left us, had not I met Mr. Simpson, of Lincoln, one day in the street, by whom I was informed that Mr. Langton, your Mamma, and yourself, had been all ill, but that you were all recovered.

'That sickness should suspend your correspondence, I did not wonder; but hoped that it would be renewed at your recovery.

'Since you will not inform us where you are, or how you live, I know not whether you desire to know any thing of us. However, I will tell you that THE CLUB subsists; but we have the loss of Burke's company since he has been engaged in publick business, in which he has gained more reputation than perhaps any man at his [first] appearance ever gained before. He made two speeches in the House for repealing the Stamp-act, which were publickly commended by Mr. Pitt, and have filled the town with wonder.

'Burke is a great man by nature, and is expected soon to attain civil greatness. I am grown greater too, for I have maintained the news-papers these many weeks; and what is greater still, I have risen every morning since New-year's day, at about eight; when I was up, I have indeed done but little; yet it is no slight advancement to obtain for so many hours more, the consciousness of being.

'I wish you were in my new study; I am now writing the first letter in it. I think it looks very pretty about me.

'Dyer is constant at THE CLUB; Hawkins is remiss; I am not over diligent. Dr. Nugent, Dr. Goldsmith, and Mr. Reynolds, are very constant. Mr. Lye is printing his Saxon and Gothick Dictionary; all THE CLUB subscribes.

'You will pay my respects to all my Lincolnshire friends. I am, dear Sir, most affectionately your's,
          'March 9, 1766.
                                                    'SAM. JOHNSON.'
Johnson's-court, Fleet-street.'

The Honourable Thomas Hervey and his lady having unhappily disagreed, and being about to separate, Johnson interfered as their friend, and wrote him a letter of expostulation, which I have not been able to find; but the substance of it is ascertained by a letter to Johnson in answer to it, which Mr. Hervey printed. The occasion of this correspondence between Dr. Johnson and Mr. Harvey, was thus related to me by Mr. Beauclerk. 'Tom Harvey had a great liking for Johnson, and in his will had left him a legacy of fifty pounds. One day he said to me, "Johnson may want this money now, more than afterwards. I have a mind to give it him directly. Will you be so good as to carry a fifty pound note from me to him?" This I positively refused to do, as he might, perhaps, have knocked me down for insulting him, and have afterwards put the note in his pocket. But I said, if Harvey would write him a letter, and enclose a fifty pound note, I should take care to deliver it. He accordingly did write him a letter, mentioning that he was only paying a legacy a little sooner. To his letter he added, "*P. S. I am going to part with my wife.*" Johnson then wrote to him, saying nothing of the note, but remonstrating with him against parting with his wife.'

In February, 1767, there happened one of the most remarkable incidents of Johnson's life, which gratified his monarchical enthusiasm, and which he loved to relate with all its circumstances, when requested by his friends. This was his being honoured by a private conversation with his Majesty, in the library at the Queen's house. He had frequently visited those splendid rooms and noble collection of books, which he used to say was more numerous and curious than he supposed any person could have made in the time which the King had employed. Mr. Barnard, the librarian, took care that he should have every accommodation that could contribute to his ease and convenience, while indulging his literary taste in that place; so that he had here a very agreeable resource at leisure hours.

His Majesty having been informed of his occasional visits, was pleased to signify a desire that he should be told when Dr. Johnson came next to the library. Accordingly, the next time that Johnson did come, as soon as he was fairly engaged with a book, on which, while he sat by the fire, he seemed quite intent, Mr. Barnard stole round to the apartment where the King was, and, in obedience to his Majesty's commands, mentioned that Dr. Johnson was then in the library. His Majesty said he was at leisure, and would go to him; upon which Mr. Barnard took one of the candles that stood on the King's table, and lighted his Majesty through a suite of rooms, till they came to a private door into the library, of which his Majesty had the key. Being entered, Mr. Barnard stepped forward hastily to Dr. Johnson, who was still in a profound study, and whispered him, 'Sir, here is the King.' Johnson started up, and stood still. His Majesty approached him, and at once was courteously easy.

His Majesty began by observing, that he understood he came sometimes to the library; and then mentioning his having heard that the Doctor had been lately at Oxford, asked him if he was not fond of going thither. To which Johnson answered, that he was indeed fond of going to Oxford sometimes, but was likewise glad to come back again. The King then asked him what they were doing at Oxford. Johnson answered, he could not much commend their diligence, but that in some respects they were mended, for they had put their press under better regulations, and were at that time printing Polybius. He was then asked whether there were better libraries at Oxford or Cambridge. He answered, he believed the Bodleian was larger than any they had at Cambridge; at the same time adding, 'I hope, whether we have more books or not than they have at Cambridge, we shall make as good use of them as they do.' Being asked whether All-Souls or Christ-Church library was the largest, he answered, 'All-Souls library is the largest we have, except the Bodleian.' 'Aye, (said the King,) that is the publick library.'

His Majesty enquired if he was then writing any thing. He answered, he was not, for he had pretty well told the world what he knew, and must now read to acquire more knowledge. The King, as it should seem with a view to urge him to rely on his own stores as an original writer, and to continue his labours, then said 'I do not think you borrow much from any body.' Johnson said, he thought he had already done his part as a writer. 'I should have thought so too, (said the King,) if you had not written so well.'—Johnson observed to me, upon this, that 'No man could have paid a handsomer compliment; and it was fit for a King to pay. It was decisive.' When asked by another friend, at Sir Joshua Reynolds's, whether he made any reply to this high compliment, he answered, 'No, Sir. When the King had said it, it was to be so. It was not for me to bandy civilities with my Sovereign.' Perhaps no man who had spent his whole life in courts could have shewn a more nice and dignified sense of true politeness, than Johnson did in this instance.

His Majesty having observed to him that he supposed he must have read a great deal; Johnson answered, that he thought more than he read; that he had read a great deal in the early part of his life, but having fallen into ill health, he had not been able to read much, compared with others: for instance, he said he had not read much, compared with Dr. Warburton. Upon which the King said, that he heard Dr. Warburton was a man of such general knowledge, that you could scarce talk with him on any subject on which he was not qualified to speak; and that his learning resembled Garrick's acting, in its universality. His Majesty then talked of the controversy between Warburton and Lowth, which he seemed to have read, and asked Johnson what he thought of it. Johnson answered, 'Warburton has most general, most scholastick learning; Lowth is the more correct scholar. I do not know which of them calls names best.' The King was pleased to say he was of the same opinion; adding, 'You do not think, then, Dr. Johnson, that there was much argument in the case.' Johnson said, he did not think there was. 'Why truly, (said the King,) when once it comes to calling names, argument is pretty well at an end.'

His Majesty then asked him what he thought of Lord Lyttelton's *History*, which was then just published. Johnson said, he thought his style pretty good, but that he had blamed Henry the Second rather too much. 'Why, (said the King,) they seldom do these things by halves.' 'No, Sir, (answered Johnson,) not to Kings.' But fearing to be misunderstood, he proceeded to explain himself; and immediately subjoined, 'That for those who spoke worse of Kings than they deserved, he could find no excuse; but that he could more easily conceive how some might speak better of them than they deserved, without any ill intention; for, as Kings had much in their power to give, those who were favoured by them would frequently, from gratitude, exaggerate their praises; and as this proceeded from a good motive, it was certainly excusable, as far as errour could be excusable.'

The King then asked him what he thought of Dr. Hill. Johnson answered, that he was an ingenious man, but had no veracity; and immediately mentioned, as an instance of it, an assertion of that writer, that he had seen objects magnified to a much greater degree by using three or four microscopes at a time, than by using one. 'Now, (added Johnson,) every one acquainted with microscopes knows, that the more of them he looks through, the less the object will appear.' 'Why, (replied the King,) this is not only telling an untruth, but telling it clumsily; for, if that be the case, every one who can look through a microscope will be able to detect him.'

'I now, (said Johnson to his friends, when relating what had passed) began to consider that I was depreciating this man in the estimation of his Sovereign, and thought it was time for me to say something that might be more favourable.' He added, therefore, that Dr. Hill was, notwithstanding, a very curious observer; and if he would have been contented to tell the world no more than he knew, he might have been a very considerable man, and needed not to have recourse to such mean expedients to raise his reputation.

The King then talked of literary journals, mentioned particularly the *Journal des Savans*, and asked Johnson if it was well done. Johnson said, it was formerly very well done, and gave some account of the persons who began it, and carried it on for some years; enlarging, at the same time, on the nature and use of such works. The King asked him if it was well done now. Johnson answered, he had no reason to think that it was. The King then asked him if there were any other literary journals published in this kingdom, except the *Monthly* and *Critical Reviews*; and on being answered there were no other, his Majesty asked which of them was the best: Johnson answered, that the *Monthly Review* was done with most care, the *Critical* upon the best principles; adding that the authours of the *Monthly Review* were enemies to the

Church. This the King said he was sorry to hear.

The conversation next turned on the Philosophical Transactions, when Johnson observed, that they had now a better method of arranging their materials than formerly. 'Aye, (said the King,) they are obliged to Dr. Johnson for that;' for his Majesty had heard and remembered the circumstance, which Johnson himself had forgot.

His Majesty expressed a desire to have the literary biography of this country ably executed, and proposed to Dr. Johnson to undertake it. Johnson signified his readiness to comply with his Majesty's wishes.

During the whole of this interview, Johnson talked to his Majesty with profound respect, but still in his firm manly manner, with a sonorous voice, and never in that subdued tone which is commonly used at the levee and in the drawing-room. After the King withdrew, Johnson shewed himself highly pleased with his Majesty's conversation, and gracious behaviour. He said to Mr. Barnard, 'Sir, they may talk of the King as they will; but he is the finest gentleman I have ever seen.' And he afterwards observed to Mr. Langton, 'Sir, his manners are those of as fine a gentleman as we may suppose Lewis the Fourteenth or Charles the Second.'

At Sir Joshua Reynolds's, where a circle of Johnson's friends was collected round him to hear his account of this memorable conversation, Dr. Joseph Warton, in his frank and lively manner, was very active in pressing him to mention the particulars. 'Come now, Sir, this is an interesting matter; do favour us with it.' Johnson, with great good humour, complied.

He told them, 'I found his Majesty wished I should talk, and I made it my business to talk. I find it does a man good to be talked to by his Sovereign. In the first place, a man cannot be in a passion—.' Here some question interrupted him, which is to be regretted, as he certainly would have pointed out and illustrated many circumstances of advantage, from being in a situation, where the powers of the mind are at once excited to vigorous exertion, and tempered by reverential awe.

During all the time in which Dr. Johnson was employed in relating to the circle at Sir Joshua Reynolds's the particulars of what passed between the King and him, Dr. Goldsmith remained unmoved upon a sopha at some distance, affecting not to join in the least in the eager curiosity of the company. He assigned as a reason for his gloom and seeming inattention, that he apprehended Johnson had relinquished his purpose of furnishing him with a Prologue to his play, with the hopes of which he had been flattered; but it was strongly suspected that he was fretting with chagrin and envy at the singular honour Dr. Johnson had lately enjoyed. At length, the frankness and simplicity of his natural character prevailed. He sprung from the sopha, advanced to Johnson, and in a kind of flutter, from imagining himself in the situation which he had just been hearing described, exclaimed, 'Well, you acquitted yourself in this conversation better than I should have done; for I should have bowed and stammered through the whole of it.'

His diary affords no light as to his employment at this time. He passed three months at Lichfield; and I cannot omit an affecting and solemn scene there, as related by himself:—

'Sunday, Oct. 18, 1767. Yesterday, Oct. 17, at about ten in the morning, I took my leave for ever of my dear old friend, Catharine Chambers, who came to live with my mother about 1724, and has been but little parted from us since. She buried my father, my brother, and my mother. She is now fifty-eight years old.

'I desired all to withdraw, then told her that we were to part for ever; that as Christians, we should part with prayer; and that I would, if she was willing, say a short prayer beside her. She expressed great desire to hear me; and held up her poor hands, as she lay in bed, with great fervour, while I prayed, kneeling by her, nearly in the following words:

'Almighty and most merciful Father, whose loving kindness is over all thy works, behold, visit, and relieve this thy servant, who is grieved with sickness. Grant that the sense of her weakness may add strength to her faith, and seriousness to her repentance. And grant that by the help of thy Holy Spirit, after the pains and labours of this short life, we may all obtain everlasting happiness, through JESUS CHRIST our Lord; for whose sake hear our prayers. Amen. Our Father, &c.

'I then kissed her. She told me, that to part was the greatest pain that she had ever felt, and that she hoped we should meet again in a better place. I expressed, with swelled eyes, and great emotion of tenderness, the same hopes. We kissed, and parted. I humbly hope to meet again, and to part no more.'

1768: ÆTAT. 59]—It appears from his notes of the state of his mind, that he suffered great perturbation and distraction in 1768. Nothing of his writing was given to the publick this year, except the Prologue to his friend Goldsmith's comedy of *The Good-natured Man*. The first lines of this Prologue are strongly characteristical of the dismal gloom of his mind; which in his case, as in the case of all who are distressed with the same malady of imagination, transfers to others its own feelings. Who could suppose it was to introduce a comedy, when Mr. Bensley solemnly began,

'Press'd with the load of life, the weary mind
Surveys the general toil of human kind.'

But this dark ground might make Goldsmith's humour shine the more.

In the spring of this year, having published my *Account of Corsica*, with the *Journal of a Tour to that Island*, I returned to London, very desirous to see Dr. Johnson, and hear him upon the subject. I found he was at Oxford, with his friend Mr. Chambers, who was now Vinerian Professor, and lived in New Inn Hall. Having had no letter from him since that in which he criticised the Latinity of my Thesis, and having been told by somebody that he was offended at my having put into my Book an extract of his letter to me at Paris, I was impatient to be with him, and therefore followed him to Oxford, where I was entertained by Mr. Chambers, with a civility which I shall ever gratefully remember. I found that Dr. Johnson had sent a letter to me to Scotland, and that I had nothing to complain of but his being more indifferent to my anxiety than I wished him to be. Instead of giving, with the circumstances of time and place, such fragments of his conversation as I preserved during this visit to Oxford, I shall throw them together in continuation.

Talking of some of the modern plays, he said *False Delicacy* was totally void of character. He praised Goldsmith's *Good-natured Man*; said, it was the best comedy that had appeared since *The Provoked Husband*, and that there had not been of late any such character exhibited on the stage as that of Croaker. I observed it was the Suspirius of his Rambler. He said, Goldsmith had owned he had borrowed it from thence. 'Sir, (continued he,) there is all the difference in the world between characters of nature and characters of manners; and *there* is the difference between the characters of Fielding and those of Richardson. Characters of manners are very entertaining; but they are to be understood by a more superficial observer than characters of nature, where a man must dive into the recesses of the human heart.'

It always appeared to me that he estimated the compositions of Richardson too highly, and that he had an unreasonable prejudice against Fielding. In comparing those two writers, he used this expression: 'that there was as great a difference between them as between a man who knew how a watch was made, and a man who could tell the hour by looking on the dial-plate.'

'I have not been troubled for a long time with authours desiring my opinion of their works. I used once to be sadly plagued with a man who wrote verses, but who literally had no other notion of a verse, but that it consisted of ten syllables. *Lay your knife and your fork, across your plate*, was to him a verse:

Lay your knife and your fork, across your plate.

As he wrote a great number of verses, he sometimes by chance made good ones, though he did not know it.'

Johnson expatiated on the advantages of Oxford for learning. 'There is here, Sir, (said he,) such a progressive emulation. The students are anxious to appear well to their tutors; the tutors are anxious to have their pupils appear well in the college; the colleges are anxious to have their students appear well in the University; and there are excellent rules of discipline in every college. That the rules are sometimes ill observed, may be true; but is nothing against the system. The members of an University may, for a season, be unmindful of their duty. I am arguing for the excellency of the institution.'

He said he had lately been a long while at Lichfield, but had grown very weary before he left it. BOSWELL. 'I wonder at that, Sir; it is your native place.' JOHNSON. 'Why, so is Scotland *your* native place.'

His prejudice against Scotland appeared remarkably strong at this time. When I talked of our advancement in literature, 'Sir, (said he,) you have learnt a little from us, and you think yourselves very great men. Hume would never have written History, had not Voltaire written it before him. He is an echo of Voltaire.' BOSWELL. 'But, Sir, we have Lord Kames.' JOHNSON. 'You *have* Lord Kames. Keep him; ha, ha, ha! We don't envy you him. Do you ever see Dr. Robertson?' BOSWELL. 'Yes, Sir.' JOHNSON. 'Does the dog talk of me?' BOSWELL. 'Indeed, Sir, he does, and loves you.' Thinking that I now had him in a corner, and being solicitous for the literary fame of my country, I pressed him for his opinion on the merit of Dr. Robertson's *History of Scotland*. But, to my surprize, he escaped.—'Sir, I love Robertson, and I won't talk of his book.'

An essay, written by Mr. Deane, a divine of the Church of England, maintaining the future life of brutes, by an explication of certain parts of the scriptures, was mentioned, and the doctrine insisted on by a gentleman who seemed fond of curious speculation. Johnson, who did not like to hear of any thing concerning a future state which was not authorised by the regular canons of orthodoxy, discouraged this talk; and being offended at its continuation, he watched an opportunity to give the gentleman a blow of reprehension. So, when the poor speculatist, with a serious metaphysical pensive face, addressed him, 'But really, Sir, when we see a very sensible dog, we don't know what to think of him;' Johnson, rolling with joy at the thought which beamed in his eye, turned quickly round, and replied, 'True, Sir: and when we see a very foolish *fellow*, we don't know what to think of *him*.' He then rose up, strided to the fire, and stood for some time laughing and exulting.

I asked him if it was not hard that one deviation from chastity should so absolutely ruin a young woman. Johnson. 'Why, no, Sir; it is the great principle which she is taught. When she has given up that principle, she has given up every notion of female honour and virtue, which are all included in chastity.'

A gentleman talked to him of a lady whom he greatly admired and wished to marry, but was afraid of her superiority of talents. 'Sir, (said he,) you need not be afraid; marry her. Before a year goes about, you'll find that reason much weaker, and that wit not so bright.' Yet the gentleman may be justified in his apprehension by one of Dr. Johnson's admirable sentences in his life of Waller: 'He doubtless praised many whom he would have been afraid to marry; and, perhaps, married one whom he would have been ashamed to praise. Many qualities contribute to domestic happiness, upon which poetry has no colours to bestow; and many airs and sallies may delight imagination, which he who flatters them never can approve.'

He praised Signor Baretti. 'His account of Italy is a very entertaining book; and, Sir, I know no man who carries his head higher in conversation than Baretti. There are strong powers in his mind. He has not, indeed, many hooks; but with what hooks he has, he grapples very forcibly.'

At this time I observed upon the dial-plate of his watch a short Greek inscription, taken from the New Testament, Νυξ γαρ ερχεται, being the first words of our SAVIOUR'S solemn admonition to the improvement of that time which is allowed us to prepare for eternity: 'the night cometh when no man can work.' He sometime afterwards laid aside this dial-plate; and when I asked him the reason, he said, 'It might do very well upon a clock which a man keeps in his closet; but to have it upon his watch which he carries about with him, and which is often looked at by others, might be censured as ostentatious.' Mr. Steevens is now possessed of the dial-plate inscribed as above.

He remained at Oxford a considerable time; I was obliged to go to London, where I received his letter, which had been returned from Scotland.

'TO JAMES BOSWELL, ESQ.

'MY DEAR BOSWELL,—I have omitted a long time to write to you, without knowing very well why. I could now tell why I should not write; for who would write to men who publish the letters of their friends, without their leave? Yet I write to you in spite of my caution, to tell you that I shall be glad to see you, and that I wish you would empty your head of Corsica, which I think has filled it rather too long. But, at all events, I shall be glad, very glad to see you. I am, Sir, yours affectionately,

'SAM. JOHNSON.'
'Oxford, March 23, 1768.'

Upon his arrival in London in May, he surprized me one morning with a visit at my lodgings in Half-Moon-street, was quite satisfied with my explanation, and was in the kindest and most agreeable frame of mind. As he had objected to a part of one of his letters being published, I thought it right to take this opportunity of asking him explicitly whether it would be improper to publish his letters after his death. His answer was, 'Nay, Sir, when I am dead, you may do as you will.'

He talked in his usual style with a rough contempt of popular liberty. 'They make a rout about *universal* liberty, without considering that all that is to be valued, or indeed can be enjoyed by individuals, is *private* liberty. Political liberty is good only so far as it produces private liberty. Now, Sir, there is the liberty of the press, which you know is a constant topick. Suppose you and I and two hundred more were restrained from printing our thoughts: what then? What proportion would that restraint upon us bear to the private happiness of the nation?'

This mode of representing the inconveniences of restraint as light and insignificant, was a kind of sophistry in which he delighted to indulge himself, in opposition to the extreme laxity for which it has been fashionable for too many to argue, when it is evident, upon reflection, that the very essence of government is restraint; and certain it is, that as government produces rational happiness, too much restraint is better than too little. But when restraint is unnecessary, and so close as to gall those who are subject to it, the people may and ought to remonstrate; and, if relief is not granted, to resist. Of this manly and spirited principle, no man was more convinced than Johnson himself.

His sincere regard for Francis Barber, his faithful negro servant, made him so desirous of his further improvement, that he now placed him at a school at Bishop Stortford, in Hertfordshire. This humane attention does Johnson's heart much honour. Out of many letters which Mr. Barber received from his master, he has preserved three, which he kindly gave me, and which I shall insert according to their dates.

'TO MR. FRANCIS BARBER.

'DEAR FRANCIS,—I have been very much out of order. I am glad to hear that you are well, and design to come soon to see you. I would have you stay at Mrs. Clapp's for the present, till I can determine what we shall do. Be a good boy.

'My compliments to Mrs. Clapp and to Mr. Fowler. I am, your's affectionately,

SAM. JOHNSON.'
'May 28, 1768.'

Soon afterwards, he supped at the Crown and Anchor tavern, in the Strand, with a company whom I collected to meet him. They were Dr. Percy, now Bishop of Dromore, Dr. Douglas, now Bishop of Salisbury, Mr. Langton, Dr. Robertson the Historian, Dr. Hugh Blair, and Mr. Thomas Davies, who wished much to be introduced to these eminent Scotch *literati*; but on the present occasion he had very little opportunity of hearing them talk, for with an excess of prudence, for which Johnson afterwards found fault with them, they hardly opened their lips, and that only to say something which they were certain would not expose them to the sword of Goliath; such was their anxiety for their fame when in the presence of Johnson. He was this evening in remarkable vigour of mind, and eager to exert himself in conversation, which he did with great readiness and fluency; but I am sorry to find that I have preserved but a small part of what passed.

He was vehement against old Dr. Mounsey, of Chelsea College, as 'a fellow who swore and talked bawdy.' 'I have been often in his company, (said Dr. Percy,) and never heard him swear or talk bawdy.' Mr. Davies, who sat next to Dr. Percy, having after this had some conversation aside with him, made a discovery which, in his zeal to pay court to Dr. Johnson, he eagerly proclaimed aloud from the foot of the table: 'O, Sir, I have found out a very good reason why Dr. Percy never heard Mounsey swear or talk bawdy; for he tells me, he never saw him but at the Duke of Northumberland's table.' 'And so, Sir, (said Johnson loudly, to Dr. Percy,) you would shield this man from the charge of swearing and talking bawdy, because he did not do so at the Duke of Northumberland's table. Sir, you might as well tell us that you had seen him hold up his hand at the Old Bailey, and he neither swore nor talked bawdy; or that you had seen him in the cart at Tyburn, and he neither swore nor talked bawdy. And is it thus, Sir, that you presume to controvert what I have related?' Dr. Johnson's animadversion was uttered in such a manner, that Dr. Percy seemed to be displeased, and soon afterwards left the company, of which Johnson did not at that time take any notice.

Swift having been mentioned, Johnson, as usual, treated him with little respect as an authour. Some of us endeavoured to support the Dean of St. Patrick's by various arguments. One in particular praised his *Conduct of the Allies*. JOHNSON. 'Sir, his *Conduct of the Allies* is a performance of very little ability.' 'Surely, Sir, (said Dr. Douglas,) you must allow it has strong facts.' JOHNSON. 'Why yes, Sir; but what is that to the merit of the composition? In the Sessions-paper of the Old Bailey, there are strong facts. Housebreaking is a strong fact; robbery is a strong fact; and murder is a *mighty* strong fact; but is great praise due to the historian of those strong facts? No, Sir. Swift has told what he had to tell distinctly enough, but that is all. He had to count ten, and he has counted it right.' Then recollecting that Mr. Davies, by acting as an *informer*, had been the occasion of his talking somewhat too harshly to his friend Dr. Percy, for which, probably, when the first ebullition was over, he felt some compunction, he took an opportunity to give him a hit; so added, with a preparatory laugh, 'Why, Sir, Tom Davies might have written *The Conduct of the Allies*.' Poor Tom being thus suddenly dragged into ludicrous notice in presence of the Scottish Doctors, to whom he was ambitious of appearing to advantage, was grievously mortified. Nor did his punishment rest here; for upon subsequent occasions, whenever he, 'statesman all over,' assumed a strutting importance, I used to hail him—'the Authour of *The Conduct of the Allies.*'

When I called upon Dr. Johnson next morning, I found him highly satisfied with his colloquial prowess the preceding evening. 'Well, (said he,) we had good talk.' BOSWELL. 'Yes, Sir; you tossed and gored several persons.'

The late Alexander, Earl of Eglintoune, who loved wit more than wine, and men of genius more than sycophants, had a great admiration of Johnson; but from the remarkable elegance of his own manners, was, perhaps, too delicately sensible of the roughness which sometimes appeared in Johnson's behaviour. One evening about this time, when his Lordship did me the honour to sup at my lodgings with Dr. Robertson and several other men of literary distinction, he regretted that Johnson had not been educated with more refinement, and lived more in polished society. 'No, no, my Lord, (said Signor Baretti,) do with him what you would, he would always have been a bear.' 'True, (answered the Earl, with a smile,) but he would have been a *dancing* bear.'

To obviate all the reflections which have gone round the world to Johnson's prejudice, by applying to him the epithet of a BEAR, let me impress upon my readers a just and happy saying of my friend Goldsmith, who knew him well: 'Johnson, to be sure, has a roughness in his manner; but no man alive has a more tender heart. *He has nothing of the bear but his skin.*'

1769: ÆTAT. 60.]—I CAME to London in the autumn, and having informed him that I was going to be married in a few months, I wished to have as much of his conversation as I could before engaging in a state of life which would probably keep me more in Scotland, and prevent me seeing him so often as when I was a single man; but I found he was at Brighthelmstone with Mr. and Mrs. Thrale.

After his return to town, we met frequently, and I continued the practice of making notes of his conversation, though not with so much assiduity as I wish I had done. At this time, indeed, I had a sufficient excuse for not being able to appropriate so much time to my Journal; for General Paoli, after Corsica had been overpowered by the monarchy of France, was now no longer at the head of his brave countrymen, but having with difficulty escaped from his native island, had sought an asylum in Great-Britain; and it was my duty, as well as my pleasure, to attend much upon him. Such particulars of Johnson's conversation at this period as I have committed to writing, I shall here introduce, without any strict attention to methodical arrangement. Sometimes short notes of different days shall be blended together, and sometimes a day may seem important enough to be separately distinguished.

He said, he would not have Sunday kept with rigid severity and gloom, but with a gravity and simplicity of behaviour.

I told him that David Hume had made a short collection of Scotticisms. 'I wonder, (said Johnson,) that *he* should find them.'

On the 30th of September we dined together at the Mitre. I attempted to argue for the superior happiness of the savage life, upon the usual fanciful topicks. JOHNSON. 'Sir, there can be nothing more false. The savages have no bodily advantages beyond those of civilised men. They have not better health; and as to care or mental uneasiness, they are not above it, but below it, like bears. No, Sir; you are not to talk such paradox: let me have no more on't. It cannot entertain, far less can it instruct. Lord Monboddo, one of your Scotch Judges, talked a great deal of such nonsense. I suffered *him*; but I will not suffer *you*.'— BOSWELL. 'But, Sir, does not Rousseau talk such nonsense?' JOHNSON. 'True, Sir, but Rousseau *knows* he is talking nonsense, and laughs at the world for staring at him.' BOSWELL. 'How so, Sir?' JOHNSON. 'Why, Sir, a man who talks nonsense so well, must know that he is talking nonsense. But I am *afraid*, (chuckling and laughing,) Monboddo does *not* know that he is talking nonsense.' BOSWELL. 'Is it wrong then, Sir, to affect singularity, in order to make people stare?' JOHNSON. 'Yes, if you do it by propagating errour: and, indeed, it is wrong in any way. There is in human nature a general inclination to make people stare; and every wise man has himself to cure of it, and does cure himself. If you wish to make people stare by doing better than others, why, make them stare till they stare their eyes out. But consider how easy it is to make people stare by being absurd. I may do it by going into a drawing-room without my shoes. You remember the gentleman in *The Spectator*, who had a commission of lunacy taken out against him for his extreme singularity, such as never wearing a wig, but a night-cap. Now, Sir, abstractedly, the night-cap was best; but, relatively, the advantage was overbalanced by his making the boys run after him.'

Talking of a London life, he said, 'The happiness of London is not to be conceived but by those who have been in it. I will venture to say, there is more learning and science within the circumference of ten miles from where we now sit, than in all the rest of the kingdom.' BOSWELL. 'The only disadvantage is the great distance at which people live from one another.' JOHNSON. 'Yes, Sir; but that is occasioned by the largeness of it, which is the cause of all the other advantages.' BOSWELL. 'Sometimes I have been in the humour of wishing to retire to a desart.' JOHNSON. 'Sir, you have desart enough in Scotland.'

Although I had promised myself a great deal of instructive conversation with him on the conduct of the married state, of which I had then a near prospect, he did not say much upon that topick. Mr. Seward heard him once say, that 'a man has a very bad chance for happiness in that state, unless he marries a woman of very strong and fixed principles of religion.' He maintained to me, contrary to the common notion, that a woman would not be the worse wife for being learned; in which, from all that I have observed of *Artemisias*, I humbly differed from him.

When I censured a gentleman of my acquaintance for marrying a second time, as it shewed a disregard of his first wife, he said, 'Not at all, Sir. On the contrary, were he not to marry again, it might be concluded that his first wife had given him a disgust to marriage; but by taking a second wife he pays the highest compliment to the first, by shewing that she made him so happy as a married man, that he wishes to be so a second time.' So ingenious a turn did he give to this delicate question. And yet, on another occasion, he owned that he once had almost asked a promise of Mrs. Johnson that she would not marry again, but had checked himself. Indeed, I cannot help thinking, that in his case the request would have been unreasonable; for if Mrs. Johnson forgot, or thought it no injury to the memory of her first love,—the husband of her youth and the father of her children,—to make a second marriage, why should she be precluded from a third, should she be so inclined? In Johnson's persevering fond appropriation of his *Tetty*, even after her decease, he seems totally to have overlooked the prior claim of the honest Birmingham trader. I presume that her having been married before had, at times, given him some uneasiness; for I remember his observing upon the marriage of one of our common friends, 'He has done a very foolish thing, Sir; he has married a widow, when he might have had a maid.'

We drank tea with Mrs. Williams. I had last year the pleasure of seeing Mrs. Thrale at Dr. Johnson's one morning, and had conversation enough with her to admire her talents, and to shew her that I was as Johnsonian as herself. Dr. Johnson had probably been kind enough to speak well of me, for this evening he delivered me a very polite card from Mr. Thrale and her, inviting me to Streatham.

On the 6th of October I complied with this obliging invitation, and found, at an elegant villa, six miles from town, every circumstance that can make society pleasing. Johnson, though quite at home, was yet looked up to with an awe, tempered by affection, and seemed to be equally the care of his host and hostess. I rejoiced at seeing him so happy.

He played off his wit against Scotland with a good humoured pleasantry, which gave me, though no bigot to national prejudices, an opportunity for a little contest with him. I having said that England was obliged to us for gardeners, almost all their good gardeners being Scotchmen. JOHNSON. 'Why, Sir, that is because gardening is much more necessary amongst you than with us, which makes so many of your people learn it. It is *all* gardening with you. Things which grow wild here, must be cultivated with great care in Scotland. Pray now (throwing himself back in his chair, and laughing,) are you ever able to bring the *sloe* to perfection?'

I boasted that we had the honour of being the first to abolish the unhospitable, troublesome, and ungracious custom of giving vails to servants. JOHNSON. 'Sir, you abolished vails, because you were too poor to be able to give them.'

Mrs. Thrale disputed with him on the merit of Prior. He attacked him powerfully; said he wrote of love like a man who had never felt it: his love verses were college verses; and he repeated the song 'Alexis shunn'd his fellow swains,' &c., in so ludicrous a manner, as to make us all wonder how any one could have been pleased with such fantastical stuff. Mrs. Thrale stood to her gun with great courage, in defence of amorous ditties, which Johnson despised, till he at last silenced her by saying, 'My dear Lady, talk no more of this. Nonsense can be defended but by nonsense.'

Mrs. Thrale then praised Garrick's talent for light gay poetry; and, as a specimen, repeated his song in *Florizel and Perdita*, and dwelt with peculiar pleasure on this line:

'I'd smile with the simple, and feed with the poor.'

JOHNSON. 'Nay, my dear Lady, this will never do. Poor David! Smile with the simple;—What folly is that? And who would feed with the poor that can help it? No, no; let me smile with the wise, and feed with the rich.' I repeated this sally to Garrick, and wondered to find his sensibility as a writer not a little irritated by it. To sooth him, I observed, that Johnson spared none of us; and I quoted the passage in Horace, in which he compares one who attacks his friends for the sake of a laugh, to a pushing ox, that is marked by a bunch of hay put upon his horns: '*foenum habet in cornu.*' 'Ay, (said Garrick vehemently,) he has a whole *mow* of it.'

He would not allow much merit to Whitefield's oratory. 'His popularity, Sir, (said be,) is chiefly owing to the peculiarity of his manner. He would be followed by crowds were he to wear a night-cap in the pulpit, or were he to preach from a tree.'

On the evening of October 10, I presented Dr. Johnson to General Paoli. I had greatly wished that two men, for whom I had the highest esteem, should meet. They met with a manly ease, mutually conscious of their own abilities, and of the abilities of each other. The General spoke Italian, and Dr. Johnson English, and understood one another very well, with a little aid of interpretation from me, in which I compared myself to an isthmus which joins two great continents. Upon Johnson's approach, the General said, 'From what I have read of your works, Sir, and from what Mr. Boswell has told me of you, I have long held you in great veneration.' The General talked of languages being formed on the particular notions and manners of a people, without knowing which, we cannot know the language. We may know the direct signification of single words; but by these no beauty of expression, no sally of genius, no wit is conveyed to the mind. All this must be by allusion to other ideas. 'Sir, (said Johnson,) you talk of language, as if you had never done any thing else but study it, instead of governing a nation.' The General said, '*Questo e un troppo gran complimento*;' this is too great a compliment. Johnson answered, 'I should have thought so, Sir, if I had not heard you talk.' The General asked him, what he thought of the spirit of infidelity which was so prevalent. JOHNSON. 'Sir, this gloom of infidelity, I hope, is only a transient cloud passing through the hemisphere, which will soon be dissipated, and the sun break forth with his usual splendour.' 'You think then, (said the General,) that they will change their principles like their clothes.' JOHNSON. 'Why, Sir, if they bestow no more thought on principles than on dress, it must be so.' The General said, that 'a great part of the fashionable infidelity was owing to a desire of shewing courage. Men who have no opportunities of shewing it as to things in this life, take death and futurity as objects on which to display it.' JOHNSON. 'That is mighty foolish affectation. Fear is one of the passions of human nature, of which it is impossible to divest it. You remember that the Emperour Charles V, when he read upon the tomb-stone of a Spanish nobleman, "Here lies one who never knew fear," wittily said, "Then he never snuffed a candle with his fingers."'

Dr. Johnson went home with me, and drank tea till late in the night. He said, 'General Paoli had the loftiest port of any man he had ever seen.' He denied that military men were always the best bred men. 'Perfect good breeding,' he observed, 'consists in having no particular mark of any profession, but a general elegance of manners; whereas, in a military man, you can commonly distinguish the *brand* of a soldier, *l'homme d'épée.*'

Dr. Johnson shunned to-night any discussion of the perplexed question of fate and free will, which I attempted to agitate. 'Sir, (said he,) we *know* our will is free, and *there's* an end on't.'

He honoured me with his company at dinner on the 16th of October, at my lodgings in Old Bond-street, with Sir Joshua Reynolds, Mr. Garrick, Dr. Goldsmith, Mr. Murphy, Mr. Bickerstaff, and Mr. Thomas Davies. Garrick played round him with a fond vivacity, taking hold of the breasts of his coat, and, looking up in his face with a lively archness, complimented him on the good health which he seemed then to enjoy; while the sage, shaking his head, beheld him with a gentle complacency. One of the company not being come at the appointed hour, I proposed, as usual upon such occasions, to order dinner to be served; adding, 'Ought six people to be kept waiting for one?' 'Why, yes, (answered Johnson, with a delicate humanity,) if the one will suffer more by your sitting down, than the six will do by waiting.' Goldsmith, to divert the tedious minutes, strutted about, bragging of his dress, and I believe was seriously vain of it, for his mind was wonderfully prone to such impressions. 'Come, come, (said Garrick,) talk no more of that. You are, perhaps, the worst—eh, eh!'—Goldsmith was eagerly attempting to interrupt him, when Garrick went on, laughing ironically, 'Nay, you will always *look* like a gentleman; but I am talking of being well or *ill drest.*' 'Well, let me tell you, (said Goldsmith,) when my tailor brought home my bloom-coloured coat, he said, "Sir, I have a favour to beg of you. When any body asks you who made your clothes, be pleased to mention John Filby, at the Harrow, in Water-lane."' JOHNSON. 'Why, Sir, that was because he knew the strange colour would attract crowds to gaze at it, and thus they might hear of him, and see how well he could make a coat even of so absurd a colour.'

After dinner our conversation first turned upon Pope. Johnson said, his characters of men were admirably drawn, those of women not so well. He repeated to us, in his forcible melodious manner, the concluding lines of the *Dunciad*. While he was talking loudly in praise of those lines, one of the company[21] ventured to say, 'Too fine for such a poem:—a poem on what?' JOHNSON, (with a disdainful look,) 'Why, on *dunces*. It was worth while being a dunce then. Ah, Sir, hadst *thou* lived in those days! It is not worth while 'being a dunce now, when there are no wits.' Bickerstaff observed, as a peculiar circumstance, that Pope's fame was higher when he was alive than it was then. Johnson said, his Pastorals were poor things, though the versification was fine. He told us, with high satisfaction, the anecdote of Pope's inquiring who was the authour of his London, and saying, he will be soon *déterré*. He observed, that in Dryden's poetry there were passages drawn from a profundity which Pope could never reach. He repeated some fine lines on love, by the former, (which I have now forgotten,) and gave great applause to the character of Zimri. Goldsmith said, that Pope's character of Addison shewed a deep knowledge of the human heart. Johnson said, that the description of the temple, in *The Mourning Bride*, was the finest poetical passage he had ever read; he recollected none in Shakspeare equal to it. 'But, (said Garrick, all alarmed for the 'God of his idolatry,') we know not the extent and variety of his powers. We are to suppose there are such passages in his works. Shakspeare must not suffer from the badness of our memories.' Johnson, diverted by this enthusiastick jealousy, went on with greater ardour: 'No, Sir; Congreve has *nature*;' (smiling on the tragick eagerness of Garrick;) but composing himself, he added, 'Sir, this is not

---

[21] Everyone guesses that 'one of the company' was Boswell.—HILL.

comparing Congreve on the whole, with Shakspeare on the whole; but only maintaining that Congreve has one finer passage than any that can be found in Shakspeare. Sir, a man may have no more than ten guineas in the world, but he may have those ten guineas in one piece; and so may have a finer piece than a man who has ten thousand pounds: but then he has only one ten-guinea piece. What I mean is, that you can shew me no passage where there is simply a description of material objects, without any intermixture of moral notions, which produces such an effect.' Mr. Murphy mentioned Shakspeare's description of the night before the battle of Agincourt; but it was observed, it had *men* in it. Mr. Davies suggested the speech of Juliet, in which she figures herself awaking in the tomb of her ancestors. Some one mentioned the description of Dover Cliff. JOHNSON. 'No, Sir; it should be all precipice,—all vacuum. The crows impede your fall. The diminished appearance of the boats, and other circumstances, are all very good descriptions; but do not impress the mind at once with the horrible idea of immense height. The impression is divided; you pass on by computation, from one stage of the tremendous space to another. Had the girl in *The Mourning Bride* said, she could not cast her shoe to the top of one of the pillars in the temple, it would not have aided the idea, but weakened it.'

Talking of a Barrister who had a bad utterance, some one, (to rouse Johnson,) wickedly said, that he was unfortunate in not having been taught oratory by Sheridan. JOHNSON. 'Nay, Sir, if he had been taught by Sheridan, he would have cleared the room.' GARRICK. 'Sheridan has too much vanity to be a good man.' We shall now see Johnson's mode of *defending* a man; taking him into his own hands, and discriminating. JOHNSON. 'No, Sir. There is, to be sure, in Sheridan, something to reprehend, and every thing to laugh at; but, Sir, he is not a bad man. No, Sir; were mankind to be divided into good and bad, he would stand considerably within the ranks of good. And, Sir, it must be allowed that Sheridan excels in plain declamation, though he can exhibit no character.'

Mrs. Montagu, a lady distinguished for having written an Essay on Shakspeare, being mentioned; REYNOLDS. 'I think that essay does her honour.' JOHNSON. 'Yes, Sir: it does *her* honour, but it would do nobody else honour. I have, indeed, not read it all. But when I take up the end of a web, and find it packthread, I do not expect, by looking further, to find embroidery. Sir, I will venture to say, there is not one sentence of true criticism in her book.' GARRICK. 'But, Sir, surely it shews how much Voltaire has mistaken Shakspeare, which nobody else has done.' Johnson. 'Sir, nobody else has thought it worth while. And what merit is there in that? You may as well praise a schoolmaster for whipping a boy who has construed ill. No, Sir, there is no real criticism in it: none shewing the beauty of thought, as formed on the workings of the human heart.'

The admirers of this Essay may be offended at the slighting manner in which Johnson spoke of it; but let it be remembered, that he gave his honest opinion unbiassed by any prejudice, or any proud jealousy of a woman intruding herself into the chair of criticism; for Sir Joshua Reynolds has told me, that when the Essay first came out, and it was not known who had written it, Johnson wondered how Sir Joshua could like it. At this time Sir Joshua himself had received no information concerning the authour, except being assured by one of our most eminent literati, that it was clear its authour did not know the Greek tragedies in the original. One day at Sir Joshua's table, when it was related that Mrs. Montagu, in an excess of compliment to the authour of a modern tragedy, had exclaimed, 'I tremble for Shakspeare;' Johnson said, 'When Shakspeare has got——for his rival, and Mrs. Montagu for his defender, he is in a poor state indeed.'

On Thursday, October 19, I passed the evening with him at his house. He advised me to complete a Dictionary of words peculiar to Scotland, of which I shewed him a specimen. 'Sir, (said he,) Ray has made a collection of north-country words. By collecting those of your country, you will do a useful thing towards the history of the language. He bade me also go on with collections which I was making upon the antiquities of Scotland. 'Make a large book; a folio.' BOSWELL. 'But of what use will it be, Sir?' JOHNSON. 'Never mind the use; do it.'

I complained that he had not mentioned Garrick in his Preface to Shakspeare; and asked him if he did not admire him. JOHNSON. 'Yes, as "a poor player, who frets and struts his hour upon the stage;"—as a shadow.' BOSWELL. 'But has he not brought Shakspeare into notice?' JOHNSON. 'Sir, to allow that, would be to lampoon the age. Many of Shakspeare's plays are the worse for being acted: *Macbeth*, for instance.' BOSWELL. 'What, Sir, is nothing gained by decoration and action? Indeed, I do wish that you had mentioned Garrick.' JOHNSON. 'My dear Sir, had I mentioned him, I must have mentioned many more: Mrs. Pritchard, Mrs. Cibber,—nay, and Mr. Cibber too; he too altered Shakspeare.' BOSWELL. 'You have read his apology, Sir?' JOHNSON. 'Yes, it is very entertaining. But as for Cibber himself, taking from his conversation all that he ought not to have said, he was a poor creature. I remember when he brought me one of his Odes to have my opinion of it; I could not bear such nonsense, and would not let him read it to the end; so little respect had I for *that great man*! (laughing.) Yet I remember Richardson wondering that I could treat him with familiarity.'

I mentioned to him that I had seen the execution of several convicts at Tyburn, two days before, and that none of them seemed to be under any concern. JOHNSON. 'Most of them, Sir, have never thought at all.' BOSWELL. 'But is not the fear of death natural to man?'

JOHNSON. 'So much so, Sir, that the whole of life is but keeping away the thoughts of it.' He then, in a low and earnest tone, talked of his meditating upon the aweful hour of his own dissolution, and in what manner he should conduct himself upon that occasion: 'I know not (said he,) whether I should wish to have a friend by me, or have it all between GOD and myself.'

Talking of our feeling for the distresses of others;—JOHNSON. 'Why, Sir, there is much noise made about it, but it is greatly exaggerated. No, Sir, we have a certain degree of feeling to prompt us to do good: more than that, Providence does not intend. It would be misery to no purpose.' BOSWELL. 'But suppose now, Sir, that one of your intimate friends were apprehended for an offence for which he might be hanged.' JOHNSON. 'I should do what I could to bail him, and give him any other assistance; but if he were once fairly hanged, I should not suffer.' BOSWELL. 'Would you eat your dinner that day, Sir?' JOHNSON. 'Yes, Sir; and eat it as if he were eating it with me. Why, there's Baretti, who is to be tried for his life to-morrow, friends have risen up for him on every side; yet if he should be hanged, none of them will eat a slice of plumb-pudding the less. Sir, that sympathetic feeling goes a very little way in depressing the mind.'

I told him that I had dined lately at Foote's, who shewed me a letter which he had received from Tom Davies, telling him that he had not been able to sleep from the concern which he felt on account of '*This sad affair of Baretti,*' begging of him to try if he could suggest any thing that might be of service; and, at the same time, recommending to him an industrious young man who kept a pickle-shop. JOHNSON. 'Ay, Sir, here you have a specimen of human sympathy; a friend hanged, and a cucumber pickled. We know not whether Baretti or the pickle-man has kept Davies from sleep; nor does he know himself. And as to his not sleeping, Sir; Tom Davies is a very great man; Tom has been upon the stage, and knows how to do those things. I have not been upon the stage, and cannot do those things.' BOSWELL. 'I have often blamed myself, Sir, for not feeling for others as sensibly as many say they do.' JOHNSON. 'Sir, don't be duped by them any more. You will find these very feeling people are not very ready to do you good. They *pay* you by *feeling.*'

BOSWELL. 'Foote has a great deal of humour?' JOHNSON. 'Yes, Sir.' BOSWELL. 'He has a singular talent of exhibiting character.' JOHNSON. 'Sir, it is not a talent; it is a vice; it is what others abstain from. It is not comedy, which exhibits the character of a species, as that of a miser gathered from many misers: it is farce, which exhibits individuals.' BOSWELL. 'Did not he think of exhibiting you, Sir?' JOHNSON. 'Sir, fear restrained him; he knew I would have broken his bones. I would have saved him the trouble of cutting off a leg; I would not have left him a leg to cut off.' BOSWELL. 'Pray, Sir, is not Foote an infidel?' JOHNSON. 'I do not know, Sir, that the fellow is an infidel; but if he be an infidel, he is an infidel as a dog is an infidel; that is to say, he has never thought upon the subject.'[22] BOSWELL. 'I suppose, Sir, he has thought superficially, and seized the first notions which occurred to his mind.' JOHNSON. 'Why then, Sir, still he is like a dog, that snatches the piece next him. Did you never observe that dogs have not the power of comparing? A dog will take a small bit of meat as readily as a large, when both are before him.'

BOSWELL. 'What do you think of Dr. Young's *Night Thoughts*, Sir?' JOHNSON. 'Why, Sir, there are very fine things in them.' BOSWELL. 'Is there not less religion in the nation now, Sir, than there was formerly?' JOHNSON. 'I don't know, Sir, that there is.' BOSWELL. 'For instance, there used to be a chaplain in every great family, which we do not find now.' JOHNSON. 'Neither do you find any of the state servants, which great families used formerly to have. There is a change of modes in the whole department of life.'

Next day, October 20, he appeared, for the only time I suppose in his life, as a witness in a Court of Justice, being called to give evidence to the character of Mr. Baretti, who having stabbed a man in the street, was arraigned at the Old Bailey for murder. Never did such a constellation of genius enlighten the awful Sessions-House, emphatically called JUSTICE HALL; Mr. Burke, Mr. Garrick, Mr. Beauclerk, and Dr. Johnson: and undoubtedly their favourable testimony had due weight with the Court and Jury. Johnson gave his evidence in a slow, deliberate, and distinct manner, which was uncommonly impressive. It is well known that Mr. Baretti was acquitted.

On the 26th of October, we dined together at the Mitre tavern. I found fault with Foote for indulging his talent of ridicule at the expence of his visitors, which I colloquially termed making fools of his company. JOHNSON. 'Why, Sir, when you go to see Foote, you do not go to see a saint: you go to see a man who will be entertained at your house, and then bring you on a publick stage; who will entertain you at his house, for the very purpose of bringing you on a publick stage. Sir, he does not make fools of his company; they whom he exposes are fools already: he only brings them into action.'

We went home to his house to tea. Mrs. Williams made it with

---

[22] When Mr. Foote was at Edinburgh, he thought fit to entertain a numerous Scotch company, with a great deal of coarse jocularity, at the expense of Dr. Johnson, imagining it would be acceptable. I felt this as not civil to me; but sat very patiently till he had exhausted his merriment on that subject; and then observed, that surely Johnson must be allowed to have some sterling wit, and that I had heard him say a very good thing of Mr. Foote himself. 'Ah, my old friend Sam (cried Foote,) no man says better things; do let us have it.' Upon which I told the above story, which produced a very loud laugh from the company. But I never saw Foote so disconcerted.—BOSWELL.

sufficient dexterity, notwithstanding her blindness, though her manner of satisfying herself that the cups were full enough appeared to me a little aukward; for I fancied she put her finger down a certain way, till she felt the tea touch it.[23] In my first elation at being allowed the privilege of attending Dr. Johnson at his late visits to this lady, which was like being *è secretioribus consiliis*, I willingly drank cup after cup, as if it had been the Heliconian spring. But as the charm of novelty went off, I grew more fastidious; and besides, I discovered that she was of a peevish temper.

There was a pretty large circle this evening. Dr. Johnson was in very good humour, lively, and ready to talk upon all subjects. Mr. Fergusson, the self-taught philosopher, told him of a new-invented machine which went without horses: a man who sat in it turned a handle, which worked a spring that drove it forward. 'Then, Sir, (said Johnson,) what is gained is, the man has his choice whether he will move himself alone, or himself and the machine too.' Dominicetti being mentioned, he would not allow him any merit. 'There is nothing in all this boasted system. No, Sir; medicated baths can be no better than warm water: their only effect can be that of tepid moisture.' One of the company took the other side, maintaining that medicines of various sorts, and some too of most powerful effect, are introduced into the human frame by the medium of the pores; and, therefore, when warm water is impregnated with salutiferous substances, it may produce great effects as a bath. This appeared to me very satisfactory. Johnson did not answer it; but talking for victory, and determined to be master of the field, he had recourse to the device which Goldsmith imputed to him in the witty words of one of Cibber's comedies: 'There is no arguing with Johnson; for when his pistol misses fire, he knocks you down with the butt end of it.' He turned to the gentleman, 'well, Sir, go to Dominicetti, and get thyself fumigated; but be sure that the steam be directed to thy *head*, for *that* is the *peccant part*.' This produced a triumphant roar of laughter from the motley assembly of philosophers, printers, and dependents, male and female.

I know not how so whimsical a thought came into my mind, but I asked, 'If, Sir, you were shut up in a castle, and a newborn child with you, what would you do?' JOHNSON. 'Why, Sir, I should not much like my company.' BOSWELL. 'But would you take the trouble of rearing it?' He seemed, as may well be supposed, unwilling to pursue the subject: but upon my persevering in my question, replied, 'Why yes, Sir, I would; but I must have all conveniencies. If I had no garden, I would make a shed on the roof, and take it there for fresh air. I should feed it, and wash it much, and with warm water to please it, not with

---

[23] Boswell afterwards learned that she felt the rising tea on the outside of the cup.— Ed.

cold water to give it pain.' BOSWELL. 'But, Sir, does not heat relax?'
JOHNSON. 'Sir, you are not to imagine the water is to be very hot. I
would not *coddle* the child. No, Sir, the hardy method of treating
children does no good. I'll take you five children from London, who
shall cuff five Highland children. Sir, a man bred in London will carry
a burthen, or run, or wrestle, as well as a man brought up in the hardiest
manner in the country.' BOSWELL. 'Good living, I suppose, makes the
Londoners strong.' JOHNSON. 'Why, Sir, I don't know that it does. Our
Chairmen from Ireland, who are as strong men as any, have been
brought up upon potatoes. Quantity makes up for quality.' BOSWELL.
'Would you teach this child that I have furnished you with, any thing?'
JOHNSON. 'No, I should not be apt to teach it.' BOSWELL. 'Would not
you have a pleasure in teaching it?' JOHNSON. 'No, Sir, I should *not*
have a pleasure in teaching it.' BOSWELL. 'Have you not a pleasure in
teaching men?—*There* I have you. You have the same pleasure in
teaching men, that I should have in teaching children.' JOHNSON. 'Why,
something about that.'

I had hired a Bohemian as my servant while I remained in London,
and being much pleased with him, I asked Dr. Johnson whether his
being a Roman Catholick should prevent my taking him with me to
Scotland. JOHNSON. 'Why no, Sir, if *he* has no objection, you can have
none.' BOSWELL. 'So, Sir, you are no great enemy to the Roman
Catholick religion.' JOHNSON. 'No more, Sir, than to the Presbyterian
religion.' BOSWELL. 'You are joking.' JOHNSON. 'No, Sir, I really think
so. Nay, Sir, of the two, I prefer the Popish.' BOSWELL. 'How so, Sir?'
JOHNSON. 'Why, Sir, the Presbyterians have no church, no apostolical
ordination.' BOSWELL. 'And do you think that absolutely essential,
Sir?' JOHNSON. 'Why, Sir, as it was an apostolical institution, I think it
is dangerous to be without it. And, Sir, the Presbyterians have no public
worship: they have no form of prayer in which they know they are to
join. They go to hear a man pray, and are to judge whether they will
join with him.'

I proceeded: 'What do you think, Sir, of Purgatory, as believed by
the Roman Catholicks?' JOHNSON. 'Why, Sir, it is a very harmless
doctrine. They are of opinion that the generality of mankind are neither
so obstinately wicked as to deserve everlasting punishment, nor so
good as to merit being admitted into the society of blessed spirits; and
therefore that God is graciously pleased to allow of a middle state,
where they may be purified by certain degrees of suffering. You see,
Sir, there is nothing unreasonable in this.' BOSWELL. 'But then, Sir,
their masses for the dead?' JOHNSON. 'Why, Sir, if it be once
established that there are souls in purgatory, it is as proper to pray for
them, as for our brethren of mankind who are yet in this life.'
BOSWELL. 'The idolatry of the Mass?' JOHNSON. 'Sir, there is no
idolatry in the Mass. They believe god to be there, and they adore him.'

BOSWELL. 'The worship of Saints?' JOHNSON. 'Sir, they do not worship saints; they invoke them; they only ask their prayers. I am talking all this time of the *doctrines* of the Church of Rome. I grant you that in *practice*, Purgatory is made a lucrative imposition, and that the people do become idolatrous as they recommend themselves to the tutelary protection of particular saints. I think their giving the sacrament only in one kind is criminal, because it is contrary to the express institution of CHRIST, and I wonder how the Council of Trent admitted it.' BOSWELL. 'Confession?' JOHNSON. 'Why, I don't know but that is a good thing. The scripture says, "Confess your faults one to another," and the priests confess as well as the laity. Then it must be considered that their absolution is only upon repentance, and often upon penance also. You think your sins may be forgiven without penance, upon repentance alone.'

When we were alone, I introduced the subject of death, and endeavoured to maintain that the fear of it might be got over. I told him that David Hume said to me, he was no more uneasy to think he should *not be* after this life, than that he *had not been* before he began to exist. JOHNSON. Sir, if he really thinks so, his perceptions are disturbed; he is mad: if he does not think so, he lies. He may tell you, he holds his finger in the flame of a candle, without feeling pain; would you believe him? When he dies, he at least gives up all he has.' BOSWELL. 'Foote, Sir, told me, that when he was very ill he was not afraid to die.' JOHNSON. 'It is not true, Sir. Hold a pistol to Foote's breast, or to Hume's breast, and threaten to kill them, and you'll see how they behave.' BOSWELL. 'But may we not fortify our minds for the approach of death?' Here I am sensible I was in the wrong, to bring before his view what he ever looked upon with horrour; for although when in a celestial frame, in his *Vanity of Human Wishes* he has supposed death to be 'kind Nature's signal for retreat,' from this state of being to 'a happier seat,' his thoughts upon this aweful change were in general full of dismal apprehensions. His mind resembled the vast amphitheatre, the Colisaeum at Rome. In the centre stood his judgement, which, like a mighty gladiator, combated those apprehensions that, like the wild beasts of the *Arena*, were all around in cells, ready to be let out upon him. After a conflict, he drives them back into their dens; but not killing them, they were still assailing him. To my question, whether we might not fortify our minds for the approach of death, he answered, in a passion, 'No, Sir, let it alone. It matters not how a man dies, but how he lives. The act of dying is not of importance, it lasts so short a time.' He added, (with an earnest look,) 'A man knows it must be so, and submits. It will do him no good to whine.'

I attempted to continue the conversation. He was so provoked, that he said, 'Give us no more of this;' and was thrown into such a state of agitation, that he expressed himself in a way that alarmed and distressed me; shewed an impatience that I should leave him, and when I was going away, called to me sternly, 'Don't let us meet tomorrow.'

I went home exceedingly uneasy. All the harsh observations which I had ever heard made upon his character, crowded into my mind; and I seemed to myself like the man who had put his head into the lion's mouth a great many times with perfect safety, but at last had it bit off.

Next morning I sent him a note, stating, that I might have been in the wrong, but it was not intentionally; he was therefore, I could not help thinking, too severe upon me. That notwithstanding our agreement not to meet that day, I would call on him in my way to the city, and stay five minutes by my watch. 'You are, (said I,) in my mind, since last night, surrounded with cloud and storm. Let me have a glimpse of sunshine, and go about my affairs in serenity and chearfulness.'

Upon entering his study, I was glad that he was not alone, which would have made our meeting more awkward. There were with him, Mr. Steevens and Mr. Tyers, both of whom I now saw for the first time. My note had, on his own reflection, softened him, for he received me very complacently; so that I unexpectedly found myself at ease, and joined in the conversation.

I whispered him, 'Well, Sir, you are now in good humour. JOHNSON. 'Yes, Sir.' I was going to leave him, and had got as far as the staircase. He stopped me, and smiling, said, 'Get you gone *in*;' a curious mode of inviting me to stay, which I accordingly did for some time longer.

This little incidental quarrel and reconciliation, which, perhaps, I may be thought to have detailed too minutely, must be esteemed as one of many proofs which his friends had, that though he might be charged with *bad humour* at times, he was always a *good-natured* man; and I have heard Sir Joshua Reynolds, a nice and delicate observer of manners, particularly remark, that when upon any occasion Johnson had been rough to any person in company, he took the first opportunity of reconciliation, by drinking to him, or addressing his discourse to him; but if he found his dignified indirect overtures sullenly neglected, he was quite indifferent, and considered himself as having done all that he ought to do, and the other as now in the wrong.

I went to him early on the morning of the tenth of November. 'Now (said he,) that you are going to marry, do not expect more from life, than life will afford. You may often find yourself out of humour, and you may often think your wife not studious enough to please you; and yet you may have reason to consider yourself as upon the whole very happily married.'

1770: ÆTAT. 61.]—DURING this year there was a total cessation of all correspondence between Dr. Johnson and me, without any coldness on either side, but merely from procrastination, continued from day to day; and as I was not in London, I had no opportunity of enjoying his company and recording his conversation. To supply this blank, I shall present my readers with some *Collectanea*, obligingly furnished to me by the Rev. Dr. Maxwell, of Falkland, in Ireland, sometime assistant preacher at the Temple, and for many years the social friend of Johnson, who spoke of him with a very kind regard.

'His general mode of life, during my acquaintance, seemed to be pretty uniform. About twelve o'clock I commonly visited him, and frequently found him in bed, or declaiming over his tea, which he drank very plentifully. He generally had a levee of morning visitors, chiefly men of letters; Hawkesworth, Goldsmith, Murphy, Langton, Steevens, Beaucherk, &c. &c., and sometimes learned ladies, particularly I remember a French lady of wit and fashion doing him the honour of a visit. He seemed to me to be considered as a kind of publick oracle, whom every body thought they had a right to visit and consult; and doubtless they were well rewarded. I never could discover how he found time for his compositions. He declaimed all the morning, then went to dinner at a tavern, where he commonly staid late, and then drank his tea at some friend's house, over which he loitered a great while, but seldom took supper. I fancy he must have read and wrote chiefly in the night, for I can scarcely recollect that he ever refused going with me to a tavern, and he often went to Ranelagh, which he deemed a place of innocent recreation.

'He frequently gave all the silver in his pocket to the poor, who watched him, between his house and the tavern where he dined. He walked the streets at all hours, and said he was never robbed, for the rogues knew he had little money, nor had the appearance of having much.

'Though the most accessible and communicative man alive; yet when he suspected he was invited to be exhibited, he constantly spurned the invitation.

'Two young women from Staffordshire visited him when I was present, to consult him on the subject of Methodism, to which they were inclined. "Come, (said he,) you pretty fools, dine with Maxwell and me at the Mitre, and we will talk over that subject;" which they did, and after dinner he took one of them upon his knee, and fondled her for half an hour together.

'Johnson was much attached to London: he observed, that a man stored his mind better there, than any where else; and that in remote situations a man's body might be feasted, but his mind was starved, and his faculties apt to degenerate, from want of exercise and competition. No place, (he said,) cured a man's vanity or arrogance so well as London; for as no man was either great or good per se, but as compared with others not so good or great, he was sure to find in the metropolis many his equals, and some his superiors. He observed, that a man in London was in less danger of falling in love indiscreetly, than any where else; for there the difficulty of deciding between the conflicting pretensions of a vast variety of objects, kept him safe. He told me, that he had frequently been offered country preferment, if he would consent to take orders; but he could not leave the improved society of the capital, or consent to exchange the exhilarating joys and splendid decorations of publick life, for the obscurity, insipidity, and uniformity of remote situations.

'Burton's *Anatomy of Melancholy*, he said, was the only book that ever took him out of bed two hours sooner than he wished to rise.

'When exasperated by contradiction, he was apt to treat his opponents with too much acrimony: as, "Sir, you don't see your way through that question:"—"Sir, you talk the language of ignorance." On my observing to him that a certain gentleman had remained silent the whole evening, in the midst of a very brilliant and learned society, "Sir, (said he,) the conversation overflowed, and drowned him."

'He observed, that the established clergy in general did not preach plain enough; and that polished periods and glittering sentences flew over the heads of the common people, without any impression upon their hearts. Something might be necessary, he observed, to excite the affections of the common people, who were sunk in languor and lethargy, and therefore he supposed that the new concomitants of methodism might probably produce so desirable an effect. The mind, like the body, he observed, delighted in change and novelty, and even in religion itself, courted new appearances and modifications. Whatever might be thought of some methodist teachers, he said, he could scarcely doubt the sincerity of that man, who travelled nine hundred miles in a month, and preached twelve times a week; for no adequate reward, merely temporal, could be given for such indefatigable labour.

'In a Latin conversation with the Père Boscovitch, at the house of Mrs. Cholmondeley, I heard him maintain the superiority of Sir Isaac Newton over all foreign philosophers, with a dignity and eloquence that surprized that learned foreigner. It being observed to him, that a rage for every thing English prevailed much in France after Lord Chatham's glorious war, he said, he did not wonder at it, for that we had drubbed those fellows into a proper reverence for us, and that their national petulance required periodical chastisement.

'Speaking of a dull tiresome fellow, whom he chanced to meet, he said, "That fellow seems to me to possess but one idea, and that is a wrong one."

'Much enquiry having been made concerning a gentleman, who had quitted a company where Johnson was, and no information being obtained; at last Johnson observed, that "he did not care to speak ill of any man behind his back, but he believed the gentleman was an *attorney*."

'A gentleman who had been very unhappy in marriage, married

immediately after his wife died: Johnson said, it was the triumph of hope over experience.

'He observed, that a man of sense and education should meet a suitable companion in a wife. It was a miserable thing when the conversation could only be such as, whether the mutton should be boiled or roasted, and probably a dispute about that.

'He did not approve of late marriages, observing that more was lost in point of time, than compensated for by any possible advantages. Even ill assorted marriages were preferable to cheerless celibacy.

'He said, foppery was never cured; it was the bad stamina of the mind, which, like those of the body, were never rectified: once a coxcomb, and always a coxcomb.

'Being told that Gilbert Cowper called him the Caliban of literature; "Well, (said he,) I must dub him the Punchinello."

'He said few people had intellectual resources sufficient to forego the pleasures of wine. They could not otherwise contrive how to fill the interval between dinner and supper.

'One evening at Mrs. Montagu's, where a splendid company was assembled, consisting of the most eminent literary characters, I thought he seemed highly pleased with the respect and attention that were shewn him, and asked him on our return home if he was not highly *gratified* by his visit:

"No, Sir, (said he,) not highly *gratified*; yet I do not recollect to have passed many evenings *with fewer objections.*"

'Though of no high extraction himself, he had much respect for birth and family, especially among ladies. He said, "adventitious accomplishments may be possessed by all ranks; but one may easily distinguish the *born gentlewoman.*"

'Speaking of Burke, he said, "It was commonly observed, he spoke too often in parliament; but nobody could say he did not speak well, though too frequently and too familiarly."

'We dined *tête à tête* at the Mitre, as I was preparing to return to Ireland, after an absence of many years. I regretted much leaving London, where I had formed many agreeable connexions: "Sir, (said he,) I don't wonder at it; no man, fond of letters, leaves London without regret. But remember, Sir, you have seen and enjoyed a great deal;— you have seen life in its highest decorations, and the world has nothing new to exhibit. No man is so well qualified to leave publick life as he who has long tried it and known it well. We are always hankering after untried situations and imagining greater felicity from them than they can afford. No, Sir, knowledge and virtue may be acquired in all countries, and your local consequence will make you some amends for the intellectual gratifications you relinquish."

'He then took a most affecting leave of me; said, he knew, it was a point of *duty* that called me away. "We shall all be sorry to lose you,"

said he: "*laudo tamen.*"'
    1771, Ætat. 62.]—

'TO SIR JOSHUA REYNOLDS, IN LEICESTER-FIELDS.

'Dear Sir,—When I came to Lichfield, I found that my portrait had been much visited, and much admired. Every man has a lurking wish to appear considerable in his native place; and I was pleased with the dignity conferred by such a testimony of your regard.

'Be pleased, therefore, to accept the thanks of, Sir, your most obliged and most humble servant,
    'Ashbourn in Derbyshire,

                              'Sam. Johnson.
    July 17, 1771.'
'Compliments to Miss Reynolds.'

In his religious record of this year, we observe that he was better than usual, both in body and mind, and better satisfied with the regularity of his conduct. But he is still 'trying his ways' too rigorously. He charges himself with not rising early enough; yet he mentions what was surely a sufficient excuse for this, supposing it to be a duty seriously required, as he all his life appears to have thought it. 'One great hindrance is want of rest; my nocturnal complaints grow less troublesome towards morning; and I am tempted to repair the deficiencies of the night.' Alas! how hard would it be if this indulgence were to be imputed to a sick man as a crime. In his retrospect on the following Easter-Eve, he says, 'When I review the last year, I am able to recollect so little done, that shame and sorrow, though perhaps too weakly, come upon me.'

In 1772 he was altogether quiescent as an authour; but it will be found from the various evidences which I shall bring together that his mind was acute, lively, and vigorous.

'TO JAMES BOSWELL, ESQ.

'Dear Sir,—That you are coming so soon to town I am very glad; and still more glad that you are coming as an advocate. I think nothing more likely to make your life pass happily away, than that consciousness of your own value, which eminence in your profession will certainly confer. If I can give you any collateral help, I hope you do not suspect that it will be wanting. My kindness for you has neither the merit of singular virtue, nor the reproach of singular prejudice. Whether to love you be right or wrong, I have many on my side: Mrs. Thrale loves you, and Mrs. Williams loves you, and what would have inclined me to love you, if I had been neutral before, you are a great favourite of Dr. Beattie.[24]

'Of Dr. Beattie I should have thought much, but that his lady puts him out of my head; she is a very lovely woman.

'The ejection which you come hither to oppose, appears very cruel, unreasonable, and oppressive. I should think there could not be much doubt of your success.

'My health grows better, yet I am not fully recovered. I believe it is held, that men do not recover very fast after threescore. I hope yet to see Beattie's College: and have not given up the western voyage. But however all this may be or not, let us try to make each other happy when we meet, and not refer our pleasure to distant times or distant places.

'How comes it that you tell me nothing of your lady? I hope to see her some time, and till then shall be glad to hear of her. I am, dear Sir, &c.

'March 15, 1772.'

'SAM. JOHNSON.'

On the 21st of March, I was happy to find myself again in my friend's study, and was glad to see my old acquaintance, Mr. Francis Barber, who was now returned home. Dr. Johnson received me with a hearty welcome; saying, 'I am glad you are come.'

I thanked him for showing civilities to Beattie. 'Sir, (said he,) I should thank *you*. We all love Beattie. Mrs. Thrale says, if ever she has another husband, she'll have Beattie. He sunk upon us that he was married; else we should have shewn his lady more civilities. She is a very fine woman. But how can you shew civilities to a nonentity? I did not think he had been married. Nay, I did not think about it one way or other; but he did not tell us of his lady till late.'

He then spoke of St. Kilda, the most remote of the Hebrides. I told him, I thought of buying it. JOHNSON. 'Pray do, Sir. We will go and pass a winter amid the blasts there. We shall have fine fish, and we will take some dried tongues with us, and some books. We will have a strong built vessel, and some Orkney men to navigate her. We must build a tolerable house: but we may carry with us a wooden house ready made, and requiring nothing but to be put up. Consider, Sir, by buying St. Kilda, you may keep the people from falling into worse hands. We must give them a clergyman, and he shall be one of Beattie's choosing. He shall be educated at Marischal College. I'll be your Lord Chancellor, or what you please.' BOSWELL. 'Are you serious, Sir, in advising me to buy St. Kilda? for if you should advise me to go to Japan, I believe I should do it.' JOHNSON. 'Why yes, Sir, I

---

[24] Boswell had given Beattie a letter of introduction to Johnson the preceding summer—Ed.

am serious.' BOSWELL. 'Why then, I'll see what can be done.'

He was engaged to dine abroad, and asked me to return to him in the evening at nine, which I accordingly did.

We drank tea with Mrs. Williams, who told us a story of second sight, which happened in Wales where she was born. He listened to it very attentively, and said he should be glad to have some instances of that faculty well authenticated. His elevated wish for more and more evidence for spirit, in opposition to the groveling belief of materialism, led him to a love of such mysterious disquisitions. He again justly observed, that we could have no certainty of the truth of supernatural appearances, unless something was told us which we could not know by ordinary means, or something done which could not be done but by supernatural power; that Pharaoh in reason and justice required such evidence from Moses; nay, that our Saviour said, 'If I had not done among them the works which none other man did, they had not had sin.'

We talked of the Roman Catholick religion, and how little difference there was in essential matters between ours and it. JOHNSON. 'True, Sir; all denominations of Christians have really little difference in point of doctrine, though they may differ widely in external forms. There is a prodigious difference between the external form of one of your Presbyterian churches in Scotland, and a church in Italy; yet the doctrine taught is essentially the same.

In the morning we had talked of old families, and the respect due to them. JOHNSON. 'Sir, you have a right to that kind of respect, and are arguing for yourself. I am for supporting the principle, and am disinterested in doing it, as I have no such right.' BOSWELL. 'Why, Sir, it is one more incitement to a man to do well.' JOHNSON. 'Yes, Sir, and it is a matter of opinion, very necessary to keep society together. What is it but opinion, by which we have a respect for authority, that prevents us, who are the rabble, from rising up and pulling down you who are gentlemen from your places, and saying, "We will be gentlemen in our turn?" Now, Sir, that respect for authority is much more easily granted to a man whose father has had it, than to an upstart, and so Society is more easily supported.' BOSWELL. 'At present, Sir, I think riches seem to gain most respect.' JOHNSON. 'No, Sir, riches do not gain hearty respect; they only procure external attention. A very rich man, from low beginnings, may buy his election in a borough; but, *cæteris paribus*, a man of family will be preferred. People will prefer a man for whose father their fathers have voted, though they should get no more money, or even less. That shows that the respect for family is not merely fanciful, but has an actual operation. If gentlemen of family would allow the rich upstarts to spend their money profusely, which they are ready enough to do, and not vie with them in expence, the upstarts would soon be at an end, and the gentlemen would remain: but if the gentlemen will vie in expence with the upstarts, which is very foolish, they must be ruined.'

On Monday, March 23, I found him busy, preparing a fourth edition of his folio Dictionary. Mr. Peyton, one of his original amanuenses, was writing for him.

He seemed also to be intent on some sort of chymical operation. I was entertained by observing how he contrived to send Mr. Peyton on an errand, without seeming to degrade him. 'Mr. Peyton,—Mr. Peyton, will you be so good as to take a walk to Temple-Bar? You will there see a chymist's shop; at which you will be pleased to buy for me an ounce of oil of vitriol; not spirit of vitriol, but oil of vitriol. It will cost three half-pence.' Peyton immediately went, and returned with it, and told him it cost but a penny.

On Saturday, March 27, I introduced to him Sir Alexander Macdonald, with whom he had expressed a wish to be acquainted. He received him very courteously.

SIR A. 'I think, Sir, almost all great lawyers, such at least as have written upon law, have known only law, and nothing else.' JOHNSON. 'Why no, Sir; Judge Hale was a great lawyer, and wrote upon law; and yet he knew a great many other things; and has written upon other things. Selden too.' SIR A. 'Very true, Sir; and Lord Bacon. But was not Lord Coke a mere lawyer?' JOHNSON. 'Why, I am afraid he was; but he would have taken it very ill if you had told him so. He would have prosecuted you for scandal.' BOSWELL. 'Lord Mansfield is not a mere lawyer. JOHNSON. 'No, Sir. I never was in Lord Mansfield's company; but Lord Mansfield was distinguished at the University. Lord Mansfield, when he first came to town, "drank champagne with the wits," as Prior says. He was the friend of Pope.' SIR A. 'Barristers, I believe, are not so abusive now as they were formerly. I fancy they had less law long ago, and so were obliged to take to abuse, to fill up the time. Now they have such a number of precedents, they have no occasion for abuse.' JOHNSON. 'Nay, Sir, they had more law long ago than they have now. As to precedents, to be sure they will increase in course of time; but the more precedents there are, the less occasion is there for law; that is to say, the less occasion is there for investigating principles.' SIR A. 'I have been correcting several Scotch accents in my friend Boswell. I doubt, Sir, if any Scotchman ever attains to a perfect English pronunciation.' JOHNSON. 'Why, Sir, few of them do, because they do not persevere after acquiring a certain degree of it. But, Sir, there can be no doubt that they may attain to a perfect English pronunciation, if they will. We find how near they come to it; and certainly, a man who conquers nineteen parts of the Scottish accent, may conquer the twentieth. But, Sir, when a man has got the better of nine tenths he grows weary, he relaxes his diligence, he finds he has corrected his accent so far as not to be disagreeable, and he no longer desires his friends to tell him when he is wrong; nor does he choose to be told. Sir, when people watch me narrowly, and I do not watch myself, they will find me out to be of a particular county. In the same manner, Dunning may be found out to be a Devonshire man. So most Scotchmen may be found out. But, Sir, little aberrations are of no disadvantage. I never catched Mallet in a Scotch accent; and yet Mallet, I suppose, was past five-and-twenty before he came to London.'

I again visited him at night. Finding him in a very good humour, I ventured to lead him to the subject of our situation in a future state, having much curiosity to know his notions on that point. . . .

BOSWELL. 'I do not know whether there are any well-attested stories of the appearance of ghosts. You know there is a famous story of the appearance of Mrs. Veal, prefixed to *Drelincourt on Death.*' JOHNSON. 'I believe, Sir, that is given up. I believe the woman declared upon her death-bed that it was a lie.' BOSWELL. 'This objection is made against the truth of ghosts appearing: that if they are in a state of happiness, it would be a punishment to them to return to this world; and if they are in a state of misery, it would be giving them a respite.' JOHNSON. 'Why, Sir, as the happiness or misery of embodied spirits does not depend upon place, but is intellectual, we cannot say that they are less happy or less miserable by appearing upon earth.'

We went down between twelve and one to Mrs. Williams's room, and drank tea. I mentioned that we were to have the remains of Mr. Gray, in prose and verse, published by Mr. Mason. JOHNSON. 'I think we have had enough of Gray. I see they have published a splendid edition of Akenside's works. One bad ode may be suffered; but a number of them together makes one sick.' BOSWELL. 'Akenside's distinguished poem is his *Pleasures of Imagination*; but for my part, I never could admire it so much as most people do.' JOHNSON. 'Sir, I could not read it through.' BOSWELL. 'I have read it through; but I did not find any great power in it.'

On Tuesday, March 31, he and I dined at General Paoli's.

Dr. Johnson went home with me to my lodgings in Conduit-street and drank tea, previous to our going to the Pantheon, which neither of us had seen before.

He said, 'Goldsmith's *Life of Parnell* is poor; not that it is poorly written, but that he had poor materials; for nobody can write the life of a man, but those who have eat and drunk and lived in social intercourse with him.'

I said, that if it was not troublesome and presuming too much, I would request him to tell me all the little circumstances of his life; what schools he attended, when he came to Oxford, when he came to London, &c. &c. He did not disapprove of my curiosity as to these particulars; but said, 'They'll come out by degrees as we talk together.'

We talked of the proper use of riches. JOHNSON. 'If I were a man of a great estate, I would drive all the rascals whom I did not like out of the county at an election.'

We then walked to the Pantheon. The first view of it did not strike us so much as Ranelagh, of which he said, the '*coup d'oeil* was the finest thing he had ever seen.' The truth is, Ranelagh is of a more beautiful form; more of it or rather indeed the whole *rotunda*, appears at once, and it is better lighted. However, as Johnson observed, we saw the Pantheon in time of mourning, when there was a dull uniformity; whereas we had seen Ranelagh when the view was enlivened with a gay profusion of colours. Mrs. Bosville, of Gunthwait, in Yorkshire, joined us, and entered into conversation with us. Johnson said to me afterwards, 'Sir, this is a mighty intelligent lady.'

I said there was not half a guinea's worth of pleasure in seeing this place. JOHNSON. 'But, Sir, there is half a guinea's worth of inferiority to other people in not having seen it.' BOSWELL. 'I doubt, Sir, whether there are many happy people here.' JOHNSON. 'Yes, Sir, there are many happy people here. There are many people here who are watching hundreds, and who think hundreds are watching them.'

Happening to meet Sir Adam Fergusson, I presented him to Dr. Johnson. Sir Adam expressed some apprehension that the Pantheon would encourage luxury. 'Sir, (said Johnson,) I am a great friend to publick amusements; for they keep people from vice. You now (addressing himself to me,) would have been with a wench, had you not been here.—O! I forgot you were married.'

Sir Adam suggested, that luxury corrupts a people, and destroys the spirit of liberty. JOHNSON. 'Sir, that is all visionary. I would not give half a guinea to live under one form of government rather than another. It is of no moment to the happiness of an individual. Sir, the danger of the abuse of power is nothing to a private man. What Frenchman is prevented from passing his life as he pleases?' SIR ADAM. 'But, Sir, in the British constitution it is surely of importance to keep up a spirit in the people, so as to preserve a balance against the crown.' JOHNSON. 'Sir, I perceive you are a vile Whig. Why all this childish jealousy of the power of the crown? The crown has not power enough. When I say that all governments are alike, I consider that in no government power can be abused long. Mankind will not bear it. If a sovereign oppresses his people to a great degree, they will rise and cut off his head. There is a remedy in human nature against tyranny, that will keep us safe under every form of government. Had not the people of France thought themselves honoured as sharing in the brilliant actions of Lewis XIV, they would not have endured him; and we may say the same of the King of Prussia's people.' Sir Adam introduced the ancient Greeks and Romans. JOHNSON. 'Sir, the mass of both of them were barbarians. The mass of every people must be barbarous where there is no printing, and consequently knowledge is not generally diffused. Knowledge is diffused among our people by the news-papers.' Sir Adam mentioned the orators, poets, and artists of Greece. JOHNSON. 'Sir, I am talking of the mass of the people. We see even what the boasted Athenians were. The little effect which Demosthenes's orations had upon them, shews that they were barbarians.'

On Sunday, April 5, after attending divine service at St. Paul's church, I found him alone.

He said, he went more frequently to church when there were prayers only, than when there was also a sermon, as the people required more an example for the one than the other; it being much easier for them to hear a sermon, than to fix their minds on prayer.

On Monday, April 6, I dined with him at Sir Alexander Macdonald's, where was a young officer in the regimentals of the Scots Royal, who talked with a vivacity, fluency, and precision so uncommon, that he attracted particular attention. He proved to be the Honourable Thomas Erskine, youngest brother to the Earl of Buchan, who has since risen into such brilliant reputation at the bar in Westminster-hall.

Fielding being mentioned, Johnson exclaimed, 'he was a blockhead;' and upon my expressing my astonishment at so strange an assertion, he said, 'What I mean by his being a blockhead is that he was a barren rascal.' BOSWELL. 'Will you not allow, Sir, that he draws very natural pictures of human life?' JOHNSON. 'Why, Sir, it is of very low life. Richardson used to say, that had he not known who Fielding was, he should have believed he was an ostler. Sir, there is more knowledge of the heart in one letter of Richardson's, than in all *Tom Jones*. I, indeed, never read *Joseph Andrews*.' ERSKINE. 'Surely, Sir, Richardson is very tedious.' JOHNSON. 'Why, Sir, if you were to read Richardson for the story, your impatience would be so much fretted that you would hang yourself. But you must read him for the sentiment, and consider the story as only giving occasion to the sentiment.'

We talked of gaming, and animadverted on it with severity. JOHNSON. 'Nay, gentlemen, let us not aggravate the matter. It is not roguery to play with a man who is ignorant of the game, while you are master of it, and so win his money; for he thinks he can play better than you, as you think you can play better than he; and the superiour skill carries it.' ERSKINE. 'He is a fool, but you are not a rogue.' JOHNSON. 'That's much about the truth, Sir. It must be considered, that a man who only does what every one of the society to which he belongs would do, is not a dishonest man. In the republick of Sparta, it was agreed, that stealing was not dishonourable, if not discovered. I do not commend a society where there is an agreement that what would not otherwise be fair, shall be fair; but I maintain, that an individual of any society, who practises what is allowed, is not a dishonest man.'

BOSWELL. 'So then, Sir, you do not think ill of a man who wins perhaps forty thousand pounds in a winter?' JOHNSON. 'Sir, I do not call a gamester a dishonest man; but I call him an unsocial man, an unprofitable man. Gaming is a mode of transferring property without producing any intermediate good. Trade gives employment to numbers, and so produces intermediate good.'

On Thursday, April 9, I called on him to beg he would go and dine with me at the Mitre tavern. He had resolved not to dine at all this day, I know not for what reason; and I was so unwilling to be deprived of his company, that I was content to submit to suffer a want, which was at first somewhat painful, but he soon made me forget it; and a man is always pleased with himself when he finds his intellectual inclinations predominate.

He observed, that to reason philosophically on the nature of prayer, was very unprofitable.

Talking of ghosts, he said, he knew one friend, who was an honest man and a sensible man, who told him he had seen a ghost, old Mr. Edward Cave, the printer at St. John's Gate. He said, Mr. Cave did not like to talk of it, and seemed to be in great horrour whenever it was mentioned. BOSWELL. 'Pray, Sir, what did he say was the appearance?' JOHNSON. 'Why, Sir, something of a shadowy being.'

On Friday, April 10, I dined with him at General Oglethorpe's, where we found Dr. Goldsmith.

I started the question whether duelling was consistent with moral duty. The brave old General fired at this, and said, with a lofty air, 'Undoubtedly a man has a right to defend his honour.' GOLDSMITH. (turning to me,) 'I ask you first, Sir, what would you do if you were affronted?' I answered I should think it necessary to fight. 'Why then, (replied Goldsmith,) that solves the question.' JOHNSON. 'No, Sir, it does not solve the question. It does not follow that what a man would do is therefore right.' I said, I wished to have it settled, whether duelling was contrary to the laws of Christianity. Johnson immediately entered on the subject, and treated it in a masterly manner; and so far as I have been able to recollect, his thoughts were these: 'Sir, as men become in a high degree refined, various causes of offence arise; which are considered to be of such importance, that life must be staked to atone for them, though in reality they are not so. A body that has received a very fine polish may be easily hurt. Before men arrive at this artificial refinement, if one tells his neighbour he lies, his neighbour tells him he lies; if one gives his neighbour a blow, his neighbour gives him a blow: but in a state of highly polished society, an affront is held to be a serious injury. It must therefore be resented, or rather a duel must be fought upon it; as men have agreed to banish from their society one who puts up with an affront without fighting a duel. Now, Sir, it is never unlawful to fight in self-defence. He, then, who fights a duel, does not fight from passion against his antagonist, but out of self-defence; to avert the stigma of the world, and to prevent himself from being driven out of society. I could wish there was not that superfluity of refinement; but while such notions prevail, no doubt a man may lawfully fight a duel.'

The General told us, that when he was a very young man, I think only fifteen, serving under Prince Eugene of Savoy, he was sitting in a company at table with a Prince of Wirtemberg. The Prince took up a glass of wine, and, by a fillip, made some of it fly in Oglethorpe's face. Here was a nice dilemma. To have challenged him instantly, might have fixed a quarrelsome character upon the young soldier: to have taken no notice of it might have been considered as cowardice. Oglethorpe, therefore, keeping his eye upon the Prince, and smiling all the time, as if he took what his Highness had done in jest, said '*Mon Prince,—*'. (I forget the French words he used, the purport however was,) 'That's a good joke; but we do it much better in England;' and threw a whole glass of wine in the Prince's face. An old General who sat by, said, '*Il a bien fait, mon Prince, vous l'avez commencé:*' and thus all ended in good humour.

Dr. Johnson said, 'Pray, General, give us an account of the siege of Belgrade.' Upon which the General, pouring a little wine upon the table, described every thing with a wet finger: 'Here we were, here were the Turks,' &c. &c. Johnson listened with the closest attention.

A question was started, how far people who disagree in a capital point can live in friendship together. Johnson said they might. Goldsmith said they could not, as they had not the *idem velle atque idem nolle*—the same likings and the same aversions. JOHNSON. 'Why, Sir, you must shun the subject as to which you disagree. For instance, I can live very well with Burke: I love his knowledge, his genius, his diffusion, and affluence of conversation; but I would not talk to him of the Rockingham party.' GOLDSMITH. 'But, Sir, when people live together who have something as to which they disagree, and which they want to shun, they will be in the situation mentioned in the story of Bluebeard: "You may look into all the chambers but one." But we should have the greatest inclination to look into that chamber, to talk of that subject.' JOHNSON. (with a loud voice,) 'Sir, I am not saying that *you* could live in friendship with a man from whom you differ as to some point: I am only saying that I could do it. You put me in mind of Sappho in Ovid.'

Goldsmith told us, that he was now busy in writing a natural history, and, that he might have full leisure for it, he had taken lodgings, at a farmer's house, near to the six milestone, on the Edgeware road, and had carried down his books in two returned post-chaises. He said, he believed the farmer's family thought him an odd character, similar to that in which the *Spectator* appeared to his landlady and her children: he was *The Gentleman.* Mr. Mickle, the translator of *The Lusiad*, and I went to visit him at this place a few days afterwards. He was not at home; but having a curiosity to see his apartment, we went in and found curious scraps of descriptions of animals, scrawled upon the wall with a black lead pencil.

On Saturday, April 11, he appointed me to come to him in the evening, when he should be at leisure to give me some assistance for the defence of Hastie, the schoolmaster of Campbelltown, for whom I was to appear in the house of Lords. When I came, I found him unwilling to exert himself. I pressed him to write down his thoughts upon the subject. He said, 'There's no occasion for my writing. I'll talk to you.' . . .

Of our friend, Goldsmith, he said, 'Sir, he is so much afraid of being unnoticed, that he often talks merely lest you should forget that he is in the company.' BOSWELL. 'Yes, he stands forward.' JOHNSON. 'True, Sir; but if a man is to stand forward, he should wish to do it not in an aukward posture, not in rags, not so as that he shall only be exposed to ridicule.' BOSWELL. 'For my part, I like very well to hear honest Goldsmith talk away carelessly.' JOHNSON. 'Why yes, Sir; but he should not like to hear himself.' . . .

On Tuesday, April 14, the decree of the Court of Session in the schoolmaster's cause was reversed in the House of Lords, after a very eloquent speech by Lord Mansfield, who shewed himself an adept in school discipline, but I thought was too rigorous towards my client. On the evening of the next day I supped with Dr. Johnson, at the Crown and Anchor tavern, in the Strand, in company with Mr. Langton and his brother-in-law, Lord Binning.

I talked of the recent expulsion of six students from the University of Oxford, who were methodists and would not desist from publickly praying and exhorting. JOHNSON. 'Sir, that expulsion was extremely just and proper. What have they to do at an University who are not willing to be taught, but will presume to teach? Where is religion to be learnt but at an University? Sir, they were examined, and found to be mighty ignorant fellows.' BOSWELL. 'But, was it not hard, Sir, to expel them, for I am told they were good beings?' JOHNSON. 'I believe they might be good beings; but they were not fit to be in the University of Oxford. A cow is a very good animal in the field; but we turn her out of a garden.' Lord Elibank used to repeat this as an illustration uncommonly happy.

Desirous of calling Johnson forth to talk, and exercise his wit, though I should myself be the object of it, I resolutely ventured to undertake the defence of convivial indulgence in wine, though he was not to-night in the most genial humour. After urging the common plausible topicks, I at last had recourse to the maxim, *in vino veritas*, a man who is well warmed with wine will speak truth. JOHNSON. 'Why,

Sir, that may be an argument for drinking, if you suppose men in general to be liars. But, Sir, I would not keep company with a fellow, who lyes as long as he is sober, and whom you must make drunk before you can get a word of truth out of him.'

At this time it appears from his *Prayers and Meditations*, that he had been more than commonly diligent in religious duties, particularly in reading the Holy Scriptures. It was Passion Week, that solemn season which the Christian world has appropriated to the commemoration of the mysteries of our redemption, and during which, whatever embers of religion are in our breasts, will be kindled into pious warmth.

I paid him short visits both on Friday and Saturday, and seeing his large folio Greek Testament before him, beheld him with a reverential awe, and would not intrude upon his time. While he was thus employed to such good purpose, and while his friends in their intercourse with him constantly found a vigorous intellect and a lively imagination, it is melancholy to read in his private register, 'My mind is unsettled and my memory confused. I have of late turned my thoughts with a very useless earnestness upon past incidents. I have yet got no command over my thoughts; an unpleasing incident is almost certain to hinder my rest.' What philosophick heroism was it in him to appear with such manly fortitude to the world while he was inwardly so distressed! We may surely believe that the mysterious principle of being 'made perfect through suffering' was to be strongly exemplified in him.

On Sunday, April 19, being Easter-day, General Paoli and I paid him a visit before dinner.

We talked of sounds. The General said, there was no beauty in a simple sound, but only in an harmonious composition of sounds. I presumed to differ from this opinion, and mentioned the soft and sweet sound of a fine woman's voice. JOHNSON. 'No, Sir, if a serpent or a toad uttered it, you would think it ugly.' BOSWELL. 'So you would think, Sir, were a beautiful tune to be uttered by one of those animals.' JOHNSON. 'No, Sir, it would be admired. We have seen fine fiddlers whom we liked as little as toads.' (laughing.)

While I remained in London this spring, I was with him at several other times, both by himself and in company. I dined with him one day at the Crown and Anchor tavern, in the Strand, with Lord Elibank, Mr. Langton, and Dr. Vansittart of Oxford. Without specifying each particular day, I have preserved the following memorable things.

I regretted the reflection in his Preface to Shakspeare against Garrick, to whom we cannot but apply the following passage: 'I collated such copies as I could procure, and wished for more, but have not found the collectors of these rarities very communicative.' I told him, that Garrick had complained to me of it, and had vindicated himself by assuring me, that Johnson was made welcome to the full use of his collection, and that he left the key of it with a servant, with orders to have a fire and every convenience for him. I found Johnson's notion was, that Garrick wanted to be courted for them, and that, on the contrary, Garrick should have courted him, and sent him the plays of his own accord. But, indeed, considering the slovenly and careless manner in which books were treated by Johnson, it could not be expected that scarce and valuable editions should have been lent to him.

A gentleman[25] having to some of the usual arguments for drinking added this: 'You know, Sir, drinking drives away care, and makes us forget whatever is disagreeable. Would not you allow a man to drink for that reason?' JOHNSON. 'Yes, Sir, if he sat next *you.*'

A learned gentleman who in the course of conversation wished to inform us of this simple fact, that the Counsel upon the circuit at Shrewsbury were much bitten by fleas, took, I suppose, seven or eight minutes in relating it circumstantially. He in a plenitude of phrase told us, that large bales of woollen cloth were lodged in the town-hall;—that by reason of this, fleas nestled there in prodigious numbers; that the lodgings of the counsel were near to the town-hall;—and that those little animals moved from place to place with wonderful agility. Johnson sat in great impatience till the gentleman had finished his tedious narrative, and then burst out (playfully however), 'It is a pity, Sir, that you have not seen a lion; for a flea has taken you such a time, that a lion must have served you a twelvemonth.'

He would not allow Scotland to derive any credit from Lord Mansfield; for he was educated in England. 'Much (said he,) may be made of a Scotchman, if he be *caught* young.'

He said, 'I am very unwilling to read the manuscripts of authours, and give them my opinion. If the authours who apply to me have money, I bid them boldly print without a name; if they have written in order to get money, I tell them to go to the booksellers, and make the best bargain they can.' BOSWELL. 'But, Sir, if a bookseller should bring you a manuscript to look at?' JOHNSON. 'Why, Sir, I would desire the bookseller to take it away.'

I mentioned a friend of mine who had resided long in Spain, and was unwilling to return to Britain. JOHNSON. 'Sir, he is attached to some woman.' BOSWELL. 'I rather believe, Sir, it is the fine climate which keeps him there.' JOHNSON. 'Nay, Sir, how can you talk so? What is *climate* to happiness? Place me in the heart of Asia, should I not be exiled? What proportion does climate bear to the complex system of human life? You may advise me to go to live at Bologna to eat sausages. The sausages there are the best in the world; they lose much by being carried.'

---

[25] The gentleman most likely is Boswell.—HILL.

On Saturday, May 9, Mr. Dempster and I had agreed to dine by ourselves at the British Coffee-house. Johnson, on whom I happened to call in the morning, said he would join us, which he did, and we spent a very agreeable day, though I recollect but little of what passed.

He said, 'Walpole was a minister given by the King to the people: Pitt was a minister given by the people to the King,—as an adjunct.'

'The misfortune of Goldsmith in conversation is this: he goes on without knowing how he is to get off. His genius is great, but his knowledge is small. As they say of a generous man, it is a pity he is not rich, we may say of Goldsmith, it is a pity he is not knowing. He would not keep his knowledge to himself.'

1773: ÆTAT. 64.]—In 1773 his only publication was an edition of his folio *Dictionary*, with additions and corrections; nor did he, so far as is known, furnish any productions of his fertile pen to any of his numerous friends or dependants, except the Preface to his old amanuensis Macbean's *Dictionary of Ancient Geography*.

'TO JAMES BOSWELL, ESQ.

'DEAR SIR,—. . . A new edition of my great *Dictionary* is printed, from a copy which I was persuaded to revise; but having made no preparation, I was able to do very little. Some superfluities I have expunged, and some faults I have corrected, and here and there have scattered a remark; but the main fabrick of the work remains as it was. I had looked very little into it since I wrote it, and, I think, I found it full as often better, as worse, than I expected.

'Baretti and Davies have had a furious quarrel; a quarrel, I think, irreconcileable. Dr. Goldsmith has a new comedy, which is expected in the spring. No name is yet given it. The chief diversion arises from a stratagem by which a lover is made to mistake his future father-in-law's house for an inn. This, you see, borders upon farce. The dialogue is quick and gay, and the incidents are so prepared as not to seem improbable. . . .

'My health seems in general to improve; but I have been troubled for many weeks with a vexatious catarrh, which is sometimes sufficiently distressful. I have not found any great effects from bleeding and physick; and am afraid, that I must expect help from brighter days and softer air.

'Write to me now and then; and whenever any good befalls you, make haste to let me know it, for no one will rejoice at it more than, dear Sir, your most humble servant,

'SAM. JOHNSON.'

'London, Feb. 24, 1773.'
'You continue to stand very high in the favour of Mrs. Thrale.'

While a former edition of my work was passing through the press, I was unexpectedly favoured with a packet from Philadelphia, from Mr. James Abercrombie, a gentleman of that country, who is pleased to honour me with very high praise of my *Life of Dr. Johnson*. To have the fame of my illustrious friend, and his faithful biographer, echoed from the New World is extremely flattering; and my grateful acknowledgements shall be wafted across the Atlantick. Mr. Abercrombie has politely conferred on me a considerable additional obligation, by transmitting to me copies of two letters from Dr. Johnson to American gentlemen.

On Saturday, April 3, the day after my arrival in London this year, I went to his house late in the evening, and sat with Mrs. Williams till he came home. I found in the *London Chronicle*, Dr. Goldsmith's apology to the publick for beating Evans, a bookseller, on account of a paragraph in a newspaper published by him, which Goldsmith thought impertinent to him and to a lady of his acquaintance. The apology was written so much in Dr. Johnson's manner, that both Mrs. Williams and I supposed it to be his; but when he came home, he soon undeceived us. When he said to Mrs. Williams, 'Well, Dr. Goldsmith's *manifesto* has got into your paper;' I asked him if Dr. Goldsmith had written it, with an air that made him see I suspected it was his, though subscribed by Goldsmith. JOHNSON. 'Sir, Dr. Goldsmith would no more have asked me to write such a thing as that for him, than he would have asked me to feed him with a spoon, or to do anything else that denoted his imbecility. I as much believe that he wrote it, as if I had seen him do it. Sir, had he shewn it to any one friend, he would not have been allowed to publish it. He has, indeed, done it very well; but it is a foolish thing well done. I suppose he has been so much elated with the success of his new comedy, that he has thought every thing that concerned him must be of importance to the publick.' BOSWELL. 'I fancy, Sir, this is the first time that he has been engaged in such an adventure.' JOHNSON. 'Why, Sir, I believe it is the first time he has *beat*; he may have *been beaten* before. This, Sir, is a new plume to him.'

At Mr. Thrale's, in the evening, he repeated his usual paradoxical declamation against action in publick speaking. 'Action can have no effect upon reasonable minds. It may augment noise, but it never can enforce argument.'

Lord Chesterfield being mentioned, Johnson remarked, that almost all of that celebrated nobleman's witty sayings were puns. He, however, allowed the merit of good wit to his Lordship's saying of Lord Tyrawley and himself, when both very old and infirm: 'Tyrawley and I have been dead these two years; but we don't choose to have it known.'

The conversation having turned on modern imitations of ancient ballads, and some one having praised their simplicity, he treated them with that ridicule which he always displayed when that subject was mentioned.

He disapproved of introducing scripture phrases into secular discourse. This seemed to me a question of some difficulty. A scripture expression may be used, like a highly classical phrase, to produce an instantaneous strong impression; and it may be done without being at all improper. Yet I own there is danger, that applying the language of our sacred book to ordinary subjects may tend to lessen our reverence for it. If therefore it be introduced at all, it should be with very great caution.

On Thursday, April 8, I sat a good part of the evening with him, but he was very silent.

Though he was not disposed to talk, he was unwilling that I should leave him; and when I looked at my watch, and told him it was twelve o'clock, he cried, What's that to you and me?' and ordered Frank to tell Mrs. Williams that we were coming to drink tea with her, which we did. It was settled that we should go to church together next day.

On the 9th of April, being Good Friday, I breakfasted with him on tea and cross-buns; *Doctor* Levet, as Frank called him, making the tea. He carried me with him to the church of St. Clement Danes, where he had his seat; and his behaviour was, as I had imaged to myself, solemnly devout. I never shall forget the tremulous earnestness with which he pronounced the awful petition in the Litany: 'In the hour of death, and at the day of judgement, good LORD deliver us.

We went to church both in the morning and evening. In the interval between the two services we did not dine; but he read in the Greek New Testament, and I turned over several of his books.

I told him that Goldsmith had said to me a few days before, 'As I take my shoes from the shoemaker, and my coat from the taylor, so I take my religion from the priest.' I regretted this loose way of talking. JOHNSON. 'Sir, he knows nothing; he has made up his mind about nothing.'

To my great surprize he asked me to dine with him on Easter-day. I never supposed that he had a dinner at his house; for I had not then heard of any one of his friends having been entertained at his table. He told me, 'I generally have a meat pye on Sunday: it is baked at a publick oven, which is very properly allowed, because one man can attend it; and thus the advantage is obtained of not keeping servants from church to dress dinners.'

April 11, being Easter-Sunday, after having attended Divine Service at St. Paul's, I repaired to Dr. Johnson's. I had gratified my curiosity much in dining with JEAN JAQUES ROUSSEAU, while he lived in the wilds of Neufchatel: I had as great a curiosity to dine with DR. SAMUEL JOHNSON, in the dusky recess of a court in Fleet-street. I supposed we should scarcely have knives and forks, and only some strange, uncouth, ill-drest dish: but I found every thing in very good order. We had no other company but Mrs. Williams and a young woman whom I did not know. As a dinner here was considered as a singular phaenomenon, and as I was frequently interrogated on the subject, my readers may perhaps be desirous to know our bill of fare. Foote, I remember, in allusion to Francis, the *negro*, was willing to suppose that our repast was *black broth*. But the fact was, that we had a very good soup, a boiled leg of lamb and spinach, a veal pye, and a rice pudding.

He owned that he thought Hawkesworth was one of his imitators, but he did not think Goldsmith was. Goldsmith, he said, had great merit. BOSWELL. 'But, Sir, he is much indebted to you for his getting so high in the publick estimation.' JOHNSON. 'Why, Sir, he has perhaps got *sooner* to it by his intimacy with me.'

Goldsmith, though his vanity often excited him to occasional competition, had a very high regard for Johnson, which he at this time expressed in the strongest manner in the Dedication of his comedy, entitled, *She Stoops to Conquer.*

He told me that he had twelve or fourteen times attempted to keep a journal of his life, but never could persevere. He advised me to do it. 'The great thing to be recorded, (said he,) is the state of your own mind; and you should write down every thing that you remember, for you cannot judge at first what is good or bad; and write immediately while the impression is fresh, for it will not be the same a week afterwards.'

I again solicited him to communicate to me the particulars of his early life. He said, 'You shall have them all for two-pence. I hope you shall know a great deal more of me before you write my Life.' He mentioned to me this day many circumstances, which I wrote down when I went home, and have interwoven in the former part of this narrative.

On Tuesday, April 13, he and Dr. Goldsmith and I dined at General Oglethorpe's. Goldsmith expatiated on the common topick, that the race of our people was degenerated, and that this was owing to luxury. JOHNSON. 'Sir, in the first place, I doubt the fact. I believe there are as many tall men in England now, as ever there were. But, secondly, supposing the stature of our people to be diminished, that is not owing to luxury; for, Sir, consider to how very small a proportion of our people luxury can reach. Our soldiery, surely, are not luxurious, who live on sixpence a day; and the same remark will apply to almost all the other classes. Luxury, so far as it reaches the poor, will do good to the race of people; it will strengthen and multiply them. Sir, no nation was ever hurt by luxury; for, as I said before, it can reach but to a very few. I admit that the great increase of commerce and manufactures hurts the military spirit of a people; because it produces a competition for something else than martial honours,—a competition for riches. It also hurts the bodies of the people; for you will observe, there is no man who works at any particular trade, but you may know him from his appearance to do so. One part or other of his body being more used than the rest, he is in some degree deformed: but, Sir, that is not luxury. A tailor sits cross-legged; but that is not luxury.' GOLDSMITH. 'Come, you're just going to the same place by another road.' JOHNSON. 'Nay, Sir, I say that is not *luxury*. Let us take a walk from Charing-cross to White-chapel, through, I suppose, the greatest series of shops in the world; what is there in any of these shops (if you except gin-shops,) that can do any human being any harm?' GOLDSMITH. 'Well, Sir, I'll accept your challenge. The very next shop to Northumberland-house is a pickle-shop.' JOHNSON. 'Well, Sir: do we not know that a maid can in one afternoon make pickles sufficient to serve a whole family for a year? nay, that five pickle-shops can serve all the kingdom? Besides, Sir, there is no harm done to any body by the making of pickles, or the eating of pickles.'

We drank tea with the ladies; and Goldsmith sung Tony Lumpkin's song in his comedy, *She Stoops to Conquer*, and a very pretty one, to an Irish tune, which he had designed for Miss Hardcastle; but as Mrs. Bulkeley, who played the part, could not sing, it was left out. He afterwards wrote it down for me, by which means it was preserved, and now appears amongst his poems. Dr. Johnson, in his way home, stopped at my lodgings in Piccadilly, and sat with me, drinking tea a second time, till a late hour.

I told him that Mrs. Macaulay said, she wondered how he could reconcile his political principles with his moral; his notions of inequality and subordination with wishing well to the happiness of all mankind, who might live so agreeably, had they all their portions of land, and none to domineer over another. JOHNSON. 'Why, Sir, I reconcile my principles very well, because mankind are happier in a state of inequality and subordination. Were they to be in this pretty state of equality, they would soon degenerate into brutes;—they would become Monboddo's nation;—their tails would grow. Sir, all would be losers were all to work for all—they would have no intellectual improvement. All intellectual improvement arises from leisure; all leisure arises from one working for another.'

Talking of the family of Stuart, he said, 'It should seem that the family at present on the throne has now established as good a right as the former family, by the long consent of the people; and that to disturb this right might be considered as culpable. At the same time I own, that it is a very difficult question, when considered with respect to the house of Stuart. To oblige people to take oaths as to the disputed right, is wrong. I know not whether I could take them: but I do not blame those who do.' So conscientious and so delicate was he upon this subject, which has occasioned so much clamour against him.

On Thursday, April 15, I dined with him and Dr. Goldsmith at General Paoli's.

I spoke of Allan Ramsay's *Gentle Shepherd*, in the Scottish dialect, as the best pastoral that had ever been written; not only abounding with beautiful rural imagery, and just and pleasing sentiments, but being a real picture of manners; and I offered to teach Dr. Johnson to understand it. 'No, Sir, (said he,) I won't learn it. You shall retain your superiority by my not knowing it.'

It having been observed that there was little hospitality in London;—JOHNSON. 'Nay, Sir, any man who has a name, or who has the power of pleasing, will be very generally invited in London. The man, Sterne, I have been told, has had engagements for three months.' GOLDSMITH. 'And a very dull fellow.' JOHNSON. 'Why, no, Sir.'

Martinelli told us, that for several years he lived much with Charles Townshend, and that he ventured to tell him he was a bad joker. JOHNSON. 'Why, Sir, thus much I can say upon the subject. One day he and a few more agreed to go and dine in the country, and each of them was to bring a friend in his carriage with him. Charles Townshend asked Fitzherbert to go with him, but told him, "You must find somebody to bring you back: I can only carry you there." Fitzherbert did not much like this arrangement. He however consented, observing sarcastically, "It will do very well; for then the same jokes will serve you in returning as in going."'

An eminent publick character being mentioned;—JOHNSON. 'I remember being present when he shewed himself to be so corrupted, or at least something so different from what I think right, as to maintain, that a member of parliament should go along with his party right or wrong. Now, Sir, this is so remote from native virtue, from scholastick virtue, that a good man must have undergone a great change before he can reconcile himself to such a doctrine. It is maintaining that you may lie to the publick; for you lie when you call that right which you think wrong, or the reverse. A friend of ours, who is too much an echo of that gentleman, observed, that a man who does not stick uniformly to a party, is only waiting to be bought. Why then, said I, he is only waiting to be what that gentleman is already.'

We talked of the King's coming to see Goldsmith's new play.—'I wish he would,' said Goldsmith; adding, however, with an affected indifference, 'Not that it would do me the least good.' JOHNSON. 'Well then, Sir, let us say it would do *him* good, (laughing.) No, Sir, this affectation will not pass;—it is mighty idle. In such a state as ours, who would not wish to please the Chief Magistrate?' GOLDSMITH. 'I *do* wish to please him. I remember a line in Dryden,—

"And every poet is the monarch's friend."

It ought to be reversed.' JOHNSON. 'Nay, there are finer lines in Dryden on this subject:—

"For colleges on bounteous Kings depend,
And never rebel was to arts a friend."'

General Paoli observed, that 'successful rebels might.' MARTINELLI. 'Happy rebellions.' GOLDSMITH. 'We have no such phrase.' GENERAL PAOLI. 'But have you not the *thing?*' GOLDSMITH. 'Yes; all our *happy* revolutions. They have hurt our constitution, and will hurt it, till we mend it by another HAPPY REVOLUTION.' I never before discovered that my friend Goldsmith had so much of the old prejudice in him.

General Paoli, talking of Goldsmith's new play, said, '*Il a fait un compliment très gracieux à une certaine grande dame;*' meaning a Duchess of the first rank.

I expressed a doubt whether Goldsmith intended it, in order that I might hear the truth from himself. It, perhaps, was not quite fair to endeavour to bring him to a confession, as he might not wish to avow positively his taking part against the Court. He smiled and hesitated. The General at once relieved him, by this beautiful image: '*Monsieur Goldsmith est comme la mer, qui jette des perles et beaucoup d'autres belles choses, sans s'en appercevoir.*' GOLDSMITH. '*Tres bien dit et très élégamment.*'

A person was mentioned, who it was said could take down in short hand the speeches in parliament with perfect exactness. JOHNSON. 'Sir, it is impossible. I remember one, Angel, who came to me to write for him a Preface or Dedication to a book upon short hand, and he professed to write as fast as a man could speak. In order to try him, I took down a book, and read while he wrote; and I favoured him, for I read more deliberately than usual. I had proceeded but a very little way, when he begged I would desist, for he could not follow me.' Hearing now for the first time of this Preface or Dedication, I said, 'What an expense, Sir, do you put us to in buying books, to which you have written Prefaces or Dedications.' JOHNSON. 'Why, I have dedicated to the Royal family all round; that is to say, to the last generation of the Royal family.' GOLDSMITH. 'And perhaps, Sir, not one sentence of wit in a whole Dedication.' JOHNSON. 'Perhaps not, Sir.' BOSWELL. 'What then is the reason for applying to a particular person to do that which any one may do as well?' JOHNSON. 'Why, Sir, one man has greater readiness at doing it than another.'

I spoke of Mr. Harris, of Salisbury, as being a very learned man, and in particular an eminent Grecian. JOHNSON. 'I am not sure of that.

His friends give him out as such, but I know not who of his friends are able to judge of it.' GOLDSMITH. 'He is what is much better: he is a worthy humane man.' JOHNSON. 'Nay, Sir, that is not to the purpose of our argument: that will as much prove that he can play upon the fiddle as well as Giardini, as that he is an eminent Grecian.' GOLDSMITH. 'The greatest musical performers have but small emoluments. Giardini, I am told, does not get above seven hundred a year.' JOHNSON. 'That is indeed but little for a man to get, who does best that which so many endeavour to do. There is nothing, I think, in which the power of art is shown so much as in playing on the fiddle. In all other things we can do something at first. Any man will forge a bar of iron, if you give him a hammer; not so well as a smith, but tolerably. A man will saw a piece of wood, and make a box, though a clumsy one; but give him a fiddle and a fiddle-stick, and he can do nothing.'

On Monday, April 19, he called on me with Mrs. Williams, in Mr. Strahan's coach, and carried me out to dine with Mr. Elphinston, at his academy at Kensington. A printer having acquired a fortune sufficient to keep his coach, was a good topick for the credit of literature. Mrs. Williams said, that another printer, Mr. Hamilton, had not waited so long as Mr. Strahan, but had kept his coach several years sooner. JOHNSON. 'He was in the right. Life is short. The sooner that a man begins to enjoy his wealth the better.'

Mr. Elphinston talked of a new book that was much admired, and asked Dr. Johnson if he had read it. JOHNSON. 'I have looked into it.' 'What, (said Elphinston,) have you not read it through?' Johnson, offended at being thus pressed, and so obliged to own his cursory mode of reading, answered tartly, 'No, Sir, do *you* read books *through*?'

On Wednesday, April 21, I dined with him at Mr. Thrale's. A gentleman attacked Garrick for being vain. JOHNSON. 'No wonder, Sir, that he is vain; a man who is perpetually flattered in every mode that can be conceived. So many bellows have blown the fire, that one wonders he is not by this time become a cinder.' BOSWELL. 'And such bellows too. Lord Mansfield with his cheeks like to burst: Lord Chatham like an Aeolus. I have read such notes from them to him, as were enough to turn his head.' JOHNSON. 'True. When he whom every body else flatters, flatters me, I then am truly happy.' MRS. THRALE. 'The sentiment is in Congreve, I think.' JOHNSON. 'Yes, Madam, in *The Way of the World*:

"If there's delight in love, 'tis when I see
That heart which others bleed for, bleed for me."

No, Sir, I should not be surprized though Garrick chained the ocean, and lashed the winds.' BOSWELL. 'Should it not be, Sir, lashed the ocean and chained the winds?' JOHNSON. 'No, Sir, recollect the original:

> *"In Corum atque Eurum solitus sævire flagellis*
> *Barbarus, Aeolia nunquam hoc in carcere passos,*
> *Ipsum compedibus qui vinxerat Ennosigaeum."*

The modes of living in different countries, and the various views with which men travel in quest of new scenes, having been talked of, a learned gentleman who holds a considerable office in the law, expatiated on the happiness of a savage life; and mentioned an instance of an officer who had actually lived for some time in the wilds of America, of whom, when in that state, he quoted this reflection with an air of admiration, as if it had been deeply philosophical: 'Here am I, free and unrestrained, amidst the rude magnificence of Nature, with this Indian woman by my side, and this gun with which I can procure food when I want it; what more can be desired for human happiness?' It did not require much sagacity to foresee that such a sentiment would not be permitted to pass without due animadversion. JOHNSON. 'Do not allow yourself, Sir, to be imposed upon by such gross absurdity. It is sad stuff; it is brutish. If a bull could speak, he might as well exclaim,— Here am I with this cow and this grass; what being can enjoy greater felicity?'

We talked of the melancholy end of a gentleman who had destroyed himself. JOHNSON. 'It was owing to imaginary difficulties in his affairs, which, had he talked with any friend, would soon have vanished.' BOSWELL. 'Do you think, Sir, that all who commit suicide are mad?' JOHNSON. 'Sir, they are often not universally disordered in their intellects, but one passion presses so upon them, that they yield to it, and commit suicide, as a passionate man will stab another.' He added, 'I have often thought, that after a man has taken the resolution to kill himself, it is not courage in him to do any thing, however desperate, because he has nothing to fear.' GOLDSMITH. 'I don't see that.' JOHNSON. 'Nay, but my dear Sir, why should not you see what every one else sees?' GOLDSMITH. 'It is for fear of something that he has resolved to kill himself; and will not that timid disposition restrain him?' JOHNSON. 'It does not signify that the fear of something made him resolve; it is upon the state of his mind, after the resolution is taken, that I argue. Suppose a man, either from fear, or pride, or conscience, or whatever motive, has resolved to kill himself; when once the resolution is taken, he has nothing to fear. He may then go and take the King of Prussia by the nose, at the head of his army. He cannot fear the rack, who is resolved to kill himself. When Eustace Budgel was walking down to the Thames, determined to drown himself, he might, if he pleased, without any apprehension of danger, have turned aside, and first set fire to St. James's palace.'

On Tuesday, April 27, Mr. Beauclerk and I called on him in the morning. As we walked up Johnson's-court, I said, 'I have a veneration for this court;' and was glad to find that Beauclerk had the same reverential enthusiasm. We found him alone. We talked of Mr. Andrew Stuart's elegant and plausible Letters to Lord Mansfield: a copy of which had been sent by the authour to Dr. Johnson. JOHNSON. 'They have not answered the end. They have not been talked of; I have never heard of them. This is owing to their not being sold. People seldom read a book which is given to them; and few are given. The way to spread a work is to sell it at a low price. No man will send to buy a thing that costs even sixpence, without an intention to read it.'

He said, 'Goldsmith should not be for ever attempting to shine in conversation: he has not temper for it, he is so much mortified when he fails. Sir, a game of jokes is composed partly of skill, partly of chance, a man may be beat at times by one who has not the tenth part of his wit. Now Goldsmith's putting himself against another, is like a man laying a hundred to one who cannot spare the hundred. It is not worth a man's while. A man should not lay a hundred to one, unless he can easily spare it, though he has a hundred chances for him: he can get but a guinea, and he may lose a hundred. Goldsmith is in this state. When he contends, if he gets the better, it is a very little addition to a man of his literary reputation: if he does not get the better, he is miserably vexed.'

Johnson's own superlative powers of wit set him above any risk of such uneasiness. Garrick had remarked to me of him, a few days before, 'Rabelais and all other wits are nothing compared with him. You may be diverted by them; but Johnson gives you a forcible hug, and shakes laughter out of you, whether you will or no.'

Goldsmith, however, was often very fortunate in his witty contests, even when he entered the lists with Johnson himself. Sir Joshua Reynolds was in company with them one day, when Goldsmith said, that he thought he could write a good fable, mentioned the simplicity which that kind of composition requires, and observed, that in most fables the animals introduced seldom talk in character. 'For instance, (said he,) the fable of the little fishes, who saw birds fly over their heads, and envying them, petitioned Jupiter to be changed into birds. The skill (continued he,) consists in making them talk like little fishes.' While he indulged himself in this fanciful reverie, he observed Johnson shaking his sides, and laughing. Upon which he smartly proceeded, 'Why, Dr. Johnson, this is not so easy as you seem to think; for if you were to make little fishes talk, they would talk like WHALES.'

On Thursday, April 29, I dined with him at General Oglethorpe's, where were Sir Joshua Reynolds, Mr. Langton, Dr. Goldsmith, and Mr. Thrale. I was very desirous to get Dr. Johnson absolutely fixed in his resolution to go with me to the Hebrides this year; and I told him that I had received a letter from Dr. Robertson the historian, upon the subject, with which he was much pleased; and now talked in such a manner of his long-intended tour, that I was satisfied he meant to fulfil his engagement.

The character of Mallet having been introduced, and spoken of slightingly by Goldsmith; JOHNSON. 'Why, Sir, Mallet had talents enough to keep his literary reputation alive as long as he himself lived; and that, let me tell you, is a good deal.' GOLDSMITH. 'But I cannot agree that it was so. His literary reputation was dead long before his natural death. I consider an authour's literary reputation to be alive only while his name will ensure a good price for his copy from the booksellers. I will get you (to Johnson,) a hundred guineas for any thing whatever that you shall write, if you put your name to it.'

Dr. Goldsmith's new play, She Stoops to Conquer, being mentioned; JOHNSON. 'I know of no comedy for many years that has so much exhilarated an audience, that has answered so much the great end of comedy—making an audience merry.'

Goldsmith having said, that Garrick's compliment to the Queen, which he introduced into the play of *The Chances*, which he had altered and revised this year, was mean and gross flattery; JOHNSON. 'Why, Sir, I would not *write*, I would not give solemnly under my hand, a character beyond what I thought really true; but a speech on the stage, let it flatter ever so extravagantly, is formular. It has always been formular to flatter Kings and Queens; so much so, that even in our church-service we have "our most religious King," used indiscriminately, whoever is King. Nay, they even flatter themselves;— "we have been graciously pleased to grant." No modern flattery, however, is so gross as that of the Augustan age, where the Emperour was deified. "*Præsens Divus habebitur Augustus.*" And as to meanness, (rising into warmth,) how is it mean in a player,—a showman,—a fellow who exhibits himself for a shilling, to flatter his Queen? The attempt, indeed, was dangerous; for if it had missed, what became of Garrick, and what became of the Queen? As Sir William Temple says of a great General, it is necessary not only that his designs be formed in a masterly manner, but that they should be attended with success. Sir, it is right, at a time when the Royal Family is not generally liked, to let it be seen that the people like at least one of them.' SIR JOSHUA REYNOLDS. 'I do not perceive why the profession of a player should be despised; for the great and ultimate end of all the employments of mankind is to produce amusement. Garrick produces more amusement than any body.' BOSWELL. 'You say, Dr. Johnson, that Garrick exhibits himself for a shilling. In this respect he is only on a footing with a lawyer who exhibits himself for his fee, and even will maintain any nonsense or absurdity, if the case requires it. Garrick refuses a play or a part which he does not like; a lawyer never refuses.' JOHNSON. 'Why, Sir, what does this prove? only that a lawyer is worse. Boswell is now like Jack in *The Tale of a Tub*, who, when he is puzzled by an argument, hangs himself. He thinks I shall cut him down, but I'll let him hang.' (laughing vociferously.) SIR JOSHUA REYNOLDS. 'Mr. Boswell thinks that the profession of a lawyer being unquestionably honourable, if he can show the profession of a player to be more honourable, he proves his argument.'

On Friday, April 30, I dined with him at Mr. Beauclerk's, where were Lord Charlemont, Sir Joshua Reynolds, and some more members of the Literary Club, whom he had obligingly invited to meet me, as I was this evening to be balloted for as candidate for admission into that distinguished society. Johnson had done me the honour to propose me, and Beauclerk was very zealous for me.

Goldsmith being mentioned; JOHNSON. 'It is amazing how little Goldsmith knows. He seldom comes where he is not more ignorant than any one else.' SIR JOSHUA REYNOLDS. 'Yet there is no man whose company is more liked.' JOHNSON. 'To be sure, Sir. When people find a man of the most distinguished abilities as a writer, their inferiour while he is with them, it must be highly gratifying to them. What Goldsmith comically says of himself is very true,—he always gets the better when he argues alone; meaning, that he is master of a subject in his study, and can write well upon it; but when he comes into company, grows confused, and unable to talk. Take him as a poet, his *Traveller* is a very fine performance; ay, and so is his *Deserted Village*, were it not sometimes too much the echo of his *Traveller*. Whether, indeed, we take him as a poet,—as a comick writer,—or as an historian, he stands in the first class.' BOSWELL. 'An historian! My dear Sir, you surely will not rank his compilation of the Roman History with the works of other historians of this age?' JOHNSON. 'Why, who are before him?' BOSWELL. 'Hume,—Robertson,—Lord Lyttelton.' JOHNSON (his antipathy to the Scotch beginning to rise). 'I have not read Hume; but, doubtless, Goldsmith's *History* is better than the *verbiage* of Robertson, or the foppery of Dalrymple.' BOSWELL. 'Will you not admit the superiority of Robertson, in whose *History* we find such penetration—such painting?' JOHNSON. 'Sir, you must consider how that penetration and that painting are employed. It is not history, it is imagination. He who describes what he never saw, draws from fancy. Robertson paints minds as Sir Joshua paints faces in a history-piece: he imagines an heroic countenance. You must look upon Robertson's work as romance, and try it by that standard. History it is not. Besides, Sir, it is the great excellence of a writer to put into his book as much as his book will hold. Goldsmith has done this in his *History*. Now Robertson might have put twice as much into his book. Robertson is like a man who has packed gold in wool: the wool takes up more room than the gold. No, Sir; I always thought Robertson would be crushed by his own weight,—would be buried under his own ornaments.

Goldsmith tells you shortly all you want to know: Robertson detains you a great deal too long. No man will read Robertson's cumbrous detail a second time; but Goldsmith's plain narrative will please again and again. I would say to Robertson what an old tutor of a college said to one of his pupils: "Read over your compositions, and where ever you meet with a passage which you think is particularly fine, strike it out." Goldsmith's abridgement is better than that of Lucius Florus or Eutropius; and I will venture to say, that if you compare him with Vertot, in the same places of the Roman History, you will find that he excels Vertot. Sir, he has the art of compiling, and of saying every thing he has to say in a pleasing manner. He is now writing a Natural History and will make it as entertaining as a Persian Tale.'

I cannot dismiss the present topick without observing, that it is probable that Dr. Johnson, who owned that he often 'talked for victory,' rather urged plausible objections to Dr. Robertson's excellent historical works, in the ardour of contest, than expressed his real and decided opinion; for it is not easy to suppose, that he should so widely differ from the rest of the literary world.

JOHNSON. 'I remember once being with Goldsmith in Westminster-abbey. While we surveyed the Poets' Corner, I said to him,

"Forsitan et nostrum nomen miscebitur istis."

when we got to Temple-bar he stopped me, pointed to the heads upon it, and slily whispered me,

"Forsitan et nostrum nomen miscebitur ISTIS."'[26]

Johnson praised John Bunyan highly. 'His *Pilgrim's Progress* has great merit, both for invention, imagination, and the conduct of the story; and it has had the best evidence of its merit, the general and continued approbation of mankind. Few books, I believe, have had a more extensive sale. It is remarkable, that it begins very much like the poem of Dante; yet there was no translation of Dante when Bunyan wrote. There is reason to think that he had read Spenser.'

A proposition which had been agitated, that monuments to eminent persons should, for the time to come, be erected in St. Paul's church as well as in Westminster-abbey, was mentioned; and it was asked, who should be honoured by having his monument first erected there. Somebody suggested Pope. JOHNSON. 'Why, Sir, as Pope was a Roman Catholick, I would not have his to be first. I think Milton's rather should have the precedence. I think more highly of him now than I did

[26] In allusion to Dr. Johnson's supposed political principles, and perhaps his own.—BOSWELL.

at twenty. There is more thinking in him and in Butler, than in any of our poets.'

The gentlemen went away to their club, and I was left at Beauclerk's till the fate of my election should be announced to me. I sat in a state of anxiety which even the charming conversation of Lady Di Beauclerk could not entirely dissipate. In a short time I received the agreeable intelligence that I was chosen. I hastened to the place of meeting, and was introduced to such a society as can seldom be found. Mr. Edmund Burke, whom I then saw for the first time, and whose splendid talents had long made me ardently wish for his acquaintance; Dr. Nugent, Mr. Garrick, Dr. Goldsmith, Mr. (afterwards Sir William) Jones, and the company with whom I had dined. Upon my entrance, Johnson placed himself behind a chair, on which he leaned as on a desk or pulpit, and with humorous formality gave me a *Charge*, pointing out the conduct expected from me as a good member of this club.

Goldsmith produced some very absurd verses which had been publickly recited to an audience for money. JOHNSON. 'I can match this nonsense. There was a poem called *Eugenio*, which came out some years ago, and concludes thus:

> "And now, ye trifling, self-assuming elves,
> Brimful of pride, of nothing, of yourselves,
> Survey Eugenio, view him o'er and o'er,
> Then sink into yourselves, and be no more."

Nay, Dryden in his poem on the Royal Society, has these lines:

> "Then we upon our globe's last verge shall go,
>   And see the ocean leaning on the sky;
> From thence our rolling neighbours we shall know,
>   And on the lunar world securely pry."'

Much pleasant conversation passed, which Johnson relished with great good humour. But his conversation alone, or what led to it, or was interwoven with it, is the business of this work.

On Saturday, May 1, we dined by ourselves at our old rendezvous, the Mitre tavern. He was placid, but not much disposed to talk. He observed that 'The Irish mix better with the English than the Scotch do; their language is nearer to English; as a proof of which, they succeed very well as players, which Scotchmen do not. Then, Sir, they have not that extreme nationality which we find in the Scotch. I will do you, Boswell, the justice to say, that you are the most *unscottified* of your countrymen. You are almost the only instance of a Scotchman that I have known, who did not at every other sentence bring in some other Scotchman.'

On Friday, May 7, I breakfasted with him at Mr. Thrale's in the Borough. While we were alone, I endeavoured as well as I could to apologise for a lady who had been divorced from her husband by act of Parliament. I said, that he had used her very ill, had behaved brutally to her, and that she could not continue to live with him without having her delicacy contaminated; that all affection for him was thus destroyed; that the essence of conjugal union being gone, there remained only a cold form, a mere civil obligation; that she was in the prime of life, with qualities to produce happiness; that these ought not to be lost; and, that the gentleman on whose account she was divorced had gained her heart while thus unhappily situated. Seduced, perhaps, by the charms of the lady in question, I thus attempted to palliate what I was sensible could not be justified; for when I had finished my harangue, my venerable friend gave me a proper check: 'My dear Sir, never accustom your mind to mingle virtue and vice. The woman's a whore, and there's an end on't.'

He described the father of one of his friends thus: 'Sir, he was so exuberant a talker at publick meeting, that the gentlemen of his county were afraid of him. No business could be done for his declamation.'

He did not give me full credit when I mentioned that I had carried on a short conversation by signs with some Esquimaux who were then in London, particularly with one of them who was a priest. He thought I could not make them understand me. No man was more incredulous as to particular facts, which were at all extraordinary; and therefore no man was more scrupulously inquisitive, in order to discover the truth.

I dined with him this day at the house of my friends, Messieurs Edward and Charles Dilly, booksellers in the Poultry: there were present, their elder brother Mr. Dilly of Bedfordshire, Dr. Goldsmith, Mr. Langton, Mr. Claxton, Reverend Dr. Mayo a dissenting minister, the Reverend Mr. Toplady, and my friend the Reverend Mr. Temple.

BOSWELL. 'I am well assured that the people of Otaheite who have the bread tree, the fruit of which serves them for bread, laughed heartily when they were informed of the tedious process necessary with us to have bread;—plowing, sowing, harrowing, reaping, threshing, grinding, baking.' JOHNSON. 'Why, Sir, all ignorant savages will laugh when they are told of the advantages of civilized life. Were you to tell men who live without houses, how we pile brick upon brick, and rafter upon rafter, and that after a house is raised to a certain height, a man tumbles off a scaffold, and breaks his neck; he would laugh heartily at our folly in building; but it does not follow that men are better without houses. No, Sir, (holding up a slice of a good loaf,) this is better than the bread tree.'

I introduced the subject of toleration. JOHNSON. 'Every society has a right to preserve publick peace and order, and therefore has a good right to prohibit the propagation of opinions which have a dangerous tendency. To say the *magistrate* has this right, is using an inadequate word: it is the *society* for which the magistrate is agent. He may be morally or theologically wrong in restraining the propagation of opinions which he thinks dangerous, but he is politically right.' MAYO. 'I am of opinion, Sir, that every man is entitled to liberty of conscience in religion; and that the magistrate cannot restrain that right.' JOHNSON. 'Sir, I agree with you. Every man has a right to liberty of conscience, and with that the magistrate cannot interfere. People confound liberty of thinking with liberty of talking; nay, with liberty of preaching. Every man has a physical right to think as he pleases; for it cannot be discovered how he thinks. He has not a moral right, for he ought to inform himself, and think justly. But, Sir, no member of a society has a right to *teach* any doctrine contrary to what the society holds to be true. The magistrate, I say, may be wrong in what he thinks: but while he thinks himself right, he may and ought to enforce what he thinks.' MAYO. 'Then, Sir, we are to remain always in errour, and truth never can prevail; and the magistrate was right in persecuting the first Christians.' JOHNSON. 'Sir, the only method by which religious truth can be established is by martyrdom. The magistrate has a right to enforce what he thinks; and he who is conscious of the truth has a right to suffer. I am afraid there is no other way of ascertaining the truth, but by persecution on the one hand and enduring it on the other.' GOLDSMITH. 'But how is a man to act, Sir? Though firmly convinced of the truth of his doctrine, may he not think it wrong to expose himself to persecution? Has he a right to do so? Is it not, as it were, committing voluntary suicide?' JOHNSON. 'Sir, as to voluntary suicide, as you call it, there are twenty thousand men in an army who will go without scruple to be shot at, and mount a breach for five-pence a day.' GOLDSMITH. 'But have they a moral right to do this?' JOHNSON. 'Nay, Sir, if you will not take the universal opinion of mankind, I have nothing to say. If mankind cannot defend their own way of thinking, I cannot defend it. Sir, if a man is in doubt whether it would be better for him to expose himself to martyrdom or not, he should not do it. He must be convinced that he has a delegation from heaven.' GOLDSMITH. 'I would consider whether there is the greater chance of good or evil upon the whole. If I see a man who had fallen into a well, I would wish to help him out; but if there is a greater probability that he shall pull me in, than that I shall pull him out, I would not attempt it. So were I to go to Turkey, I might wish to convert the Grand Signor to the Christian faith; but when I considered that I should probably be put to death without effectuating my purpose in any degree, I should keep myself quiet.' JOHNSON. 'Sir, you must consider that we have perfect and imperfect obligations. Perfect obligations, which are generally not to do something, are clear and positive; as, "thou shalt not kill?' But charity, for instance, is not definable by limits. It is a duty to give to the poor;

but no man can say how much another should give to the poor, or when a man has given too little to save his soul. In the same manner it is a duty to instruct the ignorant, and of consequence to convert infidels to Christianity; but no man in the common course of things is obliged to carry this to such a degree as to incur the danger of martyrdom, as no man is obliged to strip himself to the shirt in order to give charity. I have said, that a man must be persuaded that he has a particular delegation from heaven.' GOLDSMITH. 'How is this to be known? Our first reformers, who were burnt for not believing bread and wine to be CHRIST'—JOHNSON. (interrupting him,) 'Sir, they were not burnt for not believing bread and wine to be CHRIST, but for insulting those who did believe it. And, Sir, when the first reformers began, they did not intend to be martyred: as many of them ran away as could.' BOSWELL. 'But, Sir, there was your countryman, Elwal, who you told me challenged King George with his black-guards, and his red-guards.' JOHNSON. 'My countryman, Elwal, Sir, should have been put in the stocks; a proper pulpit for him; and he'd have had a numerous audience. A man who preaches in the stocks will always have hearers enough.' BOSWELL. 'But Elwal thought himself in the right.' JOHNSON. 'We are not providing for mad people; there are places for them in the neighbourhood.' (meaning moorfields.) MAYO. 'But, Sir, is it not very hard that I should not be allowed to teach my children what I really believe to be the truth?' JOHNSON. 'Why, Sir, you might contrive to teach your children *extrà scandalum*; but, Sir, the magistrate, if he knows it, has a right to restrain you. Suppose you teach your children to be thieves?' MAYO. 'This is making a joke of the subject.' JOHNSON. 'Nay, Sir, take it thus:—that you teach them the community of goods; for which there are as many plausible arguments as for most erroneous doctrines. You teach them that all things at first were in common, and that no man had a right to any thing but as he laid his hands upon it; and that this still is, or ought to be, the rule amongst mankind. Here, Sir, you sap a great principle in society,—property. And don't you think the magistrate would have a right to prevent you? Or, suppose you should teach your children the notion of the Adamites, and they should run naked into the streets, would not the magistrate have a right to flog 'em into their doublets?' MAYO. 'I think the magistrate has no right to interfere till there is some overt act.' BOSWELL. 'So, Sir, though he sees an enemy to the state charging a blunderbuss, he is not to interfere till it is fired off?' MAYO. 'He must be sure of its direction against the state.' JOHNSON. 'The magistrate is to judge of that.—He has no right to restrain your thinking, because the evil centers in yourself. If a man were sitting at this table, and chopping off his fingers, the magistrate, as guardian of the community, has no authority to restrain him, however he might do it from kindness as a parent.— Though, indeed, upon more consideration, I think he may; as it is probable, that he who is chopping off his own fingers, may soon proceed to chop off those of other people. If I think it right to steal Mr. Dilly's plate, I am a bad man; but he can say nothing to me. If I make an open declaration that I think so, he will keep me out of his house. If I put forth my hand, I shall be sent to Newgate. This is the gradation of thinking, preaching, and acting: if a man thinks erroneously, he may keep his thoughts to himself, and nobody will trouble him; if he preaches erroneous doctrine, society may expel him; if he acts in consequence of it, the law takes place, and he is hanged.' MAYO. 'But, Sir, ought not Christians to have liberty of conscience?' JOHNSON. 'I have already told you so, Sir. You are coming back to where you were.' BOSWELL. 'Dr. Mayo is always taking a return post-chaise, and going the stage over again. He has it at half price.' JOHNSON. 'Dr. Mayo, like other champions for unlimited toleration, has got a set of words. Sir, it is no matter, politically, whether the magistrate be right or wrong. Suppose a club were to be formed, to drink confusion to King George the Third, and a happy restoration to Charles the Third, this would be very bad with respect to the State; but every member of that club must either conform to its rules, or be turned out of it. Old Baxter, I remember, maintains, that the magistrate should "tolerate all things that are tolerable." This is no good definition of toleration upon any principle; but it shows that he thought some things were not tolerable.' TOPLADY. 'Sir, you have untwisted this difficult subject with great dexterity.'

During this argument, Goldsmith sat in restless agitation, from a wish to get in and *shine*. Finding himself excluded, he had taken his hat to go away, but remained for some time with it in his hand, like a gamester, who at the close of a long night, lingers for a little while, to see if he can have a favourable opening to finish with success. Once when he was beginning to speak, he found himself overpowered by the loud voice of Johnson, who was at the opposite end of the table, and did not perceive Goldsmith's attempt. Thus disappointed of his wish to obtain the attention of the company, Goldsmith in a passion threw down his hat, looking angrily at Johnson, and exclaiming in a bitter tone, '*Take it*.' When Toplady was going to speak, Johnson uttered some sound, which led Goldsmith to think that he was beginning again, and taking the words from Toplady. Upon which, he seized this opportunity of venting his own envy and spleen, under the pretext of supporting another person: 'Sir, (said he to Johnson,) the gentleman has heard you patiently for an hour; pray allow us now to hear him.' JOHNSON. (sternly,) 'Sir, I was not interrupting the gentleman. I was only giving him a signal of my attention. Sir, you are impertinent.' Goldsmith made no reply, but continued in the company for some time.

A gentleman present ventured to ask Dr. Johnson if there was not a material difference as to toleration of opinions which lead to action, and opinions merely speculative; for instance, would it be wrong in the magistrate to tolerate those who preach against the doctrine of the TRINITY? Johnson was highly offended, and said, 'I wonder, Sir, how a gentleman of your piety can introduce this subject in a mixed company.' He told me afterwards, that the impropriety was, that perhaps some of the company might have talked on the subject in such terms as might have shocked him; or he might have been forced to appear in their eyes a narrow-minded man. The gentleman, with submissive deference, said, he had only hinted at the question from a desire to hear Dr. Johnson's opinion upon it. JOHNSON. 'Why then, Sir, I think that permitting men to preach any opinion contrary to the doctrine of the established church tends, in a certain degree, to lessen the authority of the church, and consequently, to lessen the influence of religion.' 'It may be considered, (said the gentleman,) whether it would not be politick to tolerate in such a case.' JOHNSON. 'Sir, we have been talking of *right*: this is another question. I think it is NOT politick to tolerate in such a case.'

BOSWELL. 'Pray, Mr. Dilly, how does Dr. Leland's *History of Ireland* sell?' JOHNSON. (bursting forth with a generous indignation,) 'The Irish are in a most unnatural state; for we see there the minority prevailing over the majority. There is no instance, even in the ten persecutions, of such severity as that which the protestants of Ireland have exercised against the Catholicks. Did we tell them we have conquered them, it would be above board: to punish them by confiscation and other penalties, as rebels, was monstrous injustice. King William was not their lawful sovereign: he had not been acknowledged by the Parliament of Ireland, when they appeared in arms against him.'

He and Mr. Langton and I went together to THE CLUB, where we found Mr. Burke, Mr. Garrick, and some other members, and amongst them our friend Goldsmith, who sat silently brooding over Johnson's reprimand to him after dinner. Johnson perceived this, and said aside to some of us, 'I'll make Goldsmith forgive me;' and then called to him in a loud voice, 'Dr. Goldsmith,—something passed to-day where you and I dined; I ask your pardon.' Goldsmith answered placidly, 'It must be much from you, Sir, that I take ill.' And so at once the difference was over, and they were on as easy terms as ever, and Goldsmith rattled away as usual.

In our way to the club to-night, when I regretted that Goldsmith would, upon every occasion, endeavour to shine, by which he often exposed himself, Mr. Langton observed, that he was not like Addison, who was content with the fame of his writings, and did not aim also at excellency in conversation, for which he found himself unfit; and that he said to a lady who complained of his having talked little in company, 'Madam, I have but ninepence in ready money, but I can draw for a thousand pounds.' I observed, that Goldsmith had a great deal of gold in his cabinet, but, not content with that, was always taking out his purse. JOHNSON. 'Yes, Sir, and that so often an empty purse!'

Goldsmith's incessant desire of being conspicuous in company, was the occasion of his sometimes appearing to such disadvantage as one should hardly have supposed possible in a man of his genius. When his literary reputation had risen deservedly high, and his society was much courted, he became very jealous of the extraordinary attention which was every where paid to Johnson. One evening, in a circle of wits, he found fault with me for talking of Johnson as entitled to the honour of unquestionable superiority. 'Sir, (said he,) you are for making a monarchy of what should be a republick.'

He was still more mortified, when talking in a company with fluent vivacity, and, as he flattered himself, to the admiration of all who were present; a German who sat next him, and perceived Johnson rolling himself, as if about to speak, suddenly stopped him, saying, 'Stay, stay,—Toctor Shonson is going to say something.' This was, no doubt, very provoking, especially to one so irritable as Goldsmith, who frequently mentioned it with strong expressions of indignation.

It may also be observed, that Goldsmith was sometimes content to be treated with an easy familiarity, but, upon occasions, would be consequential and important. An instance of this occurred in a small particular. Johnson had a way of contracting the names of his friends; as Beauclerk, Beau; Boswell, Bozzy; Langton, Lanky; Murphy, Mur; Sheridan, Sherry. I remember one day, when Tom Davies was telling that Dr. Johnson said, 'We are all in labour for a name to *Goldy's* play,' Goldsmith seemed displeased that such a liberty should be taken with his name, and said, 'I have often desired him not to call me *Goldy*.' Tom was remarkably attentive to the most minute circumstance about Johnson. I recollect his telling me once, on my arrival in London, 'Sir, our great friend has made an improvement on his appellation of old Mr. Sheridan. He calls him now *Sherry derry*.'

On Monday, May 9, as I was to set out on my return to Scotland next morning, I was desirous to see as much of Dr. Johnson as I could. But I first called on Goldsmith to take leave of him. The jealousy and envy which, though possessed of many most amiable qualities, he frankly avowed, broke out violently at this interview. Upon another occasion, when Goldsmith confessed himself to be of an envious disposition, I contended with Johnson that we ought not to be angry with him, he was so candid in owning it. 'Nay, Sir, (said Johnson,) we must be angry that a man has such a superabundance of an odious quality, that he cannot keep it within his own breast, but it boils over.' In my opinion, however, Goldsmith had not more of it than other people have, but only talked of it freely.

He now seemed very angry that Johnson was going to be a

traveller; said 'he would be a dead weight for me to carry, and that I should never be able to lug him along through the Highlands and Hebrides.' Nor would he patiently allow me to enlarge upon Johnson's wonderful abilities; but exclaimed, 'Is he like Burke, who winds into a subject like a serpent?' 'But, (said I,) Johnson is the Hercules who strangled serpents in his cradle.'

I dined with Dr. Johnson at General Paoli's. He was obliged, by indisposition, to leave the company early; he appointed me, however, to meet him in the evening at Mr. (now Sir Robert) Chambers's in the Temple, where he accordingly came, though he continued to be very ill. Chambers, as is common on such occasions, prescribed various remedies to him. JOHNSON. (fretted by pain,) 'Pr'ythee don't tease me. Stay till I am well, and then you shall tell me how to cure myself.' He grew better, and talked with a noble enthusiasm of keeping up the representation of respectable families. His zeal on this subject was a circumstance in his character exceedingly remarkable, when it is considered that he himself had no pretensions to blood. I heard him once say, 'I have great merit in being zealous for subordination and the honours of birth; for I can hardly tell who was my grandfather.' He maintained the dignity and propriety of male succession, in opposition to the opinion of one of our friends, who had that day employed Mr. Chambers to draw his will, devising his estate to his three sisters, in preference to a remote heir male. Johnson called them 'three *dowdies*,' and said, with as high a spirit as the boldest Baron in the most perfect days of the feudal system, 'An ancient estate should always go to males. It is mighty foolish to let a stranger have it because he marries your daughter, and takes your name. As for an estate newly acquired by trade, you may give it, if you will, to the dog *Towser*, and let him keep his *own* name.'

I have known him at times exceedingly diverted at what seemed to others a very small sport. He now laughed immoderately, without any reason that we could perceive, at our friend's making his will; called him the *testator*, and added, 'I dare say, he thinks he has done a mighty thing. He won't stay till he gets home to his seat in the country, to produce this wonderful deed: he'll call up the landlord of the first inn on the road; and, after a suitable preface upon mortality and the uncertainty of life, will tell him that he should not delay making his will; and here, Sir, will he say, is my will, which I have just made, with the assistance of one of the ablest lawyers in the kingdom; and he will read it to him (laughing all the time). He believes he has made this will; but he did not make it: you, Chambers, made it for him. I trust you have had more conscience than to make him say, "being of sound understanding;" ha, ha, ha! I hope he has left me a legacy. I'd have his will turned into verse, like a ballad.'

Mr. Chambers did not by any means relish this jocularity upon a matter of which *pars magna fuit*, and seemed impatient till he got rid of us. Johnson could not stop his merriment, but continued it all the way till we got without the Temple-gate. He then burst into such a fit of laughter, that he appeared to be almost in a convulsion; and, in order to support himself, laid hold of one of the posts at the side of the foot pavement, and sent forth peals so loud, that in the silence of the night his voice seemed to resound from Temple-bar to Fleet-ditch.

This most ludicrous exhibition of the aweful, melancholy, and venerable Johnson, happened well to counteract the feelings of sadness which I used to experience when parting with him for a considerable time. I accompanied him to his door, where he gave me his blessing.

'TO JAMES BOSWELL, ESQ.

'DEAR SIR,—I shall set out from London on Friday the sixth of this month, and purpose not to loiter much by the way. Which day I shall be at Edinburgh, I cannot exactly tell. I suppose I must drive to an inn, and send a porter to find you.

'I am afraid Beattie will not be at his College soon enough for us, and I shall be sorry to miss him; but there is no staying for the concurrence of all conveniences. We will do as well as we can. I am, Sir, your most humble servant,
'August 3, 1773.'

'SAM. JOHNSON.'

TO JAMES BOSWELL, ESQ.

'Newcastle, Aug. 11, 1773.
'DEAR SIR, I came hither last night, and hope, but do not absolutely promise, to be in Edinburgh on Saturday. Beattie will not come so soon. I am, Sir, your most humble servant,
'My compliments to your lady.'

'SAM. JOHNSON.'

TO THE SAME.

'Mr. Johnson sends his compliments to Mr. Boswell, being just arrived at Boyd's.—Saturday night.'

His stay in Scotland was from the 18th of August, on which day he arrived, till the 22nd of November, when he set out on his return to London; and I believe ninety-four days were never passed by any man in a more vigorous exertion.[27]

---

[27] In his Journal of a Tour to the Hebrides, published the year after Johnson died,

His humane forgiving disposition was put to a pretty strong test on his return to London, by a liberty which Mr. Thomas Davies had taken with him in his absence, which was, to publish two volumes, entitled, *Miscellaneous and fugitive Pieces*, which he advertised in the news-papers, 'By the Authour of the Rambler.' In this collection, several of Dr. Johnson's acknowledged writings, several of his anonymous performances, and some which he had written for others, were inserted; but there were also some in which he had no concern whatever. He was at first very angry, as he had good reason to be. But, upon consideration of his poor friend's narrow circumstances, and that he had only a little profit in view, and meant no harm, he soon relented, and continued his kindness to him as formerly.

In the course of his self-examination with retrospect to this year, he seems to have been much dejected; for he says, January 1, 1774, 'This year has passed with so little improvement, that I doubt whether I have not rather impaired than increased my learning'; and yet we have seen how he *read*, and we know how he *talked* during that period.

He was now seriously engaged in writing an account of our travels in the Hebrides, in consequence of which I had the pleasure of a more frequent correspondence with him.

'TO BENNET LANGTON, ESQ., AT LANGTON,
NEAR SPILSBY, LINCOLNSHIRE.

'DEAR SIR,—You have reason to reproach me that I have left your last letter so long unanswered, but I had nothing particular to say. Chambers, you find, is gone far, and poor Goldsmith is gone much further. He died of a fever, exasperated, as I believe, by the fear of distress. He had raised money and squandered it, by every artifice of acquisition, and folly of expence. But let not his frailties be remembered; he was a very great man.

'I have just begun to print my Journey to the Hebrides, and am leaving the press to take another journey into Wales, whither Mr. Thrale is going, to take possession of, at least, five hundred a year, fallen to his lady. All at Streatham, that are alive, are well.

'I have never recovered from the last dreadful illness, but flatter myself that I grow gradually better; much, however, yet remains to mend. Κύριε ἐλέησον.

'If you have the Latin version of *Busy, curious, thirsty fly*, be so

---

Boswell gives a detailed account of Johnson's conversation and adventures with him throughout the journey of 1773. Partly owing to their uninterrupted association, partly to the strangeness and variation of background and circumstances, and partly to Boswell's larger leisure during the tour for the elaboration of his account, the journal is even more racy, picturesque, and interesting than any equal part of the Life. No reader who enjoys the Life should fail to read the Tour—unabridged!—Ed.

kind as to transcribe and send it; but you need not be in haste, for I shall be I know not where, for at least five weeks. I wrote the following tetastrick on poor Goldsmith:—

Τὸν τάφον εἰσοράας τὸν ‘Ολιβάροιο. κονίην
Ἄφροσι μή σεμνήν, Ξεῖνε, πόδεσσι πάτει.
Οἵσι μέμηλε φύσις, μέτρων χάρις, ‘έργα παλαιών,
Κλαίετε ποιητήν, ἱστορικόν, φυσικόν.

'Please to make my most respectful compliments to all the ladies, and remember me to young George and his sisters. I reckon George begins to shew a pair of heels.

'Do not be sullen now, but let me find a letter when I come back. I am, dear Sir, your affectionate, humble servant,

'SAM. JOHNSON.
'July 5,1774.'

In his manuscript diary of this year, there is the following entry:—

'Nov. 27. Advent Sunday. I considered that this day, being the beginning of the ecclesiastical year, was a proper time for a new course of life. I began to read the Greek Testament regularly at 160 verses every Sunday. This day I began the Acts.

'In this week I read Virgil's *Pastorals*. I learned to repeat the *Pollio* and *Gallus*. I read carelessly the first *Georgick*.'

Such evidences of his unceasing ardour, both for 'divine and human lore,' when advanced into his sixty-fifth year, and notwithstanding his many disturbances from disease, must make us at once honour his spirit, and lament that it should be so grievously clogged by its material tegument.

1775: ÆTAT. 66.]—

'MR. BOSWELL TO DR. JOHNSON.

'Edinburgh, Feb. 2,1775.

'. . . As to Macpherson,' I am anxious to have from yourself a full and pointed account of what has passed between you and him. It is confidently told here, that before your book came out he sent to you, to let you know that he understood you meant to deny the authenticity of Ossian's poems; that the originals were in his possession; that you might have inspection of them, and might take the evidence of people skilled in the Erse language; and that he hoped, after this fair offer, you would not be so uncandid as to assert that he had refused reasonable proof. That you paid no regard to his message, but published your strong attack upon him; and then he wrote a letter to you, in such terms as he thought suited to one who had not acted as a man of veracity.' . . .

What words were used by Mr. Macpherson in his letter to the venerable Sage, I have never heard; but they are generally said to have been of a nature very different from the language of literary contest. Dr. Johnson's answer appeared in the news-papers of the day, and has since been frequently re-published; but not with perfect accuracy. I give it as dictated to me by himself, written down in his presence, and authenticated by a note in his own handwriting, '*This, I think, is a true copy.*'

'MR. JAMES MACPHERSON,—I received your foolish and impudent letter. Any violence offered me I shall do my best to repel; and what I cannot do for myself, the law shall do for me. I hope I shall never be deterred from detecting what I think a cheat, by the menaces of a ruffian.

'What would you have me retract? I thought your book an imposture; I think it an imposture still. For this opinion I have given my reasons to the publick, which I here dare you to refute. Your rage I defy. Your abilities, since your Homer, are not so formidable; and what I hear of your morals, inclines me to pay regard not to what you shall say, but to what you shall prove. You may print this if you will.'

'SAM. JOHNSON.'

Mr. Macpherson little knew the character of Dr. Johnson, if he supposed that he could be easily intimidated; for no man was ever more remarkable for personal courage. He had, indeed, an aweful dread of death, or rather, 'of something after death;' and what rational man, who seriously thinks of quitting all that he has ever known, and going into a new and unknown state of being, can be without that dread? But his fear was from reflection; his courage natural. His fear, in that one instance, was the result of philosophical and religious consideration. He feared death, but he feared nothing else, not even what might occasion death. Many instances of his resolution may be mentioned. One day, at Mr. Beauclerk's house in the country, when two large dogs were fighting, he went up to them, and beat them till they separated; and at another time, when told of the danger there was that a gun might burst if charged with many balls, he put in six or seven, and fired it off against a wall. Mr. Langton told me, that when they were swimming together near Oxford, he cautioned Dr. Johnson against a pool, which was reckoned particularly dangerous; upon which Johnson directly swam into it. He told me himself that one night he was attacked in the street by four men, to whom he would not yield, but kept them all at bay, till the watch came up, and carried both him and them to the round-house. In the playhouse at Lichfield, as Mr. Garrick informed me, Johnson having for a moment quitted a chair which was placed for him between the side-scenes, a gentleman took possession of it, and when Johnson on his return civilly demanded his seat, rudely refused to give it up; upon which Johnson laid hold of it, and tossed him and the chair into the pit. Foote, who so successfully revived the old comedy, by exhibiting living characters, had resolved to imitate Johnson on the stage, expecting great profits from his ridicule of so celebrated a man. Johnson being informed of his intention, and being at dinner at Mr. Thomas Davies's the bookseller, from whom I had the story, he asked Mr. Davies 'what was the common price of an oak stick;' and being answered six-pence, 'Why then, Sir, (said he,) give me leave to send your servant to purchase me a shilling one. I'll have a double quantity; for I am told Foote means to *take me off*, as he calls it, and I am determined the fellow shall not do it with impunity. Davies took care to acquaint Foote of this, which effectually checked the wantonness of the mimick. Mr. Macpherson's menaces made Johnson provide himself with the same implement of defence; and had he been attacked, I have no doubt that, old as he was, he would have made his corporal prowess be felt as much as his intellectual.

His *Journey to the Western Islands of Scotland* is a most valuable performance. Johnson's grateful acknowledgements of kindnesses received in the course of this tour, completely refute the brutal reflections which have been thrown out against him, as if he had made an ungrateful return; and his delicacy in sparing in his book those who we find from his letters to Mrs. Thrale were just objects of censure, is much to be admired. His candour and amiable disposition is conspicuous from his conduct, when informed by Mr. Macleod, of Rasay, that he had committed a mistake, which gave that gentleman some uneasiness. He wrote him a courteous and kind letter, and inserted in the news-papers an advertisement, correcting the mistake.

As to his prejudice against the Scotch, which I always ascribed to that nationality which he observed in *them*, he said to the same gentleman, 'When I find a Scotchman, to whom an Englishman is as a Scotchman, that Scotchman shall be as an Englishman to me.' His intimacy with many gentlemen of Scotland, and his employing so many natives of that country as his amanuenses, prove that his prejudice was not virulent; and I have deposited in the British Museum, amongst other pieces of his writing, the following note in answer to one from me, asking if he would meet me at dinner at the Mitre, though a friend of mine, a Scotchman, was to be there:—

'Mr. Johnson does not see why Mr. Boswell should suppose a Scotchman less acceptable than any other man. He will be at the Mitre.'

My much-valued friend Dr. Barnard, now Bishop of Killaloc, having once expressed to him an apprehension, that if he should visit Ireland he might treat the people of that country more unfavourably than he had done the Scotch, he answered, with strong pointed double-edged wit, 'Sir, you have no reason to be afraid of me. The Irish are not in a conspiracy to cheat the world by false representations of the merits of their countrymen. No, Sir; the Irish are a FAIR PEOPLE;—they never speak well of one another.'

All the miserable cavillings against his *Journey*, in newspapers, magazines, and other fugitive publications, I can speak from certain knowledge, only furnished him with sport. At last there came out a scurrilous volume, larger than Johnson's own, filled with malignant abuse, under a name, real or fictitious, of some low man in an obscure corner of Scotland, though supposed to be the work of another Scotchman, who has found means to make himself well known both in Scotland and England. The effect which it had upon Johnson was, to produce this pleasant observation to Mr. Seward, to whom he lent the book: 'This fellow must be a blockhead. They don't know how to go about their abuse. Who will read a five-shilling book against me? No, Sir, if they had wit, they should have kept pelting me with pamphlets.'

On Tuesday, March 21, I arrived in London; and on repairing to Dr. Johnson's before dinner, found him in his study, sitting with Mr. Peter Garrick, the elder brother of David, strongly resembling him in countenance and voice, but of more sedate and placid manners. Johnson informed me, that 'though Mr. Beauclerk was in great pain, it was hoped he was not in danger, and that he now wished to consult Dr. Heberden to try the effect of a *new understanding*.' Both at this interview, and in the evening at Mr. Thrale's where he and Mr. Peter Garrick and I met again, he was vehement on the subject of the Ossian controversy; observing, 'We do not know that there are any ancient Erse manuscripts; and we have no other reason to disbelieve that there are men with three heads, but that we do not know that there are any such men.' He also was outrageous upon his supposition that my countrymen 'loved Scotland better than truth,' saying, 'All of them,— nay not all,—but *droves* of them, would come up, and attest any thing for the honour of Scotland.' He also persevered in his wild allegation, that he questioned if there was a tree between Edinburgh and the English border older than himself. I assured him he was mistaken, and suggested that the proper punishment would be that he should receive a stripe at every tree above a hundred years old, that was found within that space. He laughed, and said, 'I believe I might submit to it for a *baubee*!'

The doubts which, in my correspondence with him, I had ventured to state as to the justice and wisdom of the conduct of Great-Britain towards the American colonies, while I at the same time requested that he would enable me to inform myself upon that momentous subject, he had altogether disregarded; and had recently published a pamphlet, entitled, *Taxation no Tyranny; an answer to the Resolutions and Address of the American Congress.*

He had long before indulged most unfavourable sentiments of our fellow-subjects in America. For, as early as 1769, I was told by Dr. John Campbell, that he had said of them, 'Sir, they are a race of convicts, and ought to be thankful for any thing we allow them short of hanging.'

Of this performance I avoided to talk with him; for I had now formed a clear and settled opinion, that the people of America were well warranted to resist a claim that their fellow-subjects in the mother-country should have the entire command of their fortunes, by taxing them without their own consent; and the extreme violence which it breathed, appeared to me so unsuitable to the mildness of a christian philosopher, and so directly opposite to the principles of peace which he had so beautifully recommended in his pamphlet respecting Falkland's Islands, that I was sorry to see him appear in so unfavourable a light.

On Friday, March 24, I met him at the LITERARY CLUB, where were Mr. Beauclerk, Mr. Langton, Mr. Colman, Dr. Percy, Mr. Vesey, Sir Charles Bunbury, Dr. George Fordyce, Mr. Steevens, and Mr. Charles Fox. Before he came in, we talked of his *Journey to the Western Islands*, and of his coming away 'willing to believe the second sight,' which seemed to excite some ridicule. I was then so impressed with the truth of many of the stories of it which I had been told, that I avowed my conviction, saying, 'He is only *willing* to believe: I *do* believe. The evidence is enough for me, though not for his great mind. What will not fill a quart bottle will fill a pint bottle. I am filled with belief.' 'Are you? (said Colman,) then cork it up.'

I found his Journey the common topick of conversation in London at this time, wherever I happened to be. At one of Lord Mansfield's formal Sunday evening conversations, strangely called *Levées*, his Lordship addressed me, 'We have all been reading your travels, Mr. Boswell.' I answered, 'I was but the humble attendant of Dr. Johnson.' The Chief Justice replied, with that air and manner which none, who ever saw and heard him, can forget, 'He speaks ill of nobody but Ossian.'

Johnson was in high spirits this evening at the club, and talked with great animation and success. He attacked Swift, as he used to do upon all occasions. *The Tale of a Tub* is so much superiour to his other writings, that one can hardly believe he was the authour of it: 'there is in it such a vigour of mind, such a swarm of thoughts, so much of nature, and art, and life.' I wondered to hear him say of *Gulliver's Travels*, 'When once you have thought of big men and little men, it is very easy to do all the rest.' I endeavoured to make a stand for Swift, and tried to rouse those who were much more able to defend him; but in vain. Johnson at last, of his own accord, allowed very great merit to the inventory of articles found in the pocket of *the Man Mountain*, particularly the description of his watch, which it was conjectured was his God; as he consulted it upon all occasions. He observed, that 'Swift put his name to but two things, (after he had a name to put,) *The Plan for the Improvement of the English Language*, and the last *Drapier's Letter.*'

From Swift, there was an easy transition to Mr. Thomas Sheridan—JOHNSON. 'Sheridan is a wonderful admirer of the tragedy of *Douglas*, and presented its authour with a gold medal. Some years ago, at a coffee-house in Oxford, I called to him, "Mr. Sheridan, Mr. Sheridan, how came you to give a gold medal to Home, for writing that foolish play?" This you see, was wanton and insolent; but I *meant* to be wanton and insolent. A medal has no value but as a stamp of merit. And was Sheridan to assume to himself the right of giving that stamp? If Sheridan was magnificent enough to bestow a gold medal as an honorary reward of dramatick excellence, he should have requested one of the Universities to choose the person on whom it should be conferred. Sheridan had no right to give a stamp of merit: it was counterfeiting Apollo's coin.'

On Monday, March 27, I breakfasted with him at Mr Strahan's. He told us, that he was engaged to go that evening to Mrs. Abington's benefit. 'She was visiting some ladies whom I was visiting, and begged that I would come to her benefit. I told her I could not hear: but she insisted so much on my coming, that it would have been brutal to have refused her.' This was a speech quite characteristical. He loved to bring forward his having been in the gay circles of life; and he was, perhaps, a little vain of the solicitations of this elegant and fashionable actress. He told us, the play was to be the *The Hypocrite*, altered from Cibber's *Nonjuror*, so as to satirize the Methodists. 'I do not think (said he,) the character of *The Hypocrite* justly applicable to the Methodists, but it was very applicable to the Nonjurors.'

Mr. Strahan had taken a poor boy from the country as an apprentice, upon Johnson's recommendation. Johnson having enquired after him, said, 'Mr. Strahan, let me have five guineas on account, and I'll give this boy one. Nay if a man recommends a boy, and does nothing for him, it is sad work. Call him down.'

I followed him into the court-yard, behind Mr. Strahan's house; and there I had a proof of what I had heard him profess, that he talked alike to all. 'Some people tell you that they let themselves down to the capacity of their hearers. I never do that. I speak uniformly, in as intelligible a manner as I can.'

'Well, my boy, how do you go on?'—'Pretty well, Sir; but they are afraid I an't strong enough for some parts of the business.' JOHNSON. 'Why, I shall be sorry for it; for when you consider with how little mental power and corporeal labour a printer can get a guinea a week, it is a very desirable occupation for you. Do you hear,—take all the pains you can; and if this does not do, we must think of some other way of life for you. There's a guinea.'

Here was one of the many, many instances of his active benevolence. At the same time, the slow and sonorous solemnity with which, while he bent himself down, he addressed a little thick short-legged boy, contrasted with the boy's aukwardness and awe, could not but excite some ludicrous emotions.

I met him at Drury-lane play-house in the evening. Sir Joshua Reynolds, at Mrs. Abington's request, had promised to bring a body of wits to her benefit; and having secured forty places in the front boxes, had done me the honour to put me in the group. Johnson sat on the seat directly behind me; and as he could neither see nor hear at such a distance from the stage, he was wrapped up in grave abstraction, and seemed quite a cloud, amidst all the sunshine of glitter and gaiety. I wondered at his patience in sitting out a play of five acts, and a farce of two. He said very little; but after the prologue to *Bon Ton* had been spoken, which he could hear pretty well from the more slow and distinct utterance, he talked of prologue-writing, and observed, 'Dryden has written prologues superiour to any that David Garrick has written; but David Garrick has written more good prologues than Dryden has done. It is wonderful that he has been able to write such variety of them.'

At Mr. Beauclerk's, where I supped, was Mr. Garrick, whom I made happy with Johnson's praise of his prologues; and I suppose, in gratitude to him, he took up one of his favourite topicks, the nationality of the Scotch, which he maintained in a pleasant manner, with the aid of a little poetical fiction. 'Come, come, don't deny it: they are really national. Why, now, the Adams are as liberal-minded men as any in the world: but, I don't know how it is, all their workmen are Scotch. You are, to be sure, wonderfully free from that nationality: but so it happens, that you employ the only Scotch shoe-black in London.' He imitated the manner of his old master with ludicrous exaggeration; repeating, with pauses and half-whistlings interjected,

> '*Os homini sublime dedit,—caelumque tueri*
> *Jussit,—et erectos ad sidera—tollere vultus*';

looking downwards all the time, and, while pronouncing the four last words, absolutely touching the ground with a kind of contorted gesticulation.

Garrick, however, when he pleased, could imitate Johnson very exactly; for that great actor, with his distinguished powers of expression which were so universally admired, possessed also an admirable talent of mimickry. He was always jealous that Johnson spoke lightly of him. I recollect his exhibiting him to me one day, as if saying, 'Davy has some convivial pleasantry about him, but 'tis a futile fellow;' which he uttered perfectly with the tone and air of Johnson.

I cannot too frequently request of my readers, while they peruse my account of Johnson's conversation, to endeavour to keep in mind his deliberate and strong utterance. His mode of speaking was indeed very impressive; and I wish it could be preserved as musick is written, according to the very ingenious method of Mr. Steele, who has shewn how the recitation of Mr. Garrick, and other eminent speakers, might be transmitted to posterity *in score*.

Next day I dined with Johnson at Mr. Thrale's. He attacked Gray, calling him 'a dull fellow.' BOSWELL. 'I understand he was reserved, and might appear dull in company; but surely he was not dull in poetry.' JOHNSON. 'Sir, he was dull in company, dull in his closet, dull every where. He was dull in a new way, and that made many people think him GREAT. He was a mechanical poet.' He then repeated some ludicrous lines, which have escaped my memory, and said, 'Is not that GREAT, like his Odes?' Mrs. Thrale maintained that his Odes were melodious; upon which he exclaimed,

'Weave the warp, and weave the woof;'—

I added, in a solemn tone,

'The winding-sheet of Edward's race.'

'*There* is a good line.' 'Ay, (said he,) and the next line is a good one,' (pronouncing it contemptuously;)

'Give ample verge and room enough.'—

'No, Sir, there are but two good stanzas in Gray's poetry, which are in his *Elegy in a Country Church-yard*.' He then repeated the stanza,

'For who to dumb forgetfulness a prey,' &c.

mistaking one word; for instead of *precincts* he said *confines*. He added, 'The other stanza I forget.'

A young lady who had married a man much her inferiour in rank being mentioned, a question arose how a woman's relations should behave to her in such a situation; and, while I recapitulate the debate, and recollect what has since happened, I cannot but be struck in a manner that delicacy forbids me to express. While I contended that she ought to be treated with an inflexible steadiness of displeasure, Mrs. Thrale was all for mildness and forgiveness, and, according to the vulgar phrase, 'making the best of a bad bargain.' JOHNSON. Madam, we must distinguish. Were I a man of rank, I would not let a daughter starve who had made a mean marriage; but having voluntarily degraded herself from the station which she was originally entitled to hold, I would support her only in that which she herself had chosen; and would not put her on a level with my other daughters. You are to consider, Madam, that it is our duty to maintain the subordination of civilized society; and when there is a gross and shameful deviation from rank, it should be punished so as to deter others from the same perversion.'

On Friday, March 31, I supped with him and some friends at a tavern. One of the company[28] attempted, with too much forwardness, to rally him on his late appearance at the theatre; but had reason to repent of his temerity. 'Why, Sir, did you go to Mrs. Abington's benefit? Did you see?' JOHNSON. 'No, Sir.' 'Did you hear?' JOHNSON. 'No, Sir.' 'Why then, Sir, did you go?' JOHNSON. 'Because, Sir, she is a favourite of the publick; and when the publick cares the thousandth part for you that it does for her, I will go to your benefit too.'

Next morning I won a small bet from Lady Diana Beauclerk, by asking him as to one of his particularities, which her Ladyship laid I durst not do. It seems he had been frequently observed at the Club to put into his pocket the Seville oranges, after he had squeezed the juice of them into the drink which he made for himself. Beauclerk and Garrick talked of it to me, and seemed to think that he had a strange unwillingness to be discovered. We could not divine what he did with them; and this was the bold question to be put. I saw on his table the spoils of the preceding night, some fresh peels nicely scraped and cut into pieces. 'O, Sir, (said I,) I now partly see what you do with the squeezed oranges which you put into your pocket at the Club.' JOHNSON. 'I have a great love for them.' BOSWELL. 'And pray, Sir, what do you do with them? You scrape them, it seems, very neatly, and what next?' JOHNSON. 'Let them dry, Sir.' BOSWELL. 'And what next?' JOHNSON. 'Nay, Sir, you shall know their fate no further.' BOSWELL. 'Then the world must be left in the dark. It must be said (assuming a mock solemnity,) he scraped them, and let them dry, but what he did with them next, he never could be prevailed upon to tell.' JOHNSON. 'Nay, Sir, you should say it more emphatically:—he could not be prevailed upon, even by his dearest friends, to tell.'

He had this morning received his Diploma as Doctor of Laws from the University of Oxford. He did not vaunt of his new dignity, but I understood he was highly pleased with it.

I observed to him that there were very few of his friends so accurate as that I could venture to put down in writing what they told me as his sayings. JOHNSON. 'Why should you write down *my* sayings?' BOSWELL. 'I write them when they are good.' JOHNSON. 'Nay, you may as well write down the sayings of any one else that are

---

[28] Very likely Boswell.—HILL.

good.' But *where*, I might with great propriety have added, can I find such?

Next day, Sunday, April 2, I dined with him at Mr. Hoole's. We talked of Pope. JOHNSON. 'He wrote, his *Dunciad* for fame. That was his primary motive. Had it not been for that, the dunces might have railed against him till they were weary, without his troubling himself about them. He delighted to vex them, no doubt; but he had more delight in seeing how well he could vex them.'

His *Taxation no Tyranny* being mentioned, he said, 'I think I have not been attacked enough for it. Attack is the re-action; I never think I have hit hard, unless it rebounds.' BOSWELL. 'I don't know, Sir, what you would be at. Five or six shots of small arms in every newspaper, and repeated cannonading in pamphlets, might, I think, satisfy you. But, Sir, you'll never make out this match, of which we have talked, with a certain political lady,[29] since you are so severe against her principles.' JOHNSON. 'Nay, Sir, I have the better chance for that. She is like the Amazons of old; she must be courted by the sword. But I have not been severe upon her.' BOSWELL. 'Yes, Sir, you have made her ridiculous.' JOHNSON. 'That was already done, Sir. To endeavour to make *her* ridiculous, is like blacking the chimney.'

I talked of the cheerfulness of Fleet-street, owing to the constant quick succession of people which we perceive passing through it. JOHNSON. 'Why, Sir, Fleet-street has a very animated appearance; but I think the full tide of human existence is at Charing-cross.'

He made the common remark on the unhappiness which men who have led a busy life experience, when they retire in expectation of enjoying themselves at ease, and that they generally languish for want of their habitual occupation, and wish to return to it. He mentioned as strong an instance of this as can well be imagined. 'An eminent tallow-chandler in London, who had acquired a considerable fortune, gave up the trade in favour of his foreman, and went to live at a country-house near town. He soon grew weary, and paid frequent visits to his old shop, where he desired they might let him know their *melting-days*, and he would come and assist them; which he accordingly did. Here, Sir, was a man, to whom the most disgusting circumstance in the business to which he had been used was a relief from idleness.'

On Wednesday, April 5, I dined with him at Messieurs Dilly's, with Mr. John Scott of Amwell, the Quaker, Mr. Langton, Mr. Miller, (now Sir John,) and Dr. Thomas Campbell, an Irish clergyman, whom I took the liberty of inviting to Mr. Dilly's table, having seen him at Mr. Thrale's, and been told that he had come to England chiefly with a view to see Dr. Johnson, for whom he entertained the highest veneration. He has since published *A Philosophical Survey of the South*

---

[29] Croker identifies her as Mrs. Macaulay. See p. 119.—Ed.

of Ireland, a very entertaining book, which has, however, one fault;—that it assumes the fictitious character of an Englishman.

We talked of publick speaking—JOHNSON. 'We must not estimate a man's powers by his being able, or not able to deliver his sentiments in publick. Isaac Hawkins Browne, one of the first wits of this country, got into Parliament, and never opened his mouth. For my own part, I think it is more disgraceful never to try to speak, than to try it and fail; as it is more disgraceful not to fight, than to fight and be beaten.' This argument appeared to me fallacious; for if a man has not spoken, it may be said that he would have done very well it he had tried; whereas, if he has tried and failed, there is nothing to be said for him. 'Why then, (I asked,) is it thought disgraceful for a man not to fight, and not disgraceful not to speak in publick?' JOHNSON. 'Because there may be other reasons for a man's not speaking in publick than want of resolution: he may have nothing to say, (laughing.) Whereas, Sir, you know courage is reckoned the greatest of all virtues; because, unless a man has that virtue, he has no security for preserving any other.'

On Thursday, April 6, I dined with him at Mr. Thomas Davies's, with Mr. Hicky, the painter, and my old acquaintance Mr. Moody, the player.

Dr. Johnson, as usual, spoke contemptuously of Colley Cibber. 'It is wonderful that a man, who for forty years had lived with the great and the witty, should have acquired so ill the talents of conversation: and he had but half to furnish; for one half of what he said was oaths.' He, however, allowed considerable merit to some of his comedies, and said there was no reason to believe that the *Careless Husband* was not written by himself. Davies said, he was the first dramatick writer who introduced genteel ladies upon the stage. Johnson refuted this observation by instancing several such characters in comedies before his time. DAVIES. (trying to defend himself from a charge of ignorance,) 'I mean genteel moral characters.' 'I think (said Hicky,) gentility and morality are inseparable.' BOSWELL. 'By no means, Sir. The genteelest characters are often the most immoral. Does not Lord Chesterfield give precepts for uniting wickedness and the graces? A man, indeed, is not genteel when he gets drunk; but most vices may be committed very genteelly: a man may debauch his friend's wife genteelly: he may cheat at cards genteelly.' HICKY. 'I do not think *that* is genteel.' BOSWELL. 'Sir, it may not be like a gentleman, but it may be genteel.' JOHNSON. 'You are meaning two different things. One means exteriour grace; the other honour. It is certain that a man may be very immoral with exteriour grace. Lovelace, in *Clarissa*, is a very genteel and a very wicked character. Tom Hervey, who died t'other day, though a vicious man, was one of the genteelest men that ever lived.' Tom Davies instanced Charles the Second. JOHNSON. (taking fire at any attack upon that Prince, for whom he had an extraordinary

partiality,) 'Charles the Second was licentious in his practice; but he
always had a reverence for what was good. Charles the Second knew
his people, and rewarded merit. The Church was at no time better filled
than in his reign. He was the best King we have had from his time till
the reign of his present Majesty, except James the Second, who was a
very good King, but unhappily believed that it was necessary for the
salvation of his subjects that they should be Roman Catholicks. *He* had
the merit of endeavouring to do what he thought was for the salvation
of the souls of his subjects, till he lost a great Empire. *We*, who thought
that we should *not* be saved if we were Roman Catholicks, had the
merit of maintaining our religion, at the expence of submitting
ourselves to the government of King William, (for it could not be done
otherwise,)—to the government of one of the most worthless
scoundrels that ever existed. No; Charles the Second was not such a
man as———, (naming another King). He did not destroy his father's
will. He took money, indeed, from France: but he did not betray those
over whom he ruled: he did not let the French fleet pass ours. George
the First knew nothing, and desired to know nothing; did nothing, and
desired to do nothing: and the only good thing that is told of him is, that
he wished to restore the crown to its hereditary successor.' He roared
with prodigious violence against George the Second. When he ceased,
Moody interjected, in an Irish tone, and with a comick look, 'Ah! poor
George the Second.'

I mentioned that Dr. Thomas Campbell had come from Ireland to
London, principally to see Dr. Johnson. He seemed angry at this
observation. DAVIES. 'Why, you know, Sir, there came a man from
Spain to see Livy; and Corelli came to England to see Purcell, and
when he heard he was dead, went directly back again to Italy.'
JOHNSON. 'I should not have wished to be dead to disappoint Campbell,
had he been so foolish as you represent him; but I should have wished
to have been a hundred miles off.' This was apparently perverse; and I
do believe it was not his real way of thinking: he could not but like a
man who came so far to see him. He laughed with some complacency,
when I told him Campbell's odd expression to me concerning him:
'That having seen such a man, was a thing to talk of a century
hence,'—as if he could live so long.

We got into an argument whether the Judges who went to India
might with propriety engage in trade. Johnson warmly maintained that
they might. 'For why (he urged,) should not Judges get riches, as well
as those who deserve them less?' I said, they should have sufficient
salaries, and have nothing to take off their attention from the affairs of
the publick. JOHNSON. 'No Judge, Sir, can give his whole attention to
his office; and it is very proper that he should employ what time he has
to himself, to his own advantage, in the most profitable manner.' 'Then,
Sir, (said Davies, who enlivened the dispute by making it somewhat

dramatick,) he may become an insurer; and when he is going to the bench, he may be stopped,—"Your Lordship cannot go yet: here is a bunch of invoices: several ships are about to sail."' JOHNSON. Sir, you may as well say a Judge should not have a house; for they may come and tell him, "Your Lordship's house is on fire;" and so, instead of minding the business of his Court, he is to be occupied in getting the engine with the greatest speed. There is no end of this. Every Judge who has land, trades to a certain extent in corn or in cattle; and in the land itself, undoubtedly. His steward acts for him, and so do clerks for a great merchant. A Judge may be a farmer; but he is not to geld his own pigs. A Judge may play a little at cards for his amusement; but he is not to play at marbles, or at chuck-farthing in the Piazza. No, Sir; there is no profession to which a man gives a very great proportion of his time. It is wonderful, when a calculation is made, how little the mind is actually employed in the discharge of any profession. No man would be a Judge, upon the condition of being totally a Judge. The best employed lawyer has his mind at work but for a small proportion of his time; a great deal of his occupation is merely mechanical. I once wrote for a magazine: I made a calculation, that if I should write but a page a day, at the same rate, I should, in ten years, write nine volumes in folio, of an ordinary size and print.' BOSWELL. 'Such as Carte's *History*?' JOHNSON. 'Yes, Sir. When a man writes from his own mind, he writes very rapidly. The greatest part of a writer's time is spent in reading, in order to write: a man will turn over half a library to make one book.'

We spoke of Rolt, to whose *Dictionary of Commerce* Dr. Johnson wrote the Preface. JOHNSON. 'Old Gardner the bookseller employed Rolt and Smart to write a monthly miscellany, called *The Universal Visitor*. There was a formal written contract, which Allen the printer saw. Gardner thought as you do of the Judge. They were bound to write nothing else; they were to have, I think, a third of the profits of this sixpenny pamphlet; and the contract was for ninety-nine years. I wish I had thought of giving this to Thurlow, in the cause about Literary Property. What an excellent instance would it have been of the oppression of booksellers towards poor authours!' (smiling.) Davies, zealous for the honour of *the Trade*, said, Gardner was not properly a bookseller. JOHNSON. 'Nay, Sir; he certainly was a bookseller. He had served his time regularly, was a member of the Stationers' company, kept a shop in the face of mankind, purchased copyright, and was a *bibliopole*, Sir, in every sense. I wrote for some months in *The Universal Visitor*, for poor Smart, while he was mad, not then knowing the terms on which he was engaged to write, and thinking I was doing him good. I hoped his wits would soon return to him. Mine returned to me, and I wrote in *The Universal Visitor* no longer.'

Friday, April 7, I dined with him at a Tavern, with a numerous company.

One of the company suggested an internal objection to the antiquity of the poetry said to be Ossian's, that we do not find the wolf in it, which must have been the case had it been of that age.

The mention of the wolf had led Johnson to think of other wild beasts; and while Sir Joshua Reynolds and Mr. Langton were carrying on a dialogue about something which engaged them earnestly, he, in the midst of it, broke out, 'Pennant tells of Bears—' [what he added, I have forgotten.] They went on, which he being dull of hearing, did not perceive, or, if he did, was not willing to break off his talk; so he continued to vociferate his remarks, and *Bear* ('like a word in a catch' as Beauclerk said,) was repeatedly heard at intervals, which coming from him who, by those who did not know him, had been so often assimilated to that ferocious animal, while we who were sitting around could hardly stifle laughter, produced a very ludicrous effect. Silence having ensued, he proceeded: 'We are told, that the black bear is innocent; but I should not like to trust myself with him.' Mr. Gibbon muttered, in a low tone of voice, 'I should not like to trust myself with *you.*' This piece of sarcastick pleasantry was a prudent resolution, if applied to a competition of abilities.

Patriotism having become one of our topicks, Johnson suddenly uttered, in a strong determined tone, an apophthegm, at which many will start: 'Patriotism is the last refuge of a scoundrel.' But let it be considered, that he did not mean a real and generous love of our country, but that pretended patriotism which so many, in all ages and countries, have made a cloak for self-interest.

Mrs. Prichard being mentioned, he said, 'Her playing was quite mechanical. It is wonderful how little mind she had. Sir, she had never read the tragedy of *Macbeth* all through. She no more thought of the play out of which her part was taken, than a shoemaker thinks of the skin, out of which the piece of leather, of which he is making a pair of shoes, is cut.'

On Saturday, April 8, I dined with him at Mr. Thrale's, where we met the Irish Dr. Campbell. Johnson had supped the night before at Mrs. Abington's, with some fashionable people whom he named; and he seemed much pleased with having made one in so elegant a circle. Nor did he omit to pique his *mistress* a little with jealousy of her housewifery; for he said, (with a smile,) 'Mrs. Abington's jelly, my dear lady, was better than yours.'

Mrs. Thrale, who frequently practised a coarse mode of flattery, by repeating his *bon-mots* in his hearing, told us that he had said, a certain celebrated actor was just fit to stand at the door of an auction-room with a long pole, and cry 'Pray gentlemen, walk in;' and that a certain authour, upon hearing this, had said, that another still more celebrated actor was fit for nothing better than that, and would pick your pocket after you came out. JOHNSON. 'Nay, my dear lady, there is no wit in what our friend added; there is only abuse. You may as well say of any man that he will pick a pocket. Besides, the man who is stationed at the door does not pick people's pockets; that is done within, by the auctioneer.'

On Monday, April 10, I dined with him at General Oglethorpe's, with Mr. Langton and the Irish Dr. Campbell, whom the General had obligingly given me leave to bring with me. This learned gentleman was thus gratified with a very high intellectual feast, by not only being in company with Dr. Johnson, but with General Oglethorpe, who had been so long a celebrated name both at home and abroad.

I must, again and again, intreat of my readers not to suppose that my imperfect record of conversation contains the whole of what was said by Johnson, or other eminent persons who lived with him. What I have preserved, however, has the value of the most perfect authenticity.

He urged General Oglethorpe to give the world his Life. He said, 'I know no man whose Life would be more interesting. If I were furnished with materials, I should be very glad to write it.'

Mr. Scott of Amwell's *Elegies* were lying in the room. Dr. Johnson observed, 'They are very well; but such as twenty people might write.' Upon this I took occasion to controvert Horace's maxim,

> '———mediocribus esse poetis
> Non Di, non homines, non concessere columnae.'

For here, (I observed,) was a very middle-rate poet, who pleased many readers, and therefore poetry of a middle sort was entitled to some esteem; nor could I see why poetry should not, like every thing else, have different gradations of excellence, and consequently of value. Johnson repeated the common remark, that, 'as there is no necessity for our having poetry at all, it being merely a luxury, an instrument of pleasure, it can have no value, unless when exquisite in its kind.' I declared myself not satisfied. 'Why then, Sir, (said he,) Horace and you must settle it.' He was not much in the humour of talking.

No more of his conversation for some days appears in my journal, except that when a gentleman told him he had bought a suit of lace for his lady, he said, 'Well, Sir, you have done a good thing and a wise thing.' 'I have done a good thing, (said the gentleman,) but I do not know that I have done a wise thing.' JOHNSON. 'Yes, Sir; no money is better spent than what is laid out for domestick satisfaction. A man is pleased that his wife is drest as well as other people; and a wife is pleased that she is drest.'

On Friday, April 14, being Good-Friday, I repaired to him in the morning, according to my usual custom on that day, and breakfasted with him. I observed that he fasted so very strictly, that he did not even taste bread, and took no milk with his tea; I suppose because it is a kind of animal food.

I told him that I had been informed by Mr. Orme, that many parts of the East-Indies were better mapped than the Highlands of Scotland. JOHNSON. 'That a country may be mapped, it must be travelled over.' 'Nay, (said I, meaning to laugh with him at one of his prejudices,) can't you say, it is not *worth* mapping?'

As we walked to St. Clement's church, and saw several shops open upon this most solemn fast-day of the Christian world, I remarked, that one disadvantage arising from the immensity of London, was, that nobody was heeded by his neighbour; there was no fear of censure for not observing Good-Friday, as it ought to be kept, and as it is kept in country-towns. He said, it was, upon the whole, very well observed even in London. He, however, owned, that London was too large; but added, 'It is nonsense to say the head is too big for the body. It would be as much too big, though the body were ever so large; that is to say, though the country were ever so extensive. It has no similarity to a head connected with a body.'

Dr. Wetherell, Master of University College, Oxford, accompanied us home from church; and after he was gone, there came two other gentlemen, one of whom uttered the commonplace complaints, that by the increase of taxes, labour would be dear, other nations would undersell us, and our commerce would be ruined. JOHNSON. (smiling,) 'Never fear, Sir. Our commerce is in a very good state; and suppose we had no commerce at all, we could live very well on the produce of our own country.' I cannot omit to mention, that I never knew any man who was less disposed to be querulous than Johnson. Whether the subject was his own situation, or the state of the publick, or the state of human nature in general, though he saw the evils, his mind was turned to resolution, and never to whining or complaint.

We went again to St. Clement's in the afternoon. He had found fault with the preacher in the morning for not choosing a text adapted to the day. The preacher in the afternoon had chosen one extremely proper: 'It is finished.'

After the evening service, he said, 'Come, you shall go home with me, and sit just an hour.' But he was better than his word; for after we had drunk tea with Mrs. Williams, he asked me to go up to his study with him, where we sat a long while together in a serene undisturbed frame of mind, sometimes in silence, and sometimes conversing, as we felt ourselves inclined, or more properly speaking, as *he* was inclined; for during all the course of my long intimacy with him, my respectful attention never abated, and my wish to hear him was such, that I constantly watched every dawning of communication from that great and illuminated mind.

He again advised me to keep a journal fully and minutely, but not to mention such trifles as, that meat was too much or too little done, or that the weather was fair or rainy. He had, till very near his death, a contempt for the notion that the weather affects the human frame.

I told him that our friend Goldsmith had said to me, that he had come too late into the world, for that Pope and other poets had taken up the places in the Temple of Fame; so that, as but a few at any period can possess poetical reputation, a man of genius can now hardly acquire it. JOHNSON. 'That is one of the most sensible things I have ever heard of Goldsmith. It is difficult to get literary fame, and it is every day growing more difficult. Ah, Sir, that should make a man think of securing happiness in another world, which all who try sincerely for it may attain. In comparison of that, how little are all other things! The belief of immortality is impressed upon all men, and all men act under an impression of it, however they may talk, and though, perhaps, they may be scarcely sensible of it.' I said, it appeared to me that some people had not the least notion of immortality; and I mentioned a distinguished gentleman of our acquaintance. JOHNSON. 'Sir, if it were not for the notion of immortality, he would cut a throat to fill his pockets.' When I quoted this to Beauclerk, who knew much more of the gentleman than we did, he said, in his acid manner, 'He would cut a throat to fill his pockets, if it were not for fear of being hanged.'

He was pleased to say, 'If you come to settle here, we will have one day in the week on which we will meet by ourselves. That is the happiest conversation where there is no competition, no vanity, but a calm quiet interchange of sentiments.' In his private register this evening is thus marked, 'Boswell sat with me till night; we had some serious talk.' It also appears from the same record, that after I left him he was occupied in religious duties, in 'giving Francis, his servant, some directions for preparation to communicate; in reviewing his life, and resolving on better conduct.' The humility and piety which he discovers on such occasions, is truely edifying. No saint, however, in the course of his religious warfare, was more sensible of the unhappy failure of pious resolves, than Johnson. He said one day, talking to an acquaintance on this subject, 'Sir Hell is paved with good intentions.'

On Sunday, April 16, being Easter Day, after having attended the solemn service at St. Paul's, I dined with Dr. Johnson and Mrs. Williams. I maintained that Horace was wrong in placing happiness in *Nil admirari*, for that I thought admiration one of the most agreeable of all our feelings; and I regretted that I had lost much of my disposition to admire, which people generally do as they advance in life. JOHNSON. 'Sir, as a man advances in life, he gets what is better than admiration—judgement, to estimate things at their true value.' I still insisted that admiration was more pleasing than judgement, as love is more pleasing than friendship. The feeling of friendship is like that of being comfortably filled with roast beef; love, like being enlivened with champagne. JOHNSON. 'No, Sir; admiration and love are like being intoxicated with champagne; judgement and friendship like being enlivened. Waller has hit upon the same thought with you: but I don't believe you have borrowed from Waller. I wish you would enable yourself to borrow more.'

He then took occasion to enlarge on the advantages of reading, and combated the idle superficial notion, that knowledge enough may be acquired in conversation. 'The foundation (said he,) must be laid by reading. General principles must be had from books, which, however, must be brought to the test of real life. In conversation you never get a system. What is said upon a subject is to be gathered from a hundred people. The parts of a truth, which a man gets thus, are at such a distance from each other that he never attains to a full view.'

On Tuesday, April 15, he and I were engaged to go with Sir Joshua Reynolds to dine with Mr. Cambridge, at his beautiful villa on the banks of the Thames, near Twickenham. Dr. Johnson's tardiness was such, that Sir Joshua, who had an appointment at Richmond, early in the day, was obliged to go by himself on horseback, leaving his coach to Johnson and me. Johnson was in such good spirits, that every thing seemed to please him as we drove along.

Our conversation turned on a variety of subjects. He thought portrait-painting an improper employment for a woman. 'Publick practice of any art, (he observed,) and staring in men's faces, is very indelicate in a female.' I happened to start a question, whether, when a man knows that some of his intimate friends are invited to the house of another friend, with whom they are all equally intimate, he may join them without an invitation. JOHNSON. 'No, Sir; he is not to go when he is not invited. They may be invited on purpose to abuse him' (smiling).

As a curious instance how little a man knows, or wishes to know, his own character in the world, or, rather, as a convincing proof that Johnson's roughness was only external, and did not proceed from his heart, I insert the following dialogue. JOHNSON. 'It is wonderful, Sir, how rare a quality good humour is in life. We meet with very few good humoured men.' I mentioned four of our friends, none of whom he would allow to be good humoured. One was *acid*, another was *muddy*, and to the others he had objections which have escaped me. Then, shaking his head and stretching himself at ease in the coach, and smiling with much complacency, he turned to me and said, 'I look upon *myself* as a good humoured fellow.' The epithet *fellow*, applied to the great Lexicographer, the stately Moralist, the masterly critick, as if he had been *Sam* Johnson, a mere pleasant companion, was highly diverting; and this light notion of himself struck me with wonder. I answered, also smiling, 'No, no, Sir; that will *not* do. You are good natured, but not good humoured: you are irascible. You have not patience with folly and absurdity. I believe you would pardon them, if there were time to deprecate your vengeance; but punishment follows so quick after sentence, that they cannot escape.

I had brought with me a great bundle of Scotch magazines and news-papers, in which his *Journey to the Western Islands* was attacked in every mode; and I read a great part of them to him, knowing they would afford him entertainment. I wish the writers of them had been present: they would have been sufficiently vexed. One ludicrous imitation of his style, by Mr. Maclaurin, now one of the Scotch Judges, with the title of Lord Dreghorn, was distinguished by him from the rude mass. 'This (said he,) is the best. But I could caricature my own style much better myself.' He defended his remark upon the general insufficiency of education in Scotland; and confirmed to me the authenticity of his witty saying on the learning of the Scotch;—'Their learning is like bread in a besieged town: every man gets a little, but no man gets a full meal.' 'There is (said he,) in Scotland, a diffusion of learning, a certain portion of it widely and thinly spread. A merchant there has as much learning as one of their clergy.

No sooner had we made our bow to Mr. Cambridge, in his library, than Johnson ran eagerly to one side of the room, intent on poring over the backs of the books. Sir Joshua observed, (aside,) 'He runs to the books, as I do to the pictures: but I have the advantage. I can see much more of the pictures than he can of the books.' Mr. Cambridge, upon this, politely said, 'Dr. Johnson, I am going, with your pardon, to accuse myself, for I have the same custom which I perceive you have. But it seems odd that one should have such a desire to look at the backs of books.' Johnson, ever ready for contest, instantly started from his reverie, wheeled about, and answered, 'Sir, the reason is very plain. Knowledge is of two kinds. We know a subject ourselves, or we know where we can find information upon it. When we enquire into any subject, the first thing we have to do is to know what books have treated of it. This leads us to look at catalogues, and the backs of books in libraries.' Sir Joshua observed to me the extraordinary promptitude with which Johnson flew upon an argument. 'Yes, (said I,) he has no formal preparation, no flourishing with his sword; he is through your body in an instant.'

Johnson was here solaced with an elegant entertainment, a very accomplished family, and much good company; among whom was Mr. Harris of Salisbury, who paid him many compliments on his *Journey to the Western Islands*.

The common remark as to the utility of reading history being made;—JOHNSON. 'We must consider how very little history there is; I mean real authentick history. That certain Kings reigned, and certain battles were fought, we can depend upon as true; but all the colouring, all the philosophy of history is conjecture.' BOSWELL. 'Then, Sir, you would reduce all history to no better than an almanack, a mere chronological series of remarkable events.' Mr. Gibbon, who must at that time have been employed upon his *History*, of which he published the first volume in the following year, was present; but did not step forth in defence of that species of writing. He probably did not like to *trust* himself with JOHNSON!

The Beggar's Opera, and the common question, whether it was pernicious in its effects, having been introduced;—JOHNSON. 'As to this matter, which has been very much contested, I myself am of opinion, that more influence has been ascribed to *The Beggar's Opera*, than it in reality ever had; for I do not believe that any man was ever made a rogue by being present at its representation. At the same time I do not deny that it may have some influence, by making the character of a rogue familiar, and in some degree pleasing.' Then collecting himself as it were, to give a heavy stroke: 'There is in it such a *labefactation* of all principles, as may be injurious to morality.'

While he pronounced this response, we sat in a comical sort of restraint, smothering a laugh, which we were afraid might burst out.

We talked of a young gentleman's[30] marriage with an eminent singer, and his determination that she should no longer sing in publick, though his father was very earnest she should, because her talents would be liberally rewarded, so as to make her a good fortune. It was questioned whether the young gentleman, who had not a shilling in the world, but was blest with very uncommon talents, was not foolishly delicate, or foolishly proud, and his father truely rational without being mean. Johnson, with all the high spirit of a Roman senator, exclaimed, 'He resolved wisely and nobly to be sure. He is a brave man. Would not a gentleman be disgraced by having his wife singing publickly for hire? No, Sir, there can be no doubt here. I know not if I should not *prepare* myself for a publick singer, as readily as let my wife be one.'

Johnson arraigned the modern politicks of this country, as entirely devoid of all principle of whatever kind. 'Politicks (said he,) are now nothing more than means of rising in the world. With this sole view do men engage in politicks, and their whole conduct proceeds upon it.'

Somebody found fault with writing verses in a dead language, maintaining that they were merely arrangements of so many words, and laughed at the Universities of Oxford and Cambridge, for sending forth collections of them not only in Greek and Latin, but even in Syriac, Arabick, and other more unknown tongues. JOHNSON. 'I would have as many of these as possible; I would have verses in every language that there are the means of acquiring. Nobody imagines that an University is to have at once two hundred poets; but it should be able to show two

---

[30] Probably Richard Brinsley Sheridan, whose romantic marriage with the beautiful Elizabeth Linley took place in 1773. He became a member of the Club on Johnson's proposal. See below, p. 325.—Ed.

hundred scholars. Pieresc's death was lamented, I think, in forty languages. And I would have had at every coronation, and every death of a King, every *Gaudium*, and every *Luctus*, University verses, in as many languages as can be acquired. I would have the world to be thus told, "Here is a school where every thing may be learnt."'

Having set out next day on a visit to the Earl of Pembroke, at Wilton, and to my friend, Mr. Temple, at Mamhead, in Devonshire, and not having returned to town till the second of May, I did not see Dr. Johnson for a considerable time, and during the remaining part of my stay in London, kept very imperfect notes of his conversation, which had I according to my usual custom written out at large soon after the time, much might have been preserved, which is now irretrievably lost.

On Monday, May 8, we went together and visited the mansions of Bedlam. I had been informed that he had once been there before with Mr. Wedderburne, (now Lord Loughborough,) Mr. Murphy, and Mr. Foote; and I had heard Foote give a very entertaining account of Johnson's happening to have his attention arrested by a man who was very furious, and who, while beating his straw, supposed it was William Duke of Cumberland, whom he was punishing for his cruelties in Scotland, in 1746. There was nothing peculiarly remarkable this day; but the general contemplation of insanity was very affecting. I accompanied him home, and dined and drank tea with him.

On Friday, May 12, as he had been so good as to assign me a room in his house, where I might sleep occasionally, when I happened to sit with him to a late hour, I took possession of it this night, found every thing in excellent order, and was attended by honest Francis with a most civil assiduity. I asked Johnson whether I might go to a consultation with another lawyer upon Sunday, as that appeared to me to be doing work as much in my way, as if an artisan should work on the day appropriated for religious rest. JOHNSON. 'Why, Sir, when you are of consequence enough to oppose the practice of consulting upon Sunday, you should do it: but you may go now. It is not criminal, though it is not what one should do, who is anxious for the preservation and increase of piety, to which a peculiar observance of Sunday is a great help. The distinction is clear between what is of moral and what is of ritual obligation.'

On Saturday, May 13, I breakfasted with him by invitation, accompanied by Mr. Andrew Crosbie, a Scotch Advocate, whom he had seen at Edinburgh, and the Hon. Colonel (now General) Edward Stopford, brother to Lord Courtown, who was desirous of being introduced to him. His tea and rolls and butter, and whole breakfast apparatus were all in such decorum, and his behaviour was so courteous, that Colonel Stopford was quite surprized, and wondered at his having heard so much said of Johnson's slovenliness and roughness.

I passed many hours with him on the 17th, of which I find all my memorial is, 'much laughing.' It should seem he had that day been in a humour for jocularity and merriment, and upon such occasions I never knew a man laugh more heartily. We may suppose, that the high relish of a state so different from his habitual gloom, produced more than ordinary exertions of that distinguishing faculty of man, which has puzzled philosophers so much to explain. Johnson's laugh was as remarkable as any circumstance in his manner. It was a kind of good humoured growl. Tom Davies described it drolly enough: 'He laughs like a rhinoceros.'

'TO BENNET LANGTON, ESQ.

'DEAR SIR,—I have an old amanuensis in great distress. I have given what I think I can give, and begged till I cannot tell where to beg again. I put into his hands this morning four guineas. If you could collect three guineas more, it would clear him from his present difficulty. I am, Sir, your most humble servant,
     'May 21, 1775.'
'SAM. JOHNSON.'

After my return to Scotland, I wrote three letters to him.

'TO JAMES BOSWELL, ESQ.

'DEAR SIR,—I am returned from the annual ramble into the middle counties. Having seen nothing I had not seen before, I have nothing to relate. Time has left that part of the island few antiquities; and commerce has left the people no singularities. I was glad to go abroad, and, perhaps, glad to come home; which is, in other words, I was, I am afraid, weary of being at home, and weary of being abroad. Is not this the state of life? But, if we confess this weariness, let us not lament it, for all the wise and all the good say, that we may cure it. . . .

'Mrs. Thrale was so entertained with your *Journal*,[31] that she almost read herself blind. She has a great regard for you.

'Of Mrs. Boswell, though she knows in her heart that she does not love me, I am always glad to hear any good, and hope that she and the little dear ladies will have neither sickness nor any other affliction. But she knows that she does not care what becomes of me, and for that she may be sure that I think her very much to blame.

'Never, my dear Sir, do you take it into your head to think that I do not love you; you may settle yourself in full confidence both of my love

---

[31] My Journal of a Tour to the Hebrides, which that lady read in the original manuscript.—BOSWELL.

and my esteem; I love you as a kind man, I value you as a worthy man, and hope in time to reverence you as a man of exemplary piety. I hold you, as Hamlet has it, "in my heart of hearts," and therefore, it is little to say, that I am, Sir, your affectionate humble servant,

'SAM. JOHNSON.'

'London, Aug. 27, 1775.'

'TO MR. ROBERT LEVET.

'Paris,[32] Oct. 22, 1775.

'DEAR SIR,—We are still here, commonly very busy in looking about us. We have been to-day at Versailles. You have seen it, and I shall not describe it. We came yesterday from Fontainbleau, where the Court is now. We went to see the King and Queen at dinner, and the Queen was so impressed by Miss,[33] that she sent one of the Gentlemen to enquire who she was. I find all true that you have ever told me of Paris. Mr. Thrale is very liberal, and keeps us two coaches, and a very fine table; but I think our cookery very bad. Mrs. Thrale got into a convent of English nuns; and I talked with her through the grate, and I am very kindly used by the English Benedictine friars. But upon the whole I cannot make much acquaintance here; and though the churches, palaces, and some private houses are very magnificent, there is no very great pleasure after having seen many, in seeing more; at least the pleasure, whatever it be, must some time have an end, and we are beginning to think when we shall come home. Mr. Thrale calculates that, as we left Streatham on the fifteenth of September, we shall see it again about the fifteenth of November.

'I think I had not been on this side of the sea five days before I found a sensible improvement in my health. I ran a race in the rain this day, and beat Baretti. Baretti is a fine fellow, and speaks French, I think, quite as well as English.

'Make my compliments to Mrs. Williams; and give my love to Francis; and tell my friends that I am not lost. I am, dear Sir, your affectionate humble, &c.

'SAM. JOHNSON.'

It is to be regretted that he did not write an account of his travels in France; for as he is reported to have once said, that 'he could write the Life of a Broomstick,' so, notwithstanding so many former travellers have exhausted almost every subject for remark in that great kingdom, his very accurate observation, and peculiar vigour of thought and

---

[32] Written from a tour in France with the Thrales, Johnson's only visit to the Continent.—Ed.

[33] Miss Thrale.

illustration, would have produced a valuable work.

When I met him in London the following year, the account which he gave me of his French tour, was, 'Sir, I have seen all the visibilities of Paris, and around it; but to have formed an acquaintance with the people there, would have required more time than I could stay. I was just beginning to creep into acquaintance by means of Colonel Drumgold, a very high man, Sir, head of *L'Ecole Militaire*, a most complete character, for he had first been a professor of rhetorick, and then became a soldier. And, Sir, I was very kindly treated by the English Benedictines, and have a cell appropriated to me in their convent.'

He observed, 'The great in France live very magnificently, but the rest very miserably. There is no happy middle state as in England. The shops of Paris are mean; the meat in the markets is such as would be sent to a gaol in England: and Mr. Thrale justly observed, that the cookery of the French was forced upon them by necessity; for they could not eat their meat, unless they added some taste to it. The French are an indelicate people; they will spit upon any place. At Madame——
—'s, a literary lady of rank, the footman took the sugar in his fingers, and threw it into my coffee. I was going to put it aside; but hearing it was made on purpose for me, I e'en tasted Tom's fingers. The same lady would needs make tea *à l'Angloise*. The spout of the tea-pot did not pour freely; she had the footman blow into it. France is worse than Scotland in every thing but climate. Nature has done more for the French; but they have done less for themselves than the Scotch have done.'

It happened that Foote was at Paris at the same time with Dr. Johnson, and his description of my friend while there, was abundantly ludicrous. He told me, that the French were quite astonished at his figure and manner, and at his dress, which he obstinately continued exactly as in London;—his brown clothes, black stockings, and plain shirt. He mentioned, that an Irish gentleman said to Johnson, 'Sir, you have not seen the best French players.' JOHNSON. 'Players, Sir! I look on them as no better than creatures set upon tables and joint-stools to make faces and produce laughter, like dancing dogs.'—'But, Sir, you will allow that some players are better than others?' JOHNSON. 'Yes, Sir, as some dogs dance better than others.'

While Johnson was in France, he was generally very resolute in speaking Latin. It was a maxim with him that a man should not let himself down, by speaking a language which he speaks imperfectly. Indeed, we must have often observed how inferiour, how much like a child a man appears, who speaks a broken tongue. When Sir Joshua Reynolds, at one of the dinners of the Royal Academy, presented him to a Frenchman of great distinction, he would not deign to speak French, but talked Latin, though his Excellency did not understand it, owing, perhaps, to Johnson's English pronunciation: yet upon another occasion he was observed to speak French to a Frenchman of high rank, who spoke English; and being asked the reason, with some expression of surprise,—he answered, 'because I think my French is as good as his English.' Though Johnson understood French perfectly, he could not speak it readily, as I have observed at his first interview with General Pauli, in 1769; yet he wrote it, I imagine, pretty well.

Here let me not forget a curious anecdote, as related to me by Mr. Beauclerk, which I shall endeavour to exhibit as well as I can in that gentleman's lively manner; and in justice to him it is proper to add, that Dr. Johnson told me I might rely both on the correctness of his memory, and the fidelity of his narrative. 'When Madame de Boufflers was first in England, (said Beauclerk,) she was desirous to see Johnson. I accordingly went with her to his chambers in the Temple, where she was entertained with his conversation for some time. When our visit was over, she and I left him, and were got into Inner Temple-lane, when all at once I heard a noise like thunder. This was occasioned by Johnson, who it seems, upon a little recollection, had taken it into his head that he ought to have done the honours of his literary residence to a foreign lady of quality, and eager to shew himself a man of gallantry, was hurrying down the stair-case in violent agitation. He overtook us before we reached the Temple-gate, and brushing in between me and Madame de Boufflers, seized her hand, and conducted her to her coach. His dress was a rusty brown morning suit, a pair of old shoes by way of slippers, a little shrivelled wig sticking on the top of his head, and the sleeves of his shirt and the knees of his breeches hanging loose. A considerable crowd of people gathered round, and were not a little struck by this singular appearance.'

He spoke Latin with wonderful fluency and elegance. When Pere Boscovich was in England, Johnson dined in company with him at Sir Joshua Reynolds's, and at Dr. Douglas's, now Bishop of Salisbury. Upon both occasions that celebrated foreigner expressed his astonishment at Johnson's Latin conversation. When at Paris, Johnson thus characterised Voltaire to Freron the Journalist: '*Vir est acerrimi ingenii et paucarum literarum.*'

In the course of this year Dr. Burney informs me that 'he very frequently met Dr. Johnson at Mr. Thrale's, at Streatham, where they had many long conversations, often sitting up as long as the fire and candles lasted, and much longer than the patience of the servants subsisted.'

A few of Johnson's sayings, which that gentleman recollects, shall here be inserted.

'I never take a nap after dinner but when I have had a bad night, and then the nap takes me.'

'The writer of an epitaph should not be considered as saying nothing but what is strictly true. Allowance must be made for some degree of exaggerated praise. In lapidary inscriptions a man is not upon oath.'

'There is now less flogging in our great schools than formerly, but then less is learned there; so that what the boys get at one end they lose at the other.'

'More is learned in publick than in private schools, from emulation; there is the collision of mind with mind, or the radiation of many minds pointing to one centre. Though few boys make their own exercises, yet if a good exercise is given up, out of a great number of boys, it is made by somebody.'

'I hate by-roads in education. Education is as well known, and has long been as well known, as ever it can be. Endeavouring to make children prematurely wise is useless labour. Suppose they have more knowledge at five or six years old than other children, what use can be made of it? It will be lost before it is wanted, and the waste of so much time and labour of the teacher can never be repaid. Too much is expected from precocity, and too little performed. Miss——was an instance of early cultivation, but in what did it terminate? In marrying a little Presbyterian parson, who keeps an infant boarding-school, so that all her employment now is,

"To suckle fools, and chronicle small-beer."

She tells the children, "This is a cat, and that is a dog, with four legs and a tail; see there! you are much better than a cat or a dog, for you can speak." If I had bestowed such an education on a daughter, and had discovered that she thought of marrying such a fellow, I would have sent her to the *Congress*.'

'After having talked slightingly of musick, he was observed to listen very attentively while Miss Thrale played on the harpsichord, and with eagerness he called to her, "Why don't you dash away like Burney?" Dr. Burney upon this said to him, "I believe, Sir, we shall make a musician of you at last." Johnson with candid complacency replied, "Sir, I shall be glad to have a new sense given to me."'

'He had come down one morning to the breakfast-room, and been a considerable time by himself before any body appeared. When, on a subsequent day, he was twitted by Mrs. Thrale for being very late, which he generally was, he defended himself by alluding to the extraordinary morning, when he had been too early. "Madame, I do not like to come down to *vacuity*."'

'Dr. Burney having remarked that Mr. Garrick was beginning to look old, he said, "Why, Sir, you are not to wonder at that; no man's face has had more wear and tear."'

1776: ÆTAT. 67.]—HAVING arrived in London late on Friday, the

15th of March, I hastened next morning to wait on Dr. Johnson, at his house; but found he was removed from Johnson's-court, No. 7, to Bolt-court, No. 8, still keeping to his favourite Fleet-street. My reflection at the time upon this change as marked in my Journal, is as follows: 'I felt a foolish regret that he had left a court which bore his name;[34] but it was not foolish to be affected with some tenderness of regard for a place in which I had seen him a great deal, from whence I had often issued a better and a happier man than when I went in, and which had often appeared to my imagination while I trod its pavements, in the solemn darkness of the night, to be sacred to wisdom and piety.' Being informed that he was at Mr. Thrale's, in the Borough, I hastened thither, and found Mrs. Thrale and him at breakfast. I was kindly welcomed. In a moment he was in a full glow of conversation, and I felt myself elevated as if brought into another state of being. Mrs. Thrale and I looked to each other while he talked, and our looks expressed our congenial admiration and affection for him. I shall ever recollect this scene with great pleasure, I exclaimed to her, 'I am now, intellectually, *Hermippus redivivus*, I am quite restored by him, by transfusion of *mind*.' 'There are many (she replied) who admire and respect Mr. Johnson; but you and I *love* him.'

He seemed very happy in the near prospect of going to Italy with Mr. and Mrs. Thrale. 'But, (said he,) before leaving England I am to take a jaunt to Oxford, Birmingham, my native city Lichfield, and my old friend, Dr. Taylor's, at Ashbourn, in Derbyshire. I shall go in a few days, and you, Boswell, shall go with me.' I was ready to accompany him; being willing even to leave London to have the pleasure of his conversation.

We got into a boat to cross over to Black-friars; and as we moved along the Thames, I talked to him of a little volume, which, altogether unknown to him, was advertised to be published in a few days, under the title of *Johnsoniana, or Bon-Mots of Dr. Johnson*. JOHNSON. 'Sir, it is a mighty impudent thing.' BOSWELL. 'Pray, Sir, could you have no redress if you were to prosecute a publisher for bringing out, under your name, what you never said, and ascribing to you dull stupid nonsense, or making you swear profanely, as many ignorant relaters of your *bon-mots* do?' JOHNSON. 'No, Sir; there will always be some truth mixed with the falsehood, and how can it be ascertained how much is true and how much is false? Besides, Sir, what damages would a jury give me for having been represented as swearing?' BOSWELL. 'I think, Sir, you should at least disavow such a publication, because the world and posterity might with much plausible foundation say, "Here is a volume which was publickly advertised and came out in Dr. Johnson's own time, and, by his silence, was admitted by him to be genuine."'

---

[34] He said, when in Scotland, that he was *Johnson of that Ilk*.—BOSWELL.

JOHNSON. 'I shall give myself no trouble about the matter.'

He was, perhaps, above suffering from such spurious publications; but I could not help thinking, that many men would be much injured in their reputation, by having absurd and vicious sayings imputed to them; and that redress ought in such cases to be given.

He said, 'The value of every story depends on its being true. A story is a picture either of an individual or of human nature in general: if it be false, it is a picture of nothing. For instance: suppose a man should tell that Johnson, before setting out for Italy, as he had to cross the Alps, sat down to make himself wings. This many people would believe; but it would be a picture of nothing. ******* (naming a worthy friend of ours,) used to think a story, a story, till I shewed him that truth was essential to it.' I observed, that Foote entertained us with stories which were not true; but that, indeed, it was properly not as narratives that Foote's stories pleased us, but as collections of ludicrous images. JOHNSON. 'Foote is quite impartial, for he tells lies of every body.'

The importance of strict and scrupulous veracity cannot be too often inculcated. Johnson was known to be so rigidly attentive to it, that even in his common conversation the slightest circumstance was mentioned with exact precision. The knowledge of his having such a principle and habit made his friends have a perfect reliance on the truth of every thing that he told, however it might have been doubted if told by many others. As an instance of this, I may mention an odd incident which he related as having happened to him one night in Fleet-street. 'A gentlewoman (said he) begged I would give her my arm to assist her in crossing the street, which I accordingly did; upon which she offered me a shilling, supposing me to be the watchman. I perceived that she was somewhat in liquor.' This, if told by most people, would have been thought an invention; when told by Johnson, it was believed by his friends as much as if they had seen what passed.

We landed at the Temple-stairs, where we parted.

I found him in the evening in Mrs. Williams's room. Finding him still persevering in his abstinence from wine, I ventured to speak to him of it—JOHNSON. 'Sir, I have no objection to a man's drinking wine, if he can do it in moderation. I found myself apt to go to excess in it, and therefore, after having been for some time without it, on account of illness, I thought it better not to return to it. Every man is to judge for himself, according to the effects which he experiences. One of the fathers tells us, he found fasting made him so peevish that he did not practise it.'

Though he often enlarged upon the evil of intoxication, he was by no means harsh and unforgiving to those who indulged in occasional excess in wine. One of his friends, I well remember, came to sup at a tavern with him and some other gentlemen, and too plainly discovered that he had drunk too much at dinner. When one who loved mischief, thinking to produce a severe censure, asked Johnson, a few days afterwards, 'Well, Sir, what did your friend say to you, as an apology for being in such a situation?' Johnson answered, 'Sir, he said all that a man *should* say: he said he was sorry for it.'

I again visited him on Monday. He took occasion to enlarge, as he often did, upon the wretchedness of a sea-life. 'A ship is worse than a gaol. There is, in a gaol, better air, better company, better conveniency of every kind; and a ship has the additional disadvantage of being in danger. When men come to like a sea-life, they are not fit to live on land.'—'Then (said I) it would be cruel in a father to breed his son to the sea.' JOHNSON. 'It would be cruel in a father who thinks as I do. Men go to sea, before they know the unhappiness of that way of life; and when they have come to know it, they cannot escape from it, because it is then too late to choose another profession; as indeed is generally the case with men, when they have once engaged in any particular way of life.'

On Tuesday, March 19, which was fixed for our proposed jaunt, we met in the morning at the Somerset coffee-house in the Strand, where we were taken up by the Oxford coach. He was accompanied by Mr. Gwyn, the architect; and a gentleman of Merton College, whom we did not know, had the fourth seat. We soon got into conversation; for it was very remarkable of Johnson, that the presence of a stranger had no restraint upon his talk. I observed that Garrick, who was about to quit the stage, would soon have an easier life. JOHNSON. 'I doubt that, Sir.' BOSWELL. 'Why, Sir, he will be Atlas with the burthen off his back.' JOHNSON. 'But I know not, Sir, if he will be so steady without his load. However, he should never play any more, but be entirely the gentleman, and not partly the player: he should no longer subject himself to be hissed by a mob, or to be insolently treated by performers, whom he used to rule with a high hand, and who would gladly retaliate.' BOSWELL. 'I think he should play once a year for the benefit of decayed actors, as it has been said he means to do.' JOHNSON. 'Alas, Sir! he will soon be a decayed actor himself.'

Johnson expressed his disapprobation of ornamental architecture, such as magnificent columns supporting a portico, or expensive pilasters supporting merely their own capitals, 'because it consumes labour disproportionate to its utility.' For the same reason he satyrised statuary. 'Painting (said he) consumes labour not disproportionate to its effect; but a fellow will hack half a year at a block of marble to make something in stone that hardly resembles a man. The value of statuary is owing to its difficulty. You would not value the finest head cut upon a carrot.'

Gwyn was a fine lively rattling fellow. Dr. Johnson kept him in subjection, but with a kindly authority. The spirit of the artist, however, rose against what he thought a Gothick attack, and he made a brisk defence. 'What, Sir, will you allow no value to beauty in architecture or in statuary? Why should we allow it then in writing? Why do you take the trouble to give us so many fine allusions, and bright images, and elegant phrases? You might convey all your instruction without these ornaments.' Johnson smiled with complacency; but said, 'Why, Sir, all these ornaments are useful, because they obtain an easier reception for truth; but a building is not at all more convenient for being decorated with superfluous carved work.'

Gwyn at last was lucky enough to make one reply to Dr. Johnson, which he allowed to be excellent. Johnson censured him for taking down a church which might have stood many years, and building a new one at a different place, for no other reason but that there might be a direct road to a new bridge; and his expression was, 'You are taking a church out of the way, that the people may go in a straight line to the bridge.'—'No, Sir, (said Gwyn,) I am putting the church *in* the way, that the people may not *go out of the way*.' JOHNSON. (with a hearty loud laugh of approbation,) 'Speak no more. Rest your colloquial fame upon this.'

Upon our arrival at Oxford, Dr. Johnson and I went directly to University College, but were disappointed on finding that one of the fellows, his friend Mr. Scott, who accompanied him from Newcastle to Edinburgh, was gone to the country. We put up at the Angel inn, and passed the evening by ourselves in easy and familiar conversation. Talking of constitutional melancholy, he observed, 'A man so afflicted, Sir, must divert distressing thoughts, and not combat with them.' BOSWELL. 'May not he think them down, Sir?' JOHNSON. 'No, Sir. To attempt to *think them down* is madness. He should have a lamp constantly burning in his bed-chamber during the night, and if wakefully disturbed, take a book, and read, and compose himself to rest. To have the management of the mind is a great art, and it may be attained in a considerable degree by experience and habitual exercise.' BOSWELL. 'Should not he provide amusements for himself? Would it not, for instance, be right for him to take a course of chymistry?' JOHNSON. 'Let him take a course of chymistry, or a course of rope-dancing, or a course of any thing to which he is inclined at the time. Let him contrive to have as many retreats for his mind as he can, as many things to which it can fly from itself. Burton's *Anatomy of Melancholy* is a valuable work. It is, perhaps, overloaded with quotation. But there is great spirit and great power in what Burton says, when he writes from his own mind.'

Next morning we visited Dr. Wetherell, Master of University College, with whom Dr. Johnson conferred on the most advantageous mode of disposing of the books printed at the Clarendon press. I often had occasion to remark, Johnson loved business, loved to have his wisdom actually operate on real life.

We then went to Pembroke College, and waited on his old friend Dr. Adams, the master of it, whom I found to be a most polite, pleasing, communicative man. Before his advancement to the headship of his college, I had intended to go and visit him at Shrewsbury, where he was rector of St. Chad's, in order to get from him what particulars he could recollect of Johnson's academical life. He now obligingly gave me part of that authentick information, which, with what I afterwards owed to his kindness, will be found incorporated in its proper place in this work.

Dr. Adams told us, that in some of the Colleges at Oxford, the fellows had excluded the students from social intercourse with them in the common room. JOHNSON. 'They are in the right, Sir: there can be no real conversation, no fair exertion of mind amongst them, if the young men are by; for a man who has a character does not choose to stake it in their presence.' BOSWELL. 'But, Sir, may there not be very good conversation without a contest for superiority?' JOHNSON. 'No animated conversation, Sir, for it cannot be but one or other will come off superiour. I do not mean that the victor must have the better of the argument, for he may take the weak side; but his superiority of parts and knowledge will necessarily appear: and he to whom he thus shews himself superiour is lessened in the eyes of the young men.'

We walked with Dr. Adams into the master's garden, and into the common room. JOHNSON. (after a reverie of meditation,) 'Ay! Here I used to play at draughts with Phil. Jones and Fludyer. Jones loved beer, and did not get very forward in the church. Fludyer turned out a scoundrel, a Whig, and said he was ashamed of having been bred at Oxford. He had a living at Putney, and got under the eye of some retainers to the court at that time, and so became a violent Whig: but he had been a scoundrel all along to be sure.' BOSWELL. 'Was he a scoundrel, Sir, in any other way than that of being a political scoundrel? Did he cheat at draughts?' JOHNSON. 'Sir, we never played for *money*.'

He then carried me to visit Dr. Bentham, Canon of Christ-Church, and Divinity Professor, with whose learned and lively conversation we were much pleased. He gave us an invitation to dinner, which Dr. Johnson told me was a high honour. 'Sir, it is a great thing to dine with the Canons of Christ-Church.' We could not accept his invitation, as we were engaged to dine at University College. We had an excellent dinner there, with the Master and Fellows, it being St. Cuthbert's day, which is kept by them as a festival, as he was a saint of Durham, with which this college is much connected.

We drank tea with Dr. Horne, late President of Magdalen College, and Bishop of Norwich, of whose abilities, in different respects, the publick has had eminent proofs, and the esteem annexed to whose character was increased by knowing him personally.

We then went to Trinity College, where he introduced me to Mr. Thomas Warton, with whom we passed a part of the evening. We talked of biography—JOHNSON. 'It is rarely well executed. They only who live with a man can write his life with any genuine exactness and discrimination; and few people who have lived with a man know what to remark about him. The chaplain of a late Bishop, whom I was to assist in writing some memoirs of his Lordship, could tell me scarcely any thing.'

I said, Mr. Robert Dodsley's life should be written, as he had been so much connected with the wits of his time, and by his literary merit had raised himself from the station of a footman. Mr. Warton said, he had published a little volume under the title of *The Muse in Livery*. JOHNSON. 'I doubt whether Dodsley's brother would thank a man who should write his life: yet Dodsley himself was not unwilling that his original low condition should be recollected. When Lord Lyttelton's *Dialogues of the Dead* came out, one of which is between Apicius, an ancient epicure, and Dartineuf, a modern epicure, Dodsley said to me, "I knew Dartineuf well, for I was once his footman."'

I mentioned Sir Richard Steele having published his *Christian Hero*, with the avowed purpose of obliging himself to lead a religious life; yet, that his conduct was by no means strictly suitable. JOHNSON. 'Steele, I believe, practised the lighter vices.'

Mr. Warton, being engaged, could not sup with us at our inn; we had therefore another evening by ourselves. I asked Johnson, whether a man's being forward to make himself known to eminent people, and seeing as much of life, and getting as much information as he could in every way, was not yet lessening himself by his forwardness. JOHNSON. 'No, Sir, a man always makes himself greater as he increases his knowledge.

I censured some ludicrous fantastick dialogues between two coach-horses and other such stuff, which Baretti had lately published. He joined with me, and said, 'Nothing odd will do long. *Tristram Shandy* did not last.' I expressed a desire to be acquainted with a lady who had been much talked of, and universally celebrated for extraordinary address and insinuation. JOHNSON. 'Never believe extraordinary characters which you hear of people. Depend upon it, Sir, they are exaggerated. You do not see one man shoot a great deal higher than another.' I mentioned Mr. Burke. JOHNSON. 'Yes; Burke is an extraordinary man. His stream of mind is perpetual.' It is very pleasing to me to record, that Johnson's high estimation of the talents of this gentleman was uniform from their early acquaintance. Sir Joshua Reynolds informs me, that when Mr. Burke was first elected a member of Parliament, and Sir John Hawkins expressed a wonder at his attaining a seat, Johnson said, 'Now we who know Mr. Burke, know, that he will be one of the first men in this country.' And once, when Johnson was ill, and unable to exert himself as much as usual without fatigue, Mr. Burke having been mentioned, he said, 'That fellow calls forth all my powers. Were I to see Burke now it would kill me.' So much was he accustomed to consider conversation as a contest, and such was his notion of Burke as an opponent.

Next morning, Thursday, March 21, we set out in a post-chaise to pursue our ramble. It was a delightful day, and we rode through Blenheim park. When I looked at the magnificent bridge built by John Duke of Marlborough, over a small rivulet, and recollected the Epigram made upon it—

> 'The lofty arch his high ambition shows,
> The stream, an emblem of his bounty flows:'

and saw that now, by the genius of Brown, a magnificent body of water was collected, I said, 'They have *drowned* the Epigram.' I observed to him, while in the midst of the noble scene around us, 'You and I, Sir, have, I think, seen together the extremes of what can be seen in Britain:—the wild rough island of Mull, and Blenheim park.'

We dined at an excellent inn at Chapel-house, where he expatiated on the felicity of England in its taverns and inns, and triumphed over the French for not having, in any perfection, the tavern life. 'There is no private house, (said he,) in which people can enjoy themselves so well, as at a capital tavern. Let there be ever so great plenty of good things, ever so much grandeur, ever so much elegance, ever so much desire that every body should be easy; in the nature of things it cannot be: there must always be some degree of care and anxiety. The master of the house is anxious to entertain his guests; the guests are anxious to be agreeable to him: and no man, but a very impudent dog indeed, can as freely command what is in another man's house, as if it were his own. Whereas, at a tavern, there is a general freedom from anxiety. You are sure you are welcome: and the more noise you make, the more trouble you give, the more good things you call for, the welcomer you are. No servants will attend you with the alacrity which waiters do, who are incited by the prospect of an immediate reward, in proportion as they please. No, Sir; there is nothing which has yet been contrived by man, by which so much happiness is produced as by a good tavern or inn.'[35] He then repeated, with great emotion, Shenstone's lines:—

---

[35] Sir John Hawkins has preserved very few Memorabilia of Johnson. There is, however, to be found, in his bulky tome [p. 87], a very excellent one upon this subject:— 'In contradiction to those, who, having a wife and children, prefer domestick enjoyments to those which a tavern affords, I have heard him assert, *that a tavern chair was the throne of human felicity.*—As soon," said he, "as I enter the door of a tavern, I experience an oblivion of care, and a freedom from solicitude: when I am seated, I find

'Whoe'er has travell'd life's dull round,
  Where'er his stages may have been,
  May sigh to think he still has found
    The warmest welcome at an inn.'

In the afternoon, as we were driven rapidly along in the post-chaise, he said to me 'Life has not many things better than this.'

We stopped at Stratford-upon-Avon, and drank tea and coffee; and it pleased me to be with him upon the classick ground of Shakspeare's native place.

He spoke slightingly of Dyer's *Fleece.*—'The subject, Sir, cannot be made poetical. How can a man write poetically of serges and druggets? Yet you will hear many people talk to you gravely of that *excellent* poem, *The Fleece.*' Having talked of Grainger's *Sugar-Cane*, I mentioned to him Mr. Langton's having told me, that this poem, when read in manuscript at Sir Joshua Reynolds's, had made all the assembled wits burst into a laugh, when, after much blank-verse pomp, the poet began a new paragraph thus:—

'Now, Muse, let's sing of rats.'

And what increased the ridicule was, that one of the company, who slily overlooked the reader, perceived that the word had been originally *mice*, and had been altered to *rats*, as more dignified.

Johnson said, that Dr. Grainger was an agreeable man; a man who would do any good that was in his power. His translation of *Tibullus*, he thought, was very well done; but *The Sugar-Cane*, a poem, did not please him; for, he exclaimed, 'What could he make of a sugar-cane? One might as well write the "Parsley-bed, a Poem;" or "The Cabbage-garden, a Poem."' BOSWELL. 'You must then pickle your cabbage with the *sal atticum.*' JOHNSON. 'You know there is already *The Hop-Garden*, a Poem: and, I think, one could say a great deal about cabbage. The poem might begin with the advantages of civilized society over a rude state, exemplified by the Scotch, who had no cabbages till Oliver Cromwell's soldiers introduced them; and one might thus shew how arts are propagated by conquest, as they were by the Roman arms.' He seemed to be much diverted with the fertility of his own fancy.

I told him, that I heard Dr. Percy was writing the history of the wolf in Great-Britain. JOHNSON. 'The wolf, Sir! why the wolf? why does he not write of the bear, which we had formerly? Nay, it is said we

---

the master courteous, and the servants obsequious to my call; anxious to know and ready to supply my wants: wine there exhilarates my spirits, and prompts me to free conversation and an interchange of discourse with those whom I most love: I dogmatise and am contradicted, and in this conflict of opinions and sentiments I find delight."'—BOSWELL.

had the beaver. Or why does he not write of the grey rat, the Hanover rat, as it is called, because it is said to have come into this country about the time that the family of Hanover came? I should like to see *The History of the Grey Rat, by Thomas Percy, D. D., Chaplain in Ordinary to his Majesty,*' (laughing immoderately). BOSWELL. 'I am afraid a court chaplain could not decently write of the grey rat.' JOHNSON. 'Sir, he need not give it the name of the Hanover rat.' Thus could he indulge a luxuriant sportive imagination, when talking of a friend whom he loved and esteemed.

On Friday, March 22, having set out early from Henley, where we had lain the preceding night, we arrived at Birmingham about nine o'clock, and, after breakfast, went to call on his old schoolfellow Mr. Hector. A very stupid maid, who opened the door, told us, that 'her master was gone out; he was gone to the country; she could not tell when he would return.' In short, she gave us a miserable reception; and Johnson observed, 'She would have behaved no better to people who wanted him in the way of his profession.' He said to her, 'My name is Johnson; tell him I called. Will you remember the name?' She answered with rustick simplicity, in the Warwickshire pronunciation, 'I don't understand you, Sir.'—'Blockhead, (said he,) I'll write.' I never heard the word *blockhead* applied to a woman before, though I do not see why it should not, when there is evident occasion for it. He, however, made another attempt to make her understand him, and roared loud in her ear, '*Johnson*,' and then she catched the sound.

We next called on Mr. Lloyd, one of the people called Quakers. He too was not at home; but Mrs. Lloyd was, and received us courteously, and asked us to dinner. Johnson said to me, 'After the uncertainty of all human things at Hector's, this invitation came very well.' We walked about the town, and he was pleased to see it increasing.

Mr. Lloyd joined us in the street; and in a little while we met *Friend Hector*, as Mr. Lloyd called him. It gave me pleasure to observe the joy which Johnson and he expressed on seeing each other again. Mr. Lloyd and I left them together, while he obligingly shewed me some of the manufactures of this very curious assemblage of artificers. We all met at dinner at Mr. Lloyd's, where we were entertained with great hospitality. Mr. and Mrs. Lloyd had been married the same year with their Majesties, and like them, had been blessed with a numerous family of fine children, their numbers being exactly the same. Johnson said, 'Marriage is the best state for a man in general; and every man is a worse man, in proportion as he is unfit for the married state.'

Dr. Johnson said to me in the morning, 'You will see, Sir, at Mr. Hector's, his sister, Mrs. Careless, a clergyman's widow. She was the first woman with whom I was in love. It dropt out of my head imperceptibly; but she and I shall always have a kindness for each other.' He laughed at the notion that a man never can be really in love but once, and considered it as a mere romantick fancy.

On our return from Mr. Bolton's, Mr. Hector took me to his house, where we found Johnson sitting placidly at tea, with his *first love*; who, though now advanced in years, was a genteel woman, very agreeable, and well-bred.

Johnson lamented to Mr. Hector the state of one of their school-fellows, Mr. Charles Congreve, a clergyman, which he thus described: 'He obtained, I believe, considerable preferment in Ireland, but now lives in London, quite as a valetudinarian, afraid to go into any house but his own. He takes a short airing in his post-chaise every day. He has an elderly woman, whom he calls cousin, who lives with him, and jogs his elbow when his glass has stood too long empty, and encourages him in drinking, in which he is very willing to be encouraged; not that he gets drunk, for he is a very pious man, but he is always muddy. He confesses to one bottle of port every day, and he probably drinks more. He is quite unsocial; his conversation is quite monosyllabical: and when, at my last visit, I asked him what a clock it was? that signal of my departure had so pleasing an effect on him, that he sprung up to look at his watch, like a greyhound bounding at a hare.' When Johnson took leave of Mr. Hector, he said, 'Don't grow like Congreve; nor let me grow like him, when you are near me.'

When he again talked of Mrs. Careless to-night, he seemed to have had his affection revived; for he said, 'If I had married her, it might have been as happy for me.' BOSWELL. 'Pray, Sir, do you not suppose that there are fifty women in the world, with any one of whom a man may be as happy, as with any one woman in particular?' JOHNSON. 'Ay, Sir, fifty thousand.' BOSWELL. 'Then, Sir, you are not of opinion with some who imagine that certain men and certain women are made for each other; and that they cannot be happy if they miss their counterparts?' JOHNSON. 'To be sure not, Sir. I believe marriages would in general be as happy, and often more so, if they were all made by the Lord Chancellor, upon a due consideration of characters and circumstances, without the parties having any choice in the matter.'

I wished to have staid at Birmingham to-night, to have talked more with Mr. Hector; but my friend was impatient to reach his native city; so we drove on that stage in the dark, and were long pensive and silent. When we came within the focus of the Lichfield lamps, 'Now (said he,) we are getting out of a state of death.' We put up at the Three Crowns, not one of the great inns, but a good old fashioned one, which was kept by Mr. Wilkins, and was the very next house to that in which Johnson was born and brought up, and which was still his own property. We had a comfortable supper, and got into high spirits. I felt all my Toryism glow in this old capital of Staffordshire. I could have offered incense *genio loci*; and I indulged in libations of that ale, which Boniface, in *The Beaux Stratagem*, recommends with such an eloquent jollity.

Next morning he introduced me to Mrs. Lucy Porter, his step-daughter. She was now an old maid, with much simplicity of manner. She had never been in London. Her brother, a Captain in the navy, had left her a fortune of ten thousand pounds; about a third of which she had laid out in building a stately house, and making a handsome garden, in an elevated situation in Lichfield. Johnson, when here by himself, used to live at her house. She reverenced him, and he had a parental tenderness for her.

We then visited Mr. Peter Garrick, who had that morning received a letter from his brother David, announcing our coming to Lichfield. He was engaged to dinner, but asked us to tea, and to sleep at his house. Johnson, however, would not quit his old acquaintance Wilkins, of the Three Crowns. The family likeness of the Garricks was very striking; and Johnson thought that David's vivacity was not so peculiar to himself as was supposed. 'Sir, (said he,) I don't know but if Peter had cultivated all the arts of gaiety as much as David has done, he might have been as brisk and lively. Depend upon it, Sir, vivacity is much an art, and depends greatly on habit.' I believe there is a good deal of truth in this, notwithstanding a ludicrous story told me by a lady abroad, of a heavy German baron, who had lived much with the young English at Geneva, and was ambitious to be as lively as they; with which view, he, with assiduous exertion, was jumping over the tables and chairs in his lodgings; and when the people of the house ran in and asked, with surprize, what was the matter, he answered, '*Sh' apprens t'etre fif.*'

We dined at our inn, and had with us a Mr. Jackson, one of Johnson's schoolfellows, whom he treated with much kindness, though he seemed to be a low man, dull and untaught. He had a coarse grey coat, black waistcoat, greasy leather breeches, and a yellow uncurled wig; and his countenance had the ruddiness which betokens one who is in no haste to 'leave his can.' He drank only ale. He had tried to be a cutler at Birmingham, but had not succeeded; and now he lived poorly at home, and had some scheme of dressing leather in a better manner than common; to his indistinct account of which, Dr. Johnson listened with patient attention, that he might assist him with his advice. Here was an instance of genuine humanity and real kindness in this great man, who has been most unjustly represented as altogether harsh and destitute of tenderness. A thousand such instances might have been recorded in the course of his long life; though that his temper was warm and hasty, and his manner often rough, cannot be denied.

I saw here, for the first time, *oat ale*; and oat cakes not hard as in Scotland, but soft like a Yorkshire cake, were served at breakfast. It was pleasant to me to find, that *Oats*, the *food of horses*, were so much used as the *food of the people* in Dr. Johnson's own town. He expatiated in praise of Lichfield and its inhabitants, who, he said, were 'the most sober, decent people in England, the genteelest in proportion to their wealth, and spoke the purest English.' I doubted as to the last article of this eulogy: for they had several provincial sounds; as *there*, pronounced like *fear*, instead of like *fair*; *once* pronounced *woonse*, instead of *wunse*, or *wonse*. Johnson himself never got entirely free of those provincial accents. Garrick sometimes used to take him off, squeezing a lemon into a punch-bowl, with uncouth gesticulations, looking round the company, and calling out, 'Who's for *poonsh*?'

Very little business appeared to be going forward in Lichfield. I found however two strange manufactures for so inland a place, sail-cloth and streamers for ships; and I observed them making some saddle-cloths, and dressing sheepskins: but upon the whole, the busy hand of industry seemed to be quite slackened. 'Surely, Sir, (said I,) you are an idle set of people.' 'Sir, (said Johnson,) we are a city of philosophers, we work with our heads, and make the boobies of Birmingham work for us with their hands.'

There was at this time a company of players performing at Lichfield, The manager, Mr. Stanton, sent his compliments, and begged leave to wait on Dr. Johnson. Johnson received him very courteously, and he drank a glass of wine with us. He was a plain decent well-behaved man, and expressed his gratitude to Dr. Johnson for having once got him permission from Dr. Taylor at Ashbourne to play there upon moderate terms. Garrick's name was soon introduced. JOHNSON. 'Garrick's conversation is gay and grotesque. It is a dish of all sorts, but all good things. There is no solid meat in it: there is a want of sentiment in it. Not but that he has sentiment sometimes, and sentiment, too, very powerful and very pleasing: but it has not its full proportion in his conversation.'

When we were by ourselves he told me, 'Forty years ago, Sir, I was in love with an actress here, Mrs. Emmet, who acted Flora, in *Hob in the Well*.' What merit this lady had as an actress, or what was her figure, or her manner, I have not been informed: but, if we may believe Mr. Garrick, his old master's taste in theatrical merit was by no means refined; he was not an *elegans formarum spectator*. Garrick used to tell, that Johnson said of an actor, who played Sir Harry Wildair at Lichfield, 'There is a courtly vivacity about the fellow;' when in fact, according to Garrick's account, 'he was the most vulgar ruffian that ever went upon *boards*.'

We had promised Mr. Stanton to be at his theatre on Monday. Dr. Johnson jocularly proposed me to write a Prologue for the occasion: 'A Prologue, by James Boswell, Esq. from the Hebrides.' I was really inclined to take the hint. Methought, 'Prologue, spoken before Dr. Samuel Johnson, at Lichfield, 1776;' would have sounded as well as, 'Prologue, spoken before the Duke of York, at Oxford,' in Charles the Second's time. Much might have been said of what Lichfield had done for Shakspeare, by producing Johnson and Garrick. But I found he was averse to it.

We went and viewed the museum of Mr. Richard Green, apothecary here, who told me he was proud of being a relation of Dr. Johnson's. It was, truely, a wonderful collection, both of antiquities and natural curiosities, and ingenious works of art. He had all the articles accurately arranged, with their names upon labels, printed at his own little press; and on the staircase leading to it was a board, with the names of contributors marked in gold letters. A printed catalogue of the collection was to be had at a bookseller's. Johnson expressed his admiration of the activity and diligence and good fortune of Mr. Green, in getting together, in his situation, so great a variety of things; and Mr. Green told me that Johnson once said to him, 'Sir, I should as soon have thought of building a man of war, as of collecting such a museum.' Mr. Green's obliging alacrity in shewing it was very pleasing.

We drank tea and coffee at Mr. Peter Garrick's, where was Mrs. Aston, one of the maiden sisters of Mrs. Walmsley, wife of Johnson's first friend, and sister also of the lady of whom Johnson used to speak with the warmest admiration, by the name of Molly Aston, who was afterwards married to Captain Brodie of the navy.

On Sunday, March 24, we breakfasted with Mrs. Cobb, a widow lady, who lived in an agreeable sequestered place close by the town, called the Friary, it having been formerly a religious house. She and her niece, Miss Adey, were great admirers of Dr. Johnson; and he behaved to them with a kindness and easy pleasantry, such as we see between old and intimate acquaintance. He accompanied Mrs. Cobb to St. Mary's church, and I went to the cathedral, where I was very much delighted with the musick, finding it to be peculiarly solemn and accordant with the words of the service.

We dined at Mr. Peter Garrick's, who was in a very lively humour, and verified Johnson's saying, that if he had cultivated gaiety as much as his brother David, he might have equally excelled in it. He was to-day quite a London narrator, telling us a variety of anecdotes with that earnestness and attempt at mimicry which we usually find in the wits of the metropolis. Dr. Johnson went with me to the cathedral in the afternoon. It was grand and pleasing to contemplate this illustrious writer, now full of fame, worshipping in the 'solemn temple' of his native city.

I returned to tea and coffee at Mr. Peter Garrick's, and then found Dr. Johnson at the Reverend Mr. Seward's, Canon Residentiary, who inhabited the Bishop's palace, in which Mr. Walmsley lived, and which had been the scene of many happy hours in Johnson's early life.

On Monday, March 25, we breakfasted at Mrs. Lucy Porter's. Johnson had sent an express to Dr. Taylor's, acquainting him of our being at Lichfield, and Taylor had returned an answer that his postchaise should come for us this day. While we sat at breakfast, Dr. Johnson received a letter by the post, which seemed to agitate him very much. When he had read it, he exclaimed, 'One of the most dreadful things that has happened in my time.' The phrase *my time*, like the word *age*, is usually understood to refer to an event of a publick or general nature. I imagined something like an assassination of the King—like a gunpowder plot carried into execution—or like another fire of London. When asked, 'What is it, Sir?' he answered, 'Mr. Thrale has lost his only son!' This was, no doubt, a very great affliction to Mr. and Mrs. Thrale, which their friends would consider accordingly; but from the manner in which the intelligence of it was communicated by Johnson, it appeared for the moment to be comparatively small. I, however, soon felt a sincere concern, and was curious to observe, how Dr. Johnson would be affected. He said, 'This is a total extinction to their family, as much as if they were sold into captivity.' Upon my mentioning that Mr. Thrale had daughters, who might inherit his wealth;—'Daughters, (said Johnson, warmly,) he'll no more value his daughters than—' I was going to speak.—'Sir, (said he,) don't you know how you yourself think? Sir, he wishes to propagate his name.' In short, I saw male succession strong in his mind, even where there was no name, no family of any long standing. I said, it was lucky he was not present when this misfortune happened. JOHNSON. 'It is lucky for *me*. People in distress never think that you feel enough.' BOSWELL. 'And Sir, they will have the hope of seeing you, which will be a relief in the mean time; and when you get to them, the pain will be so far abated, that they will be capable of being consoled by you, which, in the first violence of it, I believe, would not be the case.' JOHNSON. 'No, Sir; violent pain of mind, like violent pain of body, *must* be severely felt.' BOSWELL. 'I own, Sir, I have not so much feeling for the distress of others, as some people have, or pretend to have: but I know this, that I would do all in my power to relieve them.' JOHNSON. 'Sir it is affectation to pretend to feel the distress of others, as much as they do themselves. It is equally so, as if one should pretend to feel as much pain while a friend's leg is cutting off, as he does. No, Sir; you have expressed the rational and just nature of sympathy. I would have gone to the extremity of the earth to have preserved this boy.'

He was soon quite calm. The letter was from Mr. Thrale's clerk, and concluded, 'I need not say how much they wish to see you in London.' He said, 'We shall hasten back from Taylor's.'

Mrs. Lucy Porter and some other ladies of the place talked a great deal of him when he was out of the room, not only with veneration but affection. It pleased me to find that he was so much *beloved* in his native city.

Mrs. Aston, whom I had seen the preceding night, and her sister, Mrs. Gastrel, a widow lady, had each a house and garden, and pleasure-ground, prettily situated upon Stowhill, a gentle eminence, adjoining to Lichfield. Johnson walked away to dinner there, leaving me by myself without any apology; I wondered at this want of that facility of manners, from which a man has no difficulty in carrying a friend to a house where he is intimate; I felt it very unpleasant to be thus left in solitude in a country town, where I was an entire stranger, and began to think myself unkindly deserted; but I was soon relieved, and convinced that my friend, instead of being deficient in delicacy, had conducted the matter with perfect propriety, for I received the following note in his handwriting: 'Mrs. Gastrel, at the lower house on Stowhill, desires Mr. Boswell's company to dinner at two.' I accepted of the invitation, and had here another proof how amiable his character was in the opinion of those who knew him best. I was not informed, till afterwards, that Mrs. Gastrel's husband was the clergyman who, while he lived at Stratford upon Avon, where he was proprietor of Shakspeare's garden, with Gothick barbarity cut down his mulberry-tree, and, as Dr. Johnson told me, did it to vex his neighbours. His lady, I have reason to believe, on the same authority, participated in the guilt of what the enthusiasts for our immortal bard deem almost a species of sacrilege.

After dinner Dr. Johnson wrote a letter to Mrs. Thrale on the death of her son. I said it would be very distressing to Thrale, but she would soon forget it, as she had so many things to think of. JOHNSON. 'No, Sir, Thrale will forget it first. *She* has many things that she *may* think of. *He* has many things that he *must* think of.' This was a very just remark upon the different effect of those light pursuits which occupy a vacant and easy mind, and those serious engagements which arrest attention, and keep us from brooding over grief.

In the evening we went to the Town-hall, which was converted into a temporary theatre, and saw *Theodosius*, with *The Stratford Jubilee*. I was happy to see Dr. Johnson sitting in a conspicuous part of the pit, and receiving affectionate homage from all his acquaintance. We were quite gay and merry. I afterwards mentioned to him that I condemned myself for being so, when poor Mr. and Mrs. Thrale were in such distress. JOHNSON. 'You are wrong, Sir; twenty years hence Mr. and Mrs. Thrale will not suffer much pain from the death of their son. Now, Sir, you are to consider, that distance of place, as well as distance of time, operates upon the human feelings. I would not have you be gay in the presence of the distressed, because it would shock them; but you may be gay at a distance. Pain for the loss of a friend, or of a relation whom we love, is occasioned by the want which we feel. In time the vacuity is filled with something else; or sometimes the vacuity closes up of itself.'

Mr. Seward and Mr. Pearson, another clergyman here, supt with us at our inn, and after they left us, we sat up late as we used to do in London.

Here I shall record some fragments of my friend's conversation during this jaunt.

'Marriage, Sir, is much more necessary to a man than to a woman; for he is much less able to supply himself with domestick comforts. You will recollect my saying to some ladies the other day, that I had often wondered why young women should marry, as they have so much more freedom, and so much more attention paid to them while unmarried, than when married. I indeed did not mention the *strong* reason for their marrying—the *mechanical* reason.' BOSWELL. 'Why, that *is* a strong one. But does not imagination make it much more important than it is in reality? Is it not, to a certain degree, a delusion in us as well as in women?' JOHNSON. 'Why yes, Sir; but it is a delusion that is always beginning again.' BOSWELL. 'I don't know but there is upon the whole more misery than happiness produced by that passion.' JOHNSON. 'I don't think so, Sir.'

'Never speak of a man in his own presence. It is always indelicate, and may be offensive.'

'Questioning is not the mode of conversation among gentlemen. It is assuming a superiority, and it is particularly wrong to question a man concerning himself. There may be parts of his former life which he may not wish to be made known to other persons, or even brought to his own recollection.'

'A man should be careful never to tell tales of himself to his own disadvantage. People may be amused and laugh at the time, but they will be remembered, and brought out against him upon some subsequent occasion.'

'Much may be done if a man puts his whole mind to a particular object. By doing so, Norton has made himself the great lawyer that he is allowed to be.'

On Tuesday, March 26, there came for us an equipage properly suited to a wealthy well-beneficed clergyman;—Dr. Taylor's large roomy post-chaise, drawn by four stout plump horses, and driven by two steady jolly postillions, which conveyed us to Ashbourne; where I found my friend's schoolfellow living upon an establishment perfectly corresponding with his substantial creditable equipage: his house, garden, pleasure-grounds, table, in short every thing good, and no scantiness appearing. Every man should form such a plan of living as he can execute completely. Let him not draw an outline wider than he can fill up. I have seen many skeletons of shew and magnificence which excite at once ridicule and pity. Dr. Taylor had a good estate of his own, and good preferment in the church, being a prebendary of Westminster, and rector of Bosworth. He was a diligent justice of the peace, and presided over the town of Ashbourne, to the inhabitants of which I was told he was very liberal; and as a proof of this it was mentioned to me, he had the preceding winter distributed two hundred pounds among such of them as stood in need of his assistance. He had consequently a considerable political interest in the county of Derby, which he employed to support the Devonshire family; for though the schoolfellow and friend of Johnson, he was a Whig. I could not perceive in his character much congeniality of any sort with that of Johnson, who, however, said to me, 'Sir, he has a very strong understanding.' His size, and figure, and countenance, and manner, were that of a hearty English 'Squire, with the parson super-induced: and I took particular notice of his upper servant, Mr. Peters, a decent grave man, in purple clothes, and a large white wig, like the butler or *major domo* of a Bishop.

Dr. Johnson and Dr. Taylor met with great cordiality; and Johnson soon gave him the same sad account of their school-fellow, Congreve, that he had given to Mr. Hector; adding a remark of such moment to the rational conduct of a man in the decline of life, that it deserves to be imprinted upon every mind: 'There is nothing against which an old man should be so much upon his guard as putting himself to nurse. Innumerable have been the melancholy instances of men once distinguished for firmness, resolution, and spirit, who in their latter days have been governed like children, by interested female artifice.

Dr. Taylor commended a physician who was known to him and Dr. Johnson, and said, 'I fight many battles for him, as many people in the country dislike him.' JOHNSON. 'But you should consider, Sir, that by every one of your victories he is a loser; for, every man of whom you get the better, will be very angry, and resolve not to employ him; whereas if people get the better of you in argument about him, they'll think, "We'll send for Dr. ****** nevertheless."' This was an observation deep and sure in human nature.

Next day, as Dr. Johnson had acquainted Dr. Taylor of the reason for his returning speedily to London, it was resolved that we should set out after dinner. A few of Dr. Taylor's neighbours were his guests that day.

Dr. Johnson talked with approbation of one who had attained to the state of the philosophical wise man, that is to have no want of any thing. 'Then, Sir, (said I,) the savage is a wise man.' 'Sir, (said he,) I do not mean simply being without,—but not having a want.' I maintained, against this proposition, that it was better to have fine clothes, for instance, than not to feel the want of them. JOHNSON. 'No, Sir; fine clothes are good only as they supply the want of other means of procuring respect. Was Charles the Twelfth, think you, less respected for his coarse blue coat and black stock? And you find the King of Prussia dresses plain, because the dignity of his character is sufficient.' I here brought myself into a scrape, for I heedlessly said, 'Would not *you*, Sir, be the better for velvet and embroidery?' JOHNSON. 'Sir, you put an end to all argument when you introduce your opponent himself.

no better manners? There is *your want.*' I apologised by
ad mentioned him as an instance of one who wanted as little
an in the world, and yet, perhaps, might receive some
lustre from dress.

ig left Ashbourne in the evening, we stopped to change
horses at Derby, and availed ourselves of a moment to enjoy the
conversation of my countryman, Dr. Butter, then physician there. He
was in great indignation because Lord Mountstuart's bill for a Scotch
militia had been lost. Dr. Johnson was as violent against it. 'I am glad,
(said he,) that Parliament has had the spirit to throw it out. You wanted
to take advantage of the timidity of our scoundrels;' (meaning, I
suppose, the ministry). It may be observed, that he used the epithet
scoundrel very commonly not quite in the sense in which it is generally
understood, but as a strong term of disapprobation; as when he abruptly
answered Mrs. Thrale, who had asked him how he did, 'Ready to
become a scoundrel, Madam; with a little more spoiling you will, I
think, make me a complete rascal:' he meant, easy to become a
capricious and self-indulgent valetudinarian; a character for which I
have heard him express great disgust. We lay this night at
Loughborough.

On Thursday, March 28, we pursued our journey. He said, 'It is
commonly a weak man who marries for love.' We then talked of
marrying women of fortune; and I mentioned a common remark, that a
man may be, upon the whole, richer by marrying a woman with a very
small portion, because a woman of fortune will be proportionally
expensive; whereas a woman who brings none will be very moderate in
expenses. JOHNSON. 'Depend upon it, Sir, this is not true. A woman of
fortune being used to the handling of money, spends it judiciously: but
a woman who gets the command of money for the first time upon her
marriage, has such a gust in spending it, that she throws it away with
great profusion.'

He praised the ladies of the present age, insisting that they were
more faithful to their husbands, and more virtuous in every respect,
than in former times, because their understandings were better
cultivated.

At Leicester we read in the news-paper that Dr. James was dead. I
thought that the death of an old school-fellow, and one with whom he
had lived a good deal in London, would have affected my fellow-
traveller much: but he only said, Ah! poor Jamy.' Afterwards, however,
when we were in the chaise, he said, with more tenderness, 'Since I set
out on this jaunt, I have lost an old friend and a young one;—Dr.
James, and poor Harry.' (Meaning Mr. Thrale's son.)

I enjoyed the luxury of our approach to London, that metropolis
which we both loved so much, for the high and varied intellectual
pleasure which it furnishes. I experienced immediate happiness while

whirled along with such a companion, and said to him, 'Sir, you observed one day at General Oglethorpe's, that a man is never happy for the present, but when he is drunk. Will you not add,—or when driving rapidly in a post-chaise?' JOHNSON. 'No, Sir, you are driving rapidly *from* something, or *to* something.'

Talking of melancholy, he said, 'Some men, and very thinking men too, have not those vexing thoughts. Sir Joshua Reynolds is the same all the year round. Beauclerk, except when ill and in pain, is the same. But I believe most men have them in the degree in which they are capable of having them. If I were in the country, and were distressed by that malady, I would force myself to take a book; and every time I did it I should find it the easier. Melancholy, indeed, should be diverted by every means but drinking.'

We stopped at Messieurs Dillys, booksellers in the Poultry; from whence he hurried away, in a hackney coach, to Mr. Thrale's, in the Borough. I called at his house in the evening, having promised to acquaint Mrs. Williams of his safe return; when, to my surprize, I found him sitting with her at tea, and, as I thought, not in a very good humour: for, it seems, when he had got to Mr. Thrale's, he found the coach was at the door waiting to carry Mrs. and Miss Thrale, and Signor Baretti, their Italian master, to Bath. This was not shewing the attention which might have been expected to the 'Guide, Philosopher, and Friend,' the *Imlac* who had hastened from the country to console a distressed mother, who he understood was very anxious for his return. They had, I found, without ceremony, proceeded on their intended journey. I was glad to understand from him that it was still resolved that his tour to Italy with Mr. and Mrs. Thrale should take place, of which he had entertained some doubt, on account of the loss which they had suffered; and his doubts afterwards proved to be well-founded. He observed, indeed very justly, that 'their loss was an additional reason for their going abroad; and if it had not been fixed that he should have been one of the party, he would force them out; but he would not advise them unless his advice was asked, lest they might suspect that he recommended what he wished on his own account.' I was not pleased that his intimacy with Mr. Thrale's family, though it no doubt contributed much to his comfort and enjoyment, was not without some degree of restraint: not, as has been grossly suggested, that it was required of him as a task to talk for the entertainment of them and their company; but that he was not quite at his ease; which, however, might partly be owing to his own honest pride—that dignity of mind which is always jealous of appearing too compliant.

On Sunday, March 31, I called on him, and shewed him as a curiosity which I had discovered, his *Translation of Lobo's Account of Abyssinia*, which Sir John Pringle had lent me, it being then little known as one of his works. He said, 'Take no notice of it,' or 'don't talk of it.' He seemed to think it beneath him, though done at six-and-twenty. I said to him, 'Your style, Sir, is much improved since you translated this.' He answered with a sort of triumphant smile, 'Sir, I hope it is.'

On Wednesday, April 3, in the morning I found him very busy putting his books in order, and as they were generally very old ones, clouds of dust were flying around him. He had on a pair of large gloves such as hedgers use. His present appearance put me in mind of my uncle, Dr. Boswell's description of him, 'A robust genius, born to grapple with whole libraries.'

He had been in company with Omai, a native of one of the South Sea Islands, after he had been some time in this country. He was struck with the elegance of his behaviour, and accounted for it thus: 'Sir, he had passed his time, while in England, only in the best company; so that all that he had acquired of our manners was genteel. As a proof of this, Sir, Lord Mulgrave and he dined one day at Streatham; they sat with their backs to the light fronting me, so that I could not see distinctly; and there was so little of the savage in Omai, that I was afraid to speak to either, lest I should mistake one for the other.'

We agreed to dine to-day at the Mitre-tavern after the rising of the House of Lords, where a branch of the litigation concerning the Douglas Estate, in which I was one of the counsel, was to come on.

I introduced the topick, which is often ignorantly urged, that the Universities of England are too rich; so that learning does not flourish in them as it would do, if those who teach had smaller salaries, and depended on their assiduity for a great part of their income. JOHNSON. 'Sir, the very reverse of this is the truth; the English Universities are not rich enough. Our fellowships are only sufficient to support a man during his studies to fit him for the world, and accordingly in general they are held no longer than till an opportunity offers of getting away. Now and then, perhaps, there is a fellow who grows old in his college; but this is against his will, unless he be a man very indolent indeed. A hundred a year is reckoned a good fellowship, and that is no more than is necessary to keep a man decently as a scholar. We do not allow our fellows to marry, because we consider academical institutions as preparatory to a settlement in the world. It is only by being employed as a tutor, that a fellow can obtain any thing more than a livelihood. To be sure a man, who has enough without teaching, will probably not teach; for we would all be idle if we could. In the same manner, a man who is to get nothing by teaching, will not exert himself. Gresham College was intended as a place of instruction for London; able professors were to read lectures gratis, they contrived to have no scholars; whereas, if they had been allowed to receive but sixpence a lecture from each scholar, they would have been emulous to have had many scholars. Every body will agree that it should be the interest of those who teach to have scholars and this is the case in our Universities. That they are too rich is certainly not true; for they have nothing good enough to keep a man of eminent learning with them for his life. In the foreign Universities a professorship is a high thing. It is as much almost as a man can make by his learning; and therefore we find the most learned men abroad are in the Universities. It is not so with us. Our Universities are impoverished of learning, by the penury of their provisions. I wish there were many places of a thousand a-year at Oxford, to keep first-rate men of learning from quitting the University.'

I mentioned Mr. Maclaurin's uneasiness on account of a degree of ridicule carelessly thrown on his deceased father, in Goldsmith's *History of Animated Nature*, in which that celebrated mathematician is represented as being subject to fits of yawning so violent as to render him incapable of proceeding in his lecture; a story altogether unfounded, but for the publication of which the law would give no reparation. This led us to agitate the question, whether legal redress could be obtained, even when a man's deceased relation was calumniated in a publication.

On Friday, April 5, being Good Friday, after having attended the morning service at St. Clement's Church, I walked home with Johnson. We talked of the Roman Catholick religion. JOHNSON. 'In the barbarous ages, Sir, priests and people were equally deceived; but afterwards there were gross corruptions introduced by the clergy, such as indulgencies to priests to have concubines, and the worship of images, not, indeed, inculcated, but knowingly permitted.' He strongly censured the licensed stews at Rome. BOSWELL. 'So then, Sir, you would allow of no irregular intercourse whatever between the sexes?' JOHNSON. 'To be sure I would not, Sir. I would punish it much more than it is done, and so restrain it. In all countries there has been fornication, as in all countries there has been theft; but there may be more or less of the one, as well as of the other, in proportion to the force of law. All men will naturally commit fornication, as all men will naturally steal. And, Sir, it is very absurd to argue, as has been often done, that prostitutes are necessary to prevent the violent effects of appetite from violating the decent order of life; nay, should be permitted, in order to preserve the chastity of our wives and daughters. Depend upon it, Sir, severe laws, steadily enforced, would be sufficient against those evils, and would promote marriage.'

Mr. Thrale called upon him, and appeared to bear the loss of his son with a manly composure. There was no affectation about him; and he talked, as usual, upon indifferent subjects. He seemed to me to hesitate as to the intended Italian tour, on which, I flattered myself, he and Mrs. Thrale and Dr. Johnson were soon to set out; and, therefore, I pressed it as much as I could. I mentioned, that Mr. Beauclerk had said, that Baretti, whom they were to carry with them, would keep them so long in the little towns of his own district, that they would not have time to see Rome. I mentioned this, to put them on their guard. JOHNSON. 'Sir, we do not thank Mr. Beauclerk for supposing that we are to be directed by Baretti. No, Sir; Mr. Thrale is to go, by my advice, to Mr. Jackson, (the all-knowing) and get from him a plan for seeing the most that can be seen in the time that we have to travel. We must, to be sure, see Rome, Naples, Florence, and Venice, and as much more as we can.' (Speaking with a tone of animation.)

When I expressed an earnest wish for his remarks on Italy, he said, 'I do not see that I could make a book upon Italy; yet I should be glad to get two hundred pounds, or five hundred pounds, by such a work.' This shewed both that a journal of his Tour upon the Continent was not wholly out of his contemplation, and that he uniformly adhered to that strange opinion, which his indolent disposition made him utter: 'No man but a blockhead ever wrote, except for money.' Numerous instances to refute this will occur to all who are versed in the history of literature.

He gave us one of the many sketches of character which were treasured in his mind, and which he was wont to produce quite unexpectedly in a very entertaining manner. 'I lately, (said he,) received a letter from the East Indies, from a gentleman whom I formerly knew very well; he had returned from that country with a handsome fortune, as it was reckoned, before means were found to acquire those immense sums which have been brought from thence of late; he was a scholar, and an agreeable man, and lived very prettily in London, till his wife died. After her death, he took to dissipation and gaming, and lost all he had. One evening he lost a thousand pounds to a gentleman whose name I am sorry I have forgotten. Next morning he sent the gentleman five hundred pounds, with an apology that it was all he had in the world. The gentleman sent the money back to him, declaring he would not accept of it; and adding, that if Mr.————had occasion for five hundred pounds more, he would lend it to him. He resolved to go out again to the East Indies, and make his fortune anew. He got a considerable appointment, and I had some intention of accompanying him. Had I thought then as I do now, I should have gone: but, at that time, I had objections to quitting England.'

It was a very remarkable circumstance about Johnson, whom shallow observers have supposed to have been ignorant of the world, that very few men had seen greater variety of characters; and none could observe them better, as was evident from the strong, yet nice portraits which he often drew. I have frequently thought that if he had made out what the French call *une catalogue raisonnée* of all the people who had passed under his observation, it would have afforded a very rich fund of instruction and entertainment. The suddenness with which his accounts of some of them started out in conversation, was not less pleasing than surprizing. I remember he once observed to me, 'It is wonderful, Sir, what is to be found in London. The most literary conversation that I ever enjoyed, was at the table of Jack Ellis, a money-scrivener behind the Royal Exchange, with whom I at one period used to dine generally once a week.'

Volumes would be required to contain a list of his numerous and various acquaintance, none of whom he ever forgot; and could describe and discriminate them all with precision and vivacity. He associated with persons the most widely different in manners, abilities, rank, and accomplishments. He was at once the companion of the brilliant Colonel Forrester of the Guards, who wrote *The Polite Philosopher*, and of the aukward and uncouth Robert Levet; of Lord Thurlow, and Mr. Sastres, the Italian master; and has dined one day with the beautiful, gay, and fascinating Lady Craven, and the next with good Mrs. Gardiner, the tallow-chandler, on Snow-hill.

On my expressing my wonder at his discovering so much of the knowledge peculiar to different professions, he told me, 'I learnt what I know of law, chiefly from Mr. Ballow, a very able man. I learnt some, too, from Chambers; but was not so teachable then. One is not willing to be taught by a young man.' When I expressed a wish to know more about Mr. Ballow, Johnson said, 'Sir, I have seen him but once these twenty years. The tide of life has driven us different ways.' I was sorry at the time to hear this; but whoever quits the creeks of private connections, and fairly gets into the great ocean of London, will, by imperceptible degrees, unavoidably experience such cessations of acquaintance.

'My knowledge of physick, (he added,) I learnt from Dr. James, whom I helped in writing the proposals for his *Dictionary* and also a little in the *Dictionary* itself. I also learnt from Dr. Lawrence, but was then grown more stubborn.'

A curious incident happened to-day, while Mr. Thrale and I sat with him. Francis announced that a large packet was brought to him from the post-office, said to have come from Lisbon, and it was charged *seven pounds ten shillings*. He would not receive it, supposing it to be some trick, nor did he even look at it. But upon enquiry afterwards he found that it was a real packet for him, from that very friend in the East Indies of whom he had been speaking; and the ship which carried it having come to Portugal, this packet, with others, had been put into the post-office at Lisbon.

I mentioned a new gaming-club, of which Mr. Beauclerk had given me an account, where the members played to a desperate extent. JOHNSON. 'Depend upon it, Sir, this is mere talk. *Who* is ruined by gaming? You will not find six instances in an age. There is a strange rout made about deep play: whereas you have many more people ruined

by adventurous trade, and yet we do not hear such an outcry against it.'
THRALE. 'There may be few people absolutely ruined by deep play; but
very many are much hurt in their circumstances by it.' JOHNSON. 'Yes,
Sir, and so are very many by other kinds of expence.' I had heard him
talk once before in the same manner; and at Oxford he said, 'he wished
he had learnt to play at cards.' The truth, however, is, that he loved to
display his ingenuity in argument; and therefore would sometimes in
conversation maintain opinions which he was sensible were wrong, but
in supporting which, his reasoning and wit would be most conspicuous.
He would begin thus: 'Why, Sir, as to the good or evil of card-
playing—' 'Now, (said Garrick,) he is thinking which side he shall
take.' He appeared to have a pleasure in contradiction, especially when
any opinion whatever was delivered with an air of confidence; so that
there was hardly any topick, if not one of the great truths of Religion
and Morality, that he might not have been incited to argue, either for or
against. Lord Elibank had the highest admiration of his powers. He
once observed to me, 'Whatever opinion Johnson maintains, I will not
say that he convinces me; but he never fails to shew me, that he has
good reasons for it.' I have heard Johnson pay his Lordship this high
compliment: 'I never was in Lord Elibank's company without learning
something.'

We sat together till it was too late for the afternoon service. Thrale
said he had come with intention to go to church with us. We went at
seven to evening prayers at St. Clement's church, after having drank
coffee; an indulgence, which I understood Johnson yielded to on this
occasion, in compliment to Thrale.

On Sunday, April 7, Easter-day, after having been at St. Paul's
Cathedral, I came to Dr. Johnson, according to my usual custom. It
seemed to me, that there was always something peculiarly mild and
placid in his manner upon this holy festival, the commemoration of the
most joyful event in the history of our world, the resurrection of our
LORD and SAVIOUR, who, having triumphed over death and the grave,
proclaimed immortality to mankind.

I repeated to him an argument of a lady of my acquaintance, who
maintained, that her husband's having been guilty of numberless
infidelities, released her from conjugal obligations, because they were
reciprocal. JOHNSON. 'This is miserable stuff, Sir. To the contract of
marriage, besides the man and wife, there is a third party—Society; and
if it be considered as a vow—GOD: and, therefore, it cannot be
dissolved by their consent alone. Laws are not made for particular
cases, but for men in general. A woman may be unhappy with her
husband; but she cannot be freed from him without the approbation of
the civil and ecclesiastical power. A man may be unhappy, because he
is not so rich as another; but he is not to seize upon another's property
with his own hand.' BOSWELL. 'But, Sir, this lady does not want that

the contract should be dissolved; she only argues that she may indulge herself in gallantries with equal freedom as her husband does, provided she takes care not to introduce a spurious issue into his family. You know, Sir, what Macrobius has told us of Julia.' JOHNSON. 'This lady of yours, Sir, I think, is very fit for a brothel.'

Mr. Macbean, authour of the *Dictionary of ancient Geography*, came in. He mentioned that he had been forty years absent from Scotland. 'Ah, Boswell! (said Johnson, smiling,) what would you give to be forty years from Scotland?' I said, 'I should not like to be so long absent from the seat of my ancestors.' This gentleman, Mrs. Williams, and Mr. Levet, dined with us.

Mrs. Williams was very peevish; and I wondered at Johnson's patience with her now, as I had often done on similar occasions. The truth is, that his humane consideration of the forlorn and indigent state in which this lady was left by her father, induced him to treat her with the utmost tenderness, and even to be desirous of procuring her amusement, so as sometimes to incommode many of his friends, by carrying her with him to their houses, where, from her manner of eating, in consequence of her blindness, she could not but offend the delicacy of persons of nice sensations.

After coffee, we went to afternoon service in St. Clement's church. Observing some beggars in the street as we walked along, I said to him I supposed there was no civilized country in the world, where the misery of want in the lowest classes of the people was prevented. JOHNSON. 'I believe, Sir, there is not; but it is better that some should be unhappy, than that none should be happy, which would be the case in a general state of equality.'

When the service was ended, I went home with him, and we sat quietly by ourselves.

Upon the question whether a man who had been guilty of vicious actions would do well to force himself into solitude and sadness; JOHNSON. 'No, Sir, unless it prevent him from being vicious again. With some people, gloomy penitence is only madness turned upside down. A man may be gloomy, till, in order to be relieved from gloom, he has recourse again to criminal indulgencies.'

On Wednesday, April 10, I dined with him at Mr. Thrale's, where were Mr. Murphy and some other company. Before dinner, Dr. Johnson and I passed some time by ourselves. I was sorry to find it was now resolved that the proposed journey to Italy should not take place this year. He said, 'I am disappointed, to be sure; but it is not a great disappointment.' I wondered to see him bear, with a philosophical calmness, what would have made most people peevish and fretful. I perceived, however, that he had so warmly cherished the hope of enjoying classical scenes, that he could not easily part with the scheme; for he said: 'I shall probably contrive to get to Italy some other way.

But I won't mention it to Mr. and Mrs. Thrale, as it might vex them.' I suggested, that going to Italy might have done Mr. and Mrs. Thrale good. JOHNSON. 'I rather believe not, Sir. While grief is fresh, every attempt to divert only irritates. You must wait till grief be *digested*, and then amusement will dissipate the remains of it.'

I said, I disliked the custom which some people had of bringing their children into company, because it in a manner forced us to pay foolish compliments to please their parents. JOHNSON. 'You are right, Sir. We may be excused for not caring much about other people's children, for there are many who care very little about their own children. It may be observed, that men, who from being engaged in business, or from their course of life in whatever way, seldom see their children, do not care much about them. I myself should not have had much fondness for a child of my own.' MRS. THRALE. 'Nay, Sir, how can you talk so?' JOHNSON. 'At least, I never wished to have a child.'

He talked of Lord Lyttelton's extreme anxiety as an authour; observing, that 'he was thirty years in preparing his *History*, and that he employed a man to point it for him; as if (laughing) another man could point his sense better than himself.' Mr. Murphy said, he understood his history was kept back several years for fear of Smollet. JOHNSON. 'This seems strange to Murphy and me, who never felt that anxiety, but sent what we wrote to the press, and let it take its chance.' MRS. THRALE. 'The time has been, Sir, when you felt it.' JOHNSON. 'Why, really, Madam, I do not recollect a time when that was the case.'

On Thursday, April 11, I dined with him at General Paoli's, in whose house I now resided, and where I had ever afterwards the honour of being entertained with the kindest attention as his constant guest, while I was in London, till I had a house of my own there. I mentioned my having that morning introduced to Mr. Garrick, Count Neni, a Flemish Nobleman of great rank and fortune, to whom Garrick talked of Abel Drugger as *a small part*; and related, with pleasant vanity, that a Frenchman who had seen him in one of his low characters, exclaimed, '*Comment! je ne le crois pas. Ce n'est pas Monsieur Garrick, ce Grand Homme!*' Garrick added, with an appearance of grave recollection, 'If I were to begin life again, I think I should not play those low characters.' Upon which I observed, 'Sir, you would be in the wrong; for your great excellence is your variety of playing, your representing so well, characters so very different.' JOHNSON. 'Garrick, Sir, was not in earnest in what he said; for, to be sure, his peculiar excellence is his variety; and, perhaps, there is not any one character which has not been as well acted by somebody else, as he could do it.' BOSWELL. 'Why then, Sir, did he talk so?' JOHNSON. 'Why, Sir, to make you answer as you did.' BOSWELL. 'I don't know, Sir; he seemed to dip deep into his mind for the reflection.' JOHNSON. 'He had not far to dip, Sir: he said the same thing, probably, twenty times before.'

Of a nobleman raised at a very early period to high office, he said, 'His parts, Sir, are pretty well for a Lord; but would not be distinguished in a man who had nothing else but his parts.'

A journey to Italy was still in his thoughts. He said, 'A man who has not been in Italy, is always conscious of an inferiority, from his not having seen what it is expected a man should see. The grand object of travelling is to see the shores of the Mediterranean. On those shores were the four great Empires of the world; the Assyrian, the Persian, the Grecian, and the Roman.—All our religion, almost all our law, almost all our arts, almost all that sets us above savages, has come to us from the shores of the Mediterranean.' The General observed, that 'THE MEDITERRANEAN would be a noble subject for a poem.'

We talked of translation. I said, I could not define it, nor could I think of a similitude to illustrate it; but that it appeared to me the translation of poetry could be only imitation. JOHNSON. 'You may translate books of science exactly. You may also translate history, in so far as it is not embellished with oratory, which is poetical. Poetry, indeed, cannot be translated; and, therefore, it is the poets that preserve languages; for we would not be at the trouble to learn a language, if we could have all that is written in it just as well in a translation. But as the beauties of poetry cannot be preserved in any language except that in which it was originally written, we learn the language.'

'Goldsmith (he said,) referred every thing to vanity; his virtues, and his vices too, were from that motive. He was not a social man. He never exchanged mind with you.'

We spent the evening at Mr. Hoole's. Mr. Mickle, the excellent translator of *The Lusiad*, was there. I have preserved little of the conversation of this evening. Dr. Johnson said, 'Thomson had a true poetical genius, the power of viewing every thing in a poetical light. His fault is such a cloud of words sometimes, that the sense can hardly peep through. Shiels, who compiled *Cibber's Lives of the Poets*, was one day sitting with me. I took down Thomson, and read aloud a large portion of him, and then asked,—Is not this fine? Shiels having expressed the highest admiration. Well, Sir, (said I,) I have omitted every other line.'

I related a dispute between Goldsmith and Mr. Robert Dodsley, one day when they and I were dining at Tom Davies's, in 1762. Goldsmith asserted, that there was no poetry produced in this age. Dodsley appealed to his own *Collection*, and maintained, that though you could not find a palace like Dryden's *Ode on St. Cecilia's Day*, you had villages composed of very pretty houses; and he mentioned particularly *The Spleen*. JOHNSON. 'I think Dodsley gave up the question. He and Goldsmith said the same thing; only he said it in a softer manner than Goldsmith did; for he acknowledged that there was no poetry, nothing that towered above the common mark. You may find wit and humour in verse, and yet no poetry. *Hudibras* has a profusion of these; yet it is not to be reckoned a poem. *The Spleen*, in Dodsley's Collection, on which you say he chiefly rested, is not poetry.' BOSWELL. 'Does not Gray's poetry, Sir, tower above the common mark?' JOHNSON. Yes, Sir; but we must attend to the difference between what men in general cannot do if they would, and what every man may do if he would. Sixteen-string Jack[36] towered above the common mark.' BOSWELL. 'Then, Sir, what is poetry?' JOHNSON. 'Why, Sir, it is much easier to say what it is not. We all *know* what light is; but it is not easy to *tell* what it is.'

On Friday, April 12, I dined with him at our friend Tom Davies's. He reminded Dr. Johnson of Mr. Murphy's having paid him the highest compliment that ever was paid to a layman, by asking his pardon for repeating some oaths in the course of telling a story.

Johnson and I supt this evening at the Crown and Anchor tavern, in company with Sir Joshua Reynolds, Mr. Langton, Mr. Nairne, now one of the Scotch Judges, with the title of Lord Dunsinan, and my very worthy friend, Sir William Forbes, of Pitsligo.

We discussed the question whether drinking improved conversation and benevolence. Sir Joshua maintained it did. JOHNSON. 'No, Sir: before dinner men meet with great inequality of understanding; and those who are conscious of their inferiority, have the modesty not to talk. When they have drunk wine, every man feels himself happy, and loses that modesty, and grows impudent and vociferous: but he is not improved; he is only not sensible of his defects.' Sir Joshua said the Doctor was talking of the effects of excess in wine; but that a moderate glass enlivened the mind, by giving a proper circulation to the blood. 'I am (said he,) in very good spirits, when I get up in the morning. By dinner-time I am exhausted; wine puts me in the same state as when I got up; and I am sure that moderate drinking makes people talk better.' JOHNSON. 'No, Sir; wine gives not light, gay, ideal hilarity; but tumultuous, noisy, clamorous merriment. I have heard none of those drunken,—nay, drunken is a coarse word,— none of those *vinous* flights.' SIR JOSHUA. 'Because you have sat by, quite sober, and felt an envy of the happiness of those who were drinking.' JOHNSON. 'Perhaps, contempt.—And, Sir, it is not necessary to be drunk one's self, to relish the wit of drunkenness. Do we not judge of the drunken wit, of the dialogue between Iago and Cassio, the most excellent in its kind, when we are quite sober? Wit is wit, by whatever means it is produced; and, if good, will appear so at all times. I admit that the spirits are raised by drinking, as by the common

---

[36] A noted highwayman, who after having been several times tried and acquitted, was at last hanged. He was remarkable for foppery in his dress, and particularly for wearing a bunch of sixteen strings at the knees of his breeches.—BOSWELL.

participation of any pleasure: cock-fighting, or bear-baiting, will raise the spirits of a company, as drinking does, though surely they will not improve conversation. I also admit, that there are some sluggish men who are improved by drinking; as there are fruits which are not good till they are rotten. There are such men, but they are medlars. I indeed allow that there have been a very few men of talents who were improved by drinking; but I maintain that I am right as to the effects of drinking in general: and let it be considered, that there is no position, however false in its universality, which is not true of some particular man.' Sir William Forbes said, 'Might not a man warmed with wine be like a bottle of beer, which is made brisker by being set before the fire?'—'Nay, (said Johnson, laughing,) I cannot answer that: that is too much for me.'

I observed, that wine did some people harm, by inflaming, confusing, and irritating their minds; but that the experience of mankind had declared in favour of moderate drinking. JOHNSON. 'Sir, I do not say it is wrong to produce self complacency by drinking; I only deny that it improves the mind. When I drank wine, I scorned to drink it when in company. I have drunk many a bottle by myself; in the first place, because I had need of it to raise my spirits; in the second place, because I would have nobody to witness its effects upon me.'

He told us, 'almost all his *Ramblers* were written just as they were wanted for the press; that he sent a certain portion of the copy of an essay, and wrote the remainder, while the former part of it was printing. When it was wanted, and he had fairly sat down to it, he was sure it would be done.'

He said, that for general improvement, a man should read whatever his immediate inclination prompts him to; though, to be sure, if a man has a science to learn, he must regularly and resolutely advance. He added, 'what we read with inclination makes a much stronger impression. If we read without inclination, half the mind is employed in fixing the attention; so there is but one half to be employed on what we read.' He told us, he read Fielding's *Amelia* through without stopping. He said, 'if a man begins to read in the middle of a book, and feels an inclination to go on, let him not quit it, to go to the beginning. He may perhaps not feel again the inclination.'

Soon after this day, he went to Bath with Mr. and Mrs. Thrale. I had never seen that beautiful city, and wished to take the opportunity of visiting it, while Johnson was there.

On the 26th of April, I went to Bath; and on my arrival at the Pelican inn, found lying for me an obliging invitation from Mr. and Mrs. Thrale, by whom I was agreeably entertained almost constantly during my stay. They were gone to the rooms; but there was a kind note from Dr. Johnson, that he should sit at home all the evening. I went to him directly, and before Mr. and Mrs. Thrale returned, we had by ourselves some hours of tea-drinking and talk.

I shall group together such of his sayings as I preserved during the few days that I was at Bath.

It having been mentioned, I know not with what truth, that a certain female political writer, whose doctrines he disliked, had of late become very fond of dress, sat hours together at her toilet, and even put on rouge:—Johnson. 'She is better employed at her toilet, than using her pen. It is better she should be reddening her own cheeks, than blackening other people's characters.'

He would not allow me to praise a lady then at Bath; observing, 'She does not gain upon me, Sir; I think her empty-headed.' He was, indeed, a stern critick upon characters and manners. Even Mrs. Thrale did not escape his friendly animadversion at times. When he and I were one day endeavouring to ascertain, article by article, how one of our friends could possibly spend as much money in his family as he told us he did, she interrupted us by a lively extravagant sally, on the expence of clothing his children, describing it in a very ludicrous and fanciful manner. Johnson looked a little angry, and said, 'Nay, Madam, when you are declaiming, declaim; and when you are calculating, calculate.' At another time, when she said, perhaps affectedly, 'I don't like to fly.' JOHNSON. 'With *your* wings, Madam, you *must* fly: but have a care, there are *clippers* abroad.'

On Monday, April 29, he and I made an excursion to Bristol, where I was entertained with seeing him enquire upon the spot, into the authenticity of 'Rowley's Poetry,' as I had seen him enquire upon the spot into the authenticity of 'Ossian's Poetry.' George Catcot, the pewterer, who was as zealous for Rowley, as Dr. Hugh Blair was for Ossian, (I trust my Reverend friend will excuse the comparison,) attended us at our inn, and with a triumphant air of lively simplicity called out, 'I'll make Dr. Johnson a convert.' Dr. Johnson, at his desire, read aloud some of Chatterton's fabricated verses, while Catcot stood at the back of his chair, moving himself like a pendulum, and beating time with his feet, and now and then looking into Dr. Johnson's face, wondering that he was not yet convinced. We called on Mr. Barret, the surgeon, and saw some of the *originals* as they were called, which were executed very artificially; but from a careful inspection of them, and a consideration of the circumstances with which they were attended, we were quite satisfied of the imposture, which, indeed, has been clearly demonstrated from internal evidence, by several able criticks.

Honest Catcot seemed to pay no attention whatever to any objections, but insisted, as an end of all controversy, that we should go with him to the tower of the church of St. Mary, Redcliff, and *view with our own eyes* the ancient chest in which the manuscripts were found. To this, Dr. Johnson good-naturedly agreed; and though troubled with a shortness of breathing, laboured up a long flight of steps, till we came to the place where the wonderous chest stood. '*There*, (said Cateot, with a bouncing confident credulity,) *there* is the very chest itself.' After this *ocular demonstration*, there was no more to be said. He brought to my recollection a Scotch Highlander, a man of learning too, and who had seen the world, attesting, and at the same time giving his reasons for the authenticity of Fingal:—'I have heard all that poem when I was young.'—'Have you, Sir? Pray what have you heard?'—'I have heard Ossian, Oscar, and *every one of them.*'

Johnson said of Chatterton, 'This is the most extraordinary young man that has encountered my knowledge. It is wonderful how the whelp has written such things.'

We were by no means pleased with our inn at Bristol. 'Let us see now, (said I,) how we should describe it.' Johnson was ready with his raillery. 'Describe it, Sir?—Why, it was so bad that Boswell wished to be in Scotland!'

After Dr. Johnson's return to London, I was several times with him at his house, where I occasionally slept, in the room that had been assigned to me. I dined with him at Dr. Taylor's, at General Oglethorpe's, and at General Paoli's. To avoid a tedious minuteness, I shall group together what I have preserved of his conversation during this period also, without specifying each scene where it passed, except one, which will be found so remarkable as certainly to deserve a very particular relation.

'Garrick (he observed,) does not play the part of Archer in *The Beaux Stratagem* well. The gentleman should break out through the footman, which is not the case as he does it.'

'That man is never happy for the present is so true, that all his relief from unhappiness is only forgetting himself for a little while. Life is a progress from want to want, not from enjoyment to enjoyment.'

'Lord Chesterfield's *Letters to his Son*, I think, might be made a very pretty book. Take out the immorality, and it should be put into the hands of every young gentleman. An elegant manner and easiness of behaviour are acquired gradually and imperceptibly. No man can say "I'll be genteel." There are ten genteel women for one genteel man, because they are more restrained. A man without some degree of restraint is insufferable; but we are all less restrained than women. Were a woman sitting in company to put out her legs before her as most men do, we should be tempted to kick them in.'

No man was a more attentive and nice observer of behaviour in those in whose company he happened to be, than Johnson; or, however strange it may seem to many, had a higher estimation of its refinements. Lord Eliot informs me, that one day when Johnson and he were at dinner at a gentleman's house in London, upon Lord Chesterfield's Letters being mentioned, Johnson surprized the company by this sentence: 'Every man of any education would rather be called a rascal, than accused of deficiency in *the graces.*' Mr. Gibbon, who was present, turned to a lady who knew Johnson well, and lived much with him, and in his quaint manner, tapping his box, addressed her thus: 'Don't you think, Madam, (looking towards Johnson,) that among *all* your acquaintance, you could find *one* exception?' The lady smiled, and seemed to acquiesce.

The uncommon vivacity of General Oglethorpe's mind, and variety of knowledge, having sometimes made his conversation seem too desultory, Johnson observed, 'Oglethorpe, Sir, never *completes* what he has to say.'

He on the same account made a similar remark on Patrick Lord Elibank: 'Sir, there is nothing *conclusive* in his talk.'

When I complained of having dined at a splendid table without hearing one sentence of conversation worthy of being remembered, he said, 'Sir, there seldom is any such conversation.' BOSWELL. 'Why then meet at table?' JOHNSON. 'Why, to eat and drink together, and to promote kindness; and, Sir, this is better done when there is no solid conversation; for when there is, people differ in opinion, and get into bad humour, or some of the company who are not capable of such conversation, are left out, and feel themselves uneasy. It was for this reason, Sir Robert Walpole said, he always talked bawdy at his table, because in that all could join.'

Being irritated by hearing a gentleman[37] ask Mr. Levett a variety of questions concerning him, when he was sitting by, he broke out, 'Sir, you have but two topicks, yourself and me. I am sick of both.' 'A man, (said he,) should not talk of himself, nor much of any particular person. He should take care not to be made a proverb; and, therefore, should avoid having any one topick of which people can say, "We shall hear him upon it." There was a Dr. Oldfield, who was always talking of the Duke of Marlborough. He came into a coffee-house one day, and told that his Grace had spoken in the House of Lords for half an hour. "Did he indeed speak for half an hour?" (said Belehier, the surgeon,)— "Yes."—"And what did he say of Dr. Oldfield?"—"Nothing"—"Why then, Sir, he was very ungrateful; for Dr. Oldfield could not have spoken for a quarter of an hour, without saying something of him."'

I am now to record a very curious incident in Dr. Johnson's Life, which fell under my own observation; of which *pars magna fui*, and which I am persuaded will, with the liberal-minded, be much to his credit.

My desire of being acquainted with celebrated men of every description, had made me, much about the same time, obtain an introduction to Dr. Samuel Johnson and to John Wilkes, Esq. Two men more different could perhaps not be selected out of all mankind. They

---

[37] Most likely Boswell himself.—HILL.

had even attacked one another with some asperity in their writings; yet I lived in habits of friendship with both. I could fully relish the excellence of each; for I have ever delighted in that intellectual chymistry, which can separate good qualities from evil in the same person.

Sir John Pringle, 'mine own friend and my Father's friend,' between whom and Dr. Johnson I in vain wished to establish an acquaintance, as I respected and lived in intimacy with both of them, observed to me once, very ingeniously, 'It is not in friendship as in mathematicks, where two things, each equal to a third, are equal between themselves. You agree with Johnson as a middle quality, and you agree with me as a middle quality; but Johnson and I should not agree.' Sir John was not sufficiently flexible; so I desisted; knowing, indeed, that the repulsion was equally strong on the part of Johnson; who, I know not from what cause, unless his being a Scotchman, had formed a very erroneous opinion of Sir John. But I conceived an irresistible wish, if possible, to bring Dr. Johnson and Mr. Wilkes together. How to manage it, was a nice and difficult matter.

My worthy booksellers and friends, Messieurs Dilly in the Poultry, at whose hospitable and well-covered table I have seen a greater number of literary men, than at any other, except that of Sir Joshua Reynolds, had invited me to meet Mr. Wilkes and some more gentlemen on Wednesday, May 15. 'Pray (said I,) let us have Dr. Johnson.'—'What with Mr. Wilkes? not for the world, (said Mr. Edward Dilly:) Dr. Johnson would never forgive me.'—'Come, (said I,) if you'll let me negotiate for you, I will be answerable that all shall go well.' DILLY. 'Nay, if you will take it upon you, I am sure I shall be very happy to see them both here.'

Notwithstanding the high veneration which I entertained for Dr. Johnson, I was sensible that he was sometimes a little actuated by the spirit of contradiction, and by means of that I hoped I should gain my point. I was persuaded that if I had come upon him with a direct proposal, 'Sir, will you dine in company with Jack Wilkes?' he would have flown into a passion, and would probably have answered, 'Dine with Jack Wilkes, Sir! I'd as soon dine with Jack Ketch.' I therefore, while we were sitting quietly by ourselves at his house in an evening, took occasion to open my plan thus:—'Mr. Dilly, Sir, sends his respectful compliments to you, and would be happy if you would do him the honour to dine with him on Wednesday next along with me, as I must soon go to Scotland.' JOHNSON. 'Sir, I am obliged to Mr. Dilly. I will wait upon him—' BOSWELL. 'Provided, Sir, I suppose, that the company which he is to have, is agreeable to you.' JOHNSON. 'What do you mean, Sir? What do you take me for? Do you think I am so ignorant of the world as to imagine that I am to prescribe to a gentleman what company he is to have at his table?' BOSWELL. 'I beg your pardon, Sir, for wishing to prevent you from meeting people whom you might not like. Perhaps he may have some of what he calls his patriotick friends with him.' Johnson. 'Well, Sir, and what then? What care I for his *patriotick friends*? Poh!' BOSWELL. 'I should not be surprized to find Jack Wilkes there.' Johnson. 'And if Jack Wilkes *should* be there, what is that to *me*, Sir? My dear friend, let us have no more of this. I am sorry to be angry with you; but really it is treating me strangely to talk to me as if I could not meet any company whatever, occasionally.' BOSWELL. 'Pray forgive me, Sir: I meant well. But you shall meet whoever comes, for me.' Thus I secured him, and told Dilly that he would find him very well pleased to be one of his guests on the day appointed.

Upon the much-expected Wednesday, I called on him about half an hour before dinner, as I often did when we were to dine out together, to see that he was ready in time, and to accompany him. I found him buffeting his books, as upon a former occasion, covered with dust, and making no preparation for going abroad. 'How is this, Sir? (said I.) Don't you recollect that you are to dine at Mr. Dilly's?' JOHNSON. 'Sir, I did not think of going to Dilly's: it went out of my head. I have ordered dinner at home with Mrs. Williams.' BOSWELL. 'But, my dear Sir, you know you were engaged to Mr. Dilly, and I told him so. He will expect you, and will be much disappointed if you don't come.' JOHNSON. 'You must talk to Mrs. Williams about this.'

Here was a sad dilemma. I feared that what I was so confident I had secured would yet be frustrated. He had accustomed himself to shew Mrs. Williams such a degree of humane attention, as frequently imposed some restraint upon him; and I knew that if she should be obstinate, he would not stir. I hastened down stairs to the blind lady's room, and told her I was in great uneasiness, for Dr. Johnson had engaged to me to dine this day at Mr. Dilly's, but that he had told me he had forgotten his engagement, and had ordered dinner at home. 'Yes, Sir, (said she, pretty peevishly,) Dr. Johnson is to dine at home.'—'Madam, (said I,) his respect for you is such, that I know he will not leave you unless you absolutely desire it. But as you have so much of his company, I hope you will be good enough to forego it for a day; as Mr. Dilly is a very worthy man, has frequently had agreeable parties at his house for Dr. Johnson, and will be vexed if the Doctor neglects him to-day. And then, Madam, be pleased to consider my situation; I carried the message, and I assured Mr. Dilly that Dr. Johnson was to come, and no doubt he has made a dinner, and invited a company, and boasted of the honour he expected to have. I shall be quite disgraced if the Doctor is not there.' She gradually softened to my solicitations, which were certainly as earnest as most entreaties to ladies upon any occasion, and was graciously pleased to empower me to tell Dr. Johnson, 'That all things considered, she thought he should certainly go.' I flew back to him, still in dust, and careless of what should be the event, 'indifferent in his choice to go or stay;' but as soon as I had announced to him Mrs. Williams' consent, he roared, 'Frank, a clean shirt,' and was very soon drest. When I had him fairly seated in a hackney-coach with me, I exulted as much as a fortune-hunter who has got an heiress into a post-chaise with him to set out for Gretna-Green.

When we entered Mr. Dilly's drawing room, he found himself in the midst of a company he did not know. I kept myself snug and silent, watching how he would conduct himself. I observed him whispering to Mr. Dilly, 'Who is that gentleman, Sir?'—'Mr. Arthur Lee.'— JOHNSON. 'Too, too, too,' (under his breath,) which was one of his habitual mutterings. Mr. Arthur Lee could not but be very obnoxious to Johnson, for he was not only a *patriot* but an *American*. He was afterwards minister from the United States at the court of Madrid. 'And who is the gentleman in lace?'—'Mr. Wilkes, Sir.' This information confounded him still more; he had some difficulty to restrain himself, and taking up a book, sat down upon a window-seat and read, or at least kept his eye upon it intently for some time, till he composed himself. His feelings, I dare say, were aukward enough. But he no doubt recollected his having rated me for supposing that he could be at all disconcerted by any company, and he, therefore, resolutely set himself to behave quite as an easy man of the world, who could adapt himself at once to the disposition and manners of those whom he might chance to meet.

The cheering sound of 'Dinner is upon the table,' dissolved his reverie, and we *all* sat down without any symptom of ill humour. There were present, beside Mr. Wilkes, and Mr. Arthur Lee, who was an old companion of mine when he studied physick at Edinburgh, Mr. (now Sir John) Miller, Dr. Lettsom, and Mr. Slater the druggist. Mr. Wilkes placed himself next to Dr. Johnson, and behaved to him with so much attention and politeness, that he gained upon him insensibly. No man eat more heartily than Johnson, or loved better what was nice and delicate. Mr. Wilkes was very assiduous in helping him to some fine veal. 'Pray give me leave, Sir:—It is better here—A little of the brown—Some fat, Sir—A little of the stuffing—Some gravy—Let me have the pleasure of giving you some butter—Allow me to recommend a squeeze of this orange;—or the lemon, perhaps, may have more zest.'—'Sir, Sir, I am obliged to you, Sir,' cried Johnson, bowing, and turning his head to him with a look for some time of 'surly virtue,' but, in a short while, of complacency.

Foote being mentioned, Johnson said, 'He is not a good mimick.' One of the company added, 'A merry Andrew, a buffoon.' JOHNSON. 'But he has wit too, and is not deficient in ideas, or in fertility and variety of imagery, and not empty of reading; he has knowledge enough to fill up his part. One species of wit he has in an eminent degree, that of escape. You drive him into a corner with both hands; but he's gone, Sir, when you think you have got him—like an animal that jumps over your head. Then he has a great range for wit; he never lets truth stand between him and a jest, and he is sometimes mighty coarse. Garrick is under many restraints from which Foote is free.' WILKES. 'Garrick's wit is more like Lord Chesterfield's.' JOHNSON. 'The first time I was in company with Foote was at Fitzherbert's. Having no good opinion of the fellow, I was resolved not to be pleased; and it is very difficult to please a man against his will. I went on eating my dinner pretty sullenly, affecting not to mind him. But the dog was so very comical, that I was obliged to lay down my knife and fork, throw myself back upon my chair, and fairly laugh it out. No, Sir, he was irresistible. He upon one occasion experienced, in an extraordinary degree, the efficacy of his powers of entertaining. Amongst the many and various modes which he tried of getting money, he became a partner with a small-beer brewer, and he was to have a share of the profits for procuring customers amongst his numerous acquaintance. Fitzherbert was one who took his small-beer; but it was so bad that the servants resolved not to drink it. They were at some loss how to notify their resolution, being afraid of offending their master, who they knew liked Foote much as a companion. At last they fixed upon a little black boy, who was rather a favourite, to be their deputy, and deliver their remonstrance; and having invested him with the whole authority of the kitchen, he was to inform Mr. Fitzherbert, in all their names, upon a certain day, that they would drink Foote's small-beer no longer. On that day Foote happened to dine at Fitzherbert's, and this boy served at table; he was so delighted with Foote's stories, and merriment, and grimace, that when he went down stairs, he told them, "This is the finest man I have ever seen. I will not deliver your message. I will drink his small-beer."'

Somebody observed that Garrick could not have done this. WILKES. 'Garrick would have made the small-beer still smaller. He is now leaving the stage; but he will play *Scrub* all his life.' I knew that Johnson would let nobody attack Garrick but himself, as Garrick once said to me, and I had heard him praise his liberality; so to bring out his commendation of his celebrated pupil, I said, loudly, 'I have heard Garrick is liberal.' JOHNSON. 'Yes, Sir, I know that Garrick has given away more money than any man in England that I am acquainted with, and that not from ostentatious views. Garrick was very poor when he began life; so when he came to have money, he probably was very unskilful in giving away, and saved when he should not. But Garrick began to be liberal as soon as he could; and I am of opinion, the reputation of avarice which he has had, has been very lucky for him, and prevented his having many enemies. You despise a man for avarice, but do not hate him. Garrick might have been much better attacked for living with more splendour than is suitable to a player: if they had had the wit to have assaulted him in that quarter, they might have galled him more. But they have kept clamouring about his avarice, which has rescued him from much obloquy and envy.'

Talking of the great difficulty of obtaining authentick information for biography, Johnson told us, 'When I was a young fellow I wanted to write the *Life of Dryden*, and in order to get materials, I applied to the only two persons then alive who had seen him; these were old Swinney, and old Cibber. Swinney's information was no more than this, "That at Will's coffee-house Dryden had a particular chair for himself, which was set by the fire in winter, and was then called his winter-chair; and that it was carried out for him to the balcony in summer, and was then called his summer-chair." Cibber could tell no more but "That he remembered him a decent old man, arbiter of critical disputes at Will's." You are to consider that Cibber was then at a great distance from Dryden, had perhaps one leg only in the room, and durst not draw in the other.' BOSWELL. 'Yet Cibber was a man of observation?' JOHNSON. 'I think not.' BOSWELL. 'You will allow his *Apology* to be well done.' JOHNSON. 'Very well done, to be sure, Sir. That book is a striking proof of the justice of Pope's remark:

> "Each might his several province well command,
> Would all but stoop to what they understand."'

BOSWELL. 'And his plays are good.' JOHNSON. 'Yes; but that was his trade; *l'esprit du corps*: he had been all his life among players and play-writers. I wondered that he had so little to say in conversation, for he had kept the best company, and learnt all that can be got by the ear. He abused Pindar to me, and then shewed me an Ode of his own, with an absurd couplet, making a linnet soar on an eagle's wing. I told him that when the ancients made a simile, they always made it like something real.'

Mr. Wilkes remarked, that 'among all the bold flights of Shakspeare's imagination, the boldest was making Birnamwood march to Dunsinane; creating a wood where there never was a shrub; a wood in Scotland! ha! ha! ha!' And he also observed, that 'the clannish slavery of the Highlands of Scotland was the single exception to Milton's remark of "The Mountain Nymph, sweet Liberty," being worshipped in all hilly countries.'—'When I was at Inverary (said he,) on a visit to my old friend, Archibald, Duke of Argyle, his dependents congratulated me on being such a favourite of his Grace. I said, "It is then, gentlemen, truely lucky for me; for if I had displeased the Duke, and he had wished it, there is not a Campbell among you but would have been ready to bring John Wilkes's head to him in a charger. It would have been only,

'Off with his head! So much for Aylesbury.'"

I was then member for Aylesbury.'

Mr. Arthur Lee mentioned some Scotch who had taken possession of a barren part of America, and wondered why they should choose it. JOHNSON. 'Why, Sir, all barrenness is comparative. The *Scotch* would not know it to be barren.' BOSWELL. 'Come, come, he is flattering the English. You have now been in Scotland, Sir, and say if you did not see meat and drink enough there.' JOHNSON. 'Why yes, Sir; meat and drink enough to give the enhabitants sufficient strength to run away from home.' All these quick and lively sallies were said sportively, quite in jest, and with a smile, which showed that he meant only wit. Upon this topick he and Mr. Wilkes could perfectly assimilate; here was a bond of union between them, and I was conscious that as both of them had visited Caledonia, both were fully satisfied of the strange narrow ignorance of those who imagine that it is a land of famine. But they amused themselves with persevering in the old jokes. When I claimed a superiority for Scotland over England in one respect, that no man can be arrested there for a debt merely because another swears it against him; but there must first be the judgement of a court of law ascertaining its justice; and that a seizure of the person, before judgement is obtained, can take place only, if his creditor should swear that he is about to fly from the country, or, as it is technically expressed, is *in meditatione fugoe*: WILKES. 'That, I should think, may be safely sworn of all the Scotch nation.' JOHNSON. (to Mr. Wilkes,) 'You must know, Sir, I lately took my friend Boswell and shewed him genuine civilised life in an English provincial town. I turned him loose at Lichfield, my native city, that he might see for once real civility: for you know he lives among savages in Scotland, and among rakes in London.' WILKES. 'Except when he is with grave, sober, decent people like you and me.' JOHNSON. (smiling,) 'And we ashamed of him.'

They were quite frank and easy. Johnson told the story of his asking Mrs. Macaulay to allow her footman to sit down with them, to prove the ridiculousness of the argument for the equality of mankind; and he said to me afterwards, with a nod of satisfaction, 'You saw Mr. Wilkes acquiesced.' Wilkes talked with all imaginable freedom of the ludicrous title given to the Attorney-General, *Diabolus Regis*; adding, 'I have reason to know something about that officer; for I was prosecuted for a libel.' Johnson, who many people would have supposed must have been furiously angry at hearing this talked of so lightly, said not a word. He was now, *indeed*, 'a good-humoured fellow.'

After dinner we had an accession of Mrs. Knowles, the Quaker lady, well known for her various talents, and of Mr. Alderman Lee.

Amidst some patriotick groans, somebody (I think the Alderman) said, 'Poor old England is lost.' JOHNSON. 'Sir, it is not so much to be lamented that Old England is lost, as that the Scotch have found it.' WILKES. 'Had Lord Bute governed Scotland only, I should not have taken the trouble to write his eulogy, and dedicate *Mortimer* to him.'

Mr. Wilkes held a candle to shew a fine print of a beautiful female figure which hung in the room, and pointed out the elegant contour of the bosom with the finger of an arch connoisseur. He afterwards, in a conversation with me, waggishly insisted, that all the time Johnson shewed visible signs of a fervent admiration of the corresponding charms of the fair Quaker.

This record, though by no means so perfect as I could wish, will serve to give a notion of a very curious interview, which was not only pleasing at the time, but had the agreeable and benignant effect of reconciling any animosity, and sweetening any acidity, which in the various bustle of political contest, had been produced in the minds of two men, who though widely different, had so many things in common—classical learning, modern literature, wit, and humour, and ready repartee—that it would have been much to be regretted if they had been for ever at a distance from each other.

Mr. Burke gave me much credit for this successful *negociation*; and pleasantly said, that 'there was nothing to equal it in the whole history of the *Corps Diplomatique*.'

I attended Dr. Johnson home, and had the satisfaction to hear him tell Mrs. Williams how much he had been pleased with Mr. Wilkes's company, and what an agreeable day he had passed.

I talked a good deal to him of the celebrated Margaret Caroline Rudd, whom I had visited, induced by the fame of her talents, address, and irresistible power of fascination. To a lady who disapproved of my visiting her, he said on a former occasion, 'Nay, Madam, Boswell is in the right; I should have visited her myself, were it not that they have now a trick of putting every thing into the news-papers.' This evening he exclaimed, 'I envy him his acquaintance with Mrs. Rudd.'

On the evening of the next day I took leave of him, being to set out for Scotland. I thanked him with great warmth for all his kindness. 'Sir, (said he,) you are very welcome. Nobody repays it with more.

The following letters concerning an Epitaph which he wrote for the monument of Dr. Goldsmith, in Westminster-Abbey, afford at once a proof of his unaffected modesty, his carelessness as to his own writings, and of the great respect which he entertained for the taste and judgement of the excellent and eminent person to whom they are addressed:

TO SIR JOSHUA REYNOLDS.

DEAR SIR,—I have been kept away from you, I know not well how, and of these vexatious hindrances I know not when there will be an end. I therefore send you the poor dear Doctor's epitaph. Read it first yourself; and if you then think it right, shew it to the Club. I am, you know, willing to be corrected. If you think any thing much amiss, keep it to yourself, till we come together. I have sent two copies, but prefer the card. The dates must be settled by Dr. Percy. I am, Sir, your most humble servant,
    'May 16, 1776.'

                                            'SAM. JOHNSON.'

It was, I think, after I had left London this year, that this Epitaph gave occasion to a *Remonstrance* to the MONARCH OF LITERATURE, for an account of which I am indebted to Sir William Forbes, of Pitsligo.

That my readers may have the subject more fully and clearly before them, I shall first insert the Epitaph.

OLIVARII GOLDSMITH,
Poetae, Physici, Historici,
Qui nullum fere scribendi genus
Non tetigit,
Nullum quod tetiqit non ornavit:
Sive risus essent movendi,
Sive lacrymae,
Affectuum potens at lenis dominator:
Ingenio sublimis, vividus, versatilis,
Oratione grandis, nitidus, venustus:
Hoc monumento memoriam coluit
Sodalium amor,
Amicorum fides,
Lectorum veneratio.
Natus in Hibernia Forniae Longfordiensis,
In loco cui nomen Pallas,
Nov. XXIX. MDCCXXXI;
Eblanae literis institutus;
Obiit Londini,
April IV, MDCCLXXIV.'

Sir William Forbes writes to me thus:—
    'I enclose the *Round Robin*. This *jeu d'esprit* took its rise one day at dinner at our friend Sir Joshua Reynolds's. All the company present, except myself, were friends and acquaintance of Dr. Goldsmith. The

Epitaph, written for him by Dr. Johnson, became the subject of conversation, and various emendations were suggested, which it was agreed should be submitted to the Doctor's consideration. But the question was, who should have the courage to propose them to him? At last it was hinted, that there could be no way so good as that of a *Round Robin*, as the sailors call it, which they make use of when they enter into a conspiracy, so as not to let it be known who puts his name first or last to the paper. This proposition was instantly assented to; and Dr. Barnard, Dean of Derry, now Bishop of Killaloe, drew up an address to Dr. Johnson on the occasion, replete with wit and humour, but which it was feared the Doctor might think treated the subject with too much levity. Mr. Burke then proposed the address as it stands in the paper in writing, to which I had the honour to officiate as clerk.

'Sir Joshua agreed to carry it to Dr. Johnson, who received it with much good humour,[38] and desired Sir Joshua to tell the gentlemen, that he would alter the Epitaph in any manner they pleased, as to the sense of it; but *he would never consent to disgrace the walls of Westminster Abbey with an English inscription.*

'I consider this *Round Robin* as a species of literary curiosity worth preserving, as it marks, in a certain degree, Dr. Johnson's character.'

Sir William Forbes's observation is very just. The anecdote now related proves, in the strongest manner, the reverence and awe with which Johnson was regarded, by some of the most eminent men of his time, in various departments, and even by such of them as lived most with him; while it also confirms what I have again and again inculcated, that he was by no means of that ferocious and irascible character which has been ignorantly imagined.

This hasty composition is also to be remarked as one of a thousand instances which evince the extraordinary promptitude of Mr. Burke; who while he is equal to the greatest things, can adorn the least; can, with equal facility, embrace the vast and complicated speculations of politicks, or the ingenious topicks of literary investigation.

---

[38] He however, upon seeing Dr. Warton's name to the suggestion, that the Epitaph should be in English, observed to Sir Joshua, 'I wonder that Joe Warton, a scholar by profession, should be such a fool.' He said too, 'I should have thought Mund Burke would have had more sense.' Mr. Langton, who was one of the company at Sir Joshua's, like a sturdy scholar, resolutely refused to sign the *Round Robin*. The Epitaph is engraved upon Dr. Goldsmith's monument without any alteration. At another time, when somebody endeavoured to argue in favour of its being in English, Johnson said, 'The language of the country of which a learned man was a native, is not the language fit for his epitaph, which should be in ancient and permanent language. Consider, Sir; how you should feel, were you to find at Rotterdam an epitaph upon Erasmus *in Dutch!*'— BOSWELL.

'DR. JOHNSON TO MRS. BOSWELL.

'MADAM,—You must not think me uncivil in omitting to answer the letter with which you favoured me some time ago. I imagined it to have been written without Mr. Boswell's knowledge, and therefore supposed the answer to require, what I could not find, a private conveyance.

'The difference with Lord Auchinleck is now over; and since young Alexander has appeared, I hope no more difficulties will arise among you; for I sincerely wish you all happy. Do not teach the young ones to dislike me, as you dislike me yourself; but let me at least have Veronica's kindness, because she is my acquaintance.

'You will now have Mr. Boswell home; it is well that you have him; he has led a wild life. I have taken him to Lichfield, and he has followed Mr. Thrale to Bath. Pray take care of him, and tame him. The only thing in which I have the honour to agree with you is, in loving him; and while we are so much of a mind in a matter of so much importance, our other quarrels will, I hope, produce no great bitterness. I am, Madam, your most humble servant,
     'May 16, 1776.'

                                              'SAM. JOHNSON.'

I select from his private register the following passage:

'July 25, 1776. O GOD, who hast ordained that whatever is to be desired should be sought by labour, and who, by thy blessing, bringest honest labour to good effect, look with mercy upon my studies and endeavours. Grant me, O LORD, to design only what is lawful and right; and afford me calmness of mind, and steadiness of purpose, that I may so do thy will in this short life, as to obtain happiness in the world to come, for the sake of JESUS CHRIST our Lord. Amen.'

It appears from a note subjoined, that this was composed when he 'purposed to apply vigorously to study, particularly of the Greek and Italian tongues.'

Such a purpose, so expressed, at the age of sixty-seven, is admirable and encouraging; and it must impress all the thinking part of my readers with a consolatory confidence in habitual devotion, when they see a man of such enlarged intellectual powers as Johnson, thus in the genuine earnestness of secrecy, imploring the aid of that Supreme Being, 'from whom cometh down every good and every perfect gift.'

1777: ÆTAT. 68.]—In 1777, it appears from his *Prayers and Meditations*, that Johnson suffered much from a state of mind 'unsettled and perplexed,' and from that constitutional gloom, which, together with his extreme humility and anxiety with regard to his religious state, made him contemplate himself through too dark and unfavourable a medium. It may be said of him, that he 'saw GOD in clouds.' Certain we may be of his injustice to himself in the following lamentable paragraph, which it is painful to think came from the contrite heart of this great man, to whose labours the world is so much indebted: 'When I survey my past life, I discover nothing but a barren waste of time with some disorders of body, and disturbances of the mind, very near to madness, which I hope He that made me will suffer to extenuate many faults, and excuse many deficiencies.' But we find his devotions in this year eminently fervent; and we are comforted by observing intervals of quiet, composure, and gladness.

On Easter-day we find the following emphatick prayer:

'Almighty and most merciful Father, who seest all our miseries, and knowest all our necessities, look down upon me, and pity me. Defend me from the violent incursion [incursions] of evil thoughts, and enable me to form and keep such resolutions as may conduce to the discharge of the duties which thy providence shall appoint me; and so help me, by thy Holy Spirit, that my heart may surely there be fixed, where true joys are to be found, and that I may serve thee with pure affection and a cheerful mind. Have mercy upon me, O GOD, have mercy upon me; years and infirmities oppress me, terrour and anxiety beset me. Have mercy upon me, my Creator and my Judge. [In all dangers protect me.] In all perplexities relieve and free me; and so help me by thy Holy Spirit, that I may now so commemorate the death of thy Son our Saviour JESUS CHRIST, as that when this short and painful life shall have an end, I may, for his sake, be received to everlasting happiness. Amen.'

'SIR ALEXANDER DICK TO DR. SAMUEL JOHNSON.

'Prestonfield, Feb. 17, 1777.

'SIR, I had yesterday the honour of receiving your book of your *Journey to the Western Islands of Scotland*, which you was so good as to send me, by the hands of our mutual friend, Mr. Boswell, of Auchinleck; for which I return you my most hearty thanks; and after carefully reading it over again, shall deposit in my little collection of choice books, next our worthy friend's *Journey to Corsica*. As there are many things to admire in both performances, I have often wished that no Travels or Journeys should be published but those undertaken by persons of integrity and capacity to judge well, and describe faithfully, and in good language, the situation, condition, and manners of the countries past through. Indeed our country of Scotland, in spite of the union of the crowns, is still in most places so devoid of clothing, or cover from hedges and plantations, that it was well you gave your readers a sound *Monitoire* with respect to that circumstance. The truths you have told, and the purity of the language in which they are expressed, as your *Journey* is universally read, may, and already appear to have a very good effect. For a man of my acquaintance, who has the largest nursery for trees and hedges in this country, tells me, that of late the demand upon him for these articles is doubled, and sometimes tripled. I have, therefore, listed Dr. Samuel Johnson in some of my memorandums of the principal planters and favourers of the enclosures, under a name which I took the liberty to invent from the Greek, *Papadendrion.* Lord Auchinleck and some few more are of the list. I am told that one gentleman in the shire of Aberdeen, *viz.* Sir Archibald Grant, has planted above fifty millions of trees on a piece of very wild ground at Monimusk: I must enquire if he has fenced them well, before he enters my list; for, that is the soul of enclosing. I began myself to plant a little, our ground being too valuable for much, and that is now fifty years ago; and the trees, now in my seventy-fourth year, I look up to with reverence, and shew them to my eldest son now in his fifteenth year, and they are full the height of my country-house here, where I had the pleasure of receiving you, and hope again to have that satisfaction with our mutual friend, Mr. Boswell. I shall always continue, with the truest esteem, dear Doctor, your much obliged, and obedient humble servant,

'ALEXANDER DICK.'

'TO JAMES BOSWELL, ESQ.

'DEAR SIR,—It is so long since I heard any thing from you, that I am not easy about it; write something to me next post. When you sent your last letter, every thing seemed to be mending; I hope nothing has lately grown worse. I suppose young Alexander continues to thrive, and Veronica is now very pretty company. I do not suppose the lady is yet reconciled to me, yet let her know that I love her very well, and value her very much. . . .

'Poor Beauclerk still continues very ill. Langton lives on as he used to do. His children are very pretty, and, I think, his lady loses her Scotch. Paoli I never see.

'I have been so distressed by difficulty of breathing, that I lost, as was computed, six-and-thirty ounces of blood in a few days. I am better, but not well. . . .

'Mrs. Williams sends her compliments, and promises that when you come hither, she will accommodate you as well as ever she can in the old room. She wishes to know whether you sent her book to Sir Alexander Gordon.

'My dear Boswell, do not neglect to write to me; for your kindness is one of the pleasures of my life, which I should be sorry to lose. I am, Sir, your humble servant,

'February 18, 1777.'

'SAM. JOHNSON.'

'TO DR. SAMUEL JOHNSON.

'Glasgow, April 24, 1777.

'MY DEAR SIR, . . . My wife has made marmalade of oranges for you. I left her and my daughters and Alexander all well yesterday. I have taught Veronica to speak of you thus;—Dr. John*son*, not John*ston*. I remain, my dear Sir, your most affectionate, and obliged humble servant,

'JAMES BOSWELL.'

'TO JAMES BOSWELL, ESQ.

'DEAR SIR, . . . Tell Mrs. Boswell that I shall taste her marmalade cautiously at first. *Timeo Danaos et dona ferentes.* Beware, says the Italian proverb, of a reconciled enemy. But when I find it does me no harm, I shall then receive it and be thankful for it, as a pledge of firm, and, I hope, of unalterable kindness. She is, after all, a dear, dear lady. . . .

'I am, dear Sir, your most affectionate humble servant,
'May 3, 1777.'

'SAM. JOHNSON.'

'TO JAMES BOSWELL, ESQ.

'Southill, Sept. 26, 1777.

'DEAR SIR, You will find by this letter, that I am still in the same calm retreat, from the noise and bustle of London, as when I wrote to you last. I am happy to find you had such an agreeable meeting with your old friend Dr. Johnson; I have no doubt your stock is much increased by the interview; few men, nay I may say, scarcely any man, has got that fund of knowledge and entertainment as Dr. Johnson in conversation. When he opens freely, every one is attentive to what he says, and cannot fail of improvement as well as pleasure.

'The edition of *The Poets*, now printing, will do honour to the English press; and a concise account of the life of each authour, by Dr. Johnson, will be a very valuable addition, and stamp the reputation of this edition superiour to any thing that is gone before. The first cause that gave rise to this undertaking, I believe, was owing to the little trifling edition of *The Poets*, printing by the Martins, at Edinburgh, and to be sold by Bell, in London. Upon examining the volumes which were printed, the type was found so extremely small, that many persons could not read them; not only this inconvenience attended it, but the inaccuracy of the press was very conspicuous. These reasons, as well as the idea of an invasion of what we call our Literary Property, induced the London Booksellers to print an elegant and accurate edition of all the English Poets of reputation, from Chaucer to the present time.

'Accordingly a select number of the most respectable booksellers met on the occasion; and, on consulting together, agreed, that all the proprietors of copy-right in the various Poets should be summoned together; and when their opinions were given, to proceed immediately on the business. Accordingly a meeting was held, consisting of about forty of the most respectable booksellers of London, when it was agreed that an elegant and uniform edition of *The English Poets* should be immediately printed, with a concise account of the life of each authour, by Dr. Samuel Johnson; and that three persons should be deputed to wait upon Dr. Johnson, to solicit him to undertake the Lives, *viz.*, T. Davies, Strahan, and Cadell. The Doctor very politely undertook it, and seemed exceedingly pleased with the proposal. As to the terms, it was left entirely to the Doctor to name his own: he mentioned two hundred guineas:[39] it was immediately agreed to; and a farther compliment, I believe, will be made him. A committee was likewise appointed to engage the best engravers, *viz.*, Bartolozzi, Sherwin, Hall, etc. Likewise another committee for giving directions about the paper, printing, etc., so that the whole will be conducted with spirit, and in the best manner, with respect to authourship, editorship, engravings, etc., etc. My brother will give you a list of the Poets we mean to give, many of which are within the time of the Act of Queen Anne, which Martin and Bell cannot give, as they have no property in them; the proprietors are almost all the booksellers in London, of consequence. I am, dear Sir, ever your's,

'EDWARD DILLY.'

A circumstance which could not fail to be very pleasing to Johnson occurred this year. The Tragedy of *Sir Thomas Overbury*, written by his early companion in London, Richard Savage, was brought out with alterations at Drury-lane theatre. The Prologue to it was written by Mr. Richard Brinsley Sheridan; in which, after describing very pathetically the wretchedness of

'Ill-fated Savage, at whose birth was giv'n
No parent but the Muse, no friend but Heav'n:'

he introduced an elegant compliment to Johnson on his *Dictionary*, that wonderful performance which cannot be too often or too highly

---

[39] Johnson's moderation in demanding so small a sum is extraordinary. Had he asked one thousand, or even fifteen hundred guineas, the booksellers, who knew the value of his name, would doubtless have readily given it. They have probably got five thousand guineas by this work in the course of twenty-five years.—MALONE.

praised; of which Mr. Harris, in his *Philological Inquiries*, justly and liberally observes: 'Such is its merit, that our language does not possess a more copious, learned, and valuable work.' The concluding lines of this Prologue were these:—

'So pleads the tale that gives to future times
The son's misfortunes and the parent's crimes;
There shall his fame (if own'd to-night) survive,
Fix'd by THE HAND THAT BIDS OUR LANGUAGE LIVE.'

Mr. Sheridan here at once did honour to his taste and to his liberality of sentiment, by shewing that he was not prejudiced from the unlucky difference which had taken place between his worthy father and Dr. Johnson. I have already mentioned, that Johnson was very desirous of reconciliation with old Mr. Sheridan. It will, therefore, not seem at all surprizing that he was zealous in acknowledging the brilliant merit of his son. While it had as yet been displayed only in the drama, Johnson proposed him as a member of THE LITERARY CLUB, observing, that 'He who has written the two best comedies of his age, is surely a considerable man.' And he had, accordingly, the honour to be elected; for an honour it undoubtedly must be allowed to be, when it is considered of whom that society consists, and that a single black ball excludes a candidate.

On the 23rd of June, I again wrote to Dr. Johnson, enclosing a ship-master's receipt for a jar of orange-marmalade, and a large packet of Lord Hailes's *Annals of Scotland*.

'DR. JOHNSON TO MRS. BOSWELL.

'MADAM,—Though I am well enough pleased with the taste of sweetmeats, very little of the pleasure which I received at the arrival of your jar of marmalade arose from eating it. I received it as a token of friendship, as a proof of reconciliation, things much sweeter than sweetmeats, and upon this consideration I return you, dear Madam, my sincerest thanks. By having your kindness I think I have a double security for the continuance of Mr. Boswell's, which it is not to be expected that any man can long keep, when the influence of a lady so highly and so justly valued operates against him. Mr. Boswell will tell you that I was always faithful to your interest, and always endeavoured to exalt you in his estimation. You must now do the same for me. We must all help one another, and you must now consider me, as, dear Madam, your most obliged, and most humble servant,

'July 22, 1777.'

'SAM. JOHNSON.'

'TO JAMES BOSWELL, ESQ.

'DEAR SIR,—I am this day come to Ashbourne, and have only to tell you, that Dr. Taylor says you shall be welcome to him, and you know how welcome you will be to me. Make haste to let me know when you may be expected.

'Make my compliments to Mrs. Boswell, and tell her, I hope we shall be at variance no more. I am, dear Sir, your most humble servant,
'August 30, 1777.'

'SAM. JOHNSON.'

On Sunday evening, Sept. 14, I arrived at Ashbourne, and drove directly up to Dr. Taylor's door. Dr. Johnson and he appeared before I had got out of the post-chaise, and welcomed me cordially.

I told them that I had travelled all the preceding night, and gone to bed at Leek in Staffordshire; and that when I rose to go to church in the afternoon, I was informed there had been an earthquake, of which, it seems, the shock had been felt in some degree at Ashbourne. JOHNSON. 'Sir it will be much exaggerated in popular talk: for, in the first place, the common people do not accurately adapt their thoughts to the objects; nor, secondly, do they accurately adapt their words to their thoughts: they do not mean to lie; but, taking no pains to be exact, they give you very false accounts. A great part of their language is proverbial. If anything rocks at all, they say *it rocks like a cradle*; and in this way they go on.

The subject of grief for the loss of relations and friends being introduced, I observed that it was strange to consider how soon it in general wears away. Dr. Taylor mentioned a gentleman of the neighbourhood as the only instance he had ever known of a person who had endeavoured to *retain* grief. He told Dr. Taylor, that after his Lady's death, which affected him deeply, he *resolved* that the grief, which he cherished with a kind of sacred fondness, should be lasting; but that he found he could not keep it long. JOHNSON. 'All grief for what cannot in the course of nature be helped, soon wears away; in some sooner, indeed, in some later; but it never continues very long, unless where there is madness, such as will make a man have pride so fixed in his mind, as to imagine himself a King; or any other passion in an unreasonable way: for all unnecessary grief is unwise, and therefore will not be long retained by a sound mind. If, indeed, the cause of our grief is occasioned by our own misconduct, if grief is mingled with remorse of conscience, it should be lasting.' BOSWELL. 'But, Sir, we do not approve of a man who very soon forgets the loss of a wife or a friend.' JOHNSON. 'Sir, we disapprove of him, not because he soon forgets his grief, for the sooner it is forgotten the better, but because we suppose, that if he forgets his wife or his friend soon, he has not had much affection for them.'

I was somewhat disappointed in finding that the edition of *The English Poets*, for which he was to write Prefaces and Lives, was not an undertaking directed by him: but that he was to furnish a Preface and Life to any poet the booksellers pleased. I asked him if he would do this to any dunce's works, if they should ask him. JOHNSON. 'Yes, Sir, and *say* he was a dunce.' My friend seemed now not much to relish talking of this edition.

After breakfast,[40] Johnson carried me to see the garden belonging to the school of Ashbourne, which is very prettily formed upon a bank, rising gradually behind the house. The Reverend Mr. Langley, the head-master, accompanied us.

We had with us at dinner several of Dr. Taylor's neighbours, good civil gentlemen, who seemed to understand Dr. Johnson very well, and not to consider him in the light that a certain person did, who being struck, or rather stunned by his voice and manner, when he was afterwards asked what he thought of him, answered. 'He's a tremendous companion.'

Johnson told me, that 'Taylor was a very sensible acute man, and had a strong mind; that he had great activity in some respects, and yet such a sort of indolence, that if you should put a pebble upon his chimney-piece, you would find it there, in the same state, a year afterwards.'

And here is the proper place to give an account of Johnson's humane and zealous interference in behalf of the Reverend Dr. William Dodd, formerly Prebendary of Brecon, and chaplain in ordinary to his Majesty; celebrated as a very popular preacher, an encourager of charitable institutions, and authour of a variety of works, chiefly theological. Having unhappily contracted expensive habits of living, partly occasioned by licentiousness of manners, he in an evil hour, when pressed by want of money, and dreading an exposure of his circumstances, forged a bond of which he attempted to avail himself to support his credit, flattering himself with hopes that he might be able to repay its amount without being detected. The person, whose name he thus rashly and criminally presumed to falsify, was the Earl of Chesterfield, to whom he had been tutor, and who, he perhaps, in the warmth of his feelings, flattered himself would have generously paid the money in case of an alarm being taken, rather than suffer him to fall a victim to the dreadful consequences of violating the law against forgery, the most dangerous crime in a commercial country; but the unfortunate divine had the mortification to find that he was mistaken. His noble pupil appeared against him, and he was capitally convicted.

---

[40] Next morning.—Ed.

Johnson told me that Dr. Dodd was very little acquainted with him, having been but once in his company, many years previous to this period (which was precisely the state of my own acquaintance with Dodd); but in his distress he bethought himself of Johnson's persuasive power of writing, if haply it might avail to obtain for him the Royal Mercy. He did not apply to him directly, but, extraordinary as it may seem, through the late Countess of Harrington, who wrote a letter to Johnson, asking him to employ his pen in favour of Dodd. Mr. Allen, the printer, who was Johnson's landlord and next neighbour in Bolt-court, and for whom he had much kindness, was one of Dodd's friends, of whom to the credit of humanity be it recorded, that he had many who did not desert him, even after his infringement of the law had reduced him to the state of a man under sentence of death. Mr. Allen told me that he carried Lady Harrington's letter to Johnson, that Johnson read it walking up and down his chamber, and seemed much agitated, after which he said, 'I will do what I can;'—and certainly he did make extraordinary exertions.

He this evening, as he had obligingly promised in one of his letters, put into my hands the whole series of his writings upon this melancholy occasion.

Dr. Johnson wrote in the first place, Dr. Dodd's *Speech to the Recorder of London*, at the Old-Bailey, when sentence of death was about to be pronounced upon him.

He wrote also *The Convict's Address to his unhappy Brethren*, a sermon delivered by Dr. Dodd, in the chapel of Newgate.

The other pieces mentioned by Johnson in the above-mentioned collection, are two letters, one to the Lord Chancellor Bathurst, (not Lord North, as is erroneously supposed,) and one to Lord Mansfield;— A Petition from Dr. Dodd to the King;—A Petition from Mrs. Dodd to the Queen;—Observations of some length inserted in the news-papers, on occasion of Earl Percy's having presented to his Majesty a petition for mercy to Dodd, signed by twenty thousand people, but all in vain. He told me that he had also written a petition from the city of London; 'but (said he, with a significant smile) they *mended* it.'

The last of these articles which Johnson wrote is *Dr. Dodd's last solemn Declaration*, which he left with the sheriff at the place of execution.

I found a letter to Dr. Johnson from Dr. Dodd, May 23, 1777, in which *The Convict's Address* seems clearly to be meant.

'I am so penetrated, my ever dear Sir, with a sense of your extreme benevolence towards me, that I cannot find words equal to the sentiments of my heart. . . .'

On Sunday, June 22, he writes, begging Dr. Johnson's assistance in framing a supplicatory letter to his Majesty.

This letter was brought to Dr. Johnson when in church. He stooped down and read it, and wrote, when he went home, the following letter for Dr. Dodd to the King:

'SIR,—May it not offend your Majesty, that the most miserable of men applies himself to your clemency, as his last hope and his last refuge; that your mercy is most earnestly and humbly implored by a clergyman, whom your Laws and Judges have condemned to the horrour and ignominy of a publick execution. . . .'

Subjoined to it was written as follows:—

'TO DR. DODD.

'SIR,—I most seriously enjoin you not to let it be at all known that I have written this letter, and to return the copy to Mr. Allen in a cover to me. I hope I need not tell you, that I wish it success.—But do not indulge hope.—Tell nobody.'

It happened luckily that Mr. Allen was pitched on to assist in this melancholy office, for he was a great friend of Mr. Akerman, the keeper of Newgate. Dr. Johnson never went to see Dr. Dodd. He said to me, 'it would have done *him* more harm, than good to Dodd, who once expressed a desire to see him, but not earnestly.'

All applications for the Royal Mercy having failed, Dr. Dodd prepared himself for death; and, with a warmth of gratitude, wrote to Dr. Johnson as follows:—

'June 25, *Midnight.*

'Accept, thou *great* and *good* heart, my earnest and fervent thanks and prayers for all thy benevolent and kind efforts in my behalf—Oh! Dr. Johnson! as I sought your knowledge at an early hour in life, would to heaven I had cultivated the love and acquaintance of so excellent a man!—I pray GOD most sincerely to bless you with the highest transports—the infelt satisfaction of *humane* and benevolent exertions!—And admitted, as I trust I shall be, to the realms of bliss before you, I shall hail *your* arrival there with transports, and rejoice to acknowledge that you was my Comforter, my Advocate and my *friend*! GOD *be ever with you!*'

Dr. Johnson lastly wrote to Dr. Dodd this solemn and soothing letter:—

'TO THE REVEREND DR. DODD.

'DEAR SIR,—That which is appointed to all men is now coming upon you. Outward circumstances, the eyes and the thoughts of men, are below the notice of an immortal being about to stand the trial for eternity, before the Supreme Judge of heaven and earth. Be comforted: your crime, morally or religiously considered, has no very deep dye of turpitude. It corrupted no man's principles; it attacked no man's life. It involved only a temporary and reparable injury. Of this, and of all other sins, you are earnestly to repent; and may GOD, who knoweth our frailty, and desireth not our death, accept your repentance, for the sake of his SON JESUS CHRIST our Lord.

'In requital of those well-intended offices which you are pleased so emphatically to acknowledge, let me beg that you make in your devotions one petition for my eternal welfare. I am, dear Sir, your affectionate servant,

'June 26, 1777.'

'SAM. JOHNSON.'

Under the copy of this letter I found written, in Johnson's own hand, 'Next day, June 27, he was executed.'

Tuesday, September 16, Dr. Johnson having mentioned to me the extraordinary size and price of some cattle reared by Dr. Taylor, I rode out with our host, surveyed his farm, and was shown one cow which he had sold for a hundred and twenty guineas, and another for which he had been offered a hundred and thirty. Taylor thus described to me his old schoolfellow and friend, Johnson: 'He is a man of a very clear head, great power of words, and a very gay imagination; but there is no disputing with him. He will not hear you, and having a louder voice than you, must roar you down.'

In the evening, the Reverend Mr. Seward, of Lichfield, who was passing through Ashbourne in his way home, drank tea with us. Johnson described him thus:—'Sir, his ambition is to be a fine talker; so he goes to Buxton, and such places, where he may find companies to listen to him. And, Sir, he is a valetudinarian, one of those who are always mending themselves. I do not know a more disagreeable character than a valetudinarian, who thinks he may do any thing that is for his ease, and indulges himself in the grossest freedoms: Sir, he brings himself to the state of a hog in a stye.'

Dr. Taylor's nose happening to bleed, he said, it was because he had omitted to have himself blooded four days after a quarter of a year's interval. Dr. Johnson, who was a great dabbler in physick, disapproved much of periodical bleeding. 'For (said he,) you accustom yourself to an evacuation which Nature cannot perform of herself, and therefore she cannot help you, should you, from forgetfulness or any other cause, omit it; so you may be suddenly suffocated. You may accustom yourself to other periodical evacuations, because should you omit them, Nature can supply the omission; but Nature cannot open a vein to blood you.'—'I do not like to take an emetick, (said Taylor,) for fear of breaking some small vessels.'—'Poh! (said Johnson,) if you have so many things that will break, you had better break your neck at once, and there's an end on't. You will break no small vessels:'

(blowing with high derision.)

The horrour of death which I had always observed in Dr. Johnson, appeared strong to-night. I ventured to tell him, that I had been, for moments in my life, not afraid of death; therefore I could suppose another man in that state of mind for a considerable space of time. He said, 'he never had a moment in which death was not terrible to him.' He added, that it had been observed, that scarce any man dies in publick, but with apparent resolution; from that desire of praise which never quits us. I said, Dr. Dodd seemed to be willing to die, and full of hopes of happiness. 'Sir, (said he,) Dr. Dodd would have given both his hands and both his legs to have lived. The better a man is, the more afraid he is of death, having a clearer view of infinite purity.' He owned, that our being in an unhappy uncertainty as to our salvation, was mysterious; and said, 'Ah! we must wait till we are in another state of being, to have many things explained to us.' Even the powerful mind of Johnson seemed foiled by futurity.

On Wednesday, September 17, Dr. Butter, physician at Derby, drank tea with us; and it was settled that Dr. Johnson and I should go on Friday and dine with him. Johnson said, 'I'm glad of this.' He seemed weary of the uniformity of life at Dr. Taylor's.

Talking of biography, I said, in writing a life, a man's peculiarities should be mentioned, because they mark his character. JOHNSON. 'Sir, there is no doubt as to peculiarities: the question is, whether a man's vices should be mentioned; for instance, whether it should be mentioned that Addison and Parnell drank too freely: for people will probably more easily indulge in drinking from knowing this; so that more ill may be done by the example, than good by telling the whole truth.' Here was an instance of his varying from himself in talk; for when Lord Hailes and he sat one morning calmly conversing in my house at Edinburgh, I well remember that Dr. Johnson maintained, that 'If a man is to write *A Panegyrick*, he may keep vices out of sight; but if he professes to write *A Life*, he must represent it really as it was:' and when I objected to the danger of telling that Parnell drank to excess, he said, that 'it would produce an instructive caution to avoid drinking, when it was seen, that even the learning and genius of Parnell could be debased by it.' And in the Hebrides he maintained, as appears from my *Journal*, that a man's intimate friend should mention his faults, if he writes his life.

Thursday, September 18. Last night Dr. Johnson had proposed that the crystal lustre, or chandelier, in Dr. Taylor's large room, should be lighted up some time or other. Taylor said, it should be lighted up next night. 'That will do very well, (said I,) for it is Dr. Johnson's birth-day.' When we were in the Isle of Sky, Johnson had desired me not to mention his birth-day. He did not seem pleased at this time that I mentioned it, and said (somewhat sternly,) 'he would *not* have the lustre lighted the next day.'

Some ladies, who had been present yesterday when I mentioned his birth-day, came to dinner to-day, and plagued him unintentionally, by wishing him joy. I know not why he disliked having his birth-day mentioned, unless it were that it reminded him of his approaching nearer to death, of which he had a constant dread.

I mentioned to him a friend of mine who was formerly gloomy from low spirits, and much distressed by the fear of death, but was now uniformly placid, and contemplated his dissolution without any perturbation. 'Sir, (said Johnson,) this is only a disordered imagination taking a different turn.'

He observed, that a gentleman of eminence in literature had got into a bad style of poetry of late. 'He puts (said he,) a very common thing in a strange dress till he does not know it himself, and thinks other people do not know it.' BOSWELL. 'That is owing to his being so much versant in old English poetry.' JOHNSON. 'What is that to the purpose, Sir? If I say a man is drunk, and you tell me it is owing to his taking much drink, the matter is not mended. No, Sir,———has taken to an odd mode. For example, he'd write thus:

> "Hermit hoar, in solemn cell,
>   Wearing out life's evening gray."

Gray evening is common enough; but evening gray he'd think fine.— Stay;—we'll make out the stanza:

> "Hermit hoar, in solemn cell,
>   Wearing out life's evening gray;
> Smite thy bosom, sage, and tell,
>   What is bliss? and which the way?"'

BOSWELL. 'But why smite his bosom, Sir?' JOHNSON. 'Why, to shew he was in earnest,' (smiling.)—He at an after period added the following stanza:

> 'Thus I spoke; and speaking sigh'd;
>   —Scarce repress'd the starting tear;—
> When the smiling sage reply'd—
>   —Come, my lad, and drink some beer.'

I cannot help thinking the first stanza very good solemn poetry, as also the three first lines of the second. Its last line is an excellent burlesque surprise on gloomy sentimental enquirers. And, perhaps, the advice is as good as can be given to a low-spirited dissatisfied being:—'Don't trouble your head with sickly thinking: take a cup, and be merry.'

Friday, September 19, after breakfast Dr. Johnson and I set out in Dr. Taylor's chaise to go to Derby. The day was fine, and we resolved to go by Keddlestone, the seat of Lord Scarsdale, that I might see his Lordship's fine house. I was struck with the magnificence of the building; and the extensive park, with the finest verdure, covered with deer, and cattle, and sheep, delighted me. The number of old oaks, of an immense size, filled me with a sort of respectful admiration: for one of them sixty pounds was offered. The excellent smooth gravel roads; the large piece of water formed by his Lordship from some small brooks, with a handsome barge upon it; the venerable Gothick church, now the family chapel, just by the house; in short, the grand group of objects agitated and distended my mind in a most agreeable manner. 'One should think (said I,) that the proprietor of all this *must* be happy.'—'Nay, Sir, (said Johnson,) all this excludes but one evil—poverty.'

Our names were sent up, and a well-drest elderly housekeeper, a most distinct articulator, shewed us the house; which I need not describe, as there is an account of it published in *Adam's Works in Architecture*. Dr. Johnson thought better of it to-day than when he saw it before; for he had lately attacked it violently, saying, 'It would do excellently for a town-hall. The large room with the pillars (said he,) would do for the Judges to sit in at the assizes; the circular room for a jury-chamber; and the room above for prisoners.' Still he thought the large room ill lighted, and of no use but for dancing in; and the bed-chambers but indifferent rooms; and that the immense sum which it cost was injudiciously laid out. Dr. Taylor had put him in mind of his *appearing* pleased with the house. 'But (said he,) that was when Lord Scarsdale was present. Politeness obliges us to appear pleased with a man's works when he is present. No man will be so ill bred as to question you. You may therefore pay compliments without saying what is not true. I should say to Lord Scarsdale of his large room, "My Lord, this is the most *costly* room that I ever saw;" which is true.'

Dr. Manningham, physician in London, who was visiting at Lord Scarsdale's, accompanyed us through many of the rooms, and soon afterwards my Lord himself, to whom Dr. Johnson was known, appeared, and did the honours of the house. We talked of Mr. Langton. Johnson, with a warm vehemence of affectionate regard, exclaimed, 'The earth does not bear a worthier man than Bennet Langton.' We saw a good many fine pictures, which I think are described in one of *Young's Tours*. There is a printed catalogue of them which the housekeeper put into my hand; I should like to view them at leisure. I was much struck with Daniel interpreting Nebuchadnezzar's dream by Rembrandt. We were shown a pretty large library. In his Lordship's dressing-room lay Johnson's small *Dictionary*: he shewed it to me, with some eagerness, saying, 'Look'ye! *Quoe terra nostri non plena laboris.*' He observed, also, Goldsmith's Animated Nature; and said, 'Here's our friend! The poor Doctor would have been happy to hear of this.'

In our way, Johnson strongly expressed his love of driving fast in a post-chaise. 'If (said he,) I had no duties, and no reference to futurity, I would spend my life in driving briskly in a post-chaise with a pretty woman; but she should be one who could understand me, and would add something to the conversation.' I observed, that we were this day to stop just where the Highland army did in 1745. JOHNSON. 'It was a noble attempt.' BOSWELL. 'I wish we could have an authentick history of it.' JOHNSON. 'If you were not an idle dog you might write it, by collecting from every body what they can tell, and putting down your authorities.' BOSWELL. 'But I could not have the advantage of it in my life-time.' JOHNSON. 'You might have the satisfaction of its fame, by printing it in Holland; and as to profit, consider how long it was before writing came to be considered in a pecuniary view. Baretti says, he is the first man that ever received copy-money in Italy.' I said that I would endeavour to do what Dr. Johnson suggested and I thought that I might write so as to venture to publish my *History of the Civil War in Great-Britain in* 1745 *and* 1746, without being obliged to go to a foreign press.

When we arrived at Derby, Dr. Butter accompanied us to see the manufactory of china there. I admired the ingenuity and delicate art with which a man fashioned clay into a cup, a saucer, or a tea-pot, while a boy turned round a wheel to give the mass rotundity. I thought this as excellent in its species of power, as making good verses in *its* species. Yet I had no respect for this potter. Neither, indeed, has a man of any extent of thinking for a mere verse-maker, in whose numbers, however perfect, there is no poetry, no mind. The china was beautiful, but Dr. Johnson justly observed it was too dear; for that he could have vessels of silver, of the same size, as cheap as what were here made of porcelain.

I felt a pleasure in walking about Derby such as I always have in walking about any town to which I am not accustomed. There is an immediate sensation of novelty; and one speculates on the way in which life is passed in it, which, although there is a sameness every where upon the whole, is yet minutely diversified. The minute diversities in every thing are wonderful. Talking of shaving the other night at Dr. Taylor's, Dr. Johnson said, 'Sir, of a thousand shavers, two do not shave so much alike as not to be distinguished.' I thought this not possible, till he specified so many of the varieties in shaving;— holding the razor more or less perpendicular;—drawing long or short strokes;—beginning at the upper part of the face, or the under;—at the right side or the left side. Indeed, when one considers what variety of sounds can be uttered by the windpipe, in the compass of a very small aperture, we may be convinced how many degrees of difference there may be in the application of a razor.

We dined with Dr. Butter, whose lady is daughter of my cousin Sir John Douglas, whose grandson is now presumptive heir of the noble family of Queensberry. Johnson and he had a good deal of medical conversation. Johnson said, he had somewhere or other given an account of Dr. Nichols's discourse *De Animiâ Medicâ*. He told us 'that whatever a man's distemper was, Dr. Nichols would not attend him as a physician, if his mind was not at ease; for he believed that no medicines would have any influence. He once attended a man in trade, upon whom he found none of the medicines he prescribed had any effect: he asked the man's wife privately whether his affairs were not in a bad way? She said no. He continued his attendance some time, still without success. At length the man's wife told him, she had discovered that her husband's affairs *were* in a bad way. When Goldsmith was dying, Dr. Turton said to him, "Your pulse is in greater disorder than it should be, from the degree of fever which you have: is your mind at ease?" Goldsmith answered it was not.'

Dr. Johnson told us at tea, that when some of Dr. Dodd's pious friends were trying to console him by saying that he was going to leave 'a wretched world,' he had honesty enough not to join in the cant:— 'No, no, (said he,) it has been a very agreeable world to me.' Johnson added, 'I respect Dodd for thus speaking the truth; for, to be sure, he had for several years enjoyed a life of great voluptuousness.'

He told us, that Dodd's city friends stood by him so, that a thousand pounds were ready to be given to the gaoler, if he would let him escape. He added, that he knew a friend of Dodd's, who walked about Newgate for some time on the evening before the day of his execution, with five hundred pounds in his pocket, ready to be paid to any of the turnkeys who could get him out: but it was too late; for he was watched with much circumspection. He said, Dodd's friends had an image of him made of wax, which was to have been left in his place; and he believed it was carried into the prison.

Johnson disapproved of Dr. Dodd's leaving the world persuaded that *The Convict's Address to his unhappy Brethren* was of his own writing. 'But, Sir, (said I,) you contributed to the deception; for when Mr. Seward expressed a doubt to you that it was not Dodd's own, because it had a great deal more force of mind in it than any thing known to be his, you answered,—"Why should you think so? Depend upon it, Sir, when a man knows he is to be hanged in a fortnight, it concentrates his mind wonderfully."' JOHNSON. Sir, as Dodd got it from me to pass as his own, while that could do him any good, there was an *implied promise* that I should not own it. To own it, therefore, would have been telling a lie, with the addition of breach of promise, which was worse than simply telling a lie to make it be believed it was

Dodd's. Besides, Sir, I did not *directly* tell a lie: I left the matter uncertain. Perhaps I thought that Seward would not believe it the less to be mine for what I said; but I would not put it in his power to say I had owned it.'

He said, 'Goldsmith was a plant that flowered late. There appeared nothing remarkable about him when he was young; though when he had got high in fame, one of his friends began to recollect something of his being distinguished at College. Goldsmith in the same manner recollected more of that friend's early years, as he grew a greater man.'

I mentioned that Lord Monboddo told me, he awaked every morning at four, and then for his health got up and walked in his room naked, with the window open, which he called taking *an air bath*; after which he went to bed again, and slept two hours more. Johnson, who was always ready to beat down any thing that seemed to be exhibited with disproportionate importance, thus observed: 'I suppose, Sir, there is no more in it than this, he awakes at four, and cannot sleep till he chills himself, and makes the warmth of the bed a grateful sensation.'

I talked of the difficulty of rising in the morning. Dr. Johnson told me, 'that the learned Mrs. Carter, at that period when she was eager in study, did not awake as early as she wished, and she therefore had a contrivance, that, at a certain hour, her chamber-light should burn a string to which a heavy weight was suspended, which then fell with a strong sudden noise: this roused her from sleep, and then she had no difficulty in getting up.' But I said *that* was my difficulty; and wished there could be some medicine invented which would make one rise without pain, which I never did, unless after lying in bed a very long time.

Johnson advised me to-night not to *refine* in the education of my children. 'Life (said he,) will not bear refinement: you must do as other people do.'

As we drove back to Ashbourne, Dr. Johnson recommended to me, as he had often done, to drink water only: 'For (said he,) you are then sure not to get drunk; whereas if you drink wine you are never sure.' I said, drinking wine was a pleasure which I was unwilling to give up, 'Why, Sir, (said he,) there is no doubt that not to drink wine is a great deduction from life; but it may be necessary.' He however owned, that in his opinion a free use of wine did not shorten life; and said, he would not give less for the life of a certain Scotch Lord (whom he named) celebrated for hard drinking, than for that of a sober man. 'But stay, (said he, with his usual intelligence, and accuracy of enquiry,) does it take much wine to make him drunk?' I answered, 'a great deal either of wine or strong punch.'—'Then (said he,) that is the worse.' I presume to illustrate my friend's observation thus: 'A fortress which soon surrenders has its walls less shattered than when a long and obstinate resistance is made.'

I ventured to mention a person who was as violent a Scotsman as he was an Englishman; and literally had the same contempt for an Englishman compared with a Scotsman, that he had for a Scotsman compared with an Englishman; and that he would say of Dr. Johnson, 'Damned rascal! to talk as he does of the Scotch.' This seemed, for a moment, 'to give him pause.' It, perhaps, presented his extreme prejudice against the Scotch in a point of view somewhat new to him, by the effect of *contrast*.

By the time when we returned to Ashbourne, Dr. Taylor was gone to bed. Johnson and I sat up a long time by ourselves.

On Saturday, September 20, after breakfast, when Taylor was gone out to his farm, Dr. Johnson and I had a serious conversation by ourselves on melancholy and madness.

We entered seriously upon a question of much importance to me, which Johnson was pleased to consider with friendly attention. I had long complained to him that I felt myself discontented in Scotland, as too narrow a sphere, and that I wished to make my chief residence in London, the great scene of ambition, instruction, and amusement: a scene, which was to me, comparatively speaking, a heaven upon earth. JOHNSON. 'Why, Sir, I never knew any one who had such a *gust* for London as you have: and I cannot blame you for your wish to live there: yet, Sir, were I in your father's place, I should not consent to your settling there; for I have the old feudal notions, and I should be afraid that Auchinleck would be deserted, as you would soon find it more desirable to have a country-seat in a better climate.'

I suggested a doubt, that if I were to reside in London, the exquisite zest with which I relished it in occasional visits might go off, and I might grow tired of it. JOHNSON. 'Why, Sir, you find no man, at all intellectual, who is willing to leave London. No, Sir, when a man is tired of London, he is tired of life; for there is in London all that life can afford.'

He said, 'A country gentleman should bring his lady to visit London as soon as he can, that they may have agreeable topicks for conversation when they are by themselves.'

We talked of employment being absolutely necessary to preserve the mind from wearying and growing fretful, especially in those who have a tendency to melancholy; and I mentioned to him a saying which somebody had related of an American savage, who, when an European was expatiating on all the advantages of money, put this question: 'Will it purchase *occupation*?' JOHNSON. 'Depend upon it, Sir, this saying is too refined for a savage. And, Sir, money *will* purchase occupation; it will purchase all the conveniences of life; it will purchase variety of company; it will purchase all sorts of entertainment.'

I talked to him of Forster's *Voyage to the South Seas*, which pleased me; but I found he did not like it. 'Sir, (said he,) there is a great affectation of fine writing in it.' BOSWELL. 'But he carries you along with him.' JOHNSON. 'No, Sir; he does not carry *me* along with him: he leaves me behind him: or rather, indeed, he sets me before him; for he makes me turn over many leaves at a time.'

On Sunday, September 21, we went to the church of Ashbourne, which is one of the largest and most luminous that I have seen in any town of the same size. I felt great satisfaction in considering that I was supported in my fondness for solemn publick worship by the general concurrence and munificence of mankind.

Johnson and Taylor were so different from each other, that I wondered at their preserving an intimacy. Their having been at school and college together, might, in some degree, account for this; but Sir Joshua Reynolds has furnished me with a stronger reason; for Johnson mentioned to him, that he had been told by Taylor he was to be his heir. I shall not take upon me to animadvert upon this; but certain it is, that Johnson paid great attention to Taylor. He now, however, said to me, 'Sir, I love him; but I do not love him more; my regard for him does not increase. As it is said in the Apocrypha, "his talk is of bullocks:" I do not suppose he is very fond of my company. His habits are by no means sufficiently clerical: this he knows that I see; and no man likes to live under the eye of perpetual disapprobation.'

I have no doubt that a good many sermons were composed for Taylor by Johnson. At this time I found, upon his table, a part of one which he had newly begun to write: and *Concio pro Tayloro* appears in one of his diaries. When to these circumstances we add the internal evidence from the power of thinking and style, in the collection which the Reverend Mr. Hayes has published, with the *significant* title of 'Sermons *left for publication* by the Reverend John Taylor, LL.D.,' our conviction will be complete.

I, however, would not have it thought, that Dr. Taylor, though he could not write like Johnson, (as, indeed, who could?) did not sometimes compose sermons as good as those which we generally have from very respectable divines. He shewed me one with notes on the margin in Johnson's handwriting; and I was present when he read another to Johnson, that he might have his opinion of it, and Johnson said it was 'very well.' These, we may be sure, were not Johnson's; for he was above little arts, or tricks of deception.

I mentioned to Johnson a respectable person of a very strong mind, who had little of that tenderness which is common to human nature; as an instance of which, when I suggested to him that he should invite his son, who had been settled ten years in foreign parts, to come home and pay him a visit, his answer was, 'No, no, let him mind his business. JOHNSON. 'I do not agree with him, Sir, in this. Getting money is not all a man's business: to cultivate kindness is a valuable part of the business of life.'

In the evening, Johnson, being in very good spirits, entertained us with several characteristical portraits. I regret that any of them escaped my retention and diligence. I found, from experience, that to collect my friend's conversation so as to exhibit it with any degree of its original flavour, it was necessary to write it down without delay. To record his sayings, after some distance of time, was like preserving or pickling long-kept and faded fruits, or other vegetables, which, when in that state, have little or nothing of their taste when fresh.

I shall present my readers with a series of what I gathered this evening from the Johnsonian garden.

'Did we not hear so much said of Jack Wilkes, we should think more highly of his conversation. Jack has great variety of talk, Jack is a scholar, and Jack has the manners of a gentleman. But after hearing his name sounded from pole to pole, as the phoenix of convivial felicity, we are disappointed in his company. He has always been *at me*: but I would do Jack a kindness, rather than not. The contest is now over.'

'Colley Cibber once consulted me as to one of his birthday Odes, a long time before it was wanted. I objected very freely to several passages. Cibber lost patience, and would not read his Ode to an end. When we had done with criticism, we walked over to Richardson's, the authour of Clarissa and I wondered to find Richardson displeased that I "did not treat Cibber with more *respect*." Now, Sir, to talk of *respect* for a *player*!' (smiling disdainfully.) BOSWELL. 'There, Sir, you are always heretical: you never will allow merit to a player.' JOHNSON. 'Merit, Sir! what merit? Do you respect a rope-dancer, or a ballad-singer?' BOSWELL. 'No, Sir: but we respect a great player, as a man who can conceive lofty sentiments, and can express them gracefully.' JOHNSON. 'What, Sir, a fellow who claps a hump on his back, and a lump on his leg, and cries "*I am Richard the Third*"? Nay, Sir, a ballad-singer is a higher man, for he does two things; he repeats and he sings: there is both recitation and musick in his performance: the player only recites.' BOSWELL. 'My dear Sir! you may turn anything into ridicule. I allow, that a player of farce is not entitled to respect; he does a little thing: but he who can represent exalted characters, and touch the noblest passions, has very respectable powers; and mankind have agreed in admiring great talents for the stage. We must consider, too, that a great player does what very few are capable to do: his art is a very rare faculty. *Who* can repeat Hamlet's soliloquy, "To be, or not to be," as Garrick does it?' JOHNSON. 'Any body may. Jemmy, there (a boy about eight years old, who was in the room,) will do it as well in a week.' BOSWELL. 'No, no, Sir: and as a proof of the merit of great acting, and of the value which mankind set upon it, Garrick has got a hundred thousand pounds.' JOHNSON. 'Is getting a hundred thousand pounds a proof of excellence? That has been done by a scoundrel commissary.'

This was most fallacious reasoning. I was *sure*, for once, that I had the best side of the argument. I boldly maintained the just distinction between a tragedian and a mere theatrical droll; between those who rouse our terrour and pity, and those who only make us laugh. 'If (said I,) Betterton and Foote were to walk into this room, you would respect Betterton much more than Foote.' JOHNSON. 'If Betterton were to walk into this room with Foote, Foote would soon drive him out of it. Foote, Sir, *quatenùs* Foote, has powers superiour to them all.'

On Monday, September 22, when at breakfast, I unguardedly said to Dr. Johnson, 'I wish I saw you and Mrs. Macaulay together.' He grew very angry; and, after a pause, while a cloud gathered on his brow, he burst out, 'No, Sir; you would not see us quarrel, to make you sport. Don't you know that it is very uncivil to *pit* two people against one another?' Then, checking himself, and wishing to be more gentle, he added, 'I do not say you should be hanged or drowned for this; but it *is* very uncivil.' Dr. Taylor thought him in the wrong, and spoke to him privately of it; but I afterwards acknowledged to Johnson that I was to blame, for I candidly owned, that I meant to express a desire to see a contest between Mrs. Macaulay and him; but then I knew how the contest would end; so that I was to see him triumph. JOHNSON. 'Sir, you cannot be sure how a contest will end; and no man has a right to engage two people in a dispute by which their passions may be inflamed, and they may part with bitter resentment against each other. I would sooner keep company with a man from whom I must guard my pockets, than with a man who contrives to bring me into a dispute with somebody that he may hear it. This is the great fault of———,(naming one of our friends,) endeavouring to introduce a subject upon which he knows two people in the company differ.' BOSWELL. 'But he told me, Sir, he does it for instruction.' JOHNSON. 'Whatever the motive be, Sir, the man who does so, does very wrong. He has no more right to instruct himself at such risk, than he has to make two people fight a duel, that he may learn how to defend himself.'

He found great fault with a gentleman of our acquaintance for keeping a bad table. 'Sir, (said he,) when a man is invited to dinner, he is disappointed if he does not get something good. I advised Mrs. Thrale, who has no card-parties at her house, to give sweet-meats, and such good things, in an evening, as are not commonly given, and she would find company enough come to her; for every body loves to have things which please the palate put in their way, without trouble or preparation.' Such was his attention to the *minutiae* of life and manners.

Mr. Burke's *Letter to the Sheriffs of Bristol, on the affairs of America*, being mentioned, Johnson censured the composition much, and he ridiculed the definition of a free government, *viz.* 'For any practical purpose, it is what the people think so.'—'I will let the King of France govern me on those conditions, (said he,) for it is to be governed just as I please.' And when Dr. Taylor talked of a girl being sent to a parish workhouse, and asked how much she could be obliged to work, 'Why, (said Johnson,) as much as is reasonable: and what is that? as much as *she thinks* reasonable.'

Dr. Johnson obligingly proposed to carry me to see Islam, a romantick scene, now belonging to a family of the name of Port, but formerly the seat of the Congreves. I suppose it is well described in some of the Tours. Johnson described it distinctly and vividly, at which I could not but express to him my wonder; because, though my eyes, as he observed, were better than his, I could not by any means equal him in representing visible objects. I said, the difference between us in this respect was as that between a man who has a bad instrument, but plays well on it, and a man who has a good instrument, on which he can play very imperfectly.

I recollect a very fine amphitheatre, surrounded with hills covered with woods, and walks neatly formed along the side of a rocky steep, on the quarter next the house with recesses under projections of rock, overshadowed with trees; in one of which recesses, we were told, Congreve wrote his *Old Bachelor*. We viewed a remarkable natural curiosity at Islam; two rivers bursting near each other from the rock, not from immediate springs, but after having run for many miles under ground. Plott, in his *History of Staffordshire*, gives an account of this curiosity; but Johnson would not believe it, though we had the attestation of the gardener, who said, he had put in corks, where the river *Manyfold* sinks into the ground, and had catched them in a net, placed before one of the openings where the water bursts out. Indeed, such subterraneous courses of water are found in various parts of our globe.

Talking of Dr. Johnson's unwillingness to believe extraordinary things I ventured to say, 'Sir, you come near Hume's argument against miracles, "That it is more probable witnesses should lie, or be mistaken, than that they should happen." JOHNSON. 'Why, Sir, Hume, taking the proposition simply, is right. But the Christian revelation is not proved by the miracles alone, but as connected with prophecies, and with the doctrines in confirmation of which the miracles were wrought.'

In the evening, a gentleman-farmer, who was on a visit at Dr. Taylor's, attempted to dispute with Johnson in favour of Mungo Campbell, who shot Alexander, Earl of Eglintoune, upon his having fallen, when retreating from his Lordship, who he believed was about to seize his gun, as he had threatened to do. He said, he should have done just as Campbell did. JOHNSON. 'Whoever would do as Campbell did, deserves to be hanged; not that I could, as a juryman, have found him legally guilty of murder; but I am glad they found means to convict him.' The gentleman-farmer said, 'A poor man has as much honour as a rich man; and Campbell had *that* to defend.' Johnson exclaimed, 'A poor man has no honour.' The English yeoman, not dismayed, proceeded: 'Lord Eglintoune was a damned fool to run on upon Campbell, after being warned that Campbell would shoot him if he did.' Johnson, who could not bear any thing like swearing, angrily replied, 'He was *not* a *damned* fool: he only thought too well of Campbell. He did not believe Campbell would be such a *damned* scoundrel, as to do so *damned* a thing.' His emphasis on *damned*, accompanied with frowning looks, reproved his opponent's want of decorum in *his* presence.

During this interview at Ashbourne, Johnson seemed to be more uniformly social, cheerful, and alert, than I had almost ever seen him. He was prompt on great occasions and on small. Taylor, who praised every thing of his own to excess; in short, 'whose geese were all swans,' as the proverb says, expatiated on the excellence of his bull-dog, which, he told us, was 'perfectly well shaped.' Johnson, after examining the animal attentively, thus repressed the vain-glory of our host:—'No, Sir, he is *not* well shaped; for there is not the quick transition from the thickness of the fore-part, to the *tenuity*—the thin part—behind,—which a bull-dog ought to have.' This *tenuity* was the only *hard word* that I heard him use during this interview, and it will be observed, he instantly put another expression in its place. Taylor said, a small bull-dog was as good as a large one. JOHNSON. 'No, Sir; for, in proportion to his size, he has strength: and your argument would prove, that a good bull-dog may be as small as a mouse.' It was amazing how he entered with perspicuity and keenness upon every thing that occurred in conversation. Most men, whom I know, would no more think of discussing a question about a bull-dog, than of attacking a bull.

I cannot allow any fragment whatever that floats in my memory concerning the great subject of this work to be lost. Though a small particular may appear trifling to some, it will be relished by others; while every little spark adds something to the general blaze: and to please the true, candid, warm admirers of Johnson, and in any degree increase the splendour of his reputation, I bid defiance to the shafts of ridicule, or even of malignity. Showers of them have been discharged at my *Journal of a Tour to the Hebrides*; yet it still sails unhurt along the stream of time, and, as an attendant upon Johnson,

'Pursues the triumph, and partakes the gale.'

One morning after breakfast, when the sun shone bright, we walked out together, and 'pored' for some time with placid indolence upon an artificial water-fall, which Dr. Taylor had made by building a strong dyke of stone across the river behind the garden. It was now somewhat obstructed by branches of trees and other rubbish, which had come down the river, and settled close to it. Johnson, partly from a desire to see it play more freely, and partly from that inclination to activity which will animate, at times, the most inert and sluggish mortal, took a long pole which was lying on a bank, and pushed down several parcels of this wreck with painful assiduity, while I stood quietly by, wondering to behold the sage thus curiously employed, and smiling with an humorous satisfaction each time when he carried his point. He worked till he was quite out of breath; and having found a large dead cat so heavy that he could not move it after several efforts, 'Come,' said he, (throwing down the pole,) '*you* shall take it now;' which I accordingly did, and being a fresh man, soon made the cat tumble over the cascade. This may be laughed at as too trifling to record; but it is a small characteristick trait in the Flemish picture which I give of my friend, and in which, therefore I mark the most minute particulars. And let it be remembered, that *Aesop at play* is one of the instructive apologues of antiquity.

Talking of Rochester's Poems, he said, he had given them to Mr. Steevens to castrate for the edition of the poets, to which he was to write Prefaces. Dr. Taylor (the only time I ever heard him say any thing witty) observed, that if Rochester had been castrated himself, his exceptionable poems would not have been written.' I asked if Burnet had not given a good Life of Rochester. JOHNSON. 'We have a good *Death*: there is not much *Life*.' I asked whether Prior's Poems were to be printed entire: Johnson said they were. I mentioned Lord Hailes's censure of Prior, in his Preface to a collection of *Sacred Poems*, by various hands, published by him at Edinburgh a great many years ago, where he mentions, 'those impure tales which will be the eternal opprobrium of their ingenious authour.' JOHNSON. 'Sir, Lord Hailes has forgot. There is nothing in Prior that will excite to lewdness. If Lord Hailes thinks there is, he must be more combustible than other people.' I instanced the tale of *Paulo Purganti and his Wife*. JOHNSON. Sir, there is nothing there, but that his wife wanted to be kissed when poor Paulo was out of pocket. No, Sir, Prior is a lady's book. No lady is ashamed to have it standing in her library.'

The hypochondriack disorder being mentioned, Dr. Johnson did not think it so common as I supposed. 'Dr. Taylor (said he,) is the same one day as another. Burke and Reynolds are the same; Beauclerk, except when in pain, is the same. I am not so myself; but this I do not mention commonly.'

Dr. Johnson advised me to-day, to have as many books about me as I could; that I might read upon any subject upon which I had a desire for instruction at the time. 'What you read *then* (said he,) you will remember; but if you have not a book immediately ready, and the subject moulds in your mind, it is a chance if you again have a desire to study it.' He added, 'If a man never has an eager desire for instruction, he should prescribe a task for himself. But it is better when a man reads from immediate inclination.'

He repeated a good many lines of Horace's *Odes*, while we were in the chaise. I remember particularly the Ode *Eheu fugaces.*

He told me that Bacon was a favourite authour with him; but he had never read his works till he was compiling the *English Dictionary*, in which, he said, I might see Bacon very often quoted. Mr. Seward recollects his having mentioned, that a Dictionary of the English Language might be compiled from Bacon's writings alone, and that he had once an intention of giving an edition of Bacon, at least of his English works, and writing the Life of that great man. Had he executed this intention, there can be no doubt that he would have done it in a most masterly manner.

Wishing to be satisfied what degree of truth there was in a story which a friend of Johnson's and mine had told me to his disadvantage, I mentioned it to him in direct terms; and it was to this effect: that a gentleman who had lived in great intimacy with him, shewn him much kindness, and even relieved him from a spunging-house, having afterwards fallen into bad circumstances, was one day, when Johnson was at dinner with him, seized for debt, and carried to prison; that Johnson sat still undisturbed, and went on eating and drinking; upon which the gentleman's sister, who was present, could not suppress her indignation: 'What, Sir, (said she,) are you so unfeeling, as not even to offer to go to my brother in his distress; you who have been so much obliged to him?' And that Johnson answered, 'Madam, I owe him no obligation; what he did for me he would have done for a dog.'

Johnson assured me, that the story was absolutely false: but like a man conscious of being in the right, and desirous of completely vindicating himself from such a charge, he did not arrogantly rest on a mere denial, and on his general character, but proceeded thus:—'Sir, I was very intimate with that gentleman, and was once relieved by him from an arrest; but I never was present when he was arrested, never knew that he was arrested, and I believe he never was in difficulties after the time when he relieved me. I loved him much; yet, in talking of his general character, I may have said, though I do not remember that I ever did say so, that as his generosity proceeded from no principle, but was a part of his profusion, he would do for a dog what he would do for a friend: but I never applied this remark to any particular instance, and certainly not to his kindness to me. If a profuse man, who does not value his money, and gives a large sum to a whore, gives half as much, or an equally large sum to relieve a friend, it cannot be esteemed as virtue. This was all that I could say of that gentleman; and, if said at all, it must have been said after his death. Sir, I would have gone to the world's end to relieve him. The remark about the dog, if made by me, was such a sally as might escape one when painting a man highly.'

On Tuesday, September 23, Johnson was remarkably cordial to me. It being necessary for me to return to Scotland soon, I had fixed on the next day for my setting out, and I felt a tender concern at the thought of parting with him. He had, at this time, frankly communicated to me many particulars, which are inserted in this work in their proper places; and once, when I happened to mention that the expence of my jaunt would come to much more than I had computed, he said, 'Why, Sir, if the expence were to be an inconvenience, you would have reason to regret it: but, if you have had the money to spend, I know not that you could have purchased as much pleasure with it in any other way.'

I perceived that he pronounced the word *heard*, as if spelt with a double *e, heerd*, instead of sounding it herd, as is most usually done. He said, his reason was, that if it was pronounced *herd*, there would be a single exception from the English pronunciation of the syllable *ear*, and he thought it better not to have that exception.

In the evening our gentleman-farmer, and two others, entertained themselves and the company with a great number of tunes on the fiddle. Johnson desired to have 'Let ambition fire thy mind,' played over again, and appeared to give a patient attention to it; though he owned to me that he was very insensible to the power of musick. I told him, that it affected me to such a degree, as often to agitate my nerves painfully, producing in my mind alternate sensations of pathetick dejection, so that I was ready to shed tears; and of daring resolution, so that I was inclined to rush into the thickest part of the battle. 'Sir, (said he,) I should never hear it, if it made me such a fool.'

This evening, while some of the tunes of ordinary composition were played with no great skill, my frame was agitated, and I was conscious of a generous attachment to Dr. Johnson, as my preceptor and friend, mixed with an affectionate regret that he was an old man, whom I should probably lose in a short time. I thought I could defend him at the point of my sword. My reverence and affection for him were in full glow. I said to him, 'My dear Sir, we must meet every year, if you don't quarrel with me.' JOHNSON. 'Nay, Sir, you are more likely to quarrel with me, than I with you. My regard for you is greater almost than I have words to express; but I do not choose to be always repeating it; write it down in the first leaf of your pocket-book, and never doubt of it again.'

I talked to him of misery being 'the doom of man' in this life, as displayed in his *Vanity of Human Wishes*. Yet I observed that things were done upon the supposition of happiness; grand houses were built, fine gardens were made, splendid places of publick amusement were contrived, and crowded with company. JOHNSON. 'Alas, Sir, these are all only struggles for happiness. When I first entered Ranelagh, it gave an expansion and gay sensation to my mind, such as I never experienced any where else. But, as Xerxes wept when he viewed his immense army, and considered that not one of that great multitude would be alive a hundred years afterwards, so it went to my heart to consider that there was not one in all that brilliant circle, that was not afraid to go home and think; but that the thoughts of each individual there, would be distressing when alone.'

I suggested, that being in love, and flattered with hopes of success; or having some favourite scheme in view for the next day, might prevent that wretchedness of which we had been talking. JOHNSON. 'Why, Sir, it may sometimes be so as you suppose; but my conclusion is in general but too true.'

While Johnson and I stood in calm conference by ourselves in Dr. Taylor's garden, at a pretty late hour in a serene autumn night, looking up to the heavens, I directed the discourse to the subject of a future state. My friend was in a placid and most benignant frame. 'Sir, (said he,) I do not imagine that all things will be made clear to us immediately after death, but that the ways of Providence will be explained to us very gradually.' He talked to me upon this aweful and delicate question in a gentle tone, and as if afraid to be decisive.

After supper I accompanied him to his apartment, and at my request he dictated to me an argument in favour of the negro who was then claiming his liberty, in an action in the Court of Session in Scotland. He had always been very zealous against slavery in every form, in which I, with all deference, thought that he discovered 'a zeal without knowledge.' Upon one occasion, when in company with some very grave men at Oxford, his toast was, 'Here's to the next insurrection of the negroes in the West Indies.' His violent prejudice against our West Indian and American settlers appeared whenever there was an opportunity. Towards the conclusion of his *Taxation no Tyranny*, he says, 'how is it that we hear the loudest *yelps* for liberty among the drivers of negroes?'

When I said now to Johnson, that I was afraid I kept him too late up. 'No, Sir, (said he,) I don't care though I sit all night with you.' This was an animated speech from a man in his sixty-ninth year.

Had I been as attentive not to displease him as I ought to have been, I know not but this vigil might have been fulfilled; but I unluckily entered upon the controversy concerning the right of Great-Britain to tax America, and attempted to argue in favour of our fellow-subjects on the other side of the Atlantick. I insisted that America might be very well governed, and made to yield sufficient revenue by the means of *influence*, as exemplified in Ireland, while the people might be pleased with the imagination of their participating of the British constitution, by having a body of representatives, without whose consent money could not be exacted from them. Johnson could not bear my thus opposing his avowed opinion, which he had exerted himself with an extreme degree of heat to enforce; and the violent agitation into which he was thrown, while answering, or rather reprimanding me, alarmed me so, that I heartily repented of my having unthinkingly introduced the subject. I myself, however, grew warm, and the change was great, from the calm state of philosophical discussion in which we had a little before been pleasingly employed.

We were fatigued by the contest, which was produced by my want of caution; and he was not then in the humour to slide into easy and cheerful talk. It therefore so happened, that we were after an hour or two very willing to separate and go to bed.

On Wednesday, September 24, I went into Dr. Johnson's room before he got up, and finding that the storm of the preceding night was quite laid, I sat down upon his bed-side, and he talked with as much readiness and good-humour as ever. He recommended to me to plant a considerable part of a large moorish farm which I had purchased, and he made several calculations of the expence and profit: for he delighted in exercising his mind on the science of numbers. He pressed upon me the importance of planting at the first in a very sufficient manner, quoting the saying '*In bello non licet bis errare:*' and adding, 'this is equally true in planting.'

I spoke with gratitude of Dr. Taylor's hospitality; and, as evidence that it was not on account of his good table alone that Johnson visited him often, I mentioned a little anecdote which had escaped my friend's recollection, and at hearing which repeated, he smiled. One evening, when I was sitting with him, Frank delivered this message: 'Sir, Dr. Taylor sends his compliments to you, and begs you will dine with him to-morrow. He has got a hare.'—'My compliments (said Johnson,) and I'll dine with him—hare or rabbit.'

After breakfast I departed, and pursued my journey northwards. I took my post-chaise from the Green Man, a very good inn at Ashbourne, the mistress of which, a mighty civil gentlewoman, courtseying very low, presented me with an engraving of the sign of her house; to which she had subjoined, in her own hand-writing, an address in such singular simplicity of style, that I have preserved it pasted upon one of the boards of my original Journal at this time, and shall here insert it for the amusement of my readers:—

'*M. KILLINGLEY's duty waits upon* Mr. Boswell, *is exceedingly obliged to him for this favour; whenever he comes this way, hopes for a continuance of the same. Would* Mr. Boswell *name the house to his extensive acquaintance, it would be a singular favour conferr'd on one who has it not in her power to make any other return but her most grateful thanks, and sincerest prayers for his happiness in time, and in a blessed eternity.—Tuesday morn.*'

I cannot omit a curious circumstance which occurred at Edensorinn, close by Chatsworth, to survey the magnificence of which I had gone a considerable way out of my road to Scotland. The inn was then kept by a very jolly landlord, whose name, I think, was Malton. He happened to mention that 'the celebrated Dr. Johnson had been in his house.' I inquired *who* this Dr. Johnson was, that I might hear mine host's notion of him. 'Sir, (said he,) Johnson, the great writer; *Oddity*, as they call him. He's the greatest writer in England; he writes for the ministry; he has a correspondence abroad, and lets them know what's going on.'

My friend, who had a thorough dependance upon the authenticity of my relation without any *embellishment*, as *falsehood* or *fiction* is too gently called, laughed a good deal at this representation of himself.

On Wednesday, March 18,[41] I arrived in London, and was informed by good Mr. Francis that his master was better, and was gone to Mr. Thrale's at Streatham, to which place I wrote to him, begging to know when he would be in town. He was not expected for some time; but next day having called on Dr. Taylor, in Dean's-yard, Westminster, I found him there, and was told he had come to town for a few hours. He met me with his usual kindness, but instantly returned to the writing of something on which he was employed when I came in, and on which he seemed much intent. Finding him thus engaged, I made my visit very short.

On Friday, March 20, I found him at his own house, sitting with Mrs. Williams, and was informed that the room formerly allotted to me was now appropriated to a charitable purpose; Mrs. Desmoulins, and I think her daughter, and a Miss Carmichael, being all lodged in it. Such was his humanity, and such his generosity, that Mrs. Desmoulins herself told me, he allowed her half-a-guinea a week. Let it be remembered, that this was above a twelfth part of his pension.

His liberality, indeed, was at all periods of his life very remarkable. Mr. Howard, of Lichfield, at whose father's house Johnson had in his early years been kindly received, told me, that when he was a boy at the Charter-House, his father wrote to him to go and pay a visit to Mr. Samuel Johnson, which he accordingly did, and found him in an upper room, of poor appearance. Johnson received him with much courteousness, and talked a great deal to him, as to a school-boy, of the course of his education, and other particulars. When he afterwards came to know and understand the high character of this great man, he recollected his condescension with wonder. He added, that when he was going away, Mr. Johnson presented him with half-a-guinea; and this, said Mr. Howard, was at a time when he probably had not another.

We retired from Mrs. Williams to another room. Tom Davies soon after joined us. He had now unfortunately failed in his circumstances,

---

[41] 1778.

and was much indebted to Dr. Johnson's kindness for obtaining for him many alleviations of his distress. After he went away, Johnson blamed his folly in quitting the stage, by which he and his wife got five hundred pounds a year. I said, I believed it was owing to Churchill's attack upon him,

'He mouths a sentence, as curs mouth a bone.'

JOHNSON. 'I believe so too, Sir. But what a man is he, who is to be driven from the stage by a line? Another line would have driven him from his shop.'

He returned next day to Streatham, to Mr. Thrale's; where, as Mr. Strahan once complained to me, 'he was in a great measure absorbed from the society of his old friends.' I was kept in London by business, and wrote to him on the 27th, that a separation from him for a week, when we were so near, was equal to a separation for a year, when we were at four hundred miles distance. I went to Streatham on Monday, March 30. Before he appeared, Mrs. Thrale made a very characteristical remark:—'I do not know for certain what will please Dr. Johnson: but I know for certain that it will displease him to praise any thing, even what he likes, extravagantly.'

At dinner he laughed at querulous declamations against the age, on account of luxury,—increase of London,—scarcity of provisions,—and other such topicks. 'Houses (said he,) will be built till rents fall: and corn is more plentiful now than ever it was.'

I had before dinner repeated a ridiculous story told me by an old man who had been a passenger with me in the stage-coach to-day. Mrs. Thrale, having taken occasion to allude to it in talking to me, called it 'The story told you by the old *woman*.'—'Now, Madam, (said I,) give me leave to catch you in the fact; it was not an old *woman*, but an old *man*, whom I mentioned as having told me this.' I presumed to take an opportunity, in presence of Johnson, of shewing this lively lady how ready she was, unintentionally, to deviate from exact authenticity of narration.

Next morning, while we were at breakfast, Johnson gave a very earnest recommendation of what he himself practised with the utmost conscientiousness: I mean a strict attention to truth, even in the most minute particulars. 'Accustom your children (said he,) constantly to this; if a thing happened at one window, and they, when relating it, say that it happened at another, do not let it pass, but instantly check them; you do not know where deviation from truth will end.' BOSWELL. 'It may come to the door: and when once an account is at all varied in one circumstance, it may by degrees be varied so as to be totally different from what really happened.' Our lively hostess, whose fancy was impatient of the rein, fidgeted at this, and ventured to say, 'Nay, this is too much. If Mr. Johnson should forbid me to drink tea, I would comply, as I should feel the restraint only twice a day; but little variations in narrative must happen a thousand times a day, if one is not perpetually watching.' JOHNSON. 'Well, Madam, and you *ought* to be perpetually watching. It is more from carelessness about truth than from intentional lying, that there is so much falsehood in the world.'

He was indeed so much impressed with the prevalence of falsehood, voluntary or unintentional, that I never knew any person who upon hearing an extraordinary circumstance told, discovered more of the *incredulus odi*. He would say, with a significant look and decisive tone, 'It is not so. Do not tell this again.' He inculcated upon all his friends the importance of perpetual vigilance against the slightest degrees of falsehood; the effect of which, as Sir Joshua Reynolds observed to me, has been, that all who were of his *school* are distinguished for a love of truth and accuracy, which they would not have possessed in the same degree, if they had not been acquainted with Johnson.

Talking of ghosts, he said, 'It is wonderful that five thousand years have now elapsed since the creation of the world, and still it is undecided whether or not there has ever been an instance of the spirit of any person appearing after death. All argument is against it; but all belief is for it.'

He said, 'John Wesley's conversation is good, but he is never at leisure. He is always obliged to go at a certain hour. This is very disagreeable to a man who loves to fold his legs and have out his talk, as I do.'

On Friday, April 3, I dined with him in London, in a company[42] where were present several eminent men, whom I shall not name, but distinguish their parts in the conversation by different letters.

E. 'We hear prodigious complaints at present of emigration. I am convinced that emigration makes a country more populous.' J. 'That sounds very much like a paradox.' E. 'Exportation of men, like exportation of all other commodities, makes more be produced.' JOHNSON. 'But there would be more people were there not emigration, provided there were food for more.' E. 'No; leave a few breeders, and you'll have more people than if there were no emigration.' JOHNSON. 'Nay, Sir, it is plain there will be more people, if there are more breeders. Thirty cows in good pasture will produce more calves than ten cows, provided they have good bulls.' E. 'There are bulls enough in Ireland.' JOHNSON. (smiling,) 'So, Sir, I should think from your argument.'

E. 'I believe, in any body of men in England, I should have been in the Minority; I have always been in the Minority.' P. 'The House of

---

[42] The Club. Hill identifies E. as Burke and J. as Sir Joshua Reynolds.—Ed.

Commons resembles a private company. How seldom is any man convinced by another's argument; passion and pride rise against it.' R. 'What would be the consequence, if a Minister, sure of a majority in the House of Commons, should resolve that there should be no speaking at all upon his side.' E. 'He must soon go out. That has been tried; but it was found it would not do.' . . . .

JOHNSON. 'I have been reading Thicknesse's *Travels*, which I think are entertaining.' BOSWELL. 'What, Sir, a good book?' JOHNSON. 'Yes, Sir, to read once; I do not say you are to make a study of it, and digest it; and I believe it to be a true book in his intention.'

E. 'From the experience which I have had,—and I have had a great deal,—I have learnt to think *better* of mankind.' JOHNSON. 'From my experience I have found them worse in commercial dealings, more disposed to cheat, than I had any notion of; but more disposed to do one another good than I had conceived.' J. 'Less just and more beneficent.' JOHNSON. 'And really it is wonderful, considering how much attention is necessary for men to take care of themselves, and ward off immediate evils which press upon them, it is wonderful how much they do for others. As it is said of the greatest liar, that he tells more truth than falsehood; so it may be said of the worst man, that he does more good than evil.' BOSWELL. 'Perhaps from experience men may be found *happier* than we suppose.' JOHNSON. 'No, Sir; the more we enquire, we shall find men the less happy.'

E. 'I understand the hogshead of claret, which this society was favoured with by our friend the Dean, is nearly out; I think he should be written to, to send another of the same kind. Let the request be made with a happy ambiguity of expression, so that we may have the chance of his sending *it* also as a present.' JOHNSON. 'I am willing to offer my services as secretary on this occasion.' P. 'As many as are for Dr. Johnson being secretary hold up your hands.—Carried unanimously.' BOSWELL. 'He will be our Dictator.' JOHNSON. 'No, the company is to dictate to me. I am only to write for wine; and I am quite disinterested, as I drink none; I shall not be suspected of having forged the application. I am no more than humble *scribe*.' E. 'Then you shall *pre*scribe.' BOSWELL. 'Very well. The first play of words to-day.' J. 'No, no; the *bulls* in Ireland.' JOHNSON. 'Were I your Dictator you should have no wine. It would be my business *cavere ne quid detrimenti Respublica caperet*, and wine is dangerous. Rome was ruined by luxury,' (smiling.) E. 'If you allow no wine as Dictator, you shall not have me for your master of horse.'

On Saturday, April 4, I drank tea with Johnson at Dr. Taylor's, where he had dined.

He was very silent this evening; and read in a variety of books: suddenly throwing down one, and taking up another.

He talked of going to Streatham that night. TAYLOR. 'You'll be robbed if you do: or you must shoot a highwayman. Now I would rather be robbed than do that; I would not shoot a highwayman.' JOHNSON. 'But I would rather shoot him in the instant when he is attempting to rob me, than afterwards swear against him at the Old-Bailey, to take away his life, after he has robbed me. I am surer I am right in the one case than in the other. I may be mistaken as to the man, when I swear: I cannot be mistaken, if I shoot him in the act. Besides, we feel less reluctance to take away a man's life, when we are heated by the injury, than to do it at a distance of time by an oath, after we have cooled.' BOSWELL. 'So, Sir, you would rather act from the motive of private passion, than that of publick advantage.' JOHNSON. 'Nay, Sir, when I shoot the highwayman I act from both.' BOSWELL. 'Very well, very well—There is no catching him.' JOHNSON. 'At the same time one does not know what to say. For perhaps one may, a year after, hang himself from uneasiness for having shot a man. Few minds are fit to be trusted with so great a thing.' BOSWELL. 'Then, Sir, you would not shoot him?' JOHNSON. 'But I might be vexed afterwards for that too.'

Thrale's carriage not having come for him, as he expected, I accompanied him some part of the way home to his own house. I told him, that I had talked of him to Mr. Dunning a few days before, and had said, that in his company we did not so much interchange conversation, as listen to him; and that Dunning observed, upon this, 'One is always willing to listen to Dr. Johnson:' to which I answered, 'That is a great deal from you, Sir.'—'Yes, Sir, (said Johnson,) a great deal indeed. Here is a man willing to listen, to whom the world is listening all the rest of the year.' BOSWELL. 'I think, Sir, it is right to tell one man of such a handsome thing, which has been said of him by another. It tends to increase benevolence.' JOHNSON. 'Undoubtedly it is right, Sir.'

On Tuesday, April 7, I breakfasted with him at his house. He said, 'nobody was content.' I mentioned to him a respectable person in Scotland whom he knew; and I asserted, that I really believed he was always content. JOHNSON. 'No, Sir, he is not content with the present; he has always some new scheme, some new plantation, something which is future. You know he was not content as a widower; for he married again.' BOSWELL. 'But he is not restless.' JOHNSON. 'Sir, he is only locally at rest. A chymist is locally at rest; but his mind is hard at work. This gentleman has done with external exertions. It is too late for him to engage in distant projects.' BOSWELL. 'He seems to amuse himself quite well; to have his attention fixed, and his tranquillity preserved by very small matters. I have tried this; but it would not do with me.' JOHNSON. (laughing,) 'No, Sir; it must be born with a man to be contented to take up with little things. Women have a great advantage that they may take up with little things, without disgracing themselves: a man cannot, except with fiddling. Had I learnt to fiddle, I should have done nothing else.' BOSWELL. 'Pray, Sir, did you ever play on any musical instrument?' JOHNSON. 'No, Sir. I once bought me a flagelet; but I never made out a tune.' BOSWELL. 'A flagelet, Sir!—so small an instrument? I should have liked to hear you play on the violoncello. *That* should have been *your* instrument.' JOHNSON. 'Sir, I might as well have played on the violoncello as another; but I should have done nothing else. No, Sir; a man would never undertake great things, could he be amused with small. I once tried knotting. Dempster's sister undertook to teach me; but I could not learn it.' BOSWELL. 'So, Sir; it will be related in pompous narrative, "Once for his amusement he tried knotting; nor did this Hercules disdain the distaff."' JOHNSON. 'Knitting of stockings is a good amusement. As a freeman of Aberdeen I should be a knitter of stockings.' He asked me to go down with him and dine at Mr. Thrale's at Streatham, to which I agreed. I had lent him *An Account of Scotland*, in 1702, written by a man of various enquiry, an English chaplain to a regiment stationed there. JOHNSON. 'It is sad stuff, Sir, miserably written, as books in general then were. There is now an elegance of style universally diffused. No man now writes so ill as Martin's *Account of the Hebrides* is written. A man could not write so ill, if he should try. Set a merchant's clerk now to write, and he'll do better.'

He talked to me with serious concern of a certain female friend's 'laxity of narration, and inattention to truth.'—'I am as much vexed (said he,) at the ease with which she hears it mentioned to her, as at the thing itself. I told her, "Madam, you are contented to hear every day said to you, what the highest of mankind have died for, rather than bear."—You know, Sir, the highest of mankind have died rather than bear to be told they had uttered a falsehood. Do talk to her of it: I am weary.'

BOSWELL. 'Was not Dr. John Campbell a very inaccurate man in his narrative, Sir? He once told me, that he drank thirteen bottles of port at a sitting.' JOHNSON. 'Why, Sir, I do not know that Campbell ever lied with pen and ink; but you could not entirely depend on any thing he told you in conversation: if there was fact mixed with it. However, I loved Campbell: he was a solid orthodox man: he had a reverence for religion. Though defective in practice, he was religious in principle; and he did nothing grossly wrong that I have heard.'

Talking of drinking wine, he said, 'I did not leave off wine, because I could not bear it; I have drunk three bottles of port without being the worse for it. University College has witnessed this.' BOSWELL. 'Why, then, Sir, did you leave it off?' JOHNSON. 'Why, Sir, because it is so much better for a man to be sure that he is never to be intoxicated, never to lose the power over himself. I shall not begin to drink wine again, till I grow old, and want it.' BOSWELL. 'I think, Sir, you once said to me, that not to drink wine was a great deduction from life.' JOHNSON. 'It is a diminution of pleasure, to be sure; but I do not say a diminution of happiness. There is more happiness in being rational.' BOSWELL. 'But if we could have pleasure always, should not we be happy? The greatest part of men would compound for pleasure.' JOHNSON. 'Supposing we could have pleasure always, an intellectual man would not compound for it. The greatest part of men would compound, because the greatest part of men are gross.'

I mentioned to him that I had become very weary in a company where I heard not a single intellectual sentence, except that 'a man who had been settled ten years in Minorca was become a much inferiour man to what he was in London, because a man's mind grows narrow in a narrow place.' JOHNSON. 'A man's mind grows narrow in a narrow place, whose mind is enlarged only because he has lived in a large place: but what is got by books and thinking is preserved in a narrow place as well as in a large place. A man cannot know modes of life as well in Minorca as in London; but he may study mathematicks as well in Minorca.' BOSWELL. 'I don't know, Sir: if you had remained ten years in the Isle of Col, you would not have been the man that you now are.' JOHNSON. 'Yes, Sir, if I had been there from fifteen to twenty-five; but not if from twenty-five to thirty-five.' BOSWELL. 'I own, Sir, the spirits which I have in London make me do every thing with more readiness and vigour. I can talk twice as much in London as any where else.'

Of Goldsmith he said, 'He was not an agreeable companion, for he talked always for fame. A man who does so never can be pleasing. The man who talks to unburthen his mind is the man to delight you. An eminent friend of ours is not so agreeable as the variety of his knowledge would otherwise make him, because he talks partly from ostentation.'

Soon after our arrival at Thrale's, I heard one of the maids calling eagerly on another, to go to Dr. Johnson. I wondered what this could mean. I afterwards learnt, that it was to give her a Bible, which he had brought from London as a present to her.

He was for a considerable time occupied in reading *Mémoires de Fontenelle*, leaning and swinging upon the low gate into the court, without his hat.

At dinner, Mrs. Thrale expressed a wish to go and see Scotland. JOHNSON. 'Seeing Scotland, Madam, is only seeing a worse England. It is seeing the flower gradually fade away to the naked stalk. Seeing the Hebrides, indeed, is seeing quite a different scene.'

On Thursday, April 9, I dined with him at Sir Joshua Reynolds's, with the Bishop of St. Asaph, (Dr. Shipley,) Mr. Allan Ramsay, Mr. Gibbon, Mr. Cambridge, and Mr. Langton.

Goldsmith being mentioned, Johnson observed, that it was long before his merit came to be acknowledged. That he once complained to him, in ludicrous terms of distress, 'Whenever I write any thing, the publick *make a point* to know nothing about it:' but that his *Traveller* brought him into high reputation. LANGTON. 'There is not one bad line in that poem; not one of Dryden's careless verses. SIR JOSHUA. 'I was glad to hear Charles Fox say, it was one of the finest poems in the English language.' LANGTON. 'Why was you glad? You surely had no doubt of this before.' JOHNSON. 'No; the merit of *The Traveller* is so well established, that Mr. Fox's praise cannot augment it, nor his censure diminish it.' SIR JOSHUA. 'But his friends may suspect they had too great a partiality for him.' JOHNSON. Nay, Sir, the partiality of his friends was always against him. It was with difficulty we could give him a hearing. Goldsmith had no settled notions upon any subject; so he talked always at random. It seemed to be his intention to blurt out whatever was in his mind, and see what would become of it. He was angry too, when catched in an absurdity; but it did not prevent him from falling into another the next minute. I remember Chamier, after talking with him for some time, said, "Well, I do believe he wrote this poem himself: and, let me tell you, that is believing a great deal." Chamier once asked him, what he meant by *slow*, the last word in the first line of *The Traveller,*

"Remote, unfriended, melancholy, slow."

Did he mean tardiness of locomotion? Goldsmith, who would say something without consideration, answered, "Yes." I was sitting by, and said, "No, Sir; you do not mean tardiness of locomotion; you mean, that sluggishness of mind which comes upon a man in solitude." Chamier believed then that I had written the line as much as if he had seen me write it. Goldsmith, however, was a man, who, whatever he wrote, did it better than any other man could do. He deserved a place in Westminster-Abbey, and every year he lived, would have deserved it better. He had, indeed, been at no pains to fill his mind with knowledge. He transplanted it from one place to another; and it did not settle in his mind; so he could not tell what was in his own books.'

We talked of living in the country. JOHNSON. 'No wise man will go to live in the country, unless he has something to do which can be better done in the country. For instance: if he is to shut himself up for a year to study a science, it is better to look out to the fields, than to an opposite wall. Then, if a man walks out in the country, there is nobody to keep him from walking in again: but if a man walks out in London, he is not sure when he shall walk in again. A great city is, to be sure, the school for studying life; and "The proper study of mankind is man," as Pope observes.' BOSWELL. 'I fancy London is the best place for society; though I have heard that the very first society of Paris is still beyond any thing that we have here.' JOHNSON. 'Sir, I question if in

Paris such a company as is sitting round this table could be got together in less than half a year. They talk in France of the felicity of men and women living together: the truth is, that there the men are not higher than the women, they know no more than the women do, and they are not held down in their conversation by the presence of women.'

We talked of old age. Johnson (now in his seventieth year,) said, 'It is a man's own fault, it is from want of use, if his mind grows torpid in old age.' The Bishop asked, if an old man does not lose faster than he gets. JOHNSON. 'I think not, my Lord, if he exerts himself.' One of the company rashly observed, that he thought it was happy for an old man that insensibility comes upon him. JOHNSON. (with a noble elevation and disdain,) 'No, Sir, I should never be happy by being less rational.' BISHOP OF ST. ASAPH. 'Your wish then, Sir, is Ὑηράσκειν διδασκόμενος.' JOHNSON. 'Yes, my Lord.'

This season there was a whimsical fashion in the newspapers of applying Shakspeare's words to describe living persons well known in the world; which was done under the title of *Modern Characters from Shakspeare*; many of which were admirably adapted. The fancy took so much, that they were afterwards collected into a pamphlet. Somebody said to Johnson, across the table, that he had not been in those characters. 'Yes (said he,) I have. I should have been sorry to be left out.' He then repeated what had been applied to him,

'I must borrow GARAGANTUA'S mouth.'

Miss Reynolds not perceiving at once the meaning of this, he was obliged to explain it to her, which had something of an aukward and ludicrous effect. 'Why, Madam, it has a reference to me, as using big words, which require the mouth of a giant to pronounce them. Garagantua is the name of a giant in *Rabelais*.' BOSWELL. 'But, Sir, there is another amongst them for you:

"He would not flatter Neptune for his trident,
Or Jove for his power to thunder."'

JOHNSON. 'There is nothing marked in that. No, Sir, Garagantua is the best.' Notwithstanding this ease and good humour, when I, a little while afterwards, repeated his sarcasm on Kenrick, which was received with applause, he asked, '*Who* said that?' and on my suddenly answering, *Garagantua*, he looked serious, which was a sufficient indication that he did not wish it to be kept up.

When we went to the drawing-room there was a rich assemblage. Besides the company who had been at dinner, there were Mr. Garrick, Mr. Harris of Salisbury, Dr. Percy, Dr. Burney, Honourable Mrs. Cholmondeley, Miss Hannah More, &c. &c.

After wandering about in a kind of pleasing distraction for some time, I got into a corner, with Johnson, Garrick, and Harris. GARRICK. (to Harris,) 'Pray, Sir, have you read Potter's *Æschylus*?' HARRIS. 'Yes; and think it pretty.' GARRICK. (to Johnson,) 'And what think you, Sir, of it?' JOHNSON. 'I thought what I read of it *verbiage*: but upon Mr. Harris's recommendation, I will read a play. (To Mr. Harris,) Don't prescribe two.' Mr. Harris suggested one, I do not remember which. JOHNSON. 'We must try its effect as an English poem; that is the way to judge of the merit of a translation. Translations are, in general, for people who cannot read the original.' I mentioned the vulgar saying, that Pope's *Homer* was not a good representation of the original. JOHNSON. 'Sir, it is the greatest work of the kind that has ever been produced.' BOSWELL. 'The truth is, it is impossible perfectly to translate poetry. In a different language it may be the same tune, but it has not the same tone. Homer plays it on a bassoon; Pope on a flagelet.' HARRIS. 'I think Heroick poetry is best in blank verse; yet it appears that rhyme is essential to English poetry, from our deficiency in metrical quantities. In my opinion, the chief excellence of our language is numerous prose.' JOHNSON. 'Sir William Temple was the first writer who gave cadence to English prose. Before his time they were careless of arrangement, and did not mind whether a sentence ended with an important word or an insignificant word, or with what part of speech it was concluded.'

GARRICK. 'Of all the translations that ever were attempted, I think Elphinston's *Martial* the most extraordinary. He consulted me upon it, who am a little of an epigrammatist myself, you know. I told him freely, "You don't seem to have that turn." I asked him if he was serious; and finding he was, I advised him against publishing. Why, his translation is more difficult to understand than the original. I thought him a man of some talents; but he seems crazy in this.' JOHNSON. 'Sir, you have done what I had not courage to do. But he did not ask my advice, and I did not force it upon him, to make him angry with me.' GARRICK. 'But as a friend, Sir——.' JOHNSON. 'Why, such a friend as I am with him—no.' GARRICK. 'But if you see a friend going to tumble over a precipice?' JOHNSON. 'That is an extravagant case, Sir. You are sure a friend will thank you for hindering him from tumbling over a precipice; but, in the other case, I should hurt his vanity, and do him no good. He would not take my advice. His brother-in-law, Strahan, sent him a subscription of fifty pounds, and said he would send him fifty more, if he would not publish.' GARRICK. 'What! eh! is Strahan a good judge of an Epigram? Is not he rather an *obtuse* man, eh?' JOHNSON. 'Why, Sir, he may not be a judge of an Epigram: but you see he is a judge of what is *not* an Epigram.' BOSWELL. 'It is easy for you, Mr. Garrick, to talk to an authour as you talked to Elphinston; you, who have been so long the manager of a theatre, rejecting the plays of poor authours. You are an old Judge, who have often pronounced sentence of death. You are a practiced surgeon, who have often amputated limbs; and though this may have been for the good of your patients, they cannot like you. Those who have undergone a dreadful operation, are not very fond of seeing the operator again.' GARRICK. 'Yes, I know enough of that. There was a reverend gentleman, (Mr. Hawkins,) who wrote a tragedy, the SIEGE of something, which I refused.' HARRIS. 'So, the siege was raised.' JOHNSON. 'Ay, he came to me and complained; and told me, that Garrick said his play was wrong in the *concoction*. Now, what is the concoction of a play?' (Here Garrick started, and twisted himself, and seemed sorely vexed; for Johnson told me, he believed the story was true.) GARRICK. 'I—I—I—said *first* concoction.' JOHNSON. (smiling,) 'Well, he left out *first*. And Rich, he said, refused him *in false english*: he could shew it under his hand.' GARRICK. 'He wrote to me in violent wrath, for having refused his play: "Sir, this is growing a very serious and terrible affair. I am resolved to publish my play. I will appeal to the world; and how will your judgement appear?" I answered, "Sir, notwithstanding all the seriousness, and all the terrours, I have no objection to your publishing your play; and as you live at a great distance, (Devonshire, I believe,) if you will send it to me, I will convey it to the press." I never heard more of it, ha! ha! ha!'

On Friday, April 10, I found Johnson at home in the morning. We resumed the conversation of yesterday. He put me in mind of some of it which had escaped my memory, and enabled me to record it more perfectly than I otherwise could have done. He was much pleased with my paying so great attention to his recommendation in 1763, the period when our acquaintance began, that I should keep a journal; and I could perceive he was secretly pleased to find so much of the fruit of his mind preserved; and as he had been used to imagine and say that he always laboured when he said a good thing—it delighted him, on a review, to find that his conversation teemed with point and imagery.

I said to him, 'You were yesterday, Sir, in remarkably good humour: but there was nothing to offend you, nothing to produce irritation or violence. There was no bold offender. There was not one capital conviction. It was a maiden assize. You had on your white gloves.'

He found fault with our friend Langton for having been too silent. 'Sir, (said I,) you will recollect, that he very properly took up Sir Joshua for being glad that Charles Fox had praised Goldsmith's *Traveller*, and you joined him.' JOHNSON. 'Yes, Sir, I knocked Fox on the head, without ceremony. Reynolds is too much under Fox and Burke at present. He is under the *Fox star* and the *Irish constellation*. He is always under some planet.' BOSWELL. 'There is no Fox star.' JOHNSON. 'But there is a dog star.' BOSWELL. 'They say, indeed, a fox and a dog are the same animal.'

We dined together with Mr. Scott (now Sir William Scott his Majesty's Advocate General,) at his chambers in the Temple, nobody else there. The company being small, Johnson was not in such spirits as he had been the preceding day, and for a considerable time little was said.

Talking of fame, for which there is so great a desire, I observed how little there is of it in reality, compared with the other objects of human attention. 'Let every man recollect, and he will be sensible how small a part of his time is employed in talking or thinking of Shakspeare, Voltaire, or any of the most celebrated men that have ever lived, or are now supposed to occupy the attention and admiration of the world. Let this be extracted and compressed; into what a narrow space will it go!' I then slily introduced Mr. Garrick's fame, and his assuming the airs of a great man. JOHNSON. 'Sir, it is wonderful how *little* Garrick assumes. No, Sir, Garrick *fortunam reverenter habet.* Consider, Sir: celebrated men, such as you have mentioned, have had their applause at a distance; but Garrick had it dashed in his face, sounded in his ears, and went home every night with the plaudits of a thousand in his *cranium.* Then, Sir, Garrick did not *find,* but *made* his way to the tables, the levees, and almost the bed-chambers of the great. Then, Sir, Garrick had under him a numerous body of people; who, from fear of his power, and hopes of his favour, and admiration of his talents, were constantly submissive to him. And here is a man who has advanced the dignity of his profession. Garrick has made a player a higher character.' SCOTT. 'And he is a very sprightly writer too.' JOHNSON. 'Yes, Sir; and all this supported by great wealth of his own acquisition. If all this had happened to me, I should have had a couple of fellows with long poles walking before me, to knock down every body that stood in the way. Consider, if all this had happened to Cibber or Quin, they'd have jumped over the moon—Yet Garrick speaks to *us.*' (smiling.) BOSWELL. 'And Garrick is a very good man, a charitable man.' JOHNSON. 'Sir, a liberal man. He has given away more money than any man in England. There may be a little vanity mixed; but he has shewn, that money is not his first object.' BOSWELL. 'Yet Foote used to say of him, that he walked out with an intention to do a generous action; but, turning the corner of a street, he met with the ghost of a half-penny, which frightened him.' JOHNSON. 'Why, Sir, that is very true, too; for I never knew a man of whom it could be said with less certainty to-day, what he will do to-morrow, than Garrick; it depends so much on his humour at the time.' SCOTT. 'I am glad to hear of his liberality. He has been represented as very saving.' JOHNSON. 'With his domestick saving we have nothing to do. I remember drinking tea with him long ago, when Peg Woffington made it, and he grumbled at her for making it too strong.[43] He had then begun to feel money in his purse, and did not know when he should have enough of it.'

We talked of war. JOHNSON. 'Every man thinks meanly of himself for not having been a soldier, or not having been at sea.' BOSWELL. 'Lord Mansfield does not.' JOHNSON. 'Sir, if Lord Mansfield were in a company of General Officers and Admirals who have been in service, he would shrink; he'd wish to creep under the table.' BOSWELL. 'No; he'd think he could *try* them all.' JOHNSON. 'Yes, if he could catch them: but they'd try him much sooner. No, Sir; were Socrates and Charles the Twelfth of Sweden both present in any company, and Socrates to say, "Follow me, and hear a lecture on philosophy;" and Charles, laying his hand on his sword, to say, "Follow me, and dethrone the Czar;" a man would be ashamed to follow Socrates. Sir, the impression is universal; yet it is strange.'

He talked of Mr. Charles Fox, of whose abilities he thought highly, but observed, that he did not talk much at our CLUB. I have heard Mr. Gibbon remark, 'that Mr. Fox could not be afraid of Dr. Johnson; yet he certainly was very shy of saying any thing in Dr. Johnson's presence.'

He expressed great indignation at the imposture of the Cock-lane Ghost, and related, with much satisfaction, how he had assisted in detecting the cheat, and had published an account of it in the news-papers. Upon this subject I incautiously offended him, by pressing him with too many questions, and he shewed his displeasure. I apologised, saying that 'I asked questions in order to be instructed and entertained; I repaired eagerly to the fountain; but that the moment he gave me a hint, the moment he put a lock upon the well, I desisted.'—'But, Sir, (said he), that is forcing one to do a disagreeable thing:' and he continued to rate me. 'Nay, Sir, (said I,) when you have put a lock upon the well, so that I can no longer drink, do not make the fountain of your wit play upon me and wet me.'

He sometimes could not bear being teazed with questions. I was once present when a gentleman asked so many as, 'What did you do, Sir?' 'What did you say, Sir?' that he at last grew enraged, and said, 'I will not be put to the *question*. Don't you consider, Sir, that these are not the manners of a gentleman? I will not be baited with *what*, and *why*; what is this? what is that? why is a cow's tail long? why is a fox's tail bushy?' The gentleman, who was a good deal out of countenance, said, 'Why, Sir, you are so good, that I venture to trouble you.' JOHNSON. 'Sir, my being so *good* is no reason why you should be so

---

[43] When Johnson told this little anecdote to Sir Joshua Reynolds, he mentioned a circumstance which he omitted to-day:—'Why, (said Garrick,) it is as red as blood.'— BOSWELL.

ILL.'

He talked with an uncommon animation of travelling into distant countries; that the mind was enlarged by it, and that an acquisition of dignity of character was derived from it. He expressed a particular enthusiasm with respect to visiting the wall of China. I catched it for the moment, and said I really believed I should go and see the wall of China had I not children, of whom it was my duty to take care. 'Sir, (said he,) by doing so, you would do what would be of importance in raising your children to eminence. There would be a lustre reflected upon them from your spirit and curiosity. They would be at all times regarded as the children of a man who had gone to view the wall of China. I am serious, Sir.'

When we had left Mr. Scott's, he said 'Will you go home with me?' 'Sir, (said I,) it is late; but I'll go with you for three minutes.' JOHNSON. 'Or *four*.' We went to Mrs. Williams's room, where we found Mr. Allen the printer, who was the landlord of his house in Bolt-court, a worthy, obliging man, and his very old acquaintance; and what was exceedingly amusing, though he was of a very diminutive size, he used, even in Johnson's presence, to imitate the stately periods and slow and solemn utterance of the great man.—I this evening boasted, that although I did not write what is called stenography, or short-hand, in appropriated characters devised for the purpose, I had a method of my own of writing half words, and leaving out some altogether so as yet to keep the substance and language of any discourse which I had heard so much in view, that I could give it very completely soon after I had taken it down.

On Sunday, April 12, I found him at home before dinner. He and I, and Mrs. Williams, went to dine with the Reverend Dr. Percy.

And here I shall record a scene of too much heat between Dr. Johnson and Dr. Percy, which I should have suppressed, were it not that it gave occasion to display the truely tender and benevolent heart of Johnson, who, as soon as he found a friend was at all hurt by any thing which he had 'said in his wrath,' was not only prompt and desirous to be reconciled, but exerted himself to make ample reparation.

Books of Travels having been mentioned, Johnson praised Pennant very highly, as he did at Dunvegan, in the Isle of Sky. Dr. Percy, knowing himself to be the heir male of the ancient Percies, and having the warmest and most dutiful attachment to the noble House of Northumberland, could not sit quietly and hear a man praised, who had spoken disrespectfully of Alnwick-Castle and the Duke's pleasure grounds, especially as he thought meanly of his travels. He therefore opposed Johnson eagerly. JOHNSON. 'Pennant in what he has said of Alnwick, has done what he intended; he has made you very angry.' PERCY. 'He has said the garden is *trim*, which is representing it like a citizen's parterre, when the truth is, there is a very large extent of fine turf and gravel walks.' JOHNSON. 'According to your own account, Sir, Pennant is right. It *is* trim. Here is grass cut close, and gravel rolled smooth. Is not that trim? The extent is nothing against that; a mile may be as trim as a square yard. Your extent puts me in mind of the citizen's enlarged dinner, two pieces of roast-beef, and two puddings. There is no variety, no mind exerted in laying out the ground, no trees.' PERCY. 'He pretends to give the natural history of Northumberland, and yet takes no notice of the immense number of trees planted there of late.' JOHNSON. 'That, Sir, has nothing to do with the *natural* history; that is *civil* history. A man who gives the natural history of the oak, is not to tell how many oaks have been planted in this place or that. A man who gives the natural history of the cow, is not to tell how many cows are milked at Islington. The animal is the same, whether milked in the Park or at Islington.' PERCY. 'Pennant does not describe well; a carrier who goes along the side of Loch-lomond would describe it better.' JOHNSON. 'I think he describes very well.' PERCY. 'I travelled after him.' JOHNSON. 'And *I* travelled after him.' PERCY. 'But, my good friend, you are short-sighted, and do not see so well as I do.' I wondered at Dr. Percy's venturing thus. Dr. Johnson said nothing at the time; but inflammable particles were collecting for a cloud to burst. In a little while Dr. Percy said something more in disparagement of Pennant. JOHNSON. (pointedly,) 'This is the resentment of a narrow mind, because he did not find every thing in Northumberland.' PERCY. (feeling the stroke,) 'Sir, you may be as rude as you please.' JOHNSON. 'Hold, Sir! Don't talk of rudeness; remember, Sir, you told me (puffing hard with passion struggling for a vent,) I was shortsighted. We have done with civility. We are to be as rude as we please.' PERCY. 'Upon my honour, Sir, I did not mean to be uncivil.' JOHNSON. 'I cannot say so, Sir; for I *did* mean to be uncivil, thinking *you* had been uncivil.' Dr. Percy rose, ran up to him, and taking him by the hand, assured him affectionately that his meaning had been misunderstood; upon which a reconciliation instantly took place. JOHNSON. 'My dear Sir, I am willing you shall *hang* Pennant.' PERCY. (resuming the former subject,) 'Pennant complains that the helmet is not hung out to invite to the hall of hospitality. Now I never heard that it was a custom to hang out a *helmet*.' JOHNSON. 'Hang him up, hang him up.' BOSWELL. (humouring the joke,) 'Hang out his skull instead of a helmet, and you may drink ale out of it in your hall of Odin, as he is your enemy; that will be truly ancient. *there* will be *Northern Antiquities*.' JOHNSON. 'He's a *whig*, Sir; a *sad dog*. (smiling at his own violent expressions, merely for political difference of opinion.) But he's the best traveller I ever read; he observes more things than any one else does.'

On Monday, April 13, I dined with Johnson at Mr. Langton's, where were Dr. Porteus, then Bishop of Chester, now of London, and Dr. Stinton. He was at first in a very silent mood. Before dinner he said nothing but 'Pretty baby,' to one of the children. Langton said very well to me afterwards, that he could repeat Johnson's conversation before dinner, as Johnson had said that he could repeat a complete chapter of *The Natural History of Iceland*, from the Danish of *Horrebow*, the whole of which was exactly thus:—

'CHAP. LXXII. *Concerning snakes.*

'There are no snakes to be met with throughout the whole island.'

Mr. Topham Beauclerk came in the evening, and he and Dr. Johnson and I staid to supper. It was mentioned that Dr. Dodd had once wished to be a member of THE LITERARY CLUB. JOHNSON. 'I should be sorry if any of our Club were hanged. I will not say but some of them deserve it.' BEAUCLERK. (supposing this to be aimed at persons for whom he had at that time a wonderful fancy, which, however, did not last long,) was irritated, and eagerly said, 'You, Sir, have a friend, (naming him) who deserves to be hanged; for he speaks behind their backs against those with whom he lives on the best terms, and attacks them in the newspapers. *He* certainly ought to be *kicked*.' JOHNSON. 'Sir, we all do this in some degree, "*Veniam petimus damusque vicissim.*" To be sure it may be done so much, that a man may deserve to be kicked.' BEAUCLERK. 'He is very malignant.' JOHNSON. 'No, Sir; he is not malignant. He is mischievous, if you will. He would do no man an essential injury; he may, indeed, love to make sport of people by vexing their vanity. I, however, once knew an old gentleman who was absolutely malignant. He really wished evil to others, and rejoiced at it.' BOSWELL. 'The gentleman, Mr. Beauclerk, against whom you are so violent, is, I know, a man of good principles.' BEAUCLERK. 'Then he does not wear them out in practice.'

Dr. Johnson, who, as I have observed before, delighted in discrimination of character, and having a masterly knowledge of human nature, was willing to take men as they are, imperfect and with a mixture of good and bad qualities, I suppose though he had said enough in defence of his friend, of whose merits, notwithstanding his exceptional points, he had a just value; and added no more on the subject.

On Wednesday, April 15, I dined with Dr. Johnson at Mr. Dilly's, and was in high spirits, for I had been a good part of the morning with Mr. Orme, the able and eloquent historian of Hindostan, who expressed a great admiration of Johnson. 'I do not care (said he,) on what subject Johnson talks; but I love better to hear him talk than any body. He either gives you new thoughts, or a new colouring. It is a shame to the nation that he has not been more liberally rewarded. Had I been George the Third, and thought as he did about America, I would have given

Johnson three hundred a year for his *Taxation no Tyranny* alone.' I repeated this, and Johnson was much pleased with such praise from such a man as Orme.

At Mr. Dilly's to-day were Mrs. Knowles, the ingenious Quaker lady, Miss Seward, the poetess of Lichfield, the Reverend Dr. Mayo, and the Rev. Mr. Beresford, Tutor to the Duke of Bedford. Before dinner Dr. Johnson seized upon Mr. Charles Sheridan's *Account of the late Revolution in Sweden*, and seemed to read it ravenously, as if he devoured it, which was to all appearance his method of studying. 'He knows how to read better than any one (said Mrs. Knowles;) he gets at the substance of a book directly; he tears out the heart of it.' He kept it wrapt up in the tablecloth in his lap during the time of dinner, from an avidity to have one entertainment in readiness when he should have finished another; resembling (if I may use so coarse a simile) a dog who holds a bone in his paws in reserve, while he eats something else which has been thrown to him.

The subject of cookery having been very naturally introduced at a table where Johnson, who boasted of the niceness of his palate, owned that 'he always found a good dinner,' he said, 'I could write a better book of cookery than has ever yet been written; it should be a book upon philosophical principles. Pharmacy is now made much more simple. Cookery may be made so too. A prescription which is now compounded of five ingredients, had formerly fifty in it. So in cookery, if the nature of the ingredients be well known, much fewer will do. Then as you cannot make bad meat good, I would tell what is the best butcher's meat, the best beef, the best pieces; how to choose young fowls; the proper seasons of different vegetables; and then how to roast and boil, and compound.' DILLY. 'Mrs. Glasse's *Cookery*, which is the best, was written by Dr. Hill. Half the *trade* know this.' JOHNSON. 'Well, Sir. This shews how much better the subject of cookery may be treated by a philosopher. I doubt if the book be written by Dr. Hill; for, in Mrs. Glasse's *Cookery*, which I have looked into, salt-petre and sal-prunella are spoken of as different substances whereas sal-prunella is only salt-petre burnt on charcoal; and Hill could not be ignorant of this. However, as the greatest part of such a book is made by transcription, this mistake may have been carelessly adopted. But you shall see what a Book of Cookery I shall make! I shall agree with Mr. Dilly for the copy-right.' MISS SEWARD. 'That would be Hercules with the distaff indeed.' JOHNSON. 'No, Madam. Women can spin very well; but they cannot make a good book of Cookery.'

Mrs. Knowles affected to complain that men had much more liberty allowed them than women. JOHNSON. 'Why, Madam, women have all the liberty they should wish to have. We have all the labour and the danger, and the women all the advantage. We go to sea, we build houses, we do everything, in short, to pay our court to the women.' MRS. KNOWLES. 'The Doctor reasons very wittily, but not convincingly. Now, take the instance of building; the mason's wife, if she is ever seen in liquor, is ruined; the mason may get himself drunk as often as he pleases, with little loss of character; nay, may let his wife and children starve.' JOHNSON. 'Madam, you must consider, if the mason does get himself drunk, and let his wife and children starve, the parish will oblige him to find security for their maintenance. We have different modes of restraining evil. Stocks for the men, a ducking-stool for women, and a pound for beasts. If we require more perfection from women than from ourselves, it is doing them honour. And women have not the same temptations that we have: they may always live in virtuous company; men must mix in the world indiscriminately. If a woman has no inclination to do what is wrong being secured from it is no restraint to her. I am at liberty to walk into the Thames; but if I were to try it, my friends would restrain me in Bedlam, and I should be obliged to them.' MRS. KNOWLES. 'Still, Doctor, I cannot help thinking it a hardship that more indulgence is allowed to men than to women. It gives a superiority to men, to which I do not see how they are entitled.' JOHNSON. 'It is plain, Madam, one or other must have the superiority. As Shakspeare says, "If two men ride on a horse, one must ride behind."' DILLY. 'I suppose, Sir, Mrs. Knowles would have them to ride in panniers, one on each side.' JOHNSON. 'Then, Sir, the horse would throw them both.' MRS. KNOWLES. 'Well, I hope that in another world the sexes will be equal.' BOSWELL. 'That is being too ambitious, Madam. *We* might as well desire to be equal with the angels. We shall all, I hope, be happy in a future state, but we must not expect to be all happy in the same degree. It is enough if we be happy according to our several capacities. A worthy carman will get to heaven as well as Sir Isaac Newton. Yet, though equally good, they will not have the same degrees of happiness.' JOHNSON. 'Probably not.'

Dr. Mayo having asked Johnson's opinion of Soame Jenyns's *View of the Internal Evidence of the Christian Religion*;—JOHNSON. 'I think it a pretty book; not very theological indeed; and there seems to be an affectation of ease and carelessness, as if it were not suitable to his character to be very serious about the matter.' BOSWELL. 'He may have intended this to introduce his book the better among genteel people, who might be unwilling to read too grave a treatise. There is a general levity in the age. We have physicians now with bag-wigs; may we not have airy divines, at least somewhat less solemn in their appearance than they used to be?' JOHNSON. 'Jenyns might mean as you say.' BOSWELL. '*You* should like his book, Mrs. Knowles, as it maintains, as you *friends* do, that courage is not a Christian virtue.' MRS. KNOWLES. 'Yes, indeed, I like him there; but I cannot agree with him, that friendship is not a Christian virtue.' JOHNSON. 'Why, Madam, strictly speaking, he is right. All friendship is preferring the interest of a friend, to the neglect, or, perhaps, against the interest of others; so that an old Greek said, "He that has *friends* has *no friend.*" Now Christianity recommends universal benevolence, to consider all men as our brethren, which is contrary to the virtue of friendship, as described by the ancient philosophers. Surely, Madam, your sect must approve of this; for, you call all men *friends.*' MRS. KNOWLES. 'We are commanded to do good to all men, "but especially to them who are of the household of Faith."' JOHNSON. 'Well, Madam. The household of Faith is wide enough.' MRS. KNOWLES. 'But, Doctor, our Saviour had twelve Apostles, yet there was *one* whom he *loved.* John was called "the disciple whom JESUS loved."' JOHNSON. (with eyes sparkling benignantly,) 'Very well, indeed, Madam. You have said very well.' BOSWELL. 'A fine application. Pray, Sir, had you ever thought of it?' JOHNSON. 'I had not, Sir.'

From this pleasing subject, he, I know not how or why, made a sudden transition to one upon which he was a violent aggressor; for he said, 'I am willing to love all mankind, *except an American:*' and his inflammable corruption bursting into horrid fire, he 'breathed out threatenings and slaughter;' calling them, Rascals—Robbers—Pirates;' and exclaiming, he'd 'burn and destroy them.' Miss Seward, looking to him with mild but steady astonishment, said, 'Sir, this is an instance that we are always most violent against those whom we have injured.' He was irritated still more by this delicate and keen reproach; and roared out another tremendous volley, which one might fancy could be heard across the Atlantick. During this tempest I sat in great uneasiness, lamenting his heat of temper; till, by degrees, I diverted his attention to other topicks.

Talking of Miss———, a literary lady, he said, 'I was obliged to speak to Miss Reynolds, to let her know that I desired she would not flatter me so much.' Somebody now observed, 'She flatters Garrick.' JOHNSON. 'She is in the right to flatter Garrick. She is in the right for two reasons; first, because she has the world with her, who have been praising Garrick these thirty years; and secondly, because she is rewarded for it by Garrick. Why should she flatter *me*? I can do nothing for her. Let her carry her praise to a better market. (Then turning to Mrs. Knowles.) You, Madam, have been flattering me all the evening; I wish you would give Boswell a little now. If you knew his merit as well as I do, you would say a great deal; he is the best travelling companion in the world.'

Somebody mentioned the Reverend Mr. Mason's prosecution of Mr. Murray, the bookseller, for having inserted in a collection of *Gray's Poems*, only fifty lines, of which Mr. Mason had still the exclusive property, under the statute of Queen Anne; and that Mr. Mason had persevered, notwithstanding his being requested to name his own terms of compensation. Johnson signified his displeasure at Mr.

Mason's conduct very strongly; but added, by way of shewing that he was not surprized at it, 'Mason's a Whig.' MRS. KNOWLES. (not hearing distinctly,) 'What! a Prig, Sir?' JOHNSON. 'Worse, Madam; a Whig! But he is both.'

Of John Wesley, he said, 'He can talk well on any subject.' BOSWELL. 'Pray, Sir, what has he made of his story of a ghost?' JOHNSON. 'Why, Sir, he believes it; but not on sufficient authority. He did not take time enough to examine the girl. It was at Newcastle, where the ghost was said to have appeared to a young woman several times, mentioning something about the right to an old house, advising application to be made to an attorney, which was done; and, at the same time, saying the attorneys would do nothing, which proved to be the fact. "This (says John,) is a proof that a ghost knows our thoughts." Now (laughing,) it is not necessary to know our thoughts, to tell that an attorney will sometimes do nothing. Charles Wesley, who is a more stationary man, does not believe the story. I am sorry that John did not take more pains to inquire into the evidence for it.' MISS SEWARD, (with an incredulous smile,) 'What, Sir! about a ghost?' JOHNSON. (with solemn vehemence,) 'Yes, Madam: this is a question which, after five thousand years, is yet undecided; a question, whether in theology or philosophy, one of the most important that can come before the human understanding.'

Mrs. Knowles mentioned, as a proselyte to Quakerism, Miss—— —, a young lady well known to Dr. Johnson, for whom he had shewn much affection; while she ever had, and still retained, a great respect for him. Mrs. Knowles at the same time took an opportunity of letting him know 'that the amiable young creature was sorry at finding that he was offended at her leaving the Church of England and embracing a simpler faith;' and, in the gentlest and most persuasive manner, solicited his kind indulgence for what was sincerely a matter of conscience. JOHNSON. (frowning very angrily,) 'Madam, she is an odious wench. She could not have any proper conviction that it was her duty to change her religion, which is the most important of all subjects, and should be studied with all care, and with all the helps we can get. She knew no more of the Church which she left, and that which she embraced, than she did of the difference between the Copernican and Ptolemaick systems.' MRS. KNOWLES. 'She had the New Testament before her.' JOHNSON. 'Madam, she could not understand the New Testament, the most difficult book in the world, for which the study of a life is required.' MRS. KNOWLES. 'It is clear as to essentials.' JOHNSON. 'But not as to controversial points. The heathens were easily converted, because they had nothing to give up; but we ought not, without very strong conviction indeed, to desert the religion in which we have been educated. That is the religion given you, the religion in which it may be said Providence has placed you. If you live conscientiously in that religion, you may be safe. But errour is dangerous indeed, if you err when you choose a religion for yourself.' MRS. KNOWLES. 'Must we then go by implicit faith?' JOHNSON. 'Why, Madam, the greatest part of our knowledge is implicit faith; and as to religion, have we heard all that a disciple of Confucius, all that a Mahometan, can say for himself?' He then rose again into passion, and attacked the young proselyte in the severest terms of reproach, so that both the ladies seemed to be much shocked.

We remained together till it was pretty late. Notwithstanding occasional explosions of violence, we were all delighted upon the whole with Johnson. I compared him at this time to a warm West-Indian climate, where you have a bright sun, quick vegetation, luxuriant foliage, luscious fruits; but where the same heat sometimes produces thunder, lightning, earthquakes, in a terrible degree.

April 17, being Good Friday, I waited on Johnson, as usual. I observed at breakfast that although it was a part of his abstemious discipline on this most solemn fast, to take no milk in his tea, yet when Mrs. Desmoulins inadvertently poured it in, he did not reject it. I talked of the strange indecision of mind, and imbecility in the common occurrences of life, which we may observe in some people. JOHNSON. 'Why, Sir, I am in the habit of getting others to do things for me.' BOSWELL. 'What, Sir! have you that weakness?' JOHNSON. 'Yes, Sir. But I always think afterwards I should have done better for myself.'

I expressed some inclination to publish an account of my *Travels* upon the continent of Europe, for which I had a variety of materials collected. JOHNSON. 'I do not say, Sir, you may not publish your travels; but I give you my opinion, that you would lessen yourself by it. What can you tell of countries so well known as those upon the continent of Europe, which you have visited?' BOSWELL. 'But I can give an entertaining narrative, with many incidents, anecdotes, *jeux d'esprit*, and remarks, so as to make very pleasant reading.' JOHNSON. 'Why, Sir, most modern travellers in Europe who have published their travels, have been laughed at: I would not have you added to the number. The world is now not contented to be merely entertained by a traveller's narrative; they want to learn something. Now some of my friends asked me, why I did not give some account of my travels in France. The reason is plain; intelligent readers had seen more of France than I had. *You* might have liked my travels in France, and THE CLUB might have liked them; but, upon the whole, there would have been more ridicule than good produced by them.' BOSWELL. 'I cannot agree with you, Sir. People would like to read what you say of any thing. Suppose a face has been painted by fifty painters before; still we love to see it done by Sir Joshua.' JOHNSON. 'True, Sir, but Sir Joshua cannot paint a face when he has not time to look on it.' BOSWELL. 'Sir, a sketch of any sort by him is valuable. And, Sir, to talk to you in your own style (raising my voice, and shaking my head,) you *should* have given us your travels in France. I am *sure* I am right, and *there's an end on't.*'

I said to him that it was certainly true, as my friend Dempster had observed in his letter to me upon the subject, that a great part of what was in his *Journey to the Western Islands of Scotland* had been in his mind before he left London. JOHNSON. 'Why yes, Sir, the topicks were; and books of travels will be good in proportion to what a man has previously in his mind; his knowing what to observe; his power of contrasting one mode of life with another. As the Spanish proverb says, "He, who would bring home the wealth of the Indies, must carry the wealth of the Indies with him." So it is in travelling; a man must carry knowledge with him, if he would bring home knowledge.' BOSWELL. 'The proverb, I suppose, Sir, means, he must carry a large stock with him to trade with.' JOHNSON. 'Yes, Sir.'

It was a delightful day: as we walked to St. Clement's church, I again remarked that Fleet-street was the most cheerful scene in the world. 'Fleet-street (said I,) is in my mind more delightful than Tempé.' JOHNSON. 'Ay, Sir; but let it be compared with Mull.'

There was a very numerous congregation to-day at St. Clement's church, which Dr. Johnson said he observed with pleasure.

And now I am to give a pretty full account of one of the most curious incidents in Johnson's life, of which he himself has made the following minute on this day: 'In my return from church, I was accosted by Edwards, an old fellow-collegian, who had not seen me since 1729. He knew me, and asked if I remembered one Edwards; I did not at first recollect the name, but gradually as we walked along, recovered it, and told him a conversation that had passed at an ale-house between us. My purpose is to continue our acquaintance.'

It was in Butcher-row that this meeting happened. Mr. Edwards, who was a decent-looking elderly man in grey clothes, and a wig of many curls, accosted Johnson with familiar confidence, knowing who he was, while Johnson returned his salutation with a courteous formality, as to a stranger. But as soon as Edwards had brought to his recollection their having been at Pembroke-College together nine-and-forty years ago, he seemed much pleased, asked where he lived, and said he should be glad to see him in Bolt-court. EDWARDS. 'Ah, Sir! we are old men now.' JOHNSON. (who never liked to think of being old,) 'Don't let us discourage one another.' EDWARDS. 'Why, Doctor, you look stout and hearty, I am happy to see you so; for the news-papers told us you were very ill.' JOHNSON. 'Ay, Sir, they are always telling lies of *us old fellows.*'

Wishing to be present at more of so singular a conversation as that between two fellow-collegians, who had lived forty years in London without ever having chanced to meet, I whispered to Mr. Edwards that

Dr. Johnson was going home, and that he had better accompany him now. So Edwards walked along with us, I eagerly assisting to keep up the conversation. Mr. Edwards informed Dr. Johnson that he had practised long as a solicitor in Chancery, but that he now lived in the country upon a little farm, about sixty acres, just by Stevenage in Hertfordshire, and that he came to London (to Barnard's Inn, No. 6), generally twice a week. Johnson appearing to me in a reverie, Mr. Edwards addressed himself to me, and expatiated on the pleasure of living in the country. BOSWELL. 'I have no notion of this, Sir. What you have to entertain you, is, I think, exhausted in half an hour.' EDWARDS. 'What? don't you love to have hope realized? I see my grass, and my corn, and my trees growing. Now, for instance, I am curious to see if this frost has not nipped my fruit-trees.' JOHNSON. (who we did not imagine was attending,) 'You find, Sir, you have fears as well as hopes.'—So well did he see the whole, when another saw but the half of a subject.

When we got to Dr. Johnson's house, and were seated in his library, the dialogue went on admirably. EDWARDS. 'Sir, I remember you would not let us say *prodigious* at College. For even then, Sir, (turning to me,) he was delicate in language, and we all feared him.'[44] JOHNSON. (to Edwards,) 'From your having practised the law long, Sir, I presume you must be rich.' EDWARDS. 'No, Sir; I got a good deal of money; but I had a number of poor relations to whom I gave a great part of it.' JOHNSON. 'Sir, you have been rich in the most valuable sense of the word.' EDWARDS. 'But I shall not die rich.' JOHNSON. 'Nay, sure, Sir, it is better to *live* rich than to *die* rich.' EDWARDS. 'I wish I had continued at College.' JOHNSON. 'Why do you wish that, Sir?' EDWARDS. 'Because I think I should have had a much easier life than mine has been. I should have been a parson, and had a good living, like Bloxam and several others, and lived comfortably.' JOHNSON. 'Sir, the life of a parson, of a conscientious clergyman, is not easy. I have always considered a clergyman as the father of a larger family than he is able to maintain. I would rather have Chancery suits upon my hands than the cure of souls. No, Sir, I do not envy a clergyman's life as an easy life, nor do I envy the clergyman who makes it an easy life.' Here taking himself up all of a sudden, he exclaimed, 'O! Mr. Edwards! I'll convince you that I recollect you. Do you remember our drinking together at an alehouse near Pembroke gate? At that time, you told me of the Eton boy, who, when verses on our SAVIOUR'S turning water into wine were prescribed as an exercise, brought up a single line, which was highly admired,—

---

[44] Johnson said to me afterwards, 'Sir, they respected me for my literature: and yet it was not great but by comparison. Sir, it is amazing how little literature there is in the world.'—BOSWELL.

"*Vidit et erubuit lympha pudica* DEUM,"

and I told you of another fine line in Camden's Remains, an eulogy upon one of our Kings, who was succeeded by his son, a prince of equal merit:—

"*Mira cano, Sol occubuit, nox nulla secuta est.*"'

EDWARDS. 'You are a philosopher, Dr. Johnson. I have tried too in my time to be a philosopher; but, I don't know how, cheerfulness was always breaking in.'—Mr. Burke, Sir Joshua Reynolds, Mr. Courtenay, Mr. Malone, and, indeed, all the eminent men to whom I have mentioned this, have thought it an exquisite trait of character. The truth is, that philosophy, like religion, is too generally supposed to be hard and severe, at least so grave as to exclude all gaiety.

EDWARDS. 'I have been twice married, Doctor. You, I suppose, have never known what it was to have a wife.' JOHNSON. 'Sir, I have known what it was to have a wife, and (in a solemn, tender, faultering tone) I have known what it was to *lose a wife*.—It had almost broke my heart.'

EDWARDS. 'How do you live, Sir? For my part, I must have my regular meals, and a glass of good wine. I find I require it.' JOHNSON. 'I now drink no wine, Sir. Early in life I drank wine: for many years I drank none. I then for some years drank a great deal.' EDWARDS. 'Some hogs-heads, I warrant you.' JOHNSON. 'I then had a severe illness, and left it off, and I have never begun it again. I never felt any difference upon myself from eating one thing rather than another, nor from one kind of weather rather than another. There are people, I believe, who feel a difference; but I am not one of them. And as to regular meals, I have fasted from the Sunday's dinner to the Tuesday's dinner, without any inconvenience. I believe it is best to eat just as one is hungry: but a man who is in business, or a man who has a family, must have stated meals. I am a straggler. I may leave this town and go to Grand Cairo, without being missed here or observed there.' EDWARDS. 'Don't you eat supper, Sir?' JOHNSON. 'No, Sir.' EDWARDS. 'For my part, now, I consider supper as a turnpike through which one must pass, in order to get to bed.'

JOHNSON. 'You are a lawyer, Mr. Edwards. Lawyers know life practically. A bookish man should always have them to converse with. They have what he wants.' EDWARDS. 'I am grown old: I am sixty-five.' JOHNSON. 'I shall be sixty-eight next birth-day. Come, Sir, drink water, and put in for a hundred.'

This interview confirmed my opinion of Johnson's most humane and benevolent heart. His cordial and placid behaviour to an old fellow-collegian, a man so different from himself; and his telling him that he would go down to his farm and visit him, showed a kindness of disposition very rare at an advanced age. He observed, 'how wonderful it was that they had both been in London forty years, without having ever once met, and both walkers in the street too!' Mr. Edwards, when going away, again recurred to his consciousness of senility, and looking full in Johnson's face, said to him, 'You'll find in Dr. Young,

"O my coevals! remnants of yourselves."'

Johnson did not relish this at all; but shook his head with impatience. Edwards walked off, seemingly highly pleased with the honour of having been thus noticed by Dr. Johnson. When he was gone, I said to Johnson, I thought him but a weak man. JOHNSON. 'Why, yes, Sir. Here is a man who has passed through life without experience: yet I would rather have him with me than a more sensible man who will not talk readily. This man is always willing to say what he has to say.' Yet Dr. Johnson had himself by no means that willingness which he praised so much, and I think so justly; for who has not felt the painful effect of the dreary void, when there is a total silence in a company, for any length of time; or, which is as bad, or perhaps worse, when the conversation is with difficulty kept up by a perpetual effort?

   Johnson once observed to me, 'Tom Tyers described me the best: "Sir, (said he,) you are like a ghost: you never speak till you are spoken to."'

   The gentleman whom he thus familiarly mentioned was Mr. Thomas Tyers, son of Mr. Jonathan Tyers, the founder of that excellent place of publick amusement, Vauxhall Gardens, which must ever be an estate to its proprietor, as it is peculiarly adapted to the taste of the English nation; there being a mixture of curious show,—gay exhibition, musick, vocal and instrumental, not too refined for the general ear;— for all which only a shilling is paid; and, though last, not least, good eating and drinking for those who choose to purchase that regale. Mr. Thomas Tyers was bred to the law; but having a handsome fortune, vivacity of temper, and eccentricity of mind, he could not confine himself to the regularity of practice. He therefore ran about the world with a pleasant carelessness, amusing everybody by his desultory conversation. He abounded in anecdote, but was not sufficiently attentive to accuracy. I therefore cannot venture to avail myself much of a biographical sketch of Johnson which he published, being one among the various persons ambitious of appending their names to that of my illustrious friend. That sketch is, however, an entertaining little collection of fragments. Those which he published of Pope and Addison are of higher merit; but his fame must chiefly rest upon his *Political Conferences*, in which he introduces several eminent persons delivering their sentiments in the way of dialogue, and discovers a considerable share of learning, various knowledge, and discernment of character. This much may I be allowed to say of a man who was exceedingly obliging to me, and who lived with Dr. Johnson in as easy a manner as almost any of his very numerous acquaintance.

Mr. Edwards had said to me aside, that Dr. Johnson should have been of a profession. I repeated the remark to Johnson that I might have his own thoughts on the subject. JOHNSON. 'Sir, it *would* have been better that I had been of a profession. I ought to have been a lawyer.' BOSWELL. 'I do not think, Sir, it would have been better, for we should not have had the *English Dictionary*.' JOHNSON. 'But you would have had *Reports*.' BOSWELL. 'Ay; but there would not have been another, who could have written the *Dictionary*. There have been many very good Judges. Suppose you had been Lord Chancellor; you would have delivered opinions with more extent of mind, and in a more ornamented manner, than perhaps any Chancellor ever did, or ever will do. But, I believe, causes have been as judiciously decided as you could have done.' JOHNSON. 'Yes, Sir. Property has been as well settled.'

Johnson, however, had a noble ambition floating in his mind, and had, undoubtedly, often speculated on the possibility of his supereminent powers being rewarded in this great and liberal country by the highest honours of the state. Sir William Scott informs me, that upon the death of the late Lord Lichfield, who was Chancellor of the University of Oxford, he said to Johnson, 'What a pity it is, Sir, that you did not follow the profession of the law. You might have been Lord Chancellor of Great Britain, and attained to the dignity of the peerage; and now that the title of Lichfield, your native city, is extinct, you might have had it.' Johnson, upon this, seemed much agitated; and, in an angry tone, exclaimed, 'Why will you vex me by suggesting this, when it is too late?'

But he did not repine at the prosperity of others. The late Dr. Thomas Leland, told Mr. Courtenay, that when Mr. Edmund Burke shewed Johnson his fine house and lands near Beaconsfield, Johnson coolly said, '*Non equidem invideo; miror magis.*'[45]

Yet no man had a higher notion of the dignity of literature than Johnson, or was more determined in maintaining the respect which he justly considered as due to it. Of this, besides the general tenor of his conduct in society, some characteristical instances may be mentioned.

He told Sir Joshua Reynolds, that once when he dined in a numerous company of booksellers, where the room being small, the head of the table, at which he sat, was almost close to the fire, he

---

[45] I am not entirely without suspicion that Johnson may have felt a little momentary envy; for no man loved the good things of this life better than he did and he could not but be conscious that he deserved a much larger share of them, than he ever had.—BOSWELL.

persevered in suffering a great deal of inconvenience from the heat, rather than quit his place, and let one of them sit above him.

Goldsmith, in his diverting simplicity, complained one day, in a mixed company, of Lord Camden. 'I met him (said he,) at Lord Clare's house in the country, and he took no more notice of me than if I had been an ordinary man. The company having laughed heartily, Johnson stood forth in defence of his friend. 'Nay, Gentlemen, (said he,) Dr. Goldsmith is in the right. A nobleman ought to have made up to such a man as Goldsmith; and I think it is much against Lord Camden that he neglected him.'

Nor could he patiently endure to hear that such respect as he thought due only to higher intellectual qualities, should be bestowed on men of slighter, though perhaps more amusing talents. I told him, that one morning, when I went to breakfast with Garrick, who was very vain of his intimacy with Lord Camden, he accosted me thus:—'Pray now, did you—did you meet a little lawyer turning the corner, eh?'— 'No, Sir, (said I). Pray what do you mean by the question?'—'Why, (replied Garrick, with an affected indifference, yet as if standing on tip-toe,) Lord Camden has this moment left me. We have had a long walk together.' JOHNSON. 'Well, Sir, Garrick talked very properly. Lord Camden *was a little lawyer* to be associating so familiarly with a player.'

Sir Joshua Reynolds observed, with great truth, that Johnson considered Garrick to be as it were his *property*. He would allow no man either to blame or to praise Garrick in his presence, without contradicting him.

Having fallen into a very serious frame of mind, in which mutual expressions of kindness passed between us, such as would be thought too vain in me to repeat, I talked with regret of the sad inevitable certainty that one of us must survive the other. JOHNSON. 'Yes, Sir, that is an affecting consideration. I remember Swift, in one of his letters to Pope, says, "I intend to come over, that we may meet once more; and when we must part, it is what happens to all human beings."' BOSWELL. 'The hope that we shall see our departed friends again must support the mind.' JOHNSON. 'Why yes, Sir.' BOSWELL. 'There is a strange unwillingness to part with life, independent of serious fears as to futurity. A reverend friend of ours (naming him) tells me, that he feels an uneasiness at the thoughts of leaving his house, his study, his books.' JOHNSON. 'This is foolish in *****. A man need not be uneasy on these grounds; for, as he will retain his consciousness, he may say with the philosopher, *Omnia mea mecum porto*.' BOSWELL. 'True, Sir: we may carry our books in our heads; but still there is something painful in the thought of leaving for ever what has given us pleasure. I remember, many years ago, when my imagination was warm, and I happened to be in a melancholy mood, it distressed me to think of going into a state of being in which Shakspeare's poetry did not exist. A lady whom I then much admired, a very amiable woman, humoured my fancy, and relieved me by saying, "The first thing you will meet in the other world, will be an elegant copy of Shakspeare's works presented to you."' Dr. Johnson smiled benignantly at this, and did not appear to disapprove of the notion.

We went to St. Clement's church again in the afternoon, and then returned and drank tea and coffee in Mrs. Williams's room; Mrs. Desmoulins doing the honours of the tea-table. I observed that he would not even look at a proof-sheet of his *Life of Waller* on Good-Friday.

On Saturday, April 14, I drank tea with him. He praised the late Mr. Duncombe, of Canterbury, as a pleasing man. 'He used to come to me: I did not seek much after *him*. Indeed I never sought much after any body.' BOSWELL. 'Lord Orrery, I suppose.' JOHNSON. 'No, Sir; I never went to him but when he sent for me.' BOSWELL. 'Richardson?' JOHNSON. 'Yes, Sir. But I sought after George Psalmanazar the most. I used to go and sit with him at an alehouse in the city.'

I am happy to mention another instance which I discovered of his *seeking after* a man of merit. Soon after the Honourable Daines Barrington had published his excellent *Observations on the Statutes*, Johnson waited on that worthy and learned gentleman; and, having told him his name, courteously said, 'I have read your book, Sir, with great pleasure, and wish to be better known to you.' Thus began an acquaintance, which was continued with mutual regard as long as Johnson lived.

Talking of a recent seditious delinquent, he said, 'They should set him in the pillory, that he may be punished in a way that would disgrace him.' I observed, that the pillory does not always disgrace. And I mentioned an instance of a gentleman who I thought was not dishonoured by it. JOHNSON. 'Ay, but he was, Sir. He could not mouth and strut as he used to do, after having been there. People are not willing to ask a man to their tables who has stood in the pillory.'

Johnson attacked the Americans with intemperate vehemence of abuse. I said something in their favour; and added, that I was always sorry when he talked on that subject. This, it seems, exasperated him; though he said nothing at the time. The cloud was charged with sulphureous vapour, which was afterwards to burst in thunder.—We talked of a gentleman who was running out his fortune in London; and I said, 'We must get him out of it. All his friends must quarrel with him, and that will soon drive him away.' JOHNSON. 'Nay, Sir; we'll send *you* to him. If your company does not drive a man out of his house, nothing will.' This was a horrible shock, for which there was no visible cause. I afterwards asked him why he had said so harsh a thing. JOHNSON. Because, Sir, you made me angry about the Americans.' BOSWELL.

'But why did you not take your revenge directly?' JOHNSON. (smiling,) 'Because, Sir, I had nothing ready. A man cannot strike till he has his weapons.' This was a candid and pleasant confession.

He shewed me to-night his drawing-room, very genteelly fitted up; and said, 'Mrs. Thrale sneered when I talked of my having asked you and your lady to live at my house. I was obliged to tell her, that you would be in as respectable a situation in my house as in hers. Sir, the insolence of wealth will creep out.' BOSWELL. 'She has a little both of the insolence of wealth, and the conceit of parts.' JOHNSON. 'The insolence of wealth is a wretched thing; but the conceit of parts has some foundation. To be sure it should not be. But who is without it?' BOSWELL. 'Yourself, Sir.' JOHNSON. 'Why, I play no tricks: I lay no traps.' BOSWELL. 'No, Sir. You are six feet high, and you only do not stoop.'

We talked of the numbers of people that sometimes have composed the household of great families. I mentioned that there were a hundred in the family of the present Earl of Eglintoune's father. Dr. Johnson seeming to doubt it, I began to enumerate. 'Let us see: my Lord and my Lady two.' JOHNSON. 'Nay, Sir, if you are to count by twos, you may be long enough.' BOSWELL. 'Well, but now I add two sons and seven daughters, and a servant for each, that will make twenty; so we have the fifth part already.' JOHNSON. 'Very true. You get at twenty pretty readily; but you will not so easily get further on. We grow to five feet pretty readily; but it is not so easy to grow to seven.'

On Monday, April 20, I found him at home in the morning. We talked of a gentleman who we apprehended was gradually involving his circumstances by bad management. JOHNSON. 'Wasting a fortune is evaporation by a thousand imperceptible means. If it were a stream, they'd stop it. You must speak to him. It is really miserable. Were he a gamester, it could be said he had hopes of winning. Were he a bankrupt in trade, he might have grown rich; but he has neither spirit to spend nor resolution to spare. He does not spend fast enough to have pleasure from it. He has the crime of prodigality, and the wretchedness of parsimony. If a man is killed in a duel, he is killed as many a one has been killed; but it is a sad thing for a man to lie down and die; to bleed to death, because he has not fortitude enough to sear the wound, or even to stitch it up.' I cannot but pause a moment to admire the fecundity of fancy, and choice of language, which in this instance, and, indeed, on almost all occasions, he displayed. It was well observed by Dr. Percy, now Bishop of Dromore, 'The conversation of Johnson is strong and clear, and may be compared to an antique statue, where every vein and muscle is distinct and bold. Ordinary conversation resembles an inferiour cast.'

On Saturday, April 25, I dined with him at Sir Joshua Reynolds's, with the learned Dr. Musgrave, Counsellor Leland of Ireland, son to the historian, Mrs. Cholmondeley, and some more ladies.

'Demosthenes Taylor, as he was called, (that is, the Editor of Demosthenes) was the most silent man, the merest statue of a man that I have ever seen. I once dined in company with him, and all he said during the whole time was no more than *Richard*. How a man should say only Richard, it is not easy to imagine. But it was thus: Dr. Douglas was talking of Dr. Zachary Grey, and ascribing to him something that was written by Dr. Richard Grey. So, to correct him, Taylor said, (imitating his affected sententious emphasis and nod,) *"Richard."*'

Mrs. Cholmondeley, in a high flow of spirits, exhibited some lively sallies of hyperbolical compliment to Johnson, with whom she had been long acquainted, and was very easy. He was quick in catching the *manner* of the moment, and answered her somewhat in the style of the hero of a romance, 'Madam, you crown me with unfading laurels.'

We talked of a lady's verses on Ireland. MISS REYNOLDS. 'Have you seen them, Sir?' JOHNSON. 'No, Madam. I have seen a translation from Horace, by one of her daughters. She shewed it me.' MISS REYNOLDS. 'And how was it, Sir?' JOHNSON. 'Why, very well for a young Miss's verses;—that is to say, compared with excellence, nothing; but, very well, for the person who wrote them. I am vexed at being shewn verses in that manner.' MISS REYNOLDS. 'But if they should be good, why not give them hearty praise?' JOHNSON. 'Why, Madam, because I have not then got the better of my bad humour from having been shown them. You must consider, Madam; beforehand they may be bad, as well as good. Nobody has a right to put another under such a difficulty, that he must either hurt the person by telling the truth, or hurt himself by telling what is not true.' BOSWELL. 'A man often shews his writings to people of eminence, to obtain from them, either from their good-nature, or from their not being able to tell the truth firmly, a commendation, of which he may afterwards avail himself.' JOHNSON. 'Very true, Sir. Therefore the man, who is asked by an authour, what he thinks of his work, is put to the torture, and is not obliged to speak the truth; so that what he says is not considered as his opinion; yet he has said it, and cannot retract it; and this authour, when mankind are hunting him with a cannister at his tail, can say, "I would not have published, had not Johnson, or Reynolds, or Musgrave, or some other good judge, commended the work." Yet I consider it as a very difficult question in conscience, whether one should advise a man not to publish a work, if profit be his object; for the man may say, "Had it not been for you, I should have had the money." Now you cannot be sure; for you have only your own opinion, and the publick may think very differently.' SIR JOSHUA REYNOLDS. 'You must upon such an occasion have two judgements; one as to the real value of the work, the other as to what may please the general taste at the time.' JOHNSON.

'But you can be *sure* of neither; and therefore I should scruple much to give a suppressive vote. Both Goldsmith's comedies were once refused; his first by Garrick, his second by Colman, who was prevailed on at last by much solicitation, nay, a kind of force, to bring it on. His *Vicar of Wakefield* I myself did not think would have had much success. It was written and sold to a bookseller before his *Traveller*; but published after; so little expectation had the bookseller from it. Had it been sold after the *Traveller* he might have had twice as much money for it, though sixty guineas was no mean price. The bookseller had the advantage of Goldsmith's reputation from *The Traveller* in the sale, though Goldsmith had it not in selling the copy.' SIR JOSHUA REYNOLDS. '*The Beggar's Opera* affords a proof how strangely people will differ in opinion about a literary performance. Burke thinks it has no merit.' JOHNSON. 'It was refused by one of the houses; but I should have thought it would succeed, not from any great excellence in the writing, but from the novelty, and the general spirit and gaiety of the piece, which keeps the audience always attentive, and dismisses them in good humour.'

We went to the drawing-room, where was a considerable increase of company. Several of us got round Dr. Johnson, and complained that he would not give us an exact catalogue of his works, that there might be a complete edition. He smiled, and evaded our entreaties. That he intended to do it, I have no doubt, because I have heard him say so; and I have in my possession an imperfect list, fairly written out, which he entitles *Historia Studiorum*. I once got from one of his friends a list, which there was pretty good reason to suppose was accurate, for it was written down in his presence by this friend, who enumerated each article aloud, and had some of them mentioned to him by Mr. Levett, in concert with whom it was made out; and Johnson, who heard all this, did not contradict it. But when I shewed a copy of this list to him, and mentioned the evidence for its exactness, he laughed, and said, 'I was willing to let them go on as they pleased, and never interfered.' Upon which I read it to him, article by article, and got him positively to own or refuse; and then, having obtained certainty so far, I got some other articles confirmed by him directly; and afterwards, from time to time, made additions under his sanction.

The conversation having turned on *Bon-Mots*, be quoted, from one of the *Ana*, an exquisite instance of flattery in a maid of honour in France, who being asked by the Queen what o'clock it was, answered, 'What your Majesty pleases.' He admitted that Mr. Burke's classical pun upon Mr. Wilkes's being carried on the shoulders of the mob,—

'————————*Numerisque fertur*
Lege solutus,'

was admirable; and though he was strangely unwilling to allow to that extraordinary man the talent of wit, he also laughed with approbation at another of his playful conceits; which was, that 'Horace has in one line given a description of a good desirable manour:—

> "*Est modus in rebus, sunt certi denique fines;*"

that is to say, a *modus* as to the tithes and certain *fines*.'

He observed, 'A man cannot with propriety speak of himself, except he relates simple facts; as, "I was at Richmond:" or what depends on mensuration; as, "I am six feet high." He is sure he has been at Richmond; he is sure he is six feet high: but he cannot be sure he is wise, or that he has any other excellence. Then, all censure of a man's self is oblique praise. It is in order to shew how much he can spare. It has all the invidiousness of self-praise, and all the reproach of falsehood.'

On Tuesday, April 28, he was engaged to dine at General Paoli's, where, as I have already observed, I was still entertained in elegant hospitality, and with all the ease and comfort of a home. I called on him, and accompanied him in a hackney-coach. We stopped first at the bottom of Hedgelane, into which he went to leave a letter, 'with good news for a poor man in distress,' as he told me. I did not question him particularly as to this. He himself often resembled Lady Bolingbroke's lively description of Pope; that 'he was *un politique aux choux et aux raves.*' He would say, 'I dine to-day in Grosvenor-square;' this might be with a Duke: or, perhaps, 'I dine to-day at the other end of the town:' or, 'A gentleman of great eminence called on me yesterday.' He loved thus to keep things floating in conjecture: *Omne ignotum pro magnifico est.* I believe I ventured to dissipate the cloud, to unveil the mystery, more freely and frequently than any of his friends. We stopped again at Wirgman's, the well-known *toy-shop*, in St. James's-street, at the corner of St. James's-place, to which he had been directed, but not clearly, for he searched about some time, and could not find it at first; and said, 'To direct one only to a corner shop is *toying* with one.' I suppose he meant this as a play upon the word *toy*: it was the first time that I knew him stoop to such sport. After he had been some time in the shop, he sent for me to come out of the coach, and help him to choose a pair of silver buckles, as those he had were too small. Probably this alteration in dress had been suggested by Mrs. Thrale, by associating with whom, his external appearance was much improved. He got better cloaths; and the dark colour, from which he never deviated, was enlivened by metal buttons. His wigs, too, were much better; and during their travels in France, he was furnished with a Paris-made wig, of handsome construction. This choosing of silver buckles was a negociation: 'Sir, (said he,) I will not have the ridiculous large ones now in fashion; and I will give no more than a guinea for a pair.' Such were the *principles* of the business; and, after some examination, he was fitted. As we drove along, I found him in a talking humour, of which I availed myself. BOSWELL. 'I was this morning in Ridley's shop, Sir; and was told, that the collection called *Johnsoniana* has sold very much.' JOHNSON. 'Yet the *Journey to the Hebrides* has not had a great sale.' BOSWELL. 'That is strange.' JOHNSON. 'Yes, Sir; for in that book I have told the world a great deal that they did not know before.'

BOSWELL. 'I drank chocolate, Sir, this morning with Mr. Eld; and, to my no small surprize, found him to be a *Staffordshire Whig*, a being which I did not believe had existed.' JOHNSON. 'Sir, there are rascals in all countries.' BOSWELL. 'Eld said, a Tory was a creature generated between a non-juring parson and one's grandmother.' JOHNSON. 'And I have always said, the first Whig was the Devil.' BOSWELL. 'He certainly was, Sir. The Devil was impatient of subordination; he was the first who resisted power:—

"Better to reign in Hell, than serve in Heaven."'

At General Paoli's were Sir Joshua Reynolds, Mr. Langton, Marchese Gherardi of Lombardy, and Mr. John Spottiswoode the younger, of Spottiswoode, the solicitor.

We talked of drinking wine. JOHNSON. 'I require wine only when I am alone. I have then often wished for it, and often taken it.' SPOTTISWOODE. 'What, by way of a companion, Sir?' JOHNSON. 'To get rid of myself, to send myself away. Wine gives great pleasure; and every pleasure is of itself a good. It is a good, unless counterbalanced by evil. A man may have a strong reason not to drink wine; and that may be greater than the pleasure. Wine makes a man better pleased with himself. I do not say that it makes him more pleasing to others. Sometimes it does. But the danger is, that while a man grows better pleased with himself, he may be growing less pleasing to others. Wine gives a man nothing. It neither gives him knowledge nor wit; it only animates a man, and enables him to bring out what a dread of the company had repressed. It only puts in motion what has been locked up in frost. But this may be good, or it may be bad.' SPOTTISWOODE. 'So, Sir, wine is a key which opens a box; but this box may be either full or empty.' JOHNSON. 'Nay, Sir, conversation is the key: wine is a picklock, which forces open the box and injures it. A man should cultivate his mind so as to have that confidence and readiness without wine, which wine gives.' BOSWELL. 'The great difficulty of resisting wine is from benevolence. For instance, a good worthy man asks you to taste his wine, which he has had twenty years in his cellar.' JOHNSON. 'Sir, all this notion about benevolence arises from a man's imagining himself to be of more importance to others, than he really is. They don't care a farthing whether he drinks wine or not.' SIR JOSHUA REYNOLDS. 'Yes, they do for the time.' JOHNSON. 'For the time!—If they care this minute, they forget it the next. And as for the good worthy man; how do you know he is good and worthy? No good and worthy man will insist upon another man's drinking wine. As to the wine twenty years in the cellar,—of ten men, three say this, merely because they must say something;—three are telling a lie, when they say they have had the wine twenty years;—three would rather save the wine;—one, perhaps, cares. I allow it is something to please one's company: and people are always pleased with those who partake pleasure with them. But after a man has brought himself to relinquish the great personal pleasure which arises from drinking wine, any other consideration is a trifle. To please others by drinking wine, is something only, if there be nothing against it. I should, however, be sorry to offend worthy men:—

> "Curst be the verse, how well so e'er it flow,
> That tends to make one worthy man my foe."'

BOSWELL. 'Curst be the _spring_, the _water_.' JOHNSON. 'But let us consider what a sad thing it would be, if we were obliged to drink or do any thing else that may happen to be agreeable to the company where we are.' LANGTON. 'By the same rule you must join with a gang of cut-purses.' JOHNSON. 'Yes, Sir: but yet we must do justice to wine; we must allow it the power it possesses. To make a man pleased with himself, let me tell you, is doing a very great thing;

> "_Si patriae volumus, si_ Nobis _vivere cari_."'

I was at this time myself a water-drinker, upon trial, by Johnson's recommendation. JOHNSON. 'Boswell is a bolder combatant than Sir Joshua: he argues for wine without the help of wine; but Sir Joshua with it.' SIR JOSHUA REYNOLDS. 'But to please one's company is a strong motive.' JOHNSON. (who, from drinking only water, supposed every body who drank wine to be elevated,) 'I won't argue any more with you, Sir. You are too far gone.' SIR JOSHUA. 'I should have thought so indeed, Sir, had I made such a speech as you have now done.' JOHNSON. (drawing himself in, and, I really thought blushing,) 'Nay, don't be angry. I did not mean to offend you.' SIR JOSHUA. 'At first the taste of wine was disagreeable to me; but I brought myself to drink it, that I might be like other people. The pleasure of drinking wine is so connected with pleasing your company, that altogether there is something of social goodness in it.' JOHNSON. 'Sir, this is only saying the same thing over again.' SIR JOSHUA. 'No, this is new.' JOHNSON. 'You put it in new words, but it is an old thought. This is one of the

disadvantages of wine. It makes a man mistake words for thoughts.'
BOSWELL. 'I think it is a new thought; at least, it is in a new *attitude*.'
JOHNSON. 'Nay, Sir, it is only in a new coat; or an old coat with a new
facing. (Then laughing heartily,) It is the old dog in a new doublet.—
An extraordinary instance however may occur where a man's patron
will do nothing for him, unless he will drink: *there* may be a good
reason for drinking.'

I mentioned a nobleman, who I believed was really uneasy if his
company would not drink hard. JOHNSON. 'That is from having had
people about him whom he has been accustomed to command.'
BOSWELL. 'Supposing I should be *tête-à-tête* with him at table.'
JOHNSON. 'Sir, there is no more reason for your drinking with him, than
his being sober with *you*.' BOSWELL. 'Why, that is true; for it would do
him less hurt to be sober, than it would do me to get drunk.' JOHNSON.
'Yes, Sir; and from what I have heard of him, one would not wish to
sacrifice himself to such a man. If he must always have somebody to
drink with him, he should buy a slave, and then he would be sure to
have it. They who submit to drink as another pleases, make themselves
his slaves.' Boswell. 'But, Sir, you will surely make allowance for the
duty of hospitality. A gentleman who loves drinking, comes to visit
me.' JOHNSON. 'Sir, a man knows whom he visits; he comes to the
table of a sober man.' BOSWELL. 'But, Sir, you and I should not have
been so well received in the Highlands and Hebrides, if I had not drunk
with our worthy friends. Had I drunk water only as you did, they would
not have been so cordial.' JOHNSON. 'Sir William Temple mentions that
in his travels through the Netherlands he had two or three gentlemen
with him; and when a bumper was necessary, he put it on *them*. Were I
to travel again through the islands, I would have Sir Joshua with me to
take the bumpers.' BOSWELL. 'But, Sir, let me put a case. Suppose Sir
Joshua should take a jaunt into Scotland; he does me the honour to pay
me a visit at my house in the country; I am overjoyed at seeing him; we
are quite by ourselves, shall I unsociably and churlishly let him sit
drinking by himself? No, no, my dear Sir Joshua, you shall not be
treated so, I *will* take a bottle with you.'

On Wednesday, April 29, I dined with him at Mr. Allan Ramsay's,
where were Lord Binning, Dr. Robertson the historian, Sir Joshua
Reynolds, and the Honourable Mrs. Boscawen, widow of the Admiral,
and mother of the present Viscount Falmouth; of whom, if it be not
presumptuous in me to praise her, I would say, that her manners are the
most agreeable, and her conversation the best, of any lady with whom I
ever had the happiness to be acquainted. Before Johnson came we
talked a good deal of him; Ramsay said he had always found him a
very polite man, and that he treated him with great respect, which he
did very sincerely. I said I worshipped him. ROBERTSON. 'But some of
you spoil him; you should not worship him; you should worship no

man.' BOSWELL. 'I cannot help worshipping him, he is so much superiour to other men.' ROBERTSON. In criticism, and in wit in conversation, he is no doubt very excellent; but in other respects he is not above other men; he will believe any thing, and will strenuously defend the most minute circumstance connected with the Church of England.' BOSWELL. 'Believe me, Doctor, you are much mistaken as to this; for when you talk with him calmly in private, he is very liberal in his way of thinking.' ROBERTSON. 'He and I have been always very gracious; the first time I met him was one evening at Strahan's, when he had just had an unlucky altercation with Adam Smith, to whom he had been so rough, that Strahan, after Smith was gone, had remonstrated with him, and told him that I was coming soon, and that he was uneasy to think that he might behave in the same manner to me. "No, no, Sir, (said Johnson,) I warrant you Robertson and I shall do very well." Accordingly he was gentle and good-humoured, and courteous with me the whole evening; and he has been so upon every occasion that we have met since. I have often said (laughing,) that I have been in a great measure indebted to Smith for my good reception.' BOSWELL. 'His power of reasoning is very strong, and he has a peculiar art of drawing characters, which is as rare as good portrait painting.' SIR JOSHUA REYNOLDS. 'He is undoubtedly admirable in this; but, in order to mark the characters which he draws, he overcharges them, and gives people more than they really have, whether of good or bad.'

No sooner did he, of whom we had been thus talking so easily, arrive, than we were all as quiet as a school upon the entrance of the head-master; and were very soon set down to a table covered with such variety of good things, as contributed not a little to dispose him to be pleased.

RAMSAY. 'I am old enough to have been a contemporary of Pope. His poetry was highly admired in his life-time, more a great deal than after his death.' JOHNSON. 'Sir, it has not been less admired since his death; no authours ever had so much fame in their own life-time as Pope and Voltaire; and Pope's poetry has been as much admired since his death as during his life; it has only not been as much talked of, but that is owing to its being now more distant, and people having other writings to talk of. Virgil is less talked of than Pope, and Homer is less talked of than Virgil; but they are not less admired. We must read what the world reads at the moment. It has been maintained that this superfoetation, this teeming of the press in modern times, is prejudicial to good literature, because it obliges us to read so much of what is of inferiour value, in order to be in the fashion; so that better works are neglected for want of time, because a man will have more gratification of his vanity in conversation, from having read modern books, than from having read the best works of antiquity. But it must be considered, that we have now more knowledge generally diffused; all our ladies read now, which is a great extension. Modern writers are the moons of literature; they shine with reflected light, with light borrowed from the ancients. Greece appears to me to be the fountain of knowledge; Rome of elegance.' RAMSAY. 'I suppose Homer's *Iliad* to be a collection of pieces which had been written before his time. I should like to see a translation of it in poetical prose like the book of Ruth or Job.' ROBERTSON. 'Would you, Dr. Johnson, who are master of the English language, but try your hand upon a part of it.' JOHNSON. 'Sir, you could not read it without the pleasure of verse.

Dr. Robertson expatiated on the character of a certain nobleman; that he was one of the strongest-minded men that ever lived; that he would sit in company quite sluggish, while there was nothing to call forth his intellectual vigour; but the moment that any important subject was started, for instance, how this country is to be defended against a French invasion, he would rouse himself, and shew his extraordinary talents with the most powerful ability and animation. JOHNSON. 'Yet this man cut his own throat. The true strong and sound mind is the mind that can embrace equally great things and small. Now I am told the King of Prussia will say to a servant, "Bring me a bottle of such a wine, which came in such a year; it lies in such a corner of the cellars." I would have a man great in great things, and elegant in little things.' He said to me afterwards, when we were by ourselves, 'Robertson was in a mighty romantick humour, he talked of one whom he did not know; but I *downed* him with the King of Prussia.' 'Yes, Sir, (said I,) you threw a *bottle* at his head.'

An ingenious gentleman was mentioned, concerning whom both Robertson and Ramsay agreed that he had a constant firmness of mind; for after a laborious day, and amidst a multiplicity of cares and anxieties, he would sit down with his sisters and he quite cheerful and good-humoured. Such a disposition, it was observed, was a happy gift of nature. JOHNSON. 'I do not think so; a man has from nature a certain portion of mind; the use he makes of it depends upon his own free will. That a man has always the same firmness of mind I do not say; because every man feels his mind less firm at one time than another; but I think a man's being in a good or bad humour depends upon his will.' I, however, could not help thinking that a man's humour is often uncontroulable by his will.

Next day, Thursday, April 30, I found him at home by himself. JOHNSON. 'Well, Sir, Ramsay gave us a splendid dinner. I love Ramsay. You will not find a man in whose conversation there is more instruction, more information, and more elegance, than in Ramsay's.' BOSWELL. 'What I admire in Ramsay, is his continuing to be so young.' JOHNSON. 'Why, yes, Sir, it is to be admired. I value myself upon this, that there is nothing of the old man in my conversation. I am now sixty-eight, and I have no more of it than at twenty-eight.'

BOSWELL. 'But, Sir, would not you wish to know old age? He who is never an old man, does not know the whole of human life; for old age is one of the divisions of it.' JOHNSON. 'Nay, Sir, what talk is this?' BOSWELL. 'I mean, Sir, the Sphinx's description of it;—morning, noon, and night. I would know night, as well as morning and noon.' JOHNSON. 'What, Sir, would you know what it is to feel the evils of old age? Would you have the gout? Would you have decrepitude?'— Seeing him heated, I would not argue any farther; but I was confident that I was in the right. I would, in due time, be a Nestor, an elder of the people; and there *should* be some difference between the conversation of twenty-eight and sixty-eight. A grave picture should not be gay. There is a serene, solemn, placid old age. JOHNSON. 'Mrs. Thrale's mother said of me what flattered me much. A clergyman was complaining of want of society in the country where he lived; and said, "They talk of *runts*;" (that is, young cows). "Sir, (said Mrs. Salusbury,) Mr. Johnson would learn to talk of runts:" meaning that I was a man who would make the most of my situation, whatever it was.' He added, 'I think myself a very polite man.'

On Saturday, May 2, I dined with him at Sir Joshua Reynolds's, where there was a very large company, and a great deal of conversation; but owing to some circumstance which I cannot now recollect, I have no record of any part of it, except that there were several people there by no means of the Johnsonian school; so that less attention was paid to him than usual, which put him out of humour; and upon some imaginary offence from me, he attacked me with such rudeness, that I was vexed and angry, because it gave those persons an opportunity of enlarging upon his supposed ferocity, and ill treatment of his best friends. I was so much hurt, and had my pride so much roused, that I kept away from him for a week; and, perhaps, might have kept away much longer, nay, gone to Scotland without seeing him again, had not we fortunately met and been reconciled. To such unhappy chances are human friendships liable.

On Friday, May 8, I dined with him at Mr. Langton's. I was reserved and silent, which I suppose he perceived, and might recollect the cause. After dinner when Mr. Langton was called out of the room, and we were by ourselves, he drew his chair near to mine, and said, in a tone of conciliating courtesy, 'Well, how have you done?' Boswell. 'Sir, you have made me very uneasy by your behaviour to me when we were last at Sir Joshua Reynolds's. You know, my dear Sir, no man has a greater respect and affection for you, or would sooner go to the end of the world to serve you. Now to treat me so—.' He insisted that I had interrupted him, which I assured him was not the case; and proceeded—'But why treat me so before people who neither love you nor me?' JOHNSON. 'Well, I am sorry for it. I'll make it up to you twenty different ways, as you please.' BOSWELL. 'I said to-day to Sir

Joshua, when he observed that you *tossed* me sometimes—I don't care how often, or how high he tosses me, when only friends are present, for then I fall upon soft ground: but I do not like falling on stones, which is the case when enemies are present.—I think this a pretty good image, Sir.' JOHNSON. 'Sir, it is one of the happiest I have ever heard.'

The truth is, there was no venom in the wounds which he inflicted at any time, unless they were irritated by some malignant infusion by other hands. We were instantly as cordial again as ever, and joined in hearty laugh at some ludicrous but innocent peculiarities of one of our friends. BOSWELL. 'Do you think, Sir, it is always culpable to laugh at a man to his face?' JOHNSON. 'Why, Sir, that depends upon the man and the thing. If it is a slight man, and a slight thing, you may; for you take nothing valuable from him.'

When Mr. Langton returned to us, the 'flow of talk' went on. An eminent authour being mentioned;—JOHNSON. 'He is not a pleasant man. His conversation is neither instructive nor brilliant. He does not talk as if impelled by any fulness of knowledge or vivacity of imagination. His conversation is like that of any other sensible man. He talks with no wish either to inform or to hear, but only because he thinks it does not become——to sit in a company and say nothing.'

Mr. Langton having repeated the anecdote of Addison having distinguished between his powers in conversation and in writing, by saying 'I have only nine-pence in my pocket; but I can draw for a thousand pounds;'—JOHNSON. 'He had not that retort ready, Sir; he had prepared it before-hand.' LANGTON. (turning to me,) 'A fine surmise. Set a thief to catch a thief.'

JOHNSON. 'I shall be at home to-morrow.' BOSWELL. 'Then let us dine by ourselves at the Mitre, to keep up the old custom, "the custom of the manor," the custom of the mitre.' JOHNSON. 'Sir, so it shall be.'

On Saturday, May 9, we fulfilled our purpose of dining by ourselves at the Mitre, according to old custom. There was, on these occasions, a little circumstance of kind attention to Mrs. Williams, which must not be omitted. Before coming out, and leaving her to dine alone, he gave her her choice of a chicken, a sweetbread, or any other little nice thing, which was carefully sent to her from the tavern, ready-drest.

On Tuesday, May 12, I waited on the Earl of Marchmont, to know if his Lordship would favour Dr. Johnson with information concerning Pope, whose Life he was about to write. Johnson had not flattered himself with the hopes of receiving any civility from this nobleman; for he said to me, when I mentioned Lord Marchmont as one who could tell him a great deal about Pope,—'Sir, he will tell *me* nothing.' I had the honour of being known to his Lordship, and applied to him of myself, without being commissioned by Johnson. His Lordship behaved in the most polite and obliging manner, promised to tell all he recollected about Pope, and was so very courteous as to say, 'Tell Dr. Johnson I have a great respect for him, and am ready to shew it in any way I can. I am to be in the city to-morrow, and will call at his house as I return.' His Lordship however asked, 'Will he write the Lives of the Poets impartially? He was the first that brought Whig and Tory into a Dictionary. And what do you think of his definition of Excise? Do you know the history of his aversion to the word *transpire*?' Then taking down the folio *Dictionary*, he shewed it with this censure on its secondary sense: '"To escape from secrecy to notice; a sense lately innovated from France, without necessity." The truth was Lord Bolingbroke, who left the Jacobites, first used it; therefore, it was to be condemned. He should have shewn what word would do for it, if it was unnecessary.' I afterwards put the question to Johnson: 'Why, Sir, (said he,) *get abroad*.' BOSWELL. 'That, Sir, is using two words.' JOHNSON. 'Sir, there is no end of this. You may as well insist to have a word for old age.' BOSWELL. 'Well, Sir, Senectus.' JOHNSON. 'Nay, Sir, to insist always that there should be one word to express a thing in English, because there is one in another language, is to change the language.'

I proposed to Lord Marchmont that he should revise Johnson's *Life of Pope*: 'So (said his Lordship,) you would put me in a dangerous situation. You know he knocked down Osborne the bookseller.'

Elated with the success of my spontaneous exertion to procure material and respectable aid to Johnson for his very favourite work, *The Lives of the Poets*, I hastened down to Mr. Thrale's at Streatham, where he now was, that I might insure his being at home next day; and after dinner, when I thought he would receive the good news in the best humour, I announced it eagerly: 'I have been at work for you to-day, Sir. I have been with Lord Marchmont. He bade me tell you he has a great respect for you, and will call on you to-morrow at one o'clock, and communicate all he knows about Pope.'—Here I paused, in full expectation that he would be pleased with this intelligence, would praise my active merit, and would be alert to embrace such an offer from a nobleman. But whether I had shewn an over-exultation, which provoked his spleen; or whether he was seized with a suspicion that I had obtruded him on Lord Marchmont, and humbled him too much; or whether there was any thing more than an unlucky fit of ill-humour, I know not; but, to my surprize, the result was,—JOHNSON. 'I shall not be in town to-morrow. I don't care to know about Pope.' MRS. THRALE. (surprized as I was, and a little angry,) 'I suppose, Sir, Mr. Boswell thought, that as you are to write *Pope's Life*, you would wish to know about him.' JOHNSON. 'Wish! why yes. If it rained knowledge I'd hold out my hand; but I would not give myself the trouble to go in quest of it.' There was no arguing with him at the moment. Some time afterwards he said, 'Lord Marchmont will call on me, and then I shall call on Lord Marchmont.' Mr. Thrale was uneasy at his unaccountable caprice; and told me, that if I did not take care to bring about a meeting between Lord Marchmont and him, it would never take place, which would be a great pity. I sent a card to his Lordship, to be left at Johnson's house, acquainting him, that Dr. Johnson could not be in town next day, but would do himself the honour of waiting on him at another time. I give this account fairly, as a specimen of that unhappy temper with which this great and good man had occasionally to struggle, from something morbid in his constitution. Let the most censorious of my readers suppose himself to have a violent fit of the tooth-ach, or to have received a severe stroke on the shin-bone, and when in such a state to be asked a question; and if he has any candour, he will not be surprized at the answers which Johnson sometimes gave in moments of irritation, which, let me assure them, is exquisitely painful. But it must not be erroneously supposed that he was, in the smallest degree, careless concerning any work which he undertook, or that he was generally thus peevish. It will be seen, that in the following year he had a very agreeable interview with Lord Marchmont, at his Lordship's house; and this very afternoon he soon forgot any fretfulness, and fell into conversation as usual.

JOHNSON. 'How foolish was it in Pope to give all his friendship to Lords, who thought they honoured him by being with him; and to choose such Lords as Burlington, and Cobham, and Bolingbroke! Bathurst was negative, a pleasing man; and I have heard no ill of Marchmont; and then always saying, "I do not value you for being a Lord;" which was a sure proof that he did. I never say, I do not value Boswell more for being born to an estate, because I do not care.' BOSWELL. 'Nor for being a Scotchman?' JOHNSON. 'Nay, Sir, I do value you more for being a Scotchman. You are a Scotchman without the faults of a Scotchman. You would not have been so valuable as you are, had you not been a Scotchman.'

Amongst the numerous prints pasted on the walls of the dining-room at Streatham, was Hogarth's 'Modern Midnight Conversation.' I asked him what he knew of Parson Ford, who makes a conspicuous figure in the riotous group. JOHNSON. 'Sir, he was my acquaintance and relation, my mother's nephew. He had purchased a living in the country, but not simoniacally. I never saw him but in the country. I have been told he was a man of great parts; very profligate, but I never heard he was impious.' BOSWELL. 'Was there not a story of his ghost having appeared?' JOHNSON. 'Sir, it was believed. A waiter at the Hummums, in which house Ford died, had been absent for some time, and returned, not knowing that Ford was dead. Going down to the cellar, according to the story, he met him; going down again he met him a second time. When he came up, he asked some of the people of the house what Ford could be doing there. They told him Ford was dead. The waiter took a fever, in which he lay for some time. When he recovered, he said he had a message to deliver to some women from Ford; but he was not to tell what, or to whom. He walked out; he was followed; but somewhere about St. Paul's they lost him. He came back, and said he had delivered the message, and the women exclaimed, "Then we are all undone!" Dr. Pellet, who was not a credulous man, inquired into the truth of this story, and he said, the evidence was irresistible. My wife went to the Hummums; (it is a place where people get themselves cupped.) I believe she went with intention to hear about this story of Ford. At first they were unwilling to tell her; but, after they had talked to her, she came away satisfied that it was true. To be sure the man had a fever; and this vision may have been the beginning of it. But if the message to the women, and their behaviour upon it, were true as related, there was something supernatural. That rests upon his word; and there it remains.'

I staid all this day[46] with him at Streatham. He talked a great deal, in very good humour.

Looking at Messrs. Dilly's splendid edition of Lord Chesterfield's miscellaneous works, he laughed, and said, 'Here now are two speeches ascribed to him, both of which were written by me: and the best of it is, they have found out that one is like Demosthenes, and the other like Cicero.'

BOSWELL. 'Is not modesty natural?' JOHNSON. 'I cannot say, Sir, as we find no people quite in a state of nature; but I think the more they are taught, the more modest they are. The French are a gross, ill-bred, untaught people; a lady there will spit on the floor and rub it with her foot. What I gained by being in France was, learning to be better satisfied with my own country. Time may be employed to more advantage from nineteen to twenty-four almost in any way than in travelling; when you set travelling against mere negation, against doing nothing, it is better to be sure; but how much more would a young man improve were he to study during those years. Indeed, if a young man is wild, and must run after women and bad company, it is better this should be done abroad, as, on his return, he can break off such connections, and begin at home a new man, with a character to form, and acquaintances to make. How little does travelling supply to the conversation of any man who has travelled; how little to Beauclerk!' BOSWELL. 'What say you to Lord———?' JOHNSON. 'I never but once heard him talk of what he had seen, and that was of a large serpent in one of the Pyramids of Egypt.' BOSWELL. 'Well, I happened to hear him tell the same thing, which made me mention him.'

I talked of a country life. JOHNSON. 'Were I to live in the country, I would not devote myself to the acquisition of popularity; I would live in a much better way, much more happily; I would have my time at my

---

own command.' BOSWELL. 'But, Sir, is it not a sad thing to be at a distance from all our literary friends?' JOHNSON. 'Sir, you will by and by have enough of this conversation, which now delights you so much.'

As he was a zealous friend of subordination, he was at all times watchful to repress the vulgar cant against the manners of the great; 'High people, Sir, (said he,) are the best; take a hundred ladies of quality, you'll find them better wives, better mothers, more willing to sacrifice their own pleasure to their children than a hundred other women. Tradeswomen (I mean the wives of tradesmen) in the city, who are worth from ten to fifteen thousand pounds, are the worst creatures upon the earth, grossly ignorant, and thinking viciousness fashionable. Farmers, I think, are often worthless fellows. Few lords will cheat; and, if they do, they'll be ashamed of it: farmers cheat and are not ashamed of it: they have all the sensual vices too of the nobility, with cheating into the bargain. There is as much fornication and adultery among farmers as amongst noblemen.' BOSWELL. 'The notion of the world, Sir, however is, that the morals of women of quality are worse than those in lower stations.' JOHNSON. 'Yes, Sir, the licentiousness of one woman of quality makes more noise than that of a number of women in lower stations; then, Sir, you are to consider the malignity of women in the city against women of quality, which will make them believe any thing of them, such as that they call their coachmen to bed. No, Sir, so far as I have observed, the higher in rank, the richer ladies are, they are the better instructed and the more virtuous.'

On Tuesday, May 19, I was to set out for Scotland in the evening. He was engaged to dine with me at Mr. Dilly's, I waited upon him to remind him of his appointment and attend him thither; he gave me some salutary counsel, and recommended vigorous resolution against any deviation from moral duty. BOSWELL. 'But you would not have me to bind myself by a solemn obligation?' JOHNSON. (much agitated,) 'What! a vow—O, no, Sir, a vow is a horrible thing, it is a snare for sin. The man who cannot go to Heaven without a vow—may go—' Here, standing erect, in the middle of his library, and rolling grand, his pause was truly a curious compound of the solemn and the ludicrous; he half-whistled in his usual way, when pleasant, and he paused, as if checked by religious awe. Methought he would have added—to Hell—but was restrained. I humoured the dilemma. 'What! Sir, (said I,) *In caelum jusseris ibit?*' alluding to his imitation of it,—

'And bid him go to Hell, to Hell he goes.'

We had a quiet comfortable meeting at Mr. Dilly's; nobody there but ourselves. My illustrious friend and I parted with assurances of affectionate regard.

Mr. Langton has been pleased, at my request, to favour me with some particulars of Dr. Johnson's visit to Warley-camp, where this gentleman was at the time stationed as a Captain in the Lincolnshire militia. I shall give them in his own words in a letter to me.

'It was in the summer of the year 1778, that he complied with my invitation to come down to the Camp at Warley, and he staid with me about a week; the scene appeared, notwithstanding a great degree of ill health that he seemed to labour under, to interest and amuse him, as agreeing with the disposition that I believe you know he constantly manifested towards enquiring into subjects of the military kind. He sate, with a patient degree of attention, to observe the proceedings of a regimental court-martial, that happened to be called, in the time of his stay with us; and one night, as late as at eleven o'clock, he accompanied the Major of the regiment in going what are styled the Rounds, where he might observe the forms of visiting the guards, for the seeing that they and their sentries are ready in their duty on their several posts. He took occasion to converse at times on military topicks, one in particular, that I see the mention of, in your *Journal of a Tour to the Hebrides*, which lies open before me, as to gun-powder; which he spoke of to the same effect, in part, that you relate.

'On one occasion, when the regiment were going through their exercise, he went quite close to the men at one of the extremities of it, and watched all their practices attentively; and, when he came away, his remark was, "The men indeed do load their muskets and fire with wonderful celerity." He was likewise particular in requiring to know what was the weight of the musquet balls in use, and within what distance they might be expected to take effect when fired off.

'In walking among the tents, and observing the difference between those of the officers and private men, he said that the superiority of accommodation of the better conditions of life, to that of the inferiour ones, was never exhibited to him in so distinct a view. The civilities paid to him in the camp were, from the gentlemen of the Lincolnshire regiment, one of the officers of which accommodated him with a tent in which he slept; and from General Hall, who very courteously invited him to dine with him, where he appeared to be very well pleased with his entertainment, and the civilities he received on the part of the General; the attention likewise, of the General's aide-de-camp, Captain Smith, seemed to be very welcome to him, as appeared by their engaging in a great deal of discourse together.'

We surely cannot but admire the benevolent exertions of this great and good man, especially when we consider how grievously he was afflicted with bad health, and how uncomfortable his home was made by the perpetual jarring of those whom he charitably accommodated under his roof. He has sometimes suffered me to talk jocularly of his group of females, and call them his *Seraglio*. He thus mentions them, together with honest Levett, in one of his letters to Mrs. Thrale:

'Williams hates every body; Levett hates Desmoulins, and does not love Williams; Desmoulins hates them both; Poll[47] loves none of them.'[48]

In 1779, Johnson gave the world a luminous proof that the vigour of his mind in all its faculties, whether memory, judgement, or imagination, was not in the least abated; for this year came out the first four volumes of his *Prefaces, biographical and critical, to the most eminent of the English Poets*, published by the booksellers of London. The remaining volumes came out in the year 1780. The Poets were selected by the several booksellers who had the honorary copy right, which is still preserved among them by mutual compact, notwithstanding the decision of the House of Lords against the perpetuity of Literary Property. We have his own authority, that by his recommendation the poems of Blackmore, Watts, Pomfret, and Yalden, were added to the collection.

On the 22nd of January, I wrote to him on several topicks, and mentioned that as he had been so good as to permit me to have the proof sheets of his *Lives of the Poets*, I had written to his servant, Francis, to take care of them for me.

On the 23rd of February I wrote to him again, complaining of his silence, as I had heard he was ill, and had written to Mr. Thrale, for information concerning him; and I announced my intention of soon being again in London.

'TO JAMES BOSWELL, ESQ.

'DEAR SIR,—Why should you take such delight to make a bustle, to write to Mr. Thrale that I am negligent, and to Francis to do what is so very unnecessary. Thrale, you may be sure, cared not about it; and I shall spare Francis the trouble, by ordering a set both of the *Lives* and *Poets* to dear Mrs. Boswell,[49] in acknowledgement of her marmalade. Persuade her to accept them, and accept them kindly. If I thought she would receive them scornfully, I would send them to Miss Boswell, who, I hope, has yet none of her mamma's ill-will to me. . . .

'Mrs. Thrale waits in the coach. I am, dear Sir, &c.,
'March 13, 1779.'

'SAM. JOHNSON.'

This letter crossed me on the road to London, where I arrived on Monday, March 15, and next morning at a late hour, found Dr. Johnson

---

[47] Miss Carmichael.
[48] A year later he wrote: At Bolt-court there is much malignity, but of late little hostility.'—Ed.
[49] He sent a set elegantly bound and gilt, which was received as a very handsome present.—BOSWELL.

sitting over his tea, attended by Mrs. Desmoulins, Mr. Levett, and a clergyman, who had come to submit some poetical pieces to his revision. It is wonderful what a number and variety of writers, some of them even unknown to him, prevailed on his good-nature to look over their works, and suggest corrections and improvements. My arrival interrupted for a little while the important business of this true representative of Bayes; upon its being resumed, I found that the subject under immediate consideration was a translation, yet in manuscript, of the *Carmen Seculare* of Horace, which had this year been set to musick, and performed as a publick entertainment in London, for the joint benefit of monsieur Philidor and Signor Baretti. When Johnson had done reading, the authour asked him bluntly, 'If upon the whole it was a good translation?' Johnson, whose regard for truth was uncommonly strict, seemed to be puzzled for a moment, what answer to make; as he certainly could not honestly commend the performance: with exquisite address he evaded the question thus, 'Sir, I do not say that it may not be made a very good translation.' Here nothing whatever in favour of the performance was affirmed, and yet the writer was not shocked. A printed *Ode to the Warlike Genius of Britain*, came next in review; the bard was a lank bony figure, with short black hair; he was writhing himself in agitation, while Johnson read, and shewing his teeth in a grin of earnestness, exclaimed in broken sentences, and in a keen sharp tone, 'Is that poetry, Sir?—Is it *Pindar?*' JOHNSON. 'Why, Sir, there is here a great deal of what is called poetry.' Then, turning to me, the poet cried, 'My muse has not been long upon the town, and (pointing to the *Ode*) it trembles under the hand of the great critick.' Johnson, in a tone of displeasure, asked him, 'Why do you praise Anson?' I did not trouble him by asking his reason for this question. He proceeded, 'Here is an errour, Sir; you have made Genius feminine.' 'Palpable, Sir; (cried the enthusiast,) I know it. But (in a lower tone,) it was to pay a compliment to the Duchess of Devonshire, with which her Grace was pleased. She is walking across Coxheath, in the military uniform, and I suppose her to be the Genius of Britain.' JOHNSON. 'Sir, you are giving a reason for it; but that will not make it right. You may have a reason why two and two should make five; but they will still make but four.'

Although I was several times with him in the course of the following days, such it seems were my occupations, or such my negligence, that I have preserved no memorial of his conversation till Friday, March 26, when I visited him. He said he expected to be attacked on account of his *Lives of the Poets*. 'However (said he,) I would rather be attacked than unnoticed. For the worst thing you can do to an authour is to be silent as to his works. An assault upon a town is a bad thing; but starving it is still worse; an assault may be unsuccessful; you may have more men killed than you kill; but if you starve the town, you are sure of victory.'

Talking of a friend of ours associating with persons of very discordant principles and characters; I said he was a very universal man, quite a man of the world. JOHNSON. 'Yes, Sir; but one may be so much a man of the world as to be nothing in the world. I remember a passage in Goldsmith's *Vicar of Wakefield,* which he was afterwards fool enough to expunge: "I do not love a man who is zealous for nothing."' BOSWELL. 'That was a fine passage.' JOHNSON. 'Yes, Sir: there was another fine passage too, which be struck out: "When I was a young man, being anxious to distinguish myself, I was perpetually starting new propositions. But I soon gave this over; for, I found that generally what was new was false."' I said I did not like to sit with people of whom I had not a good opinion. JOHNSON. 'But you must not indulge your delicacy too much; or you will be a *tête-à-tête* man all your life.'

During my stay in London this spring, I find I was unaccountably negligent in preserving Johnson's sayings, more so than at any time when I was happy enough to have an opportunity of hearing his wisdom and wit. There is no help for it now. I must content myself with presenting such scraps as I have. But I am nevertheless ashamed and vexed to think how much has been lost. It is not that there was a bad crop this year; but that I was not sufficiently careful in gathering it in. I, therefore, in some instances can only exhibit a few detached fragments.

Talking of the wonderful concealment of the authour of the celebrated letters signed *Junius*; he said, 'I should have believed Burke to be Junius, because I know no man but Burke who is capable of writing these letters; but Burke spontaneously denied it to me. The case would have been different had I asked him if he was the authour; a man so questioned, as to an anonymous publication, may think he has a right to deny it.'

On Wednesday, March 31, when I visited him, and confessed an excess of which I had very seldom been guilty; that I had spent a whole night in playing at cards, and that I could not look back on it with satisfaction; instead of a harsh animadversion, he mildly said, 'Alas, Sir, on how few things can we look back with satisfaction.'

On Friday, April 2, being Good-Friday, I visited him in the morning as usual; and finding that we insensibly fell into a train of ridicule upon the foibles of one of our friends, a very worthy man, I, by way of a check, quoted some good admonition from *The Government of the Tongue,* that very pious book. It happened also remarkably enough, that the subject of the sermon preached to us to-day by Dr. Burrows, the rector of St. Clement Danes, was the certainty that at the last day we must give an account of 'the deeds done in the body;' and, amongst various acts of culpability he mentioned evil-speaking. As we were moving slowly along in the crowd from church, Johnson jogged my elbow, and said, 'Did you attend to the sermon?' 'Yes, Sir, (said I,) it was very applicable to *us.*' He, however, stood upon the defensive. 'Why, Sir, the sense of ridicule is given us, and may be lawfully used. The authour of *The Government of the Tongue* would have us treat all men alike.'

In the interval between morning and evening service, he endeavoured to employ himself earnestly in devotional exercises; and as he has mentioned in his *Prayers and Meditations,* gave me *Les Pensées de Paschal,* that I might not interrupt him. I preserve the book with reverence. His presenting it to me is marked upon it with his own hand, and I have found in it a truly divine unction. We went to church again in the afternoon.

On Wednesday, April 7, I dined with him at Sir Joshua Reynolds's. I have not marked what company was there. Johnson harangued upon the qualities of different liquors; and spoke with great contempt of claret, as so weak, that a man would be drowned by it before it made him drunk.' He was persuaded to drink one glass of it, that he might judge, not from recollection, which might be dim, but from immediate sensation. He shook his head, and said, 'Poor stuff! No, Sir, claret is the liquor for boys; port for men; but he who aspires to be a hero (smiling), must drink brandy. In the first place, the flavour of brandy is most grateful to the palate; and then brandy will do soonest for a man what drinking *can* do for him. There are, indeed, few who are able to drink brandy. That is a power rather to be wished for than attained. And yet, (proceeded he,) as in all pleasure hope is a considerable part, I know not but fruition comes too quick by brandy. Florence wine I think the worst; it is wine only to the eye; it is wine neither while you are drinking it, nor after you have drunk it; it neither pleases the taste, nor exhilarates the spirits.' I reminded him how heartily he and I used to drink wine together, when we were first acquainted; and how I used to have a head-ache after sitting up with him. He did not like to have this recalled, or, perhaps, thinking that I boasted improperly, resolved to have a witty stroke at me: 'Nay, Sir, it was not the *wine* that made your head ache, but the *sense* that I put into it.' BOSWELL. 'What, Sir! will sense make the head ache?' JOHNSON. 'Yes, Sir, (with a smile,) when it is not used to it.'—No man who has a true relish of pleasantry could be offended at this; especially if Johnson in a long intimacy had given him repeated proofs of his regard and good estimation. I used to say, that as he had given me a thousand pounds in praise, he had a good right now and then to take a guinea from me.

On Thursday, April 8, I dined with him at Mr. Allan Ramsay's, with Lord Graham and some other company. We talked of Shakspeare's witches. JOHNSON. 'They are beings of his own creation; they are a compound of malignity and meanness, without any abilities; and are quite different from the Italian magician. King James says in his *Daemonology*, 'Magicians command the devils: witches are their servants. The Italian magicians are elegant beings.' RAMSAY. 'Opera witches, not Drury-lane witches.' Johnson observed, that abilities might be employed in a narrow sphere, as in getting money, which he said he believed no man could do, without vigorous parts, though concentrated to a point. RAMSAY. 'Yes, like a strong horse in a mill; he pulls better.'

Lord Graham, while he praised the beauty of Lochlomond, on the banks of which is his family seat, complained of the climate, and said he could not bear it. JOHNSON. 'Nay, my Lord, don't talk so: you may bear it well enough. Your ancestors have borne it more years than I can tell.' This was a handsome compliment to the antiquity of the House of Montrose. His Lordship told me afterwards, that he had only affected to complain of the climate; lest, if he had spoken as favourably of his country as he really thought, Dr. Johnson might have attacked it. Johnson was very courteous to Lady Margaret Macdonald. 'Madam, (said he,) when I was in the Isle of Sky, I heard of the people running to take the stones off the road, lest Lady Margaret's horse should stumble.'

Lord Graham commended Dr. Drummond at Naples, as a man of extraordinary talents; and added, that he had a great love of liberty. JOHNSON. 'He is *young*, my Lord; (looking to his Lordship with an arch smile,) all *boys* love liberty, till experience convinces them they are not so fit to govern themselves as they imagined. We are all agreed as to our own liberty; we would have as much of it as we can get; but we are not agreed as to the liberty of others: for in proportion as we take, others must lose. I believe we hardly wish that the mob should have liberty to govern us. When that was the case some time ago, no man was at liberty not to have candles in his windows.' RAMSAY. 'The result is, that order is better than confusion.' JOHNSON. 'The result is, that order cannot be had but by subordination.'

On Friday, April 16, I had been present at the trial of the unfortunate Mr. Hackman, who, in a fit of frantick jealous love, had shot Miss Ray, the favourite of a nobleman. Johnson, in whose company I dined to-day with some other friends, was much interested by my account of what passed, and particularly with his prayer for the mercy of heaven. He said, in a solemn fervid tone, 'I hope he *shall* find mercy.'

This day a violent altercation arose between Johnson and Beauclerk, which having made much noise at the time, I think it proper, in order to prevent any future misrepresentation, to give a minute account of it.

In talking of Hackman, Johnson argued, as Judge Blackstone had done, that his being furnished with two pistols was a proof that he meant to shoot two persons. Mr. Beauclerk said, 'No; for that every wise man who intended to shoot himself, took two pistols, that he might be sure of doing it at once. Lord——— ———' cook shot himself with one pistol, and lived ten days in great agony. Mr.———, who loved buttered muffins, but durst not eat them because they disagreed with his stomach, resolved to shoot himself; and then he eat three buttered muffins for breakfast, before shooting himself, knowing that he should not be troubled with indigestion: *he* had two charged pistols; one was found lying charged upon the table by him, after he had shot himself with the other.' 'Well, (said Johnson, with an air of triumph,) you see here one pistol was sufficient.' Beauclerk replied smartly, 'Because it happened to kill him.' And either then or a very little afterwards, being piqued at Johnson's triumphant remark, added, 'This is what you don't know, and I do.' There was then a cessation of the dispute; and some minutes intervened, during which, dinner and the glass went on cheerfully; when Johnson suddenly and abruptly exclaimed, 'Mr. Beauclerk, how came you to talk so petulantly to me, as "This is what you don't know, but what I know"? One thing *I* know, which *you* don't seem to know, that you are very uncivil.' BEAUCLERK. 'Because *you* began by being uncivil, (which you always are.)' The words in parenthesis were, I believe, not heard by Dr. Johnson. Here again there was a cessation of arms. Johnson told me, that the reason why he waited at first some time without taking any notice of what Mr. Beauclerk said, was because he was thinking whether he should resent it. But when he considered that there were present a young Lord and an eminent traveller, two men of the world with whom he had never dined before, he was apprehensive that they might think they had a right to take such liberties with him as Beauclerk did, and therefore resolved he would not let it pass; adding, that 'he would not appear a coward.' A little while after this, the conversation turned on the violence of Hackman's temper. Johnson then said, 'It was his business to *command* his temper, as my friend, Mr. Beauclerk, should have done some time ago.' BEAUCLERK. 'I should learn of *you*, Sir.' JOHNSON. 'Sir, you have given *me* opportunities enough of learning, when I have been in *your* company. No man loves to be treated with contempt.' BEAUCLERK. (with a polite inclination towards Johnson,) 'Sir, you have known me twenty years, and however I may have treated others, you may be sure I could never treat you with contempt.' JOHNSON. 'Sir, you have said more than was necessary.' Thus it ended; and Beauclerk's coach not having come for him till very late, Dr. Johnson and another gentleman sat with him a long time after the rest of the company were gone; and he and I dined at Beauclerk's on the Saturday se'nnight following.

After this tempest had subsided, I recollect the following particulars of his conversation:—

'I am always for getting a boy forward in his learning; for that is a sure good. I would let him at first read *any* English book which happens to engage his attention; because you have done a great deal when you have brought him to have entertainment from a book. He'll get better books afterwards.'

'To be contradicted, in order to force you to talk, is mighty unpleasing. You *shine*, indeed; but it is by being *ground*.'

On Saturday, April 24, I dined with him at Mr. Beauclerk's, with Sir Joshua Reynolds, Mr. Jones, (afterwards Sir William,) Mr. Langton, Mr. Steevens, Mr. Paradise, and Dr. Higgins. I mentioned that Mr. Wilkes had attacked Garrick to me, as a man who had no friend. 'I believe he is right, Sir. Οἱ φίλοι, οὐ φίλος—He had friends, but no friend. Garrick was so diffused, he had no man to whom he wished to unbosom himself. He found people always ready to applaud him, and that always for the same thing: so he saw life with great uniformity.' I took upon me, for once, to fight with Goliath's weapons, and play the sophist.—Garrick did not need a friend, as he got from every body all he wanted. What is a friend? One who supports you and comforts you, while others do not. Friendship, you know, Sir, is the cordial drop, "to make the nauseous draught of life go down:" but if the draught be not nauseous, if it be all sweet, there is no occasion for that drop.' JOHNSON. 'Many men would not be content to live so. I hope I should not. They would wish to have an intimate friend, with whom they might compare minds, and cherish private virtues. One of the company mentioned Lord Chesterfield, as a man who had no friend. JOHNSON. 'There were more materials to make friendship in Garrick, had he not been so diffused.' BOSWELL. 'Garrick was pure gold, but beat out to thin leaf. Lord Chesterfield was tinsel.' JOHNSON. 'Garrick was a very good man, the cheerfullest man of his age; a decent liver in a profession which is supposed to give indulgence to licentiousness; and a man who gave away, freely, money acquired by himself. He began the world with a great hunger for money; the son of a half-pay officer, bred in a family, whose study was to make four-pence do as much as others made four-pence halfpenny do. But, when he had got money, he was very liberal.' I presumed to animadvert on his eulogy on Garrick, in his Lives of the Poets. 'You say, Sir, his death eclipsed the gaiety of nations.' JOHNSON. 'I could not have said more nor less. It is the truth; *eclipsed*, not *extinguished*; and his death *did* eclipse; it was like a storm.' BOSWELL. 'But why nations? Did his gaiety extend farther than his own nation?' JOHNSON. 'Why, Sir, some exaggeration must be allowed. Besides, nations may be said—if we allow the Scotch to be a nation, and to have gaiety,—which they have not. *You* are an exception, though. Come, gentlemen, let us candidly admit that there is one Scotchman who is cheerful.' BEAUCLERK. 'But he is a very unnatural Scotchman.' I, however, continued to think the compliment to Garrick hyperbolically untrue. His acting had ceased some time before his death; at any rate he had acted in Ireland but a short time, at an early period of his life, and never in Scotland. I objected also to what appears an anticlimax of praise, when contrasted with the preceding panegyrick,—'and diminished the public stock of harmless pleasure!'—'Is not *harmless pleasure* very tame?' JOHNSON. 'Nay, Sir, harmless pleasure is the highest praise. Pleasure is a word of dubious import; pleasure is in general dangerous, and pernicious to virtue; to be able therefore to furnish pleasure that is harmless, pleasure pure and unalloyed, is as great a power as man can possess.' This was, perhaps, as ingenious a defence as could be made; still, however, I was not satisfied.

Talking of celebrated and successful irregular practisers in physick; he said, 'Taylor was the most ignorant man I ever knew; but sprightly. Ward the dullest. Taylor challenged me once to talk Latin with him; (laughing). I quoted some of Horace, which he took to be a part of my own speech. He said a few words well enough.' BEAUCLERK. 'I remember, Sir, you said that Taylor was an instance how far impudence could carry ignorance.' Mr. Beauclerk was very entertaining this day, and told us a number of short stories in a lively elegant manner, and with that air of *the world* which has I know not what impressive effect, as if there were something more than is expressed, or than perhaps we could perfectly understand. As Johnson and I accompanied Sir Joshua Reynolds in his coach, Johnson said, 'There is in Beauclerk a predominance over his company, that one does not like. But he is a man who has lived so much in the world, that he has a short story on every occasion; he is always ready to talk, and is never exhausted.'

Soon after this time a little incident occurred, which I will not suppress, because I am desirous that my work should be, as much as is consistent with the strictest truth, an antidote to the false and injurious notions of his character, which have been given by others, and therefore I infuse every drop of genuine sweetness into my biographical cup.

'TO DR. JOHNSON.

'MY DEAR SIR,—I am in great pain with an inflamed foot, and obliged to keep my bed, so am prevented from having the pleasure to dine at Mr. Ramsay's to-day, which is very hard; and my spirits are sadly sunk. Will you be so friendly as to come and sit an hour with me in the evening. I am ever your most faithful, and affectionate humble servant,

'South Audley-street, Monday, April 26.'

'JAMES BOSWELL.'

'TO MR. BOSWELL.

'Mr. Johnson laments the absence of Mr. Boswell, and will come to him.—Harley-street.'

He came to me in the evening, and brought Sir Joshua Reynolds. I need scarcely say, that their conversation, while they sate by my bedside, was the most pleasing opiate to pain that could have been administered.

Johnson being now better disposed to obtain information concerning Pope than he was last year, sent by me to my Lord Marchmont a present of those volumes of his *Lives of the Poets* which were at this time published, with a request to have permission to wait on him; and his Lordship, who had called on him twice, obligingly appointed Saturday, the first of May, for receiving us.

On that morning Johnson came to me from Streatham, and after drinking chocolate at General Paoli's, in South-Audley-street, we proceeded to Lord Marchmont's in Curzon-street. His Lordship met us at the door of his library, and with great politeness said to Johnson, 'I am not going to make an encomium upon *myself*, by telling you the high respect I have for *you*, Sir.' Johnson was exceedingly courteous; and the interview, which lasted about two hours, during which the Earl communicated his anecdotes of Pope, was as agreeable as I could have wished. When we came out, I said to Johnson, that considering his Lordship's civility, I should have been vexed if he had again failed to come. 'Sir, (said he,) I would rather have given twenty pounds than not have come.' I accompanied him to Streatham, where we dined, and returned to town in the evening.

He had, before I left London, resumed the conversation concerning the appearance of a ghost at Newcastle upon Tyne, which Mr. John Wesley believed, but to which Johnson did not give credit. I was, however, desirous to examine the question closely, and at the same time wished to be made acquainted with Mr. John Wesley; for though I differed from him in some points, I admired his various talents, and loved his pious zeal. At my request, therefore, Dr. Johnson gave me a letter of introduction to him.

'TO THE REVEREND MR. JOHN WESLEY.

'SIR,—Mr. Boswell, a gentleman who has been long known to me, is desirous of being known to you, and has asked this recommendation, which I give him with great willingness, because I think it very much to be wished that worthy and religious men should be acquainted with each other. I am, Sir, your most humble servant,

'May 3, 1779.'

'SAM. JOHNSON.'

Mr. Wesley being in the course of his ministry at Edinburgh, I presented this letter to him, and was very politely received. I begged to have it returned to me, which was accordingly done. His state of the evidence as to the ghost did not satisfy me.

My readers will not be displeased at being told every slight circumstance of the manner in which Dr. Johnson contrived to amuse his solitary hours. He sometimes employed himself in chymistry, sometimes in watering and pruning a vine, sometimes in small experiments, at which those who may smile, should recollect that there are moments which admit of being soothed only by trifles.[50]

My friend Colonel James Stuart, second son of the Earl of Bute, who had distinguished himself as a good officer of the Bedfordshire militia, had taken a publick-spirited resolution to serve his country in its difficulties, by raising a regular regiment, and taking the command of it himself. This, in the heir of the immense property of Wortley, was highly honourable. Having been in Scotland recruiting, he obligingly asked me to accompany him to Leeds, then the head-quarters of his corps; from thence to London for a short time, and afterwards to other places to which the regiment might be ordered. Such an offer, at a time of the year when I had full leisure, was very pleasing; especially as I was to accompany a man of sterling good sense, information, discernment, and conviviality; and was to have a second crop in one year of London and Johnson. Of this I informed my illustrious friend, in characteristical warm terms, in a letter dated the 30th of September, from Leeds.

On Monday, October 4, I called at his house before he was up. He sent for me to his bedside, and expressed his satisfaction at this incidental meeting, with as much vivacity as if he had been in the gaiety of youth. He called briskly, 'Frank, go and get coffee, and let us breakfast IN SPLENDOUR.'

On Sunday, October 10, we dined together at Mr. Strahan's. The conversation having turned on the prevailing practice of going to the East-Indies in quest of wealth;—JOHNSON. 'A man had better have ten thousand pounds at the end of ten years passed in England, than twenty

---

[50] In one of his manuscript Diaries, there is the following entry, which marks his curious minute attention: 'July 26, 1768. I shaved my nail by accident in whetting the knife, about an eighth of an inch from the bottom, and about a fourth from the top. This I measure that I may know the growth of nails; the whole is about five eighths of an inch.' Another of the same kind appears, 'Aug. 7, 1779, *Partem brachii dextri carpo proximum et cutem pectoris circa mamillam dextram rasi, ut notum fieret quanto temporis pili renovarentur.*' And, 'Aug. 15, 1773. I cut from the vine 41 leaves, which weighed five oz. and a half, and eight scruples:—I lay them upon my bookcase, to see what weight they will lose by drying.'—BOSWELL.

thousand pounds at the end of ten years passed in India, because you must compute what you *give* for money; and a man who has lived ten years in India, has given up ten years of social comfort and all those advantages which arise from living in England. The ingenious Mr. Brown, distinguished by the name of *Capability Brown*, told me, that he was once at the seat of Lord Clive, who had returned from India with great wealth; and that he shewed him at the door of his bed-chamber a large chest, which he said he had once had full of gold; upon which Brown observed, "I am glad you can bear it so near your bed-chamber."'

We talked of the state of the poor in London.—JOHNSON. 'Saunders Welch, the Justice, who was once High-Constable of Holborn, and had the best opportunities of knowing the state of the poor, told me, that I under-rated the number, when I computed that twenty a week, that is, above a thousand a year, died of hunger; not absolutely of immediate hunger; but of the wasting and other diseases which are the consequences of hunger. This happens only in so large a place as London, where people are not known. What we are told about the great sums got by begging is not true: the trade is overstocked. And, you may depend upon it, there are many who cannot get work. A particular kind of manufacture fails: those who have been used to work at it, can, for some time, work at nothing else. You meet a man begging; you charge him with idleness: he says, "I am willing to labour. Will you give me work?"—"I cannot."—"Why, then you have no right to charge me with idleness."'

We left Mr. Strahan's at seven, as Johnson had said he intended to go to evening prayers. As we walked along, he complained of a little gout in his toe, and said, 'I shan't go to prayers to-night; I shall go to-morrow: Whenever I miss church on a Sunday, I resolve to go another day. But I do not always do it.' This was a fair exhibition of that vibration between pious resolutions and indolence, which many of us have too often experienced.

I went home with him, and we had a long quiet conversation. BOSWELL. 'Why, Sir, do people play this trick which I observe now, when I look at your grate, putting the shovel against it to make the fire burn?' JOHNSON. 'They play the trick, but it does not make the fire burn. *There* is a better; (setting the poker perpendicularly up at right angles with the grate.) In days of superstition they thought, as it made a cross with the bars, it would drive away the witch.'

BOSWELL. 'By associating with you, Sir, I am always getting an accession of wisdom. But perhaps a man, after knowing his own character—the limited strength of his own mind, should not be desirous of having too much wisdom, considering, *quid valeant humeri*, how little he can carry.' JOHNSON. 'Sir, be as wise as you can; let a man be *aliis laetus, sapiens sibi*:

"Though pleas'd to see the dolphins play,
I mind my compass and my way."

You may be wise in your study in the morning, and gay in company at a tavern in the evening. Every man is to take care of his own wisdom and his own virtue, without minding too much what others think.'

He said, 'Dodsley first mentioned to me the scheme of an English Dictionary; but I had long thought of it.' BOSWELL. 'You did not know what you were undertaking.' JOHNSON. 'Yes, Sir, I knew very well what I was undertaking,—and very well how to do it,—and have done it very well.' BOSWELL. 'An excellent climax! and it *has* availed you. In your Preface you say, "What would it avail me in this gloom of solitude?" You have been agreeably mistaken.'

In his *Life of Milton* he observes, 'I cannot but remark a kind of respect, perhaps unconsciously, paid to this great man by his biographers: every house in which he resided is historically mentioned, as if it were an injury to neglect naming any place that he honoured by his presence.' I had, before I read this observation, been desirous of shewing that respect to Johnson, by various inquiries. Finding him this evening in a very good humour, I prevailed on him to give me an exact list of his places of residence, since he entered the metropolis as an authour, which I subjoin in a note.[51]

On Tuesday, October 12, I dined with him at Mr. Ramsay's, with Lord Newhaven, and some other company, none of whom I recollect, but a beautiful Miss Graham, a relation of his Lordship's, who asked Dr. Johnson to hob or nob with her. He was flattered by such pleasing attention, and politely told her, he never drank wine; but if she would drink a glass of water, he was much at her service. She accepted. 'Oho, Sir! (said Lord Newhaven,) you are caught.' JOHNSON. 'Nay, I do not see *how* I am *caught*; but if I am caught, I don't want to get free again. If I am caught, I hope to be kept.' Then when the two glasses of water were brought, smiling placidly to the young lady, he said, 'Madam, let us *reciprocate*.'

Lord Newhaven and Johnson carried on an argument for some time, concerning the Middlesex election. Johnson said, 'Parliament may be considered as bound by law as a man is bound where there is nobody to tie the knot. As it is clear that the House of Commons may expel and expel again and again, why not allow of the power to

---

[51] 1. Exeter-street, off Catherine-street, Strand. 2. Greenwich. 3. Woodstock-street, near Hanover-square. 4. Castle-street, Cavendish-square, No. 6. 5. Strand. 6. Boswell-Court. 7. Strand, again. 8. Bow-street. 9. Holborn. 10. Fetter-lane. 11. Holborn, again. 12. Gough-square. 13. Staple Inn. 14. Gray's Inn. 15. Inner Temple-lane, No. 1. 16. Johnson's-court, No. 7. 17. Bolt-court. No. 8.—BOSWELL.

incapacitate for that parliament, rather than have a perpetual contest kept up between parliament and the people.' Lord Newhaven took the opposite side; but respectfully said, 'I speak with great deference to you, Dr. Johnson; I speak to be instructed.' This had its full effect on my friend. He bowed his head almost as low as the table, to a complimenting nobleman; and called out, 'My Lord, my Lord, I do not desire all this ceremony; let us tell our minds to one another quietly.' After the debate was over, he said, 'I have got lights on the subject to-day, which I had not before.' This was a great deal from him, especially as he had written a pamphlet upon it.

Of his fellow-collegian, the celebrated Mr. George Whitefield, he said, 'Whitefield never drew as much attention as a mountebank does; he did not draw attention by doing better than others, but by doing what was strange. Were Astley to preach a sermon standing upon his head on a horse's back, he would collect a multitude to hear him; but no wise man would say he had made a better sermon for that. I never treated Whitefield's ministry with contempt; I believe he did good. He had devoted himself to the lower classes of mankind, and among them he was of use. But when familiarity and noise claim the praise due to knowledge, art, and elegance, we must beat down such pretensions.'

What I have preserved of his conversation during the remainder of my stay in London at this time, is only what follows: I told him that when I objected to keeping company with a notorious infidel, a celebrated friend of ours said to me, 'I do not think that men who live laxly in the world, as you and I do, can with propriety assume such an authority. Dr. Johnson may, who is uniformly exemplary in his conduct. But it is not very consistent to shun an infidel to-day, and get drunk to-morrow.' JOHNSON. 'Nay, Sir, this is sad reasoning. Because a man cannot be right in all things, is he to be right in nothing? Because a man sometimes gets drunk, is he therefore to steal? This doctrine would very soon bring a man to the gallows.'

He, I know not why, shewed upon all occasions an aversion to go to Ireland, where I proposed to him that we should make a tour. JOHNSON. 'It is the last place where I should wish to travel.' BOSWELL. 'Should you not like to see Dublin, Sir?' JOHNSON. 'No, Sir! Dublin is only a worse capital.' BOSWELL. 'Is not the Giant's-Causeway worth seeing?' JOHNSON. 'Worth seeing? yes; but not worth going to see.'

Yet he had a kindness for the Irish nation, and thus generously expressed himself to a gentleman from that country, on the subject of an UNION which artful Politicians have often had in view—'Do not make an union with us, Sir. We should unite with you, only to rob you. We should have robbed the Scotch, if they had had any thing of which we could have robbed them.'

Of an acquaintance of ours, whose manners and every thing about him, though expensive, were coarse, he said, 'Sir, you see in him vulgar prosperity.'

A foreign minister of no very high talents, who had been in his company for a considerable time quite overlooked, happened luckily to mention that he had read some of his *Rambler* in Italian, and admired it much. This pleased him greatly; he observed that the title had been translated, *Il Genio errante*, though I have been told it was rendered more ludicrously, *Il Vagabondo*; and finding that this minister gave such a proof of his taste, he was all attention to him, and on the first remark which he made, however simple, exclaimed, '*The Ambassadour says well*—His Excellency observes—' And then he expanded and enriched the little that had been said, in so strong a manner, that it appeared something of consequence. This was exceedingly entertaining to the company who were present, and many a time afterwards it furnished a pleasant topick of merriment: 'The Ambassadour says well,' became a laughable term of applause, when no mighty matter had been expressed.

I left London on Monday, October 15, and accompanied Colonel Stuart to Chester, where his regiment was to lye for some time.

1780: ÆTAT. 71.]—In 1780, the world was kept in impatience for the completion of his *Lives of the Poets*, upon which he was employed so far as his indolence allowed him to labour.

His friend Dr. Lawrence having now suffered the greatest affliction to which a man is liable, and which Johnson himself had felt in the most severe manner; Johnson wrote to him in an admirable strain of sympathy and pious consolation.

'TO DR. LAWRENCE.

'DEAR SIR,—At a time when all your friends ought to shew their kindness, and with a character which ought to make all that know you your friends, you may wonder that you have yet heard nothing from me.

'I have been hindered by a vexatious and incessant cough, for which within these ten days I have been bled once, fasted four or five times, taken physick five times, and opiates, I think, six. This day it seems to remit.

'The loss, dear Sir, which you have lately suffered, I felt many years ago, and know therefore how much has been taken from you, and how little help can be had from consolation. He that outlives a wife whom he has long loved, sees himself disjoined from the only mind that has the same hopes, and fears, and interest; from the only companion with whom he has shared much good or evil; and with whom he could set his mind at liberty, to retrace the past or anticipate the future. The continuity of being is lacerated; the settled course of sentiment and action is stopped; and life stands suspended and motionless, till it is driven by external causes into a new channel. But the time of suspense is dreadful.

'Our first recourse in this distressed solitude, is, perhaps for want of habitual piety, to a gloomy acquiescence in necessity. Of two mortal beings, one must lose the other; but surely there is a higher and better comfort to be drawn from the consideration of that Providence which watches over all, and a belief that the living and the dead are equally in the hands of God, who will reunite those whom he has separated; or who sees that it is best not to reunite. I am, dear Sir, your most affectionate, and most humble servant,

'January 20, 1780.'

'SAM. JOHNSON.'

On the 2nd of May I wrote to him, and requested that we might have another meeting somewhere in the North of England, in the autumn of this year.

From Mr. Langton I received soon after this time a letter, of which I extract a passage, relative both to Mr. Beauclerk and Dr. Johnson.

'The melancholy information you have received concerning Mr. Beauclerk's death is true. Had his talents been directed in any sufficient degree as they ought, I have always been strongly of opinion that they were calculated to make an illustrious figure; and that opinion, as it had been in part formed upon Dr. Johnson's judgment, receives more and more confirmation by hearing what, since his death, Dr. Johnson has said concerning them; a few evenings ago, he was at Mr. Vesey's, where Lord Althorpe, who was one of a numerous company there, addressed Dr. Johnson on the subject of Mr. Beauclerk's death, saying, "Our CLUB has had a great loss since we met last." He replied, "A loss, that perhaps the whole nation could not repair!" The Doctor then went on to speak of his endowments, and particularly extolled the wonderful ease with which he uttered what was highly excellent. He said, that "no man ever was so free when he was going to say a good thing, from a LOOK that expressed that it was coming; or, when he had said it, from a look that expressed that it had come." At Mr. Thrale's, some days before when we were talking on the same subject, he said, referring to the same idea of his wonderful facility, "That Beauclerk's talents were those which he had felt himself more disposed to envy, than those of any whom he had known."

'On the evening I have spoken of above, at Mr. Vesey's, you would have been much gratified, as it exhibited an instance of the high importance in which Dr. Johnson's character is held, I think even beyond any I ever before was witness to. The company consisted chiefly of ladies, among whom were the Duchess Dowager of Portland, the Duchess of Beaufort, whom I suppose from her rank I must name before her mother Mrs. Boscawen, and her elder sister Mrs. Lewson, who was likewise there; Lady Lucan, Lady Clermont, and others of note both for their station and understandings. Among the gentlemen were Lord Althorpe, whom I have before named, Lord Macartney, Sir Joshua Reynolds, Lord Lucan, Mr. Wraxal, whose book you have probably seen, *The Tour to the Northern Parts of Europe*; a very agreeable ingenious man; Dr. Warren, Mr. Pepys, the Master in Chancery, whom I believe you know, and Dr. Barnard, the Provost of Eton. As soon as Dr. Johnson was come in and had taken a chair, the company began to collect round him, till they became not less than four, if not five, deep; those behind standing, and listening over the heads of those that were sitting near him. The conversation for some time was chiefly between Dr. Johnson and the Provost of Eton, while the others contributed occasionally their remarks.'

On his birth-day, Johnson has this note: 'I am now beginning the seventy-second year of my life, with more strength of body, and greater vigour of mind, than I think is common at that age.' But still he complains of sleepless nights and idle days, and forgetfulness, or neglect of resolutions. He thus pathetically expresses himself,—'Surely I shall not spend my whole life with my own total disapprobation.'

Mr. Macbean, whom I have mentioned more than once, as one of Johnson's humble friends, a deserving but unfortunate man, being now oppressed by age and poverty, Johnson solicited the Lord Chancellor Thurlow, to have him admitted into the Charterhouse. I take the liberty to insert his Lordship's answer, as I am eager to embrace every occasion of augmenting the respectable notion which should ever be entertained of my illustrious friend:—

'TO DR. SAMUEL JOHNSON.

'London, October 24, 1780.

'SIR,

'I have this moment received your letter, dated the 19th, and returned from Bath.

'In the beginning of the summer I placed one in the Chartreux, without the sanction of a recommendation so distinct and so authoritative as yours of Macbean; and I am afraid, that according to the establishment of the House, the opportunity of making the charity so good amends will not soon recur. But whenever a vacancy shall happen, if you'll favour me with notice of it, I will try to recommend him to the place, even though it should not be my turn to nominate. I am, Sir, with great regard, your most faithful and obedient servant,

'THURLOW.'

Being disappointed in my hopes of meeting Johnson this year, so that I could hear none of his admirable sayings, I shall compensate for this want by inserting a collection of them, for which I am indebted to my worthy friend Mr. Langton, whose kind communications have been separately interwoven in many parts of this work. Very few articles of this collection were committed to writing by himself, he not having that habit; which he regrets, and which those who know the numerous opportunities he had of gathering the rich fruits of *Johnsonian* wit and wisdom, must ever regret. I however found, in conversations with him, that a good store of *Johnsoniana* was treasured in his mind; and I compared it to Herculaneum, or some old Roman field, which when dug, fully rewards the labour employed. The authenticity of every article is unquestionable. For the expression, I, who wrote them down in his presence, am partly answerable.

'There is nothing more likely to betray a man into absurdity than *condescension*; when he seems to suppose his understanding too powerful for his company.'

'Having asked Mr. Langton if his father and mother had sat for their pictures, which he thought it right for each generation of a family to do, and being told they had opposed it, he said, "Sir, among the anfractuosities of the human mind, I know not if it may not be one, that there is a superstitious reluctance to sit for a picture."'

'John Gilbert Cooper related, that soon after the publication of his *Dictionary*, Garrick being asked by Johnson what people said of it, told him, that among other animadversions, it was objected that he cited authorities which were beneath the dignity of such a work, and mentioned Richardson. "Nay, (said Johnson,) I have done worse than that: I have cited *thee*, David."'

'When in good humour he would talk of his own writings with a wonderful frankness and candour, and would even criticise them with the closest severity. One day, having read over one of his *Ramblers*, Mr. Langton asked him, how he liked that paper; he shook his head, and answered, "too wordy." At another time, when one was reading his tragedy of *Irene* to a company at a house in the country, he left the room; and somebody having asked him the reason of this, he replied, "Sir, I thought it had been better."'

'He related, that he had once in a dream a contest of wit with some other person, and that he was very much mortified by imagining that his opponent had the better of him. "Now, (said he,) one may mark here the effect of sleep in weakening the power of reflection; for had not my judgement failed me, I should have seen, that the wit of this supposed antagonist, by whose superiority I felt myself depressed, was as much furnished by me, as that which I thought I had been uttering in my own character."'

'Of Sir Joshua Reynolds, he said, "Sir, I know no man who has passed through life with more observation than Reynolds."'

'He repeated to Mr. Langton, with great energy, in the Greek, our

SAVIOUR'S gracious expression concerning the forgiveness of Mary Magdalen, 'Η πίστις σου σέσωκέ σε πορεύου εἰς εἰρήνην. "Thy faith hath saved thee; go in peace." He said, "the manner of this dismission is exceedingly affecting."'

'Talking of the Farce of *High Life below Stairs*, he said, "Here is a Farce, which is really very diverting when you see it acted; and yet one may read it, and not know that one has been reading any thing at all."'

'He used at one time to go occasionally to the green room of Drury-lane Theatre, where he was much regarded by the players, and was very easy and facetious with them. He had a very high opinion of Mrs. Clive's comick powers, and conversed more with her than with any of them. He said, "Clive, Sir, is a good thing to sit by; she always understands what you say." And she said of him, "I love to sit by Dr. Johnson; he always entertains me." One night, when *The Recruiting Officer* was acted, he said to Mr. Holland, who had been expressing an apprehension that Dr. Johnson would disdain the works of Farquhar; "No, Sir, I think Farquhar a man whose writings have considerable merit."'

'His friend Garrick was so busy in conducting the drama, that they could not have so much intercourse as Mr. Garrick used to profess an anxious wish that there should be. There might, indeed, be something in the contemptuous severity as to the merit of acting, which his old preceptor nourished in himself, that would mortify Garrick after the great applause which he received from the audience. For though Johnson said of him, "Sir, a man who has a nation to admire him every night, may well be expected to be somewhat elated;" yet he would treat theatrical matters with a ludicrous slight. He mentioned one evening, "I met David coming off the stage, drest in a woman's riding-hood, when he acted in *The Wonder*; I came full upon him, and I believe he was not pleased."'

'Once he asked Tom Davies, whom he saw drest in a fine suit of clothes, "And what art thou to-night?" Tom answered, "The Thane of Ross;" (which it will be recollected is a very inconsiderable character.) "O brave!" said Johnson.

'Of Mr. Longley, at Rochester, a gentleman of very considerable learning, whom Dr. Johnson met there, he said, "My heart warms towards him. I was surprised to find in him such a nice acquaintance with the metre in the learned languages; though I was somewhat mortified that I had it not so much to myself, as I should have thought."'

'Talking of the minuteness with which people will record the sayings of eminent persons, a story was told, that when Pope was on a visit to Spence at Oxford, as they looked from the window they saw a Gentleman Commoner, who was just come in from riding, amusing himself with whipping at a post. Pope took occasion to say, "That young gentleman seems to have little to do." Mr. Beauclerk observed, "Then, to be sure, Spence turned round and wrote that down;" and went on to say to Dr. Johnson, "Pope, Sir, would have said the same of you, if he had seen you distilling." JOHNSON. "Sir, if Pope had told me of my distilling, I would have told him of his grotto."'

'He would allow no settled indulgence of idleness upon principle, and always repelled every attempt to urge excuses for it. A friend one day suggested, that it was not wholesome to study soon after dinner. JOHNSON. "Ah, Sir, don't give way to such a fancy. At one time of my life I had taken it into my head that it was not wholesome to study between breakfast and dinner."'

'Dr. Goldsmith, upon occasion of Mrs. Lennox's bringing out a play, said to Dr. Johnson at THE CLUB, that a person had advised him to go and hiss it, because she had attacked Shakspeare in her book called *Shakspeare Illustrated*. JOHNSON. "And did not you tell him he was a rascal?" GOLDSMITH. "No, Sir, I did not. Perhaps he might not mean what he said." JOHNSON. "Nay, Sir, if he lied, it is a different thing." Colman slily said, (but it is believed Dr. Johnson did not hear him,) "Then the proper expression should have been,—Sir, if you don't lie, you're a rascal."'

'His affection for Topham Beauclerk was so great, that when Beauclerk was labouring under that severe illness which at last occasioned his death, Johnson said, (with a voice faultering with emotion,) "Sir, I would walk to the extent of the diameter of the earth to save Beauclerk."'

'Johnson was well acquainted with Mr. Dossie, authour of a treatise on Agriculture; and said of him, "Sir, of the objects which the Society of Arts have chiefly in view, the chymical effects of bodies operating upon other bodies, he knows more than almost any man." Johnson, in order to give Mr. Dossie his vote to be a member of this Society, paid up an arrear which had run on for two years. On this occasion he mentioned a circumstance as characteristick of the Scotch. "One of that nation, (said he,) who had been a candidate, against whom I had voted, came up to me with a civil salutation. Now, Sir, this is their way. An Englishman would have stomached it, and been sulky, and never have taken further notice of you; but a Scotchman, Sir, though you vote nineteen times against him, will accost you with equal complaisance after each time, and the twentieth time, Sir, he will get your vote."'

'Talking on the subject of toleration, one day when some friends were with him in his study, he made his usual remark, that the State has a right to regulate the religion of the people, who are the children of the State. A clergyman having readily acquiesced in this, Johnson, who loved discussion, observed, "But, Sir, you must go round to other States than your own. You do not know what a Bramin has to say for himself. In short, Sir, I have got no further than this: Every man has a right to utter what he thinks truth, and every other man has a right to knock him down for it. Martyrdom is the test."'

'Goldsmith one day brought to THE CLUB a printed Ode, which he, with others, had been hearing read by its authour in a publick room at the rate of five shillings each for admission. One of the company having read it aloud, Dr. Johnson said, "Bolder words and more timorous meaning, I think never were brought together."

'Talking of Gray's *Odes*, he said, "They are forced plants raised in a hot-bed; and they are poor plants; they are but cucumbers after all." A gentleman present, who had been running down Ode-writing in general, as a bad species of poetry, unluckily said, "Had they been literally cucumbers, they had been better things than Odes."—"Yes, Sir, (said Johnson,) for a *hog*."'

'It is very remarkable, that he retained in his memory very slight and trivial, as well as important things. As an instance of this, it seems that an inferiour domestick of the Duke of Leeds had attempted to celebrate his Grace's marriage in such homely rhimes as he could make; and this curious composition having been sung to Dr. Johnson he got it by heart, and used to repeat it in a very pleasant manner. Two of the stanzas were these:—

"When the Duke of Leeds shall married be
To a fine young lady of high quality,
How happy will that gentlewoman be
In his Grace of Leeds's good company.

She shall have all that's fine and fair,
And the best of silk and satin shall wear;
And ride in a coach to take the air,
And have a house in St. James's-square."

To hear a man, of the weight and dignity of Johnson, repeating such humble attempts at poetry, had a very amusing effect. He, however, seriously observed of the last stanza repeated by him, that it nearly comprized all the advantages that wealth can give.'

'An eminent foreigner, when he was shewn the British Museum, was very troublesome with many absurd inquiries. "Now there, Sir, (said he,) is the difference between an Englishman and a Frenchman. A Frenchman must be always talking, whether he knows any thing of the matter or not; an Englishman is content to say nothing, when he has nothing to say."

'His unjust contempt for foreigners was, indeed, extreme. One evening, at old Slaughter's coffee-house, when a number of them were talking loud about little matters, he said, "Does not this confirm old

Meynell's observation—*For any thing I see, foreigners are fools.*"'

'He said, that once, when he had a violent tooth-ache, a Frenchman accosted him thus:—"*Ah, Monsieur vous etudiez trop.*"'

'Colman, in a note on his translation of *Terence*, talking of Shakspeare's learning, asks, "What says Farmer to this? What says Johnson?" Upon this he observed, "Sir, let Farmer answer for himself: *I* never engaged in this controversy. I always said, Shakspeare had Latin enough to grammaticise his English."'

'A clergyman, whom he characterised as one who loved to say little oddities, was affecting one day, at a Bishop's table, a sort of slyness and freedom not in character, and repeated, as if part of *The Old Man's Wish*, a song by Dr. Walter Pope, a verse bordering on licentiousness. Johnson rebuked him in the finest manner, by first shewing him that he did not know the passage he was aiming at, and thus humbling him:

"Sir, that is not the song: it is thus." And he gave it right. Then looking stedfastly on him, "Sir, there is a part of that song which I should wish to exemplify in my own life:—

"May I govern my passions with absolute sway!"'

'He used frequently to observe, that men might be very eminent in a profession, without our perceiving any particular power of mind in them in conversation. "It seems strange (said he,) that a man should see so far to the right, who sees so short a way to the left. Burke is the only man whose common conversation corresponds with the general fame which he has in the world. Take up whatever topick you please, he is ready to meet you."'

'Mr. Langton, when a very young man, read Dodsley's *Cleone, a Tragedy*, to him, not aware of his extreme impatience to be read to. As it went on he turned his face to the back of his chair, and put himself into various attitudes, which marked his uneasiness. At the end of an act, however, he said, "Come let's have some more, let's go into the slaughter-house again, Lanky. But I am afraid there is more blood than brains."

'Snatches of reading (said he,) will not make a Bentley or a Clarke. They are, however, in a certain degree advantageous. I would put a child into a library (where no unfit books are) and let him read at his choice. A child should not be discouraged from reading any thing that he takes a liking to, from a notion that it is above his reach. If that be the ease, the child will soon find it out and desist; if not, he of course gains the instruction; which is so much the more likely to come, from the inclination with which he takes up the study.'

'A gentleman who introduced his brother to Dr. Johnson was earnest to recommend him to the Doctor's notice, which he did by saying, "When we have sat together some time, you'll find my brother grow very entertaining."—"Sir, (said Johnson,) I can wait."'

'In the latter part of his life, in order to satisfy himself whether his mental faculties were impaired, he resolved that he would try to learn a new language, and fixed upon the Low Dutch, for that purpose, and this he continued till he had read about one half of *Thomas à Kempis*; and finding that there appeared no abatement of his power of acquisition, he then desisted, as thinking the experiment had been duly tried.'

'Mr. Langton and he having gone to see a Freemason's funeral procession, when they were at Rochester, and some solemn musick being played on French horns, he said, "This is the first time that I have ever been affected by musical sounds;" adding, "that the impression made upon him was of a melancholy kind." Mr. Langton saying, that this effect was a fine one,—JOHNSON. "Yes, if it softens the mind, so as to prepare it for the reception of salutary feelings, it may be good: but inasmuch as it is melancholy *per se*, it is bad."'

'Goldsmith had long a visionary project, that some time or other when his circumstances should be easier, he would go to Aleppo, in order to acquire a knowledge as far as might be of any arts peculiar to the East, and introduce them into Britain. When this was talked of in Dr. Johnson's company, he said, "Of all men Goldsmith is the most unfit to go out upon such an inquiry; for he is utterly ignorant of such arts as we already possess, and consequently could not know what would be accessions to our present stock of mechanical knowledge. Sir, he would bring home a grinding barrow, which you see in every street in London, and think that he had furnished a wonderful improvement."'

'Greek, Sir, (said he,) is like lace; every man gets as much of it as he can.'

'Johnson one day gave high praise to Dr. Bentley's verses in Dodsley's *Collection*, which he recited with his usual energy. Dr. Adam Smith, who was present, observed in his decisive professorial manner, "Very well—Very well." Johnson however added, "Yes, they *are* very well, Sir; but you may observe in what manner they are well. They are the forcible verses of a man of a strong mind, but not accustomed to write verse; for there is some uncouthness in the expression."'

'Drinking tea one day at Garrick's with Mr. Langton, he was questioned if he was not somewhat of a heretick as to Shakspeare; said Garrick, "I doubt he is a little of an infidel."—"Sir, (said Johnson,) I will stand by the lines I have written on Shakspeare in my Prologue at the opening of your Theatre." Mr. Langton suggested, that in the line

"And panting Time toil'd after him in vain,"

Johnson might have had in his eye the passage in *The Tempest*, where Prospero says of Miranda,

> "———She will outstrip all praise,
> And make it halt behind her."

Johnson said nothing. Garrick then ventured to observe, "I do not think that the happiest line in the praise of Shakspeare." Johnson exclaimed (smiling,) "Prosaical rogues! next time I write, I'll make both time and space pant."'

'It is well known that there was formerly a rude custom for those who were sailing upon the Thames, to accost each other as they passed, in the most abusive language they could invent, generally, however, with as much satirical humour as they were capable of producing. Addison gives a specimen of this ribaldry, in Number 383 of *The Spectator*, when Sir Roger de Coverly and he are going to Spring-garden. Johnson was once eminently successful in this species of contest; a fellow having attacked him with some coarse raillery, Johnson answered him thus, "Sir, your wife, *under pretence of keeping a bawdy-house*, is a receiver of stolen goods." One evening when he and Mr. Burke and Mr. Langton were in company together, and the admirable scolding of Timon of Athens was mentioned, this instance of Johnson's was quoted, and thought to have at least equal excellence.'

'As Johnson always allowed the extraordinary talents of Mr. Burke, so Mr. Burke was fully sensible of the wonderful powers of Johnson. Mr. Langton recollects having passed an evening with both of them, when Mr. Burke repeatedly entered upon topicks which it was evident he would have illustrated with extensive knowledge and richness of expression; but Johnson always seized upon the conversation, in which, however, he acquitted himself in a most masterly manner. As Mr. Burke and Mr. Langton were walking home, Mr. Burke observed that Johnson had been very great that night; Mr. Langton joined in this, but added, he could have wished to hear more from another person; (plainly intimating that he meant Mr. Burke.) "O, no (said Mr. Burke,) it is enough for me to have rung the bell to him."'

'Beauclerk having observed to him of one of their friends, that he was aukward at counting money, "Why, Sir, (said Johnson,) I am likewise aukward at counting money. But then, Sir, the reason is plain; I have had very little money to count."'

'Goldsmith, upon being visited by Johnson one day in the Temple, said to him with a little jealousy of the appearance of his accommodation, "I shall soon be in better chambers than these." Johnson at the same time checked him and paid him a handsome compliment, implying that a man of his talents should be above attention to such distinctions,—"Nay, Sir, never mind that. *Nil te quaesiveris extra.'''*

'When Mr. Vesey was proposed as a member of THE LITERARY CLUB, Mr. Burke began by saying that he was a man of gentle manners. "Sir, (said Johnson,) you need say no more. When you have said a man of gentle manners; you have said enough."'

'The late Mr. Fitzherbert told Mr. Langton that Johnson said to him, "Sir, a man has no more right to *say* an uncivil thing, than to *act* one; no more right to say a rude thing to another than to knock him down"'

'Richardson had little conversation, except about his own works, of which Sir Joshua Reynolds said he was always willing to talk, and glad to have them introduced. Johnson when he carried Mr. Langton to see him, professed that he could bring him out into conversation, and used this allusive expression, "Sir, I can make him *rear*." But he failed; for in that interview Richardson said little else than that there lay in the room a translation of his *Clarissa* into German.'

'Once when somebody produced a newspaper in which there was a letter of stupid abuse of Sir Joshua Reynolds, of which Johnson himself came in for a share,—"Pray," said he, "let us have it read aloud from beginning to end;" which being done, he with a ludicrous earnestness, and not directing his look to any particular person, called out, "Are we alive after all this satire!"'

'Of Dr. Goldsmith he said, "No man was more foolish when he had not a pen in his hand, or more wise when he had."'

'An observation of Bathurst's may be mentioned, which Johnson repeated, appearing to acknowledge it to be well founded, namely, it was somewhat remarkable how seldom, on occasion of coming into the company of any new person, one felt any wish or inclination to see him again.'

1781: ÆTAT. 72.]—In 1781 Johnson at last completed his *Lives of the Poets*, of which he gives this account: 'Some time in March I finished the *Lives of the Poets*, which I wrote in my usual way, dilatorily and hastily, unwilling to work, and working with vigour and haste.' In a memorandum previous to this, he says of them: 'Written, I hope, in such a manner as may tend to the promotion of piety.'

The booksellers, justly sensible of the great additional value of the copy-right, presented him with another hundred pounds, over and above two hundred, for which his agreement was to furnish such prefaces as he thought fit.

As he was so good as to make me a present of the greatest part of the original and indeed only manuscript of this admirable work, I have an opportunity of observing with wonder, the correctness with which he rapidly struck off such glowing composition.

The Life of COWLEY he himself considered as the best of the whole, on account of the dissertation which it contains on the

Metaphysical Poets.

While the world in general was filled with admiration of Johnson's Lives of the Poets, there were narrow circles in which prejudice and resentment were fostered, and from which attacks of different sorts issued against him. By some violent Whigs he was arraigned of injustice to Milton; by some Cambridge men of depreciating Gray; and his expressing with a dignified freedom what he really thought of George, Lord Lyttelton, gave offence to some of the friends of that nobleman, and particularly produced a declaration of war against him from Mrs. Montagu, the ingenious Essayist on Shakspeare, between whom and his Lordship a commerce of reciprocal compliments had long been carried on. In this war the smaller powers in alliance with him were of course led to engage, at least on the defensive, and thus I for one was excluded from the enjoyment of 'A Feast of Reason,' such as Mr. Cumberland has described, with a keen, yet just and delicate pen, in his *Observer*. These minute inconveniences gave not the least disturbance to Johnson. He nobly said, when I talked to him of the feeble, though shrill outcry which had been raised, 'Sir, I considered myself as entrusted with a certain portion of truth. I have given my opinion sincerely; let them shew where they think me wrong.'

I wrote to him in February, complaining of having been troubled by a recurrence of the perplexing question of Liberty and Necessity;— and mentioning that I hoped soon to meet him again in London.

'TO JAMES BOSWELL, ESQ.

'DEAR SIR,—I hoped you had got rid of all this hypocrisy of misery. What have you to do with Liberty and Necessity? Or what more than to hold your tongue about it? Do not doubt but I shall be most heartily glad to see you here again, for I love every part about you but your affectation of distress.

'I have at last finished my *Lives*, and have laid up for you a load of copy, all out of order, so that it will amuse you a long time to set it right. Come to me, my dear Bozzy, and let us be as happy as we can. We will go again to the Mitre, and talk old times over. I am, dear Sir, yours affectionately,

'March 14, 1781.'

'SAM. JOHNSON.'

On Monday, March 19, I arrived in London, and on Tuesday, the 20th, met him in Fleet-street, walking, or rather indeed moving along; for his peculiar march is thus described in a very just and picturesque manner, in a short Life of him published very soon after his death:— 'When he walked the streets, what with the constant roll of his head, and the concomitant motion of his body, he appeared to make his way by that motion, independent of his feet.' That he was often much stared at while he advanced in this manner, may easily be believed; but it was not safe to make sport of one so robust as he was. Mr. Langton saw him one day, in a fit of absence, by a sudden start, drive the load off a porter's back, and walk forward briskly, without being conscious of what he had done. The porter was very angry, but stood still, and eyed the huge figure with much earnestness, till he was satisfied that his wisest course was to be quiet, and take up his burthen again.

Our accidental meeting in the street after a long separation was a pleasing surprize to us both. He stepped aside with me into Falcon-court, and made kind inquiries about my family, and as we were in a hurry going different ways, I promised to call on him next day; he said he was engaged to go out in the morning. 'Early, Sir?' said I. JOHNSON. 'Why, Sir, a London morning does not go with the sun.'

I waited on him next evening, and he gave me a great portion of his original manuscript of his *Lives of the Poets*, which he had preserved for me.

I found on visiting his friend, Mr. Thrale, that he was now very ill, and had removed, I suppose by the solicitation of Mrs. Thrale, to a house in Grosvenor-square. I was sorry to see him sadly changed in his appearance.

He told me I might now have the pleasure to see Dr. Johnson drink wine again, for he had lately returned to it. When I mentioned this to Johnson, he said, 'I drink it now sometimes, but not socially.' The first evening that I was with him at Thrale's, I observed he poured a large quantity of it into a glass, and swallowed it greedily. Every thing about his character and manners was forcible and violent; there never was any moderation; many a day did he fast, many a year did he refrain from wine; but when he did eat, it was voraciously; when he did drink wine, it was copiously. He could practise abstinence, but not temperance.

Mrs. Thrale and I had a dispute, whether Shakspeare or Milton had drawn the most admirable picture of a man[52] I was for Shakspeare; Mrs. Thrale for Milton; and after a fair hearing, Johnson decided for my opinion.

I told him of one of Mr. Burke's playful sallies upon Dean Marlay: 'I don't like the Deanery of Ferns, it sounds so like a *barren* title.'— 'Dr. *Heath* should have it;' said I. Johnson laughed, and condescending to trifle in the same mode of conceit, suggested Dr. *Moss*.

He said, 'Mrs. Montagu has dropt me. Now, Sir, there are people whom one should like very well to drop, but would not wish to be dropped by.' He certainly was vain of the society of ladies, and could make himself very agreeable to them, when he chose it; Sir Joshua

---

[52] The passages considered, according to Boswell's note, were the portrait of Hamlet's father (Ham. 3. 4. 55-62), and the portrait of Adam (P. L. 4. 300-303).—Ed.

Reynolds agreed with me that he could. Mr. Gibbon, with his usual sneer, controverted it, perhaps in resentment of Johnson's having talked with some disgust of his ugliness, which one would think a *philosopher* would not mind. Dean Marlay wittily observed, 'A lady may be vain, when she can turn a wolf-dog into a lap-dog.'

His notion of the duty of a member of Parliament, sitting upon an election-committee, was very high; and when he was told of a gentleman upon one of those committees, who read the newspapers part of the time, and slept the rest, while the merits of a vote were examined by the counsel; and as an excuse, when challenged by the chairman for such behaviour, bluntly answered, 'I had made up my mind upon that case.'—Johnson, with an indignant contempt, said, 'If he was such a rogue as to make up his mind upon a case without hearing it, he should not have been such a fool as to tell it.' 'I think (said Mr. Dudley Long, now North,) the Doctor has pretty plainly made him out to be both rogue and fool.'

Johnson's profound reverence for the Hierarchy made him expect from bishops the highest degree of decorum; he was offended even at their going to taverns; 'A bishop (said he,) has nothing to do at a tippling-house. It is not indeed immoral in him to go to a tavern; neither would it be immoral in him to whip a top in Grosvenor-square. But, if he did, I hope the boys would fall upon him, and apply the whip to *him*. There are gradations in conduct; there is morality,—decency,—propriety. None of these should be violated by a bishop. A bishop should not go to a house where he may meet a young fellow leading out a wench.' BOSWELL. 'But, Sir, every tavern does not admit women.' JOHNSON. 'Depend upon it, Sir, any tavern will admit a well-drest man and a well-drest woman; they will not perhaps admit a woman whom they see every night walking by their door, in the street. But a well-drest man may lead in a well-drest woman to any tavern in London. Taverns sell meat and drink, and will sell them to any body who can eat and can drink. You may as well say that a mercer will not sell silks to a woman of the town.'

He also disapproved of bishops going to routs, at least of their staying at them longer than their presence commanded respect. He mentioned a particular bishop. 'Poh! (said Mrs. Thrale,) the Bishop of———is never minded at a rout.' BOSWELL. 'When a bishop places himself in a situation where he has no distinct character, and is of no consequence, he degrades the dignity of his order.' JOHNSON. 'Mr. Boswell, Madam has said it as correctly as it could be.'

Johnson and his friend, Beauclerk, were once together in company with several clergymen, who thought that they should appear to advantage, by assuming the lax jollity of *men of the world*; which, as it may be observed in similar cases, they carried to noisy excess. Johnson, who they expected would be *entertained*, sat grave and silent for some time; at last, turning to Beauclerk, he said, by no means in a whisper, 'This merriment of parsons is mighty offensive.'

On Friday, March 30, I dined with him at Sir Joshua Reynolds's, with the Earl of Charlemont, Sir Annesley Stewart, Mr. Eliot of Port-Eliot, Mr. Burke, Dean Marlay, Mr. Langton; a most agreeable day, of which I regret that every circumstance is not preserved; but it is unreasonable to require such a multiplication of felicity.

Mr. Eliot mentioned a curious liquor peculiar to his country, which the Cornish fishermen drink. They call it *Mahogany*; and it is made of two parts gin, and one part treacle, well beaten together. I begged to have some of it made, which was done with proper skill by Mr. Eliot. I thought it very good liquor; and said it was a counterpart of what is called *Athol Porridge* in the Highlands of Scotland, which is a mixture of whisky and honey. Johnson said, 'that must be a better liquor than the Cornish, for both its component parts are better.' He also observed, '*Mahogany* must be a modern name; for it is not long since the wood called mahogany was known in this country.' I mentioned his scale of liquors;—claret for boys,—port for men,—brandy for heroes. 'Then (said Mr. Burke,) let me have claret: I love to be a boy; to have the careless gaiety of boyish days.' JOHNSON. 'I should drink claret too, if it would give me that; but it does not: it neither makes boys men, nor men boys. You'll be drowned by it, before it has any effect upon you.'

I ventured to mention a ludicrous paragraph in the newspapers, that Dr. Johnson was learning to dance of Vestris. Lord Charlemont, wishing to excite him to talk, proposed in a whisper, that he should be asked, whether it was true. 'Shall I ask him?' said his Lordship. We were, by a great majority, clear for the experiment. Upon which his Lordship very gravely, and with a courteous air said, 'Pray, Sir, is it true that you are taking lessons of Vestris?' This was risking a good deal, and required the boldness of a General of Irish Volunteers to make the attempt. Johnson was at first startled, and in some heat answered, 'How can your Lordship ask so simple a question?' But immediately recovering himself, whether from unwillingness to be deceived, or to appear deceived, or whether from real good humour, he kept up the joke: 'Nay, but if any body were to answer the paragraph, and contradict it, I'd have a reply, and would say, that he who contradicted it was no friend either to Vestris or me. For why should not Dr. Johnson add to his other powers a little corporeal agility? Socrates learnt to dance at an advanced age, and Cato learnt Greek at an advanced age. Then it might proceed to say, that this Johnson, not content with dancing on the ground, might dance on the rope; and they might introduce the elephant dancing on the rope.'

On Sunday, April 1, I dined with him at Mr. Thrale's, with Sir Philip Jennings Clerk and Mr. Perkins, who had the superintendence of Mr. Thrale's brewery, with a salary of five hundred pounds a year. Sir

Philip had the appearance of a gentleman of ancient family, well advanced in life. He wore his own white hair in a bag of goodly size, a black velvet coat, with an embroidered waistcoat, and very rich laced ruffles; which Mrs. Thrale said were old fashioned, but which, for that reason, I thought the more respectable, more like a Tory; yet Sir Philip was then in Opposition in Parliament. 'Ah, Sir, (said Johnson,) ancient ruffles and modern principles do not agree.' Sir Philip defended the Opposition to the American war ably and with temper, and I joined him. He said, the majority of the nation was against the ministry. JOHNSON. '*I*, Sir, am against the ministry; but it is for having too little of that, of which Opposition thinks they have too much. Were I minister, if any man wagged his finger against me, he should be turned out; for that which it is in the power of Government to give at pleasure to one or to another, should be given to the supporters of Government. If you will not oppose at the expence of losing your place, your opposition will not be honest, you will feel no serious grievance; and the present opposition is only a contest to get what others have. Sir Robert Walpole acted as I would do. As to the American war, the *sense* of the nation is *with* the ministry. The majority of those who can *understand* is with it; the majority of those who can only *hear*, is against it; and as those who can only hear are more numerous than those who can understand, and Opposition is always loudest, a majority of the rabble will be for Opposition.'

This boisterous vivacity entertained us; but the truth in my opinion was, that those who could understand the best were against the American war, as almost every man now is, when the question has been coolly considered.

Mrs. Thrale gave high praise to Mr. Dudley Long, (now North). JOHNSON. 'Nay, my dear lady, don't talk so. Mr. Long's character is very *short*. It is nothing. He fills a chair. He is a man of genteel appearance, and that is all. I know nobody who blasts by praise as you do: for whenever there is exaggerated praise, every body is set against a character. They are provoked to attack it. Now there is Pepys; you praised that man with such disproportion, that I was incited to lessen him, perhaps more than he deserves. His blood is upon your head. By the same principle, your malice defeats itself; for your censure is too violent. And yet, (looking to her with a leering smile,) she is the first woman in the world, could she but restrain that wicked tongue of hers;—she would be the only woman, could she but command that little whirligig.'

Upon the subject of exaggerated praise I took the liberty to say, that I thought there might be very high praise given to a known character which deserved it, and therefore it would not be exaggerated. Thus, one might say of Mr. Edmund Burke, He is a very wonderful man. JOHNSON. 'No, Sir, you would not be safe if another man had a mind perversely to contradict. He might answer, "Where is all the wonder? Burke is, to be sure, a man of uncommon abilities, with a great quantity of matter in his mind, and a great fluency of language in his mouth. But we are not to be stunned and astonished by him." So you see, Sir, even Burke would suffer, not from any fault of his own, but from your folly.'

Mrs. Thrale mentioned a gentleman who had acquired a fortune of four thousand a year in trade, but was absolutely miserable, because he could not talk in company; so miserable, that he was impelled to lament his situation in the street to ******, whom he hates, and who he knows despises him. 'I am a most unhappy man, (said he). I am invited to conversations. I go to conversations; but, alas! I have no conversation.' JOHNSON. 'Man commonly cannot be successful in different ways. This gentleman has spent, in getting four thousand pounds a year, the time in which he might have learnt to talk; and now he cannot talk.' Mr. Perkins made a shrewd and droll remark: 'If he had got his four thousand a year as a mountebank, he might have learnt to talk at the same time that he was getting his fortune.'

Some other gentlemen came in. The conversation concerning the person whose character Dr. Johnson had treated so slightingly, as he did not know his merit, was resumed. Mrs. Thrale said, 'You think so of him, Sir, because he is quiet, and does not exert himself with force. You'll be saying the same thing of Mr. ***** there, who sits as quiet— .' This was not well-bred; and Johnson did not let it pass without correction. 'Nay, Madam, what right have you to talk thus? Both Mr. ***** and I have reason to take it ill. *You* may talk so of Mr. *****; but why do you make *me* do it? Have I said anything against Mr. *****? You have set him, that I might shoot him: but I have not shot him.'

One of the gentlemen said, he had seen three folio volumes of Dr. Johnson's sayings collected by me. 'I must put you right, Sir, (said I,) for I am very exact in authenticity. You could not see folio volumes, for I have none: you might have seen some in quarto and octavo. This is inattention which one should guard against.' JOHNSON. 'Sir, it is a want of concern about veracity. He does not know that he saw *any* volumes. If he had seen them he could have remembered their size.'

Mr. Thrale appeared very lethargick to-day. I saw him again on Monday evening, at which time he was not thought to be in immediate danger; but early in the morning of Wednesday, the 4th, he expired. Johnson was in the house, and thus mentions the event: 'I felt almost the last flutter of his pulse, and looked for the last time upon the face that for fifteen years had never been turned upon me but with respect and benignity.' Upon that day there was a *Call* of THE LITERARY CLUB; but Johnson apologised for his absence by the following note:—

'MR. JOHNSON knows that Sir Joshua Reynolds and the other

gentlemen will excuse his incompliance with the call, when they are told that Mr. Thrale died this morning.—Wednesday.'

Mr. Thrale's death was a very essential loss to Johnson, who, although he did not foresee all that afterwards happened, was sufficiently convinced that the comforts which Mr. Thrale's family afforded him, would now in a great measure cease. He, however, continued to shew a kind attention to his widow and children as long as it was acceptable; and he took upon him, with a very earnest concern, the office of one of his executors, the importance of which seemed greater than usual to him, from his circumstances having been always such, that he had scarcely any share in the real business of life. His friends of THE CLUB were in hopes that Mr. Thrale might have made a liberal provision for him for his life, which, as Mr. Thrale left no son, and a very large fortune, it would have been highly to his honour to have done; and, considering Dr. Johnson's age, could not have been of long duration; but he bequeathed him only two hundred pounds, which was the legacy given to each of his executors. I could not but be somewhat diverted by hearing Johnson talk in a pompous manner of his new office, and particularly of the concerns of the brewery, which it was at last resolved should be sold. Lord Lucan tells a very good story, which, if not precisely exact, is certainly characteristical: that when the sale of Thrale's brewery was going forward, Johnson appeared bustling about, with an ink-horn and pen in his button-hole, like an excise-man; and on being asked what he really considered to be the value of the property which was to be disposed of, answered, 'We are not here to sell a parcel of boilers and vats, but the potentiality of growing rich, beyond the dreams of avarice.'

On Friday, April 6, he carried me to dine at a club, which, at his desire, had been lately formed at the Queen's Arms, in St. Paul's Church-yard. He told Mr. Hoole, that he wished to have a *City Club*, and asked him to collect one; but, said he, 'Don't let them be *patriots*.' The company were to-day very sensible, well-behaved men.

On Friday, April 13, being Good-Friday, I went to St. Clement's church with him as usual. There I saw again his old fellow-collegian, Edwards, to whom I said, 'I think, Sir, Dr. Johnson and you meet only at Church.'—'Sir, (said he,) it is the best place we can meet in, except Heaven, and I hope we shall meet there too.' Dr. Johnson told me, that there was very little communication between Edwards and him, after their unexpected renewal of acquaintance. 'But, (said he, smiling), he met me once, and said, "I am told you have written a very pretty book called *The Rambler*." I was unwilling that he should leave the world in total darkness, and sent him a set.'

Mr. Berrenger visited him to-day, and was very pleasing. We talked of an evening society for conversation at a house in town, of which we were all members, but of which Johnson said, 'It will never do, Sir. There is nothing served about there, neither tea, nor coffee, nor lemonade, nor any thing whatever; and depend upon it, Sir, a man does not love to go to a place from whence he comes out exactly as he went in.' I endeavoured, for argument's sake, to maintain that men of learning and talents might have very good intellectual society, without the aid of any little gratifications of the senses. Berrenger joined with Johnson, and said, that without these any meeting would be dull and insipid. He would therefore have all the slight refreshments; nay, it would not be amiss to have some cold meat, and a bottle of wine upon a side-board. 'Sir, (said Johnson to me, with an air of triumph,) Mr. Berrenger knows the world. Every body loves to have good things furnished to them without any trouble. I told Mrs. Thrale once, that as she did not choose to have card tables, she should have a profusion of the best sweetmeats, and she would be sure to have company enough come to her.'

On Sunday, April 15, being Easter-day, after solemn worship in St. Paul's church, I found him alone; Dr. Scott of the Commons came in.

We talked of the difference between the mode of education at Oxford, and that in those Colleges where instruction is chiefly conveyed by lectures. JOHNSON. 'Lectures were once useful; but now, when all can read, and books are so numerous, lectures are unnecessary. If your attention fails, and you miss a part of a lecture, it is lost; you cannot go back as you do upon a book.' Dr. Scott agreed with him. 'But yet (said I), Dr. Scott, you yourself gave lectures at Oxford.' He smiled. 'You laughed (then said I,) at those who came to you.'

Dr. Scott left us, and soon afterwards we went to dinner. Our company consisted of Mrs. Williams, Mrs. Desmoulins, Mr. Levett, Mr. Allen, the printer, and Mrs. Hall, sister of the Reverend Mr. John Wesley, and resembling him, as I thought, both in figure and manner. Johnson produced now, for the first time, some handsome silver salvers, which he told me he had bought fourteen years ago; so it was a great day. I was not a little amused by observing Allen perpetually struggling to talk in the manner of Johnson, like the little frog in the fable blowing himself up to resemble the stately ox.

He mentioned a thing as not unfrequent, of which I had never heard before,—being *called*, that is, hearing one's name pronounced by the voice of a known person at a great distance, far beyond the possibility of being reached by any sound uttered by human organs. 'An acquaintance, on whose veracity I can depend, told me, that walking home one evening to Kilmarnock, he heard himself called from a wood, by the voice of a brother who had gone to America; and the next packet brought accounts of that brother's death.' Macbean asserted that this inexplicable *calling* was a thing very well known. Dr. Johnson said, that one day at Oxford, as he was turning the key of his chamber, he heard his mother distinctly call *Sam*. She was then at Lichfleld; but nothing ensued. This phaenomenon is, I think, as wonderful as any other mysterious fact, which many people are very slow to believe, or rather, indeed, reject with an obstinate contempt.

Some time after this, upon his making a remark which escaped my attention, Mrs. Williams and Mrs. Hall were both together striving to answer him. He grew angry, and called out loudly, 'Nay, when you both speak at once, it is intolerable.' But checking himself, and softening, he said, 'This one may say, though you *are* ladies.' Then he brightened into gay humour, and addressed them in the words of one of the songs in *The Beggar's Opera*:—

'But two at a time there's no mortal can bear.'

'What, Sir, (said I,) are you going to turn Captain Macheath?' There was something as pleasantly ludicrous in this scene as can be imagined. The contrast between Macheath, Polly, and Lucy—and Dr. Samuel Johnson, blind, peevish Mrs. Williams, and lean, lank, preaching Mrs. Hall, was exquisite.

On Friday, April 20, I spent with him one of the happiest days that I remember to have enjoyed in the whole course of my life. Mrs. Garrick, whose grief for the loss of her husband was, I believe, as sincere as wounded affection and admiration could produce, had this day, for the first time since his death, a select party of his friends to dine with her. The company was Miss Hannah More, who lived with her, and whom she called her Chaplain; Mrs. Boscawen, Mrs. Elizabeth Carter, Sir Joshua Reynolds, Dr. Burney, Dr. Johnson, and myself. We found ourselves very elegantly entertained at her house in the Adelphi, where I have passed many a pleasing hour with him 'who gladdened life.' She looked well, talked of her husband with complacency, and while she cast her eyes on his portrait, which hung over the chimney-piece, said, that 'death was now the most agreeable object to her.' The very semblance of David Garrick was cheering.

We were all in fine spirits; and I whispered to Mrs. Boscawen, 'I believe this is as much as can be made of life.' In addition to a splendid entertainment, we were regaled with Lichfield ale, which had a peculiar appropriated value. Sir Joshua, and Dr. Burney, and I, drank cordially of it to Dr. Johnson's health; and though he would not join us, he as cordially answered, 'Gentlemen, I wish you all as well as you do me.'

The general effect of this day dwells upon my mind in fond remembrance; but I do not find much conversation recorded. What I have preserved shall be faithfully given.

One of the company mentioned Mr. Thomas Hollis, the strenuous Whig, who used to send over Europe presents of democratical books, with their boards stamped with daggers and caps of liberty. Mrs. Carter said, 'He was a bad man. He used to talk uncharitably.' JOHNSON. 'Poh! poh! Madam; who is the worse for being talked of uncharitably? Besides, he was a dull poor creature as ever lived: and I believe he would not have done harm to a man whom he knew to be of very opposite principles to his own. I remember once at the Society of Arts, when an advertisement was to be drawn up, he pointed me out as the man who could do it best. This, you will observe, was kindness to me. I however slipt away, and escaped it.'

Mrs. Carter having said of the same person, 'I doubt he was an Atheist.' JOHNSON. 'I don't know that. He might perhaps have become one, if he had had time to ripen, (smiling.) He might have *exuberated* into an Atheist.'

Sir Joshua Reynolds praised *Mudge's Sermons*. JOHNSON. 'Mudge's Sermons are good, but not practical. He grasps more sense than he can hold; he takes more corn than he can make into meal; he opens a wide prospect, but it is so distant, it is indistinct. I love *Blair's Sermons*. Though the dog is a Scotchman, and a Presbyterian, and every thing he should not be, I was the first to praise them. Such was my candour,' (smiling.) MRS. BOSCAWEN. 'Such his great merit to get the better of all your prejudices.' JOHNSON. 'Why, Madam, let us compound the matter; let us ascribe it to my candour, and his merit.'

In the evening we had a large company in the drawing-room, several ladies, the Bishop of Killaloe, Dr. Percy, Mr. Chamberlayne, of the Treasury, &c. &c.

Talking of a very respectable authour, he told us a curious circumstance in his life, which was, that he had married a printer's devil. REYNOLDS. 'A printer's devil, Sir! Why, I thought a printer's devil was a creature with a black face and in rags.' JOHNSON. 'Yes, Sir. But I suppose, he had her face washed, and put clean clothes on her. (Then looking very serious, and very earnest.) And she did not disgrace him; the woman had a bottom of good sense.' The word *bottom* thus introduced, was so ludicrous when contrasted with his gravity, that most of us could not forbear tittering and laughing; though I recollect that the Bishop of Killaloe kept his countenance with perfect steadiness, while Miss Hannah More slyly hid her face behind a lady's back who sat on the same settee with her. His pride could not bear that any expression of his should excite ridicule, when he did not intend it; he therefore resolved to assume and exercise despotick power, glanced sternly around, and called out in a strong tone, 'Where's the merriment?' Then collecting himself, and looking aweful, to make us feel how he could impose restraint, and as it were searching his mind for a still more ludicrous word, he slowly pronounced, 'I say the *woman* was *fundamentally* sensible;' as if he had said, hear this now, and laugh if you dare. We all sat composed as at a funeral.

He and I walked away together; we stopped a little while by the rails of the Adelphi, looking on the Thames, and I said to him with some emotion that I was now thinking of two friends we had lost, who once lived in the buildings behind us, Beauclerk and Garrick. 'Ay, Sir, (said he, tenderly,) and two such friends as cannot be supplied.'

For some time after this day I did not see him very often, and of the conversation which I did enjoy, I am sorry to find I have preserved but little. I was at this time engaged in a variety of other matters, which required exertion and assiduity, and necessarily occupied almost all my time.

On Tuesday, May 8, I had the pleasure of again dining with him and Mr. Wilkes, at Mr. Dilly's. No *negociation* was now required to bring them together; for Johnson was so well satisfied with the former interview, that he was very glad to meet Wilkes again, who was this day seated between Dr. Beattie and Dr. Johnson; (between *Truth* and *Reason*, as General Paoli said, when I told him of it.) WILKES. 'I have been thinking, Dr. Johnson, that there should be a bill brought into parliament that the controverted elections for Scotland should be tried in that country, at their own Abbey of Holy-Rood House, and not here; for the consequence of trying them here is, that we have an inundation of Scotchmen, who come up and never go back again. Now here is Boswell, who is come up upon the election for his own county, which will not last a fortnight.' JOHNSON. 'Nay, Sir, I see no reason why they should be tried at all; for, you know, one Scotchman is as good as another.' WILKES. 'Pray, Boswell, how much may be got in a year by an Advocate at the Scotch bar?' BOSWELL. 'I believe two thousand pounds.' WILKES. 'How can it be possible to spend that money in Scotland?' JOHNSON. 'Why, Sir, the money may be spent in England: but there is a harder question. If one man in Scotland gets possession of two thousand pounds, what remains for all the rest of the nation?' WILKES. 'You know, in the last war, the immense booty which Thurot carried off by the complete plunder of seven Scotch isles; he re-embarked with *three and six-pence.*' Here again Johnson and Wilkes joined in extravagant sportive raillery upon the supposed poverty of Scotland, which Dr. Beattie and I did not think it worth our while to dispute.

The subject of quotation being introduced, Mr. Wilkes censured it as pedantry. JOHNSON. 'No, Sir, it is a good thing; there is a community of mind in it. Classical quotation is the parole of literary men all over the world.'

He gave us an entertaining account of *Bet Flint*, a woman of the town, who, with some eccentrick talents and much effrontery, forced herself upon his acquaintance. 'Bet (said he,) wrote her own Life in verse, which she brought to me, wishing that I would furnish her with a Preface to it, (laughing.) I used to say of her that she was generally slut and drunkard; occasionally, whore and thief. She had, however, genteel lodgings, a spinnet on which she played, and a boy that walked before her chair. Poor Bet was taken up on a charge of stealing a counterpane, and tried at the Old Bailey. Chief Justice————, who loved a wench, summed up favourably, and she was acquitted. After which Bet said, with a gay and satisfied air, "Now that the counterpane is *my own*, I shall make a petticoat of it.'"

Talking of oratory, Mr. Wilkes described it as accompanied with all the charms of poetical expression. JOHNSON. 'No, Sir; oratory is the power of beating down your adversary's arguments, and putting better in their place.' WILKES. 'But this does not move the passions.' JOHNSON. 'He must be a weak man, who is to be so moved.' WILKES. (naming a celebrated orator,) 'Amidst all the brilliancy of————'s imagination, and the exuberance of his wit, there is a strange want of *taste*. It was observed of Apelles's Venus, that her flesh seemed as if she had been nourished by roses: his oratory would sometimes make one suspect that he eats potatoes and drinks whisky.'

Mr. Wilkes said to me, loud enough for Dr. Johnson to hear, 'Dr. Johnson should make me a present of his *Lives of the Poets*, as I am a poor patriot, who cannot afford to buy them.' Johnson seemed to take no notice of this hint; but in a little while, he called to Mr. Dilly, 'Pray, Sir, be so good as to send a set of my *Lives* to Mr. Wilkes, with my compliments.' This was accordingly done; and Mr. Wilkes paid Dr. Johnson a visit, was courteously received, and sat with him a long time.

The company gradually dropped away. Mr. Dilly himself was called down stairs upon business; I left the room for some time; when I returned, I was struck with observing Dr. Samuel Johnson and John Wilkes, Esq., literally *tête-à-tête*; for they were reclined upon their chairs, with their heads leaning almost close to each other, and talking earnestly, in a kind of confidential whisper, of the personal quarrel between George the Second and the King of Prussia. Such a scene of perfectly easy sociality between two such opponents in the war of political controversy, as that which I now beheld, would have been an excellent subject for a picture. It presented to my mind the happy days which are foretold in Scripture, when the lion shall lie down with the kid.

After this day there was another pretty long interval, during which Dr. Johnson and I did not meet. When I mentioned it to him with regret, he was pleased to say, 'Then, Sir, let us live double.'

About this time it was much the fashion for several ladies to have evening assemblies, where the fair sex might participate in conversation with literary and ingenious men, animated by a desire to please. These societies were denominated *Blue-stocking Clubs*, the origin of which title being little known, it may be worth while to relate it. One of the most eminent members of those societies, when they first commenced, was Mr. Stillingfleet, whose dress was remarkably grave, and in particular it was observed, that he wore *blue stockings*. Such was the excellence of his conversation, that his absence was felt as so great a loss, that it used to be said, 'We can do nothing without the blue stockings;' and thus by degrees the title was established. Miss Hannah More has admirably described a *Blue-stocking Club*, in her Bas Bleu, a poem in which many of the persons who were most conspicuous there are mentioned.

Johnson was prevailed with to come sometimes into these circles, and did not think himself too grave even for the lively Miss Monckton (now Countess of Corke), who used to have the finest *bit of blue* at the house of her mother, Lady Galway. Her vivacity enchanted the Sage, and they used to talk together with all imaginable ease. A singular instance happened one evening, when she insisted that some of Sterne's writings were very pathetick. Johnson bluntly denied it. 'I am sure (said she,) they have affected ME.' 'Why, (said Johnson, smiling, and rolling himself about,) that is, because, dearest, you're a dunce.' When she some time afterwards mentioned this to him, he said with equal truth and politeness; 'Madam, if I had thought so, I certainly should not have said it.'

Another evening Johnson's kind indulgence towards me had a pretty difficult trial. I had dined at the Duke of Montrose's with a very agreeable party, and his Grace, according to his usual custom, had circulated the bottle very freely. Lord Graham and I went together to Miss Monckton's, where I certainly was in extraordinary spirits, and above all fear or awe. In the midst of a great number of persons of the first rank, amongst whom I recollect with confusion, a noble lady of the most stately decorum, I placed myself next to Johnson, and thinking myself now fully his match, talked to him in a loud and boisterous manner, desirous to let the company know how I could contend with *Ajax*. I particularly remember pressing him upon the value of the pleasures of the imagination, and as an illustration of my argument, asking him, 'What, Sir, supposing I were to fancy that the—— (naming the most charming Duchess in his Majesty's dominions) were in love with me, should I not be very happy?' My friend with much address evaded my interrogatories, and kept me as quiet as possible; but it may easily be conceived how he must have felt. However, when a few days afterwards I waited upon him and made an apology, he behaved with the most friendly gentleness.

While I remained in London this year, Johnson and I dined together at several places. I recollect a placid day at Dr. Butter's, who had now removed from Derby to Lower Grosvenor-street, London; but of his conversation on that and other occasions during this period, I neglected to keep any regular record, and shall therefore insert here some miscellaneous articles which I find in my Johnsonian notes.

His disorderly habits, when 'making provision for the day that was passing over him,' appear from the following anecdote, communicated to me by Mr. John Nichols:—'In the year 1763, a young bookseller, who was an apprentice to Mr. Whiston, waited on him with a subscription to his *Shakspeare*: and observing that the Doctor made no entry in any book of the subscriber's name, ventured diffidently to ask, whether he would please to have the gentleman's address, that it might be properly inserted in the printed list of subscribers. "*I shall print no list of subscribers*;" said Johnson, with great abruptness: but almost immediately recollecting himself, added, very complacently, "Sir, I have two very cogent reasons for not printing any list of subscribers;— one, that I have lost all the names,—the other, that I have spent all the money."

Johnson could not brook appearing to be worsted in argument, even when he had taken the wrong side, to shew the force and dexterity of his talents. When, therefore, he perceived that his opponent gained ground, he had recourse to some sudden mode of robust sophistry. Once when I was pressing upon him with visible advantage, he stopped me thus:—'My dear Boswell, let's have no more of this; you'll make nothing of it. I'd rather have you whistle a Scotch tune.'

Care, however, must be taken to distinguish between Johnson when he 'talked for victory,' and Johnson when he had no desire but to inform and illustrate. 'One of Johnson s principal talents (says an eminent friend of his) was shewn in maintaining the wrong side of an argument, and in a splendid perversion of the truth. If you could contrive to have his fair opinion on a subject, and without any bias from personal prejudice, or from a wish to be victorious in argument, it was wisdom itself, not only convincing, but overpowering.'

He had, however, all his life habituated himself to consider conversation as a trial of intellectual vigour and skill; and to this, I think, we may venture to ascribe that unexampled richness and brilliancy which appeared in his own. As a proof at once of his eagerness for colloquial distinction, and his high notion of this eminent friend, he once addressed him thus:— '——, we now have been several hours together; and you have said but one thing for which I envied you.'

Goldsmith could sometimes take adventurous liberties with him, and escape unpunished. Beauclerk told me that when Goldsmith talked of a project for having a third Theatre in London, solely for the exhibition of new plays, in order to deliver authours from the supposed tyranny of managers, Johnson treated it slightingly; upon which Goldsmith said, 'Ay, ay, this may be nothing to you, who can now shelter yourself behind the corner of a pension;' and that Johnson bore this with good-humour.

Johnson had called twice on the Bishop of Killaloe before his Lordship set out for Ireland, having missed him the first time. He said,

'It would have hung heavy on my heart if I had not seen him. No man ever paid more attention to another than he has done to me; and I have neglected him, not wilfully, but from being otherwise occupied. Always, Sir, set a high value on spontaneous kindness. He whose inclination prompts him to cultivate your friendship of his own accord, will love you more than one whom you have been at pains to attach to you.'

I asked him if he was not dissatisfied with having so small a share of wealth, and none of those distinctions in the state which are the objects of ambition. He had only a pension of three hundred a year. Why was he not in such circumstances as to keep his coach? Why had he not some considerable office? JOHNSON. 'Sir, I have never complained of the world; nor do I think that I have reason to complain. It is rather to be wondered at that I have so much. My pension is more out of the usual course of things than any instance that I have known. Here, Sir, was a man avowedly no friend to Government at the time, who got a pension without asking for it. I never courted the great; they sent for me; but I think they now give me up. They are satisfied; they have seen enough of me.'

Strange, however, it is, to consider how few of the great sought his society; so that if one were disposed to take occasion for satire on that account, very conspicuous objects present themselves. His noble friend, Lord Elibank, well observed, that if a great man procured an interview with Johnson, and did not wish to see him more, it shewed a mere idle curiosity, and a wretched want of relish for extraordinary powers of mind. Mrs. Thrale justly and wittily accounted for such conduct by saying, that Johnson's conversation was by much too strong for a person accustomed to obsequiousness and flattery; it was *mustard in a young child's mouth*!

On Saturday, June 2, I set out for Scotland, and had promised to pay a visit in my way, as I sometimes did, at Southill, in Bedfordshire, at the hospitable mansion of 'Squire Dilly, the elder brother of my worthy friends, the booksellers, in the Poultry. Dr. Johnson agreed to be of the party this year, with Mr. Charles Dilly and me, and to go and see Lord Bute's seat at Luton Hoe. He talked little to us in the carriage, being chiefly occupied in reading Dr. Watson's second volume of *Chemical Essays*, which he liked very well, and his own *Prince of Abyssinia*, on which he seemed to be intensely fixed; having told us, that he had not looked at it since it was first published. I happened to take it out of my pocket this day, and he seized upon it with avidity.

We stopped at Welwyn, where I wished much to see, in company with Dr. Johnson, the residence of the authour of *Night Thoughts*, which was then possessed by his son, Mr. Young. Here some address was requisite, for I was not acquainted with Mr. Young, and had I proposed to Dr. Johnson that we should send to him, he would have checked my wish, and perhaps been offended. I therefore concerted with Mr. Dilly, that I should steal away from Dr. Johnson and him, and try what reception I could procure from Mr. Young; if unfavourable, nothing was to be said; but if agreeable, I should return and notify it to them. I hastened to Mr. Young's, found he was at home, sent in word that a gentleman desired to wait upon him, and was shewn into a parlour, where he and a young lady, his daughter, were sitting. He appeared to be a plain, civil, country gentleman; and when I begged pardon for presuming to trouble him, but that I wished much to see his place, if he would give me leave; he behaved very courteously, and answered, 'By all means, Sir; we are just going to drink tea; will you sit down?' I thanked him, but said, that Dr. Johnson had come with me from London, and I must return to the inn and drink tea with him; that my name was Boswell, I had travelled with him in the Hebrides. 'Sir, (said he,) I should think it a great honour to see Dr. Johnson here. Will you allow me to send for him?' Availing myself of this opening, I said that 'I would go myself and bring him, when he had drunk tea; he knew nothing of my calling here.' Having been thus successful, I hastened back to the inn, and informed Dr. Johnson that 'Mr. Young, son of Dr. Young, the authour of *Night Thoughts*, whom I had just left, desired to have the honour of seeing him at the house where his father lived.' Dr. Johnson luckily made no inquiry how this invitation had arisen, but agreed to go, and when we entered Mr. Young's parlour, he addressed him with a very polite bow, 'Sir, I had a curiosity to come and see this place. I had the honour to know that great man, your father.' We went into the garden, where we found a gravel walk, on each side of which was a row of trees, planted by Dr. Young, which formed a handsome Gothick arch; Dr. Johnson called it a fine grove. I beheld it with reverence.

We sat some time in the summer-house, on the outside wall of which was inscribed, '*Ambulantes in horto audiebant vocem Dei*;' and in reference to a brook by which it is situated, '*Vivendi rectè qui prorogat horam*,' &c. I said to Mr. Young, that I had been told his father was cheerful. 'Sir, (said he,) he was too well-bred a man not to be cheerful in company; but he was gloomy when alone. He never was cheerful after my mother's death, and he had met with many disappointments.' Dr. Johnson observed to me afterwards, 'That this was no favourable account of Dr. Young; for it is not becoming in a man to have so little acquiescence in the ways of Providence, as to be gloomy because he has not obtained as much preferment as he expected; nor to continue gloomy for the loss of his wife. Grief has its time.' The last part of this censure was theoretically made. Practically, we know that grief for the loss of a wife may be continued very long, in proportion as affection has been sincere. No man knew this better than Dr. Johnson.

Upon the road we talked of the uncertainty of profit with which authours and booksellers engage in the publication of literary works. JOHNSON. 'My judgement I have found is no certain rule as to the sale of a book.' BOSWELL. 'Pray, Sir, have you been much plagued with authours sending you their works to revise?' JOHNSON. 'No, Sir; I have been thought a sour, surly fellow.' BOSWELL. 'Very lucky for you, Sir,—in that respect.' I must however observe, that notwithstanding what he now said, which he no doubt imagined at the time to be the fact, there was, perhaps, no man who more frequently yielded to the solicitations even of very obscure authours, to read their manuscripts, or more liberally assisted them with advice and correction.

He found himself very happy at 'Squire Dilly's, where there is always abundance of excellent fare, and hearty welcome.

On Sunday, June 3, we all went to Southill church, which is very near to Mr. Dilly's house. It being the first Sunday of the month, the holy sacrament was administered, and I staid to partake of it. When I came afterwards into Dr. Johnson's room, he said, 'You did right to stay and receive the communion; I had not thought of it.' This seemed to imply that he did not choose to approach the altar without a previous preparation, as to which good men entertain different opinions, some holding that it is irreverent to partake of that ordinance without considerable premeditation.

Although upon most occasions I never heard a more strenuous advocate for the advantages of wealth, than Dr. Johnson: he this day, I know not from what caprice, took the other side. 'I have not observed (said he,) that men of very large fortunes enjoy any thing extraordinary that makes happiness. What has the Duke of Bedford? What has the Duke of Devonshire? The only great instance that I have ever known of the enjoyment of wealth was, that of Jamaica Dawkins, who, going to visit Palmyra, and hearing that the way was infested by robbers, hired a troop of Turkish horse to guard him.'

Dr. Gibbons, the Dissenting minister, being mentioned, he said, 'I took to Dr. Gibbons.' And addressing himself to Mr. Charles Dilly, added, 'I shall be glad to see him. Tell him, if he'll call on me, and dawdle over a dish of tea in an afternoon, I shall take it kind.'

The Reverend Mr. Smith, Vicar of Southill, a very respectable man, with a very agreeable family, sent an invitation to us to drink tea. I remarked Dr. Johnson's very respectful politeness. Though always fond of changing the scene, he said, 'We must have Mr. Dilly's leave. We cannot go from your house, Sir, without your permission.' We all went, and were well satisfied with our visit.

When I observed that a housebreaker was in general very timorous; JOHNSON. 'No wonder, Sir; he is afraid of being shot getting *into* a house, or hanged when he has got *out* of it.'

He told us, that he had in one day written six sheets of a translation from the French, adding, 'I should be glad to see it now. I wish that I had copies of all the pamphlets written against me, as it is said Pope had. Had I known that I should make so much noise in the world, I should have been at pains to collect them. I believe there is hardly a day in which there is not something about me in the newspapers.'

On Monday, June 4, we all went to Luton-Hoe, to see Lord Bute's magnificent seat, for which I had obtained a ticket. As we entered the park, I talked in a high style of my old friendship with Lord Mountstuart, and said, 'I shall probably be much at this place.' The Sage, aware of human vicissitudes, gently checked me: 'Don't you be too sure of that.' He made two or three peculiar observations; as when shewn the botanical garden, 'Is not *every* garden a botanical garden?' When told that there was a shrubbery to the extent of several miles: 'That is making a very foolish use of the ground; a little of it is very well.' When it was proposed that we should walk on the pleasure-ground; 'Don't let us fatigue ourselves. Why should we walk there? Here's a fine tree, let's get to the top of it.' But upon the whole, he was very much pleased. He said, 'This is one of the places I do not regret having come to see. It is a very stately place, indeed; in the house magnificence is not sacrificed to convenience, nor convenience to magnificence. The library is very splendid: the dignity of the rooms is very great; and the quantity of pictures is beyond expectation, beyond hope.'

It happened without any previous concert, that we visited the seat of Lord Bute upon the King's birthday; we dined and drank his Majesty's health at an inn, in the village of Luton.

In the evening I put him in mind of his promise to favour me with a copy of his celebrated Letter to the Earl of Chesterfield, and he was at last pleased to comply with this earnest request, by dictating it to me from his memory; for he believed that he himself had no copy. There was an animated glow in his countenance while he thus recalled his high-minded indignation.

On Tuesday, June 5, Johnson was to return to London. He was very pleasant at breakfast; I mentioned a friend of mine having resolved never to marry a pretty woman. JOHNSON. 'Sir it is a very foolish resolution to resolve not to marry a pretty woman. Beauty is of itself very estimable. No, Sir, I would prefer a pretty woman, unless there are objections to her. A pretty woman may be foolish; a pretty woman may be wicked; a pretty woman may not like me. But there is no such danger in marrying a pretty woman as is apprehended: she will not be persecuted if she does not invite persecution. A pretty woman, if she has a mind to be wicked, can find a readier way than another; and that is all.'

At Shefford I had another affectionate parting from my revered friend, who was taken up by the Bedford coach and carried to the metropolis. I went with Messieurs Dilly, to see some friends at Bedford; dined with the officers of the militia of the county, and next day proceeded on my journey.

Johnson's charity to the poor was uniform and extensive, both from inclination and principle. He not only bestowed liberally out of his own purse, but what is more difficult as well as rare, would beg from others, when he had proper objects in view. This he did judiciously as well as humanely. Mr. Philip Metcalfe tells me, that when he has asked him for some money for persons in distress, and Mr. Metcalfe has offered what Johnson thought too much, he insisted on taking less, saying, 'No, no, Sir; we must not *pamper* them.'

I am indebted to Mr. Malone, one of Sir Joshua Reynolds's executors, for the following note, which was found among his papers after his death, and which, we may presume, his unaffected modesty prevented him from communicating to me with the other letters from Dr. Johnson with which he was pleased to furnish me. However slight in itself, as it does honour to that illustrious painter, and most amiable man, I am happy to introduce it.

'TO SIR JOSHUA REYNOLDS.

'DEAR SIR,—It was not before yesterday that I received your splendid benefaction. To a hand so liberal in distributing, I hope nobody will envy the power of acquiring. I am, dear Sir, your obliged and most humble servant,
   'June 23, 1781.'

                             'SAM. JOHNSON.'

The following curious anecdote I insert in Dr. Burney's own words:—

'Dr. Burney related to Dr. Johnson the partiality which his writings had excited in a friend of Dr. Burney's, the late Mr. Bewley, well known in Norfolk by the name of the *Philosopher of Massingham*: who, from the *Ramblers* and Plan of his *Dictionary*, and long before the authour's fame was established by the *Dictionary* itself, or any other work, had conceived such a reverence for him, that he urgently begged Dr. Burney to give him the cover of the first letter he had received from him, as a relick of so estimable a writer. This was in 1755. In 1760, when Dr. Burney visited Dr. Johnson at the Temple in London, where he had then chambers, he happened to arrive there before he was up; and being shewn into the room where he was to breakfast, finding himself alone, he examined the contents of the apartment, to try whether he could undiscovered steal anything to send to his friend Bewley, as another relick of the admirable Dr. Johnson. But finding nothing better to his purpose, he cut some bristles off his hearth-broom, and enclosed them in a letter to his country enthusiast, who received them with due reverence. The Doctor was so sensible of the honour done him by a man of genius and science, to whom he was an utter stranger, that he said to Dr. Burney, "Sir, there is no man possessed of the smallest portion of modesty, but must be flattered with the admiration of such a man. I'll give him a set of my *Lives*, if he will do me the honour to accept of them." In this he kept his word; and Dr. Burney had not only the pleasure of gratifying his friend with a present more worthy of his acceptance than the segment from the hearth-broom, but soon after of introducing him to Dr. Johnson himself in Bolt-court, with whom he had the satisfaction of conversing a considerable time, not a fortnight before his death; which happened in St. Martin's-street, during his visit to Dr. Burney, in the house where the great Sir Isaac Newton had lived and died before.'

In one of his little memorandum-books is the following minute:—
'August 9, 3 P.M., ÆTAT. 72, in the summer-house at Streatham.

'After innumerable resolutions formed and neglected, I have retired hither, to plan a life of greater diligence, in hope that I may yet be useful, and be daily better prepared to appear before my Creator and my Judge, from whose infinite mercy I humbly call for assistance and support.

'My purpose is,

'To pass eight hours every day in some serious employment.

'Having prayed, I purpose to employ the next six weeks upon the Italian language, for my settled study.'

In autumn he went to Oxford, Birmingham, Lichfield, and Ashbourne, for which very good reasons might be given in the conjectural yet positive manner of writers, who are proud to account for every event which they relate. He himself, however, says, 'The motives of my journey I hardly know; I omitted it last year, and am not willing to miss it again.'

But some good considerations arise, amongst which is the kindly recollection of Mr. Hector, surgeon at Birmingham: 'Hector is likewise an old friend, the only companion of my childhood that passed through the school with me. We have always loved one another; perhaps we may be made better by some serious conversation, of which however I have no distinct hope.' He says too, 'At Lichfield, my native place, I hope to shew a good example by frequent attendance on publick worship.'

1782: ÆTAT. 73.]—In 1782, his complaints increased, and the history of his life this year, is little more than a mournful recital of the variations of his illness, in the midst of which, however, it will appear from his letters, that the powers of his mind were in no degree impaired.

At a time when he was less able than he had once been to sustain a shock, he was suddenly deprived of Mr. Levett, which event he thus communicated to Dr. Lawrence:—

'SIR,—Our old friend, Mr. Levett, who was last night eminently cheerful, died this morning. The man who lay in the same room, hearing an uncommon noise, got up and tried to make him speak, but without effect, he then called Mr. Holder, the apothecary, who, though when he came he thought him dead, opened a vein, but could draw no blood. So has ended the long life of a very useful and very blameless man. I am, Sir, your most humble servant,
        'Jan. 17, 1782.'

'SAM. JOHNSON.'

In one of his memorandum-books in my possession, is the following entry:—'January 20, Sunday. Robert Levett was buried in the church-yard of Bridewell, between one and two in the afternoon. He died on Thursday 17, about seven in the morning, by an instantaneous death. He was an old and faithful friend; I have known him from about 46. *Commendavi.* May GOD have mercy on him. May he have mercy on me.'

On the 30th of August, I informed him that my honoured father had died that morning; a complaint under which he had long laboured having suddenly come to a crisis, while I was upon a visit at the seat of Sir Charles Preston, from whence I had hastened the day before, upon receiving a letter by express.

In answer to my next letter, I received one from him, dissuading me from hastening to him as I had proposed; what is proper for publication is the following paragraph, equally just and tender:—'One expence, however, I would not have you to spare: let nothing be omitted that can preserve Mrs. Boswell, though it should be necessary to transplant her for a time into a softer climate. She is the prop and stay of your life. How much must your children suffer by losing her.'

My wife was now so much convinced of his sincere friendship for me, and regard for her, that, without any suggestion on my part, she wrote him a very polite and grateful letter:—

'DR. JOHNSON TO MRS. BOSWELL.

'DEAR LADY,—I have not often received so much pleasure as from your invitation to Auchinleck. The journey thither and back is, indeed, too great for the latter part of the year; but if my health were fully recovered, I would suffer no little heat and cold, nor a wet or a rough road to keep me from you. I am, indeed, not without hope of seeing Auchinleek again; but to make it a pleasant place I must see its lady well, and brisk, and airy. For my sake, therefore, among many greater reasons, take care, dear Madam, of your health, spare no expence, and want no attendance that can procure ease, or preserve it. Be very careful to keep your mind quiet; and do not think it too much to give an account of your recovery to, Madam, yours, &c.

'London, Sept. 7, 1782.'

'SAM. JOHNSON.'

The death of Mr. Thrale had made a very material alteration with respect to Johnson's reception in that family. The manly authority of the husband no longer curbed the lively exuberance of the lady; and as her vanity had been fully gratified, by having the Colossus of Literature attached to her for many years, she gradually became less assiduous to please him. Whether her attachment to him was already divided by another object, I am unable to ascertain; but it is plain that Johnson's penetration was alive to her neglect or forced attention; for on the 6th of October this year, we find him making a 'parting use of the library' at Streatham, and pronouncing a prayer, which he composed on leaving Mr. Thrale's family:—

'Almighty God, Father of all mercy, help me by thy grace, that I may, with humble and sincere thankfulness, remember the comforts and conveniences which I have enjoyed at this place; and that I may resign them with holy submission, equally trusting in thy protection when thou givest, and when thou takest away. Have mercy upon me, O Lord, have mercy upon me.

'To thy fatherly protection, O Lord, I commend this family. Bless, guide, and defend them, that they may so pass through this world, as finally to enjoy in thy presence everlasting happiness, for Jesus Christ's sake. Amen.'

One cannot read this prayer, without some emotions not very favourable to the lady whose conduct occasioned it.

In one of his memorandum-books I find, 'Sunday, went to church at Streatham. *Templo valedixi cam osculo.*'

He met Mr. Philip Metcalfe often at Sir Joshua Reynolds's, and other places, and was a good deal with him at Brighthelmston this autumn, being pleased at once with his excellent table and animated conversation. Mr. Metcalfe shewed him great respect, and sent him a note that he might have the use of his carriage whenever he pleased. Johnson (3rd October, 1782) returned this polite answer:—'Mr. Johnson is very much obliged by the kind offer of the carriage, but he has no desire of using Mr. Metcalfe's carriage, except when he can have the pleasure of Mr. Metcalfe's company.' Mr. Metcalfe could not but be highly pleased that his company was thus valued by Johnson, and he frequently attended him in airings. They also went together to Chichester, and they visited Petworth, and Cowdry, the venerable seat of the Lords Montacute. 'Sir, (said Johnson,) I should like to stay here four-and-twenty hours. We see here how our ancestors lived.'

'TO SIR JOSHUA REYNOLDS.

'DEAR SIR,—I heard yesterday of your late disorder, and should think ill of myself if I had heard of it without alarm. I heard likewise of your recovery, which I sincerely wish to be complete and permanent. Your country has been in danger of losing one of its brightest ornaments, and I of losing one of my oldest and kindest friends: but I hope you will still live long, for the honour of the nation: and that more enjoyment of your elegance, your intelligence, and your benevolence, is still reserved for, dear Sir, your most affectionate, &c.
'Brighthelmston, Nov. 14, 1782.'

                                                    'SAM. JOHNSON.'

1783: ÆTAT. 74.]—In 1783, he was more severely afflicted than ever, as will appear in the course of his correspondence; but still the same ardour for literature, the same constant piety, the same kindness for his friends, and the same vivacity both in conversation and writing, distinguished him.

On Friday, March 21, having arrived in London the night before, I was glad to find him at Mrs. Thrale's house, in Argyll-street, appearances of friendship between them being still kept up. I was shewn into his room, and after the first salutation he said, 'I am glad you are come. I am very ill.' He looked pale, and was distressed with a difficulty of breathing; but after the common inquiries he assumed his usual strong animated style of conversation. Seeing me now for the first time as a *Laird*, or proprietor of land, he began thus: 'Sir, the superiority of a country-gentleman over the people upon his estate is very agreeable; and he who says he does not feel it to be agreeable, lies; for it must be agreeable to have a casual superiority over those who are by nature equal with us.' BOSWELL. 'Yet, Sir, we see great proprietors of land who prefer living in London.' JOHNSON. 'Why, Sir, the pleasure of living in London, the intellectual superiority that is enjoyed there, may counterbalance the other. Besides, Sir, a man may prefer the state of the country-gentleman upon the whole, and yet there may never be a moment when he is willing to make the change to quit London for it.'

He talked with regret and indignation of the factious opposition to Government at this time, and imputed it in a great measure to the Revolution. 'Sir, (said he, in a low voice, having come nearer to me, while his old prejudices seemed to be fermenting in his mind,) this Hanoverian family is *isolée* here. They have no friends. Now the Stuarts had friends who stuck by them so late as 1745. When the right of the King is not reverenced, there will not be reverence for those appointed by the King.'

He repeated to me his verses on Mr. Levett, with an emotion which gave them full effect; and then he was pleased to say, 'You must be as much with me as you can. You have done me good. You cannot think how much better I am since you came in.

He sent a message to acquaint Mrs. Thrale that I was arrived. I had not seen her since her husband's death. She soon appeared, and favoured me with an invitation to stay to dinner, which I accepted. There was no other company but herself and three of her daughters, Dr. Johnson, and I. She too said, she was very glad I was come, for she was going to Bath, and should have been sorry to leave Dr. Johnson before I came. This seemed to be attentive and kind; and I who had not been informed of any change, imagined all to be as well as formerly. He was little inclined to talk at dinner, and went to sleep after it; but when he joined us in the drawing-room, he seemed revived, and was again himself.

Talking of conversation, he said, 'There must, in the first place, be knowledge, there must be materials; in the second place, there must be a command of words; in the third place, there must be imagination, to place things in such views as they are not commonly seen in; and in the fourth place, there must be presence of mind, and a resolution that is not to be overcome by failures: this last is an essential requisite; for want of it many people do not excel in conversation. Now I want it: I throw up the game upon losing a trick.' I wondered to hear him talk thus of himself, and said, 'I don't know, Sir, how this may be; but I am sure you beat other people's cards out of their hands.' I doubt whether he heard this remark. While he went on talking triumphantly, I was fixed in admiration, and said to Mrs. Thrale, 'O, for short-hand to take this down!' 'You'll carry it all in your head, (said she;) a long head is as good as short-hand.'

It has been observed and wondered at, that Mr. Charles Fox never talked with any freedom in the presence of Dr. Johnson, though it is well known, and I myself can witness, that his conversation is various, fluent, and exceedingly agreeable. Johnson's own experience, however, of that gentleman's reserve was a sufficient reason for his going on thus: 'Fox never talks in private company; not from any determination not to talk, but because he has not the first motion. A man who is used to the applause of the House of Commons, has no wish for that of a private company. A man accustomed to throw for a thousand pounds, if set down to throw for sixpence, would not be at the pains to count his dice. Burke's talk is the ebullition of his mind; he does not talk from a desire of distinction, but because his mind is full.'

After musing for some time, he said, 'I wonder how I should have any enemies; for I do harm to nobody.' BOSWELL. 'In the first place, Sir, you will be pleased to recollect, that you set out with attacking the

Scotch; so you got a whole nation for your enemies.' JOHNSON. 'Why, I own, that by my definition of *oats* I meant to vex them.' BOSWELL. 'Pray, Sir, can you trace the cause of your antipathy to the Scotch?' JOHNSON. 'I cannot, Sir.' BOSWELL. 'Old Mr. Sheridan says, it was because they sold Charles the First.' JOHNSON. 'Then, Sir, old Mr. Sheridan has found out a very good reason.'

I had paid a visit to General Oglethorpe in the morning,[53] and was told by him that Dr. Johnson saw company on Saturday evenings, and he would meet me at Johnson's that night. When I mentioned this to Johnson, not doubting that it would please him, as he had a great value for Oglethorpe, the fretfulness of his disease unexpectedly shewed itself; his anger suddenly kindled, and he said, with vehemence, 'Did not you tell him not to come? Am I to be *hunted* in this manner?' I satisfied him that I could not divine that the visit would not be convenient, and that I certainly could not take it upon me of my own accord to forbid the General.

I found Dr. Johnson in the evening in Mrs. Williams's room, at tea and coffee with her and Mrs. Desmoulins, who were also both ill; it was a sad scene, and he was not in very good humour. He said of a performance that had lately come out, 'Sir, if you should search all the madhouses in England, you would not find ten men who would write so, and think it sense.'

I was glad when General Oglethorpe's arrival was announced, and we left the ladies. Dr. Johnson attended him in the parlour, and was as courteous as ever.

On Sunday, March 23, I breakfasted with Dr. Johnson, who seemed much relieved, having taken opium the night before. He however protested against it, as a remedy that should be given with the utmost reluctance, and only in extreme necessity. I mentioned how commonly it was used in Turkey, and that therefore it could not be so pernicious as he apprehended. He grew warm and said, 'Turks take opium, and Christians take opium; but Russel, in his *Account of Aleppo*, tells us, that it is as disgraceful in Turkey to take too much opium, as it is with us to get drunk. Sir, it is amazing how things are exaggerated. A gentleman was lately telling in a company where I was present, that in France as soon as a man of fashion marries, he takes an opera girl into keeping; and this he mentioned as a general custom. "Pray, Sir, (said I,) how many opera girls may there be?" He answered, "About fourscore." "Well then, Sir, (said I,) you see there can be no more than fourscore men of fashion who can do this."'

Mrs. Desmoulins made tea; and she and I talked before him upon a topick which he had once borne patiently from me when we were by ourselves,—his not complaining of the world, because he was not

---

[53] March 22.—Ed.

called to some great office, nor had attained to great wealth. He flew into a violent passion, I confess with some justice, and commanded us to have done. 'Nobody, (said he,) has a right to talk in this manner, to bring before a man his own character, and the events of his life, when he does not choose it should be done. I never have sought the world; the world was not to seek me. It is rather wonderful that so much has been done for me. All the complaints which are made of the world are unjust. I never knew a man of merit neglected: it was generally by his own fault that he failed of success. A man may hide his head in a hole: he may go into the country, and publish a book now and then, which nobody reads, and then complain he is neglected. There is no reason why any person should exert himself for a man who has written a good book: he has not written it for any individual. I may as well make a present to the postman who brings me a letter. When patronage was limited, an authour expected to find a Maecenas, and complained if he did not find one. Why should he complain? This Maecenas has others as good as he, or others who have got the start of him.'

On the subject of the right employment of wealth, Johnson observed, 'A man cannot make a bad use of his money, so far as regards Society, if he does not hoard it; for if he either spends it or lends it out, Society has the benefit. It is in general better to spend money than to give it away; for industry is more promoted by spending money than by giving it away. A man who spends his money is sure he is doing good with it: he is not so sure when he gives it away. A man who spends ten thousand a year will do more good than a man who spends two thousand and gives away eight.'

In the evening I came to him again. He was somewhat fretful from his illness. A gentleman asked him, whether he had been abroad to-day. 'Don't talk so childishly, (said he.) You may as well ask if I hanged myself to-day.' I mentioned politicks. Johnson. 'Sir, I'd as soon have a man to break my bones as talk to me of publick affairs, internal or external. I have lived to see things all as bad as they can be.'

He said, 'Goldsmith's blundering speech to Lord Shelburne, which has been so often mentioned, and which he really did make to him, was only a blunder in emphasis: "I wonder they should call your Lordship *Malagrida*, for Malagrida was a very good man;" meant, I wonder they should use *Malagrida* as a term of reproach.'

Soon after this time I had an opportunity of seeing, by means of one of his friends, a proof that his talents, as well as his obliging service to authours, were ready as ever. He had revised *The Village*, an admirable poem, by the Reverend Mr. Crabbe. Its sentiments as to the false notions of rustick happiness and rustick virtue were quite congenial with his own; and he had taken the trouble not only to suggest slight corrections and variations, but to furnish some lines, when he thought he could give the writer's meaning better than in the words of the manuscript.

On Sunday, March 30, I found him at home in the evening, and had the pleasure to meet with Dr. Brocklesby, whose reading, and knowledge of life, and good spirits, supply him with a never-failing source of conversation.

I shall here insert a few of Johnson's sayings, without the formality of dates, as they have no reference to any particular time or place.

'The more a man extends and varies his acquaintance the better.' This, however, was meant with a just restriction; for, he on another occasion said to me, 'Sir, a man may be so much of every thing, that he is nothing of any thing.'

'It is a very good custom to keep a journal for a man's own use; he may write upon a card a day all that is necessary to be written, after he has had experience of life. At first there is a great deal to be written, because there is a great deal of novelty; but when once a man has settled his opinions, there is seldom much to be set down.'

Talking of an acquaintance of ours, whose narratives, which abounded in curious and interesting topicks, were unhappily found to be very fabulous; I mentioned Lord Mansfield's having said to me, 'Suppose we believe one *half* of what he tells.' JOHNSON. 'Ay; but we don't know *which* half to believe. By his lying we lose not only our reverence for him, but all comfort in his conversation.' BOSWELL. 'May we not take it as amusing fiction?' JOHNSON. 'Sir, the misfortune is, that you will insensibly believe as much of it as you incline to believe.'

It is remarkable, that notwithstanding their congeniality in politicks, he never was acquainted with a late eminent noble judge, whom I have heard speak of him as a writer, with great respect. Johnson, I know not upon what degree of investigation, entertained no exalted opinion of his Lordship's intellectual character. Talking of him to me one day, he said, 'It is wonderful, Sir, with how little real superiority of mind men can make an eminent figure in publick life.' He expressed himself to the same purpose concerning another law-Lord, who, it seems, once took a fancy to associate with the wits of London; but with so little success, that Foote said, 'What can he mean by coming among us? He is not only dull himself, but the cause of dullness in others.' Trying him by the test of his colloquial powers, Johnson had found him very defective. He once said to Sir Joshua Reynolds, 'This man now has been ten years about town, and has made nothing of it;' meaning as a companion. He said to me, 'I never heard any thing from him in company that was at all striking; and depend upon it, Sir, it is when you come close to a man in conversation, that you discover what his real abilities are; to make a speech in a publick assembly is a knack. Now I honour Thurlow, Sir; Thurlow is a fine fellow; he fairly puts his mind to yours.'

After repeating to him some of his pointed, lively sayings, I said,

'It is a pity, Sir, you don't always remember your own good things, that you may have a laugh when you will.' JOHNSON. 'Nay, Sir, it is better that I forget them, that I may be reminded of them, and have a laugh on their being brought to my recollection.'

When I recalled to him his having said as we sailed up Loch-lomond, 'That if he wore any thing fine, it should be *very* fine;' I observed that all his thoughts were upon a great scale. JOHNSON. 'Depend upon it, Sir, every man will have as fine a thing as he can get; as a large diamond for his ring.' BOSWELL. 'Pardon me, Sir: a man of a narrow mind will not think of it, a slight trinket will satisfy him:

> "*Nec sufferre queat majoris pondera gemmae.*"'

I told him I should send him some Essays which I had written, which I hoped he would be so good as to read, and pick out the good ones. JOHNSON. 'Nay, Sir, send me only the good ones; don't make *me* pick them.'

As a small proof of his kindliness and delicacy of feeling, the following circumstance may be mentioned: One evening when we were in the street together, and I told him I was going to sup at Mr. Beauclerk's, he said, 'I'll go with you.' After having walked part of the way, seeming to recollect something, he suddenly stopped and said, 'I cannot go,—but *I do not love Beauclerk the less.*'

On the frame of his portrait, Mr. Beauclerk had inscribed,—

> '————Ingenium ingens
> Inculto latet hoc sub corpore.'

After Mr. Beauclerk's death, when it became Mr. Langton's property, he made the inscription be defaced. Johnson said complacently, 'It was kind in you to take it off;' and then after a short pause, added, 'and not unkind in him to put it on.'

He said, 'How few of his friends' houses would a man choose to be at when he is sick.' He mentioned one or two. I recollect only Thrale's.

He observed, 'There is a wicked inclination in most people to suppose an old man decayed in his intellects. If a young or middle-aged man, when leaving a company, does not recollect where he laid his hat, it is nothing; but if the same inattention is discovered in an old man, people will shrug up their shoulders, and say, "His memory is going."'

Sir Joshua Reynolds communicated to me the following particulars:—

Johnson thought the poems published as translations from Ossian had so little merit, that he said, 'Sir, a man might write such stuff for ever, if he would *abandon* his mind to it.'

He said, 'A man should pass a part of his time with *the laughers*, by which means any thing ridiculous or particular about him might be presented to his view, and corrected.' I observed, he must have been a bold laugher who would have ventured to tell Dr. Johnson of any of his particularities.[54]

Dr. Goldsmith said once to Dr. Johnson, that he wished for some additional members to THE LITERARY CLUB, to give it an agreeable variety; for (said he,) there can now be nothing new among us: we have travelled over one another's minds. Johnson seemed a little angry, and said, 'Sir, you have not travelled over *my* mind, I promise you.' Sir Joshua, however, thought Goldsmith right; observing, that 'when people have lived a great deal together, they know what each of them will say on every subject. A new understanding, therefore, is desirable; because though it may only furnish the same sense upon a question which would have been furnished by those with whom we are accustomed to live, yet this sense will have a different colouring; and colouring is of much effect in every thing else as well as in painting.'

Johnson used to say that he made it a constant rule to talk as well as he could both as to sentiment and expression, by which means, what had been originally effort became familiar and easy. The consequence of this, Sir Joshua observed, was, that his common conversation in all companies was such as to secure him universal attention, as something above the usual colloquial style was expected.

Yet, though Johnson had this habit in company, when another mode was necessary, in order to investigate truth, he could descend to a language intelligible to the meanest capacity. An instance of this was witnessed by Sir Joshua Reynolds, when they were present at an examination of a little blackguard boy, by Mr. Saunders Welch, the late Westminster Justice. Welch, who imagined that he was exalting himself in Dr. Johnson's eyes by using big words, spoke in a manner that was utterly unintelligible to the boy; Dr. Johnson perceiving it, addressed himself to the boy, and changed the pompous phraseology into colloquial language. Sir Joshua Reynolds, who was much amused by this procedure, which seemed a kind of reversing of what might have been expected from the two men, took notice of it to Dr. Johnson, as they walked away by themselves. Johnson said, that it was continually the case; and that he was always obliged to *translate* the Justice's swelling diction, (smiling,) so as that his meaning might be understood by the vulgar, from whom information was to be obtained.

---

[54] I am happy, however, to mention a pleasing instance of his enduring with great gentleness to hear one of his most striking particularities pointed out:—Miss Hunter, a niece of his friend Christopher Smart, when a very young girl, struck by his extraordinary motions, said to him, Pray, Dr. Johnson, why do you make such strange gestures?' From bad habit, he replied. 'Do you, my dear, take care to guard against bad habits.' This I was told by the young lady's brother at Margate.—BOSWELL.

Sir Joshua once observed to him, that he had talked above the capacity of some people with whom they had been in company together. 'No matter, Sir, (said Johnson;) they consider it as a compliment to be talked to, as if they were wiser than they are. So true is this, Sir, that Baxter made it a rule in every sermon that he preached, to say something that was above the capacity of his audience.'

Johnson's dexterity in retort, when he seemed to be driven to an extremity by his adversary, was very remarkable. Of his power in this respect, our common friend, Mr. Windham of Norfolk, has been pleased to furnish me with an eminent instance. However unfavourable to Scotland, he uniformly gave liberal praise to George Buchanan, as a writer. In a conversation concerning the literary merits of the two countries, in which Buchanan was introduced, a Scotchman, imagining that on this ground he should have an undoubted triumph over him, exclaimed, 'Ah, Dr. Johnson, what would you have said of Buchanan, had he been an Englishman?' 'Why, Sir, (said Johnson, after a little pause,) I should *not* have said of Buchanan, had he been an *Englishman*, what I will now say of him as a *Scotchman*,—that he was the only man of genius his country ever produced.'

Though his usual phrase for conversation was *talk*, yet he made a distinction; for when he once told me that he dined the day before at a friend's house, with 'a very pretty company;' and I asked him if there was good conversation, he answered, 'No, Sir; we had *talk* enough, but no *conversation*; there was nothing *discussed*.'

Such was his sensibility, and so much was he affected by pathetick poetry, that, when he was reading Dr. Beattie's *Hermit* in my presence, it brought tears into his eyes.

Mr. Hoole told him, he was born in Moorfields, and had received part of his early instruction in Grub-street. 'Sir, (said Johnson, smiling,) you have been *regularly* educated.' Having asked who was his instructor, and Mr. Hoole having answered, 'My uncle, Sir, who was a taylor;' Johnson, recollecting himself, said, 'Sir, I knew him; we called him the *metaphysical taylor*. He was of a club in Old-street, with me and George Psalmanazar, and some others: but pray, Sir, was he a good taylor?' Mr. Hoole having answered that he believed he was too mathematical, and used to draw squares and triangles on his shop-board, so that he did not excel in the cut of a coat;—'I am sorry for it (said Johnson,) for I would have every man to be master of his own business.'

In pleasant reference to himself and Mr. Hoole, as brother authours, he often said, 'Let you and I, Sir, go together, and eat a beef-steak in Grub-street.'

He said to Sir William Scott, 'The age is running mad after innovation; all the business of the world is to be done in a new way; men are to be hanged in a new way; Tyburn itself is not safe from the fury of innovation.' It having been argued that this was an improvement,—'No, Sir, (said he, eagerly,) it is *not* an improvement: they object that the old method drew together a number of spectators. Sir, executions are intended to draw spectators. If they do not draw spectators they don't answer their purpose. The old method was most satisfactory to all parties; the publick was gratified by a procession; the criminal was supported by it. Why is all this to be swept away?' I perfectly agree with Dr. Johnson upon this head, and am persuaded that executions now, the solemn procession being discontinued, have not nearly the effect which they formerly had. Magistrates both in London, and elsewhere, have, I am afraid, in this had too much regard to their own case.

Johnson's attention to precision and clearness in expression was very remarkable. He disapproved of parentheses; and I believe in all his voluminous writings, not half a dozen of them will be found. He never used the phrases *the former* and *the latter*, having observed, that they often occasioned obscurity; he therefore contrived to construct his sentences so as not to have occasion for them, and would even rather repeat the same words, in order to avoid them. Nothing is more common than to mistake surnames when we hear them carelessly uttered for the first time. To prevent this, he used not only to pronounce them slowly and distinctly, but to take the trouble of spelling them; a practice which I have often followed; and which I wish were general.

Such was the heat and irritability of his blood, that not only did he pare his nails to the quick; but scraped the joints of his fingers with a pen-knife, till they seemed quite red and raw.

The heterogeneous composition of human nature was remarkably exemplified in Johnson. His liberality in giving his money to persons in distress was extraordinary. Yet there lurked about him a propensity to paultry saving. One day I owned to him that 'I was occasionally troubled with a fit of *narrowness.*' 'Why, Sir, (said he,) so am I. *But I do not tell it.*' He has now and then borrowed a shilling of me; and when I asked for it again, seemed to be rather out of humour. A droll little circumstance once occurred: as if he meant to reprimand my minute exactness as a creditor, he thus addressed me;—'Boswell, *lend* me sixpence—*not to be repaid.*'

This great man's attention to small things was very remarkable. As an instance of it, he one day said to me, 'Sir, when you get silver in change for a guinea, look carefully at it; you may find some curious piece of coin.'

Though a stern *true-born Englishman*, and fully prejudiced against all other nations, he had discernment enough to see, and candour enough to censure, the cold reserve too common among Englishmen towards strangers: 'Sir, (said he,) two men of any other nation who are shewn into a room together, at a house where they are both visitors, will immediately find some conversation. But two Englishmen will probably go each to a different window, and remain in obstinate silence. Sir, we as yet do not enough understand the common rights of humanity.'

Johnson, for sport perhaps, or from the spirit of contradiction, eagerly maintained that Derrick had merit as a writer. Mr. Morgann[55] argued with him directly, in vain. At length he had recourse to this device. 'Pray, Sir, (said he,) whether do you reckon Derrick or Smart the best poet?' Johnson at once felt himself roused; and answered, 'Sir, there is no settling the point of precedency between a louse and a flea.'

He was pleased to say to me one morning when we were left alone in his study, 'Boswell, I think I am easier with you than with almost any body.'

He would not allow Mr. David Hume any credit for his political principles, though similar to his own; saying of him, 'Sir, he was a Tory by chance.'

His acute observation of human life made him remark, 'Sir, there is nothing by which a man exasperates most people more, than by displaying a superiour ability or brilliancy in conversation. They seem pleased at the time; but their envy makes them curse him in their hearts.'

Johnson's love of little children, which he discovered upon all occasions, calling them 'pretty dears,' and giving them sweetmeats, was an undoubted proof of the real humanity and gentleness of his disposition.

His uncommon kindness to his servants, and serious concern, not only for their comfort in this world, but their happiness in the next, was another unquestionable evidence of what all, who were intimately acquainted with him, knew to be true.

Nor would it be just, under this head, to omit the fondness which he shewed for animals which he had taken under his protection. I never shall forget the indulgence with which he treated Hodge, his cat: for whom he himself used to go out and buy oysters, lest the servants having that trouble should take a dislike to the poor creature. I am, unluckily, one of those who have an antipathy to a cat, so that I am uneasy when in the room with one; and I own, I frequently suffered a good deal from the presence of this same Hodge. I recollect him one day scrambling up Dr. Johnson's breast, apparently with much satisfaction, while my friend smiling and half-whistling, rubbed down his back, and pulled him by the tail; and when I observed he was a fine cat, saying, 'Why yes, Sir, but I have had cats whom I liked better than this;' and then as if perceiving Hodge to be out of countenance, adding, 'but he is a very fine cat, a very fine cat indeed.'

---

[55] Author of the *Essay on the Character of Falstaff.*—Ed.

3444444.4.

4444444444444

This reminds me of the ludicrous account which he gave Mr. Langton, of the despicable state of a young Gentleman of good family. 'Sir, when I heard of him last, he was running about town shooting cats.' And then in a sort of kindly reverie, he bethought himself of his own favourite cat, and said, 'But Hodge shan't be shot; no, no, Hodge shall not be shot.'

On Thursday, April 10, I introduced to him, at his house in Bolt-court, the Honourable and Reverend William Stuart, son of the Earl of Bute; a gentleman truly worthy of being known to Johnson; being, with all the advantages of high birth, learning, travel, and elegant manners, an exemplary parish priest in every respect.

After some compliments on both sides, the tour which Johnson and I had made to the Hebrides was mentioned. JOHNSON. 'I got an acquisition of more ideas by it than by any thing that I remember. I saw quite a different system of life.' BOSWELL. 'You would not like to make the same journey again?' JOHNSON. 'Why no, Sir; not the same: it is a tale told. Gravina, an Italian critick, observes, that every man desires to see that of which he has read; but no man desires to read an account of what he has seen: so much does description fall short of reality. Description only excites curiosity: seeing satisfies it. Other people may go and see the Hebrides.' BOSWELL. 'I should wish to go and see some country totally different from what I have been used to; such as Turkey, where religion and every thing else are different.' JOHNSON. 'Yes, Sir; there are two objects of curiosity,—the Christian world, and the Mahometan world. All the rest may be considered as barbarous.' BOSWELL. 'Pray, Sir, is the *Turkish Spy* a genuine book?' JOHNSON. 'No, Sir. Mrs. Manley, in her *Life*, says that her father wrote the first two volumes: and in another book, *Dunton's Life and Errours*, we find that the rest was written by one Sault, at two guineas a sheet, under the direction of Dr. Midgeley.'

About this time he wrote to Mrs. Lucy Porter, mentioning his bad health, and that he intended a visit to Lichfield. 'It is, (says he,) with no great expectation of amendment that I make every year a journey into the country; but it is pleasant to visit those whose kindness has been often experienced.'

On April 18, (being Good-Friday,) I found him at breakfast, in his usual manner upon that day, drinking tea without milk, and eating a cross-bun to prevent faintness; we went to St. Clement's church, as formerly. When we came home from church, he placed himself on one of the stone-seats at his garden-door, and I took the other, and thus in the open air and in a placid frame of mind, he talked away very easily. JOHNSON. 'Were I a country gentleman, I should not be very hospitable, I should not have crowds in my house.' BOSWELL. 'Sir Alexander Dick tells me, that he remembers having a thousand people in a year to dine at his house: that is, reckoning each person as one, each time that he dined there.' JOHNSON. 'That, Sir, is about three a day.' BOSWELL. 'How your statement lessens the idea.' JOHNSON. 'That, Sir, is the good of counting. It brings every thing to a certainty, which before floated in the mind indefinitely.'

BOSWELL. 'I wish to have a good walled garden.' JOHNSON. 'I don't think it would be worth the expence to you. We compute in England, a park wall at a thousand pounds a mile; now a garden-wall must cost at least as much. You intend your trees should grow higher than a deer will leap. Now let us see; for a hundred pounds you could only have forty-four square yards, which is very little; for two hundred pounds, you may have eighty-four square yards, which is very well. But when will you get the value of two hundred pounds of walls, in fruit, in your climate? No, Sir, such contention with Nature is not worth while. I would plant an orchard, and have plenty of such fruit as ripen well in your country. My friend, Dr. Madden, of Ireland, said, that "in an orchard there should be enough to eat, enough to lay up, enough to be stolen, and enough to rot upon the ground." Cherries are an early fruit, you may have them; and you may have the early apples and pears.' BOSWELL. 'We cannot have nonpareils.' JOHNSON. 'Sir, you can no more have nonpareils than you can have grapes.' BOSWELL. 'We have them, Sir; but they are very bad.' JOHNSON. 'Nay, Sir, never try to have a thing merely to shew that you *cannot* have it. From ground that would let for forty shillings you may have a large orchard; and you see it costs you only forty shillings. Nay, you may graze the ground when the trees are grown up; you cannot while they are young.' BOSWELL. 'Is not a good garden a very common thing in England, Sir?' JOHNSON. 'Not so common, Sir, as you imagine. In Lincolnshire there is hardly an orchard; in Staffordshire very little fruit.' BOSWELL. 'Has Langton no orchard?' JOHNSON. 'No, Sir.' BOSWELL. 'How so, Sir?' JOHNSON. 'Why, Sir, from the general negligence of the county. He has it not, because nobody else has it.' BOSWELL. 'A hot-house is a certain thing; I may have that.' JOHNSON. 'A hot-house is pretty certain; but you must first build it, then you must keep fires in it, and you must have a gardener to take care of it.' BOSWELL. 'But if I have a gardener at any rate?—' JOHNSON. 'Why, yes.' BOSWELL. 'I'd have it near my house; there is no need to have it in the orchard.' JOHNSON. 'Yes, I'd have it near my house. I would plant a great many currants; the fruit is good, and they make a pretty sweetmeat.'

I record this minute detail, which some may think trifling, in order to shew clearly how this great man, whose mind could grasp such large and extensive subjects, as he has shewn in his literary labours, was yet well-informed in the common affairs of life, and loved to illustrate them.

Talking of the origin of language; JOHNSON. 'It must have come by inspiration. A thousand, nay, a million of children could not invent a language. While the organs are pliable, there is not understanding enough to form a language; by the time that there is understanding enough, the organs are become stiff. We know that after a certain age we cannot learn to pronounce a new language. No foreigner, who comes to England when advanced in life, ever pronounces English tolerably well; at least such instances are very rare. When I maintain that language must have come by inspiration, I do not mean that inspiration is required for rhetorick, and all the beauties of language; for when once man has language, we can conceive that he may gradually form modifications of it. I mean only that inspiration seems to me to be necessary to give man the faculty of speech; to inform him that he may have speech; which I think he could no more find out without inspiration, than cows or hogs would think of such a faculty.' WALKER. 'Do you think, Sir, that there are any perfect synonimes in any language?' JOHNSON. 'Originally there were not; but by using words negligently, or in poetry, one word comes to be confounded with another.'

He talked of Dr. Dodd. 'A friend of mine, (said he,) came to me and told me, that a lady wished to have Dr. Dodd's picture in a bracelet, and asked me for a motto. I said, I could think of no better than *Currat Lex*. I was very willing to have him pardoned, that is, to have the sentence changed to transportation: but, when he was once hanged, I did not wish he should be made a saint.'

Mrs. Burney, wife of his friend Dr. Burney, came in, and he seemed to be entertained with her conversation.

Garrick's funeral was talked of as extravagantly expensive. Johnson, from his dislike to exaggeration, would not allow that it was distinguished by any extraordinary pomp. 'Were there not six horses to each coach?' said Mrs. Burney. JOHNSON. 'Madam, there were no more six horses than six phoenixes.'

Time passed on in conversation till it was too late for the service of the church at three o'clock. I took a walk, and left him alone for some time; then returned, and we had coffee and conversation again by ourselves.

We went to evening prayers at St. Clement's, at seven, and then parted.

On Sunday, April 20, being Easter-day, after attending solemn service at St. Paul's, I came to Dr. Johnson, and found Mr. Lowe, the painter, sitting with him. Mr. Lowe mentioned the great number of new buildings of late in London, yet that Dr. Johnson had observed, that the number of inhabitants was not increased. JOHNSON. Why, Sir, the bills of mortality prove that no more people die now than formerly; so it is plain no more live. The register of births proves nothing, for not one tenth of the people of London are born there.' BOSWELL. 'I believe, Sir, a great many of the children born in London die early.' JOHNSON.

'Why, yes, Sir.' BOSWELL. 'But those who do live, are as stout and strong people as any: Dr. Price says, they must be naturally stronger to get through.' JOHNSON. 'That is system, Sir. A great traveller observes, that it is said there are no weak or deformed people among the Indians; but he with much sagacity assigns the reason of this, which is, that the hardship of their life as hunters and fishers does not allow weak or diseased children to grow up. Now had I been an Indian, I must have died early; my eyes would not have served me to get food. I indeed now could fish, give me English tackle; but had I been an Indian I must have starved, or they would have knocked me on the head, when they saw I could do nothing.' BOSWELL. 'Perhaps they would have taken care of you: we are told they are fond of oratory, you would have talked to them.' JOHNSON. Nay, Sir, I should not have lived long enough to be fit to talk; I should have been dead before I was ten years old. Depend upon it, Sir, a savage, when he is hungry, will not carry about with him a looby of nine years old, who cannot help himself. They have no affection, Sir.' BOSWELL. 'I believe natural affection, of which we hear so much, is very small.' JOHNSON. 'Sir, natural affection is nothing: but affection from principle and established duty is sometimes wonderfully strong.' LOWE. 'A hen, Sir, will feed her chickens in preference to herself.' JOHNSON. 'But we don't know that the hen is hungry; let the hen be fairly hungry, and I'll warrant she'll peck the corn herself. A cock, I believe, will feed hens instead of himself; but we don't know that the cock is hungry.' BOSWELL. 'And that, Sir, is not from affection but gallantry. But some of the Indians have affection.' JOHNSON. 'Sir, that they help some of their children is plain; for some of them live, which they could not do without being helped.'

I dined with him; the company were, Mrs. Williams, Mrs. Desmoulins, and Mr. Lowe. He seemed not to be well, talked little, grew drowsy soon after dinner, and retired, upon which I went away.

Having next day gone to Mr. Burke's seat in the country, from whence I was recalled by an express, that a near relation of mine had killed his antagonist in a duel, and was himself dangerously wounded, I saw little of Dr. Johnson till Monday, April 28, when I spent a considerable part of the day with him, and introduced the subject, which then chiefly occupied my mind. JOHNSON. 'I do not see, Sir, that fighting is absolutely forbidden in Scripture; I see revenge forbidden, but not self-defence.' BOSWELL. 'The Quakers say it is; "Unto him that smiteth thee on one cheek, offer him also the other."' JOHNSON. 'But stay, Sir; the text is meant only to have the effect of moderating passion; it is plain that we are not to take it in a literal sense. We see this from the context, where there are other recommendations, which I warrant you the Quaker will not take literally; as, for instance, "From him that would borrow of thee, turn thou not away." Let a man whose credit is bad, come to a Quaker, and say, "Well, Sir, lend me a hundred pounds;" he'll find him as unwilling as any other man. No, Sir, a man may shoot the man who invades his character, as he may shoot him who attempts to break into his house.[56] So in 1745, my friend, Tom Gumming, the Quaker, said, he would not fight, but he would drive an ammunition cart; and we know that the Quakers have sent flannel waistcoats to our soldiers, to enable them to fight better.' BOSWELL. 'When a man is the aggressor, and by ill-usage forces on a duel in which he is killed, have we not little ground to hope that he is gone into a state of happiness?' JOHNSON. 'Sir, we are not to judge determinately of the state in which a man leaves this life. He may in a moment have repented effectually, and it is possible may have been accepted by GOD.'

Upon being told that old Mr. Sheridan, indignant at the neglect of his oratorical plans, had threatened to go to America; JOHNSON. 'I hope he will go to America.' BOSWELL. 'The Americans don't want oratory.' JOHNSON. 'But we can want Sheridan.'

On Monday, April 29, I found him at home in the forenoon, and Mr. Seward with him. Horace having been mentioned; BOSWELL. 'There is a great deal of thinking in his works. One finds there almost every thing but religion.' SEWARD. 'He speaks of his returning to it, in his Ode *Parcus Deorum cultor et infrequens.*' JOHNSON. 'Sir, he was not in earnest: this was merely poetical.' BOSWELL. 'There are, I am afraid, many people who have no religion at all.' SEWARD. 'And sensible people too.' JOHNSON. 'Why, Sir, not sensible in that respect. There must be either a natural or a moral stupidity, if one lives in a total neglect of so very important a concern. SEWARD. 'I wonder that there should be people without religion.' JOHNSON. 'Sir, you need not wonder at this, when you consider how large a proportion of almost every man's life is passed without thinking of it. I myself was for some years totally regardless of religion. It had dropped out of my mind. It was at an early part of my life. Sickness brought it back, and I hope I have never lost it since.' BOSWELL. 'My dear Sir, what a man must you have been without religion! Why you must have gone on drinking, and swearing, and—' JOHNSON (with a smile,) 'I drank enough and swore enough, to be sure.' SEWARD. 'One should think that sickness and the view of death would make more men religious.' JOHNSON. 'Sir, they do not know how to go about it: they have not the first notion. A man who has never had religion before, no more grows religious when he is sick,

---

[56] I think it necessary to caution my readers against concluding that in this or any other conversation of Dr. Johnson, they have his serious and deliberate opinion on the subject of duelling. In my Journal of a Tour to the Hebrides, 3rd edit. p. 386 [p. 366, Oct. 24], it appears that he made this frank confession:—'Nobody at times, talks more laxly than I do;' and, ib., p. 231 [Sept. 19, 1773], 'He fairly owned he could not explain the rationality of duelling.' We may, therefore, infer, that he could not think that justifiable, which seems so inconsistent with the spirit of the Gospel.—BOSWELL.

than a man who has never learnt figures can count when he has need of calculation.'

I mentioned Dr. Johnson's excellent distinction between liberty of conscience and liberty of teaching. JOHNSON. 'Consider, Sir; if you have children whom you wish to educate in the principles of the Church of England, and there comes a Quaker who tries to pervert them to his principles, you would drive away the Quaker. You would not trust to the predomination of right, which you believe is in your opinions; you would keep wrong out of their heads. Now the vulgar are the children of the State. If any one attempts to teach them doctrines contrary to what the State approves, the magistrate may and ought to restrain him.' SEWARD. 'Would you restrain private conversation, Sir?' JOHNSON. 'Why, Sir, it is difficult to say where private conversation begins, and where it ends. If we three should discuss even the great question concerning the existence of a Supreme Being by ourselves, we should not be restrained; for that would be to put an end to all improvement. But if we should discuss it in the presence of ten boarding-school girls, and as many boys, I think the magistrate would do well to put us in the stocks, to finish the debate there.'

'How false (said he,) is all this, to say that in ancient times learning was not a disgrace to a Peer as it is now. In ancient times a Peer was as ignorant as any one else. He would have been angry to have it thought he could write his name. Men in ancient times dared to stand forth with a degree of ignorance with which nobody would dare now to stand forth. I am always angry when I hear ancient times praised at the expence of modern times. There is now a great deal more learning in the world than there was formerly; for it is universally diffused. You have, perhaps, no man who knows as much Greek and Latin as Bentley; no man who knows as much mathematicks as Newton: but you have many more men who know Greek and Latin, and who know mathematicks.'

On Thursday, May 1, I visited him in the evening along with young Mr. Burke. He said, 'It is strange that there should be so little reading in the world, and so much writing. People in general do not willingly read, if they can have any thing else to amuse them. There must be an external impulse; emulation, or vanity, or avarice. The progress which the understanding makes through a book, has more pain than pleasure in it. Language is scanty, and inadequate to express the nice gradations and mixtures of our feelings. No man reads a book of science from pure inclination. The books that we do read with pleasure are light compositions, which contain a quick succession of events. However, I have this year read all Virgil through. I read a book of the *Aeneid* every night, so it was done in twelve nights, and I had great delight in it. The *Georgicks* did not give me so much pleasure, except the fourth book. The *Eclogues* I have almost all by heart. I do not think the story of the *Aeneid* interesting. I like the story of the Odyssey much better; and this not on account of the wonderful things which it contains; for there are wonderful things enough in the *Aeneid*;—the ships of the Trojans turned to sea-nymphs,—the tree at Polydorus's tomb dropping blood. The story of the *Odyssey* is interesting, as a great part of it is domestick. It has been said, there is pleasure in writing, particularly in writing verses. I allow you may have pleasure from writing, after it is over, if you have written well; but you don't go willingly to it again. I know when I have been writing verses, I have run my finger down the margin, to see how many I had made, and how few I had to make.'

He seemed to be in a very placid humour, and although I have no note of the particulars of young Mr. Burke's conversation, it is but justice to mention in general, that it was such that Dr. Johnson said to me afterwards, 'He did very well indeed; I have a mind to tell his father.'

I have no minute of any interview with Johnson till Thursday, May 15, when I find what follows:—BOSWELL. 'I wish much to be in Parliament, Sir.' JOHNSON. 'Why, Sir, unless you come resolved to support any administration, you would be the worse for being in Parliament, because you would be obliged to live more expensively.' BOSWELL. 'Perhaps, Sir, I should be the less happy for being in Parliament. I never would sell my vote, and I should be vexed if things went wrong.' JOHNSON. 'That's cant, Sir. It would not vex you more in the house, than in the gallery: publick affairs vex no man.' BOSWELL. 'Have not they vexed yourself a little, Sir? Have not you been vexed by all the turbulence of this reign, and by that absurd vote of the house of Commons, "That the influence of the Crown has increased, is increasing, and ought to be diminished?"' Johnson. 'Sir, I have never slept an hour less, nor eat an ounce less meat. I would have knocked the factious dogs on the head, to be sure; but I was not *vexed*.' BOSWELL. 'I declare, Sir, upon my honour, I did imagine I was vexed, and took a pride in it; but it WAS, perhaps, cant; for I own I neither ate less, nor slept less.' JOHNSON. 'My dear friend, clear your *mind* of cant. You may *talk* as other people do: you may say to a man, "Sir, I am your most humble servant." You are not his most humble servant. You may say, "These are bad times; it is a melancholy thing to be reserved to such times." You don't mind the times. You tell a man, "I am sorry you had such bad weather the last day of your journey, and were so much wet." You don't care six-pence whether he is wet or dry. You may *talk* in this manner; it is a mode of talking in Society: but don't *think* foolishly.'

Here he discovered a notion common enough in persons not much accustomed to entertain company, that there must be a degree of elaborate attention, otherwise company will think themselves neglected; and such attention is no doubt very fatiguing. He proceeded: 'I would not, however, be a stranger in my own county; I would visit my neighbours, and receive their visits; but I would not be in haste to return visits. If a gentleman comes to see me, I tell him he does me a great deal of honour. I do not go to see him perhaps for ten weeks; then we are very complaisant to each other. No, Sir, you will have much more influence by giving or lending money where it is wanted, than by hospitality.'

On Saturday, May 17, I saw him for a short time. Having mentioned that I had that morning been with old Mr. Sheridan, he remembered their former intimacy with a cordial warmth, and said to me, 'Tell Mr. Sheridan, I shall be glad to see him, and shake hands with him.' BOSWELL. 'It is to me very wonderful that resentment should be kept up so long.' JOHNSON. 'Why, Sir, it is not altogether resentment that he does not visit me; it is partly falling out of the habit,—partly disgust, as one has at a drug that has made him sick. Besides, he knows that I laugh at his oratory.'

Another day I spoke of one of our friends, of whom he, as well as I, had a very high opinion. He expatiated in his praise; but added, 'Sir, he is a cursed Whig, a *bottomless* Whig, as they all are now.'

On Monday, May 26, I found him at tea, and the celebrated Miss Burney, the authour of *Evelina* and *Cecilia*, with him. I asked if there would be any speakers in Parliament, if there were no places to be obtained. JOHNSON. 'Yes, Sir. Why do you speak here? Either to instruct and entertain, which is a benevolent motive; or for distinction, which is a selfish motive.' I mentioned *Cecilia*. JOHNSON. (with an air of animated satisfaction,) 'Sir, if you talk of *Cecilia*, talk on.'

We talked of Mr. Barry's exhibition of his pictures. JOHNSON. 'Whatever the hand may have done, the mind has done its part. There is a grasp of mind there which you find nowhere else.'

I asked whether a man naturally virtuous, or one who has overcome wicked inclinations, is the best. JOHNSON. 'Sir, to *you*, the man who has overcome wicked inclinations is not the best. He has more merit to *himself*: I would rather trust my money to a man who has no hands, and so a physical impossibility to steal, than to a man of the most honest principles. There is a witty satirical story of Foote. He had a small bust of Garrick placed upon his bureau. "You may be surprized (said he,) that I allow him to be so near my gold;—but you will observe he has no hands."'

On Friday, May 29, being to set out for Scotland next morning, I passed a part of the day with him in more than usual earnestness; as his health was in a more precarious state than at any time when I had parted from him. He, however, was quick and lively, and critical as usual. I mentioned one who was a very learned man. JOHNSON. 'Yes, Sir, he has a great deal of learning; but it never lies straight. There is never one idea by the side of another; 'tis all entangled: and their he drives it so aukwardly upon conversation.'

He said, 'Get as much force of mind as you can. Live within your income. Always have something saved at the end of the year. Let your imports be more than your exports, and you'll never go far wrong.

I assured him, that in the extensive and various range of his acquaintance there never had been any one who had a more sincere respect and affection for him than I had. He said, 'I believe it, Sir. Were I in distress, there is no man to whom I should sooner come than to you. I should like to come and have a cottage in your park, toddle about, live mostly on milk, and be taken care of by Mrs. Boswell. She and I are good friends now; are we not?'

He embraced me, and gave me his blessing, as usual when I was leaving him for any length of time. I walked from his door to-day, with a fearful apprehension of what might happen before I returned.

My anxious apprehensions at parting with him this year, proved to be but too well founded; for not long afterwards he had a dreadful stroke of the palsy, of which there are very full and accurate accounts in letters written by himself, to shew with what composure of mind, and resignation to the Divine Will, his steady piety enabled him to behave.

'TO MR. EDMUND ALLEN.

'DEAR SIR,—It has pleased GOD, this morning, to deprive me of the powers of speech; and as I do not know but that it may be his further good pleasure to deprive me soon of my senses, I request you will on the receipt of this note, come to me, and act for me, as the exigencies of my case may require. I am, sincerely yours,
      'June 17, 1783.'

                                                            'SAM. JOHNSON.'

Two days after he wrote thus to Mrs. Thrale:—

'On Monday, the 16th, I sat for my picture, and walked a considerable way with little inconvenience. In the afternoon and evening I felt myself light and easy, and began to plan schemes of life. Thus I went to bed, and in a short time waked and sat up, as has been long my custom, when I felt a confusion and indistinctness in my head, which lasted, I suppose, about half a minute. I was alarmed, and prayed God, that however he might afflict my body, he would spare my understanding. This prayer, that I might try the integrity of my faculties, I made in Latin verse. The lines were not very good, but I knew them not to be very good: I made them easily, and concluded myself to be unimpaired in my faculties.

'Soon after I perceived that I had suffered a paralytick stroke, and that my speech was taken from me. I had no pain, and so little dejection in this dreadful state, that I wondered at my own apathy, and considered that perhaps death itself, when it should come, would excite less horrour than seems now to attend it.

'In order to rouse the vocal organs, I took two drams. Wine has been celebrated for the production of eloquence. I put myself into violent motion, and I think repeated it; but all was vain. I then went to bed, and strange as it may seem, I think slept. When I saw light, it was time to contrive what I should do. Though God stopped my speech, he left me my hand; I enjoyed a mercy which was not granted to my dear friend Lawrence, who now perhaps overlooks me as I am writing, and rejoices that I have what he wanted. My first note was necessarily to my servant, who came in talking, and could not immediately comprehend why he should read what I put into his hands.

'I then wrote a card to Mr. Allen, that I might have a discreet friend at hand, to act as occasion should require. In penning this note, I had some difficulty; my hand, I knew not how nor why, made wrong letters. I then wrote to Dr. Taylor to come to me, and bring Dr. Heberden; and I sent to Dr. Brocklesby, who is my neighbour. My physicians are very friendly, and give me great hopes; but you may imagine my situation. I have so far recovered my vocal powers, as to repeat the Lord's Prayer with no very imperfect articulation. My memory, I hope, yet remains as it was; but such an attack produces solicitude for the safety of every faculty.'

'TO MR. THOMAS DAVIES.

'DEAR SIR,—I have had, indeed, a very heavy blow; but GOD, who yet spares my life, I humbly hope will spare my understanding, and restore my speech. As I am not at all helpless, I want no particular assistance, but am strongly affected by Mrs. Davies's tenderness; and when I think she can do me good, shall be very glad to call upon her. I had ordered friends to be shut out; but one or two have found the way in; and if you come you shall be admitted: for I know not whom I can see, that will bring more amusement on his tongue, or more kindness in his heart. I am, &c.

'June 18, 1783.'

'SAM. JOHNSON.'

It gives me great pleasure to preserve such a memorial of Johnson's regard for Mr. Davies, to whom I was indebted for my introduction to him. He indeed loved Davies cordially, of which I shall give the following little evidence. One day when he had treated him with too much asperity, Tom, who was not without pride and spirit, went off in a passion; but he had hardly reached home when Frank, who had been sent after him, delivered this note:—'Come, come, dear Davies, I am always sorry when we quarrel; send me word that we are friends.'

Such was the general vigour of his constitution, that he recovered from this alarming and severe attack with wonderful quickness; so that in July he was able to make a visit to Mr. Langton at Rochester, where he passed about a fortnight, and made little excursions as easily as at any time of his life. In August he went as far as the neighbourhood of Salisbury, to Heale, the seat of William Bowles, Esq., a gentleman whom I have heard him praise for exemplary religious order in his family. In his diary I find a short but honourable mention of this visit:—'August 28, I came to Heale without fatigue. 30, I am entertained quite to my mind.'

While he was here he had a letter from Dr. Brocklesby, acquainting him of the death of Mrs. Williams, which affected him a good deal. Though for several years her temper had not been complacent, she had valuable qualities, and her departure left a blank in his house. Upon this occasion he, according to his habitual course of piety, composed a prayer.

I shall here insert a few particulars concerning him, with which I have been favoured by one of his friends.

'He spoke often in praise of French literature. "The French are excellent in this, (he would say,) they have a book on every subject." From what he had seen of them he denied them the praise of superiour politeness, and mentioned, with very visible disgust, the custom they have of spitting on the floors of their apartments. "This, (said the Doctor), is as gross a thing as can well be done; and one wonders how any man, or set of men, can persist in so offensive a practice for a whole day together; one should expect that the first effort towards civilization would remove it even among savages."

'Chymistry was always an interesting pursuit with Dr. Johnson. Whilst he was in Wiltshire, he attended some experiments that were made by a physician at Salisbury, on the new kinds of air. In the course of the experiments frequent mention being made of Dr. Priestley, Dr. Johnson knit his brows, and in a stern manner inquired, "Why do we hear so much of Dr. Priestley?" He was very properly answered, "Sir, because we are indebted to him for these important discoveries." On this Dr. Johnson appeared well content; and replied, "Well, well, I believe we are; and let every man have the honour he has merited."'

'A friend was one day, about two years before his death, struck with some instance of Dr. Johnson's great candour. "Well, Sir, (said he,) I will always say that you are a very candid man." "Will you, (replied the Doctor,) I doubt then you will be very singular. But, indeed, Sir, (continued he,) I look upon myself to be a man very much misunderstood. I am not an uncandid, nor am I a severe man. I sometimes say more than I mean, in jest; and people are apt to believe me serious: however, I am more candid than I was when I was younger. As I know more of mankind I expect less of them, and am ready now to call a man *a good man*, upon easier terms than I was formerly.'"

On his return from Heale he wrote to Dr. Burney:—

'I came home on the 18th at noon to a very disconsolate house. You and I have lost our friends; but you have more friends at home. My domestick companion is taken from me. She is much missed, for her acquisitions were many, and her curiosity universal; so that she partook of every conversation. I am not well enough to go much out; and to sit, and eat, or fast alone, is very wearisome. I always mean to send my compliments to all the ladies.'

His fortitude and patience met with severe trials during this year. The stroke of the palsy has been related circumstantially; but he was also afflicted with the gout, and was besides troubled with a complaint which not only was attended with immediate inconvenience, but threatened him with a chirurgical operation, from which most men would shrink. The complaint was a *sarcocele*, which Johnson bore with uncommon firmness, and was not at all frightened while he looked forward to amputation. He was attended by Mr. Pott and Mr. Cruikshank.

Happily the complaint abated without his being put to the torture of amputation. But we must surely admire the manly resolution which he discovered while it hung over him.

He this autumn received a visit from the celebrated Mrs. Siddons. He gives this account of it in one of his letters to Mrs. Thrale:—

'Mrs. Siddons, in her visit to me, behaved with great modesty and propriety, and left nothing behind her to be censured or despised. Neither praise nor money, the two powerful corrupters of mankind, seem to have depraved her. I shall be glad to see her again. Her brother Kemble calls on me, and pleases me very well. Mrs. Siddons and I talked of plays; and she told me her intention of exhibiting this winter the characters of Constance, Catharine, and Isabella, in Shakspeare.'

Mr. Kemble has favoured me with the following minute of what passed at this visit:—

'When Mrs. Siddons came into the room, there happened to be no chair ready for her, which he observing, said with a smile, "Madam, you who so often occasion a want of seats to other people, will the more easily excuse the want of one yourself."

'Having placed himself by her, he with great good-humour entered upon a consideration of the English drama; and, among other inquiries, particularly asked her which of Shakspeare's characters she was most pleased with. Upon her answering that she thought the character of Queen Catharine, in *Henry the Eighth*, the most natural:—"I think so too, Madam, (said he;) and whenever you perform it, I will once more hobble out to the theatre myself." Mrs. Siddons promised she would do herself the honour of acting his favourite part for him; but many circumstances happened to prevent the representation of *King Henry the Eighth* during the Doctor's life.

'In the course of the evening he thus gave his opinion upon the merits of some of the principal performers whom he remembered to have seen upon the stage. "Mrs. Porter in the vehemence of rage, and Mrs. Clive in the sprightliness of humour, I have never seen equalled. What Clive did best, she did better than Garrick; but could not do half so many things well; she was a better romp than any I ever saw in nature. Pritchard, in common life, was a vulgar ideot; she would talk of her *gownd*: but, when she appeared upon the stage, seemed to be inspired by gentility and understanding. I once talked with Colley Cibber, and thought him ignorant of the principles of his art. Garrick, Madam; was no declaimer; there was not one of his own scene-shifters who could not have spoken *To be, or not to be*, better than he did; yet he was the only actor I ever saw, whom I could call a master both in tragedy and comedy; though I liked him best in comedy. A true conception of character, and natural expression of it, were his distinguished excellencies." Having expatiated, with his usual force and eloquence, on Mr. Garrick's extraordinary eminence as an actor, he concluded with this compliment to his social talents: "And after all, Madam, I thought him less to be envied on the stage than at the head of a table."'

Johnson, indeed, had thought more upon the subject of acting than might be generally supposed. Talking of it one day to Mr. Kemble, he said, 'Are you, Sir, one of those enthusiasts who believe yourself transformed into the very character you represent?' Upon Mr. Kemble's answering that he had never felt so strong a persuasion himself; 'To be sure not, Sir, (said Johnson;) the thing is impossible. And if Garrick really believed himself to be that monster, Richard the Third, he deserved to be hanged every time he performed it.'

I find in this, as in former years, notices of his kind attention to Mrs. Gardiner, who, though in the humble station of a tallow-chandler upon Snow-hill, was a woman of excellent good sense, pious, and charitable. She told me, she had been introduced to him by Mrs. Masters, the poetess, whose volumes he revised, and, it is said, illuminated here and there with a ray of his own genius. Mrs. Gardiner was very zealous for the support of the Ladies' charity-school, in the parish of St. Sepulchre. It is confined to females; and, I am told, it afforded a hint for the story of *Betty Broom* in *The Idler*.

The late ingenious Mr. Mickle, some time before his death, wrote me a letter concerning Dr. Johnson, in which he mentions,—'I was upwards of twelve years acquainted with him, was frequently in his company, always talked with ease to him, and can truly say, that I never received from him one rough word.'

Mr. Mickle reminds me in this letter of a conversation, at dinner one day at Mr. Hoole's with Dr. Johnson, when Mr. Nicol the King's bookseller and I attempted to controvert the maxim, 'better that ten guilty should escape, than one innocent person suffer;' and were answered by Dr. Johnson with great power of reasoning and eloquence. I am very sorry that I have no record of that day: but I well recollect my illustrious friend's having ably shewn, that unless civil institutions insure protection to the innocent, all the confidence which mankind should have in them would be lost.

Notwithstanding the complication of disorders under which Johnson now laboured, he did not resign himself to despondency and discontent, but with wisdom and spirit endeavoured to console and amuse his mind with as many innocent enjoyments as he could procure. Sir John Hawkins has mentioned the cordiality with which he insisted that such of the members of the old club in Ivy-lane as survived, should meet again and dine together, which they did, twice at a tavern and once at his house: and in order to insure himself society in the evening for three days in the week, he instituted a club at the Essex Head, in Essex-street, then kept by Samuel Greaves, an old servant of Mr. Thrale's.

'TO SIR JOSHUA REYNOLDS.

'DEAR SIR,—It is inconvenient to me to come out, I should else have waited on you with an account of a little evening Club which we are establishing in Essex-street, in the Strand, and of which you are desired to be one. It will be held at the Essex Head, now kept by an old servant of Thrale's. The company is numerous, and, as you will see by the list, miscellaneous. The terms are lax, and the expences light. Mr. Barry was adopted by Dr. Brocklesby, who joined with me in forming the plan. We meet thrice a week, and he who misses forfeits two-pence.

'If you are willing to become a member, draw a line under your name. Return the list. We meet for the first time on Monday at eight. I am, &c.

'Dec. 4, 1783.'

'SAM. JOHNSON.'

It did not suit Sir Joshua to be one of this Club. But when I mention only Mr. Daines Barrington, Dr. Brocklesby, Mr. Murphy, Mr. John Nichols, Mr. Cooke, Mr. Joddrel, Mr. Paradise, Dr. Horsley, Mr. Windham,[57] I shall sufficiently obviate the misrepresentation of it by

---

[57] I was in Scotland when this Club was founded, and during all the winter. Johnson, however, declared I should be a member, and invented a word upon the

Sir John Hawkins, as if it had been a low ale-house association, by which Johnson was degraded. Johnson himself, like his namesake Old Ben, composed the Rules of his Club.

In the end of this year he was seized with a spasmodick asthma of such violence, that he was confined to the house in great pain, being sometimes obliged to sit all night in his chair, a recumbent posture being so hurtful to his respiration, that he could not endure lying in bed; and there came upon him at the same time that oppressive and fatal disease, a dropsy. It was a very severe winter, which probably aggravated his complaints; and the solitude in which Mr. Levett and Mrs. Williams had left him, rendered his life very gloomy. Mrs. Desmoulins, who still lived, was herself so very ill, that she could contribute very little to his relief. He, however, had none of that unsocial shyness which we commonly see in people afflicted with sickness. He did not hide his head from the world, in solitary abstraction; he did not deny himself to the visits of his friends and acquaintances; but at all times, when he was not overcome by sleep, was ready for conversation as in his best days.

'TO MRS. LUCY PORTER, IN LICHFIELD.

'DEAR MADAM,—You may perhaps think me negligent that I have not written to you again upon the loss of your brother; but condolences and consolations are such common and such useless things, that the omission of them is no great crime: and my own diseases occupy my mind, and engage my care. My nights are miserably restless, and my days, therefore, are heavy. I try, however, to hold up my head as high as I can.

'I am sorry that your health is impaired; perhaps the spring and the summer may, in some degree, restore it: but if not, we must submit to the inconveniences of time, as to the other dispensations of Eternal Goodness. Pray for me, and write to me, or let Mr. Pearson write for you. I am, &c.

'London, Nov. 29, 1783.'

'SAM. JOHNSON.'

1784: ÆTAT. 75.]—And now I am arrived at the last year of the life of SAMUEL JOHNSON, a year in which, although passed in severe indisposition, he nevertheless gave many evidences of the continuance of those wondrous powers of mind, which raised him so high in the

---

occasion: Boswell (said he,) is a very *clubable* man.' When I came to town I was proposed by Mr. Barrington, and chosen. I believe there are few societies where there is better conversation or more decorum, several of us resolved to continue it after our great founder was removed by death. Other members were added; and now, above eight years since that loss, we go on happily.—BOSWELL.

intellectual world. His conversation and his letters of this year were in no respect inferiour to those of former years.

In consequence of Johnson's request that I should ask our physicians about his case, and desire Sir Alexander Dick to send his opinion, I transmitted him a letter from that very amiable Baronet, then in his eighty-first year, with his faculties as entire as ever; and mentioned his expressions to me in the note accompanying it: 'With my most affectionate wishes for Dr. Johnson's recovery, in which his friends, his country, and all mankind have so deep a stake:' and at the same time a full opinion upon his case by Dr. Gillespie, who, like Dr. Cullen, had the advantage of having passed through the gradations of surgery and pharmacy, and by study and practice had attained to such skill, that my father settled on him two hundred pounds a year for five years, and fifty pounds a year during his life, as an *honorarium* to secure his particular attendance.

I also applied to three of the eminent physicians who had chairs in our celebrated school of medicine at Edinburgh, Doctors Cullen, Hope, and Monro.

All of them paid the most polite attention to my letter, and its venerable object. Dr. Cullen's words concerning him were, 'It would give me the greatest pleasure to be of any service to a man whom the publick properly esteem, and whom I esteem and respect as much as I do Dr. Johnson.' Dr. Hope's, 'Few people have a better claim on me than your friend, as hardly a day passes that I do not ask his opinion about this or that word.' Dr. Monro's, 'I most sincerely join you in sympathizing with that very worthy and ingenious character, from whom his country has derived much instruction and entertainment.'

'TO THE REVEREND DR. TAYLOR,
ASHBOURNE, DERBYSHIRE.

'DEAR SIR,—What can be the reason that I hear nothing from you? I hope nothing disables you from writing. What I have seen, and what I have felt, gives me reason to fear every thing. Do not omit giving me the comfort of knowing, that after all my losses I have yet a friend left.

'I want every comfort. My life is very solitary and very cheerless. Though it has pleased GOD wonderfully to deliver me from the dropsy, I am yet very weak, and have not passed the door since the 13th of December. I hope for some help from warm weather, which will surely come in time.

'I could not have the consent of the physicians to go to church yesterday; I therefore received the holy sacrament at home, in the room where I communicated with dear Mrs. Williams, a little before her death. O! my friend, the approach of death is very dreadful. I am afraid to think on that which I know I cannot avoid. It is vain to look round and round for that help which cannot be had. Yet we hope and hope, and fancy that he who has lived to-day may live to-morrow. But let us learn to derive our hope only from GOD.

'In the mean time, let us be kind to one another. I have no friend now living but you and Mr. Hector, that was the friend of my youth. Do not neglect, dear Sir, yours affectionately,

'London, Easter-Monday, April 12, 1784.'

'SAM. JOHNSON.'

What follows is a beautiful specimen of his gentleness and complacency to a young lady his god-child, one of the daughters of his friend Mr. Langton, then I think in her seventh year. He took the trouble to write it in a large round hand, nearly resembling printed characters, that she might have the satisfaction of reading it herself. The original lies before me, but shall be faithfully restored to her; and I dare say will be preserved by her as a jewel as long as she lives.

'TO MISS JANE LANGTON, IN ROCHESTER, KENT.

'MY DEAREST MISS JENNY,—I am sorry that your pretty letter has been so long without being answered; but, when I am not pretty well, I do not always write plain enough for young ladies. I am glad, my dear, to see that you write so well, and hope that you mind your pen, your book, and your needle, for they are all necessary. Your books will give you knowledge, and make you respected; and your needle will find you useful employment when you do not care to read. When you are a little older, I hope you will be very diligent in learning arithmetick, and, above all, that through your whole life you will carefully say your prayers, and read your Bible. I am, my dear, your most humble servant,

'May 10, 1784.'

'SAM. JOHNSON.'

On Wednesday, May 5, I arrived in London, and next morning had the pleasure to find Dr. Johnson greatly recovered. I but just saw him; for a coach was waiting to carry him to Islington, to the house of his friend the Reverend Mr. Strahan, where he went sometimes for the benefit of good air, which, notwithstanding his having formerly laughed at the general opinion upon the subject, he now acknowledged was conducive to health.

One morning afterwards, when I found him alone, he communicated to me, with solemn earnestness, a very remarkable circumstance which had happened in the course of his illness, when he was much distressed by the dropsy. He had shut himself up, and employed a day in particular exercises of religion—fasting, humiliation, and prayer. On a sudden he obtained extraordinary relief, for which he looked up to Heaven with grateful devotion. He made no direct inference from this fact; but from his manner of telling it, I could perceive that it appeared to him as something more than an incident in the common course of events. For my own part, I have no difficulty to avow that cast of thinking, which by many modern pretenders to wisdom is called *superstitious*. But here I think even men of dry rationality may believe, that there was an intermediate interposition of Divine Providence, and that 'the fervent prayer of this righteous man' availed.

On Saturday, May 15, I dined with him at Dr. Brocklesby's, where were Colonel Vallancy, Mr. Murphy, and that ever-cheerful companion Mr. Devaynes, apothecary to his Majesty. Of these days, and others on which I saw him, I have no memorials, except the general recollection of his being able and animated in conversation, and appearing to relish society as much as the youngest man. I find only these three small particulars:—When a person was mentioned, who said, 'I have lived fifty-one years in this world without having had ten minutes of uneasiness;' he exclaimed, 'The man who says so, lies: he attempts to impose on human credulity.' The Bishop of Exeter in vain observed, that men were very different. His Lordship's manner was not impressive, and I learnt afterwards that Johnson did not find out that the person who talked to him was a Prelate; if he had, I doubt not that he would have treated him with more respect; for once talking of George Psalmanazar, whom he reverenced for his piety, he said, 'I should as soon think of contradicting a BISHOP.' One of the company[58] provoked him greatly by doing what he could least of all bear, which was quoting something of his own writing, against what he then maintained. 'What, Sir, (cried the gentleman,) do you say to

> "The busy day, the peaceful night,
>   Unfelt, uncounted, glided by?"'—

Johnson finding himself thus presented as giving an instance of a man who had lived without uneasiness, was much offended, for he looked upon such a quotation as unfair. His anger burst out in an unjustifiable retort, insinuating that the gentleman's remark was a sally of ebriety; 'Sir, there is one passion I would advise you to command: when you have drunk out that glass, don't drink another.' Here was exemplified what Goldsmith said of him, with the aid of a very witty image from one of Cibber's Comedies: 'There is no arguing with Johnson; for if his pistol misses fire, he knocks you down with the butt end of it.' Another was this: when a gentleman of eminence in the literary world was violently censured for attacking people by anonymous paragraphs in

---

[58] Boswell himself, likely enough.—HILL.

news-papers; he, from the spirit of contradiction as I thought, took up his defence, and said, 'Come, come, this is not so terrible a crime; he means only to vex them a little. I do not say that I should do it; but there is a great difference between him and me; what is fit for Hephaestion is not fit for Alexander.' Another, when I told him that a young and handsome Countess had said to me, 'I should think that to be praised by Dr. Johnson would make one a fool all one's life;' and that I answered, 'Madam, I shall make him a fool to-day, by repeating this to him,' he said, 'I am too old to be made a fool; but if you say I am made a fool, I shall not deny it. I am much pleased with a compliment, especially from a pretty woman.'

On the evening of Saturday, May 15, he was in fine spirits, at our Essex-Head Club. He told us, 'I dined yesterday at Mrs. Garrick's, with Mrs. Carter, Miss Hannah More, and Miss Fanny Burney. Three such women are not to be found: I know not where I could find a fourth, except Mrs. Lennox, who is superiour to them all.' BOSWELL. 'What! had you them all to yourself, Sir?' JOHNSON. 'I had them all as much as they were had; but it might have been better had there been more company there.' BOSWELL. 'Might not Mrs. Montagu have been a fourth?' JOHNSON. 'Sir, Mrs. Montagu does not make a trade of her wit; but Mrs. Montagu is a very extraordinary woman; she has a constant stream of conversation, and it is always impregnated; it has always meaning.' BOSWELL. 'Mr. Burke has a constant stream of conversation.' JOHNSON. 'Yes, Sir; if a man were to go by chance at the same time with Burke under a shed, to shun a shower, he would say—"this is an extraordinary man." If Burke should go into a stable to see his horse drest, the ostler would say—"we have had an extraordinary man here."' BOSWELL. 'Foote was a man who never failed in conversation. If he had gone into a stable—' JOHNSON. 'Sir, if he had gone into a stable, the ostler would have said, "here has been a comical fellow"; but he would not have respected him.' BOSWELL. 'And, Sir, the ostler would have answered him, would have given him as good as he brought, as the common saying is.' JOHNSON. 'Yes, Sir; and Foote would have answered the ostler.—When Burke does not descend to be merry, his conversation is very superiour indeed. There is no proportion between the powers which he shews in serious talk and in jocularity. When he lets himself down to that, he is in the kennel.' I have in another place opposed, and I hope with success, Dr. Johnson's very singular and erroneous notion as to Mr. Burke's pleasantry. Mr. Windham now said low to me, that he differed from our great friend in this observation; for that Mr. Burke was often very happy in his merriment. It would not have been right for either of us to have contradicted Johnson at this time, in a Society all of whom did not know and value Mr. Burke as much as we did. It might have occasioned something more rough, and at any rate would probably have checked the flow of Johnson's good-humour. He called to us with a sudden air of exultation, as the thought started into his mind, 'O! Gentlemen, I must tell you a very great thing. The Empress of Russia has ordered the *Rambler* to be translated into the Russian language: so I shall be read on the banks of the Wolga. Horace boasts that his fame would extend as far as the banks of the Rhone; now the Wolga is farther from me than the Rhone was from Horace.' BOSWELL. 'You must certainly be pleased with this, Sir.' JOHNSON. 'I am pleased, Sir, to be sure. A man is pleased to find he has succeeded in that which he has endeavoured to do.'

One of the company mentioned his having seen a noble person driving in his carriage, and looking exceedingly well, notwithstanding his great age. JOHNSON. 'Ah, Sir; that is nothing. Bacon observes, that a stout healthy old man is like a tower undermined.'

On Sunday, May 16, I found him alone; he talked of Mrs. Thrale with much concern, saying, 'Sir, she has done every thing wrong, since Thrale's bridle was off her neck;' and was proceeding to mention some circumstances which have since been the subject of publick discussion, when he was interrupted by the arrival of Dr. Douglas, now Bishop of Salisbury.

In one of his little manuscript diaries, about this time, I find a short notice, which marks his amiable disposition more certainly than a thousand studied declarations.—'Afternoon spent cheerfully and elegantly, I hope without offence to GOD or man; though in no holy duty, yet in the general exercise and cultivation of benevolence.'

On Monday, May 17, I dined with him at Mr. Dilly's, where were Colonel Vallancy, the Reverend Dr. Gibbons, and Mr. Capel Lofft, who, though a most zealous Whig, has a mind so full of learning and knowledge, and so much exercised in various departments, and withal so much liberality, that the stupendous powers of the literary Goliath, though they did not frighten this little David of popular spirit, could not but excite his admiration. There was also Mr. Braithwaite of the Post-office, that amiable and friendly man, who, with modest and unassuming manners, has associated with many of the wits of the age. Johnson was very quiescent to-day. Perhaps too I was indolent. I find nothing more of him in my notes, but that when I mentioned that I had seen in the King's library sixty-three editions of my favourite *Thomas à Kempis*, amongst which it was in eight languages, Latin, German, French, Italian, Spanish, English, Arabick, and Armenian, he said, he thought it unnecessary to collect many editions of a book, which were all the same, except as to the paper and print; he would have the original, and all the translations, and all the editions which had any variations in the text. He approved of the famous collection of editions of *Horace* by Douglas, mentioned by Pope, who is said to have had a closet filled with them; and he added, every man should try to collect one book in that manner, and present it to a publick library.'

On Wednesday, May 19, I sat a part of the evening with him, by ourselves. I observed, that the death of our friends might be a consolation against the fear of our own dissolution, because we might have more friends in the other world than in this. He perhaps felt this as a reflection upon his apprehension as to death; and said, with heat, 'How can a man know *where* his departed friends are, or whether they will be his friends in the other world? How many friendships have you known formed upon principles of virtue? Most friendships are formed by caprice or by chance, mere confederacies in vice or leagues in folly.'

We talked of our worthy friend Mr. Langton. He said, 'I know not who will go to Heaven if Langton does not. Sir, I could almost say, *Sit anima mea cum Langtono.*' I mentioned a very eminent friend as a virtuous man. JOHNSON. 'Yes, Sir; but————has not the evangelical virtue of Langton.————, I am afraid, would not scruple to pick up a wench.'

He however charged Mr. Langton with what he thought want of judgment upon an interesting occasion. 'When I was ill, (said he,) I desired he would tell me sincerely in what he thought my life was faulty. Sir, he brought me a sheet of paper, on which he had written down several texts of Scripture, recommending christian charity. And when I questioned him what occasion I had given for such an animadversion, all that he could say amounted to this,—that I sometimes contradicted people in conversation. Now what harm does it do to any man to be contradicted?' BOSWELL. 'I suppose he meant the *manner* of doing it; roughly,—and harshly.' JOHNSON. 'And who is the worse for that?' BOSWELL. 'It hurts people of weak nerves.' JOHNSON. 'I know no such weak-nerved people.' Mr. Burke, to whom I related this conference, said, 'It is well, if when a man comes to die, he has nothing heavier upon his conscience than having been a little rough in conversation.'

Johnson, at the time when the paper was presented to him, though at first pleased with the attention of his friend, whom he thanked in an earnest manner, soon exclaimed, in a loud and angry tone, 'What is your drift, Sir?' Sir Joshua Reynolds pleasantly observed, that it was a scene for a comedy, to see a penitent get into a violent passion and belabour his confessor.

He had dined that day at Mr. Hoole's, and Miss Helen Maria Williams being expected in the evening, Mr. Hoole put into his hands her beautiful *Ode on the Peace*: Johnson read it over, and when this elegant and accomplished young lady was presented to him, he took her by the hand in the most courteous manner, and repeated the finest stanza of her poem; this was the most delicate and pleasing compliment he could pay. Her respectable friend, Dr. Kippis, from whom I had this anecdote, was standing by, and was not a little gratified.

Miss Williams told me, that the only other time she was fortunate enough to be in Dr. Johnson's company, he asked her to sit down by him, which she did, and upon her inquiring how he was, he answered, 'I am very ill indeed, Madam. I am very ill even when you are near me; what should I be were you at a distance?'

He had now a great desire to go to Oxford, as his first jaunt after his illness; we talked of it for some days, and I had promised to accompany him. He was impatient and fretful to-night, because I did not at once agree to go with him on Thursday. When I considered how ill he had been, and what allowance should be made for the influence of sickness upon his temper, I resolved to indulge him, though with some inconvenience to myself, as I wished to attend the musical meeting in honour of Handel, in Westminster-Abbey, on the following Saturday.

In the midst of his own diseases and pains, he was ever compassionate to the distresses of others, and actively earnest in procuring them aid, as appears from a note to Sir Joshua Reynolds, of June, in these words:—'I am ashamed to ask for some relief for a poor man, to whom, I hope, I have given what I can be expected to spare. The man importunes me, and the blow goes round. I am going to try another air on Thursday.'

On Thursday, June 3, the Oxford post-coach took us up in the morning at Bolt-court. The other two passengers were Mrs. Beresford and her daughter, two very agreeable ladies from America; they were going to Worcestershire, where they then resided. Frank had been sent by his master the day before to take places for us; and I found, from the waybill, that Dr. Johnson had made our names be put down. Mrs. Beresford, who had read it, whispered me, 'Is this the great Dr. Johnson?' I told her it was; so she was then prepared to listen. As she soon happened to mention in a voice so low that Johnson did not hear it, that her husband had been a member of the American Congress, I cautioned her to beware of introducing that subject, as she must know how very violent Johnson was against the people of that country. He talked a great deal, but I am sorry I have preserved little of the conversation. Miss Beresford was so much charmed, that she said to me aside, 'How he does talk! Every sentence is an essay.' She amused herself in the coach with knotting; he would scarcely allow this species of employment any merit. 'Next to mere idleness (said he,) I think knotting is to be reckoned in the scale of insignificance; though I once attempted to learn knotting. Dempster's sister (looking to me,) endeavoured to teach me it; but I made no progress.'

I was surprised at his talking without reserve in the publick post-coach of the state of his affairs; 'I have (said he,) about the world I think above a thousand pounds, which I intend shall afford Frank an annuity of seventy pounds a year.' Indeed his openness with people at a first interview was remarkable. He said once to Mr. Langton, 'I think I am like Squire Richard in *The Journey to London*, "*I'm never strange in a strange place.*'" He was truly *social*. He strongly censured what is much too common in England among persons of condition,—maintaining an absolute silence, when unknown to each other; as for instance, when occasionally brought together in a room before the master or mistress of the house has appeared. 'Sir, that is being so uncivilised as not to understand the common rights of humanity.'

At the inn where we stopped he was exceedingly dissatisfied with some roast mutton which we had for dinner. The ladies I saw wondered to see the great philosopher, whose wisdom and wit they had been admiring all the way, get into ill-humour from such a cause. He scolded the waiter, saying, 'It is as bad as bad can be: it is ill-fed, ill-killed, ill-kept, and ill-drest.'

He bore the journey very well, and seemed to feel himself elevated as he approached Oxford, that magnificent and venerable seat of learning, Orthodoxy, and Toryism. Frank came in the heavy coach, in readiness to attend him; and we were received with the most polite hospitality at the house of his old friend Dr. Adams, Master of Pembroke College, who had given us a kind invitation. Before we were set down, I communicated to Johnson, my having engaged to return to London directly, for the reason I have mentioned, but that I would hasten back to him again. He was pleased that I had made this journey merely to keep him company. He was easy and placid with Dr. Adams, Mrs. and Miss Adams, and Mrs. Kennicot, widow of the learned Hebraean, who was here on a visit. He soon dispatched the inquiries which were made about his illness and recovery, by a short and distinct narrative; and then assuming a gay air, repeated from Swift,—

> 'Nor think on our approaching ills,
> And talk of spectacles and pills.'

I fulfilled my intention by going to London, and returned to Oxford on Wednesday the 9th of June, when I was happy to find myself again in the same agreeable circle at Pembroke College, with the comfortable prospect of making some stay. Johnson welcomed my return with more than ordinary glee.

Next morning at breakfast, he pointed out a passage in Savage's *Wanderer*, saying, 'These are fine verses.' 'If (said he,) I had written with hostility of Warburton in my *Shakspeare*, I should have quoted this couplet:—

> "Here Learning, blinded first and then beguil'd,
> Looks dark as Ignorance, as Fancy wild."

You see they'd have fitted him to a *T*,' (smiling.) DR. ADAMS. 'But you did not write against Warburton.' JOHNSON. No, Sir, I treated him with great respect both in my Preface and in my Notes.'

After dinner, when one of us talked of there being a great enmity between Whig and Tory;—Johnson. 'Why not so much, I think, unless when they come into competition with each other. There is none when they are only common acquaintance, none when they are of different sexes. A Tory will marry into a Whig family, and a Whig into a Tory family, without any reluctance. But indeed, in a matter of much more concern than political tenets, and that is religion, men and women do not concern themselves much about difference of opinion; and ladies set no value on the moral character of men who pay their addresses to them; the greatest profligate will be as well received as the man of the greatest virtue, and this by a very good woman, by a woman who says her prayers three times a day.' Our ladies endeavoured to defend their sex from this charge; but he roared them down! 'No, no, a lady will take Jonathan Wild as readily as St. Austin, if he has threepence more; and, what is worse, her parents will give her to him. Women have a perpetual envy of our vices; they are less vicious than we, not from choice, but because we restrict them; they are the slaves of order and fashion; their virtue is of more consequence to us than our own, so far as concerns this world.'

Miss Adams mentioned a gentleman of licentious character, and said, 'Suppose I had a mind to marry that gentleman, would my parents consent?' JOHNSON. 'Yes, they'd consent, and you'd go. You'd go though they did not consent.' MISS ADAMS. 'Perhaps their opposing might make me go.' JOHNSON. 'O, very well; you'd take one whom you think a bad man, to have the pleasure of vexing your parents. You put me in mind of Dr. Barrowby, the physician, who was very fond of swine's flesh. One day, when he was eating it, he said, "I wish I was a Jew." "Why so? (said somebody;) the Jews are not allowed to eat your favourite meat." "Because, (said he,) I should then have the gust of eating it, with the pleasure of sinning."' Johnson then proceeded in his declamation.

Miss Adams soon afterwards made an observation that I do not recollect, which pleased him much: he said with a good-humoured smile, 'That there should be so much excellence united with so much *depravity*, is strange.'

Indeed, this lady's good qualities, merit, and accomplishments, and her constant attention to Dr. Johnson, were not lost upon him. She happened to tell him that a little coffeepot, in which she had made his coffee, was the only thing she could call her own. He turned to her with a complacent gallantry, 'Don't say so, my dear; I hope you don't reckon my heart as nothing.'

On Friday, June 11, we talked at breakfast, of forms of prayer.

JOHNSON. 'I know of no good prayers but those in the *Book of Common Prayer.*' DR. ADAMS. (in a very earnest manner:) 'I wish, Sir, you would compose some family prayers.' JOHNSON. 'I will not compose prayers for you, Sir, because you can do it for yourself. But I have thought of getting together all the books of prayers which I could, selecting those which should appear to me the best, putting out some, inserting others, adding some prayers of my own, and prefixing a discourse on prayer.' We all now gathered about him, and two or three of us at a time joined in pressing him to execute this plan. He seemed to be a little displeased at the manner of our importunity, and in great agitation called out, 'Do not talk thus of what is so aweful. I know not what time GOD will allow me in this world. There are many things which I wish to do.' Some of us persisted, and Dr. Adams said, 'I never was more serious about any thing in my life.' JOHNSON. 'Let me alone, let me alone; I am overpowered.' And then he put his hands before his face, and reclined for some time upon the table.

Dr. Johnson and I went in Dr. Adams's coach to dine with Dr. Nowell, Principal of St. Mary Hall, at his beautiful villa at Iffley, on the banks of the Isis, about two miles from Oxford. While we were upon the road, I had the resolution to ask Johnson whether he thought that the roughness of his manner had been an advantage or not, and if he would not have done more good if he had been more gentle. I proceeded to answer myself thus: 'Perhaps it has been of advantage, as it has given weight to what you said: you could not, perhaps, have talked with such authority without it.' JOHNSON. 'No, Sir; I have done more good as I am. Obscenity and Impiety have always been repressed in my company.' BOSWELL. 'True, Sir; and that is more than can be said of every Bishop. Greater liberties have been taken in the presence of a Bishop, though a very good man, from his being milder, and therefore not commanding such awe. Yet, Sir, many people who might have been benefited by your conversation, have been frightened away. A worthy friend of ours has told me, that he has often been afraid to talk to you.' JOHNSON. 'Sir, he need not have been afraid, if he had any thing rational to say. If he had not, it was better he did not talk.'

We talked of a certain clergyman of extraordinary character, who by exerting his talents in writing on temporary topicks, and displaying uncommon intrepidity, had raised himself to affluence. I maintained that we ought not to be indignant at his success; for merit of every sort was entitled to reward. JOHNSON. 'Sir, I will not allow this man to have merit. No, Sir; what he has is rather the contrary; I will, indeed, allow him courage, and on this account we so far give him credit. We have more respect for a man who robs boldly on the highway, than for a fellow who jumps out of a ditch, and knocks you down behind your back. Courage is a quality so necessary for maintaining virtue, that it is always respected, even when it is associated with vice.'

Mr. Henderson, with whom I had sauntered in the venerable walks of Merton College, and found him a very learned and pious man, supped with us. Dr. Johnson surprised him not a little, by acknowledging with a look of horrour, that he was much oppressed by the fear of death. The amiable Dr. Adams suggested that GOD was infinitely good. JOHNSON. 'That he is infinitely good, as far as the perfection of his nature will allow, I certainly believe; but it is necessary for good upon the whole, that individuals should be punished. As to an *individual*, therefore, he is not infinitely good; and as I cannot be *sure* that I have fulfilled the conditions on which salvation is granted, I am afraid I may be one of those who shall be damned.' (looking dismally). DR. ADAMS. 'What do you mean by damned?' JOHNSON. (passionately and loudly,) 'Sent to Hell, Sir, and punished everlastingly!' DR. ADAMS. 'I don't believe that doctrine.' JOHNSON. 'Hold, Sir, do you believe that some will be punished at all?' DR. ADAMS. 'Being excluded from Heaven will be a punishment; yet there may be no great positive suffering.' JOHNSON. Well, Sir; but, if you admit any degree of punishment, there is an end of your argument for infinite goodness simply considered; for, infinite goodness would inflict no punishment whatever. There is not infinite goodness physically considered; morally there is.' BOSWELL. 'But may not a man attain to such a degree of hope as not to be uneasy from the fear of death?' JOHNSON. 'A man may have such a degree of hope as to keep him quiet. You see I am not quiet, from the vehemence with which I talk; but I do not despair.' MRS. ADAMS. 'You seem, Sir, to forget the merits of our Redeemer.' JOHNSON. 'Madam, I do not forget the merits of my Redeemer; but my Redeemer has said that he will set some on his right hand and some on his left.' He was in gloomy agitation, and said, 'I'll have no more on't.' If what has now been stated should be urged by the enemies of Christianity, as if its influence on the mind were not benignant, let it be remembered, that Johnson's temperament was melancholy, of which such direful apprehensions of futurity are often a common effect. We shall presently see that when he approached nearer to his aweful change, his mind became tranquil, and he exhibited as much fortitude as becomes a thinking man in that situation.

From the subject of death we passed to discourse of life, whether it was upon the whole more happy or miserable. Johnson was decidedly for the balance of misery: in confirmation of which I maintained, that no man would choose to lead over again the life which he had experienced. Johnson acceded to that opinion in the strongest terms.

On Sunday, June 13, our philosopher was calm at breakfast. There was something exceedingly pleasing in our leading a College life, without restraint, and with superiour elegance, in consequence of our living in the Master's house, and having the company of ladies. Mrs. Kennicot related, in his presence, a lively saying of Dr. Johnson to Miss

Hannah More, who had expressed a wonder that the poet who had written *Paradise Lost* should write such poor Sonnets:—'Milton, Madam, was a genius that could cut a Colossus from a rock; but could not carve heads upon cherry-stones.'

On Monday, June 14, and Tuesday, 15, Dr. Johnson and I dined, on one of them, I forget which, with Mr. Mickle, translator of the *Lusiad*, at Wheatley, a very pretty country place a few miles from Oxford; and on the other with Dr. Wetherell, Master of University College. From Dr. Wetherell's he went to visit Mr. Sackville Parker, the bookseller; and when he returned to us, gave the following account of his visit, saying, 'I have been to see my old friend, Sack Parker; I find he has married his maid; he has done right. She had lived with him many years in great confidence, and they had mingled minds; I do not think he could have found any wife that would have made him so happy. The woman was very attentive and civil to me; she pressed me to fix a day for dining with them, and to say what I liked, and she would be sure to get it for me. Poor Sack! He is very ill, indeed. We parted as never to meet again. It has quite broke me down.' This pathetic narrative was strangely diversified with the grave and earnest defence of a man's having married his maid. I could not but feel it as in some degree ludicrous.

In the morning of Tuesday, June 15, while we sat at Dr. Adams's, we talked of a printed letter from the Reverend Herbert Croft, to a young gentleman who had been his pupil, in which he advised him to read to the end of whatever books he should begin to read. JOHNSON. 'This is surely a strange advice; you may as well resolve that whatever men you happen to get acquainted with, you are to keep to them for life. A book may be good for nothing; or there may be only one thing in it worth knowing; are we to read it all through? These Voyages, (pointing to the three large volumes of *Voyages to the South Sea*, which were just come out) *who* will read them through? A man had better work his way before the mast, than read them through; they will be eaten by rats and mice, before they are read through. There can be little entertainment in such books; one set of Savages is like another.' BOSWELL. 'I do not think the people of Otaheite can be reckoned Savages.' JOHNSON. 'Don't cant in defence of Savages.' BOSWELL. 'They have the art of navigation.' JOHNSON. 'A dog or a cat can swim.' BOSWELL. 'They carve very ingeniously.' JOHNSON. 'A cat can scratch, and a child with a nail can scratch.' I perceived this was none of the *mollia tempora fandi*; so desisted.

Upon his mentioning that when he came to College he wrote his first exercise twice over; but never did so afterwards; MISS ADAMS. 'I suppose, Sir, you could not make them better?' JOHNSON. 'Yes, Madam, to be sure, I could make them better. Thought is better than no thought.' MISS ADAMS. 'Do you think, Sir, you could make your

Ramblers better?' JOHNSON. 'Certainly I could.' BOSWELL. 'I'll lay a bet, Sir, you cannot.' JOHNSON. 'But I will, Sir, if I choose. I shall make the best of them you shall pick out, better.' BOSWELL. 'But you may add to them. I will not allow of that.' JOHNSON. 'Nay, Sir, there are three ways of making them better;—putting out,—adding,—or correcting.'

During our visit at Oxford, the following conversation passed between him and me on the subject of my trying my fortune at the English bar: Having asked whether a very extensive acquaintance in London, which was very valuable, and of great advantage to a man at large, might not be prejudicial to a lawyer, by preventing him from giving sufficient attention to his business;—JOHNSON. 'Sir, you will attend to business, as business lays hold of you. When not actually employed, you may see your friends as much as you do now. You may dine at a Club every day, and sup with one of the members every night; and you may be as much at publick places as one who has seen them all would wish to be. But you must take care to attend constantly in Westminster-Hall; both to mind your business, as it is almost all learnt there, (for nobody reads now;) and to shew that you want to have business. And you must not be too often seen at publick places, that competitors may not have it to say, "He is always at the Playhouse or at Ranelagh, and never to be found at his chambers." And, Sir, there must be a kind of solemnity in the manner of a professional man. I have nothing particular to say to you on the subject. All this I should say to any one; I should have said it to Lord Thurlow twenty years ago.'

On Wednesday, June 19, Dr. Johnson and I returned to London; he was not well to-day, and said very little, employing himself chiefly in reading Euripides. He expressed some displeasure at me, for not observing sufficiently the various objects upon the road. 'If I had your eyes, Sir, (said he,) I should count the passengers.' It was wonderful how accurate his observation of visual objects was, notwithstanding his imperfect eyesight, owing to a habit of attention. That he was much satisfied with the respect paid to him at Dr. Adams's is thus attested by himself: 'I returned last night from Oxford, after a fortnight's abode with Dr. Adams, who treated me as well as I could expect or wish; and he that contents a sick man, a man whom it is impossible to please, has surely done his part well.'

After his return to London from this excursion, I saw him frequently, but have few memorandums: I shall therefore here insert some particulars which I collected at various times.

It having been mentioned to Dr. Johnson that a gentleman who had a son whom he imagined to have an extreme degree of timidity, resolved to send him to a publick school, that he might acquire confidence;—'Sir, (said Johnson,) this is a preposterous expedient for removing his infirmity; such a disposition should be cultivated in the shade. Placing him at a publick school is forcing an owl upon day.'

Speaking of a gentleman whose house was much frequented by low company; 'Rags, Sir, (said he,) will always make their appearance where they have a right to do it.'

Of the same gentleman's mode of living, he said, 'Sir, the servants, instead of doing what they are bid, stand round the table in idle clusters, gaping upon the guests; and seem as unfit to attend a company, as to steer a man of war.'

A dull country magistrate gave Johnson a long tedious account of his exercising his criminal jurisdiction, the result of which was his having sentenced four convicts to transportation. Johnson, in an agony of impatience to get rid of such a companion, exclaimed, 'I heartily wish, Sir, that I were a fifth.'

Johnson was present when a tragedy was read, in which there occurred this line:—

'Who rules o'er freemen should himself be free.'

The company having admired it much, 'I cannot agree with you (said Johnson). It might as well be said,—

'Who drives fat oxen should himself be fat.'

Johnson having argued for some time with a pertinacious gentleman; his opponent, who had talked in a very puzzling manner, happened to say, 'I don't understand you, Sir:' upon which Johnson observed, 'Sir, I have found you an argument; but I am not obliged to find you an understanding.'

Talking to me of Horry Walpole, (as Horace late Earl of Orford was often called,) Johnson allowed that he got together a great many curious little things, and told them in an elegant manner. Mr. Walpole thought Johnson a more amiable character after reading his *Letters to Mrs. Thrale*: but never was one of the true admirers of that great man. We may suppose a prejudice conceived, if he ever heard Johnson's account to Sir George Staunton, that when he made the speeches in parliament for the *Gentleman's Magazine*, 'he always took care to put Sir Robert Walpole in the wrong, and to say every thing he could against the electorate of Hanover.' The celebrated *Heroick Epistle*, in which Johnson is satyrically introduced, has been ascribed both to Mr. Walpole and Mr. Mason. One day at Mr. Courtenay's, when a gentleman expressed his opinion that there was more energy in that poem than could be expected from Mr. Walpole; Mr. Warton, the late Laureat, observed, 'It may have been written by Walpole, and *buckram'd* by Mason.'

Sir Joshua Reynolds having said that he took the altitude of a man's taste by his stories and his wit, and of his understanding by the remarks which he repeated; being always sure that he must be a weak man who quotes common things with an emphasis as if they were oracles; Johnson agreed with him; and Sir Joshua having also observed that the real character of a man was found out by his amusements,— Johnson added, 'Yes, Sir; no man is a hypocrite in his pleasures.'

I have mentioned Johnson's general aversion to a pun. He once, however, endured one of mine. When we were talking of a numerous company in which he had distinguished himself highly, I said, 'Sir, you were a COD surrounded by smelts. Is not this enough for you? at a time too when you were not *fishing* for a compliment?' He laughed at this with a complacent approbation. Old Mr. Sheridan observed, upon my mentioning it to him, 'He liked your compliment so well, he was willing to take it with *pun sauce*.' For my own part, I think no innocent species of wit or pleasantry should be suppressed; and that a good pun may be admitted among the smaller excellencies of lively conversation.

Mr. Burke uniformly shewed Johnson the greatest respect; and when Mr. Townshend, now Lord Sydney, at a period when he was conspicuous in opposition, threw out some reflection in parliament upon the grant of a pension to a man of such political principles as Johnson; Mr. Burke, though then of the same party with Mr. Townshend, stood warmly forth in defence of his friend, to whom, he justly observed, the pension was granted solely on account of his eminent literary merit. I am well assured, that Mr. Townshend's attack upon Johnson was the occasion of his 'hitching in a rhyme;' for, that in the original copy of Goldsmith's character of Mr. Burke, in his *Retaliation*, another person's name stood in the couplet where Mr. Townshend is now introduced:—

> 'Though fraught with all learning kept straining his throat,
> To persuade *Tommy Townshend* to lend him a vote.'

It may be worth remarking, among the *minutiae* of my collection, that Johnson was once drawn to serve in the militia, the Trained Bands of the City of London, and that Mr. Rackstrow, of the Museum in Fleet-street, was his Colonel. It may be believed he did not serve in person; but the idea, with all its circumstances, is certainly laughable. He upon that occasion provided himself with a musket, and with a sword and belt, which I have seen hanging in his closet.

An authour of most anxious and restless vanity being mentioned, 'Sir, (said he,) there is not a young sapling upon Parnassus more severely blown about by every wind of criticism than that poor fellow.'

The difference, he observed, between a well-bred and an ill-bred man is this: 'One immediately attracts your liking, the other your aversion. You love the one till you find reason to hate him; you hate the other till you find reason to love him.'

A foppish physician once reminded Johnson of his having been in company with him on a former occasion; 'I do not remember it, Sir.' The physician still insisted; adding that he that day wore so fine a coat that it must have attracted his notice. 'Sir, (said Johnson,) had you been dipt in Pactolus I should not have noticed you.'

He seemed to take a pleasure in speaking in his own style; for when he had carelessly missed it, he would repeat the thought translated into it. Talking of the Comedy of *The Rehearsal*, he said, 'It has not wit enough to keep it sweet.' This was easy; he therefore caught himself, and pronounced a more round sentence; 'It has not vitality enough to preserve it from putrefaction.'

Though he had no taste for painting, he admired much the manner in which Sir Joshua Reynolds treated of his art, in his *Discourses to the Royal Academy*. He observed one day of a passage in them, 'I think I might as well have said this myself:' and once when Mr. Langton was sitting by him, he read one of them very eagerly, and expressed himself thus:—'Very well, Master Reynolds; very well, indeed. But it will not be understood.'

When I observed to him that Painting was so far inferiour to Poetry, that the story or even emblem which it communicates must be previously known, and mentioned as a natural and laughable instance of this, that a little Miss on seeing a picture of Justice with the scales, had exclaimed to me, 'See, there's a woman selling sweetmeats;' he said, 'Painting, Sir, can illustrate, but cannot inform.'

No man was more ready to make an apology when he had censured unjustly, than Johnson. When a proof-sheet of one of his works was brought to him, he found fault with the mode in which a part of it was arranged, refused to read it, and in a passion desired that the compositor might be sent to him. The compositor was Mr. Manning, a decent sensible man, who had composed about one half of his *Dictionary*, when in Mr. Strahan's printing-house; and a great part of his *Lives of the Poets*, when in that of Mr. Nichols; and who (in his seventy-seventh year), when in Mr. Baldwin's printing-house, composed a part of the first edition of this work concerning him. By producing the manuscript, he at once satisfied Dr. Johnson that he was not to blame. Upon which Johnson candidly and earnestly said to him, 'Mr. Compositor, I ask your pardon. Mr. Compositor, I ask your pardon, again and again.'

His generous humanity to the miserable was almost beyond example. The following instance is well attested:—Coming home late one night, he found a poor woman lying in the street, so much exhausted that she could not walk; he took her upon his back, and carried her to his house, where he discovered that she was one of those wretched females who had fallen into the lowest state of vice, poverty, and disease. Instead of harshly upbraiding her, he had her taken care of with all tenderness for a long time, at considerable expence, till she was restored to health, and endeavoured to put her into a virtuous way of living.

He once in his life was known to have uttered what is called a *bull*: Sir Joshua Reynolds, when they were riding together in Devonshire, complained that he had a very bad horse, for that even when going down hill he moved slowly step by step. 'Ay (said Johnson,) and when he *goes* up hill, he *stands still.*'

He had a great aversion to gesticulating in company. He called once to a gentleman who offended him in that point, 'Don't *attitudenise.*' And when another gentleman thought he was giving additional force to what he uttered, by expressive movements of his hands, Johnson fairly seized them, and held them down.

Mr. Steevens, who passed many a social hour with him during their long acquaintance, which commenced when they both lived in the Temple, has preserved a good number of particulars concerning him, most of which are to be found in the department of Apothegms, &c. in the Collection of *Johnson's Works*. But he has been pleased to favour me with the following, which are original:—

'Dr. Johnson once assumed a character in which perhaps even Mr. Boswell never saw him. His curiosity having been excited by the praises bestowed on the celebrated Torre's fireworks at Marybone-Gardens, he desired Mr. Steevens to accompany him thither. The evening had proved showery; and soon after the few people present were assembled, publick notice was given, that the conductors to the wheels, suns, stars, &c., were so thoroughly water-soaked, that it was impossible any part of the exhibition should be made. "This is a mere excuse, (says the Doctor,) to save their crackers for a more profitable company. Let us but hold up our sticks, and threaten to break those coloured lamps that surround the Orchestra, and we shall soon have our wishes gratified. The core of the fireworks cannot be injured; let the different pieces be touched in their respective centers, and they will do their offices as well as ever." Some young men who overheard him, immediately began the violence he had recommended, and an attempt was speedily made to fire some of the wheels which appeared to have received the smallest damage; but to little purpose were they lighted, for most of them completely failed. The authour of *The Rambler*, however, may be considered, on this occasion, as the ringleader of a successful riot, though not as a skilful pyrotechnist.'

'It has been supposed that Dr. Johnson, so far as fashion was concerned, was careless of his appearance in publick. But this is not altogether true, as the following slight instance may show:— Goldsmith's last Comedy was to be represented during some court-mourning: and Mr. Steevens appointed to call on Dr. Johnson, and carry him to the tavern where he was to dine with others of the Poet's friends. The Doctor was ready dressed, but in coloured cloaths; yet being told that he would find every one else in black, received the intelligence with a profusion of thanks, hastened to change his attire, all the while repeating his gratitude for the information that had saved him from an appearance so improper in the front row of a front box. "I would not (added he,) for ten pounds, have seemed so retrograde to any general observance."

'He would sometimes found his dislikes on very slender circumstances. Happening one day to mention Mr. Flexman, a Dissenting Minister, with some compliment to his exact memory in chronological matters; the Doctor replied, "Let me hear no more of him, Sir. That is the fellow who made the Index to my *Ramblers*, and set down the name of Milton thus: Milton, MR. John."'

In the course of this work a numerous variety of names has been mentioned, to which many might be added. I cannot omit Lord and Lady Lucan, at whose house he often enjoyed all that an elegant table and the best company can contribute to happiness; he found hospitality united with extraordinary accomplishments, and embellished with charms of which no man could be insensible.

On Tuesday, June 22, I dined with him at THE LITERARY CLUB, the last time of his being in that respectable society. The other members present were the Bishop of St. Asaph, Lord Eliot, Lord Palmerston, Dr. Fordyce, and Mr. Malone. He looked ill; but had such a manly fortitude, that he did not trouble the company with melancholy complaints. They all shewed evident marks of kind concern about him, with which he was much pleased, and he exerted himself to be as entertaining as his indisposition allowed him.

The anxiety of his friends to preserve so estimable a life, as long as human means might be supposed to have influence, made them plan for him a retreat from the severity of a British winter, to the mild climate of Italy. This scheme was at last brought to a serious resolution at General Paoli's, where I had often talked of it. One essential matter, however, I understood was necessary to be previously settled, which was obtaining such an addition to his income, as would be sufficient to enable him to defray the expence in a manner becoming the first literary character of a great nation, and independent of all his other merits, the Authour of THE DICTIONARY OF THE ENGLISH LANGUAGE. The person to whom I above all others thought I should apply to negociate this business, was the Lord Chancellor, because I knew that he highly valued Johnson, and that Johnson highly valued his Lordship; so that it was no degradation of my illustrious friend to solicit for him the favour of such a man. I have mentioned what Johnson said of him to me when he was at the bar; and after his Lordship was advanced to the seals, he said of him, 'I would prepare myself for no man in England but Lord Thurlow. When I am to meet with him I should wish to know a day before.' How he would have prepared himself I cannot conjecture. Would he have selected certain topicks, and considered them in every view so as to be in readiness to argue them at all points? and what may we suppose those topicks to have been? I once started the curious inquiry to the great man who was the subject of this compliment: he smiled, but did not pursue it.

I first consulted with Sir Joshua Reynolds, who perfectly coincided in opinion with me; and I therefore, though personally very little known to his Lordship, wrote to him, stating the case, and requesting his good offices for Dr. Johnson. I mentioned that I was obliged to set out for Scotland early in the following week, so that if his Lordship should have any commands for me as to this pious negociation, he would be pleased to send them before that time; otherwise Sir Joshua Reynolds would give all attention to it.

This application was made not only without any suggestion on the part of Johnson himself, but was utterly unknown to him, nor had he the smallest suspicion of it. Any insinuations, therefore, which since his death have been thrown out, as if he had stooped to ask what was superfluous, are without any foundation. But, had he asked it, it would not have been superfluous; for though the money he had saved proved to be more than his friends imagined, or than I believe he himself, in his carelessness concerning worldly matters, knew it to be, had he travelled upon the Continent, an augmentation of his income would by no means have been unnecessary.

On Thursday, June 24, I dined with him at Mr. Dilly's, where were the Rev. Mr. (now Dr.) Knox, master of Tunbridge-school, Mr. Smith, Vicar of Southill, Dr. Beattie, Mr. Pinkerton, authour of various literary performances, and the Rev. Dr. Mayo. At my desire old Mr. Sheridan was invited, as I was earnest to have Johnson and him brought together again by chance, that a reconciliation might be effected. Mr. Sheridan happened to come early, and having learned that Dr. Johnson was to be there, went away; so I found, with sincere regret, that my friendly intentions were hopeless. I recollect nothing that passed this day, except Johnson's quickness, who, when Dr. Beattie observed, as something remarkable which had happened to him, that he had chanced to see both No. 1, and No. 1000, of the hackney-coaches, the first and the last; 'Why, Sir, (said Johnson,) there is an equal chance for one's seeing those two numbers as any other two.'

On Friday, June 25, I dined with him at General Paoli's, where, he says in one of his letters to Mrs. Thrale, 'I love to dine.' There was a variety of dishes much to his taste, of all which he seemed to me to eat so much, that I was afraid he might be hurt by it; and I whispered to the General my fear, and begged he might not press him. 'Alas! (said the General,) see how very ill he looks; he can live but a very short time. Would you refuse any slight gratifications to a man under sentence of death? There is a humane custom in Italy, by which persons in that melancholy situation are indulged with having whatever they like best to eat and drink, even with expensive delicacies.'

On Sunday, June 27, I found him rather better. I mentioned to him a young man who was going to Jamaica with his wife and children, in expectation of being provided for by two of her brothers settled in that island, one a clergyman, and the other a physician. JOHNSON. 'It is a wild scheme, Sir, unless he has a positive and deliberate invitation. There was a poor girl, who used to come about me, who had a cousin in Barbadoes, that, in a letter to her, expressed a wish she should come out to that Island, and expatiated on the comforts and happiness of her situation. The poor girl went out: her cousin was much surprised, and asked her how she could think of coming. "Because, (said she,) you invited me." "Not I," answered the cousin. The letter was then produced. "I see it is true, (said she,) that I did invite you: but I did not think you would come." They lodged her in an out-house, where she passed her time miserably; and as soon as she had an opportunity she returned to England. Always tell this, when you hear of people going abroad to relations, upon a notion of being well received. In the case which you mention, it is probable the clergyman spends all he gets, and the physician does not know how much he is to get.'

We this day dined at Sir Joshua Reynolds's, with General Paoli, Lord Eliot, (formerly Mr. Eliot, of Port Eliot,) Dr. Beattie, and some other company. Talking of Lord Chesterfield;—JOHNSON. 'His manner was exquisitely elegant, and he had more knowledge than I expected.' BOSWELL. 'Did you find, Sir, his conversation to be of a superiour style?' JOHNSON. 'Sir, in the conversation which I had with him I had the best right to superiority, for it was upon philology and literature.' Lord Eliot, who had travelled at the same time with Mr. Stanhope, Lord Chesterfield's natural son, justly observed, that it was strange that a man who shewed he had so much affection for his son as Lord Chesterfield did, by writing so many long and anxious letters to him, almost all of them when he was Secretary of State, which certainly was a proof of great goodness of disposition, should endeavour to make his son a rascal. His Lordship told us, that Foote had intended to bring on the stage a father who had thus tutored his son, and to shew the son an honest man to every one else, but practising his father's maxims upon him, and cheating him. JOHNSON. 'I am much pleased with this design; but I think there was no occasion to make the son honest at all. No; he should be a consummate rogue: the contrast between honesty and knavery would be the stronger. It should be contrived so that the father should be the only sufferer by the son's villainy, and thus there would be poetical justice.'

A young gentleman present took up the argument against him, and maintained that no man ever thinks of the *nose of the mind*, not adverting that though that figurative sense seems strange to us, as very unusual, it is truly not more forced than Hamlet's 'In my *mind's eye*, Horatio.' He persisted much too long, and appeared to Johnson as putting himself forward as his antagonist with too much presumption; upon which he called to him in a loud tone, 'What is it you are contending for, if you *be* contending?' And afterwards imagining that the gentleman retorted upon him with a kind of smart drollery, he said, 'Mr. ***** it does not become you to talk so to me. Besides, ridicule is not your talent; you have *there* neither intuition nor sagacity.' The gentleman protested that he had intended no improper freedom, but had the greatest respect for Dr. Johnson. After a short pause, during which we were somewhat uneasy,—JOHNSON. 'Give me your hand, Sir. You were too tedious, and I was too short.' MR. *****. 'Sir, I am honoured by your attention in any way.' JOHNSON. 'Come, Sir, let's have no more of it. We offended one another by our contention; let us not offend the company by our compliments.'

He now said, 'He wished much to go to Italy, and that he dreaded passing the winter in England.' I said nothing; but enjoyed a secret satisfaction in thinking that I had taken the most effectual measures to make such a scheme practicable.

On Monday, June 28, I had the honour to receive from the Lord Chancellor the following letter:—

'TO JAMES BOSWELL, ESQ.

'SIR,—I should have answered your letter immediately, if (being much engaged when I received it) I had not put it in my pocket, and forgot to open it till this morning.

'I am much obliged to you for the suggestion; and I will adopt and press it as far as I can. The best argument, I am sure, and I hope it is not likely to fail, is Dr. Johnson's merit. But it will be necessary, if I should be so unfortunate as to miss seeing you, to converse with Sir Joshua on the sum it will be proper to ask,—in short, upon the means of setting him out. It would be a reflection on us all, if such a man should perish for want of the means to take care of his health. Yours, &c.

'THURLOW.'

This letter gave me a very high satisfaction; I next day went and shewed it to Sir Joshua Reynolds, who was exceedingly pleased with it. He thought that I should now communicate the negociation to Dr. Johnson, who might afterwards complain if the attention with which he had been honoured, should be too long concealed from him. I intended to set out for Scotland next morning; but Sir Joshua cordially insisted that I should stay another day, that Johnson and I might dine with him, that we three might talk of his Italian Tour, and, as Sir Joshua expressed himself, 'have it all out.' I hastened to Johnson, and was told by him that he was rather better to-day. BOSWELL. 'I am very anxious about you, Sir, and particularly that you should go to Italy for the winter, which I believe is your own wish.' JOHNSON. 'It is, Sir.' BOSWELL. 'You have no objection, I presume, but the money it would require.' JOHNSON. 'Why, no, Sir.' Upon which I gave him a particular account of what had been done, and read to him the Lord Chancellor's letter. He listened with much attention; then warmly said, 'This is taking prodigious pains about a man.' 'O! Sir, (said I, with most sincere affection,) your friends would do every thing for you.' He paused, grew more and more agitated, till tears started into his eyes, and he exclaimed with fervent emotion, 'GOD bless you all.' I was so affected that I also shed tears. After a short silence, he renewed and extended his grateful benediction, 'GOD bless you all, for JESUS CHRIST'S sake.' We both remained for some time unable to speak. He rose suddenly and quitted the room, quite melted in tenderness. He staid but a short time, till he had recovered his firmness; soon after he returned I left him, having first engaged him to dine at Sir Joshua Reynolds's, next day. I never was again under that roof which I had so long reverenced.

On Wednesday, June 30, the friendly confidential dinner with Sir Joshua Reynolds took place, no other company being present. Had I known that this was the last time that I should enjoy in this world, the conversation of a friend whom I so much respected, and from whom I derived so much instruction and entertainment, I should have been deeply affected. When I now look back to it, I am vexed that a single word should have been forgotten.

Both Sir Joshua and I were so sanguine in our expectations, that we expatiated with confidence on the liberal provision which we were sure would be made for him, conjecturing whether munificence would be displayed in one large donation, or in an ample increase of his pension. He himself catched so much of our enthusiasm, as to allow himself to suppose it not impossible that our hopes might in one way or other be realised. He said that he would rather have his pension doubled than a grant of a thousand pounds; 'For, (said he,) though probably I may not live to receive as much as a thousand pounds, a man would have the consciousness that he should pass the remainder of his life in splendour, how long soever it might be.' Considering what a moderate proportion an income of six hundred pounds a year bears to innumerable fortunes in this country, it is worthy of remark, that a man so truly great should think it splendour.

As an instance of extraordinary liberality of friendship, he told us, that Dr. Brocklesby had upon this occasion offered him a hundred a year for his life. A grateful tear started into his eye, as he spoke this in a faultering tone.

Sir Joshua and I endeavoured to flatter his imagination with agreeable prospects of happiness in Italy. 'Nay, (said he,) I must not expect much of that; when a man goes to Italy merely to feel how he breathes the air, he can enjoy very little.'

Our conversation turned upon living in the country, which Johnson, whose melancholy mind required the dissipation of quick successive variety, had habituated himself to consider as a kind of mental imprisonment. 'Yet, Sir, (said I,) there are many people who are content to live in the country.' JOHNSON. 'Sir, it is in the intellectual world as in the physical world; we are told by natural philosophers that a body is at rest in the place that is fit for it; they who are content to live in the country, are *fit* for the country.'

Talking of various enjoyments, I argued that a refinement of taste was a disadvantage, as they who have attained to it must be seldomer pleased than those who have no nice discrimination, and are therefore satisfied with every thing that comes in their way. JOHNSON. 'Nay, Sir; that is a paltry notion. Endeavour to be as perfect as you can in every respect.'

I accompanied him in Sir Joshua Reynolds's coach, to the entry of Bolt-court. He asked me whether I would not go with him to his house; I declined it, from an apprehension that my spirits would sink. We bade adieu to each other affectionately in the carriage. When he had got down upon the foot-pavement, he called out, 'Fare you well;' and without looking back, sprung away with a kind of pathetick briskness, if I may use that expression, which seemed to indicate a struggle to conceal uneasiness, and impressed me with a foreboding of our long, long separation.

I remained one day more in town, to have the chance of talking over my negociation with the Lord Chancellor; but the multiplicity of his Lordship's important engagements did not allow of it; so I left the management of the business in the hands of Sir Joshua Reynolds.

Soon after this time Dr. Johnson had the mortification of being informed by Mrs. Thrale, that, 'what she supposed he never believed,' was true; namely, that she was actually going to marry Signor Piozzi, an Italian musick-master. He endeavoured to prevent it; but in vain. If she would publish the whole of the correspondence that passed between Dr. Johnson and her on the subject, we should have a full view of his real sentiments. As it is, our judgement must be biassed by that characteristick specimen which Sir John Hawkins has given us: 'Poor Thrale! I thought that either her virtue or her vice would have restrained her from such a marriage. She is now become a subject for her enemies to exult over; and for her friends, if she has any left, to forget, or pity.'

It must be admitted that Johnson derived a considerable portion of happiness from the comforts and elegancies which he enjoyed in Mr. Thrale's family; but Mrs. Thrale assures us he was indebted for these to her husband alone, who certainly respected him sincerely.

Having left the *pious negociation*, as I called it, in the best hands, I shall here insert what relates to it. Johnson wrote to Sir Joshua Reynolds on July 6, as follows:—

'I am going, I hope, in a few days, to try the air of Derbyshire, but hope to see you before I go. Let me, however, mention to you what I have much at heart. If the Chancellor should continue his attention to Mr. Boswell's request, and confer with you on the means of relieving my languid state, I am very desirous to avoid the appearance of asking money upon false pretences. I desire you to represent to his Lordship, what, as soon as it is suggested, he will perceive to be reasonable,— That, if I grow much worse, I shall be afraid to leave my physicians, to suffer the inconveniences of travel, and pine in the solitude of a foreign country; That, if I grow much better, of which indeed there is now little appearance, I shall not wish to leave my friends and my domestick comforts; for I do not travel, for pleasure or curiosity; yet if I should recover, curiosity would revive. In my present state, I am desirous to make a struggle for a little longer life, and hope to obtain some help from a softer climate. Do for me what you can.'

By a letter from Sir Joshua Reynolds I was informed, that the Lord Chancellor had called on him, and acquainted him that the application had not been successful; but that his Lordship, after speaking highly in praise of Johnson, as a man who was an honour to his country, desired Sir Joshua to let him know, that on granting a mortgage of his pension, he should draw on his Lordship to the amount of five or six hundred pounds; and that his Lordship explained the meaning of the mortgage to be, that he wished the business to be conducted in such a manner, that Dr. Johnson should appear to be under the least possible obligation. Sir Joshua mentioned, that he had by the same post communicated all this to Dr. Johnson.

How Johnson was affected upon the occasion will appear from what he wrote to Sir Joshua Reynolds:—

'Ashbourne, Sept. 9. Many words I hope are not necessary between you and me, to convince you what gratitude is excited in my heart by the Chancellor's liberality, and your kind offices. . . .

'I have enclosed a letter to the Chancellor, which, when you have read it, you will be pleased to seal with a head, or any other general seal, and convey it to him: had I sent it directly to him, I should have seemed to overlook the favour of your intervention.'

'TO THE LORD HIGH CHANCELLOR.

'MY LORD,—After a long and not inattentive observation of mankind, the generosity of your Lordship's offer raises in me not less wonder than gratitude. Bounty, so liberally bestowed, I should gladly receive, if my condition made it necessary; for, to such a mind, who would not be proud to own his obligations? But it has pleased GOD to restore me to so great a measure of health, that if I should now appropriate so much of a fortune destined to do good, I could not escape from myself the charge of advancing a false claim. My journey to the continent, though I once thought it necessary, was never much encouraged by my physicians; and I was very desirous that your Lordship should be told of it by Sir Joshua Reynolds, as an event very uncertain; for if I grew much better, I should not be willing, if much worse, not able, to migrate. Your Lordship was first solicited without my knowledge; but, when I was told that you were pleased to honour me with your patronage, I did not expect to hear of a refusal; yet, as I have had no long time to brood hope, and have not rioted in imaginary opulence, this cold reception has been scarce a disappointment; and, from your Lordship's kindness, I have received a benefit, which only men like you are able to bestow. I shall now live *mihi carior*, with a higher opinion of my own merit. I am, my Lord, your Lordship's most obliged, most grateful, and most humble servant,
'September, 1784.'

'SAM. JOHNSON.'

Upon this unexpected failure I abstain from presuming to make any remarks, or to offer any conjectures.

Let us now contemplate Johnson thirty years after the death of his wife, still retaining for her all the tenderness of affection.

'TO THE REVEREND MR. BAGSHAW, AT BROMLEY.

'SIR,—Perhaps you may remember, that in the year 1753, you committed to the ground my dear wife. I now entreat your permission to lay a stone upon her; and have sent the inscription, that, if you find it proper, you may signify your allowance.

'You will do me a great favour by showing the place where she lies, that the stone may protect her remains.

'Mr. Ryland will wait on you for the inscription, and procure it to be engraved. You will easily believe that I shrink from this mournful office. When it is done, if I have strength remaining, I will visit Bromley once again, and pay you part of the respect to which you have a right from, Reverend Sir, your most humble servant,

'July 12, 1784.'

'SAM. JOHNSON.'

Next day he set out on a jaunt to Staffordshire and Derbyshire, flattering himself that he might be in some degree relieved.

During his absence from London he kept up a correspondence with several of his friends, from which I shall select what appears to me proper for publication, without attending nicely to chronological order.

TO DR. BROCKLESBY, he writes, Ashbourne, Sept. 9:—

'Do you know the Duke and Duchess of Devonshire? And have you ever seen Chatsworth? I was at Chatsworth on Monday: I had indeed seen it before, but never when its owners were at home; I was very kindly received, and honestly pressed to stay: but I told them that a sick man is not a fit inmate of a great house. But I hope to go again some time.'

Sept. 11. 'I think nothing grows worse, but all rather better, except sleep, and that of late has been at its old pranks. Last evening, I felt what I had not known for a long time, an inclination to walk for amusement; I took a short walk, and came back again neither breathless nor fatigued. This has been a gloomy, frigid, ungenial summer, but of late it seems to mend; I hear the heat sometimes mentioned, but I do not feel it:

> "Praeterea minimus gelido jam in corpore sanguis
> Febre calet sola.—"

I hope, however, with good help, to find means of supporting a winter at home, and to hear and tell at the Club what is doing, and what ought to be doing in the world. I have no company here, and shall naturally come home hungry for conversation. To wish you, dear Sir, more leisure, would not be kind; but what leisure you have, you must bestow upon me.'

Lichfield, Sept. 29. 'On one day I had three letters about the air-balloon: yours was far the best, and has enabled me to impart to my friends in the country an idea of this species of amusement. In amusement, mere amusement, I am afraid it must end, for I do not find that its course can be directed so as that it should serve any purposes of communication; and it can give no new intelligence of the state of the air at different heights, till they have ascended above the height of mountains, which they seem never likely to do. I came hither on the 27th. How long I shall stay I have not determined. My dropsy is gone, and my asthma much remitted, but I have felt myself a little declining these two days, or at least to-day; but such vicissitudes must be expected. One day may be worse than another; but this last month is far better than the former; if the next should be as much better than this, I shall run about the town on my own legs.'

October 25. 'You write to me with a zeal that animates, and a tenderness that melts me. I am not afraid either of a journey to London, or a residence in it. I came down with little fatigue, and am now not weaker. In the smoky atmosphere I was delivered from the dropsy, which I consider as the original and radical disease. The town is my element;[59] there are my friends, there are my books, to which I have not yet bid farewell, and there are my amusements. Sir Joshua told me long ago that my vocation was to publick life, and I hope still to keep my station, till GOD shall bid me *Go in peace.*'

TO SIR JOSHUA REYNOLDS:—

Ashbourne, Sept. 2. '. . . I still continue by God's mercy to mend. My breath is easier, my nights are quieter, and my legs are less in bulk, and stronger in use. I have, however, yet a great deal to overcome, before I can yet attain even an old man's health. Write, do write to me now and then; we are now old acquaintance, and perhaps few people have lived so much and so long together, with less cause of complaint on either side. The retrospection of this is very pleasant, and I hope we shall never think on each other with less kindness.'

Sept. 9. 'I could not answer your letter before this day, because I went on the sixth to Chatsworth, and did not come back till the post was gone. Many words, I hope, are not necessary between you and me, to convince you what gratitude is excited in my heart, by the Chancellor's liberality and your kind offices. I did not indeed expect that what was asked by the Chancellor would have been refused, but since it has, we will not tell that any thing has been asked. I have enclosed a letter to the Chancellor which, when you have read it, you will be pleased to seal with a head, or other general seal, and convey it to him; had I sent it directly to him, I should have seemed to overlook the favour of your intervention. I do not despair of supporting an English winter. At Chatsworth, I met young Mr. Burke, who led me very commodiously into conversation with the Duke and Duchess. We had a very good morning. The dinner was publick.'

---

[59] His love of London continually appears. In a letter from him to Mrs. Smart, wife of his friend the Poet, which is published in a well-written life of him, prefixed to an edition of his Poems, in 1791, there is the following sentence:—'To one that has passed so many years in the pleasures and opulence of London, there are few places that can give much delight.' Once, upon reading that line in the curious epitaph quoted in *The Spectator*, 'Born in New-England, did in London die;' he laughed and said, 'I do not wonder at this. It would have been strange, if born in London, he had died in New-England.'—BOSWELL.

Sept. 18. 'I have three letters this day, all about the balloon, I could have been content with one. Do not write about the balloon, whatever else you may think proper to say.'

It may be observed, that his writing in every way, whether for the publick, or privately to his friends, was by fits and starts; for we see frequently, that many letters are written on the same day. When he had once overcome his aversion to begin, he was, I suppose, desirous to go on, in order to relieve his mind from the uneasy reflection of delaying what he ought to do.

We now behold Johnson for the last time, in his native city, for which he ever retained a warm affection, and which, by a sudden apostrophe, under the word Lich, he introduces with reverence, into his immortal Work, THE ENGLISH DICTIONARY:—*Salve, magna parens*! While here, he felt a revival of all the tenderness of filial affection, an instance of which appeared in his ordering the grave-stone and inscription over Elizabeth Blaney[60] to be substantially and carefully renewed.

To Mr. Henry White, a young clergyman, with whom he now formed an intimacy, so as to talk to him with great freedom, he mentioned that he could not in general accuse himself of having been an undutiful son. 'Once, indeed, (said he,) I was disobedient; I refused to attend my father to Uttoxeter-market. Pride was the source of that refusal, and the remembrance of it was painful. A few years ago, I desired to atone for this fault; I went to Uttoxeter in very bad weather, and stood for a considerable time bareheaded in the rain, on the spot where my father's stall used to stand. In contrition I stood, and I hope the penance was expiatory.'

'I told him (says Miss Seward) in one of my latest visits to him, of a wonderful learned pig, which I had seen at Nottingham; and which did all that we have observed exhibited by dogs and horses. The subject amused him. "Then, (said he,) the pigs are a race unjustly calumniated. *Pig* has, it seems, not been wanting to *man*, but *man* to *pig*. We do not allow *time* for his education, we kill him at a year old." Mr. Henry White, who was present, observed that if this instance had happened in or before Pope's time, he would not have been justified in instancing the swine as the lowest degree of groveling instinct. Dr. Johnson seemed pleased with the observation, while the person who made it proceeded to remark, that great torture must have been employed, ere the indocility of the animal could have been subdued. "Certainly, (said the Doctor;) but, (turning to me,) how old is your pig?" I told him, three years old. "Then, (said he,) the pig has no cause to complain; he would have been killed the first year if he had not been *educated*, and protracted existence is a good recompence for very considerable

---

[60] His mother.—Ed.

degrees of torture.'''

As Johnson had now very faint hopes of recovery, and as Mrs. Thrale was no longer devoted to him, it might have been supposed that he would naturally have chosen to remain in the comfortable house of his beloved wife's daughter, and end his life where he began it. But there was in him an animated and lofty spirit, and however complicated diseases might depress ordinary mortals, all who saw him, beheld and acknowledged the *invictum animum Catonis*. Such was his intellectual ardour even at this time, that he said to one friend, 'Sir, I look upon every day to be lost, in which I do not make a new acquaintance;' and to another, when talking of his illness, 'I will be conquered; I will not capitulate.' And such was his love of London, so high a relish had he of its magnificent extent, and variety of intellectual entertainment, that he languished when absent from it, his mind having become quite luxurious from the long habit of enjoying the metropolis; and, therefore, although at Lichfield, surrounded with friends, who loved and revered him, and for whom he had a very sincere affection, he still found that such conversation as London affords, could be found no where else. These feelings, joined, probably, to some flattering hopes of aid from the eminent physicians and surgeons in London, who kindly and generously attended him without accepting fees, made him resolve to return to the capital.

From Lichfield he came to Birmingham, where he passed a few days with his worthy old schoolfellow, Mr. Hector, who thus writes to me:—'He was very solicitous with me to recollect some of our most early transactions, and transmit them to him, for I perceive nothing gave him greater pleasure than calling to mind those days of our innocence. I complied with his request, and he only received them a few days before his death. I have transcribed for your inspection, exactly the minutes I wrote to him.' This paper having been found in his repositories after his death, Sir John Hawkins has inserted it entire, and I have made occasional use of it and other communications from Mr. Hector, in the course of this Work. I have both visited and corresponded with him since Dr. Johnson's death, and by my inquiries concerning a great variety of particulars have obtained additional information. I followed the same mode with the Reverend Dr. Taylor, in whose presence I wrote down a good deal of what he could tell; and he, at my request, signed his name, to give it authenticity. It is very rare to find any person who is able to give a distinct account of the life even of one whom he has known intimately, without questions being put to them. My friend Dr. Kippis has told me, that on this account it is a practice with him to draw out a biographical catechism.

Johnson then proceeded to Oxford, where he was again kindly received by Dr. Adams.

He arrived in London on the 16th of November, and next day sent to Dr. Burney the following note, which I insert as the last token of his remembrance of that ingenious and amiable man, and as another of the many proofs of the tenderness and benignity of his heart:—

'MR. JOHNSON, who came home last night, sends his respects to dear Dr. Burney, and all the dear Burneys, little and great.'

Having written to him, in bad spirits, a letter filled with dejection and fretfulness, and at the same time expressing anxious apprehensions concerning him, on account of a dream which had disturbed me; his answer was chiefly in terms of reproach, for a supposed charge of 'affecting discontent, and indulging the vanity of complaint.' It, however, proceeded,—

'Write to me often, and write like a man. I consider your fidelity and tenderness as a great part of the comforts which are yet left me, and sincerely wish we could be nearer to each other. . . . My dear friend, life is very short and very uncertain; let us spend it as well as we can. My worthy neighbour, Allen, is dead. Love me as well as you can. Pay my respects to dear Mrs. Boswell. Nothing ailed me at that time; let your superstition at last have an end.'

Feeling very soon, that the manner in which he had written might hurt me, he two days afterwards, July 28, wrote to me again, giving me an account of his sufferings; after which, he thus proceeds:—

'Before this letter, you will have had one which I hope you will not take amiss; for it contains only truth, and that truth kindly intended. . . . *Spartam quam nactus es orna*; make the most and best of your lot, and compare yourself not with the few that are above you, but with the multitudes which are below you.'

Yet it was not a little painful to me to find, that . . . he still persevered in arraigning me as before, which was strange in him who had so much experience of what I suffered. I, however, wrote to him two as kind letters as I could; the last of which came too late to be read by him, for his illness encreased more rapidly upon him than I had apprehended; but I had the consolation of being informed that he spoke of me on his death-bed, with affection, and I look forward with humble hope of renewing our friendship in a better world.

Soon after Johnson's return to the metropolis, both the asthma and dropsy became more violent and distressful.

During his sleepless nights he amused himself by translating into Latin verse, from the Greek, many of the epigrams in the *Anthologia*. These translations, with some other poems by him in Latin, he gave to his friend Mr. Langton, who, having added a few notes, sold them to the booksellers for a small sum, to be given to some of Johnson's relations, which was accordingly done; and they are printed in the collection of his works.

A very erroneous notion has circulated as to Johnson's deficiency in the knowledge of the Greek language, partly owing to the modesty with which, from knowing how much there was to be learnt, he used to mention his own comparative acquisitions. When Mr. Cumberland talked to him of the Greek fragments which are so well illustrated in *The Observer*, and of the Greek dramatists in general, he candidly acknowledged his insufficiency in that particular branch of Greek literature. Yet it may be said, that though not a great, he was a good Greek scholar. Dr. Charles Burney, the younger, who is universally acknowledged by the best judges to be one of the few men of this age who are very eminent for their skill in that noble language, has assured me, that Johnson could give a Greek word for almost every English one; and that although not sufficiently conversant in the niceties of the language, he upon some occasions discovered, even in these, a considerable degree of critical acumen. Mr. Dalzel, Professor of Greek at Edinburgh, whose skill in it is unquestionable, mentioned to me, in very liberal terms, the impression which was made upon him by Johnson, in a conversation which they had in London concerning that language. As Johnson, therefore, was undoubtedly one of the first Latin scholars in modern times, let us not deny to his fame some additional splendour from Greek.

The ludicrous imitators of Johnson's style are innumerable. Their general method is to accumulate hard words, without considering, that, although he was fond of introducing them occasionally, there is not a single sentence in all his writings where they are crowded together, as in the first verse of the following imaginary Ode by him to Mrs. Thrale, which appeared in the newspapers:—

> '*Cervisial coctor's viduate* dame,
> *Opin'st* thou this gigantick frame,
> *Procumbing* at thy shrine:
> Shall, *catenated* by thy charms,
> A captive in thy *ambient* arms,
> *Perennially* be thine?'

This, and a thousand other such attempts, are totally unlike the original, which the writers imagined they were turning into ridicule. There is not similarity enough for burlesque, or even for caricature.

'TO MR. GREEN, APOTHECARY, AT LICHFIELD.

'DEAR SIR,—I have enclosed the Epitaph for my Father, Mother, and Brother, to be all engraved on the large size, and laid in the middle aisle in St. Michael's church, which I request the clergyman and churchwardens to permit.

'The first care must be to find the exact place of interment, that the stone may protect the bodies. Then let the stone be deep, massy, and hard; and do not let the difference of ten pounds, or more, defeat our purpose.

'I have enclosed ten pounds, and Mrs. Porter will pay you ten more, which I gave her for the same purpose. What more is wanted shall be sent; and I beg that all possible haste may be made, for I wish to have it done while I am yet alive. Let me know, dear Sir, that you receive this. I am, Sir, your most humble servant,
    'Dec. 2, 1784.'

'SAM. JOHNSON.'

Death had always been to him an object of terrour; so that, though by no means happy, he still clung to life with an eagerness at which many have wondered. At any time when he was ill, he was very much pleased to be told that he looked better. An ingenious member of the *Eumelian Club*, informs me, that upon one occasion when he said to him that he saw health returning to his cheek, Johnson seized him by the hand and exclaimed, 'Sir, you are one of the kindest friends I ever had.'

Dr. Heberden, Dr. Brocklesby, Dr. Warren, and Dr. Butter, physicians, generously attended him, without accepting any fees, as did Mr. Cruikshank, surgeon; and all that could be done from professional skill and ability, was tried, to prolong a life so truly valuable. He himself, indeed, having, on account of his very bad constitution, been perpetually applying himself to medical inquiries, united his own efforts with those of the gentlemen who attended him; and imagining that the dropsical collection of water which oppressed him might be drawn off by making incisions in his body, he, with his usual resolute defiance of pain, cut deep, when he thought that his surgeon had done it too tenderly.[61]

About eight or ten days before his death, when Dr. Brocklesby paid him his morning visit, he seemed very low and desponding, and said, 'I have been as a dying man all night.' He then emphatically broke out in the words of Shakspeare:—

'Can'st thou not minister to a mind diseas'd;
Pluck from the memory a rooted sorrow;
Raze out the written troubles of the brain;
And, with some sweet oblivious antidote,
Cleanse the stuff'd bosom of that perilous stuff,

---

[61] This bold experiment, Sir John Hawkins has related in such a manner as to suggest a charge against Johnson of intentionally hastening his end; a charge so very inconsistent with his character in every respect, that it is injurious even to refute it, as Sir John has thought it necessary to do. It is evident, that what Johnson did in hopes of relief, indicated an extraordinary eagerness to retard his dissolution.—BOSWELL.

Which weighs upon the heart?'

To which Dr. Brocklesby readily answered, from the same great poet:—

> '—therein the patient
> Must minister to himself.'

Johnson expressed himself much satisfied with the application.

On another day after this, when talking on the subject of prayer, Dr. Brocklesby repeated from Juvenal,—

> '*Orandum est, ut sit mens sana in corpore sano,*'

and so on to the end of the tenth satire; but in running it quickly over, he happened, in the line,

> '*Qui spatium vitae extremum inter munera ponat,*'

to pronounce *supremum* for *extremum*; at which Johnson's critical ear instantly took offence, and discoursing vehemently on the unmetrical effect of such a lapse, he shewed himself as full as ever of the spirit of the grammarian.

Having no near relations, it had been for some time Johnson's intention to make a liberal provision for his faithful servant, Mr. Francis Barber, whom he looked upon as particularly under his protection, and whom he had all along treated truly as an humble friend. Having asked Dr. Brocklesby what would be a proper annuity to a favourite servant, and being answered that it must depend on the circumstances of the master; and, that in the case of a nobleman, fifty pounds a year was considered as an adequate reward for many years' faithful service; 'Then, (said Johnson,) shall I be *nobilissimus*, for I mean to leave Frank seventy pounds a year, and I desire you to tell him so.' It is strange, however, to think, that Johnson was not free from that general weakness of being averse to execute a will, so that he delayed it from time to time; and had it not been for Sir John Hawkins's repeatedly urging it, I think it is probable that his kind resolution would not have been fulfilled. After making one, which, as Sir John Hawkins informs us, extended no further than the promised annuity, Johnson's final disposition of his property was established by a Will and Codicil.

The consideration of numerous papers of which he was possessed, seems to have struck Johnson's mind, with a sudden anxiety, and as they were in great confusion, it is much to be lamented that he had not entrusted some faithful and discreet person with the care and selection of them; instead of which, he in a precipitate manner, burnt large masses of them, with little regard, as I apprehend, to discrimination. Not that I suppose we have thus been deprived of any compositions which he had ever intended for the publick eye; but, from what escaped the flames, I judge that many curious circumstances relating both to himself and other literary characters have perished.

Two very valuable articles, I am sure, we have lost, which were two quarto volumes, containing a full, fair, and most particular account of his own life, from his earliest recollection. I owned to him, that having accidentally seen them, I had read a great deal in them; and apologizing for the liberty I had taken, asked him if I could help it. He placidly answered, 'Why, Sir, I do not think you could have helped it.' I said that I had, for once in my life, felt half an inclination to commit theft. It had come into my mind to carry off those two volumes, and never see him more. Upon my inquiring how this would have affected him, 'Sir, (said he,) I believe I should have gone mad.'

During his last illness, Johnson experienced the steady and kind attachment of his numerous friends. Mr. Hoole has drawn up a narrative of what passed in the visits which he paid him during that time, from the 10th of November to the 13th of December, the day of his death, inclusive, and has favoured me with a perusal of it, with permission to make extracts, which I have done. Nobody was more attentive to him than Mr. Langton, to whom he tenderly said, *Te teneam moriens deficiente manu*. And I think it highly to the honour of Mr. Windham, that his important occupations as an active statesman did not prevent him from paying assiduous respect to the dying Sage whom he revered, Mr. Langton informs me, that, 'one day he found Mr. Burke and four or five more friends sitting with Johnson. Mr. Burke said to him, "I am afraid, Sir, such a number of us may be oppressive to you." "No, Sir, (said Johnson,) it is not so; and I must be in a wretched state, indeed, when your company would not be a delight to me." Mr. Burke, in a tremulous voice, expressive of being very tenderly affected, replied, "My dear Sir, you have always been too good to me." Immediately afterwards he went away. This was the last circumstance in the acquaintance of these two eminent men.'

The following particulars of his conversation within a few days of his death, I give on the authority of Mr. John Nichols:—

'He said, that the Parliamentary Debates were the only part of his writings which then gave him any compunction: but that at the time he wrote them, he had no conception he was imposing upon the world, though they were frequently written from very slender materials, and often from none at all,—the mere coinage of his own imagination. He never wrote any part of his works with equal velocity. Three columns of the *Magazine*, in an hour, was no uncommon effort, which was faster than most persons could have transcribed that quantity.

'Of his friend Cave, he always spoke with great affection. "Yet (said he,) Cave, (who never looked out of his window, but with a view to the *Gentleman's Magazine*,) was a penurious pay-master; he would contract for lines by the hundred, and expect the long hundred; but he was a good man, and always delighted to have his friends at his table."

'He said at another time, three or four days only before his death, speaking of the little fear he had of undergoing a chirurgical operation, "I would give one of these legs for a year more of life, I mean of comfortable life, not such as that which I now suffer;"—and lamented much his inability to read during his hours of restlessness; "I used formerly, (he added,) when sleepless in bed, *to read like a Turk*."

'Whilst confined by his last illness, it was his regular practice to have the church-service read to him, by some attentive and friendly Divine. The Rev. Mr. Hoole performed this kind office in my presence for the last time, when, by his own desire, no more than the Litany was read; in which his responses were in the deep and sonorous voice which Mr. Boswell has occasionally noticed, and with the most profound devotion that can be imagined. His hearing not being quite perfect, he more than once interrupted Mr. Hoole, with "Louder, my dear Sir, louder, I entreat you, or you pray in vain!"—and, when the service was ended, he, with great earnestness, turned round to an excellent lady who was present, saying, "I thank you, Madam, very heartily, for your kindness in joining me in this solemn exercise. Live well, I conjure you; and you will not feel the compunction at the last, which I now feel." So truly humble were the thoughts which this great and good man entertained of his own approaches to religious perfection.'

Amidst the melancholy clouds which hung over the dying Johnson, his characteristical manner shewed itself on different occasions.

When Dr. Warren, in the usual style, hoped that he was better; his answer was, 'No, Sir; you cannot conceive with what acceleration I advance towards death.'

A man whom he had never seen before was employed one night to sit up with him. Being asked next morning how he liked his attendant, his answer was, 'Not at all, Sir: the fellow's an ideot; he is as aukward as a turn-spit when first put into the wheel, and as sleepy as a dormouse.'

Mr. Windham having placed a pillow conveniently to support him, he thanked him for his kindness, and said, 'That will do,—all that a pillow can do.'

He requested three things of Sir Joshua Reynolds:—To forgive him thirty pounds which he had borrowed of him; to read the Bible; and never to use his pencil on a Sunday. Sir Joshua readily acquiesced.

Johnson, with that native fortitude, which, amidst all his bodily distress and mental sufferings, never forsook him, asked Dr.

Brocklesby, as a man in whom he had confidence, to tell him plainly whether he could recover. 'Give me (said he,) a direct answer.' The Doctor having first asked him if he could hear the whole truth, which way soever it might lead, and being answered that he could, declared that, in his opinion, he could not recover without a miracle. 'Then, (said Johnson,) I will take no more physick, not even my opiates; for I have prayed that I may render up my soul to GOD unclouded.' In this resolution he persevered, and, at the same time, used only the weakest kinds of sustenance. Being pressed by Mr. Windham to take somewhat more generous nourishment, lest too low a diet should have the very effect which he dreaded, by debilitating his mind, he said, 'I will take any thing but inebriating sustenance.'

The Reverend Mr. Strahan, who was the son of his friend, and had been always one of his great favourites, had, during his last illness, the satisfaction of contributing to soothe and comfort him. That gentleman's house, at Islington, of which he is Vicar, afforded Johnson, occasionally and easily, an agreeable change of place and fresh air; and he attended also upon him in town in the discharge of the sacred offices of his profession.

Mr. Strahan has given me the agreeable assurance, that, after being in much agitation, Johnson became quite composed, and continued so till his death.

Dr. Brocklesby, who will not be suspected of fanaticism, obliged me with the following account:—

'For some time before his death, all his fears were calmed and absorbed by the prevalence of his faith, and his trust in the merits and *propitiation* of JESUS CHRIST.'

Johnson having thus in his mind the true Christian scheme, at once rational and consolatory, uniting justice and mercy in the DIVINITY, with the improvement of human nature, previous to his receiving the Holy Sacrament in his apartment, composed and fervently uttered this prayer:—

'Almighty and most merciful Father, I am now as to human eyes, it seems, about to commemorate, for the last time, the death of thy Son JESUS CHRIST, our Saviour and Redeemer. Grant, O LORD, that my whole hope and confidence may be in his merits, and thy mercy; enforce and accept my imperfect repentance; make this commemoration available to the confirmation of my faith, the establishment of my hope, and the enlargement of my charity; and make the death of thy Son JESUS CHRIST effectual to my redemption. Have mercy upon me, and pardon the multitude of my offences. Bless my friends; have mercy upon all men. Support me, by thy Holy Spirit, in the days of weakness, and at the hour of death; and receive me, at my death, to everlasting happiness, for the sake of JESUS CHRIST. Amen.'

Having, as has been already mentioned, made his will on the 8th and 9th of December, and settled all his worldly affairs, he languished till Monday, the 13th of that month, when he expired, about seven o'clock in the evening, with so little apparent pain that his attendants hardly perceived when his dissolution took place.

Of his last moments, my brother, Thomas David, has furnished me with the following particulars:—

'The Doctor, from the time that he was certain his death was near, appeared to be perfectly resigned, was seldom or never fretful or out of temper, and often said to his faithful servant, who gave me this account, "Attend, Francis, to the salvation of your soul, which is the object of greatest importance:" he also explained to him passages in the Scripture, and seemed to have pleasure in talking upon religious subjects.

'On Monday, the 13th of December, the day on which he died, a Miss Morris, daughter to a particular friend of his, called, and said to Francis, that she begged to be permitted to see the Doctor, that she might earnestly request him to give her his blessing. Francis went into his room, followed by the young lady, and delivered the message. The Doctor turned himself in the bed, and said, "GOD bless you, my dear!" These were the last words he spoke. His difficulty of breathing increased till about seven o'clock in the evening, when Mr. Barber and Mrs. Desmoulins, who were sitting in the room, observing that the noise he made in breathing had ceased, went to the bed, and found he was dead.'

About two days after his death, the following very agreeable account was communicated to Mr. Malone, in a letter by the Honourable John Byng, to whom I am much obliged for granting me permission to introduce it in my work.

'DEAR SIR,—Since I saw you, I have had a long conversation with Cawston, who sat up with Dr. Johnson, from nine o'clock, on Sunday evening, till ten o'clock, on Monday morning. And, from what I can gather from him, it should seem, that Dr. Johnson was perfectly composed, steady in hope, and resigned to death. At the interval of each hour, they assisted him to sit up in his bed, and move his legs, which were in much pain; when he regularly addressed himself to fervent prayer; and though, sometimes, his voice failed him, his senses never did, during that time. The only sustenance he received, was cyder and water. He said his mind was prepared, and the time to his dissolution seemed long. At six in the morning, he inquired the hour, and, on being informed, said that all went on regularly, and he felt he had but a few hours to live.

'At ten o'clock in the morning, he parted from Cawston, saying, "You should not detain Mr. Windham's servant:—I thank you; bear my remembrance to your master." Cawston says, that no man could appear more collected, more devout, or less terrified at the thoughts of the approaching minute.

'This account, which is so much more agreeable than, and somewhat different from, yours, has given us the satisfaction of thinking that that great man died as he lived, full of resignation, strengthened in faith, and joyful in hope.'

A few days before his death, he had asked Sir John Hawkins, as one of his executors, where he should be buried; and on being answered, 'Doubtless, in Westminster-Abbey,' seemed to feel a satisfaction, very natural to a Poet; and indeed in my opinion very natural to every man of any imagination, who has no family sepulchre in which he can be laid with his fathers. Accordingly, upon Monday, December 20, his remains were deposited in that noble and renowned edifice; and over his grave was placed a large blue flag-stone, with this inscription:—

'SAMUEL JOHNSON, LL.D.
Obiit XIII *die Decembris,*
Anno Domini
M.DCC.LXXXIV.
Ætatis suae LXXV.'

His funeral was attended by a respectable number of his friends, particularly such of the members of the LITERARY CLUB as were then in town; and was also honoured with the presence of several of the Reverend Chapter of Westminster. Mr. Burke, Sir Joseph Banks, Mr. Windham, Mr. Langton, Sir Charles Bunbury, and Mr. Colman, bore his pall. His school-fellow, Dr. Taylor, performed the mournful office of reading the burial service.

I trust, I shall not be accused of affectation, when I declare, that I find myself unable to express all that I felt upon the loss of such a 'Guide, Philosopher, and Friend.' I shall, therefore, not say one word of my own, but adopt those of an eminent friend, which he uttered with an abrupt felicity, superior to all studied compositions:—'He has made a chasm, which not only nothing can fill up, but which nothing has a tendency to fill up. Johnson is dead. Let us go to the next best:—there is nobody; no man can be said to put you in mind of Johnson.'

THE END

Made in United States
North Haven, CT
26 March 2022

17586063R00259